**DATE DUE**

|  |  |  |  |
|---|---|---|---|
|  |  |  |  |
|  |  |  |  |
|  |  |  |  |
|  |  |  |  |
|  |  |  |  |
|  |  |  |  |
|  |  |  |  |
|  |  |  |  |
|  |  |  |  |
|  |  |  |  |
|  |  |  |  |
|  |  |  |  |
|  |  |  |  |
|  |  |  |  |
|  |  |  |  |
|  |  |  |  |
|  |  |  |  |
|  |  |  |  |

*UNITED STATES ARMY IN WORLD WAR II*

# The Technical Services

# THE CORPS OF ENGINEERS: THE WAR AGAINST GERMANY

*by*

*Alfred M. Beck*
*Abe Bortz*
*Charles W. Lynch*
*Lida Mayo*
*and*
*Ralph F. Weld*

MILITARY INSTRVCTION

*CENTER OF MILITARY HISTORY*

*UNITED STATES ARMY*

*WASHINGTON, D.C., 1985*

*U.S. Army Center of Military History*

# Brig. Gen. Douglas Kinnard, USA (Ret.), Chief of Military History

| | |
|---|---|
| Chief Historian | David F. Trask |
| Chief, Histories Division | Col. James W. Dunn |
| Editor in Chief | John W. Elsberg |

**Library of Congress Cataloging in Publication Data**

The Corps of Engineers.

(United States Army in World War II: the technical services)
  Bibliography: p.
  Includes index.
  1. World War, 1939–1945—Regimental histories—
United States. 2. United States. Army. Corps of
Engineers—History. 3. World War, 1939–1945—Campaigns—
Europe. 4. World War, 1939–1945—Campaigns—Africa,
North. I. Beck, Alfred M., 1939–      . II. Series:
United States Army in World War II.

D769.33.C67 1985          940.54'12'73          84–11376

First Printing—CMH Pub 10–22

. . . to Those Who Served

# History of

# THE CORPS OF ENGINEERS

Troops and Equipment
Construction in the United States
The War Against Germany
The War Against Japan

# Foreword

In this, the last volume dealing with the performance of the Corps of Engineers during World War II, the Corps' support of the war in the European and North African theaters is recounted in detail.

This narrative makes clear the indispensible role of the military engineer at the fighting front and his part in maintaining Allied armies in the field against European Axis powers. American engineers carried the fight to enemy shores by their mastery of amphibious warfare. In building and repairing road and rail nets for the fighting forces, they wrote their own record of achievement. In supporting combat and logistical forces in distant lands, these technicians of war transferred to active theaters many of the construction and administrative functions of the peacetime Corps, so heavily committed to public works at home.

The authors of this volume have reduced a highly complex story to a comprehensive yet concise account of American military engineers in the two theaters of operations where the declared main enemy of the war was brought to unconditional surrender. The addition of this account to the official U.S. Army in World War II series closes the last remaining gaps in the history of the technical services in that conflict.

Washington, D.C.  
21 June 1984

DOUGLAS KINNARD  
Brigadier General, USA (Ret.)  
Chief of Military History

# The Authors

Alfred M. Beck received his M.A. and Ph.D. degrees from Georgetown University. He has held several research and supervisory positions in the U.S. Army Center of Military History and the Historical Division, Office of the Chief of Engineers.

Abe Bortz received his Ph.D. degree from Harvard University in 1951. After working for twelve years for the Historical Division, Office of the Chief of Engineers, he has served since 1963 as the historian of the Social Security Administration, Baltimore, Maryland. He is the author of *Social Security Sources in Federal Records*.

Charles W. Lynch received his M.A. degree from the University of West Virginia in 1948. He worked for the Historical Division, Office of the Chief of Engineers, from 1951 to 1963 before transferring to the U.S. Army Materiel Command, the predecessor of the U.S. Army Materiel Development and Readiness Command. He retired from the federal service in 1980.

Lida Mayo was a graduate of Randolph-Macon Woman's College. She served as a historian at the Military Air Transport Service from 1946 to 1950 and from 1950 to 1962 at the Office of the Chief of Ordnance, where she was the chief historian until that office merged with the Office, Chief of Military History, the predecessor of the U.S. Army Center of Military History. She is the author of *The Ordnance Department: On Beachhead and Battlefront* and coauthor of *The Ordnance Department: Planning Munitions for War*, both in the U.S. Army in World War II series. Her commercially published works include *Henry Clay, Rustics in Rebellion, Bloody Buna*, and a number of journal articles. She retired from federal service in 1971 and died in 1978.

Ralph F. Weld received his Ph.D. degree from Columbia University in 1938. He worked as a historian with the Historical Division, Office of the Chief of Engineers, from 1951 to 1958, when he retired from the federal service. He continued to serve the Historical Division on short assignments until 1964. He is the author of *Brooklyn Is America* and was on the editorial staff of the *Columbia Encyclopedia*.

# Preface

This volume is the fourth in the series dealing with the activities of the U.S. Army Corps of Engineers during World War II. As a companion to an earlier history of American military engineering in the war against Japan, this book recounts the engineer role in the campaigns in North Africa, Italy, and western and central Europe that wrested those areas from German and Italian control.

Because of the thin neutrality to which the United States government clung in 1941, the first introduction of American engineer elements into England was clandestine, but even with the earliest American theater command existing only in embryo, the need for engineers was implicit in Allied strategy. The Anglo-American decision in March 1941 to deal first with Germany as the most dangerous enemy required the construction of strategic bomber bases and huge troop cantonments in England, all with the object of bringing Allied might to bear against Germany from the west. The story of how this was accomplished necessarily concerns itself with organizational structures, operating procedures, statistical data, and descriptions of vast logistical effort. The redirection of the entire strategy in 1942 to a second theater in the Mediterranean brought American engineer troops to their first encounters with a determined and skilled adversary in that part of the world and to a sober realization of their own strengths and weaknesses in combat. In sustained operations across two continents and through two and a half years of war, these engineers carried out the basic mission of the military engineer in the field.

With the measured assurance of doctrinal literature, the 1943 edition of the engineer Field Manual 5–6, *Operations of Field Engineer Units*, defined the engineer's task as support of other Army combat and supply elements, increasing the power of forces by construction or destruction to facilitate the movement of friendly troops and to impede that of the enemy. To assert, however, that American engineers handily fulfilled this mandate in Europe and North Africa is to overlook constant trial and error and relearning from past experience. By the end of the war engineer officers and men well understood the meaning of the ancient poet who declared that the immortals had put sweat and a long, steep way before excellence.

Many hands have shaped the mass of material on which this history is based into a comprehensive whole. The first half of the manuscript, roughly through the end of the Italian campaign, was completed by Abe Bortz, William Lynch, and Ralph Weld, all of whom worked for the Corps of Engineers Historical Office. Lida Mayo set in place most of the draft chapters covering operations in northwest Europe and Germany. I added several chapters and recast virtually the entire manuscript, working under the discerning eye of Robert W. Coakley, a historian of surpassing ability and a guiding spirit in the process of transforming a rough product into a viable history worthy of print.

The publication of a work of even such cooperative authorship as this one would be impossible without the able assistance of a number of fine editors who brought this book from manuscript to printed page. Joyce W. Hardyman and Edith M. Boldan began this labor, but the heavier burden fell to Catherine A. Heerin and Diane L. Sedore, whose respect for the English language and attention to detail made this account consistently readable. Their patience in the tedious process of preparing a book and their good humor in dealing with its last author were unfailing.

The maps presented in the volume are the work of Charles L. Brittle, who took vague requests for illustrations and created a series of visual aids to guide the reader through a sometimes complicated text. Howell C. Brewer, Jr., lent his hand to this effort by producing the organization charts shown in the narrative. Arthur S. Hardyman, who directed the graphic work, also gave valuable advice on the choice of photographs that complement the text.

For all the advice and support rendered by this willing staff of assistants, the final responsibility for the content of this history remains that of the authors. Collectively they bear the burden of errors of fact or omission.

Washington, D.C.                                                    ALFRED M. BECK
5 January 1984

# Contents

# Charts

# Maps

# Illustrations

All illustrations are from Department of Defense files.

# THE CORPS OF ENGINEERS:
# THE WAR AGAINST GERMANY

# CHAPTER I

# Introduction

On the eve of American involvement in World War II, the U.S. Army Corps of Engineers had 150 years of experience in national wars and in statutory assignment to civil works projects outside the Army. Its veteran officers could hark back to an unprecedented performance in World War I, when the Corps had expanded from 2,454 officers and enlisted men to nearly 300,000—174,000 in France alone when the Armistice was signed.[1]

In unexpected measure their works on the Continent from 1917 to 1919 enlarged upon traditional engineer functions, especially as they applied to facilitating troop movement. In several ports where the French government turned over wharfage to incoming American forces, the 17th and 18th Engineer Regiments, two of the first nine engineer regiments to arrive, constructed additions to docks, erected depots, and then laid new rail lines linking the facilities to the French national system and the Zone of the Advance that included the front line itself. An entire regiment spent the war in forestry operations, providing much of the lumber for rail ties, housing, and hospitals for the American Expeditionary Forces. In forward areas engineers braved the same fire as the infantry to build narrow-gauge rail nets for supply and troop movement, to dig complex trench systems, to string wire, to install bridging, and even to engage the enemy. Engineer flash- and sound-ranging equipment helped direct counterbattery artillery fire. Chemical engineers, the forerunners of an independent postwar Chemical Corps, released gas employed against the Germans in the trenches and developed protective devices and procedures against enemy gas attacks. Elaborate camouflage screens and nets manufactured and painted with the help of French labor masked American equipment and concealed preparations for forthcoming operations.

Falling within the usual definitions of engineer work in war, these activities covered a far wider technical range than ever before in American military engineering experience. So complex and extensive had the operations become, in fact, that one regimental commander declared that the military engineer had died and his close relative, the civil engineer, had taken his

---

[1] *Historical Report of the Chief Engineer, American Expeditionary Forces, 1917–1919* (Washington, 1919), pp. 12–13. The report excludes from the engineer troop strength in France the separate Transportation Corps, another 60,000 men who functioned only indirectly under the chief engineer of the American Expeditionary Forces.

place.[2] For all their accomplishments in forging smooth lines of communications from the rear to the front and in providing invaluable services between, the engineers fought in a war distinguished by the lack of forward movement of the front itself until the final months of the conflict.

Events in Europe in the spring of 1940 effectively demonstrated that harnessing the internal combustion engine to new tactics gave much more range and speed to military operations.[3] The German defeat of France in six weeks and the narrow escape of the British Expeditionary Force at Dunkirk proved the superiority of the *Wehrmacht*. Coordinated with aerial attacks that destroyed ground obstacles and threw enemy rear areas into confusion, massed armor assaults on narrow fronts offered the antidote to static trench warfare and allowed rapid decision on the battlefield.

German success with these tactics and the subsequent bombing campaign against Great Britain converted a fitful American rearmament into a real mobilization. Congress appropriated more funds for national defense than the Army could readily absorb with its limited plans to defend the western hemisphere from Axis infiltration or overt military advances in 1940. Like the rest of the Army under this largesse, the engineers accelerated their recovery from twenty years of impoverishment. Though the Corps had been heavily committed to civil works through the two

preceding decades, its separate military units were few and scattered across the continental United States and its overseas possessions. Given time to develop additional combat and support units along older organizational lines, the engineers could expand as they had in World War I and take up again their recognized general functions of bridge, rail, and road construction or maintenance; port rehabilitation; and more specialized work in camouflage, water supply, map production, mine warfare, forestry, and the administrative work necessary to support combat forces. But even if engineer elements remained divided into general and special units, the engineers could not simply reactivate old units under this framework in anticipation of a new conflict. The modern method of war generated new missions and demanded new organizational structures, new units, and new types of equipment to accommodate the revolution in tactics.

A reorganization of the Army was already under way.[4] Field testing of revisions in the basic organization of the infantry division began in 1937 with a reduction of infantry regiments from four to three to create a flexible and more easily maneuvered force. The organic engineer unit in the smaller division was a battalion rather than an engineer combat regiment. Numerical strength varied in the experiments, but three companies became the eventual standard for engineer battalions assigned to infantry divisions. Respond-

[2] William B. Parsons, *American Engineers in France* (New York: D. Appleton and Company, 1920), p. 5.

[3] Lt. Col. Paul W. Thompson, *What You Should Know About The Army Engineers* (New York: W. W. Norton & Company, 1942), pp. 9–10.

[4] Blanche D. Coll, Jean E. Keith, and Herbert E. Rosenthal, *The Corps of Engineers: Troops and Equipment*, United States Army in World War II (Washington, 1958), pp. 1–63. Unless otherwise noted, the following is based on this source.

ing to events in Europe in 1940, the Army also developed two armored divisions from its small, scattered and experimental, mechanized and armored elements and provided each division with an organic engineer battalion, eventually numbering 712 men. In imitation of the German organization for panzer divisions, the American engineer armored unit had four companies, one a bridge company equipped with a large variety of military bridging. A reconnaissance platoon of the battalion's headquarters company was to scout ahead of the advancing division to determine the need for bridge and demolition work or the best detours around obstacles.

Engineer regiments, either for general service or for combat support, survived as separate entities attached to field armies or to corps headquarters. Consisting of two battalions and various supporting companies, these larger units assumed many of the rear-area tasks formerly left to divisional units. The more heavily equipped general service regiment was to perform general construction, maintenance, or bridge work on main routes of communications, and military construction once the engineers assumed that responsibility from the Quartermaster Corps. The combat regiment, with twenty-four machine guns in its normal equipment, was more heavily armed for work in the combat zone but had less heavy machinery than the general service regiment. It was particularly suited to support divisional units in forward areas and had a special role in large-scale assault river crossings.[5]

---

[5] Thompson, *What You Should Know About the Army Engineers*, pp. 61–62.

Experiments produced new equipment for the revised engineer organizations. In the search for easily transported and rapidly emplaced bridging, the armored force engineers copied the German inflatable ponton system and produced a 25-ton ponton treadway bridge for tanks. Other tests showed the British-designed Bailey bridge to be lighter and more adaptable to a war of movement than the standard American H−10 and H−20 girder bridges. Repeated experience with construction equipment convinced the engineers of the value of heavier and larger bulldozers, scrapers, cranes, and trucks, though the conflicting demands of the American industrial mobilization often made these items hard to procure in the desired quantities. As a result, an engineer unit Table of Organization and Equipment (TOE) immediately before American entry into the war called for much less heavy equipment than eventually proved necessary. Demands for additional heavy equipment of new design arose as the engineers encountered conditions that overtaxed the standard machinery they brought with them to the theaters of war. A new battery-operated magnetic mine detector enabled the engineers rapidly to unearth mines that impeded the advance of friendly troops, but there was little advance intelligence on the nature of Axis mines or the doctrine governing German mine warfare. Engineer map production techniques improved remarkably with the use of aerial photography employing specialized multilens cameras and multiplex interpretation systems.

Given the heavy use of tactical aviation and the then-current theories of bombardment aviation, the engineers also expected to support the Army Air Forces in any future conflict. Established immediately after the spring maneuvers of 1940, the engineer aviation regiment (66 officers and 2,200 enlisted men) consisted of three battalions that could be employed independently. Within two years of its inception, the unit had the highly specialized mission of constructing large rear-area bomber bases and hasty forward fields for tactical aircraft. The regiment carried with it all the necessary earth-moving, paving, and construction machinery and was adequately armed to thwart an enemy airborne attack on the installation under construction. The unit used another idea from abroad—long, narrow steel plank sections, perforated to reduce their weight and linked together to form temporary runways on poor or unstable soil.

The motorization and mechanization of modern armies and the addition of aerial components dictated increased consumption of gasoline and oil in future operations. The engineers met this likelihood with another innovation that eventually proved its value in the theaters of war in North Africa and Europe. The Quartermaster Corps had distributed petroleum products in containers transported to using troops by rail and truck. Though the engineers did not displace this method entirely, they took over and improved pipelines to lessen the load on vehicles in combat and communications zones. A highly specialized unit, the engineer petro-leum distribution company, came into existence to build and operate pipelines from major ports to the immediate rear areas of the field armies.

An engineer role in amphibious warfare was not considered until shortly before the Japanese attack on Pearl Harbor. In all the likely arenas of the obviously approaching war, an advancing army would have to move across expanses of open water. In the Pacific, where the American possessions and the Japanese homeland were islands, the ability to seize objectives depended upon operations across beaches. In Europe, it was apparent by mid-1940 that Axis control of every major port would make similar operations necessary. Though the Army began amphibious training for two infantry divisions in June 1940 and established a research committee to examine possible roles for amphibian engineers, special units for the purpose were still in the future.[6]

By mid-1941, the Corps of Engineers had embarked upon an ambitious program of revising its military units and equipment. Though not fully ready to fight in an overseas theater, the engineers had done much to adapt to the realities of modern combat and combat support. This process continued as a shadow American staff structure took shape in England.

---

[6] Coll, Keith, and Rosenthal, *The Corps of Engineers: Troops and Equipment*, p. 357.

# CHAPTER II

# The Engineers Cross the Atlantic 1941–1942

In the late spring of 1941 a few American officers in civilian clothes slipped into London and established a small headquarters in a building near the American embassy on Grosvenor Square. They might have been attaches of the embassy, as far as the general public could tell. Their name, Special Observer Group (SPOBS), like their attire, concealed rather than expressed their functions, for they had much more urgent business than to act as neutral observers of the military effort of a friendly nation at war. They were organized as a military staff complete with G–1 (personnel), G–2 (intelligence), G–3 (plans and operations), and G–4 (logistics and supply), together with a full complement of special staff officers. The group was located in England so that close liaison with the British High Command would be in effect should American quasi-neutrality suddenly shift into active belligerence. The group's mission was to coordinate plans, so far as circumstances permitted, for American participation in the war, and to receive, house, and equip American forces.

The engineer officer of the Special Observer Group was Lt. Col. Donald A. Davison, who had been the General Headquarters (GHQ) Air Force staff engineer in Washington.[1] Barely a year had passed since Colonel Davison had organized the 21st Engineer Aviation Regiment, the Army's first engineer aviation unit. He was an obvious choice for the SPOBS staff, for the group was to be concerned first of all with planning facilities for future air operations and air defense. The emphasis on air power was apparent also in the choice of Maj. Gen. James E. Chaney, AC, to head the group, and of Brig. Gen. Joseph T. McNarney, AC, as General Chaney's chief of staff.

The Special Observer Group at first numbered eighteen officers and eleven enlisted men. While the task of planning the transportation of U.S. Army troops, their location in the United Kingdom, and their shelter involved the entire SPOBS staff and their opposites in the British Army, much of the work fell to the engineer officer. Construction planning for the U.S. Army in the British Isles was the responsibility of five officers: General McNarney; Lt. Col. George W. Griner, Jr., ACofS, G–4; Lt. Col. John E. Dahlquist, ACofS,

---

[1] Promoted to colonel 26 June 1941 and to brigadier general on 16 April 1942.

G—1; Lt. Col. Charles L. Bolte, ACofS for Plans; and Colonel Davison. In November 1941 Colonel Davison also began to function as a member of a new technical committee, which represented an expansion of the duties of the Special Observer Group and a step toward closer liaison with the British.[2]

### Reconnaissance

For many weeks in 1941, Davison and officers of the group toured those areas to which American forces would be sent if the United States entered the war. SPOBS activities were guided by the basic American war plan, RAINBOW—5, and an agreement designated ABC—1, which resulted from meetings held early in 1941 by representatives of the British Chiefs of Staff, the Chief of Staff of the U.S. Army, and the U.S. Chief of Naval Operations. Features of ABC—1 relating specifically to initial American activities in the European theater included provisions for the defense of bases in Scotland and Northern Ireland to be used by U.S. naval forces, the establishment of a U.S. bomber command to operate from England, the dispatch of a U.S. token force for the defense of Britain, and American relief of the British garrison in Iceland.

Between 27 May and 21 November

1941, representatives of the Special Observer Group attended eight meetings of the Operational Planning Section of the British Joint Planning Staff; the group had its first meeting with the British Air Ministry on 6 June. These meetings promoted practical cooperation between the SPOBS staff and British officers. Soon after the 27 May meeting the British War Office submitted a list of questions to General Chaney concerning accommodations for U.S. troops. This questionnaire brought up many points considered in detail by officers who in the summer and fall of 1941 inspected areas in Northern Ireland, Scotland, and Kent where the token force probably would be located. The British had already undertaken much of the construction necessary for the accommodation of American troops in those areas, but much more needed to be done to extend and improve roads and to provide housing and other necessary structures for the troops.

The rush of events following Pearl Harbor outdated the recommendations and detailed planning that resulted from these tours. Colonel Davison and the other SPOBS officers nevertheless obtained valuable information concerning resources, equipment, housing, and British methods. Most important, the inspection tours promoted the practical teamwork with the British that was later so essential to the war effort. After the inspection tour of Northern Ireland in July 1941, the surveyors reported to the War Department that the chief engineering problem in Ulster was to provide housing for the approximately 27,000 troops envisaged in RAINBOW—5. The British would be able to supply all the Nissen huts required, and crushed rock and cement could be

---

[2] Capt S. J. Thurman et al., The Special Observer Group Prior to the Activation of the European Theater of Operations, Oct 44, OCE, ETOUSA, Hist Sect; Henry G. Elliott, The Administrative and Logistical History of the European Theater of Operations, vol. I, "The Predecessor Commands: The Special Observers (SPOBS) and the United States Army Forces in the British Isles (USAFBI)," Mar 46, in CMH; Roland G. Ruppenthal, Logistical Support of the Armies, Volume I: May 1941—September 1944, United States Army in World War II (Washington, 1953), pp. 13—113. Unless otherwise indicated, this chapter is based on these sources.

obtained in England.[3] Lumber and quarrying machinery were scarce, however, and hardware would have to come from the United States. One engineer aviation battalion and a general service or combat engineer regiment would be needed to do general construction and airfield maintenance.[4]

The plans for Northern Ireland were eventually carried out with minor deviations, but this was not the case for most of the other areas surveyed in the United Kingdom. After American entry into the war the bases in Northern Ireland became more important than those in Scotland as a new war strategy gave less relative weight to air defense and offense and more to preparations for invasion of the Continent.

The SPOBS officers surveyed three widely separated sites for prospective Army installations in Scotland: Gare Loch, Loch Ryan, and Ayr Airdrome. SPOBS estimated that new construction would be necessary to support some 6,000 troops: about 860 Nissens for housing; a hospital at Ayr; and 27 storage Nissens distributed among the three areas. An American contractor was then at work on U.S. Navy installations at Gare Loch and Loch Ryan at opposite ends of the Firth of Clyde. In view of the serious labor problem in the United Kingdom, the officers suggested three alternatives: concluding an agreement with the Navy to extend its contracts to cover the Army construction; letting new Army contracts with the same companies; or shipping one engineer general service regiment to Scotland ahead of the first convoy to put up the hospital and troop barracks using British Nissen huts.[5]

The proposed token force area in England lay southeast of London, near Wrotham in Kent. SPOBS officers checked the site during late August and early September, recommending that an engineer unit, with a planned strength of 543 men of the 7,600 in the token force, bring all TOE equipment. Engineers in this district would support an infantry regiment in the field, build many new roads, and maintain or widen the narrow, winding roads in the area. The SPOBS report pointed out that supplies for the building of field fortifications and obstacles should be sent from the United States.[6]

SPOBS officers also inspected a contemplated supply or base area near Birmingham and a proposed bomber command site in Huntingdonshire, both in the Midlands. General Chaney sent to the War Department in the summer and fall of 1941 a series of reports, based largely on studies and estimates prepared by Colonel Davison, that summed up the surveys from an engineering standpoint. A report of 17 December 1941 summarized Colonel Davison's recommendations for construction. Although dated ten days after Pearl Harbor, the report was based on the earlier concept of air strategy that had governed all SPOBS activity in the United Kingdom in 1941.

---

[3] The Nissen hut was a prefabricated half cylinder of corrugated iron with a cement floor. It was named after its designer, Lt. Col. P. N. Nissen (1871–1930).

[4] Annex 4 (Engr) to Rpt on Northern Ireland, Special Observer Group, 3 Sep 41, Hist Sect, Intel Div, OCE ETOUSA.

[5] OCE ETOUSA Hist Rpt 7, Field and Service Force Construction (United Kingdom), 1946, pp. 16–18, Liaison Sect, Intel Div, ETOUSA Adm file 547. This is one of twenty historical reports prepared by the OCE Intelligence Division during 1945–46.

[6] Summary of Annex 4 to Rpt on Token Force Area, 4 Sep 41, AG 381–Kent 'Area, Token Force, OCE ETOUSA Hist Records.

Unlike the earlier ones, the 17 December report took for granted the arrival of American troops in Britain. Britain's limited material and labor resources were already severely strained, and it was obvious that supplemental American labor and materials would be needed. Starting construction before the troops arrived was essential, but the threat of enemy submarines and a shipping shortage dictated moving only a minimum of materials from the United States. Since troop labor was desirable only if civilian labor was not available, the final report pointed out that the War Department would have to determine policy, proportions of skilled and unskilled civilian and troop labor, and many details relating to materials, contracts, and transportation. Matters relating to sites, construction details, and utilities would have to be handled in the United Kingdom.[7]

The report provided figures on housing already available together with estimates of housing that would have to be built. Somewhat more than 11,000 standard 16-by-36-foot quartering huts were needed, as well as nearly 500 40-by-100-foot storage and shop buildings, and 442 ordnance igloos. Buildings for 10,000 hospital beds would also have to be built. Hard-surface paving construction for airfield access roads and for aircraft hardstandings added up to 182 miles.

Colonel Davison was better acquainted than anyone else with the engineering problems that the Army had to face in Britain and had studied all the proposed sites in detail. He knew

the views of the SPOBS staff and those of the British War Office. Accordingly, on General Chaney's recommendation, he went to Washington in January 1942 to help plan the movement of troops and their accommodation in Britain.[8]

### Iceland

In June 1941 SPOBS engineers also undertook a survey of locations in Iceland, where an American occupation was imminent. Construction of facilities began before Pearl Harbor as Americans moved in July 1941 to replace the British on the island.[9]

Iceland had great strategic importance. The British occupied the island in May 1940 to prevent its seizure by the Germans, in whose hands it would have formed a base for attack on English soil and on the British shipping lifeline. Britain had acted quickly to develop air and naval bases in Iceland to protect the North Atlantic convoy routes. Yet by the summer of 1941 British reverses in the western Sahara prompted plans to withdraw the Iceland garrison for use in the desert and elsewhere. Talks begun in February 1941 during the British-American ABC–1 meeting set the stage for a timely invitation from the Icelandic *Althing* (Parliament) for American troops to replace the British. Thus, belligerent Britain proposed to leave the defense of neutral Iceland to the quasi-neutral United States.[10]

---

[7] Summaries of SPOBS Planning, pp. 16–24; Rpt, Chaney to TAG, 17 Dec 41, AG 381 (Great Britain, U.S. troops in UK), OCE ETOUSA Hist Records.

[8] Msg 24, Chaney to TAG, 22 Jan 42, Northern Ireland Const Prog, OCE ETOUSA Hist Records.

[9] On the planning for and occupation of Iceland in 1941, see Stetson Conn, Rose C. Engelman, and Byron Fairchild, *Guarding the United States and Its Outposts*, United States Army in World War II (Washington, 1964), pp. 459–531.

[10] Lt Col William L. Thorkelson, "The Occupation of Iceland During World War II, Including the Post

On 11 June 1941, Colonel Davison and seven officers arrived on the island and by 18 June could report that from an engineering standpoint Iceland had little to offer. Without trees there was no lumber. Practically all supplies had to move through the poorly equipped port of Reykjavik. Ships exceeding 470 feet in length and 21 feet in draft could not moor alongside the two quays that served the harbor. The climate offered a mean winter temperature of 30°F and a summer mean of 52°F, but rainfall of nearly fifty inches a year and midwinter winds of eighty miles per hour made working and living conditions severe. Only volcanic rock, gravel, and sand were abundant on the bleak island. Two airdromes built by the British were usable immediately but required work to conform to American standards and expansion to accommodate heavier American traffic. Added to Reykjavik Field in the city itself and the Kaldadharnes Airdrome, some thirty-five miles southeast of the capital, were other rudimentary fields such as Keflavik, on a windswept point of land twenty-five miles southwest of Reykjavik. A grass field with a runway 1,000 yards long and 50 yards wide, it was suitable for emergency use only. The SPOBS officers believed that another

site sixty miles southeast of the capital, known as the Oddi Airdrome, gave promise of immediate development. Two other fields were too remote even to be visited on the hasty tour: Melgerdhi in the north, 13 1/2 miles from Akureyri, and another emergency field at Hoefn in the southeast.

Voluminous, if spotty, collections of similar data reached Washington from military and naval teams scanning the island's facilities. A Navy party came over from Greenland looking for likely naval air patrol bases, and another Army-Marine Corps party arrived after Colonel Davison's departure. General Chaney sent the SPOBS report to Washington with Lt. Col. George W. Griner, Jr., the SPOBS G–4 who had accompanied Davison. War Department planners compiled the information for the projected occupation of Iceland under the code name INDIGO.[11]

After some changes in planning and a revision in the concept of the operation that committed American troops to the reinforcement and not to the relief of the British 49th Infantry Division on the island, a convoy with the 4,400 officers and enlisted men of the 1st Provisional Brigade (Marines) under Brig. Gen. John Marston, USMC, arrived at Reykjavik on 7 July 1941. Army engineer troops reached that port on 6 August 1941 as part of the first echelon of Task Force 4 (92 officers and

War Economic and Social Effects," M.A. Thesis, Syracuse University, 1949, pp. 16–17, in CMH. Iceland authorities, doubtful about Britain's staying power in the war with Germany, had already approached the American Consul in Iceland in December 1940 with suggestions for including Iceland within the "Monroe Doctrine area." Thurman, The Special Observer Group Prior to the Activation of the European Theater of Operations, p. 49; The Adm and Log Hist of the ETO, vol. I, "The Predecessor Commands," pp. 36–37; Wesley F. Craven and James L. Cate, eds., "The U.S. Army Air Forces in World War II," vol. I, *Plans and Early Operations: January 1939 to August 1942* (Chicago: University of Chicago Press, 1948), pp. 122–23, 342–48.

[11] Thorkelson, "Occupation of Iceland," p. 5; Rpt, Maj Gen James E. Chaney to CofEngrs, HQ, SPOBS, 19 Jun 41, partially quoted in OCE ETOUSA Hist Rpt 17, Engineering in Iceland, Aug 45, app. 2, Liaison Sect, Intel Div, ETOUSA Adm file 547; The Adm and Log Hist of the ETO, vol. I, "The Predecessor Commands," pp. 40–45. An emergency field was eventually built near Oddi. Rpt, Oddi Emergency Strip, Construction and Installation, Aug 42–45; Conn, Engelman, and Fairchild, *Guarding the United States and Its Outposts*, pp. 472–73.

GENERAL BONESTEEL

1,125 enlisted men), the first U.S. Army contingent to reach Iceland. The force consisted of the 33d Pursuit Squadron, which flew in from the U.S.S. *Wasp* offshore; an air base squadron; and a number of special service detachments to contribute to the air defense of Iceland. Engineer elements were two companies of the 21st Engineer Aviation Regiment, soon to be redesignated the 824th Engineer Aviation Battalion. On 16 September 1941, the 2d Battalion, 5th Engineer Combat Regiment, arrived with the second echelon of Task Force 4; the entire American force in Iceland became the Iceland Base Command on the same day. The command, under Maj. Gen. Charles H. Bonesteel, remained directly subordinate to the field force commander in Washington, General George C. Marshall. Because of British strategic responsibility for Iceland, General Chaney continued to argue for the inclusion of the Ameri-

can garrison in Iceland under his control, but his viewpoint did not prevail until the summer of the following year.[12]

During the first days in Iceland, the engineer troops lived in tents previously erected by the Marines, and other units moved into Nissen huts provided by the British. For a few days after the landing of the 2d Battalion, 5th Engineer Combat Regiment, there was considerable confusion. The base engineer, Lt. Col. Clarence N. Iry, who had come with the Marine brigade, reported much equipment broken by careless loading and handling. The material and specialized equipment for an entire refrigerated warehouse were damaged beyond recovery. Navy pressure for quick unloading did not improve matters since there was no covered storage space in Reykjavik waterfront areas and too little dump space elsewhere. In the confusion the property of various units went widely astray; several weeks passed before the engineer battalion located all its belongings and assembled them in one place.[13]

The engineers took up a building, repair, and maintenance program well begun by the British. At first their work supplemented that of the Royal Engineers, and not until late in 1942 did they replace their British counterparts

[12] Rpt, Maj Gen C. H. Bonesteel to AG, WD, 30 Apr 43, sub: Report on Historical Data, Overseas Bases, 314.7 Hist, 1942–43; The Adm and Log Hist of the ETO, vol. I, "The Predecessor Commands," pp. 43–50; Rpt, Base Engr in GHQ, U.S. Army, INDIGO, to the Engr, 1 Sep 41, OCE 381 (INDIGO) Gr Pt; IBC Record of Events, 14 Jul 41–20 Jun 42, p. 16; OCE ETOUSA Hist Rpt 17, Engineering in Iceland, pp. 8–9; Ruppenthal, *Logistical Support of the Armies, Volume I*, p. 19.

[13] Ltr, Lt Col Iry to Col George Mayo, CE, 10 Aug 41, E 381 (INDIGO) 89, WD, OQMG; Rpt, Base Engr in GHQ, U.S. Army, INDIGO, to the Engr, 1 Sep 41; 1st Lt Walter H. Heldt (commanding 21st Engrs [Avn]) to CO, HQ, IBCAF, 314.7 Hist Records, 1941–43.

CONSTRUCTION SUPPLIES AT REYKJAVIK HARBOR, OCTOBER 1941

entirely. But the main construction activities of the war years were already evident: building airdromes, improving communications and supply facilities, and constructing adequate camp and hospital accommodations. The program, originally limited to the more settled part of Iceland in the vicinity of Reykjavik, extended gradually to remote regions along the northern and eastern coasts.

The principal problems of construction lay in the forbidding terrain, high winds, poor communications, and the consequent difficulties of supply. Outside the southwestern corner of the country, the roads—or the lack of them—made long-distance hauling of bulk supplies impossible. Iceland had no railroads. Though most shipments

funneled through Reykjavik and then moved on to these outposts by smaller craft, vessels from the United States occasionally touched at Akureyri, Seydhisfjordhur and Budhareyri, ports that had remained ice free year-round since 1918. Other than the rock, sand, and gravel obtained locally, all engineer supplies came from the United States and Britain. Nissen hutting, coal, and coke were the principal supplies from Britain; the Boston Port of Embarkation handled the remainder of the Iceland garrison's needs including the interior fittings for the huts and any necessary equipment.[14]

---

[14] Rad, Navy Dept to AG, for Gross from Consul Reykjavik, 21 Jul 41, AG 320.2; Unsigned British Rpt to Dir of Movements, War Office, 18 Aug 41, cited in

ENGINEER TROOPS DUMPING FILL AT MEEKS FIELD, KEFLAVIK

For storage and quarters the engineers followed the British example and used Nissen huts that could withstand the wind. Standard warehouse and barracks construction could not stand up to the elements, and even the huts suffered when gales ripped the metal sheeting from the frames. The men banked earth and stone against the sides of the structures to anchor and insulate them and slung sandbags on cables across the arched roofs for stability. Any loose material outside in open storage had to be staked.[15]

During the first weeks after Task Force 4 arrived, the engineers rushed to complete troop housing and covered storage and pushed to extend the docks in Reykjavik harbor. Nearly everywhere they struggled with a subsoil of soggy peat covered with lava rock. As autumn drew on, they moved ahead with expanding airdromes on the island.

By late 1941 American engineers had gradually taken over airfield construction from the British. Reykjavik Field was under development by a force of 2,500 British engineers and Icelandic workmen when the 21st Engineer Aviation Regiment arrived with its heavier construction equipment. The Ameri-

---

Adm 53, IBC Hist; Msg, Chaney to WD, 9 Aug 41, AG 320.2; Msg, Whitcomb [Consul in Reykjavik] to Scowden, G—4, WD. The convoy that carried the first echelon of Task Force 4 to Iceland deposited 11,000 tons of stores at Reykjavik, including vehicles, meats, vegetables, dairy products, coal, and coke.
[15] OCE ETOUSA Hist Rpt 17, Engineering in Ice-

land, app. 8, G—4 Rpt, IBC, and app. 10, Unit Hist, 475th Engr Co.

cans took over the western side of the field, their first responsibility being a foundation for a British prefabricated hangar. In November the British pulled out of all work at the site except for some road work on their side of the airdrome. At the end of the year, the 21st was in full control of the operation and supervised the contracted Icelandic labor on the perimeter roads surrounding the base. The departure of the Royal Engineers in November and December 1941 also brought the 21st to the Kaldadharnes site, and survey parties began laying out what became the largest airfield in Iceland at Keflavik.[16]

The last of the Marine contingent left Iceland in March, and by mid-1942 the Iceland Base Command numbered 35,000 Army officers and enlisted men, with the requirement for engineer support growing steadily. With the 824th Engineer Aviation Battalion—an offshoot of the former 21st Engineer Aviation Regiment—engaged in airfield work, the 5th Engineer Combat Regiment built most of the troop quarters, laundries, kitchens, refrigeration and ice plants, and hospitals for the garrison until the arrival of the 7th Engineer Combat Battalion in May 1942. Work on roads to connect the outposts established by or taken over from the British on the northern and eastern coasts developed in stride with housing

and airdrome construction. *(Map 1)*[17]

The limited stretches of hard-topped roads in the Reykjavik area remained serviceable, but the gravel tracks elsewhere took a constant beating from heavy Army traffic. The 5th Engineer Combat Regiment regraded and metalized surfaces where necessary and applied a top course of red lava rock mixed with a finer crushed grade of the lava, a composite also used for the hardstandings, taxi strips, and service access roads around the airfields.[18]

The 824th Engineer Aviation Battalion still employed hundreds of Icelanders on the perimeter roads and hangar aprons at the Reykjavik Field but gradually centered its efforts on the huge complex at Keflavik. On the wind-swept peninsula, two separate fields—Meeks Field for bombers and Patterson Field for fighter aircraft—took shape, both ready for operation in early 1943. Work here was carried on by the 824th in early 1942 and then taken over by a U.S. Navy contractor. Navy Seabees also arrived to work under Army engineer supervision after the civilian contractor returned to the United States. Beset by high winds that scoured the featureless landscape, the engineers devised expedients in the final phases of runway construction. When the wind churned the powdery top surfaces of newly graded runway beds into dust storms, they laid on liquid asphalt. But with September frosts, the asphalt cooled

[16] Rpt, Base Engr, IBC, to the Engr, GHQ, U.S. Army, Oct 41, OCE (12– 3–41), 381 (INDIGO) 225/2; Rpt, Base Engr, IBC, to the Engr, GHQ, U.S. Army, 6 Dec 41, 381 (INDIGO) 267/1; Lt Col D. A. Morris, Notes on Aviation Engineer Operations in Iceland, July 1941 to October 1942, in USAAF pamphlet, Excerpts From Overseas Letters and Memoranda, 1943, pp. 5–9, Ft. Belvoir, Va., Engr Sch Lib; Capt Reginald J. B. Page (21st Engrs [Avn]) to CO, HQ, IBCAF, Camp Tripoli, Iceland, 314.7 Hist Records, 1941–43.

[17] IBC, ACofS, G–2, Record of Events, 14 Jun 41–30 Jun 42, pp. 12–19, 314.7 Hist, 1942–43; Rpt, Analysis of Engineer Activities in Various Theaters of Operations, Based on Troop Basis, 1 Mar 43, 381 (Gen) 661/1, Doc 77446, Intel files, Ft. Belvoir, Va., Engr Sch Lib.

[18] Base Engr, INDIGO, to CG, SOS, Monthly Progress Rpt for May 42, OCE (7–4–42), 381 (INDIGO) 431.

MAP 1

and coagulated before it could penetrate the lava deeply enough to stabilize it. Later experiments with a porous-
mix base produced a runway rugged
enough to take heavy Navy patrol craft
and Army bombers on the ferry run to
England.[19]

The Iceland Base Command converted Iceland into a great protective
bastion for the convoy routes to Europe.
Engineer-constructed facilities on the
island housed American defense forces
that guaranteed one outpost on the way

to the embattled United Kingdom, which
became the principal focus of American interest in the Atlantic area after
Pearl Harbor.

### Magnet Force

With the United States an active belligerent, on 2 January 1942, the U.S.
Army replaced SPOBS with U.S. Army
Forces, British Isles (USAFBI), a more
formal headquarters that was initially
only SPOBS in uniform. But creation
of the headquarters made the American officers full partners of their opposites on the British staff.

On 5 January 1942, the War Department placed the engineers in charge of
all overseas construction, but it was Feb-

---

[19] Keflavik Project Report, vol. I, Construction, 1943,
pp. 7–10, 600.1; Rpt, Dir, Atlantic Div, BuY&D, to
Chf, BuY&D, 18 Jun 45, Naval Facilities in Iceland;
Morris, Notes on Aviation Engineer Operations in
Iceland, p. 6; Craven and Cate, *Plans and Early Opera-
tions: January 1939 to August 1942*, p. 346.

ruary before Colonel Davison, still in Washington, got Army approval for a USAFBI construction program. Pressures to bolster home defenses and desperate attempts to stop the Japanese in the Pacific were absorbing the energies of Washington officials, and still another month went by before Colonel Davison could obtain facts and figures from the Office of the Chief of Engineers (OCE) concerning labor, materials, and shipping requirements. This was hardly accomplished before the War Department called upon USAFBI to reduce estimated construction to the minimum, despite General Chaney's repeated warnings that more construction, especially housing, would be required than had been planned in December.[20]

ABC–1 and RAINBOW–5 provided for sending an American token force to England, but America's new belligerent status and British needs brought some changes. New plans called for the earliest possible dispatch of 105,000 men (the MAGNET Force) to Northern Ireland. For tactical purposes, the force was to be organized as V Corps, made up of the 1st Armored and the 32d, 34th, and 37th Infantry Divisions, with supply and service troops as well as air units. Of the total, 13,310 were to be engineers. Engineer plans for MAGNET Force gave detailed instructions on landing, administration, depot operations, and supply levels, with heavy reliance on the British for accommodations and supplies. From January to June 1942 engineers in the United Kingdom

concentrated on installng the MAGNET Force in Northern Ireland.[21]

American troops and aircraft went to Northern Ireland to defend Ulster from air raid or invasion, to lift morale in the United States and in the United Kingdom, and to release British troops for action in the threatened areas of the Near East and Africa.[22] But carrying out deployments to Northern Ireland on the scale envisaged in MAGNET Force proved inexpedient because of the initial deployments of shipping to meet the Japanese onslaught in the Pacific. Decisions concerning the size and makeup of the final MAGNET Force changed from time to time during the early part of 1942. On 2 January the War Department set the first contingent at 14,000; a week later the figure was increased to 17,300, but on 12 January it was reduced to 4,100 in order to speed troop movements to the Pacific.[23]

This American strategic uncertainty after Pearl Harbor led to contradictions in events in the British Isles. Though the decision to defeat Germany first remained unquestioned, the implied troop buildup in Britain did not necessarily flow from that decision. Rather, as American leaders attempted to meet the demands of a two-front global war, engineer work in Northern Ireland was determined by the exigencies of the moment and not by a comprehensive

---

[20] WD Ltr, sub: War Department Construction Policy (Theaters of Operation), 5 Jan 42, AG 600.12 (1–3–42) MO–D–M; Cbl, Chaney to TAG, 22 Jan 42, Northern Ireland Const Prog, OCE ETOUSA Hist Records.

[21] Gen Annex 9 (Engr) to Operational Plan, Northern Ireland Theater; Ltr, OCE to Engr, GHQ, 2 Jan 42, sub: Northern Ireland Base Section Supplies, 1004 Engr files, NIBS.
[22] ETO Gen Bd Rpt 128, Logistical Build-up in the British Isles, 1946, p. 47.
[23] Cbl 491, Marshall to Milattache, LDN, 7 Feb 42, Northern Ireland Const Prog.

GENERAL CHANEY, AMBASSADOR JOHN G. WINANT, AND GENERAL HARTLE *inspect American installations in Ulster, Northern Ireland, February 1942.*

construction program supporting a strategic plan.[24]

MAGNET Force started with little notice. An advance party under Col. Edward H. Heavey left New York secretly on 6 January 1942; with it was Lt. Col. Donald B. Adams, the V Corps engineer. The party sailed from Halifax on a Norwegian ship and reached Scotland on the nineteenth. Colonel Adams and the other officers went to London for a week of briefing, and the rest of the party moved on to Belfast. A brigadier of the Royal Engineers guided Adams almost from the day he reached Northern Ireland, acquainting him with British Army methods and with the type of work demanded of him in Northern Ireland.[25]

On 24 January the U.S. Army Northern Ireland Forces formally came into existence. The first troop contingent, under Maj. Gen. Russell P. Hartle of the 34th Infantry Division, arrived on the twenty-sixth. The troop strength of 4,100 set for 12 January was not reached; a USAFBI report of 15 February showed 3,904 troops and 12 civilians in Ulster. By mid-March, after the second increment had arrived, U.S. Army Northern Ireland Forces totaled 11,039 officers and enlisted men. This force included two engineer combat

---

[24] Ltr, Adams to Chaney, 15 May 42, Engr files, NIBS.

[25] Interv with Gen Adams.

battalions and three separate companies of engineers.

The third and fourth increments arrived on 12 and 18 May respectively. The fourth, 10,000 troops aboard the *Queen Mary,* had to go ashore in lighters, for the great vessel was too large for Belfast harbor. Meanwhile, the 32d and 37th Infantry Divisions had been diverted to the Pacific, and at the end of May V Corps consisted of the 34th Infantry Division, the 1st Armored Division, and some corps units. No engineer construction units were in the theater. The final engineer component consisted of a combat regiment, two combat battalions, and four service companies. During May, MAGNET Force reached its peak of 30,000 U.S. Army troops in Northern Ireland, some 70,000 fewer than called for originally.[26]

U.S. Army engineers had to undertake relatively little construction, for nearly all the American troops brought to Northern Ireland moved into camps British units had vacated. British engineer officers made the arrangements and furnished moveable equipment and supplies such as furniture, light bulbs, and coal. Each camp commander appointed an American utility officer to be responsible for camp maintenance and to provide fuel, equipment, and waste disposal service. Arrangements were made to have American soldiers admitted to hospitals serving British and Canadian units.[27]

The Americans depended on the British for additional construction nec-essary to house U.S. troops. In fact, the British did most of the planning as well as the building. The first U.S. Army engineer organizations, which settled in Walworth Camp in County Londonderry on Lough Foyle, did not receive their organic equipment, including vehicles, until weeks after the troops arrived. With the "force mark" system, each unit's equipment was coded before shipment overseas; men and supplies went on different ships, the equipment usually on slower moving vessels. This system plagued almost all engineer units arriving in the United Kingdom during 1942. Yet almost as soon as the first engineer troops landed, the War Department called for a complete construction program for U.S. Army forces scheduled to arrive in Northern Ireland. March was over before Colonel Adams could submit a detailed study, for he had little more than a skeleton engineering staff.[28]

At first, the most essential projects were building and enlarging engineer depots. The V Corps commanders established a new depot at Desertmartin in the southern part of County Londonderry and decided to enlarge an existing depot at Ballyclare in Antrim north of Belfast, adapting it to American use. Once a site was picked, the engineers were to design the depot—type of building construction, layout of buildings and access roads, railroad service, and

[26] Ibid.; ETO Gen Bd Rpt 128, Logistical Build-up in the British Isles, p. 43; Ltr, Adams to Chaney, 15 May 42.

[27] Memo, Bonesteel for G–4, 9 Mar 42, Northern Ireland Const Prog.

[28] Cbl 410, Marshall to USAFBI, 26 Jan 42, Northern Ireland Const Prog; Mtg, British Ministry of Commerce with American Reps, 1942–43, 1009 Sup Cont, MofC, Engr files, NIBS; Rpt, Force Engr, NIF, to OCE, 9 May 42, sub: USANIF Engr Tech Rpt No. 5, Engr files, NIBS; Rpt, Force Engr, NIF, to OCE, 3 Feb 42, sub: Periodic Engr Rpts as of 1 Feb 42; ETO Gen Bd Rpt 128, Logistical Build-up in the British Isles, p. 47.

concrete hardstandings. They undertook little actual construction, however.[29]

Work on enlarging the depot at Ballyclare and force headquarters near Wilmont, south of Belfast, began early in February. After the Ballyclare construction was finished, a company of the 107th Engineer Battalion (Combat) remained there to operate the depot, aided by work and guard details from the 467th Engineer Maintenance Company. From 1 March to 31 August the 112th Engineers (originally a combat battalion and in June enlarged and redesignated a combat regiment) worked at Desertmartin except for three weeks in late March and early April when it furnished troops to make repairs at force headquarters. Such units as the 112th Engineer Combat Regiment, Company A of the 109th Engineer Combat Battalion, the 467th Engineer Shop Company, the 427th Engineer Dump Truck Company, and the 397th Engineer Depot Company chiefly enlarged existing facilities to meet American standards and needs.[30]

By May the supply situation, except for organizational equipment, was comparatively satisfactory. As early as 20 February, engineer items were sixth on the shipping priority list (below post exchange supplies) and using units, upon their arrival from America, requisitioned engineer supplies almost immediately. Day-by-day requirements determined the use of supplies, for the engineers had no experience and no directives to guide them. Yet by May, Colonel Adams could report that engineer supplies were generally adequate. Originally, a system was established to maintain a sixty- to ninety-day level of supplies, taking into account not only those troops already in Northern Ireland, but also those due to arrive within the next sixty days. Some of these supplies came from the United States without requisition, others by specific requisition, still others by requisition of British military supplies, and a certain amount by local purchase. Incoming supplies went to the engineer depots at Desertmartin and Ballyclare, and some equipment went to Moneymore General Depot, a British depository taken over for U.S. Army use in County Londonderry west of Lough Neagh.[31]

Shortages of organizational equipment persisted, in part because of the delays caused by the force mark system; at the end of March organizations in the theater had only 25 percent of their equipment. Five months later, 85 percent was on hand, but by this time Northern Ireland had declined in significance. Some of the equipment was entirely too light for the construction demands made on it.[32]

On the whole, the engineers sent to Northern Ireland had had scanty training in the United States except in basic military subjects, and overseas they had little chance to learn their jobs. The

---

[29] Ltrs, Hartle to COC, BFNI, 29 Jan and 3 Feb 42, 1001 Engr Depot E−510, Engr files, NIBS; Interv with Gen Adams.

[30] Rpt, Force Engr, NIF, to OCE, 17 Feb 42, sub: Interim Report, O&T Br files, OCE; Ibid., 3 Feb 42, sub: Periodic Engr Rpts as of 1 Feb 42; Ltr, Adams to Chaney, 15 May 42; Engr Tech Rpt 9, NIBS to OCE, SOS, 7 Sep 42, Incl 3; Rpt, Engr, NIBS, 26 Nov 42, Engr files, NIBS.

[31] Rpt, Force Engr, NIF, to OCE, 9 May 42, sub: USANIF Engr Tech Rpt No. 5; Interv with Gen Adams; Cbl, Marshall to SPOBS, 20 Feb 42, 3.00 USAFBI Planning, OCE ETOUSA Hist Records; Rpt, Engr, NIBS, 26 Nov 42.

[32] Rpt, Force Engr, NIBS, to G−4, NIF, 3 Apr 42, sub: Monthly Rpt on Engr Equipment and Supplies, 1004 Sup Misc, 1942, Engr files, NIBS.

112th Engineers, a combat battalion redesignated a regiment in August 1942, was constantly engaged in construction and was able to give only 10 percent of its time to training outside of that received on the job. Though valuable, such work did not train the unit for the many other missions of a combat regiment in which it had had no real instruction since September 1941. Thirty percent of the men in one battalion had recently transferred from the infantry, and many of the enlisted men in the unit had never learned any engineer specialties.[33] The men of the 107th Engineer Battalion (Combat) at Ballyclare were supposed to be undergoing training, but they were called on so often to enlarge force headquarters and rehabilitate the Quartermaster Depot at Antrim that little time remained.[34]

Even when time was available, the lack of space hindered training. Agricultural land could not easily be withdrawn from production to provide room for military training. Engineer organizations were unfamiliar with British Army procedures even though after February 1942 Royal Engineer schools were open to American troops. The first attempt to teach British ways was limited, but eventually such instruction became an essential part of U.S. Army engineer training.[35]

On 1 June 1942, the Northern Ireland Base Command (Provisional) was formed to relieve V Corps of supply and administrative problems so that it could, as the highest ground force command in the United Kingdom, devote its full time to tactical preparations. The arrangement was short-lived; the command soon became part of a Services of Supply in the newly formed European Theater of Operations under the more normal designation of a base section. The decisions that led to the formation of the theater presaged the decline in importance of Northern Ireland as a base. By the summer of 1942 the main combat forces in the MAGNET Force (the 1st Armored and 34th Infantry Divisions) had been earmarked for an invasion of North Africa, and U.S. construction in Ulster ceased completely.[36]

Limited though they were in scope, the engineering tasks in Northern Ireland were often difficult to accomplish. The damp, cold weather depressed troops fresh from camps in the southern states, and the men complained about British food. Equally telling were the insufficient, inadequate, and frequently unfamiliar tools. The early period in Northern Ireland was, for the engineers, a time of stumbling forward. Yet worthwhile lessons were learned, especially in planning construction and in establishing a supply system. As valu-

---

[33] The 112th Engineers was formed in August 1942 on a nucleus of one battalion from the 112th Engineers, 37th Division, Ohio National Guard, and another from the 107th Engineers, 32d Division, Wisconsin National Guard. The two battalions had had little or no training for the type of construction required in Northern Ireland.

[34] Ltr, Adams to Chaney, 15 May 42; ETO Gen Bd Rpt 128, Logistical Build-up in the British Isles, p. 47.

[35] Hist 397th Engr Depot Co; Rpt, Force Engr, NIF, to OCE, 17 Feb 42, sub: Interim Report; Interv with Col Anson D. Marston.

[36] On 21 October 1942 there were only 292 U.S. Army engineer personnel left in Northern Ireland. SOS ETOUSA Statistical Summaries XIV, 26 Oct 42, 319.25; Rpt, Engr, NIBS, to OCE, 9 Jul 42, sub: Engr Tech Rpt No. 7, ETOUSA, 600 NI Gen, Engr files, NIBS; ETOUSA GO 17, 17 Jul 42; SOS ETOUSA GO 79, 9 Dec 42; Thore Bengston, Historical Resume of Engineer Activities in the British Isles.

able as anything was the day-by-day cooperation with the British.[37]

### The Bolero Plan

Outside of Northern Ireland, the entire engineer force in the British Isles on 1 April 1942 consisted of Maj. Charles H. Bonesteel III, the officer in charge; a lieutenant detailed from the British Army; and two enlisted men on loan from the American embassy. Colonel Davison was still in the United States. A larger engineer buildup awaited fundamental decisions on strategy that would determine troop and support requirements. In April these decisions came, though they were to be changed again in August.

In mid-April 1942, General George C. Marshall, U.S. Army Chief of Staff, and Harry Hopkins, President Roosevelt's personal representative, on a special mission in London won British approval of an American plan for a cross-Channel invasion in 1943. Under the original code name BOLERO, the operation was to have three phases—a preparatory buildup in the British Isles, a cross-Channel movement and seizure of beachheads, and finally a general advance into German-occupied Europe. The plan also provided for an emergency invasion of Europe in 1942 if the Germans were critically weakened or if a Soviet collapse seemed imminent. By early July the code name BOLERO had come to designate only the buildup or preparatory phase; the emergency operation in 1942 was designated SLEDGEHAMMER, and the full-scale 1943 invasion was designated ROUNDUP.

BOLERO envisaged the development of the United Kingdom as a massive American base for a future invasion and for an immediate air offensive. It changed the dimensions of the American task in the British Isles and shifted emphasis from Northern Ireland to England. Between April and August 1942 it gave the American buildup purpose and direction, but the original BOLERO concept did not last long enough to permit buildup plans to take final form. In the end neither ROUNDUP nor SLEDGEHAMMER proved feasible. In late July a new strategic decision for an invasion of North Africa (TORCH) made any cross-Channel invasion in 1942 or 1943 all but impossible and placed the BOLERO buildup in limbo. The engineer story in England during spring and summer of 1942 is inextricably tied to the changes in direction that resulted from these strategic decisions.[38]

At the very least, the BOLERO plan gave impetus to the development of an American planning and support organization in the British Isles and laid the groundwork for the massive buildup for an invasion in 1943–44. As a first step, combined BOLERO committees were established in Washington and London, the task of the London committee being to "prepare plans and make administrative preparations for the reception, accommodation and maintenance of United States forces in the United Kingdom and for the devel-

---

[37] ETO Gen Bd Rpt 128, Logistical Build-up in the British Isles, pp. 11–12.

[38] For background on ROUNDUP planning, see Gordon A. Harrison, *Cross-Channel Attack*, United States Army in World War II (Washington, 1951), pp. 1–45. A detailed study of strategic plans is in Maurice Matloff and Edwin M. Snell, *Strategic Planning for Coalition Warfare, 1941–1942*, United States Army in World War II (Washington, 1953), pp. 32–62.

opment of the United Kingdom in accordance with the requirements of the 'ROUNDUP' plan." During 1942 the committee produced three separate BOLERO troop bases—referred to as key plans—which provided general guides for the buildup, including U.S. Army engineers. The first BOLERO Key Plan appeared on 31 May 1942; a comprehensive revision based on much more detailed studies followed on 25 July; and a third plan was published in late November reflecting the adjustments required by the TORCH decision.[39]

Each of the plans was based on forecasts of American troops to be sent to the United Kingdom and included estimates of personnel and hospital accommodations, depot storage, and special structures they would require, together with British advice on where the facilities would be found or built. All these plans suffered from the lack of a firm invasion troop basis, a target date, or a specific landing zone, but they did represent tentative bases on which buildup operations could proceed. The original plan brought to London by General Marshall called for thirty U.S. divisions included within a total of about one million men, all to be in the United Kingdom in time for the spring 1943 invasion. The BOLERO Key Plan of 31 May called for 1,049,000 U.S. troops in Britain, but for not nearly so many divisions on account of the need for air and service troops. The second BOLERO Plan of July provided a troop basis of 1,147,000. The third plan in November, reflecting the abandonment of hope for a 1943 invasion, set the short-

term goal for April 1943 at 427,000 men, although it optimistically retained the long-term goal of the first plan— 1,049,000. As 1942 ended, however, in the face of a continuing drain for the operation in North Africa and an acute shipping shortage, neither the long- nor the short-term goal seemed attainable. BOLERO thus proceeded with uncertainty in 1942 and was subject to constant changes.[40]

As the central planning agency in the United Kingdom, the BOLERO Combined Committee in London was concerned with high-level policy only. Subcommittees took care of intergovernmental planning for specific tasks such as troop housing, hospitals, and depots. Various permanent British and American agencies in direct cooperation undertook the day-to-day work, and these agencies set up special machinery that dealt with specific problems. To the U.S. Army engineers, the most important British official at this stage of the war was Maj. Gen. Richard M. Wooten, Deputy Quartermaster General (Liaison) of the War Office. Under his command were two sections: a planning group concerned with receiving and housing troops and another dealing with entertainment and morale.[41]

Most American ground troops were to be stationed in southern England and

[39] DQMG(L) Paper 1, Administrative Planning, etc., for BOLERO and ROUNDUP, 1943, ETO Adm files, BOLERO Misc.

[40] Ruppenthal, *Logistical Support of the Armies, Volume I*, pp. 66, 106; BOLERO Key Plans, BOLERO Publications, ETO Hist Sect, Adm file 50, BOLERO; DQMG(L) Paper 8, 2d ed., Key Plan, 5 Jun 42, BOLERO Publications, OCE ETOUSA Hist Records.

[41] Maj. Gen. C. R. Moore, *Final Report of Chief Engineer European Theater of Operations 1942–1945*, p. 231 (cited hereafter as Moore, *Final Report*); Mtgs, British War Cabinet, BOLERO Combined Committee (London), OCE ETOUSA Hist Records; F. M. Albrecht, "Engineer Aspects of Operation BOLERO," *The Military Engineer*, XLII, no. 286 (March–April 1950), 116.

were assigned positions in that area (the British Southern Command) west of the principal British forces, for the Continental invasion plan provided that the Americans were to be on the right, the British on the left, when they went ashore in France. This meant that thousands of British troops already on the right would have to move east to new areas. Immediately after publication of the first BOLERO Plan, representatives of the two armies met to plan the necessary transfers.[42]

But other problems were not so easily settled. Housing standards included such matters as the size, shape, and equipment of structures, materials to be used, and sewage facilities. These difficulties were the product of two different standards of living; Americans were reluctant to accept many standards that seemed to the British entirely adequate. Another problem concerned airfield specifications and materials. These differences surfaced when the British turned over their own accommodations to American forces and drew up plans for new structures. The British view was understandable, for one of BOLERO's chief aims was to limit new construction and expansion to the barest minimum. Moreover, all the BOLERO installations were to be returned to the British after they had served their purpose for the Americans.

### Creation of the Services of Supply

BOLERO required a large American military organization to handle the proposed massive buildup in the United Kingdom. On 2 May General Chaney cabled the War Department outlining his own ideas on a Services of Supply (SOS) to be organized for this purpose and requested personnel to man it. He indicated that General Davison was his choice as SOS commander. To head a construction division under Davison, he suggested Col. Thomas B. Larkin or Col. Stanley L. Scott, and his choice for Davison's successor as chief engineer was Col. William F. Tompkins. But the War Department had its own ideas. General Marshall had already chosen another engineer officer, Maj. Gen. John C. H. Lee, to head the theater SOS, and by 5 May Lee was busily engaged in recruiting an SOS staff in Washington. On 14 May Marshall sent a directive to Chaney stipulating that the organization of the theater SOS was to parallel that of the SOS recently formed under Lt. Gen. Brehon B. Somervell in the United States and was to be given far broader powers than Chaney proposed. The theater headquarters was to retain "a minimum of supply and administrative services" under the SOS.[43]

General Lee, a strong-minded, even controversial man, entered the theater on 24 May like a whirlwind, determined to carry out the Marshall directive. His approach provoked spirited resistance among General Chaney's staff, most of whom believed that the theater chiefs of technical services could function properly only if they were directly under the theater commander. Chaney had already established an SOS com-

---

[42] Memo, HQ, USAFBI, for CofS, USAFBI, 11 Jun 42, sub: Conf with HQ, Southern Command, 10 Jun 42. Other meetings of DQMG(L) and U.S. Army representatives took place on 2, 4, and 24 July 1942. See Ltr, HQ, Southern Command, sub: Operational Control of U.S. Forces, Adm file 50, BOLERO, ETOUSA Hist Sect.

[43] Ltr, Marshall to CG, USAFBI, 14 May 42, OCE ETOUSA Hist Records.

GENERAL LEE

mand in anticipation of General Lee's arrival. The two officers appeared to have reached agreement on the command during transatlantic telephone conversations in which General Davison took part as well. But after Lee began operations in London on 24 May, it developed that his conception of the scope of his command far exceeded what General Chaney had vaguely staked out for him. As dynamic an organizer as he was a forceful personality, General Lee eventually acquired a special train, which he called "Alive," to enable him to make quick trips to solve knotty problems and to hold command-level conferences in complete privacy.[44]

For all his determination and dynamism, General Lee was not to have his way entirely. On 8 June 1942, the War Department formally established the European Theater of Operations, U.S. Army (ETOUSA), to succeed the USAFBI command. General Chaney retained command temporarily but on 24 June was succeeded by Maj. Gen. Dwight D. Eisenhower, also General Marshall's personal choice. Before Eisenhower's arrival Chaney had already tried to resolve the jurisdiction of the SOS by a compromise arrangement reflected in ETOUSA Circular 2 of 13 June 1942. Eleven of eighteen theater special staff sections, including all the technical services, were placed under the SOS commander, but he was to carry out his functions "under directives issued

---

[44] USAFBI GO 17, 24 May 42; ETO Adm File 16, Alive-Special Train.

by the theater commander," and there were other clauses to assure that the theater command retained control of theater-wide functions. The theater staff sections under the SOS were to maintain liaison offices at theater headquarters. The broad grant of authority to General Lee was thus diluted by the dual nature of the relationship of his technical service chiefs to the SOS and to the theater command. The result was a division of supply and administrative functions between the SOS and Headquarters, ETOUSA.

On assuming command, General Eisenhower made only small changes in the arrangement. ETOUSA General Order 19 of 20 July 1942 actually reduced the number of staff sections directly under SOS control, probably the result of the removal of SOS headquarters from London to Cheltenham, physically separating it from ETOUSA headquarters. The engineers, as well as the other technical services, remained under the SOS with their headquarters, in effect, divided between London and Cheltenham. It was, in the words of the theater's logistical historian, "a compromise solution which . . . resulted in the creation of overlapping agencies and much duplication of effort." If Eisenhower had an impulse to change the arrangement, he was soon absorbed in planning for TORCH, an operation of which he was to be Allied commander, and General Order 19 was to govern SOS-ETOUSA relationships for another year.[45]

*The Engineer Pyramid*

Within this framework, the Engineer Service in the ETOUSA finally took shape. When General Lee first began assembling his SOS staff in the United States, he asked General Davison to be his chief engineer. The office Davison was to head really had had its start earlier. In March 1942, while Davison was still in the United States, eight engineer officers and twenty-one enlisted men sailed for Britain to add some flesh to the skeleton force then under Major Bonesteel. Additional personnel came with General Davison when he returned to England in April, and others soon followed. In early June their distribution was uncertain; no one knew how many engineers were to make up the total force in the chief's office, nor, indeed, whether there was to be one chief engineer.[46]

Officially, the Engineer Service, SOS, ETOUSA, came into existence on 1 July 1942. The various divisions were set up the next day: Supply, Administration and Personnel, Construction, Quartering, Intelligence, and Operations and Training. (*Chart 1*) General Davison's tenure as head of the service ended late in July when General Lee, carrying out a plan to decentralize his command, organized base sections in the United Kingdom and made Davison commanding officer of Western Base Section. Brig. Gen. Thomas B. Larkin (promoted 23 May 1942) then became chief engineer, but was called away in September to plan for TORCH and then to command the SOS to be established in North Africa. Larkin was titular chief

---

[45] Ruppenthal, *Logistical Support of the Armies, Volume I*, p. 44. The account of the evolution of the ETOUSA command structure is drawn from pp. 32–44.

[46] Bengsten, Hist Resume; Lee Diary, entries 7 and 8 May 42, Adm files 102, ETOUSA Hist Sect.

CHART 1—OFFICE OF THE CHIEF ENGINEER, ETOUSA, 1 JULY 1942

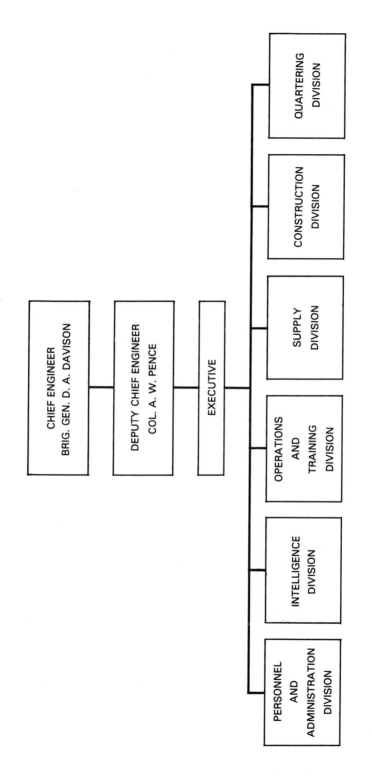

CHIEF ENGINEER
BRIG. GEN. D. A. DAVISON

DEPUTY CHIEF ENGINEER
COL. A. W. PENCE

EXECUTIVE

PERSONNEL AND ADMINISTRATION DIVISION

INTELLIGENCE DIVISION

OPERATIONS AND TRAINING DIVISION

SUPPLY DIVISION

CONSTRUCTION DIVISION

QUARTERING DIVISION

As of 1 July 1942

engineer until 2 November, but, in fact, he was replaced on 15 September by Col. (later Maj. Gen.) Cecil R. Moore as acting chief engineer, ETOUSA. With the landings in North Africa, Moore became chief engineer, ETOUSA, on 9 November, and was named to the same job for SOS on 23 November 1942.[47]

Colonel Moore, widely known as "Dinty," served as chief engineer until the end of the war in Europe. Born 3 July 1894, Moore entered the Army from Virginia Polytechnic Institute in 1917 and served overseas in World War I. The period between the two wars found him active on various dam projects, primarily in the Pacific Northwest where, for a time, he served as the Portland district engineer under General Lee, then chief of the North Pacific Engineer Division. In 1940 he was in charge of the building of camps, depots, and hospitals in the Pacific Northwest, and he left this task to go to the European theater. Arriving in the United Kingdom in July 1942, for some time he did double duty in OCE and as commander of Eastern Base Section.[48]

During its hectic first months, the Engineer Service, SOS, ETOUSA, was plagued by these rapid changes in leadership, uncertainties about its functions, division of its staff between London and Cheltenham, and continuous personnel shortages. When General Davison took over, he found that an SOS directive placed the engineers, along with the other technical services, under the supervision of G–4, SOS, and that the Requirements Branch of G–4 had responsibility to "prepare policies, plans and directives for the formulation and execution of supply and construction projects in terms of type, quantities, and time schedules." This function, as far as construction was concerned, seemed to belong rightfully to the chief engineer; but only in December was it officially transferred, although the engineers had long before assumed it in practice.[49]

The move of SOS to Cheltenham, a famous watering spot in the Gloucestershire countryside some ninety miles west of London, accentuated the difficulties of coordination between theater and SOS engineer sections. The chief engineer and his division chiefs were perforce commuters between Cheltenham and London in their efforts to coordinate work between the two complementary but often overlapping engineer sections. Maintaining two staffs worsened the manpower shortages of the engineer force in the United Kingdom, a force that did not have all its authorized officers until 15 May 1943 and enlisted men until mid-September.[50]

The shortages affected the progress of all the engineer command's work. Besides construction, for which American engineers relied so heavily upon the British, the SOS command as of 13 June 1942 was responsible for railroad operations, quartering and utilities, and

[47] ETOUSA GO 19, 20 Jul 42; SOS ETOUSA GO 1, 20 Jul 42; SOS ETOUSA Cirs, 1, 1 Jul 42; 2, 2 Jul 42; and 3, 20 Jul 42; OCE ETOUSA Hist Rpt 1, Organization, Administration, and Personnel (United Kingdom), 1946, p. 6, Liaison Sect, Intel Div, ETOUSA Adm file 547.

[48] Moore, *Final Report*, p. 13.

[49] SOS, Initial Directive for the Organization of the SOS, ETO, 23 Jun 42, and SOS Cir 63, 14 Dec 42; both in Compilation of Directives Relating to Engineer Services, OCE ETOUSA Hist Records. Comments by Brig Gen F. M. Albrecht.

[50] OCE ETOUSA Hist Rpt 1, Organization, Administration, and Personnel, p. 23. For more details, see ch. III.

for all the boats and landing craft scheduled to arrive with incoming amphibian engineer units. In August the new Transportation Corps (TC) took over the railroads, but the engineers still had too few men to procure fire-fighting equipment for the transportation service, acquire cranes, lumber, and real estate, and build fuel pumping installations. Col. Arthur W. Pence, who had arrived with General Lee to be the deputy chief engineer of SOS ETOUSA found the personnel situation highly confused. He could only commiserate for the moment with General Davison that the twenty officers available for the Office of the Chief Engineer in the Services of Supply command were not enough to do the job.[51]

Despite personnel and organizational problems during 1942 the engineer parts were gradually building into a working machine, as the development of the "static force," or regional organization, demonstrated. The need for district organization such as existed in the United States was appreciated by engineer officers—Colonel Pence, for example—even before General Lee had decided to set up such a system. On 9 June General Lee asked the War Department for personnel to make up twelve engineer district offices, and the engineers began to establish such an organization on 3 July. This engineer machinery was absorbed on 20 July by

GENERAL LARKIN

General Lee's reorganization of the entire SOS. He established four base sections, roughly paralleling a British military division of the United Kingdom. (*Map 2*) These jurisdictions—the Northern Ireland, Eastern, Western, and Southern Base Sections—were divided into districts which, in turn, were divided into areas. Each organization, from the base section down, had its own engineer.[52]

General Lee's aim was to employ the base sections and their subdivisions as instruments of the parent SOS to secure centralized control and decentralized operation of the whole field organization. The base sections became the

---

[51] ETOUSA Cir 2, 13 Jun 42; SOS ETOUSA Initial Directive for the Organization of SOS, ETO; OCE ETOUSA Cir 1, 1 Jul 42, sub: Responsibility of the Construction and Real Estate Activities; SOS ETOUSA Procurement Directive 5, 17 Jul 42; 8, 19 Aug 42; 11, 18 Sep 42; and 14, 2 Nov 42; OCE ETOUSA Cir 22 (O&T), 16 Sep 42; SOS ETOUSA Cir 13, 19 Aug 42; Ltr, Pence to Col J. S. Gorlinski, OCE, Wash D.C., 4 Jun 42; all in OCE ETOUSA Hist Records.

[52] ETOUSA GO 19, 20 Jul 42; SOS ETOUSA Cirs 1, 1 Jul 42; 2, 2 Jul 42; and 3, 20 Jul 42; SOS GO 10, 20 Jul 42; Ltr, Pence to Gorlinski, 4 Jun 42; OCE ETOUSA Hist Rpt 1, Organization, Administration, and Personnel, p. 4.

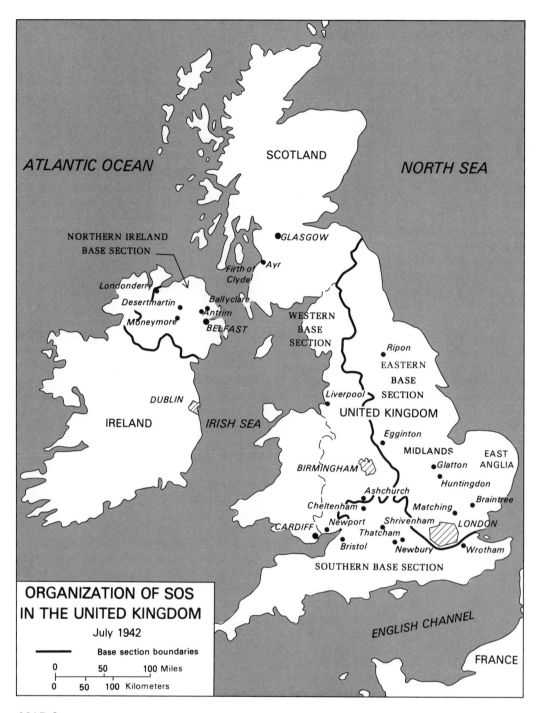

ATLANTIC OCEAN

NORTH SEA

SCOTLAND

NORTHERN IRELAND
BASE SECTION

•GLASGOW

Firth of
Clyde

•Ayr

Londonderry•

Desertmartin•
•Ballyclare

•Antrim
Moneymore•

BELFAST

WESTERN
BASE
SECTION

•Ripon

EASTERN
BASE
SECTION

DUBLIN

•Liverpool

UNITED KINGDOM

IRELAND

IRISH SEA

•Egginton

MIDLANDS

EAST
ANGLIA

BIRMINGHAM

•Glatton

•Huntingdon

•Ashchurch

Cheltenham•

•Matching

•Braintree

CARDIFF

•Newport

Shrivenham

LONDON

Thatcham•

Bristol•

•Newbury

•Wrotham

SOUTHERN BASE SECTION

ENGLISH CHANNEL

FRANCE

ORGANIZATION OF SOS
IN THE UNITED KINGDOM

July 1942

Base section boundaries

0        50        100 Miles

0     50    100 Kilometers

*MAP 2*

offices of record, while the districts were primarily offices of supervision. The base section, district, and area staffs were known as the static force, and each worked in close liaison with its local counterpart in the British Army. Two of the four base section commanders first appointed by General Lee—General Davison and Colonel Moore—were engineers.[53]

The base section engineer was not only a member of the base section commander's special staff but was also the representative with the base section of the chief engineer, SOS. This created a difficult problem: the division of authority between the chief engineer and the base section commander. When the field system came into being, "technical control" was reserved to the chief of each service, but the concept was so vague that it satisfied no one. For months, the matter troubled the entire SOS organization, and it was never completely settled. In August Headquarters, SOS, attempted to clarify the situation for the engineers. New construction and base repair shops were removed from the base section commanders' jurisdiction, and Colonel Moore, chief engineer, obtained authority to deal directly with his representatives in the base sections on these matters. Nevertheless, the engineers were told to keep the base section commanders informed concerning progress. Although on paper Colonel Moore had direct authority over new construction, in practice both he and the base section commanders expected the base section engineers to assume responsibility; leav-

ing a large measure of authority to these subordinate officers made it possible to avoid controversy.[54]

### Roundup Planning

In addition to organizing a base in the United Kingdom for an Allied invasion of the Continent, it was necessary to plan for the operation itself. A ROUNDUP Administrative Planning Staff was set up for joint planning, holding its first meeting on 29 May 1942. Of the forty original sections, several were of special concern to the engineers: port salvage and repair, development of communication lines, shops and utilities, water supply, bridging, and construction and maintenance of airfields. A U.S. Joint Staff Planners decision on the jurisdiction over landing craft also made the engineers in the theater responsible for training boat crews for amphibious operations in Europe.[55]

As deputy chief engineer at Headquarters, ETOUSA, Col. Elmer E. Barnes headed the engineer planners for ROUNDUP; it was July before he obtained even a limited number of officers for his staff. While chiefly concerned with ROUNDUP planning, Barnes' organization also maintained contact with the British on all engineer matters, prepared studies on construction requirements for the Construction Division of OCE, SOS, and maintained

---

[53] Memo, Harwood for Moore, 30 Jul 42, Min of Mtgs 1942, USFET, Engr Sect; SOS ETOUSA Cir 3, 20 Jul 42.

[54] Comments by Gen Moore on MS, Engineer Operations in Europe and Africa; SOS GO 10, 20 Jul 42; SOS ETOUSA Cirs 3, 20 Jul 42, and 12, 17 Aug 42.

[55] Incl, Appreciation of ROUNDUP, Adm Plng Situation, 4 May 43, w/ Memo, OCE for Port, Gen Const, Communications, Utilities & POL Sections of the Plng Br, Const and Quartering Div, 20 May 43, OCE ETOUSA Hist Records; Mins, U.S. Joint Staff Planners, 20 Apr 42, ABC 334, JSP Min, sec. 1 (2–13–42).

liaison with the Operations and Training and Supply Divisions of OCE, SOS. Finally, Barnes' office coordinated engineer activities with other arms and services represented at ETOUSA headquarters in London.[56]

Colonel Barnes and his subordinates faced a chronic shortage of officers and the lack of a basic operational plan for ROUNDUP in 1942. The engineer section at Headquarters, ETOUSA, unavoidably lost time and wasted effort because everything had to be referred for approval to OCE, SOS, at Cheltenham. For example, the officer dealing with expected construction requirements on the Continent after the invasion would have to send his plan and estimates to Cheltenham for approval and suggestions, wait for the revision, and then return his second draft for final approval.[57]

When TORCH preparations went into full swing, ROUNDUP planning was virtually shelved, to be taken up again as circumstances permitted. Key personnel were assigned to the North African invasion, and a Pentagon directive of 18 November that prohibited stockpiling of supplies and equipment for ROUNDUP beyond that required for the 427,000-man force further handicapped Barnes. The British, who insisted on going on with their ROUNDUP planning, wanted to continue stockpiling standardized supplies to be used by British and American forces. In one case they tried to obtain a particular item of petroleum, oil, and lubricants (POL) equipment from the United States, but because of the new American policy they had to continue manufacturing and using their own product.[58]

G–4, ETOUSA, continued a semblance of planning by requiring from each of the services a maintenance program for a theoretical Continental operation. The engineers also prepared their part of an invasion plan, an exercise that eventually proved its value in helping to determine the necessary engineer nonstandard heavy construction—Class IV—supplies and the adequacy of the engineer troop basis.[59]

As important as any aspect of this work was the experience gained in working with the British. Estimating requirements, for example, led to the establishment of a joint stockpile which cut down duplication and made supply facilities more flexible. The tremendous tonnages involved and the long periods required for production made the importance of the joint stockpile apparent. Close liaison also promoted standardization of equipment. For example, the U.S. Army in December 1942 requisitioned from the British ROUNDUP stocks 20,000 standard 16-foot-wide

---

[56] History of the Engineer Service, p. 6, ETO Adm file 547, Engrs; Chron. of Events (OCE ETOUSA); Memo, Barnes for Moore, 10 Jul 42, Orgn for ETO Engr Sect, OCE ETOUSA Hist Records; Rpt, OCE ETOUSA CG to ETOUSA, 8 Aug 42, 319.1 OCE Rpts to CG, EUCOM Engr files; OCE ETOUSA Hist Rpt 1, Organization, Administration, and Personnel, app. 25; Memo, Harwood for Barnes, 15 Sep 42, 316 Office Methods, EUCOM Engr files.

[57] Memo, Barnes for Moore, 10 Jul 42; Incl, Appreciation of ROUNDUP w/Memo; Memo, Lord for Moore, 2 Nov 42, SOS and OCE Organization, OCE ETOUSA Hist Records.

[58] Ltr, Lee to Somervell, 17 Nov 42, ETO 381 ROUNDUP, Jul–Nov 42; Weekly Rpt, London Repr, OCE, 12 Oct and 7 Dec 42, 319.1 Engr Sect, ETO London Repr Rpts, OCE ETOUSA Hist Records.

[59] Ltr, 18 Dec 42, sub: Engr Operational Plans in Connection with G–4 Directing for ROUNDUP Planning, Engr Sect, ETOUSA; Incl, Appreciation of ROUNDUP w/Memo; Rpt, A Total Tonnage Schedule for the Nov 42 G–4 Problem, etc., Amphibious Sect, Engr Sect, ETO, ROUNDUP, OCE ETOUSA.

Nissen huts, 6 million square feet of 24-foot-wide Nissen hutting, 2,000 Bailey bridges, 25 million sandbags, large quantities of barbed wire, and other supplies. These requisitions were "on paper" for future delivery and represented a part of planning for the actual invasion. In road and general construction, where the problems were more or less peculiar to each force, joint action extended only to the standardization of materials. In addition to its other benefits, standardization in any form tends to reduce costs. The good relations established at planning meetings were of incalculable importance for the future.[60]

In connection with POL distribution, port reconstruction, and beach and port operations, the engineers in the various ROUNDUP administrative planning sections in 1942 accomplished worthwhile planning. Less was achieved in regard to water supply and amphibious operations, little on bridging problems, and almost nothing on airfield construction and maintenance.[61]

When OCE, ETOUSA, conducted a drastic self-examination in the fall and winter of 1942, it discovered that SOS personnel concerned themselves too much with matters in which they should not have been involved beyond coordinating details after receiving broad operational plans from London. The ETOUSA section was further embarrassed by difficulty in securing well-qualified personnel, probably because current needs, especially for construction, seemed much more important than rather indefinite planning for ROUNDUP. These were not the criticisms of Barnes alone, but also of other important officials at SOS headquarters.[62]

In the meantime, through the last few months of 1942, Colonel Barnes' group broadened its field, not only in planning for the future, but also in presenting the SOS and ETOUSA engineer view on any new procedures adopted in the theater. Finally, in November, Col. Royal B. Lord, then chief of the Operations and Training Division, declared that "the time has arrived to put *all* planning under Colonel Barnes."[63]

Near the end of 1942, most officers in OCE could agree that the rather artificial separation of ETOUSA and SOS headquarters impeded efficient operations.[64] Yet despite the problem of the drain that TORCH imposed on engineer personnel and resources in the United Kingdom, by the end of the year very real progress had been made in building an organization that would play an important role in preparing for the cross-Channel invasion in 1943 and 1944. Although many problems were left unsolved, the machinery for the buildup to come was put together in

---

[60] Mtgs, BOLERO Combined Committee (London); Moore, *Final Report*, p. 38; Daily Jnl, entry 12 Dec 42, Supply Div, OCE ETOUSA, EUCOM Engr files.
[61] Rpt, Engr Sect, ETOUSA, 22 Nov 42, sub: Summary of POL Activities (1 Jul–15 Nov 42), and Folder, Total Tonnage Schedule for Nov 42 Problem ROUNDUP, both in OCE ETOUSA Hist Records, Appreciation of ROUNDUP.

[62] O&T Informal Memo, 23 Oct 42, on relations between ETO and SOS, file Organization Oct–Dec 42, OCE ETOUSA Hist Records; Memo, Milwit for Harwood, 5 Nov 42, SOS and OCE Organization, OCE ETOUSA Hist Records; Memo, Moore for Reybold, 30 Nov 42, sub: Engr Problems in ETO, 381 War Plans (Jun 42–Jul 43), EUCOM Engr files.
[63] Memo, Barnes for Moore, 12 Oct 42, 319.1 ETO (weekly), Jul 42–Apr 43, EUCOM Engr files; Memo, Lord for Moore, 2 Nov 42.
[64] Memo, Col Harwood for Div Chfs, OCE, 12 Nov 42, w/replies and related material in file Organization Oct–Dec 42, OCE ETOUSA Hist Records.

the spring and summer of 1942. Repeated changes in SOS and engineer troop allotments upset planning, but the organization, hurriedly assembled in a strange land under the stress of war, worked reasonably well in carrying out a quartering and construction program across the British Isles.

# CHAPTER III

# The Engineer Machine in Motion in the United Kingdom, 1942

The engineer force in the United Kingdom spent the months following the formal organization of the theater command struggling to fulfill its obligations under the BOLERO Plan, which was beset by problems of organization and direction, supply, personnel, methodology, weather, and geography. Efficient management was difficult if not impossible given uncertain goals, insufficient personnel, and a bifurcate theater structure. The TORCH decision disrupted the BOLERO program before it could build up any momentum and scattered the engineer effort. Nevertheless, an important beginning was made in 1942 in creating a base in England for an eventual cross-Channel invasion, and the engineer effort was no small part of that accomplishment.[1]

## Personnel

Engineers formed part of the ground

and air force troop bases as well as that of the Services of Supply, but the service force engineers were supposed to do most of the static force construction work. Service engineers in the force sent to Northern Ireland had been outnumbered by combat engineers, who consequently had to do construction work for which they had not been trained. In an effort to avoid such a situation in the whole United Kingdom buildup, the Office of the Chief of Engineers (OCE) in Washington asked the War Department to provide 16,000 men immediately for twelve general service regiments and ten dump truck companies. They were to be sent overseas with a minimum of basic military training. Late in March General Chaney asked for three general service regiments and for a like number of engineer aviation battalions to assist the British in building those airfields to be turned over to the American air force. Early in May 1942 the Office of the Chief of Engineers (OCE), USAFBI, made its first formal requisition for ten general service regiments (13,000 men) and ten engineer aviation battalions (7,000 men) to arrive in the theater between June and October. Not counting aviation battalions, USAFBI then expected there would be some 40,330

---

[1] Unless otherwise indicated this chapter is based on Min of Mtgs, Jun–Dec 42, USFET Engr 337; Rpts, 1942–44, EUCOM Engr file 319.1; and related documents in the following EUCOM Engr files: 321 Engrs, 381 Supply 1942–43, 381 BOLERO, 381 War Plans, 400 Maintenance, 475 Engr Equipment, and Daily Jnl (Supply and Adm Services), Jun 42–Jul 43. Other sources used throughout, but not always separately cited, are Moore, *Final Report*, and Ruppenthal, *Logistical Support of the Armies, Volume I*.

U.S. Army engineers in Britain at the time of the Continental invasion. Of these, the two largest groups would be combat units (11,394 men) and general service units (17,626 men).[2]

These calculations were soon outdated by those surrounding the formal inception of the BOLERO program. The first tentative BOLERO troop basis drawn up in Washington in early May contemplated a force of 1,042,000 for ROUNDUP, about 25 percent service troops. Later in May the War Department prescribed priorities for shipment—first air units, then essential SOS units, then ground forces, followed by additional service units to prepare for more ground force troops. Within these general lines, the theater was expected to prescribe priorities for particular types of units. The scheme was logical enough, but it broke down in practice in the face of shipping shortages, lack of trained service troops, and finally the midsummer shift in strategy.

Early in June 1942 (coincident with the first BOLERO Key Plan) the War Department submitted to ETOUSA a more detailed breakdown of a troop basis that totaled 1,071,060 men. The War Department allotted just over 104,000 engineers to the theater: 31,648 in a total of 279,145 troops for the Services of Supply; 54,380 in a ground force troop strength of 585,565; and 18,909 aviation engineers in an Air Forces strength of 206,400. General Davison argued for increases in all categories to raise the total engi-

neer troop strength to about 147,000, but he received no concessions. Indeed, on the premise that the command could use quartermaster units for many jobs, the SOS allocation was reduced to 29,500.[3]

The Operations and Training Division of the Office of the Chief of Engineers (OCE), ETOUSA, had made Davison's estimates, using the capabilities of engineer units against the tasks to be performed. For example, depot troop requirements were calculated from the number of depots and the tonnage to be handled, and maintenance companies from the number of pieces of equipment to be kept in condition. But calculations depended on the troop basis figure, which constantly changed. Not until the fall of 1943 could a definite ETO troop basis be evolved for either SOS or combat engineers. Furthermore, the value of these tentative troop bases was questionable because the number of trained engineer troops to support the forces involved was so limited. Planning for aviation engineer units was originally based on one air force, the Eighth, which included interceptor, bomber, fighter, and service commands. After TORCH, a decision came to have two air forces, strategic and tactical. The Air Forces estimated the number of engineer aviation battalions required, although the chief engineer concurred in the proposed total.[4]

---

[2] Memo, O&T Br, Trp Dir, OCE, for CofEngrs, 11 Mar 42; Ltr, CG, USAFBI, 2 Apr 42; Memo, O&T Div for CofS, USAFBI, 5 May 42; and BOLERO Movement Schedule, 9 May 42; all in OCE ETOUSA Hist Records.

[3] Memo, Davison for Baker, 25 Jun 42; Memo, Davison for Pence, 1 Jul 42; and Memo, SOS, ETOUSA, 14 Jul 42, sub: Troop Requirements; all in 321 Engrs, 1942 (Jun–Sep), EUCOM Engr files.

[4] Moore, *Final Report*, pp. 42–45; OCE ETOUSA Hist Rpt 4, Troops (United Kingdom), 1946, p. 17, Liaison Sect, Intel Div, ETOUSA Adm file 547; Albrecht, "Engineer Aspects of Operation BOLERO," pp. 119–20.

The problem of the shifting troop basis was compounded by that of finding units to fulfill the plan of the moment. Before Pearl Harbor the U.S. Army had few trained service units, and after that day the great cry was for combat forces. The War Department was slow to recognize the need for service forces and to start their training.[5] At a May SOS conference in Washington Colonel Larkin said that a half-trained man in the theater was better than no man at all. Accepting this philosophy, the War Department authorized the early shipment of 10,000 service troops to the ETO, many of whom were indeed half trained.

Already plagued by the lack of trained units and an acute shipping shortage, the whole BOLERO schedule was thrown off by TORCH. In August word came from the War Department that no more SOS engineers were to be stationed in the United Kingdom, while many of the units there were alerted for movement to North Africa. In September a new tentative troop basis was published by G–4, ETO, based on the adjustment for TORCH and the 427,000-man force reflected in the third BOLERO Plan. In this plan engineers were to provide 45,000 men or 10.5 percent of the total force—16,600 in an SOS force of 106,000; 6,000 in a ground force of 159,000; and 23,000 aviation engineers in an Air Forces strength of 157,000.

The actualities were somewhat different. On 1 July 1942, of 58,845 Americans in the ETO, then chiefly in Northern Ireland, only 2,150 were engineers. By November the ETO total was 255,155 and the number of engineers had risen to more than 40,000, but 18,554 of them had left England for North Africa by January 1943. The 21,858 left represented 20 percent of the remaining ETOUSA command, a percentage in line with General Lee's policy to deploy engineers to the United Kingdom early to prepare the way for air and ground forces. But the actual number of engineers was still well below the 45,000 authorized to be there in the next two months and was insufficient to perform tasks under the 427,000-man plan, much less the long-range plan for a million-man force. Moreover, organizing new units such as pipeline companies and separate water supply companies for TORCH, as well as transfers to fill units alerted for North Africa, left the remaining engineer units in the United Kingdom with a shortage of 3,000 men.[6]

The problems of requisitioning engineers and of supervising assignment and promotion in the Office of the Chief of Engineers (OCE), SOS, were the concern of the Personnel and Administration Division, OCE, organized in July 1942. The division's first chief

---

[5] On the overall problem of service troops in the troop basis in 1942, see Richard M. Leighton and Robert W. Coakley, *Global Logistics and Strategy, 1940–43* (Washington, 1956), pp. 346–52, and Kent Roberts Greenfield, Robert R. Palmer, and Bell I. Wiley, *The Organization of Ground Combat Troops* (Washington, 1947), pp. 159–260; both in the United States Army in World War II series.

[6] Folder, Engr Serv in UK; OCE ETOUSA Hist Rpt 4, Troops, app. 2; SOS ETOUSA Statistical Summary XII, 12 Oct; XIV, 26 Oct; and XV, 2 Nov; Statistical Summaries, 319.25, EUCOM Engr files; ETO Gen Bd Rpt 128, Logistical Build-up in the British Isles, p. 47; RG 741, Gen Bd 401/13, Logistical Buildup in the UK, EUCOM Engr files; Ltr, OCE, SOS ETOUSA, to SOS ETOUSA, 19 Dec 42, sub: New Engineer Troop Basis, 320.3, EUCOM Engr files; Memo, Moore for Reybold, 30 Nov 42, sub: Engr Problems in ETO.

was Maj. J. M. Franey, soon succeeded by Maj. Beryl C. Brooks. The division initially edited the consolidated personnel requisitions which engineer units submitted and then transmitted them to G–1, SOS, whence they went to G–1, ETOUSA, and finally to the War Department. This procedure proved cumbersome and slow, and OCE, SOS, ordered engineer units to submit monthly requisitions directly to G–1, SOS, with OCE assisting in a staff capacity to process the requisitions through G–1.[7]

The division had difficulty in obtaining authorized personnel. Requisitioning officers and enlisted men by name took too long. Early in 1942 many officers assigned to OCE and to base sections came from a reserve pool; many others were former engineer division and district officers from the Zone of the Interior (ZI). The 342d, 332d, and 341st Engineer General Service Regiments, among the earliest engineer units dispatched to Britain, were filled with men experienced in civilian construction work, obtained under special OCE recruiting authority.[8]

In July 1942 General Larkin had complained of a lack of military experience among engineer officers, and in October Colonel Moore found that 84 of 271 officers in the base sections and in OCE, ETOUSA, had no previous military experience. Among the remaining 187 officers, 170 were from the National Guard or the Officers Reserve Corps with little active military experience. Of seventeen Regular Army officers, four were quite young and six were tapped for the impending TORCH operation. Only seven experienced officers remained to handle the eleven important jobs of chief engineer, chief engineer's deputy, executive, division chiefs, supervisor of engineer schools, and three base section engineer posts. SOS engineer units averaged one regular or former regular per regiment, and sometimes he was of junior grade. Most of the remaining officers were commissioned in the Army of the United States (AUS).[9]

Aviation engineer units lacked skilled construction personnel. The total construction experience among thirty-two officers of one aviation battalion added up to two years, while few battalions had an experienced unit engineering officer. Conditions were no better in the lower ranks, and inexperienced officers had to do much of the work of even more inexperienced noncommissioned officers. To remedy the situation Colonel Moore recommended that the post of engineering officer in an engineer aviation battalion be raised

---

[7] OCE ETOUSA Hist Rpt 1, Organization, Administration, and Personnel, pp. 5, 17, 21–23 and app. 2; Memo, OCE, SOS ETOUSA (Personnel and Adm Div), for Col Harwood, 14 Nov 42, Organization, Oct–Dec 42; OCE, SOS ETOUSA, Cir 2, 2 Jul 42, Orgn Charts, ETOUSA SOS Commands.

[8] Ltr, Col Harwood to Col William W. Bessell, Jr., OCE, WD, 321.02 Engr Officers (27 Jul–31 Oct 42), EUCOM Engr files; Interv, Dr. John S. G. Shotwell with Col William W. Bessell, Jr., 9 Sep 50.

[9] Ltr, Larkin to OCE, WD, 30 Jul 42, sub: Engr Supplies, Equipment, Personnel, and Units, 381 War Plans (Jul 42–Jul 43), EUCOM Engr files; Memo, OCE, SOS ETOUSA, for G–1, ETOUSA, 13 Oct 42, 321 Engr Officers, EUCOM Engr files; AUS, Army of the United States, refers to the temporary military organization established in wartime encompassing the Regular Army, the National Guard while in federal service, the organized reserves, all draftees, and officers specially appointed in the wartime establishment but not in any particular component. The last was the category in which civil engineers in great demand for war zone or domestic projects received commissions and rank in the military organizations they were joining at home or overseas.

from the rank of captain to that of major.[10]

TORCH drew heavily on experienced units and key officers with executive and administrative ability. The Offices of the Chief of Engineers, SOS, and ETOUSA, and the base sections gave TORCH sixty-five officers, including Generals Larkin and Davison and Colonel Pence and Lt. Col. Howard H. Reed of the Supply Division. Headquarters, ETOUSA, alerted four battalions of aviation engineers for North Africa. To bring these units to full strength, SOS had to draw on the remaining twelve battalions for both officers and enlisted men. For example, the 830th gave 30 men per company to the 814th; the 809th, also bound for North Africa, drew 105 men from the 832d and 57 from the 825th. Engineer general service regiments and combat battalions also helped fill out alerted units.

## Training

The problems created by personnel shortages and transfers were compounded by the inadequate training of engineers in the theater. Many engineer troops lacked not only specialist training but even adequate basic training. The Corps of Engineers' size doubled in the first six months of U.S. participation in World War II, and training new personnel for urgent demands was impossible.[11]

Colonel Lord, deputy chief engineer, ETOUSA, concluded in December 1942 that basic training had to be completed in the United States. He did not stand alone in this judgment, although it was in conflict with Colonel Larkin's belief that a half-trained man was better than no man.[12] Many half-trained engineer troops reached the ETO. Six general service regiments arrived in the Eastern Base Section area in the summer of 1942; they had received an average of ten weeks' basic training between their organization in the United States and their departure for a port of embarkation. Losses of cadres for newly formed units weakened many engineer organizations shortly before they went overseas. Some engineer unit officers, even commanders, were transferred to other units after reaching the port of embarkation. However necessary it was to build up a large force, the immediate effect on particular units was one of incalculable harm.[13]

Many units were brought up to strength only at the port of embarkation. In 1942 the 397th Engineer Depot Company arrived at Fort Dix, a staging area for the New York Port of Embarkation (POE), with 4 officers and 68 enlisted men, picking up an additional 104 enlisted men at Dix. In another case the 830th Engineer Aviation Battalion received 82 percent of its enlisted

---

[10] Memo, Moore for Reybold, 30 Nov 42, sub: Reply to Questionnaire, 381 War Plans (Jun 42–Jul 43), EUCOM Engr files; Unit Hist, 818th Engr Avn Bn.

[11] OCE ETOUSA Hist Rpt 4, Troops, pp. 2–3; Greenfield, Palmer, and Wiley, *The Organization of Ground Combat Troops*, p. 203; Ann Rpt, OCE, WD, 1942, p. 3; See Coll, Keith, and Rosenthal, *The Corps of Engineers: Troops and Equipment*, chs. 5, 7, 11, 15, 16 for detailed treatment of engineer training in the Zone of the Interior.

[12] Ltr, Col R. B. Lord, Dep Chf Engr, ETOUSA, to Col J. H. Carruth, G–3, ETOUSA, 26 Dec 42; Memo, Col Albrecht, Construction Div, for Col R. B. Lord, 13 Jan 43, 325.51 Policies and Plans, EUCOM Engr files; Lee Diary, entry for 18 May 42.

[13] Hists: 470th Engr Maint Co; 98th, 344th, 346th Engr GS Rgts; 424th, 433d, 434th Engr Dump Truck Cos; 397th, 450th Engr Depot Cos; 817th, 818th, 819th, 831st, 834th Avn Bns; Ltr, Lt Col James E. Walsh to CofEngrs, 28 Dec 43, sub: Operation of GS Rgt, D1784, Engr Sch Lib; Bennett interv.

men and 50 percent of its officers between 29 July and 9 August 1942, before entraining for Fort Dix on 11 August. Units manned in such fashion could hardly be characterized as cohesive.

The hope persisted that basic training could be completed in the United Kingdom and that the troops could learn their special skills on the job. Good construction experience could be gained, as could some training for amphibious operations, but not for such combat skills as laying and removing mines, booby traps, and other obstacles and rapidly building and reinforcing bridges. Engineer aviation units, which were kept busy constructing permanent bomber bases, could not be trained for building hasty airfields in forward areas. Reports on North African operations later highlighted such deficiencies.[14]

The chief of engineers in Washington formally recognized the vital need for training, but practical considerations prevented rapid solutions. A supply plan issued in September 1942 left a loophole for tired construction units in England, then working seven days a week on day and night shifts, by providing that training be carried on with minimum interference to unit duties and tasks. Thus during 1942, training was overshadowed—first by the buildup and then by preparations for TORCH. In practice, the time spent on training varied from one hour in eight to one in ten. Some troops took one hour for five days, then four hours on the sixth day. Two aviation battalions, the 818th and the 825th, worked ten hours a day and set aside one day a week for training. Later, these and other units trained on Sundays. Some general service regiments alerted for North Africa trained one battalion for a week while the other battalion continued construction work; but, in general, training schedules, no matter how elaborate on paper, had little actual meaning.

The chief obstacle was the buildup. Each hour spent away from actual work delayed buildup goals. The official viewpoint—that training was a diversion—affected the attitude of all personnel. Even after TORCH started, the engineer troops remaining in England had construction or other urgent tasks to perform, and realistic training was nearly impossible.[15]

There were other obstacles. Space was limited in the British Isles; lumber to build training quarters was scarce and equipment hard to come by. Some units fell back on their own resources. The 434th Engineer Dump Truck Company, for example, set up its own crane operator school, while other units did the same for brickwork, plumbing, steel construction, and electrical equipment installation. Engineers from various units received valuable military training at schools for enlisted men set up at Shrivenham, Berkshire, in what became known as the American School Center.

Just as important was the training offered by the British. Perhaps the best

---

[14] Memo, Col Albrecht for Col Lord, 13 Jan 43; Interv, Lt Col S. A. McMillion with Col Albrecht, 11 Dec 43.

[15] Memo, CofEngrs and CG, SOS, WD, for G–4, SOS ETOUSA, 23 Sep 42, sub: Revision of Supply Plan, ETO, 381 Supply 1942–43, EUCOM Engr files; Blueprint, 343d Engr GS Rgt, 15 Sep 42 entry, Col R. M. Edgar's personal files; Memo, OCE, SBS, SOS ETOUSA, Lt R. A. Cosgrove for Lt Col C. J. Barker, 12 Aug 42, sub: Field Notes From Southern Base Section, 600 Rpts, 20 Jun 42–29 Jul 43, EUCOM Engr files.

British school open to American engineers was the School of Military Engineering at Ripon, Yorkshire, which gave instruction in field work, bridging, electrical and mechanical work, military duties, and bomb disposal. Here U.S. Army engineers learned the value of the Bailey bridge. Courses ranged from two to five weeks, and after a time American instructors, including engineers, augmented the staff.[16] Other British institutions open to U.S. Army engineers included the railroad engineering school, the British staff college, a school that devoted special attention to camouflage, a fire-fighting school, a military intelligence school, and a diving school. By the end of 1942, 47 engineer officers and 185 enlisted men were attending British or American military training schools in England.

## Supply

The engineers in the United Kingdom during 1942 were supplied by the United States and by local procurement in Britain, from which came the largest tonnages. Generals Chaney and Davison recognized the need for extensive reciprocal aid from the British, and on 25 May, Headquarters, USAFBI, established a General Purchasing Board and a Board of Contracts and Adjustments.

Made up of representatives of the chiefs of each American service, the General Purchasing Board issued procurement directives, outlined local procurement procedure, and provided information on available materials. Before submitting requisitions for materials from the United States, each service sent copies to the general purchasing agent (GPA), who determined if British materials were available.[17]

Local procurement took one of three forms: materials that came direct from British resources, articles that Britain manufactured from material shipped from the United States, or substitutes. This third form of procurement took place when American materials went to British overseas forces, principally in the Pacific, and were exchanged for materials produced in the British Isles. The British and Americans did not work out a final procurement system until mid-October; until then lack of clearly defined procedures inhibited procurement under reverse lend-lease. The engineers frequently found it impossible to obtain needed items through the seventeen official British agencies involved and turned to local British businessmen, a procedure which often led to disagreements with the general purchasing agent. As late as January 1943 Col. Douglas C. MacKeachie, the GPA, criticized the engineers for constantly ignoring "most of the policies established for procurement in the UK." He declared that there had been a waste of "crucial tonnage" because the

---

[16] Ltr, Lt Col James E. Walsh to CofEngrs, 28 Dec 43, sub: Operations GS Rgts; Rpt, Engr Office, USANIF, to Engr, ETOUSA, 17 Feb 42, sub: Interim Rpt, Engr USANIF, O&T Br, OCE, Northern Ireland file; Ltr, Maj H. C. Trask to Base Sect Engr, NIBS, 14 Sep 42, sub: SME (Sch of Military Engineering, Brit), 103−SME−Ripon 1942−43, EUCOM Engr files; Memo, OCE, SOS ETOUSA, for Col D. B. Adams, Chf, O&T Div, OCE, SOS, 15 Aug 42, sub: Officers and Enlisted Men Attending British Schools, 321.02 Engr Officers (27 Jul 42−31 Oct 42), EUCOM Engr files.

[17] HQ, USAFBI, 25 May 42, Establishment of a Gen Purchasing Bd and a Bd of Contracts and Adjustments in the British Isles for the European Area; and HQ, SOS ETOUSA, 17 Jun 42, Function of the Gen Purchasing Bd and the Bd of Contracts and Adjustments; both in USFET, Engr 008 Precedents, 1942.

engineers did not follow up, and he felt their laxity in figuring requirements for reverse lend-lease items had made it difficult for the British to plan production. The engineer defense against this criticism was that procurement policy remained ill-defined until mid-October. In any case, Colonel MacKeachie admitted that Colonel Moore, the chief engineer of SOS and ETOUSA, had generally worked out satisfactory procedures by January 1943.[18]

During the last seven months of 1942 the British provided the engineers with 211,150 long (2,240-pound) tons of supplies under reverse lend-lease, not including large quantities of construction materials for sheltering and servicing American troops. Much of this material was shipped to North Africa to support American forces. Among other important items the engineers received or requisitioned were Bailey bridges, Sommerfeld track (a matting made of wire netting reinforced with steel), lumber, and essential tools and spare parts. Thousands of British civilian clerks and laborers worked on construction, depot supply, storage, and other projects. At one time, more than 27,760 civilians contributed to the BOLERO program and 20,000 to the separate air force engineer development.[19] Two factors inhibited reciprocal aid; the first was the limited quantity of raw materials available in the United Kingdom and the second was that U.S. Army equipment was standardized to American specifications so as to make substitution often impossible.[20]

During 1942 the engineers received from the United States some 75,400 tons of supplies representing 11,100 items in the Engineer Supply Catalog. The second half of the year saw 58,000 tons arrive, the peak month being August, when 26,000 tons reached Britain. But this tonnage fell far short of projected figures in BOLERO planning, and again, some quantities were siphoned off to North Africa. From the start and throughout 1942, no definite priority or allocation system existed.[21]

In July 1942 the Engineer Service, SOS, set up a Supply Division headed by Lt. Col. Thomas DeF. Rogers to receive, store, and distribute engineer supplies and equipment. The division's early days were marked with confusion, for none of the personnel initially assigned had any experience in engineer supply operations. Ultimately the division established a depot and shop branch as well as planning, procurement, requirements, and transportation branches. Supply Division sent a representative to London to maintain liaison with the General Purchasing Board and sundry British agencies; this office gradually evolved into the Procurement Branch. Liaison with OCE in Washington was not always good, as evidenced by Supply Division's lack of catalogs,

---

[18] HQ, SOS, Min of Orgl Mtg of . . . Gen Purchasing Bd, 26 Jun 42, USFET, Engr 400.12 Procurement, 1942; HQ, SOS, Final Rpt of Col D. C. MacKeachie, GPA, 319.1 Rpts, 1943, EUCOM Engr files; Interv, Shotwell with Col T. D. Rogers, 24 Sep 50; Moore, *Final Report*, pp. 189–91.

[19] App. A to Memo, HQ, SOS ETOUSA, for Chiefs, Staff Secs and Servs, 20 Feb 43; AMS Min of Mtg, BOLERO Combined Committee, London, 18 Jul 42; Interv, Shotwell with Col George W. Bennett; Memo, Moore for CG, SOS ETOUSA, 11 Jan 43, 325.51 Policies and Plans, EUCOM Engr files.

[20] Interv, Shotwell with Col A. W. Pence.
[21] SOS ETOUSA Statistical Summary XXI, 14 Dec 42, pp. 15ff; Cbl, Marshall to SPOBS, 20 Feb 42, sub: Shipment of Supplies, USAFBI Planning folder 3.00.

nomenclature lists, TOEs, and TBAs. Another difficulty was the failure of the Construction and Planning Division of OCE, SOS, to recognize that it, and not Supply Division, was responsible for submitting initial lists of requirements. Supply Division worked out a comprehensive engineer supply plan in October, but by December the North African operation had rendered it obsolete and had robbed the division of some of its more experienced officers.[22]

Not until December did SOS, GPA, and other agencies concerned establish a stable system for securing engineer supplies from the United States. Under this system requisitions went from the Supply Division to the deputy chief engineer, SOS, and then to G–4, SOS. The general purchasing agent received a copy of each requisition to determine whether the materials were available in the United Kingdom. If not, the requisitions went to the Overseas Supply Division in the New York port. Supply Division, OCE, in Washington checked the quantities requisitioned and either approved them or made arbitrary cuts depending upon available stocks.

In the normal requisitioning cycle 90 to 120 days passed between the time Supply Division, OCE, processed a requisition and when the articles were issued at a depot. This length of time often meant that requirements could be outdated by the time requisitions

were filled. In July 1942 the War Department authorized a sixty-day level for Class II engineer supplies (organizational equipment to fill TOE and TBA allowances of units) and Class IV items (construction supplies) needed for special projects. The sixty-day level was prescribed as the "minimum amount to be held as a reserve" over and above quantities required for normal operations, but in practice this level could not be maintained and shortages persisted throughout 1942.

Even the calculation of requirements to meet that level was disrupted by TORCH. Requirements for Class II depended upon numbers and types of units, and the North African invasion drained units from the United Kingdom and left the future troop basis uncertain; the requirements for Class IV supply in North Africa were obviously different from those in the British Isles. TORCH seriously depleted British resources, took essential material from U.S. Army engineer units remaining in the United Kingdom, and practically exhausted depot stocks of Class IV supplies in the theater.

Realizing that the lead time for production and delivery of most special project material was twelve to eighteen months, Colonel Moore, in December, sought to rebuild Class IV stockpiles in the United Kingdom and appointed a board to estimate future requirements and delivery schedules. The move seemed to fly in the face of a Somervell directive dated 18 November 1942, stating that no supplies were to be sent to Britain beyond those necessary to equip the 427,000 men scheduled to be in England by spring 1943. But General Somervell hardly intended this figure to be sacrosanct, for an ultimate cross-

---

[22] Moore, *Final Report*, pp. 22ff; Interv, Shotwell with Rogers, 24 Sep 50; Ltr, Moore to Col C. Rodney Smith, OCE, WD, 21 Dec 42, sub: Shortage of Supply Officers, 475 Engr Equip, Dec 42–Dec 43, EUCOM Engr files; Ltr, OCE, SOS ETOUSA, 13 Oct 42, sub: Supply Plan, 300 Supply Plan, EUCOM Engr files; OCE ETOUSA Hist Rpt 3, Supply, (United Kingdom), 1946, Liaison Sect, Intel Div, ETOUSA Adm file 547, and OCE ETOUSA Hist Rpt 1, Organization, Administration, and Personnel, app. 2.

Channel invasion was still the principal tenet of American strategy.[23]

One of the most frequent complaints of engineer units was that their Class II equipment did not reach them until weeks after they arrived in the United Kingdom. Most troop transports carried little or no equipment, sending it instead by slow-moving freighters. It was almost impossible to bring men and equipment together simultaneously in the United Kingdom. When units were still in camp in the United States they needed their equipment for training. Taking the equipment from the men at least a month before departure would have been necessary for it to arrive overseas at the same time as the troops, and even then there would have been no guarantee. Some equipment was lost in ports or depots or sent to the bottom by German submarines. The 817th Engineer Aviation Battalion, on its arrival in July 1942, had 1 transit, 100 axes, and 100 shovels for 800 men, while several other units had nothing but jeeps. Two months after their arrival in late summer, four engineer aviation battalions had received less than one-third of their heavy equipment. Borrowing British equipment alleviated problems somewhat, but such loans

were limited. The lack of tools was a major factor in retarding construction.[24]

The War Department or Headquarters, ETOUSA, regulated the supply and issue of many scarce items. Those under War Department allocation regulation were known as *controlled* items; those in short supply in ETO were designated *critical* items by the theater command. Throughout 1942 the supply of items in both categories remained unsatisfactory, and as late as mid-December such engineer equipment as air compressors, generators, welding sets, compasses, mine detectors, gas cylinders, gas pipeline supplies, pumps, D−7 tractors with angledozers, and truck-mounted cranes remained in short supply.[25]

Nevertheless, by the end of 1942 U.S. Army engineer units in England had received 90 percent of their heavy construction equipment from the United States and 70 percent of their general-purpose vehicles. But few additional engineer troops had been stationed in the United Kingdom since 1 September, and some serious shortages remained—a result of the unavoidable time lag in manufacturing heavy equipment in the United States and an unforeseen heavy demand for it in all theaters. Too few Class II items were arriving, and only about 27 percent of items not under special controls were

[23] Ltr, HQ, SOS ETOUSA, to CG, ETOUSA, 13 Dec 42, sub: Policy in Procurement of Engineer Supplies to Support Future Operations, 381 Supply 1942–43, EUCOM Engr files; Interv, Col Barnes, 7 Nov 50; Memo, OCE, SOS ETOUSA, for Col Elmer E. Barnes, 6 Nov 42, sub: Engineer Class IV Supplies, 400 General (Nov 42–Feb 43), EUCOM Engr files; Lt Herbert French, The Administrative and Logistical History of the European Theater of Operations, vol. III, "Troop and Supply Buildup in the UK Prior to D-Day," p. 70, in CMH; Leighton and Coakley, *Global Logistics and Strategy, 1940–43*, pp. 322–36 and app. F.

[24] Unit Hist, 470th Engr Maint Co; Interv, Col B. D. Cassidy; Adm and Log Hist of the ETO, vol. III, "Troop and Supply Buildup in the UK Prior to D-Day," p. 155; Ltr, Moore to CE, WD, 31 Oct 42, sub: Equipment for Avn Bns, 475 Engr Equip, Oct–Nov 42, EUCOM Engr files.

[25] Memo, OCE, SOS ETOUSA, for G−4, SOS ETOUSA, 11 Dec 42, sub: Critical Items, atchd to Memo, sub: G−4 Logistical Book, 325.51 Policies and Plans, EUCOM Engr files.

available for initial issue requirements. With shortages already prevalent, SOS had to equip units alerted for TORCH by stripping equipment from units scheduled to remain in England.[26]

Many other supply problems arose. Poor packing in the United States often resulted in saltwater damage. Improper handling caused more loss, and worn or used supplies showed up all too frequently. Sometimes various parts of equipment arrived in separate containers, and in other cases some parts never arrived at all. Vague and ambiguous ship manifests caused countless hours to be spent in sorting equipment. Equipment lost for long periods had to be requisitioned again. Spare parts in large quantities left the United States, yet months later some units had not received a single box. In July a machine training detachment (a captain and twelve sergeants) began working at Liverpool, the chief freight port, supervising the unloading and loading of all engineer equipment and greatly reduced the confusion. This and other steps improved matters so that by November engineer equipment reached the proper units ten days after it landed.[27]

The depot system serving American forces in the United Kingdom expanded slowly, laboring under the same organizational, geographic, and manpower restraints that hobbled the entire ETOUSA operation in its early stages. The engineers had specified areas for supply in general depots, or they set up their own depots. The system began to take shape with Desertmartin in Northern Ireland and eventually amounted to ten installations in the first year. As shipments from the United States increased, American planners in the theater moved depot operations into large warehouses in Liverpool, Bristol, and other smaller ports on Britain's west coast. In June 1942 the British turned over to U.S. Army control, under the general command of Chief Quartermaster Brig. Gen. Robert McG. Littlejohn, several existing British Army depots, among them a recently constructed facility at Ashchurch, just south of Liverpool. Engineer supply in the summer of 1942 was concentrated at this general depot and at a former Royal Ordnance depot at Thatcham-Newbury, sixty miles due west of London, also shared with other service arms. A small, exclusively engineer depot was established in British quarters at Huntingdon, sixty miles north of London, to supply airfield construction units in the Eastern Base Section with building materials. But the planned storage capacity for the troop buildup under BOLERO still awaited construction. If the consolidation of supply requests was the province of the quartermaster, providing the storage space and the physical fixtures was the responsibility of the chief engineer.[28]

---

[26] Rpt, OCE, SOS ETOUSA, 7 Jan 43, sub: Status Rpt, CE 319.1, Status Rpts, OCE, Dec 42–Jul 43; Unit Hist, 470th Engr Maint Co; Rpt, HQ, EBS, 12 Apr 44, sub: Rpt of Activities of the Eastern Base Section, Hist of the Office of the Base Section Engr, EUCOM Engr files; Ltr, OCE, ETOUSA (C. Rodney Smith), to Engr, SOS ETOUSA, 22 Sep 42, sub: Maint of Engr 319.1 (9–11–42), QG14–1942–44, USFET Engr files.

[27] Entries Aug–Oct 42 in Quartering Div, OCE, ETOUSA, Daily Jnl and Supply Div Daily Jnl, EUCOM Engr files; Ltr, OCE, ETOUSA (C. Rodney Smith), to Engr, SOS ETOUSA, 22 Sep 42, sub: Maint of Engr Equipment in the ETO, Supplies Misc 1942, file 1004, NIBS Engr files; Interv, Col A. L. Hartfield, 19 Sep 50.

[28] Moore, *Final Report*, pp. 179–80; Ruppenthal, *Logistical Support of the Armies, Volume I*, p. 152.

Decisions on the location of new depots were complicated by the necessity to share buildings with the British and by the lack of space at more desirable sites. The threat of German air attack induced the British government to disperse depot installations in unlikely spots. American engineers followed this principle to some extent, but, also influenced by the plan for a large BOLERO static force, they gave some thought to locating the depots so as to support both the buildup and the subsequent invasion of Europe.

By the end of 1942, the engineers had constructed additional depots in the English interior. All of them suffered problems of transport. Interdepot shipments were made impractical by circuitous and slow rail service and by an inventory system that failed to show changes in the location of material; by fall of 1942, theater policy forbade movement of materiel between the depots. In September the Thatcham-Newbury installation had 85,000 tons of engineer supplies on hand with the 450th Engineer Depot Company there handling the supply needs of the Southern Base Section. The Engineer Section at Ashchurch not only became a spare parts repository but also took care of the general engineer supply for western and northern England. Though limited in space, another general depot associated with Cardiff and Newport on the Bristol Channel was the only port depot in the system and contributed in the fall of 1942 to the direct flow of materiel into the Southern Base Section from the United States.

Shortages in trained supply technicians and the absence of a standard nomenclature list for items of supply posed other problems. Through the summer, the 450th Engineer Depot Company at Thatcham-Newbury, complemented by British civilians, was the only unit in the country handling engineer depot supplies. The civilians were largely untrained in wholesale stock management, and the depot company found conditions and procedures totally different. The demands of TORCH were particularly felt here. Six depot companies were scheduled to arrive in England by the end of the year; of the two that came, one shipped out immediately for Africa, and the experienced 450th found itself in Algeria in late November 1942. Stock records and daily tally-in and -out cards were unreliable. Illegible and ambivalent notations made some records useless, and inventories at various locations differed in the description of identical items until the ETOUSA chief engineer's office produced a standard depot manual in February 1943 and a combined British-American nomenclature list the following month. Difficulties in stock and depot control brought the direct attention of the chief engineer to the lowest levels of the command, an undesirable situation since directives and verbal instructions then bypassed the base section commands having jurisdiction over the areas in which individual depots were located.[29]

Another serious problem in 1942 was equipment maintenance. Normally, five echelons of repair existed for heavy engineer and other equipment. The using

---

[29] Moore, *Final Report*, p. 180; Ltr, Col J. S. Gorlinski, O&T Br, Trps Div, OCE, WD, to Col Chorpening, Supply Div, OCE, WD, 2 Jul 42, sub: Depot Companies for BOLERO, 381 BOLERO, folio I, O&T Div (Rec-Ret), OCE files; Supply Div, OCE, SOS ETOUSA, 1 Sep 42, Control Folder, and SOS ETOUSA GO 7, 11 Jul 42.

units took care of first and second echelons, mainly preventive maintenance such as lubrication, cleaning, tightening, and minor replacements. Engineer maintenance companies took care of third and fourth echelon work, which involved major assembly replacements and technical repairs; engineer heavy shop companies undertook fifth echelon maintenance—salvaging, rebuilding, and reconditioning. This was the prescribed procedure, but under conditions existing in Britain in 1942 the engineers could not fully implement it. Maintenance operations were slow in getting under way and proved unsatisfactory throughout the period.[30]

The 467th Engineer Maintenance Company, the first engineer maintenance unit to arrive in the theater, reached Northern Ireland in March 1942 as a skeleton organization made up of company headquarters and one maintenance platoon. In early November the unit moved to the Eastern Base Section where it performed not only third and fourth echelon maintenance for which it was trained but also fifth echelon work. In August, after only a few weeks of training, the 470th Engineer Maintenance Company arrived from the United States as a complete unit and set up at Ashchurch. With only half of its equipment, the company had to borrow tools and parts from the 471st Engineer Maintenance Company, which had arrived in England at the same time. Moreover, the company repeatedly had to provide cadres for new units. OCE, SOS, never issued any directives defining the company's functions, and few engineer troops outside

the immediate Ashchurch area were aware that it existed and that it could aid them. The company left England for North Africa late in November 1942.

The October supply plan had called for maintenance shops at Ashchurch, Shrivenham in Berkshire, and Braintree in Essex. For lack of equipment, these shops were not close to operating at full capacity by the year's end. Individual engineer units felt shortages in maintenance equipment just as acutely as did the shops. Aviation and other engineer units constantly called for mobile shops, tools, and tool sets. Though schedules called for maintenance machinery to be used eight to ten hours a day, shortages compelled engineer units to use them at times for more than twenty hours.

Despite these handicaps the engineers took on considerable maintenance work and occasionally the duties of the Ordnance Department. In the late fall of 1942, engineers in the Southern Base Section were responsible not only for maintaining engineer equipment but also for operating most of the motor vehicles. Even with shortages of repair parts and operating manuals, most men did their best to keep their equipment in good condition. The dearth of facilities and tools forced men to do things on their own, to employ expedients, and to learn the intricacies of each tool, machine, or vehicle. On the other hand, losses and damages inevitably resulted because so many operators lacked adequate training.[31]

---

[30] Engr Supply Precedents, Engr Sch Lib text, pp. 222–26, Engr Sch Lib.

[31] Ltr, OCE, SOS ETOUSA, 13 Oct 42, sub: Supply Plan, 400 Supply Plan, EUCOM Engr files; Ltr, OCE, ETOUSA (C. Rodney Smith), to Engr, SOS ETOUSA, 22 Sep 42, sub: Maint of Engr Equipment in the ETO, Supplies Misc 1942; Ltr, OCE, SOS ETOUSA, to OCE,

A critical shortage of spare parts became apparent early. Although in June the War Department had authorized a year's automatic supply of spare parts for overseas operations, OCE, WD, reported that spare parts stock for the following six months would not be ready for shipment until October and that a balanced twelve-month depot stock, then being assembled, would not be ready until the close of the year. Nor were the prospects brighter that units overseas would soon get a three- to six-month supply of critical spare parts. The situation became so serious in the Eastern Base Section that depots issued some items only upon presentation of the parts to be replaced. In September, OCE, SOS, formed a spare parts depot on the nucleus of an engineer base equipment company at Ashchurch, with subdepots at Egginton in Derbyshire and Huntingdon in Huntingdonshire. October saw some improvement, but stocks were far from balanced.[32]

The quality of equipment provided to the engineer units was good, though some was unsuited for larger tasks. The earth auger and the medium tractor with angledozer proved too light for much of the work for which they were used, and they frequently broke down. The 1 1/2-ton dump truck was also inadequate and wore out much sooner than the larger and more rugged 2 1/2-ton truck. But with their heavy graders, bulldozers, paving machines, post-hole diggers, and other efficient machinery, American engineers could usually outperform British engineers, who generally had lighter equipment, although the British machines often excelled in muddy conditions.[33]

## Intelligence

In late 1942 engineer intelligence was still unprepared for the tasks looming ahead. Intelligence functions were related to ROUNDUP, but Continental operations were a hope for the future rather than an imminent reality. To staff officers responsible for building up engineer forces in the United Kingdom, intelligence and mapping appeared less urgent than construction. When the intelligence organization of OCE, SOS, became an independent division in midsummer 1942, its staff consisted of only a few officers and even fewer enlisted men. Lt. Col. Herbert Milwit, formerly with the 30th Engineer Topographic Battalion and an expert in mapping and photogrammetry, remained division chief throughout the war in Europe. Not until December 1942 did sufficient personnel arrive in Britain to make possible more than extremely limited operations.[34]

In spite of the importance of map-

WD, 13 Jan 43, sub: Maint of Engr Equipment in ETO, 400, 402, EUCOM Engr files.

[32] Ltr, AGO, WD, 11 Jun 42, sub: Automotive Parts Policy, Engr Cons, EUCOM Engr files; Ltr, OCE, ETOUSA (C. Rodney Smith), to Engr, SOS ETOUSA, 22 Sep 42, sub: Maint of Engr Equipment in the ETO, Supplies Misc 1942; Interv, Col A. L. Hartfield, 19 Sep 50; Ltr, Engr Sect, ETOUSA, to G–4, SOS ETOUSA, 8 Oct 42, sub: Initial GIV Periodic Rpt, 319.1 GIV Monthly Rpt, 1942–43–44, USFET Engr files.

[33] Memo, SOS, WD, and Ltr, CofEngrs, 17 Aug 42, sub: Recommended Changes in Engr Equipment, ETO 400.34, OCE C and R files; Rpt, USANI Base Command (Prov), Office of Base Engr, to CofEngrs, USANIBC, in Engr Tech Rpt No. 7, 600 NI Gen (Current), NIBS Engr files; Albrecht, "Engineer Aspects of Operation BOLERO," p. 119.

[34] OCE ETOUSA Hist Rpt 5, Intelligence and Topography (United Kingdom), 1946, pp. 1–10, Liaison Sect, Intel Div, ETOUSA Adm file 547; Intel Div, OCE, SOS ETOUSA, Status Rpts for Sep, Oct, Nov, and Dec 1942 and Jan 1943, EUCOM Engr files.

ping as a branch of engineer intelligence, Americans in the European theater at first assumed little responsibility for it. In May 1942 the British and Americans concluded the Loper-Hotine Agreement to divide mapping responsibility throughout the world. The British agreed to take care of most of Western Europe and the Middle East, leaving North and South America, the Far East, and the Pacific to the Americans. The Directorate of Military Survey of the British War Office provided Americans with maps, equipment, housing, and storage facilities. This British agency also aided in training a small but vital engineer model makers detachment, whose model beaches were to prove useful in planning amphibious operations.[35]

The Loper-Hotine Agreement recognized that the British would require American help in compiling and reproducing maps for American forces and in providing photomaps for those parts of northwest Europe not covered by reliable large-scale maps. The agreement also specified that American topographic units and staffs would support major American forces. Though American topographical battalions arrived in Britain in the latter part of 1942 without adequate equipment, by the close of the year Colonel Milwit's units were producing maps in considerable quantities and were building up a worthwhile map library.[36]

COLONEL MILWIT

For a time, relations with the British were better than with the Army Air Forces. OCE, WD, had arranged with the Air Forces at Wright Field outside Dayton, Ohio, to train a B−17 squadron to carry out photomapping in cooperation with the engineers. After months of negotiating over the type of plane, the need for an escort, and the flying altitude, the scheme failed. Engineer mapmakers thus had to rely upon the slower, less accurate methods of the Royal Air Force.[37]

[35] OCE, SOS ETOUSA, Topo Memo No. 1, 15 Oct 43, Topographic Experience in the Theaters; Intel Div, OCE, SOS ETOUSA, General Mission statement, 4 Oct 44, sub: Model Makers Detachment, Model Makers Detachment folder; Coll, Keith, and Rosenthal, *The Corps of Engineers: Troops and Equipment,* pp. 445ff.
[36] OCE ETOUSA Hist Rpt 5, Intelligence and Topography, pp. 3−5 and app. 9; Ltr, Col Loper to Capt G. F. Hahas, Survey Liaison Office, HQ, WASC,

13 Jan 44, 061.01 Mapping, Intel Div, OCE, SOS; Ltr, Milwit, 14 Aug 53.
[37] Memo, Milwit for Conrad, G−2, AAF, ETOUSA, 20 Dec 42, sub: Trimetrogen Topographic Mapping, and Ltr, Air Ministry (BR) to Milwit, S 2898, 1/A.D. Maps; both General 061, EUCOM Engr files. OCE ETOUSA Hist Rpt 5, Intelligence and Topography, pp. 15−19 and apps. 5, 10, 11, 12.

## Construction

As the BOLERO plans developed, it became apparent that without considerable assistance the British would not be able to house the American force scheduled to arrive in the United Kingdom. General Davison pointed out in June of 1942 that the difference between what the Americans would need and what the British could provide in new and existing facilities would constitute the engineer construction program. Determining American needs was difficult because of the uncertainty in 1942 as to how many American troops would come, when they would come, and how they would be used in the invasion. The orderly development of the quartering and construction programs—at first in separate divisions but in mid-October combined—suffered because of these uncertainties.[38]

Until enough American "static force" engineers arrived, the British handled everything connected with quartering. British Army and Air Force officers met U.S. Army units as they arrived, directed them to assigned areas, and arranged for various services, including utilities, medical facilities, and the Navy-Army-Air Force Institution (NAAFI, the British equivalent of the post exchange). In at least one instance a British advance party remained with the U.S. troops to aid in maintaining equipment and drawing supplies, to make the Americans familiar with British military procedure, and to provide laundry, shoe repair, and tailoring services. In the early summer of 1942, when the SOS was too new and undermanned to handle these matters, such British assistance was vital.[39]

Americans gradually took over many of these functions, though the British role remained great. Aviation engineer battalions which had to construct sites on grain fields or pastureland without facilities (mostly in Eastern Base Section) put up tents for those who came next. In Southern and Western Base Sections, the British could usually turn over existing facilities, at least for the early arrivals. To meet U.S. Army requirements, however, these facilities often had to be altered or enlarged by either the British or the Engineer Construction Division. If no housing existed, one or the other had to put up new structures.[40]

The Engineer Construction Division, a subsidiary of the chief engineer's office at Cheltenham, was set up in mid-June with two officers and two enlisted men headed by Col. Frank M. Albrecht. As more officers arrived in the ETO the organization grew, and in October it absorbed the Quartering Division. Before TORCH, tasks consisted mainly of planning and liaison. In designing and constructing buildings the British predominated because they ultimately were to own all installations. In some cases, especially in airfield construction, Americans attempted to lower British specifications in the interest of speed and economy, but, in general, the British held to their point of view.

---

[38] Memo, Davison for Lee, 28 Jun 42, 400 General (May–Oct 42), EUCOM Engr files; OCE ETOUSA Hist Rpt 8, Quartering (United Kingdom), 1946, pp. 5–6, Liaison Sect, Intel Div, ETOUSA Adm file 547.

[39] OCE ETOUSA Hist Rpt 8, Quartering, pp. 13–17.

[40] Ltr, Henderson to Air Ministry, 8 Aug 42, sub: Advance Parties for Engr Bn (Avn) and Ltr, Maj T. F. Bengston, XO, C&T Div, to Base Sect Engr, 27 Aug 42, sub: Transmittal of Orders to Arriving Organizations; both in 321 Engrs, EUCOM Engr files.

General Lee's policy of centralized control and decentralized operations governed administrative procedures in building facilities of all types. Engineer officers of the "static force" had authority to approve or disapprove construction projects in accordance with estimated costs. Unit utility offices could approve maintenance and utility projects originating within such units as ground force battalions if the projects cost less than $825, which at World War II exchange rates amounted to £100. American district engineers could authorize projects involving less than $20,600, while base section engineers could approve new construction costing under $164,800. For projects above $164,800 the base section engineers had to secure the approval of the chief engineer, SOS, ETOUSA.

Since all installations were ultimately to be turned over to the British, area, district, or base section engineers had to obtain approval for each project from their opposites in the local British military hierarchy. The British were reluctant to delegate the authority to approve even minor construction, and some projects costing as little as $410 had to go to the War Office for approval.

General Lee constantly pressed the War Office to modify the British system, arguing that new construction costing less than $164,800 could and should be disposed of at a much lower level than the War Office. Not until well into the fall of 1942 did the War Office acquiesce. Thereafter, British commanders had the same approval powers as American base section, district, and area commanders.[41]

Under the new arrangement, if a camp, depot, or hospital was to cost more than $164,800 the chief engineer asked the British War Office to recommend suitable sites, and the base section engineer then selected a site board. For camp and hospital sites, such boards included an engineer, a medical officer, and representatives of each unit, arm, or service concerned. The board inspected the proposed sites and reported their selection to the chief engineer. Although only the chief engineer or his representative had authority to request sites or facilities from the British, OCE made no objection to informal agreements, subject to the chief engineer's approval, entered into by other arms and services.[42]

Differences between American and British methods, organization, and nomenclature posed seemingly endless problems. A requisition was an "indent," a monkey wrench was a "spanner"; nails were designated by length rather than weight, rope by circumference rather than diameter. Large American trucks had difficulty traversing the narrow, sharply curved British roads. American electrical equipment would not

---

[41] Memo, Albrecht for Moore, 1 Oct 42, 600–A–Con, EUCOM Engr files: Jnl entry 1430, 14 Oct 42,

C&Q Div, OCE, SOS, Oct–Dec 42; Ltr, Albrecht to Base Sect Engr, EBS, 30 Oct 42, sub: Requests for Construction Work, 337 (Min of Mtgs 1943), USFET Engr Serv files; SOS ETOUSA Cir 12, 17 Aug 42, sub: Instructions Concerning Base Sections; MS, Maj Gen A.G.B. Smyser, Engineer Eighth Air Force History. For the general construction story, see OCE ETOUSA Hist Rpt 6, Air Force Construction (United Kingdom), 1946, Liaison Sect, Intel Div, ETOUSA Adm file 547, and OCE ETOUSA Hist Rpt 7, Field and Service Force Construction. These two reports are general sources for the remainder of this section.

[42] Ltr, Larkin to CG, AA Comd, ETOUSA, 30 Jul 42, sub: Construction, Utilities Work, and Use of Facilities, 600–N–General, EUCOM Engr files. These instructions were repeated almost verbatim in the subsequent Ltr, Moore to CG, V Corps, 1 Dec 42, same sub, 600 General, 1–31 Dec 42, EUCOM Engr files.

operate on British current; the USAAF required more hardstandings, quarters, and facilities than RAF airdromes provided; and American commanders found British special facilities for noncoms hard to reconcile with U.S. Army practices.[43]

A problem stemmed from the fact that the Air Ministry was a separate arm of the British War Office. The engineers wanted to separate the USAAF from construction channels—a policy that found little favor with either the Air Forces or the British Air Ministry. With ETOUSA support General Lee finally succeeded in his efforts to coordinate all U.S. construction under one office, gaining by fall both Air Forces and British Air Ministry acquiescence. The Air Forces stated requirements; the engineers did the construction. The Air Ministry agreed not only to deal directly with the engineers but to grant its subordinate commands powers of approval paralleling those of the American static force.[44]

Another general working agreement was that American engineer units would undertake the larger construction projects to make better use of their heavy equipment. ETOUSA also agreed that U.S. Army camps would remain as small as possible so that local municipal utility systems could serve them. The British and Americans prepared standard layouts for camps for 600, 750, 1,000, and 1,250 men and hospitals for 750 and 1,000 beds. The need for conserving shipping space, the scarcity of wood, and the necessity for speed in construction all dictated the choice of 16-foot-wide Nissen huts for housing and 35-foot-wide Iris huts for storage and shop space. The British agreed to manufacture these units from billet steel imported from the United States. The huts provided good semipermanent quarters that could be erected easily and quickly.[45]

As the machinery for construction and quartering evolved, the Engineer Construction Division and engineer construction units turned their energies toward camps and depots in the Southern Base Section and air installations in the Eastern Base Section. In March 1942 the British indicated that they would need help in providing fields for American Air Forces; General Davison immediately cabled Washington for ten aviation engineer battalions and soon afterwards raised the number to twenty. The first of these battalions arrived in June. Late in July Eighth Air Force set its requirements at 98 airdromes, of which the British already had built 52; they would build 29 more and the U.S. aviation engineers

[43] MS, Lt Gen J.C.H. Lee, Invasion Prelude—The SOS in Britain, 10 Apr 44; Hist 332d Engr GS Rgt, 1 Jan–31 Dec 44, Supply Sect; Memo, 1st Lt E. W. McCall for Chf, Reqts Br, sub: Trip Rpt, 319.1 Rpts, EUCOM Engr Sect; Moore, *Final Report*, p. 238.

[44] Ltr, Larkin to CG, AAF, 10 Aug 42, sub: Construction and Utility Work w/1st Ind, 25 Aug 42, and Memo, Albrecht for Moore, 10 Oct 42; both in 600–A–Gen, EUCOM Engr files. Ltr, Albrecht to Wooten, 18 Sep 42, sub: Command Approval of Construction Projects, 600 Gen 43, EUCOM Engr files.

[45] Engr 817, SU–RE, Jun 42–5 Jul 45, Air Univ, Maxwell Field, Ala; OCE ETOUSA Cir 6, 16 Jul 42, extracted from OCE ETOUSA Hist Rpt 7, Field and Service Force Construction, pp. 58–59. This directive provided the working basis for U.S. and British agencies concerned with construction. The British counterpart was reproduced in OCE ETOUSA Cir 10, 27 Jul 42; Incl 3, Scales of Accommodations, 1st Ind, Albrecht to Col G. A. Lincoln, Chf, Planning Control Br, G–4, 10 Dec 42, sub: Construction Program; OCE ETOUSA Hist Rpt 7, Field and Service Force Construction, app. 7.

MEN OF THE 829TH ENGINEER AVIATION BATTALION ERECT NISSEN HUTTING

17. By 1 September the U.S. figure had risen unofficially to 38.[46]

Although the construction program was neither formally approved nor coordinated, by 1 September unofficial figures listed new camps for 77,346 men, 53 hospitals, and 16 convertible camps, in addition to the 38 new airdromes. SOS building operations were already well under way. Eight general

service regiments had arrived and were employed on thirty-one projects. Five of these regiments were in Southern Base Section, one building railroad spurs and four building shelters. By contrast, little had been done in Western Base Section. Although three general service regiments arrived there in August and began shelter construction, in September all were diverted to TORCH.[47] In Eastern Base Section the 809th Engineer Aviation Battalion, the first SOS engineer unit to do construc-

---

[46] Ltr, Gen Carl Spaatz, CG, 8th AF, 8 AF 600.1 to CG, ETOUSA, Jul 42, sub: Eighth Air Force Airdrome Construction Program; Ltr, Gen Larkin to CofEngrs, Washington, D.C., 30 Jul 42, sub: Engineer Supplies, Equipment, Personnel, and Units, 381 War Plans (Jun 42–Jul 43), EUCOM Engr Sect; Ruppenthal, *Logistical Support of the Armies, Volume I*, pp. 38, 95, 113; MS, Notes on Staff and Command Conference, 17 May 43, p. 6, Engr Serv in the ETO, Hist Br Liaison Sect.

[47] Station List, Engr Units, 9 Sep 42, Disposition Lists; Engr Units and files, and OCE, SOS, Sitrep, 1 Aug 42; OCE ETOUSA Hist Rpt 7, Field and Service Force Construction, p. 71; His Rcd of Engr Serv, WBS, 20 Jul 42–15 Mar 44; OCE ETOUSA Hist Rpt 4, Troops, app. 22, sheet 1.

PAVING TRAIN AT AN AMERICAN BOMBER FIELD IN ENGLAND

tion in England, began work at Glatton Airdrome on 5 July. By September sixteen aviation battalions were at work in that area, although only six had been at their job sites more than a few days.[48]

The British heavy bomber airdrome was accepted as the standard for each field to be constructed by the Americans, with few modifications and a relatively tight clamp on local adjustments. Three runways, each 150 feet wide, were set in a generally triangular form with intersecting legs. The main runway was 6,000 feet long, the other two 4,200 feet each. A fifty-foot perimeter

track encircling the runways connected some fifty hardstandings. In addition, at each field a 2,500-man "village" had to be built complete with utilities such as sewage—no small problem in the flat lands of East Anglia. At Matching Airdrome buildings included 214 Nissen huts (16 by 36 feet) arranged in seven living sites, with attendant washhouses and latrines. The technical site adjacent to the runways included some forty-odd buildings for administration, operations, and maintenance. Other structures included hospitals, recreation halls, and messes. Away from these areas was a "danger site," where a score of buildings housed bombs, fuses, and other ordnance.

Agreement on layouts and construction standards was a minor issue com-

---

[48] Status Rpts, Col Moore to CG, ETOUSA, 31 Oct 42 (dated 8 Nov 42) and 30 Nov 42 (dated 6 Dec 42), both 319.1 Rpts, OCE Rpts to CG, EUCOM Engr files.

pared to problems in the actual work. Though the Air Ministry provided airfield and village construction plans and arranged for locally supplied materials, British equipment was often too light and too little. Other considerations plagued the Americans—a lack of experienced construction workers, strange British nomenclature and methods, rains beginning in mid-October that turned fields into bogs and company areas into quagmires, and finally the disruptions of TORCH. Because of delays in the arrival of the heavy organizational equipment, aviation battalions began clearing land with hand tools; one unit had only a small-scale map to locate and chart the runways it was to construct. All units had to train men on the job. Even those with some construction training were at a loss in the United Kingdom where virtually no construction was of wood—every piece came under the control of a separate British Timber Control Board. One unit traded food for enough lumber to build concrete pouring forms. The corrugated curved steel Nissen, Iris, and Romney huts were enclosed at the ends with masonry, and a number of structures on airdromes were entirely of brick. Engineer units had to train large numbers of masons, using men experienced in the trade as teachers.[49]

Even when heavy equipment arrived

more regularly in late 1942, aviation engineer battalions had few men familiar with it. Operators needed intensive training. One method divided the labor into specialized tasks: one company handled the runway preparation and paving; another roads and taxiways; and the third the huts, drainage systems, and ancillary tasks. Methods and schedules varied from battalion to battalion, but nearly all worked double shifts to take advantage of the long summer days. As daylight hours shortened in the fall, units worked under lights; two, and sometimes three, shifts kept the vital heavy equipment running day and night.

Engineer aviation units were armed and organized to defend their airfields should the need arise. In the early days men marched to work with their rifles, stacking them at the job site. Alerts and blackouts punctuated the nighttime work as German bombers passed over on their way to metropolitan areas, but airdrome construction proceeded with little interference. Some attempt was made to disguise the characteristic outline of runways with a wood chip covering and that of buildings with paint, but camouflage did not become an important consideration.

In the end, the progress demanded of the engineer aviation battalions in the first year of construction work in England proved beyond those partially trained, underequipped, and often undermanned units. Airfields that OCE, SOS, originally estimated would take one battalion six months to build took a year or more.[50]

---

[49] Unit histories of sixteen engineer aviation battalions in the United Kingdom before December 1942, especially those of the 809th, the 817th, the 818th, and the 826th and histories of the 833d and 834th; Memo, Lt Col H. H. Reed, Actg Chf, Supply Div, SOS, for XO, Engr Serv, 4 Sep 42, sub: Revision of Supply Plan, ETO; Unit Hist, 332d Engr GS Rgt, 1 Jan 44–31 Oct 44, Supply Sect; Ltr, Albrecht to Base Engr, EBS, 20 Oct 42; Memo, Moore for Reybold, 30 Nov 42, sub: Engr Problems in ETO; Memo, Moore for Lee 12 Nov 42.

[50] Moore, *Final Report,* pp. 259–61; Work Like Hell, Play Like Hell, p. 11, Engr 825–Hi, Apr 42–Aug 45; Engr 833–Hi, 10 Aug 42–25 Sep 45, Air Univ.

The decision to invade North Africa dealt a blow to BOLERO construction from which it did not recover until well into the spring of 1943. In September, just when the arrival of more engineer construction units made possible an increase in building activity, many of the engineer units were alerted for TORCH; others had to support the offensive, mainly in depot operations, because TORCH called for a greatly increased volume of supplies from the United Kingdom.[51]

The diversion of supplies and troops for North Africa dictated new means for tapping the labor supply. Early in October SOS, ETOUSA, provided for labor pools in each of the base sections, with a general service regiment or equivalent serving as a nucleus on which to form organizations for freight handling and various other tasks at depots and similar installations. Aviation engineers also performed these duties. On 1 October Colonel Adams of the Operations and Training Division, OCE, SOS, reported that three aviation battalions had just arrived but had only 20 percent of their heavy construction equipment. General Littlejohn, General Lee's deputy, pointed to this as a justification for adding these units to the labor pools, emphasizing that 5,000 SOS engineers had already been diverted from construction.[52]

In November the British, who were scraping the bottom of their own construction labor barrel, removed 2,843 pioneer troops from depot work. Colonel Albrecht of the Construction Division, OCE, SOS, argued to no avail that it was ridiculous to transfer unskilled pioneer labor to construction if this forced more skilled American units to perform unskilled work. At the end of November, a peak of 4,000 SOS, 1,160 aviation, and 1,100 ground forces engineers were in labor pools. Large numbers continued at depot work through March 1943. In spite of repeated requests from the chief engineer, ETOUSA, for more civilian aid, the British could do little. And, with apologies, Colonel Moore had to explain to the Eighth Air Force that the success of TORCH depended upon keeping aviation engineers on unskilled depot work.[53]

General Lee recognized that returning engineers to construction or build-up tasks should have high priority, with aviation engineers heading the list, as soon as the TORCH emergency passed. In the meantime, as the labor pool system functioned, engineers had to do the work of other services. They carried on the entire operations of many ord-

[51] Ltr, Albrecht, 4 Nov 53; OCE ETOUSA Hist Rpt 7, Field and Service Force Construction, p. 73; Memo, Moore for Brig Gen E. S. Hughes, 17 Nov 42, BC 1, BOLERO Combined Committee.

[52] Ltr, SOS ETOUSA to Chfs of Supply Services, Base Sect COs, and Depot COs, 9 Oct 42, sub: Labor Pools for Depot Opns, 319.1 Rpts (Labor), Sep–Nov 42, EUCOM Engr files; Ltr, OCE, SOS ETOUSA, Col Donald B. Adams, Chf, O&T Div, to Col E. E. Barnes, London OCE Rep, 1 Oct 42, sub: Rpt on Engr Bns (Avn) and Airport Cons, 322.030; Ltr, SOS ETOUSA, Littlejohn, to CG, Eighth Air Force, 4 Oct

42, sub: Use of Avn Bns; both in 321 Avn Units, EUCOM Engr files. Ltr, SOS ETOUSA to CG, ETOUSA, 6 Oct 42, sub: SOS Troop and Labor Situation, BOLERO SOS Overall Plan.

[53] Ltr, SOS ETOUSA to CG, ETOUSA, 6 Oct 42, sub: SOS Troop and Labor Situation; Memo, Albrecht for Chf Engr, 1 Nov 42, and Memo, Cons Div for CE, 14 Nov 42; both in 231.4 Custodian (Labor), EUCOM Engr files. OCE ETOUSA Hist Rpt 4, Troops, app. 2, sheets 4–8; Memo, OCE ETOUSA for G–4, SOS ETOUSA, 24 Oct 42, sub: SOS Troops and Labor Situation, 321 Aviation Units, EUCOM Engr files; Ltr, HQ, VIII Bomber Command, to CG, Eighth Air Force, sub: Proposed Status List, w/4th Ind, OCE, SOS, to CG, Eighth Air Force, 10 Oct 42.

HOSPITAL CONSTRUCTION EMPLOYING PREFABRICATED CONCRETE ROOF TRUSSES

nance depots, and they supplied a large part of the personnel for quartermaster depots. The labor pool system originally established for the TORCH emergency aided materially in getting the North African invasion on its way in time. But the system seemed to have expanded beyond reason. With only 105,000 troops in the entire theater, Colonel Moore could not understand why it was necessary to have 15,500 men (not all of them engineers) carrying on supply functions.[54]

In the spring of 1943, SOS abolished the labor pool system and engineer units returned to their normal jobs. Although necessary, labor pools had markedly affected ETO construction progress. ROUNDUP plans had to be thrust aside, and work on airfields, depots, troop accommodations, and hospitals was thrown off schedule. Some construction had continued, but on a greatly reduced scale. Morale dropped and disciplinary problems increased, because men were doing jobs with which they were not familiar and for which they had no training. Moreover, many units had to be divided into small groups, with a resulting loss of unit integrity and pride.[55]

[54] Ltr, Lee to CG, Eighth Air Force, 12 Nov 42, sub: Engr Avn Bns, and 1st Ind, Eighth Air Force to CG, SOS, 4 Jan 43; both in 320.2 General, EUCOM Engr files. Memo, Moore for Reybold, 30 Nov 42, sub: Engr Problems in the ETO.

[55] Memo, OCE, SOS ETOUSA, for Col W. G. Weaver, Actg CofS, SOS, ETOUSA, 17 Dec 42, sub:

The British continued to execute their part of BOLERO construction, largely by contract, but the future of the American program hung in the balance. Many doubted that construction on the scale of the long-range BOLERO Plan would ever be needed. The general agreement was that additional camp construction would not be necessary during the winter, but depot and airfield programs were not substantially decreased. The engineers could not cope with this construction program so they sought a clear statement of responsibilities. Lacking such a state-

ment, they used General Somervell's order of 17 November, which sharply limited materials and supplies to the new, short-term 427,000-man troop basis. But this order did not look beyond the spring of 1943 and placed the Americans in the awkward position of seeming to block preparations in the United Kingdom for a cross-Channel attack. The ETOUSA publication in mid-January 1943 of a modified construction program left this situation basically unchanged. The unqualified revival of the buildup had to await agreement on a strategic program for 1943−44.[56]

---

Attachment of Engr Troops to Other Services, 321 Engrs, EUCOM Engr files; Ltr, Office of the Engr, Southern Base Sect, to Chf Engr, ETOUSA, 20 Oct 42, sub: Progress on Construction; Memo, Col R. B. Lord for Chf Engr, 24 Jan 43, 231.4 Custodian (Labor), EUCOM Engr files.

[56] Ltr, Albrecht, 4 Nov 53; Ltr, Moore to Base Sect Engrs, 13 Jan 43, sub: Modifying Plan for BOLERO Construction Program w/related papers, 600 Gen, 1 Jun 43−31 Aug 43, and 600−A−Gen; Memo, Moore for Reybold, 30 Nov 42, sub: Engr Problems in ETO, w/related papers; Ltr, Lee to Somervell, 17 Nov 42.

# CHAPTER IV

# The Engineers in the Invasion of North Africa

While the BOLERO program in the United Kingdom took second place, Allied planners turned their attention to an assault on the periphery of German power and began detailed consideration of landings in North Africa. The hurried planning for TORCH offered an object lesson in disorderly preparation and brilliant improvisation. Though the timetable called for landings before the end of the year, the force envisaged did not have an overall command until the Combined Chiefs of Staff named General Eisenhower Commander in Chief, Allied Expeditionary Force, on 13 August 1942. The Allied Force Headquarters (AFHQ) that Eisenhower headed came into existence officially only on 12 September but was already a closely integrated organization. General Sir Kenneth A. N. Anderson commanded the British ground forces and Admiral Sir Andrew B. Cunningham the naval forces. The various general and special staff sections were Allied organizations, with American and British officers interspersed throughout in various positions of command and subordination. Maj. Gen. Humfrey Gale (British) became the chief administrative officer at AFHQ. Of three task forces, Western Task Force (WTF), which was to sail directly from the United States to Casablanca, was under Maj. Gen. George S. Patton, Jr. Center Task Force (CTF), with the primary mission of capturing the port of Oran, was under Maj. Gen. Lloyd R. Fredendall. Eastern Task Force (ETF), with responsibility for seizing Algiers and the Blida and Maison Blanche Airfields, was largely British but retained an American commander, Maj. Gen. Charles W. Ryder, to confuse the French defenders of North Africa as to the nationality of the invading force.[1]

## Engineer Plans and Preparations

The Engineer Section of AFHQ came into being when Col. Frank O. Bowman arrived in London toward the end of August 1942. This small section worked closely with the Engineer Section of Center Task Force, headed by Col. Mark M. Boatner, Jr., of the 591st Engineer Boat Regiment, in preparing plans for the CTF landing at Oran. AFHQ's G-4 section was responsible

---

[1] Leighton and Coakley, *Global Logistics and Strategy, 1940–43*, p. 455; George F. Howe, *Northwest Africa: Seizing the Initiative in the West*, United States Army in World War II (Washington, 1957), pp. 15, 32–35.

for planning engineer supply, and under G–4 were SOS groups attached to the two U.S. task forces. The Center Task Force (II Corps), SOS, assembled in England under Brig. Gen. Thomas B. Larkin, former ETOUSA chief engineer. After the landings, Larkin's organization was to become the Mediterranean Base Section.

Western Task Force planning took place in the United States. Its Engineer Section, headed by Col. John F. Conklin, developed along the lines of an augmented corps-level engineer organization. The section received valuable assistance from OCE (which was just one block away), particularly the Supply Division, and from the Army Map Service.[2]

Early in the fall the first elements of the future Atlantic Base Section (initially designated SOS Task Force A) assembled in the United States under Brig. Gen. Arthur R. Wilson as the SOS for the Western Task Force. The Engineer Section, SOS, WTF, under Col. Francis H. Oxx, obtained considerable aid from the Plans and Distribution Division, OCE, WD, as well as from engineers of WTF themselves. OCE, WD, was responsible for engineer supply for the first four WTF convoys, the engineer allocation being 2,000 tons per convoy. The engineers planned that requisitions would be submitted first to the New York Port of Embarkation (NYPOE); in case of losses at sea, NYPOE would determine priority of replacement and shipment.[3]

The fact that Allied forces were to undertake the landings complicated

supply planning for TORCH in the United Kingdom. Most of the engineer Class IV items (heavy construction equipment) would come from the British, while the remainder of Class IV and all Class II and V items would come from American sources. A joint stockpile established in England helped to avoid confusion and duplication. British elements would handle logistics for WTF, while SOS, ETOUSA, would supply the CTF and the American components of the ETF. After late December (about D plus 40) supplies for all American elements of TORCH were to come directly from the United States. Planners expected to build up supplies in North Africa to a 14-day level by D plus 30, a 30-day level by D plus 60, and a 45-day level by D plus 90. Classes II, IV, and V items were to be resupplied automatically for the first two months because the task forces could not be expected to establish adequate inventory control and requisition procedures until base sections became operational. Estimates by the chiefs of the technical services at ASF, WD, were to form the basis for the automatic resupply program, but the plan also permitted limited requisitioning from the NYPOE.

From the engineers' point of view, one of the most disturbing events during the planning was a high-level decision to cut authorized vehicle allocations. Cutting the number of vehicles by 50 percent freed the drivers and crews for duties in fighting formations. The cut applied not only to the engineers' trucks but also to special engineer vehicles of all types. Maj. Gen. Mark W. Clark, deputy commander in chief for TORCH, believed the decision would not seriously affect the WTF, whose primary mission was to establish and de-

---

[2]Ltr, Col John A. Chambers to EHD, 5 Apr 56.
[3] History of Atlantic Base Section to June 1, 1943 vol. I, p. 5, in CMH.

fend a line of communications, but the 50 percent cut meant a reduction of 10,000 vehicles for Center Task Force alone. Afterwards, Brig. Gen. Donald A. Davison, Colonel Bowman's successor as AFHQ engineer, observed that engineers without vehicles became merely underarmed and improperly trained infantry, unable to perform their technical missions.[4]

Supply plans had to be made before information concerning important phases of the invasion was available. Arriving at a fixed troop basis was fundamental, but the Allies could not come to an agreement on one until planning was well along. Even after a figure for the total invasion force was at hand the allocations among service, ground, and air forces changed continually. Furthermore, no outline plan of attack became available until long after supply preparations were under way.

Requirements for special engineer equipment included such diverse items as bulldozers, tractors with detachable angledozers, amphibious tractors, mines and mine detectors, beach and airfield landing mats, camouflage equipment and supplies, lighting plants, well-digging machinery, water trucks, water cans (by the thousands), hand carts, portable air compressors, fumigation vaults, asphalt, magnifying glasses, unbleached cotton sheeting, cotton sack, cord, rope, insect repellent, cable cutters, and grappling hooks. As it turned out, the engineers managed to satisfy most of their supply demands except for vehicles. On 17 October engineer units of CTF reported that they had

secured 80 percent of their supply requirements, and on 22 October the 1st Engineer Amphibian Brigade reported 99 percent of its engineer equipment on hand. However, many of the missing items were important ones.

The engineers of both task forces understood in general, but not in detail, what clearing obstacles from the beaches would involve. They were, for example, unable to obtain sea-level, offshore photographs of the Barbary coastline.[5] British photo reconnaissance of some of the beaches proved helpful, and plans were adjusted after submarines went in close for a final investigation.

The engineers knew that the rainy season would begin about the time of D-day and that mud would limit the use of roads and airfields. They also knew there were few rivers to cross, so they would need little bridging equipment. However, they would need much machinery to maintain and repair roads, airfields, and railroads. The meager natural resources of North Africa would not aid construction, and the engineers would have to maintain water supply, sewage, gas, electricity, and transit systems.[6]

Requirements for certain items of supply had to be studied in collaboration with other services. The Engineer Section, SOS, WTF, worked with the Transportation Section in requisitioning railway equipment and petroleum pipeline and negotiated the procurement of the pipeline. Many unknowns remained. The engineers had to esti-

---

[4]Memo, D. A. Davison, 3 Jan 43, sub: Lessons of Opn TORCH (hereafter cited as Davison Memo), 381 War Plans (Jun 42–Jul 43), 300.162 AFHQ Engr Sect.

[5]Samuel Eliot Morison, "History of the United States Naval Operations in World War II," vol. II, *Operations in North African Waters* (Boston: Little, Brown and Company, 1950), p. 26.

[6]AFHQ (U.S.) Engr Sect (Sept–Oct 42); Ltr, Brig Gen W. A. Carter to EHD, 8 Feb 56.

mate the amount of pipe that would be needed to transport petroleum products to storage tanks in cities and at airfields in North Africa. They had to consider, among other things, the probable amount of petroleum that would have to be moved by rail or truck as well as the probable storage facilities, and their estimate had to be based on intelligent guesswork rather than on specific knowledge.[7]

The American high command had barely begun to appreciate the practicability and utility of a military pipeline system when the United States became .involved in the war.[8] Well before TORCH began, the Army had placed orders with American industry for equipment needed to build military pipelines. Military requirements called for materials that could be easily transported and readily erected in the field, and during the year of peace the petroleum industry had produced such equipment. From the military standpoint, the important development was the "victaulic" coupling, named for one of the fabricators, the Victaulic Company of America. This coupling consisted of a gas-resistant gasket of synthetic rubber and a metal clamp. The gasket fit into grooves cut around the ends of two lengths of piping and was held in place by the clamp, a two-piece steel collar bolted tight to hold the gasket. This type of coupling could be fitted more quickly and was less rigid than either threaded or welded joints. The steel welded-seam

pipe came in twenty-foot lengths. Early in the war this standard length was four inches in inside diameter and weighed 168 pounds. American industry later developed a four-inch pipe—"invasion tubing"—which weighed only sixty-eight pounds per length.

The engineers adapted other items of military pipeline equipment from the most portable items in commercial oil fields—pumps, engines, ship discharge hoses, fittings, and storage tanks. The Army used six sizes (ranging from 100-barrel to 10,000-barrel capacity) of bolted steel tanks for semiportable storage. These tanks, consisting of shaped steel plates fitted together with bolts, could be shipped "knocked down" as sets—complete with valves and fittings—for onsite assembly.[9]

Maps were essential to the success of the North Africa invasion. The British Geographical Section, General Staff, supplied most of the maps CTF and ETF used. The Intelligence Division, OCE, SOS, ETOUSA, helped distribute the maps—some 500,000 items weighing approximately forty tons. Twenty tons were sorted, wrapped, and bundled in coded rolls for distribution aboard ships. Some 400,000 additional photomaps required careful handling and packing.[10]

---

[7] History of Atlantic Base Section to June 1, 1943, vol. II, ch. XIV, p. 4.

[8] Ltr, C. W. Karstens to Maj Gen A. C. Smith, 29 Jan 54, with attached comments signed by Karstens; see Coll, Keith, and Rosenthal, *The Corps of Engineers: Troops and Equipment*, pp. 418ff.

[9] Many factors could vary the amount of gasoline actually pumped through a pipeline; six-inch pipe had a rated capacity of 400 gallons a minute, or 480,000 gallons in a normal (20-hour) operating day. Engineer School Special Text (ST−5−350−1), Military Pipeline Systems (Fort Belvoir, Va., 1950), pp. 23, 32, 198.

[10] Ltr, Col Martin Hotine, Geographical Sect, General Staff, to Col Herbert Milwit, 27 Nov 42, 319 Chf Engr, EUCOM Engr files; Status Rpt, 4 Nov 42, Intel Div, 319.1 Rpts, EUCOM Engr files; Coll, Keith, and Rosenthal, *The Corps of Engineers: Troops and Equipment*, pp. 445−46; OCE ETOUSA Hist Rpt 5, Intelligence and Topography, pp. 31−32.

The engineers in WTF did not have enough maps, and on short notice reproduction alone posed serious problems, not the least of which was security. The Army Map Service reproduced maps for WTF at its plant just outside Washington, D.C., but even there security risks existed, for only a few of the 800 workers could be screened in time. The maps were then taken to Hampton Roads by a detachment from the 66th Engineer Topographic Company, which kept them under constant surveillance. The 1:25,000-scale maps of the beachheads, issued to the troops before they sailed, had place names blacked out and carried a false north. Only the commanding generals of the individual subtask forces received true maps before departure from the United States. Each of the subtask forces making up the WTF had an attached mobile mapmaking detachment from the 66th Engineer Topographic Company, and each detachment carried a 250-pound reserve stock of maps. WTF sailed with some sixty tons of maps of many different types—ground force maps on a scale of six inches to the mile, air corps target maps, colored mosaics of such harbors as Port-Lyautey and Casablanca and the airdrome of Safi—and hundreds of photographs.[11]

The hurried attempt to produce maps for TORCH had poor results. On both sides of the Atlantic, maps of the target areas had to be printed from available sources, and little opportunity existed to bring them up to date or to produce them at the scales required for ground and close air support operations. In some cases major military operations had to be based on 1:200,000-scale maps with ground configuration shown by spot elevations and hachures. Low-grade photomaps, neither rectified for tilt nor matched for tone, substituted for large-scale maps of limited areas. The lack of good base maps of the target area, coupled with too little lead time, ruled out satisfactory maps for the North Africa invasion, while the secrecy that enveloped invasion plans severely limited the amount of map work that could be undertaken in time.[12]

British and American agencies aided each other in preparing intelligence material vital to TORCH; one example was a bulky work that the Strategic Engineer Studies Section in the Strategic Intelligence Branch, OCE, WD, compiled in September 1942. Material came from the British as well as from American construction companies, consular agents, geologists, even people who sent postcards depicting scenes in North Africa. The volumes contained a wealth of information on North Africa, including descriptions of roads and railroads, port facilities, bridge capacities, water supply, construction materials, forests, airfields, electric power, and the layout of known minefields.[13]

Engineer beach models were in great demand on both sides of the Atlantic. Large plaster of paris models were made at Fort Belvoir, Virginia, and models of Moroccan beaches came to the United States from England. The British model beaches originated from

---

[11]OCE ETOUSA Hist Rpt 5, Intelligence and Topography, app. 5; "The North African Campaign," *Reader's Digest* (February 1943), 98–99; Hist 66th Engr Topo Co; Engr Comment on Map Supply Opn TORCH, TF 3–0.3 (47844), 8–11 Nov 42, apps. 8 and 2; Maj William C. Frierson, Preparations for TORCH, pp. 1–3, 63.

[12]Ltr, Col Herbert Milwit to EHD, 31 Jan 56.
[13]Coll, Keith, and Rosenthal, *The Corps of Engineers: Troops and Equipment*, p. 450.

information the British Inter-Service Information Series (ISIS) gleaned from reports by the British military staff. Two American engineer officers who, posing as airline officials, had visited Bathurst on the western coast of Africa early in 1942 furnished useful information, particularly on coastal surf. Other information came from tourist guidebooks and from recent visitors to North Africa. Some of the model beaches depicted the terrain a mile or more inland.[14]

### Engineer Amphibian Brigades

Engineer training for the invasion of North Africa concentrated heavily on methods of landing on hostile shores. Japanese occupation of Pacific islands and German control of nearly all the worthwhile harbors on the European continent forced the War Department's attention to the possibility of Army beach crossings and to means of invasion and logistical support that did not rely entirely on seizing strongly defended ports at the outset. Amphibious warfare had been the preserve of the Navy for two decades before American entry into the new conflict, and, in fact, had become the *raison d'etre* of the U.S. Marine Corps. An agreement in 1935 defined the responsibilities of each service in landing operations and limited the Army to stevedoring at established ports. Clearly based on the experience of World War I, in which the Navy could deliver goods to French ports that were intact and secure from enemy

interdiction, the arrangement was now passe. Though the issue remained open throughout the war, the Navy continued to lobby for the exclusive right to operate across beaches. However, the Army did take over a large share of this function in the spring of 1942 because the Navy could not supply smaller landing craft or provide enough men to operate boats or train other coxswains and crews. Out of the necessity to prepare for Army amphibious operations grew the engineer amphibian brigades.

The Army's earliest conceptions for the brigades in 1942 reemphasized an ancient method of moving troops onto a hostile shore. The Navy's prewar experimentation with amphibious operations relied almost entirely upon a ship-to-shore method of deployment to the beach in which combat troops and cargo were unloaded offshore into smaller craft that made the run from deeper water to the shore. Hazardous under any circumstances, the ship-to-shore system was a near impossibility at night and in heavy seas. With the introduction of larger, shallow-draft vessels that could plow up to the beach and disgorge men and equipment dry-shod, Army and Navy planners could readily see the advantage of the shore-to-shore amphibious operations. The shore-to-shore alternative treated each operation as a major river crossing and presupposed that landing craft making the assault would embark units and equipment on the near, or friendly, shore and transport them directly, without the confusion of a deepwater transfer, to the far, or hostile, shore. Unsaddled with earlier doctrine in the field, the Army favored the latter method as the means of crossing the Channel to the

[14] H. H. Dunham, U.S. Army Transportation and the Conquest of North Africa, Jan 45, pp. 42, 80, in CMH; Ltr, Milwit to EHD, 31 Jan 56, and Interv, Maj Gen Frank O. Bowman, 9 Feb 56.

Continent. Though the major landings of the war employed combinations of both methods, Army engineer training, organization, and equipment in the amphibian brigades created in 1942 followed shore-to-shore doctrine.[15]

The Army started relatively late to form amphibian units. Formally established on 10 June 1942 under Col. Daniel Noce, the Engineer Amphibian Command as an SOS organization paralleled an Army Ground Forces command, the Amphibious Training Command, at Camp Edwards, Massachusetts. The Engineer Amphibian Command specified the organizational shape of the first units, the 1st and 2d Engineer Amphibian Brigades, activated on 15 and 20 June, respectively. Each consisted of a boat regiment, a shore regiment, and support units. Later additions to the standard TOE included signal units and a quartermaster battalion. Each shore regiment consisted of three battalions; each battalion included two far-shore companies responsible for marking and organizing hostile beaches and moving supplies across them to invading forces and one near-shore company charged with loading combat troops and materiel. The Army made constant changes in the standard unit composition in an attempt to perfect the concept and to provide the brigades with a flexible structure to meet the conditions of the assault. The 2d, 3d, and 4th Brigades, eventually known as engineer special brigades, each had three boat and shore regiments. Because no larger craft were available when Colonel Noce took over the Engineer Amphibian Command,

the engineers had as standard equipment 36-foot LCVPs and 50-foot LCM–3s. Though experimentation with the 50-foot boat produced the LCM–6, a longer, more commodious, and slightly faster boat using the originally designed engines, the command knew that none of its models was a match for the choppy waters of the English Channel and none could negotiate larger expanses of open ocean. Engineer amphibian training at Camp Edwards and later at Camp Carrabelle on the Florida Gulf Coast centered on the 36- and 50-foot craft as they became available from Navy stocks or from factories. But even before the 105-foot LCT–5 became available, the Navy reemphasized its prerogatives on amphibious warfare units and on training responsibilities in that field.[16]

In July 1942 the Navy reaffirmed the validity of the 1935 agreement, arguing for control of amphibious operations. Though it could not prevail everywhere—the Army retained command and control of the brigades for the most part in the Southwest Pacific—the Navy officially took over all boats and maintained its responsibility for training boat crews elsewhere outside the United States. Thus, the Army's Amphibious Corps, Atlantic Fleet, consisting of the 3d and 9th Infantry Divisions and the 2d Armored Division, under Maj. Gen. Jonathan W. Anderson, was subordinate for training to Rear Adm. H. Kent Hewitt, though it was a part of General Patton's Western Task Force. A King-Marshall agreement then delineated the

---

[15] Morison, *Operations in North African Waters*, pp. 270–71; Coll, Keith, and Rosenthal, *The Corps of Engineers: Troops and Equipment*, p. 362.

[16] Coll, Keith, and Rosenthal, *The Corps of Engineers: Troops and Equipment*, pp. 364–65; Brig. Gen. William F. Heavey, *Down Ramp! The Story of the Army Amphibian Engineers* (Washington: Infantry Journal Press, 1947), p. 12.

Navy's responsibility for operating and maintaining all landing boats in the European Theater of Operations. The agreement worked to the detriment of the 1st Engineer Amphibian Brigade when it arrived in the theater on 17 August 1942, only six weeks after its formation, to complete its training with the 1st Infantry Division. It interfered further with the assault training schedule for the Center Task Force laid out in a meeting on 25 August among British Lt. Gen. K. A. N. Anderson, Vice Adm. J. Hughes-Hallett, and Maj. Gen. J. C. Hayden and American Maj. Gen. Mark W. Clark.

The engineer brigade, under Col. Henry C. Wolfe, operated in England under a number of constraints, much as the engineer units that had preceded it into the theater. Most obvious as a source of grief was the command structure resulting from the Army-Navy agreements. ETOUSA headquarters, following the lead from home, established the Maritime Command under Rear Adm. Andrew C. Bennett to provide naval supervision for the brigade's activity. The Maritime Command, hastily put together on 11 August while the brigade was still at sea, had virtually no personnel experienced in amphibious warfare and no equipment to carry out training exercises. Admiral Bennett, acting with no clear statement of the scope of his command, was forced to ask Colonel Wolfe for several of his boat crews to train junior naval officers in small boat handling so that they, in turn, could teach future Navy crews. Bennett's command also resorted to splitting up the brigade elements. The unit, designed as an integral organization of 366 officers, 21 warrant officers, and 7,013 enlisted men to support an entire division, found itself spread on both sides of Britain's North Channel. Though later designated principal military landing officer for Center Task Force, Colonel Wolfe served on Bennett's staff once the Maritime Command headquarters had moved from London to Rosneath, Scotland. His own headquarters company and the 531st Engineer Shore Regiment went to Londonderry while two battalions of the 591st Engineer Boat Regiment settled in Belfast with the brigade medical battalion. The brigade managed to secure some basic training and shake down its organization, but it received no training in far-shore unloading, and much of its equipment arrived after delays at six widely scattered ports aboard sixty-five different ships.[17]

When Brig. Gen. Daniel Noce toured the amphibian training centers in the United Kingdom in September, he found them all inadequate. Constant rain reduced training time; the terrain behind the available beaches was not suited to the brigade's needs; landing beaches were too constricted, windswept, and rocky. Noce saw boat crews cautiously approach the beach for fear of damaging their craft instead of coming in rapidly as they would have to do under enemy fire. A lack of tools, equipment, and personnel hampered the training program, and campsites for the men were poor. Large unit training was infeasible with the small facilities available. A reserve of boats had to

[17]ETOUSA GO 27, 11 Aug 42; Heavey, *Down Ramp! The Story of the Army Amphibian Engineers*, pp. 10–19; Memo, Engr Sect, ETOUSA, for Brig Gen T. B. Larkin, Chf Engr, 24 Aug 42, sub: Weekly Rpt of Activities, 319.1 ETOUSA, EUCOM files; 1st Engr Amphib Bde, Rpt of Opns with Center Task Force, 29 Nov 42.

GENERAL NOCE *(Photograph taken in 1944.)*

hatch crew experience. Because of British manpower shortages, one battalion was to supply 35-man hatch crews for ten of the twenty-three cargo vessels in the assault wave to the CTF. Two officers and fifteen enlisted men of the maintenance company of the 591st Engineer Boat Regiment received some excellent training in repairing landing craft when they were attached to British naval contingents of the ETF at Inverary on Loch Fyne, Scotland. The men of the brigade's 561st Boat Maintenance Company had earlier repaired approximately one hundred landing craft at the U.S. naval base at Rosneath, in the Glasgow area. The company was fortunate in having the necessary equipment to do the job.[19]

For units other than boat maintenance and stevedore crews, training in the United Kingdom consisted chiefly of physical conditioning and instruction in infantry fundamentals. Only eight weeks were available between the time units were alerted for TORCH and moved to the port area for final rehearsal, and for some engineer units construction work interrupted even that short period.

Training in the 19th Engineer Combat Regiment and the 16th Armored Engineer Battalion (the 1st Armored Division's organic engineer unit) may be taken as an example. The 19th Engineer Combat Regiment had sufficient physical hardening but received no ammunition or mines for training and no instruction in the use of the Bailey bridge, British explosives, or antitank

be overhauled and carefully protected against damage in preparation for TORCH, which took the craft temporarily from training use. The brigade's engineers spent considerable time assembling new craft shipped in crates from the United States. Much of this production went to equip British units before American engineer organizations received their standard equipment. Between 22 September and 5 October, all landing craft were withdrawn from training units to be prepared for the invasion.[18]

In various parts of the United Kingdom the brigade's 591st Engineer Boat Regiment received some infantry training and considerable stevedore and

---

[18] Memo, AFHQ for Gen Clark, 26 Sep 42, sub: Observation at Amphibian Training Centers in Scotland by Brig Gen Daniel Noce, EAC 353 (Training); Ltr, Lt Col John B. Webb to EHD, 23 Apr 56.

[19] Ltr, Col Kenneth W. Kennedy to EHD, 9 Apr 56; Heavey, *Down Ramp! The Story of the Army Amphibian Engineers*, pp. 20–21.

mines.[20] The 16th Armored Engineer Battalion fared somewhat better. While stationed in Northern Ireland, the 16th received some comprehensive bridge and ferry training. The unit used the British Bailey bridge, its value having been recognized by officers who attended the British military engineering school. The 16th, likewise, became familiar with other British equipment, including Sommerfeld track, mines, booby traps, and demolitions. The battalion also launched a treadway bridge from a modified maracaibo boat off Newcastle.[21]

During the summer and fall of 1942, engineer units went through invasion rehearsal drills in both the United States and the United Kingdom. In the Zone of the Interior the WTF split into three subtask forces, X, Y, and Z, and carried out amphibious drills. Since loading went slowly, supplies were delayed, and because beach capacity was limited, one subtask force began rehearsals while the others continued loading. From the start there were mixups because loads were stowed aboard wrong ships and ammunition and gasoline were not unloaded for fear of explosions and fire. The result was a landing exercise limited to the loading and unloading of vehicles and other bulky items. While Y was loading, X and Z forces participated in the same type of exercise. Another serious deficiency was a lack of rigorous night training, which was to prove costly during the landings. The value of all WTF exercises also was limited by the fact that they took place during near ideal conditions—a tide that varied little and a relatively calm sea—hardly the situation to be expected along the Atlantic coast of North Africa.[22]

CTF and ETF held rehearsals like those of the WTF on 19–20 October near Loch Linnhe on the northwest coast of Scotland. Their objectives were to practice landing-craft techniques at night, rehearse the seizure of objectives up to ten miles inland, test communication among groups landing on a wide front, and promote cooperation among carrier-borne aircraft, naval bombardment vessels, and ground troops. The engineers gained some experience in laying out shore installations and communications but learned almost nothing about unloading vehicles and supplies. The rehearsals were final; no opportunity existed to correct errors.[23] Only the experience of an actual invasion could provide an understanding of the problems involved, and only then would it be clear that a close-knit beach organization was required to coordinate the work of engineer shore regiments and of the Navy.[24]

### The Landings

#### Western Task Force

WTF had the mission of taking the

---

[20] Hist 19th Engr C Rgt; AFHQ, compilation Rpts Opn Torch, CTF, Incl 1, 29 Dec 42, Lesson from Opn Torch, HQ, 19th Engr Rgt.

[21] Hist 16th Armd Engr Bn. The forerunner of the LST, the maracaibo was converted from shallow-draft oil tankers used on Lake Maracaibo in Venezuela.

[22] Leighton and Coakley, *Global Logistics and Strategy, 1940–43*, p. 444; Dunham, U.S. Army Transportation and the Conquest, pp. 35–37, 73–78; Interv, Shotwell and Gardes with Chabbock, 4 Nov 50; U.S. Atlantic Fleet Amphib Force to CofS Amphib Force, 18 Nov 42, sub: Observation of Landing Opns at Port Lyautey, EAC folder African campaign.

[23] Ltr, Brig Gen John F. Conklin, 25 Jan 56; The Administrative and Logistical History of the European Theater of Operations, vol. IV, "Operations Torch and the ETO," pp. 61–62, in CMH; 1st Engr Amphib Bde, Rpt of Opns with Center Task Force.

[24] Ltr, Col John A. Chambers to EHD, 5 Apr 56.

port and adjacent airfield at Casablanca and then establishing communication with CTF at Oran. If Spain should intercede, the WTF was to join with Center Task Force and secure Spanish Morocco. Casablanca itself was too strongly defended to be taken by direct frontal assault. Instead, it was to be captured from the rear with three subtask forces landing close enough to the city to take it before reinforcements could arrive. This plan required the early use of medium or heavy tanks, for which a port was essential since landing craft to carry such heavy loads were not then available. Also, if land-based aircraft were to support the attack, an airfield had to be captured quickly.

The three subtask forces were called BRUSHWOOD, GOALPOST, and BLACKSTONE. The first, commanded by Maj. Gen. Jonathan W. Anderson and made up of the 3d Infantry Division, a portion of the 2d Armored Division, and supporting troops, was to provide the main blow by capturing Fedala, a resort thirteen miles north of Casablanca, and then moving on to Casablanca. Maj. Gen. Lucian K. Truscott, Jr., headed the GOALPOST force, which was made up of part of the 9th Infantry Division and elements of the 2d Armored Division along with supporting units. Its goals were the capture of Mehdia (eighty miles from Casablanca) and the Port-Lyautey Airfield with its hard-surfaced runways. BLACKSTONE, the third subtask force, was under Maj. Gen. Ernest N. Harmon and had parts of the 9th Infantry and 2d Armored Divisions. Its initial mission was the capture of Safi, a small port about 150 miles south of Casablanca. *(Map 3)*

The main engineer forces of the WTF were distributed among the three task forces. The 1st and 3d Battalions of the 36th Engineer Combat Regiment were with BRUSHWOOD, and the 1st and 2d Battalions of the 540th Engineers were with GOALPOST and BLACKSTONE, respectively. All were to act as shore parties. The 15th Engineer Combat Battalion (9th Division) with GOALPOST, the 10th Battalion (3d Division) with BRUSHWOOD, and elements of the 17th Armored Engineer Battalion (2d Armored Division) with BLACKSTONE were to carry out normal combat engineer duties. The 2d Battalion of the 20th Engineer Combat Regiment, assigned to BRUSHWOOD, was to remain on board ship as a reserve force to be called in when needed.[25]

The main objective of the Western Task Force on D-day was Fedala, where landing beaches were exposed to the double hazard of enfilading coastal defense batteries and dangerously high surf. When successive waves of landing craft approached the shore, many swept off course to founder on reefs or rocks. Others, only partly unloaded and stranded during ebb tide, were not able to retract because following landing craft were too close. The pounding surf wrecked many stranded craft. The inadequacy of the shore parties, made up chiefly of combat engineers of the 36th Engineers assisted by naval beach parties, also created dangerous delays.

The toll of landing craft was high at the Fedala beachhead, and the landing of troops and supplies became badly disorganized. Barely more than 1 percent of the supplies was ashore as late as 1700 on D-day. Engineer officers, badly needed on the beaches to control

---

[25]HQ, WTF, Engr, 8 Jan 43, sub: Engr Annex to Final Rpt of Opns of WTF, 8 Nov 42.

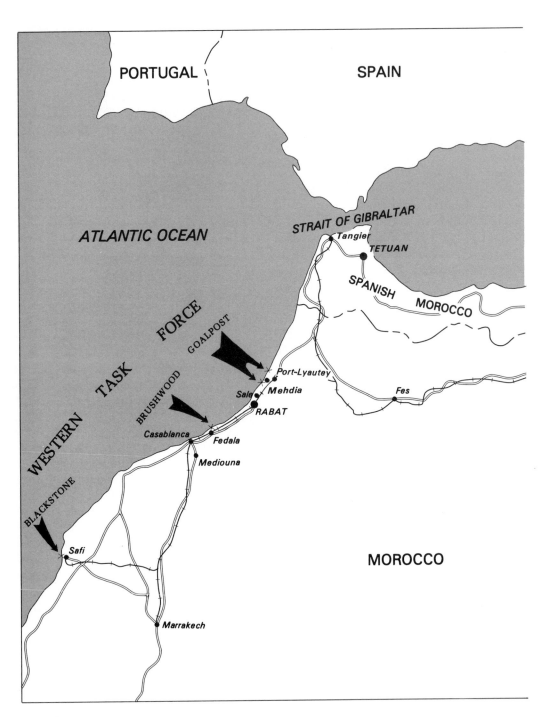

*MAP 3*

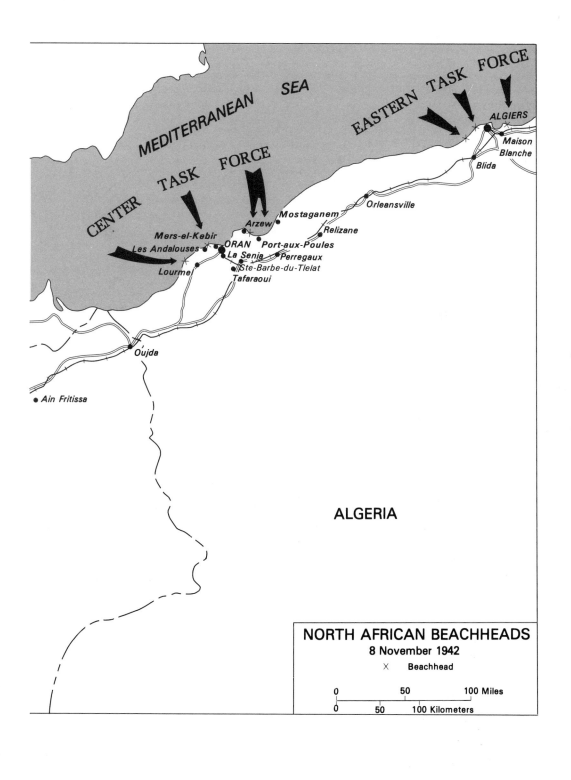

MEDITERRANEAN SEA

EASTERN TASK FORCE

CENTER TASK FORCE

ALGIERS
Maison
Blanche
Blida

Orleansville

Mostaganem
Arzew
Relizane

Mers-el-Kebir
Les Andalouses
ORAN  Port-aux-Poules
La Senia
Perregaux
Lourmel
Ste-Barbe-du-Tlelat
Tafaraoui

Oujda

Ain Fritissa

ALGERIA

## NORTH AFRICAN BEACHHEADS
### 8 November 1942
×  Beachhead

| 0 | | 50 | 100 Miles |
|---|---|---|---|
| 0 | 50 | 100 Kilometers | |

WRECKED AND BROACHED LANDING CRAFT AT FEDALA, FRENCH MOROCCO

and direct the engineers of the shore parties, could not get ashore. No centralized coordination of supply activities for the different landing operations existed. The G–4 section of WTF did not get ashore at Fedala until the third morning, and the G–4 himself was not with this group of only two officers and three enlisted men. General Patton, however, was at the beach before daylight on D plus 1 and remained there until after noon because of his disgust over conditions. He condemned what seemed to him the lack of enterprise of the Army shore parties and took measures to divert the small craft from the beaches, where they had to fight the menacing surf, to the port of Fedala.

The chaos with which the Western Task Force had to contend drove home the lesson that trained service troops should always accompany invasion forces to assume the burden of supply and service functions, allowing the task force commander to concentrate on tactical problems. As it was, Patton had held back SOS Task Force A, and the SOS did not reach Casablanca until 24 December.[26]

The employment of engineers as provisional assault and defensive units in the Western Task Force was exemplified by the experience of Company C, 15th Engineer Combat Battalion and 1st Battalion, 540th Engineer Shore Regiment, supporting a regimental com-

[26]History of Atlantic Base Section to June 1, 1943, vol. I, ch. XIV, p. 9.

bat team of the 9th Infantry Division in GOALPOST—the attack on Mehdia north of Casablanca and on Port-Lyautey Airfield. In addition to weapons and hand tools, the engineers in the assault carried mine detectors, bangalore torpedoes, and flame throwers to enable them to push through minefields and other obstacles and to reduce pillboxes.

A provisional assault company of engineers made up of detachments from Company C, 15th Engineer Combat Battalion, the 540th Engineer Shore Regiment, and the 871st Engineer Aviation Battalion participated in an attack on 10 November on the Kasba, an old stone fortress that stood on a cliff above the mouth of the Sebou River and blocked the approach to Mehdia and the airfield upriver. Shouting French defenders stood on the walls firing down at the Americans but American infantry attacks along the ridge and engineer attacks along the river took the Kasba. Then a small detachment from Company C of the 15th Engineer Battalion rendered the fort's guns useless. The destroyer *Dallas,* with a special raiding detachment aboard including part of a Company C platoon, then entered the Sebou, and, after the engineers had removed a cable net, proceeded upriver and captured Port-Lyautey Airfield. After the destroyer's guns had silenced enemy artillery, the engineers began repairs on the airfield. That afternoon, the 888th Airborne Engineer Aviation Company relieved Company C's elements.

After the occupation of Casablanca on D plus 4, supply operations began to center there, and an almost hopeless tangle quickly developed. The first task of the WTF engineers was to resolve this problem, and the 175th Engineer General Service Regiment tackled the job. The regiment reached Casablanca on 16 November 1942 in the D plus 5 convoy and found a dump location that was eventually to be expanded to 160 acres. All supplies brought ashore, whether engineer, quartermaster, or ordnance, went into this dump, where, before any systematic attempt could be made to institute depot procedures, more supplies of all sorts began arriving. Every type of vehicle that could be used for the purpose, including jeeps, was pressed into service to move supplies from the ships. The rush to unload was so great that materials were cast off railroad cars and trucks without system or order, and there were times after the December rains began when supplies stood a foot deep in water.

The 175th Engineer General Service Regiment had the extraordinarily difficult task of operating the engineer depot under such chaotic conditions, and it had to undertake an around-the-clock job for which it was not trained. For days the regiment had no opportunity to rest and no chance to consolidate its units. The engineer depot office force was housed in a sixteen-foot tent during the first week. For more than a month supplies of all description spread over the dump area without adequate shelter, while guards had to be posted to prevent pilfering by natives. The engineers improvised shelter for perishables by turning landing barges upside down. Late in December warehouse construction was possible, and the engineer dump, which the 175th operated throughout the winter months, gradually began to assume the characteristics of an orderly depot.[27]

---

[27]Hist 175th Engr GS Rgt, Feb 42–Oct 45.

*Center Task Force*

The mission of Center Task Force, consisting of the 1st Infantry Division, Combat Command B of the 1st Armored Division, and the 1st Ranger Battalion, was to capture Oran and its adjacent airfields, to establish communication with the WTF, and, in the event of Spanish intervention, to cooperate with General Patton in securing Spanish Morocco. Finally, CTF was to establish communications with ETF at Orleansville, Algeria. Around Oran, four landings were scheduled, with a frontal assault on the port itself as the key objective. The Ranger battalion was to develop the smaller port of Arzew, thirty miles east of Oran, while Combat Command B, designated Task Force Red, and the 16th and 18th Regimental Combat Teams of the 1st Infantry Division went ashore on Beach Z, just east of Arzew. Armored forces were to slice inland to seize the airfields at Tafaraoui and La Senia, as the 16th and 18th Regimental Combat Teams closed Oran from the east. The 26th Regimental Combat Team, 1st Infantry Division, was to land at Les Andalouses and advance on Oran from the west. The fourth group, a smaller component of Combat Command B, was to come ashore at Mersa Bou Zedjar, move inland to Lourmel, seize the airstrip there, and then advance on the La Senia Airfield just south of Oran. Brig. Gen. Henry C. Wolfe, commanding the much-dispersed 1st Engineer Amphibian Brigade, was to operate Arzew as a port and bring supplies and troops across the adjacent Beach Z. He gave the responsibility for unloading the D-day convoy to the 531st Engineer Shore Regiment, which was to co-operate with Royal Navy units on the beaches.[28]

The 531st Engineer Shore Regiment, attached to the 1st Infantry Division, provided one battalion at Les Andalouses and two battalions at Arzew. The 2d Battalion of the 591st Engineer Boat Regiment had shore engineer support duty for Combat Command B of the 1st Armored Division, split between two beaches. The 1st Battalion of the 591st furnished hatch crews, while the 16th Armored Engineer Battalion (1st Armored Division) and the 1st Engineer Combat Battalion (1st Division) were to carry out normal combat engineer functions.[29]

The experience of Company F of the 591st Engineer Boat Regiment illustrated much that was learned about combat engineer support at Oran. Attached to Force GREEN (Combat Command B of the 1st Armored Division), Company F supervised the landing of men and supplies at Mersa Bou Zedjar (called X-Ray Beach), some twenty-eight miles west of Oran. Its 9 officers and 186 enlisted men, commanded by Capt. Kenneth W. Kennedy, were to aid in landing 108 officers, 2,158 enlisted men, 409 wheeled vehicles, 54 tracked vehicles, and 430 tons of supplies. The company organized into a headquarters platoon of 2 officers and 30 enlisted men; a defense platoon of 1 officer and 40 enlisted men; a medical detachment of 1 officer and 6 aid men; and 2 construction and unloading platoons, each composed of 55 enlisted

[28] 1st Engr Amphib Bde, Lessons from Opn TORCH, 30 Dec 42, Incl 1 to Rpts on Opn TORCH, CTF, 16 Jan 43.

[29] 1st Engr Amphib Bde, Rpt of Opns with Center Task Force; Hists, 1st Engr C Bn and 16th Armd Engr Bn.

men, one with 3 officers and the other with 2. Available landing craft consisted of 10 LCAs, 14 LCP(R)s, 4 LCM(I)s, 2 LCM(III)s, and 1 LST.[30]

Plans called for routing all vehicles off the LST directly onto a road leading to the village of Bou Zadjar. As soon as waterproofing could be removed, the vehicles were to move out along the road. All other vehicles coming ashore were to gather in an assembly area for removal of waterproofing, and this initial assembly area was also to serve as a dump to keep both beaches clear. At night wheeled vehicles were to be guided across the beach to the area by a line of shaded green lights held by guides, while tracked vehicles were to be guided to the same area by orange lights along another route. Personnel could follow either color.

A high rocky point divided X-Ray Beach into two sections, Green and White beaches, about a fifteen-minute walk apart. Company F had to be split into two complete units, each with its own defense and construction sections, unloading details, and even medical detachments. Green Beach was 100 yards long and almost 30 yards deep and rose steeply to high sand dunes and a hill of 500 feet. The only possible exit was to the east, a climb up a steep grade over deep sand. Because of sandbars, landing craft had to be halted 300 yards from the beach. Much of White Beach was difficult for landings because of a narrow approach and dangerous rocks in the water along the shore.

During the landings little went according to plan. When the operation started at 0145, the weather was clear and the surf moderate. Captain Kennedy and the men of his company headquarters, who were supposed to land on Green Beach at H plus 15 minutes, were ten minutes late. They remained alone on the beach for almost an hour, because the British naval beach party, which was to put the markers in place, had not yet landed. The contingents of the shore party that were to land at H-hour disembarked on Green Beach at H plus 90 minutes and White Beach at H plus 30 minutes.

Captain Kennedy and his group met no French opposition. They carried out the reconnaissance which was to have been directed by the missing assistant shore party commanders on the beach and for some distance inland. When the markers were finally put down, the first few waves of landing craft failed to land between them, and many craft were damaged and vehicles mired. Early in the operation an LCP(R) caught fire and lit up the area for miles around, revealing the site of operations. The vessel finally sank under the fire of a .50-caliber machine gun of Company F, but for some time thereafter oil continued to burn.

At approximately H plus 3 the naval beach party notified the engineers it wanted to land its maracaibo on Green Beach according to plan. To unload at this spot Company A of the 16th Armored Engineer Battalion had to erect 300 feet of treadway bridging, as expected. At H plus 4 the maracaibo was almost ready for unloading, but no Sommerfeld track for preparing an exit road was yet on hand. Without this flexible mat as a base, trucks would sink to their axles in the sand. By the time

---

[30] This account for Company F derives from Capt Kenneth W. Kennedy, Rpt on Amphib Opn by Co F, 591st Engr Boat Rgt, 27 Feb 43, in Hist 591st Engr Boat Rgt, 1943–44; Ltr, Lt Col Kenneth W. Kennedy to EHD, 9 Apr 56.

the track arrived from White Beach and was in place, it was H plus 5, four hours behind schedule.

Landing craft continued to founder, and at noon on D-day Captain Kennedy had to close the beach. From that hour all landing operations took place at better protected White Beach. But White Beach had only two narrow exits, and in one of these, seventy-five yards from the landing points, only tracked vehicles could be used. By H plus 6, 1,500 barracks bags and other supplies had been dumped on the sands, and too little room remained to put down Sommerfeld tracks; as a result, all supplies had to be carried from the water's edge on sleds. At 1300 the first combat unit had moved out with its equipment, but an hour and a half later the beach had become completely blocked by gasoline cans, barracks bags, and ammunition.

By 1800, with the aid of Arabs and twenty-five men from units already ashore, Kennedy and his men finally had relieved the congestion. It was then possible to lay Sommerfeld track and get two trucks on the beach simultaneously. Thereafter, the beach remained clear, and by 1900 enough equipment was ashore to send an additional combat unit forward.

Captain Kennedy called for thirty men from units already ashore to aid in a night unloading shift. As darkness fell, with serials coming in more slowly and inexperienced crews contributing to the boat casualties, the whole operation lagged further behind schedule. Next morning, 9 November, unloading continued at a still slower pace as the number of serviceable landing craft dwindled. Naval forces tried to compensate for the small craft losses by loading an LST directly from the cargo vessels and then beaching it. As another expedient, a ponton bridge served as a floating lighter to bring ashore some twenty light tanks. That night nearly all the LCMs had their propellers tangled with landing lines or had broached. Broached craft lay broadside to the sea on the sand and open to the pounding surf; even undamaged, they were of no use until they could be pushed off the shore and put back into action. Not until 1900 on 10 November was the beach closed and beach operations declared complete—twenty-three hours behind time.

With little training in shore operations, with only three vehicles at its disposal, and with the many problems of unloading, Company F managed to accomplish its task by dint of continuous hard work and cooperation with the British beach party—the fruit of joint exercises in the United Kingdom. Since a definite line of responsibility between the two had not been drawn, each could, and did, perform almost identical tasks; the shore party aiding, for instance, in retracting the boats from the beach and the beach party helping to unload the boats.

While the Rangers were capturing the French fort above Arzew and silencing Arzew's harbor defenses, the 1st Infantry Division (less the 26th Regimental Combat Team) landed on the beaches adjacent to Arzew, the 531st Engineer Shore Regiment (less the 3d Battalion) assisting. Supplies began to come ashore, with ammunition given top priority. The 531st Engineer Shore Regiment had enough trucks to clear the beaches initially but did not have the manpower to keep up the pace without relief, and unloading slowed perceptibly after D-day. However, tonnage stacked along and near the beaches was never in danger of getting wet since the tide in the Mediterranean varied only about a foot. The 1st Division's capture of the port of Arzew decreased dependence upon the beaches, and by D plus 3 ships were at dockside being unloaded rapidly. The beaches then closed and 531st Engineer Shore Regiment personnel, along with their trucks, became available for unloading parties in the town. .

The lack of trained supply personnel was a serious handicap from the beginning. After the armistice with the French, the confusion increased with a scramble to secure sites for depots and dumps. By D plus 3 staff officers were "scurrying in all directions" to find locations for supplies coming in from "the tangled mess at Arzew" and to get ready for those discharged from a convoy arriving that day.[31]

The first echelon of the Mediterranean Base Section (MBS) organization came ashore near Oran on 11 November. Within a month, with the arrival of later echelons and service troops from the United States, this base section was operating with comparative smoothness. Its Engineer Service consisted of three groups of men that left England on 12, 22, and 27 November. During November the first two groups, totaling fifteen officers and thirty-eight enlisted men detached from SOS, ETO-USA, served as part of the II Corps engineer's staff. Upon landing at Oran their most immediate jobs were acquiring real estate, establishing water points

and engineer depots, and handling gasoline and oils from ship-to-shore storage and tank cars.

On 8 December, two days after the third group arrived, and the day MBS was activated, Headquarters, Engineer Service, MBS, was formally set up to incorporate all three groups. During December the Engineer Service had an average strength of fifty-seven officers, one warrant officer, and sixty-three enlisted men assigned and four officers and enlisted men attached.[32]

*Eastern Task Force*

Two hundred fifty miles to the east was the Eastern Assault Force (EAF), at first under the command of General Ryder of the 34th Division, later the nucleus of the British First Army under Lt. Gen. K. A. N. Anderson. This attack force, after occupying Algiers and adjacent airfields, was to establish communication with CTF at Orleansville, southwest of Algiers, and to advance toward Tunis. For the seizure of Algiers, EAF devised a plan like that CTF employed. The landings were to take place outside the Bay of Algiers, on beaches west and east of the city, while two smaller groups were to take Maison Blanche Airfield, ten miles southeast of Algiers, and Blida Airfield, twenty-nine miles southwest of the city. A special landing party (TERMINAL) prepared to make a direct assault on the port itself to forestall sabotage of harbor installations. EAF was about one-half American, chiefly the 39th Regimental Combat Team (9th Division) and the 168th Regi-

[31]Ltr, Brig Gen W. A. Carter, Engr, U.S. Army Forces, Far East, and Eighth U.S. Army (Rear), to Lt Col David M. Matheson, Chf, 8 Feb 56.

[32] Rpt, HQ, MBS, Ofc of the Engr, to ACofS, G-2, 17 Dec 42, sub: Organization Hist, Engr Service, 10-30 Nov 42, 314.7 History 1942-48, Ofc of Engr, North African Service Command.

mental Combat Team (34th Division). Company C of the 109th Engineer Combat Battalion was with the 168th Regimental Combat Team; Company A of the 15th Engineers (9th Division) and the 2d Battalion of the 36th Engineers were with the 39th Regimental Combat Team.[33] U.S. engineers participated less in ETF than in the WTF and CTF landings, nor were they needed as much, for Algiers was captured on D-day.

*The Assessment*

The invasion of North Africa, by far the largest amphibious operation attempted to that time, developed in a very brief time, and from the very beginning much went wrong. In a number of instances, as on Green Beach at Oran, unloading fell hours behind schedule. Engineer units landed three, five, even ten and more hours behind schedule. Not only were inexperienced troops late in disembarking from the transports, but equally inexperienced Royal Navy crews, approaching the coast in darkness from points far offshore, beached their craft many yards—even miles—from designated landing spots. In one extreme case a landing craft missed its mark by twelve miles. Some of the landings were so scattered that supplies were spread out all along the beaches, and the small engineer shore parties had difficulty governing the flow to advancing troops inland.

Another delaying factor was the poor seamanship of Navy crews in handling landing craft at the beaches. All three task forces had high losses: WTF lost

34.3 percent of its craft, CTF 28 percent, and EAF 94 percent. So many boats broached or swamped that schedules for following boat waves fell apart. The Navy claimed, with some justice, that help from those on shore, including engineers, might have reduced the losses; nevertheless, one of the chief causes of boat losses was the failure of the naval beach parties to place markers properly or in time to guide the boats. In some cases the beach parties emplaced no markers at all.[34]

The division of responsibility between the two services was not well defined, especially as to the time and place at which the beach commander was to transfer his authority to the shore commander. Naval officials afterwards complained that the engineers refused to aid in unloading supplies and clearing boats from the beaches; the engineers made similar criticisms of certain naval personnel. Both accusations had some basis; neither service clearly understood the other's particular problems or duties.

A better preventive measure might

---

[33]The Adm and Log Hist of the ETO, vol. IV, "Operations TORCH and the ETO," p. 86; AFHQ, Outline Opn TORCH, an. 4, ETF.

[34]The following assessment of engineer operations on 9–11 November 1942 is based on Operation, 1st Prov Bde (WTF), an. 3; Rpts of 1st Engr Amphib Bde (CTF); 591st Engr Boat Rgt; Co F, 36th Engr C Bn; Co A, 15th Engr C Bn; 109th Engr C Bn; 19th Engr C Bn; 3d Inf Div, an. 2; U.S. Atlantic Fleet Amphib Force (Port Lyautey), an. 8, app. 1; Rpts by Lt Col C. F. Tank, CE (WTF), 18 Jan 43; A. R. Wilson (Atlantic Base Sect), 17 Jan 43; Brig Gen S. C. Godfrey (HQ, USAAF, Ofc Dir of Base Services, Engr Sect), 4 Jan 43; all in folder African Campaign, FAC. Davison Memo; Hists, 1st Engr Spec Bde, Jan 42–Sep 45; 591st Engr Boat Rgt, 1943–44; 561st Engr Boat Maint Co; 19th Engr C Rgt; Morison, *Operations in North African Waters;* Intervs with Lt Col Houghton, 30 May 50; Lt Col Chubbock, 4 Nov 50; Lt Col Philip Y. Browning; and Col William Powers, 13 Feb 51; Ltrs, Lt Col J. B. Chubbock, 12 Mar 56; Col A.T.W. Moore, 9 Mar 56; Col R. C. Brown, 20 Mar 56; Col John A. Chambers, 5 Apr 56; Lt Col Kenneth W. Kennedy, 9 Apr 56.

well have been experience: more training exercises before the landing. If a strict division of responsibility was indeed essential, it should have been clear to all. On the other hand, the difficulty might have been overcome had sufficient authority been given one individual. This did not happen. Engineer shore party commanders were uncertain of their authority and did not know how to meet the inevitable unexpected developments. The WTF task force engineer, who might have directed the landing activities, did not arrive ashore until the emergency had passed. At Fedala, Safi, and Mehdia experienced SOS personnel, who might have made it possible to use the ports earlier, also remained aboard ship.

Worse still was the situation at the Bay of Arzew. Units involved in the operation included the 1st Infantry Division; a port battalion operating with shore, boat, and combat engineer units; and a naval unit, all with no clear divisions of responsibility among them. Communication here and elsewhere between the men at the port and the vessels lying offshore was far from perfect. Engineer shore parties depended upon the naval beach parties for communications with the ships. This may explain complaints that landing craft appeared to be idle, lying at anchor or merely cruising about, when they were needed to land men and equipment. Communication was also poor among elements ashore. Loudspeakers often could not be heard above the firing, the shouting, and the din of the beaches. In such an intricate operation many things could go awry, and many did; even British accents over loudspeakers confused the relatively few Americans on EAF beaches.

At all the beaches, when the engineers were ready to move supplies to more permanent dumps they faced an acute transportation shortage, one that should have been expected after the 50 percent cut in vehicles. For many engineer units (already understrength to perform all their assigned tasks efficiently), this cut had created another handicap: many engineers of the shore parties were specialists, whereas landing operations with little transportation and heavy equipment called for unskilled labor. General Noce of the Engineer Amphibian Command later recommended that the shore parties be enlarged by as much as 30 percent.

The bulldozer was the most valuable means of moving supplies and equipment across the beaches; too few were available and many arrived too late or not at all. Some vehicles landed without their drivers, or drivers landed without their vehicles. The whole unloading process lagged when a great deal more than anticipated had to be done by hand.

Some of the blame for the delay could be charged to loading and some to unloading. Often combat, shore, aviation, and service engineers found that their equipment had not been combat loaded at all, especially in the CTF shipping. Combat loading meant that troops were shipped with their equipment and were ready for combat when they disembarked. Though not economical in terms of ship space, the practice was all important in saving time during operations ashore. Convoy-loaded equipment had to be assembled for use after being deposited on the beach. Moreover, ship unloading plans often did not coincide with actual loadings, while priority lists for unloading were all too often ignored. In one case the lighters unloading the U.S.S. *Leedstown* were ordered to report to the U.S.S. *Chase* when only half the prime movers loaded on the *Leedstown*—equipment badly needed to clear the beaches—had been landed. One battalion of the 36th Engineer Combat Regiment lost most of its equipment and tools when the *Leedstown* was torpedoed on D plus 2. Hatch crews frequently were not familiar with their ships. (Later criticism pointed out that these crews should have had 60 percent more men.) Yet there were instances of rapid and efficient work. The 1st Battalion of the 591st Boat Regiment received a commendation from the commanding general, Communications Zone, NATOUSA, for the work of its hatch crews and unloading details on ten of the CTF's twenty-three transports.

Part of the delay in unloading undoubtedly could be attributed to the inexperience of officers and men, and sometimes delays had serious consequences. By H plus 96 the 1st Engineer Amphibian Brigade should have landed 80 percent of its assigned cargo and all of its assigned personnel. Actually, only 75 percent of the vehicles and 35 percent of the total cargo were ashore on schedule, although all personnel had landed. In this instance, and in several others, the forward movement of combat troops was retarded.

Engineers made many errors during the early phases onshore. Through ignorance or demands for speedy unloading, they often set up dumps too close to the water's edge and then had to move them when the tides came in. Training exercises which had taken place in ideal tide conditions and calm seas both in the United States and in the United Kingdom did little to prepare the engineers for the Moroccan tides, rising as much as fourteen feet, or for the rough seas that interrupted unloading at several beaches. Had the engineers been more familiar with conditions, they could have closed beaches sooner, moved on to the captured ports, and saved boats and equipment.

Another cause for delay in getting supplies forward, at least in the Casablanca area, was piling all items—engineer, signal, medical, ordnance, and the five different classes—into common dumps. This mingling made it difficult to find certain much-needed supplies quickly, and the engineers claimed that they had neither the time nor the manpower to sort supplies properly. Even in dumps where segregation was attempted, faded package markings often hindered distribution. Frequently, supplies belonging to combat and shore party engineers were thrown together with those belonging to aviation engineers. The shore party engineers complained that packaging materials and crates were often too flimsy; corrugated paper or cardboard containers proved of no value whatever. Another complaint was that too often equipment was shipped in boxes too large and bulky for easy handling.

Unloading and other shore operations could have proceeded with much greater dispatch had full advantage been taken of native labor. The engineers made some effort to employ local workers on the beaches and at the ports; the 591st Boat Regiment, by doing so, cut discharge time in half at the Arzew quays. But the Americans were too trustful and lax in supervision. At Safi, natives thronged the beaches, unloading landing craft for a cigarette,

MOROCCAN LABOR GANG AT CASABLANCA HARBOR

a can of food, a piece of cloth. Two days later tons of ammunition and rations were found on Arab fishing vessels. American planning and preparations had made too little provision for using this vast labor pool or studying its peculiarities. Civilian workers wanted to be paid in goods, not in local currency. Nor did they look with favor upon the weekly pay system, and many quit in disgust after a day's work. Once the engineers arranged to pay in cloth, sugar, tea, bread, and the like, willing workers became available.

The engineers' slowness to begin salvaging equipment lost or damaged on the beaches, in turn, slowed unloading. The engineers were not trained for salvage work, nor had they been assigned it in the plans. But they did help to recover a considerable amount of equip-ment and supplies. Some tractors used in futile attempts to salvage equipment from the water were lost. LCVPs proved inadequate; tank lighters, although better adapted, were little used. Sleds of wood or metal, some of them improvised, proved most useful on the beaches. A sled designed to carry larger loads would have been more useful, and a reserve of sleds, cables, and chains would have improved salvage work and general movement of equipment and supplies.

A further impediment to rapid progress on the beaches was the inadequacy of the maps issued to the shore engineers. These maps indicated the contour of the terrain only a short distance behind the beaches, and the information was sometimes inaccurate. In several areas engineers found unexpectedly high dunes that obstructed egress to the inland plateau and that forced them in one case to build a road with a hairpin turn; at Blue Beach (Mehdia-Plage) engineers had to construct a road through a mile of deep, soft sand.

Troops and equipment moved off the various beaches on quickly improvised roads and bridges substantial enough to withstand heavy military traffic but emplaced in a constant struggle with poor construction material, equipment, procedure, and inexperience. In general, engineers concluded that the British Sommerfeld track, chicken wire netting, and cyclone wire were all inadequate, for they sank into the soft sand after traffic passed over them. They found cyclone wire of some value, provided burlap bags were used as a base. The bulldozer, the most useful piece of equipment landed, was put to various uses such as clearing exits through sand dunes and other obstacles, pulling equipment from lighters and across the beaches, and afterwards building and repairing roads as well as runways at airfields. Unfortunately, some bulldozers proved mechanically defective. Waterproofing would have increased their utility, and they all should have been equipped with winches, so effective in pulling out mired vehicles. Light cranes, had they been present to operate with the bulldozers, would have made unloading, as well as rescuing stranded boats and vehicles, more efficient. A lack of spare parts was still another factor in cutting down the effective use of vehicles and other engineer equipment, even some weapons.

Shore party engineers complained of the heavy individual load of equipment they had to carry, a problem common to all troops in the TORCH operation.

Much might have been left behind for later shipment or left on board ship to be distributed at a more convenient time. Engineer officers and noncommissioned officers complained especially of the heavy submachine gun. On many occasions soldiers were forced to jump into the water some distance out to keep boats from broaching. Men burdened with their heavy loads stumbled and fell in the surf trying to wade ashore through water that was in some places two to four feet deep.

In summing up his observations during TORCH somewhat later, an experienced engineer officer entered an oft-repeated plea for enough service troops, including guard units, fire-fighting units, bomb disposal companies, depot companies, and labor units, especially in the early waves of an invasion force. "When this is not done, either combat troops must be diverted to service tasks for which they are not trained, [thus reducing] the effective combat strength by more men than would have been necessary if trained service troops had been available; or the combat troops will not be supplied, in which case they cease to be effective."[35]

The dilemma was classic and continuing. The experience the engineers gained in the invasion of North Africa stood them well in future landings in the Mediterranean and European theaters and made superior veterans of them. Lessons derived on the littered beaches were enlarged upon in new procedures and organizations, but many had to be learned again in the face of far stronger resistance than the French defenders offered in Algeria and Morocco.

---

[35]Rpt, Col Morris W. Gilland, Dep Engr, MBS, to CG, MBS, 27 Dec 42, sub: Lessons from Opn TORCH, Pence Papers, Dec 42–Jan 43, MBS.

# CHAPTER V

# The Tunisian Campaign

As soon as the Allies concluded an armistice with the French, British units of the Eastern Task Force struck by air, sea, and land toward Tunis. With this port in Allied hands, the Axis hold on North Africa would be broken. On 12 November 1942, British commandos and paratroopers converged on Bone, 135 miles west of Tunis, but German units had begun flying into Tunisia from Sicily and the mainland of Italy three days earlier; by the twelfth they were arriving by sea.[1] Before the month was out the British 78th Division with its Blade Force (which resembled a U.S. armored combat command and included an American armored battalion) drove to the outskirts of Djedeida, less than sixteen miles from Tunis. But five months would pass before the Allies reached Tunis. The rapid Axis buildup and a lack of air support (Allied planes were mired in the mud of fair-weather fields) brought the British offensive to a halt. By Christmas Day AFHQ had canceled immediate attack plans, for a much larger push was in prospect. The Allies were faced with building suffi-

cient strength in Tunisia to crush the expanded German and Italian forces.

The British First Army, moving over the long land route east from Algiers, built up its strength in the hill country around Bedja. Elements of the American II Corps arrived from faraway Oran to take up positions east of Tebessa whence they could threaten central Tunisia; poorly equipped French forces were deployed along the Eastern Dorsal as a link between the British and the Americans. By mid-January II Corps elements had concentrated in the Tebessa-Kasserine region, and on the eighteenth the enemy began exerting pressure against the center of the Allied line, which the French held. These operations, continuing until early February, pulled additional American units into action but weakened Allied defensive positions along the Eastern Dorsal. The stage was being set for a swift, hard blow by enemy armored units, and the *German-Italian Panzer Army* had reached a strong defensive position (the Mareth Line) near the southeastern Tunisian border. Since it would be weeks before the British Eighth Army under General Sir Bernard L. Montgomery could mount an offensive against this position from the east, German panzer units from the north and south teamed up for an assault designed to overrun II

---

[1] For a detailed account of combat operations in Tunisia, see Howe, *Northwest Africa*, pp. 277ff, which provided background material for this account. For more general treatment, see Commander in Chief's Dispatch, North African Campaign, 1942–43 (hereafter cited as Eisenhower Dispatch).

Corps and force the British First Army into a general withdrawal westward.

The main attack poured through Faid Pass on 14 February, sweeping elements of the U.S. 1st Armored Division before it and isolating American troops on solitary mountains. When the assault began, three U.S. divisions were in Tunisia, all rather fully committed along some one hundred miles of front. Before it ended eight days later, enemy tanks had swept through Kasserine Pass and struck some seventy miles deep into II Corps territory, coming dangerously close to a large Allied supply dump at Tebessa and a key road center at Thala. Allied armored reinforcements, along with increasing support from the XII Air Support Command (U.S.) and Montgomery's buildup against the Mareth Line in southeastern Tunisia, combined to compel a German withdrawal, which began 23 February.

Two more phases of the campaign, both offensive, followed for II Corps in Tunisia. On 17 March the bulk of II Corps, aided by air strikes, pushed through Gafsa toward Maknassy and Gabes. This limited offensive was timed to draw off German reserves from the Mareth Line while Montgomery cracked through from the south. Montgomery's offensive began on 20 March and during the next three weeks drove the enemy back into a small bridgehead around Tunis and Bizerte.

Squeezed out of the action by Eighth Army's advance, II Corps moved north across the British First Army supply lines to take over British 5 Corps positions near Bedja. On 24 April the American force began the final phase of the Tunisian campaign, an attack through the hills near the north coast of Tunisia toward Bizerte. On its right, the British First Army, also driving eastward, pressed the attack on Tunis in conjunction with Eighth Army, pushing north from positions near Enfidaville. On 7 May American units first entered Bizerte. Tunis fell to the British, and by the thirteenth organized Axis resistance in Africa had ended.

Engineer support of air and ground operations in Tunisia had to take into account the terrain and the weather. In central Tunisia, where the main American effort took place, the terrain was quite different from the hilly area around Bizerte and Tunis in the north, where the British First Army began its buildup. From a wide, semi-arid plateau of sandstone and clay rose two ridgelines, the Eastern and Western Dorsals, which came together at a point south of Pont-du-Fahs. The Eastern Dorsal extended almost due south from Pont-du-Fahs for over 125 miles to Maknassy; the bolder Western Dorsal angled away to the southwest toward Feriana. Clay roads snaked through at a few points and two ribbons of asphalt macadam crossed to the sea, one through  Sbeitla to Sfax, the other through Gafsa to Gabes. Except for bits of verdure, the landscape offered little color. Central Tunisia had no perennial streams and few trees except for a pine forest that hugged the hills from Bou Chebka through Kasserine Pass and north toward Thala.

Control of the passes through the two ridgelines was the key to hundreds of square miles of wadi-scarred tableland that lay between. Once through the passes, armor could range cross-country with comparative ease during dry weather. During the winter months rainfall turned the flats into mud and made vehicular movement difficult on all but a few hard-topped roads.

By the time II Corps began to move into Tunisia early in January, the rainy season was more than a month old. Northern Tunisia and Algeria have an annual rainfall of about twenty-five to thirty inches, almost all between late November and early March. These rains were instrumental in keeping Allied planes on the ground and halting the first Allied drive on Bizerte and Tunis. The nearest hard-surfaced Allied airfield was a small one near Bone, in Algeria. Allied planes at hastily graded airstrips nearer the front soon became hopelessly mired in mud, whereas Axis planes, flying from hard-surfaced airfields only minutes from the battleground, ranged virtually unopposed over the front. Until drier fields could be found or all-weather ones built, Allied airpower could do little toward winning superiority or cutting the enemy's air and sea supply routes from Sicily.[2]

### Aviation Engineer Support

The North African invasion employed American aviation engineer units available in England or summarily assembled in the United States, and in the days after the successful landings they foundered amid a number of uncontrolled circumstances. The 809th, 814th, 815th, and 817th Engineer Avia-

tion Battalions landed with the Center Task Force. From the United States came a battalion of the 21st Engineer Aviation Regiment, the prototype of its kind, and the 887th Engineer Airborne Company and the 888th Airborne Engineer Aviation Company. With the exception of the 21st Engineer Aviation Regiment, the units were hastily formed and sketchily trained. The 809th, though experienced in airfield construction in England, had to draw 150 enlisted men from the 832d and 157 from the 825th in the United Kingdom to achieve its allotted strength. The 887th and the 888th were thrown together in the United States just weeks before the convoy sailed, and none of the units had any inkling of the conditions of forward airfield construction in a fluid campaign.

Charged first with resurfacing damaged runways near the larger cities within the landing zones, the American units were to support air operations including patrols over Allied lines of communications along the coast west of Algiers; east of that city, according to the invasion plan, British Airdrome Construction Groups were responsible for forward fields supporting the move toward Tunisia. Within this division of labor, the American aviation engineers were to construct six fields ringing the borders of Spanish Morocco on the possibility that the Axis might mount an offensive against the Allied bridgehead through the Iberian peninsula and into the Spanish dependency.

Aside from training deficiencies, the aviation engineers' foremost problem was the fate of their equipment, especially that coming from England. Loaded on different ships from the units, with some ships sailing in different

[2] Eisenhowever Dispatch; General Omar N. Bradley, *A Soldier's Story* (New York: Holt, 1951), p. 22; Ltr, Col W. A. Carter, 8 Feb 56; Wesley Frank Craven and James Lea Cate, eds., "The U.S. Army Air Forces in World War II," vol. II, *Europe: TORCH to POINT-BLANK* (Chicago: University of Chicago Press, 1949), pp. 91, 116.

convoys, engineer paraphernalia from heavy machinery to hand tools often failed to arrive with the troops. The 815th's equipment was lost at sea off Oran with a torpedoed vessel, and the ship transporting part of the 809th's belongings returned to England with engine trouble two days after sailing with the invasion convoy. Heavy construction equipment was often diverted to other use or to other engineer units as it came ashore. Some of the 809th's materiel arrived intact because members of the battalion traveled on the same ship and supervised its unloading, but the unit's trucks, in a later convoy, arrived stripped of spare tires, all canvas supports, and the tools packed aboard them for embarkation. As late as January 1943, the 2d Battalion of the 21st Engineer Aviation Regiment, working at Craw Field near Port-Lyautey, had to use secondhand French tools or improvised equipment. All the necessary equipment did not arrive until March 1943.[3]

The existing airfields in North Africa were ill-suited for the heavy invasion traffic. Of the French fields in the landing areas, only four had hard-surfaced runways: those at Port-Lyautey on the Moroccan coast north of Rabat; at Tafaraoui near Oran; at Maison Blanche, close to Algiers in the Eastern Task Force zone; and at Bone, fifty miles short of the Tunisian border. With its main strip and a crosswind leg, Tafaraoui became the focus for incoming American aircraft of all description

belonging to Brig. Gen. James H. Doolittle's Twelfth Air Force, and the resulting glut of planes on the field slowed operations to a crawl. When the seasonal rains commenced in late November, everything in the dispersal areas off the runways sank into mud "like liquid reinforced concrete of bottomless depth."

In an attempt to give maneuvering room to some 285 mired planes, the Twelfth Air Force flew its B–26 mediums to Maison Blanche, where the 809th Engineer Aviation Battalion, leaving two detachments behind at Tafaraoui and other smaller dirt fields in the area, began work on 29 November on a second runway, taking up where the French builders of an intersecting runway to the main macadam strip had left off. The same insidious mud hampered operations; however, the engineers were able to lay gravel-clay taxiways and hardstands in a large dispersal area.

German air resistance to further Allied advances into Tunisia also brought a radical change to the arrangement that confined American aviation construction to the area west of Algiers. When General K. A. N. Anderson declared on 4 December that a lack of air cover had cost him the opportunity to move further against the Germans, American aviation engineers were already heading eastward in an attempt to bring Allied air power closer to the front lines.

British efforts to construct airfields behind their advancing lines suffered even more from inadequate heavy equipment than did the American efforts. Beginning on 20 November, detachments of a British airdrome construction unit attempted to build a fighter

---

[3] Craven and Cate, *Europe: TORCH to POINTBLANK*, pp. 117–18; Hist 809th Engr Avn Bn; Rpt, Brig Gen S. C. Godfrey to CG, AAF, 4 Jan 43, sub: Report on Airdomes and Avn Engrs in North Africa, OCE 370.2 (MTO), hereafter cited as Godfrey Rpt; Hist 2d Bn, 21st Engr Avn Rgt, 8 Nov 42–1 Jul 43, Engr 21 HI, Maxwell AFB.

field in Tunisia in the neighborhood of Souk el Arba, eighty miles west of Tunis, but the December rains defeated them. Their Sommerfeld mat, well-suited to English sod fields, sank out of sight in the Tunisian mud, and pierced steel plank was in short supply in the theater. They had better success with the sandy soil nearby at Souk el Khemis, but the British still had too few fields to support a concentrated aerial offensive against German strength in Tunisia.[4]

Early December marked the wholesale departure of American aviation engineers from northwest Africa for sites in eastern Algeria. On 2 December, acting on French advice that dry weather prevailed there, Brig. Gen. Donald A. Davison flew to Telergma, a village by a large bowl on a 3,500-foot-high plateau in the mountains southwest of Constantine. On the field guarded by French troops, Davison found a platoon of the 809th Engineer Aviation Battalion already working, having reached the prospective field by forced march from Maison Blanche. Another company of the battalion moved in by plane and truck, and, assisted by several hundred Algerians, the engineers scraped out a compacted earth runway that began handling B−26 traffic just ten days after Davison's first visit. With this single runway, a well-drained strip of loam, caliche, and gravel, the 809th, the first American unit of its kind to work east of Algiers, began developing a complex of medium bomber fields in the Telergma area.[5]

Heavy bombers found a home farther south on the fringes of the Sahara at Biskra, a winter resort. Though Biskra and Telergma lay close to rail lines, the disruption in French train control and traffic forced most supply to the bases, especially Biskra, to go by air. Accordingly, the engineer unit chosen to develop the Biskra base was the 887th Airborne Engineer Aviation Company, its troops and light, air-transportable equipment carried to the site from Morocco, a thousand miles away, in fifty-six aircraft. Landing on 13 December, the company completed two new fields of compacted earth for B−17s and B−24s in four days to give the heavies a dry toehold within easy striking range of the enemy. Apparently vindicating the faith placed in the airborne aviation engineer concept by its developers in Washington, the 887th's performance still could not redeem the failure of its sister company flown into Tebessa from Port-Lyautey to expand and improve advance fields at what became a main supply base in the drive into Tunisia. Here the 888th Airborne Engineer Aviation Company's midget bulldozers could do little in the rough terrain, and the company took two long weeks to carve out a single runway, though it was supposed to recondition dirt fields lying as far away as Gafsa, across the Tunisian border. Eventually the 814th Engineer Aviation Battalion took over the job.[6]

The aviation engineers shared their problems of lost and inadequate equipment with other engineer units but

[4] Interv, A−2 with Brig Gen Donald A. Davison, 1 Jun 43, 142.052−38, 8 Jun 43, USAF Hist Div Archives; Hist Sect, AAFC MTO, History of the Aviation Engineers in the MTO, 12 Jun 46, Maxwell AFB, hereafter cited as Avn Engrs in MTO; Godfrey Rpt.

[5] Davison interv, 1 Jun 43; Avn Engrs in MTO, pp. 12−14; Hist 809th Engr Avn Bn.

[6] Unit Hists, 887th, 888th Abn Engr Cos, and 814th Engr Avn Bn; Wesley Frank Craven and James L. Cate, eds., "The U.S. Army Air Forces in World War II," vol. VII, *Services Around the World* (Chicago: University of Chicago Press, 1958), pp. 249−50.

wrestled with problems of command structure peculiar to them. From the outset it was not clear whether the Corps of Engineers or the Army Air Forces (AAF) would control the aviation engineers. Field service regulations for 1942 did not fix responsibility for building airfields in the theater of operations, but in October 1942 AFHQ gave the job to the engineer, Twelfth Air Force, with the ruling that the aviation engineers were "an organic part of the air force." Following the invasion, the Twelfth Air Force engineer, Col. John O. Colonna, assumed operational control of all the American aviation engineers in North Africa. In the consolidation after the invasion, administrative control of the aviation engineers passed to individual commanders of service areas established at Casablanca, Oran, and Constantine, subordinate, in turn, to the new XII Air Force Service Command (AFSC), of which Colonel Colonna was also the engineer. Chafing under the division of control over the aviation engineers, Colonna saw to it that Twelfth Air Force issued orders for airfield construction directly to the constructing units without going through the service command. But the service command area commanders, in guarding their own prerogatives, frequently countermanded orders from Twelfth Air Force. The divided control created obvious and serious delays in construction projects for the aviation engineers.[7]

On 30 December 1942, Brig. Gen. Thomas B. Larkin, commanding the newly established Mediterranean Base Section, proposed that all requests for new airfield construction be submitted to base section commanders through AFHQ and be carried out by base section engineers, arguing that logistical agencies should control all construction, including that of airfields. Colonna strongly opposed this stand and recommended that the aviation engineers be removed from the administrative control of the service command and transferred into the Twelfth Air Force. While conceding that Services of Supply (SOS) control might be feasible in a static situation, Colonna was convinced that base section control would not work in a fluid situation like that in North Africa. He also opposed a proposal General Davison made to General Eisenhower on 13 February 1943 that all engineer troops, including aviation engineers, be placed under the chief engineer, AFHQ; Colonna pointed out that airfield construction was "intimately associated with shifting strategic and tactical situations" and should be "directly under the Air Force Commander."[8]

Davison's plan found no effective support. The activation on 18 February of the Northwest African Air Forces (NAAF) under the command of Maj. Gen. Carl W. Spaatz with Colonna as aviation engineer provided an opportunity to keep airfield construction under the control of the Air Forces. In addition, the fast-moving situation after the German breakthrough at Kasserine converted Davison to the principle of Air Forces control; early in March Davison joined Spaatz's staff as aviation engineer, with Colonna as his deputy.

A growing concern in Washington lest the AAF should, in effect, detach

---

[7] AFHQ Opn Memo 27, as quoted in Avn Engrs in MTO.

[8] Avn Engrs in MTO, p. 16.

the aviation engineers from their organic connection with the Corps of Engineers and thus from their administrative subordination to Army Service Forces (ASF), the new name taken by the SOS on 12 March 1943, led to an ASF proposal in the spring of 1943 to abolish the aviation engineers and to reorganize all engineer construction under ASF. But the AAF was firm in opposing any such solution. Moreover, by April 1943 the AAF had become too important an element of the armed forces and its performance in North Africa too impressive a demonstration of its potential for successful opposition on a matter that it held vital to its functions in a theater of war. The hotly contested argument reached a firm solution only at the end of 1943.

In the closing two months of the campaign in North Africa, the aviation engineers improved and expanded the rear area construction and provided new fields, especially fighter fields, for swiftly changing tactical situations. For example, five fields the 814th Engineer Aviation Battalion built in the Sbeitla area were usable in seventy-two hours and complete in four days. By the end of March, with the arrival of 837th, 838th, and 845th Engineer Aviation Battalions and the 3d Battalion of the 21st Engineer Aviation Regiment, the American construction force in the theater amounted to nearly 9,000 troops, three times the number in the British Airdrome Construction Groups active around the Souk el Arba–Souk el Khemis area. With ten American battalions and two separate companies available in North Africa, engineers established a first priority for fields behind the front, a secondary importance for the bomber fields in western Algeria

and eastern Morocco. The new arrivals worked in the rear area but also were involved in transferring the large bomber base at Biskra, an untenable site in the heat and dust storms of the spring, to constantly expanding facilities at Telergma. The 814th carried most of the responsibility for forward airfield construction, though British engineers from Souk el Arba added their manpower to the projects, and in late April two platoons from the 21st Engineer Aviation Regiment scraped out a dry weather field at Djebel Abiod, on the coast north of Souk el Khemis and eighty miles west of Tunis.[9]

The arrival in Tunisia in the spring of heavy machinery necessary for airfield construction over and above the Table of Basic Allowance (TBA) of the aviation engineer battalions made possible such accomplishments. Another important factor was a Northwest African Air Forces order of 5 March setting forth new and realistic specifications for airfield construction. The new specifications called for the barest essentials—in the forward areas, one earth runway per field, with loop taxiways and dispersed hardstands. The directive also assumed that no buildings would be required, that bomb and gasoline dump areas would be served by existing roads, and that occupying troops would provide dugouts and trenches. Construction shortcuts and heavy machinery used on a scale unknown in any other Army found their first combined application to aerial warfare in the Tunisian campaign. Heavy bomber and fighter airfield construction could keep pace with the move-

---

[9] Davison Interv; Hist 2d Bn, 21st Engr Avn Rgt, 8 Nov 42–1 Jul 43.

ment of the ground forces in a rapidly developing campaign. In May General Spaatz stressed the contribution of the aviation engineers to the impressive performance of the AAF in North Africa. He termed the Air Forces and its aviation engineers a team able to "work smoothly and efficiently during the stress of battle."[10]

The heavy equipment set the American engineers apart from the British Airdrome Construction Groups in their achievements; even with 3,000 British airdrome engineers in Tunisia, their efforts remained concentrated around their two main RAF bases at Souk el Khemis and Souk el Arba, the complex there consisting of around a dozen fields. This compared with the American construction of over a hundred fields throughout the theater.[11]

Their efficiency was all the more remarkable since the frustrating division of control over the aviation engineers continued until the end of the campaign in North Africa. The planning, the preparation of construction standards, and the issuance of work directives were in the hands of the engineer, NAAF, but the execution of all engineer work for the Air Forces and the administration of aviation engineers was the responsibility of the engineer of the North African Air Service Command (NAASC), an NAAF subordinate command that came into being along with NAAF in February 1943. The dual command hampered the pro-

curement of heavy equipment and spare parts. Orders had to be processed through the service command staff, causing delay and confusion, and the divided control interfered with replacement and rotation of personnel and promotion of officers. At times "the aviation engineer officers and men considered themselves . . . neglected and forgotten troops not belonging to any particular command."[12]

The unsatisfactory command arrangements in North Africa were an object lesson to planners in England concerned with the employment of aviation engineers in the coming invasion of Europe. During the spring of 1943 the planners undertook studies aimed at resolving problems of administration, discipline, and supply, and in August 1943 Col. Rudolf E. Smyser, Jr., engineer of the Eighth Air Force, went to North Africa to study the command situation in the Mediterranean Theater of Operations (MTO). His observations confirmed his opinion that all engineer aviation units should be under the complete administrative as well as operational control of a single agency subordinate only to the Air Forces, a conclusion that played an important part in the later creation of the IX Engineer Command in England. General Davison convinced Lt. Gen. Carl W. Spaatz of the necessity of setting up a separate aviation engineer command, and the XII Air Force Engineer Command, MTO (Provisional)—changed 1 January 1944 to Army Air Forces Engineer Command, MTO (Provisional)—came into being.[13]

---

[10] AAFC MTO, Hist of Policies Affecting Avn Engrs in the Mediterranean Campaign, p. 22; Col. A. E. Harris, "Colonel Harris Reporting" [feature column], *The Air Force Engineer*, no. 17 (November 1944), 15; Ltr, Spaatz to CG, AAF, 6 May 43, MTO Comd–Engr 638.129, Jan–Jun 43, 900.3, EUCOM Engr files.

[11] Craven and Cate, *Europe: TORCH to POINT-BLANK*, p. 170.

[12] Avn Engrs in MTO, p. 19.

[13] Col R. E. Smyser, Jr., Origin of the IX Engineer [Air Force] Command; 1st Lt. Lloyd F. Latendresse, "Narrative History," *The History of IX Engineer Command* (Wiesbaden, Germany, 1945), pp. 11ff.

COLONEL SMYSER

*Petroleum, Oil, and Lubricants Supply*

Engineer construction for POL supply was of several types: pipelines from ship to shore, bulk storage tanks and connecting pipelines, and extensive lines with pumping units leading toward the front. In North Africa existing port facilities had to be improved, tank farms had to be built at convenient points, and many miles of pipeline had to be constructed. Initially, no centralized control for the distribution and use of POL projects existed in North Africa, for each task force of TORCH was responsible for its own POL supply. Confusion, duplication of effort, and waste resulted. Gradually, early chaos gave way to an integrated system of control and the establishment of a common Allied POL pool from which products could be released to the

British and American armed forces as well as to the French military and civilian agencies.[14]

The 2602d Engineer Petroleum Distribution Company, which reached Oran on the D plus 3 convoy, immediately went to work to rehabilitate and operate existing French POL facilities at the port. Next, the company installed a seven-mile-long, four-inch victaulic pipeline from the Victor Hugo Storage Depot at Oran to airfields at La Senia and Tafaraoui. The same convoy also brought fifty miles of four-inch pipe that had reached England just in time to be loaded for TORCH. Delayed for weeks by heavy rains, the engineers eventually erected bolted steel tanks at the airfields for aviation gasoline; they also installed feeder lines and dispensing racks to service Air Forces trucks. The available storage at La Senia amounted to 462,000 gallons, at Tafaraoui 651,000 gallons. Another four-inch line, from Arzew to Perregaux, furnished a truck convoy connection with the airfields in the latter area. Such construction exemplified what was soon to be undertaken in other port areas in Algeria and Morocco.[15]

On 24 December 1942, a conference on petroleum supply, held at Algiers, determined the network of pipelines in Algeria and Tunisia. From the port of Philippeville a six-inch pipeline was to run to the heart of the airfield region in eastern Algeria, with bulk storage at

---

[14] Rpt, Capt M. D. Altgelt to Lt Col S. A. Potter, Jr., Chf, C&A Planning, OCE, SOS ETOUSA, covering trip to North Africa (POL Inspection). The paragraphs relating to administration in this section are largely based on this report.

[15] Ltr, Lt Col Cabel Gwathmey, Engr, MBS, to Engr, MTOUSA, 6 Dec 44; Engr MTOUSA file 679.11, Pipeline History, 1944 and 1945; Engr Sch Spec Text (ST–5–350–1), Military Pipeline Systems, 1950.

Ouled Rahmoun and lateral four-inch lines from there west to the Telergma fields and east to Tebessa. Eventually, the planners envisaged extending the Tebessa pipeline branch east to the port of Sousse and southeast to the port of Sfax. The ports of Bizerte, Tabarka, and Tunis would also be used.

Extensive pipeline construction got under way in earnest in February 1943, when two parallel four-inch lines were built from Philippeville to Ouled Rahmoun, one of them a V−80 line for motor gasoline.[16] This project included plans for erecting bolted steel tanks for bulk storage at existing airfields and for building a tanker unloading line and a tank farm at Philippeville. Execution involved coordinating the activities of American engineers, French Army contractors, and local labor, and assembling extensive and complicated equipment as well as obtaining rights-of-way. The pipeline engineers had to supplement materials at Mediterranean Base Section (MBS) with additional stocks requisitioned from the Atlantic Base Section (ABS) and the Royal Engineers.[17]

By 18 February pipe extended more than twenty miles, with construction actually complete for only some three miles. Then the work virtually halted until more pipe and other materials arrived in the forward area. The fate of the project hung on transporting bulky and easily damaged materials from the base sections in spite of severely limited cargo space and enemy air and naval interference. To complete the system, additional materials had to be shipped by risky sea routes because of the bottlenecks in overland transportation.

The 2004th Engineer Petroleum Distribution Company completed the project in mid-April, and on the sixteenth the first American tanker discharged its 64,000-barrel cargo into storage tanks at Philippeville. Pumps took the aircraft fuel fifty-five miles through the pipeline to Ouled Rahmoun. In this construction job alone the engineers could claim a solid share in neutralizing the enemy's air menace and hastening his final capitulation in North Africa.

On the same day that gasoline first flowed to Ouled Rahmoun, the 702d Engineer Petroleum Distribution Company began work on a second important pipeline, closer to the front. This line ran southeast from the port of Bone in Algeria to Souk el Arba, Tunisia, with a branch line to Souk el Khemis. The whole system, involving ninety miles of four-inch pipe and nine pump stations, was completed in a month. During construction, petroleum engineers had the help of the 144th Native Labor Company, a working force of uncertain value, which furnished an average of 148 men a day.

Neither enemy action nor hostile natives impeded construction. The only necessary road work was that through mountains. Ample tools and supplies were on hand. Pipe had to be hauled an average of sixty-six miles, but the 702d Engineer Company had a fleet of forty-five vehicles, including twenty-five 2 1/2-ton trucks and ten pole trailers. The weather was cool, rainfall moderate. Enlisted men engaged in all phases

---

[16] History of the Eastern Base Section, Jun−Sep 43.

[17] Memo, Engr, MBS, for Engr Pipeline Co (Sep) (Prov), 10 Jan 43, sub: Movement of Troops; Memo, Maj C. L. Lockett for Col Donald B. Adams, Engr, MBS, 14 Jan 43; Memo, Col Morris W. Gilland, XO, MBS, for Pipeline Co (Sep) (Prov), 10 Jan 43; all in Oil-Pipeline (Gen), vol. I, 679.11, MBS file.

GASOLINE STORAGE AT PORT-LYAUTEY

of the operation, including such skilled engineering jobs as coupling, testing, tying-in and connecting, and working on pump stations. Natives did work requiring no special skill or training, such as clearing and grading for the main line to Souk el Arba, stringing pipes, and ditching and backfilling.

At the other extreme of the communication line, in French Morocco, the Army Transport Command and the North African Training Comand at Marrakech in March 1943 estimated their combined need for gasoline to be 800,000 to 1,200,000 gallons per month. Rail tank cars to haul this amount were urgently needed elsewhere, and the obvious solution to the problem was a pipeline from Casa-

blanca to Marrakech. Since materials were locally available to build this system, including terminal storage at Marrakech, the engineers laid a four-inch line 160 miles long. Four-inch lines from Casablanca and Fedala also supplied airfields at Mediouna, Sale, and Port-Lyautey, and another line connected Casablanca and Fedala. The 345th General Service Regiment, a unit that had no previous experience in building pipelines, did the work.[18]

---

[18] Rpt on Pipeline, Bone to Souk el Arba, AFHQ Engr Sect, 21 Jul 43; Ltr, M. F. Grant, AG, ABS, to CG, SOS, NATOUSA, 13 Mar 43, sub: Pipeline to Marrakech, Oil-Pipeline (Gen), vol. I, 679.11, ABS file; Rgtl Jnl and Hist 345th Engr GS Rgt.

## Ground Support

Before the Kasserine breakthrough, the total combat engineer force with II Corps was three divisional battalions serving with the 1st and 34th Infantry Divisions and the 1st Armored Division, and, as corps troops, the 19th Engineer Combat Regiment. During the three weeks between the German withdrawal from Kasserine and II Corps' attack on Gafsa, other engineer units joined II Corps: Company B of the 601st Engineer Camouflage Battalion, the 15th Engineer Combat Battalion (9th Infantry Division), the 175th Engineer General Service Regiment, the 518th Engineer Water Supply Company, and the 62d Engineer Topographic Company. A few days after the II Corps' attack on Gafsa started, the 20th Engineer Combat Regiment arrived from Casablanca, followed late in March by a platoon of the 470th Engineer Maintenance Company. Shortly before the Tunisian campaign ended, the 10th Engineer Combat Battalion (3d Infantry Division) also joined II Corps.[19]

Since the Allied forces were on the offensive during most of the Tunisian campaign, the most important engineer function was to provide and maintain roads over which motorized ground troops could roll and to keep these roads clear of enemy mines. This function turned around in mid-February, when the Germans struck through the Faid and Kasserine Passes. At that time the engineers worked on roads leading to the rear, sowed mines in the path of the enemy, erected roadblocks, and fought as infantry. On the north, for

example, the 109th Engineer Combat Battalion made possible the withdrawal of its parent 34th Infantry Division to Sbiba; on the south, the 19th Engineer Combat Regiment fought as infantry at Kasserine. (*Map 4*)

At daylight on 7 February the 109th Engineer Combat Battalion pulled into a bivouac near Maktar after a six-day trip through the mountains from Tlemcen, near Oran. A cold rain had changed intermittently to snow at night, and the lead trucks found the twisting clay roads into the bivouac area slippery with mud and clogged with broken-down French vehicles. German aircraft strafed the end of the convoy, still on the road at daybreak.

For a few days the battalion improved bivouac area roads and reconnoitered. The first task was to improve the road-net for troops holding the Pichon–Fondouk el Aouareb Pass area, a critical opening where many thought the impending German attack would come. Engineer reconnaissance found a 35-mile trail across semi-desert flats, rock-ribbed ridges, and sand dunes from Sbiba east to El Ala that could be made passable for six-by-six trucks in a week. By 14 February the companies of the 109th had spread out along the route. Men of Company C, responsible for the middle section of the road, discovered warm springs near their bivouac, and many had their first good bath in more than two weeks.

On the night of 16 February, Maj. Vernon L. Watkins, the battalion executive officer, carried alarming news over the rough route. German armor had cut the main road forward (Sbeitla–Hadjeb el Aioun) and, while the front could bend without serious loss, a break that allowed mobile enemy units into

[19] Rpt of Engr Opns, Lt Col W. A. Carter, II Corps, 15 Mar–10 Apr, dated 1 May 43.

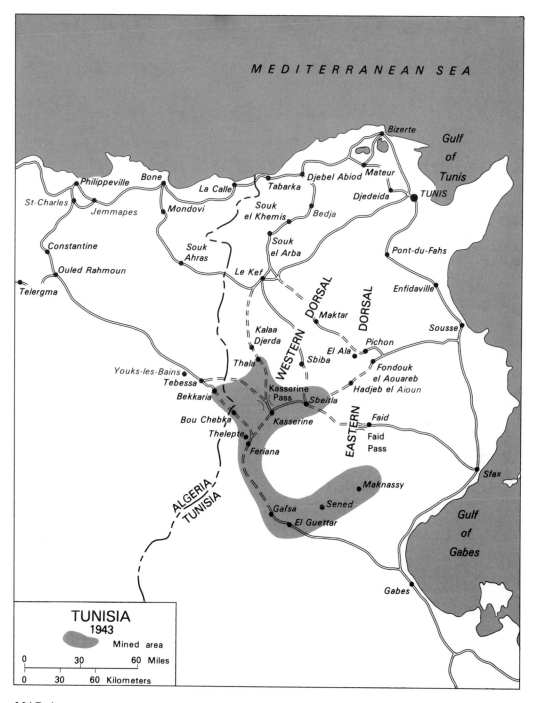

MEDITERRANEAN SEA

Bizerte

Gulf
of
Tunis

Bone          Djebel Abiod   Mateur
Philippeville        La Calle    Tabarka              TUNIS
St-Charles                                  Djedeida
Jemmapes      Mondovi          Souk          Bedja
                        el Khemis
Constantine           Souk          Souk              Pont-du-Fahs
                      Ahras       el Arba
Ouled Rahmoun              Le Kef              Enfidaville
Telergma                                    DORSAL

                                   DORSAL
                                         Maktar         Sousse
                          Kalaa
                          Djerda       El Ala   Pichon
                                WESTERN   Sbiba
Youks-les-Bains      Thala            Fondouk
Tebessa                      Kasserine    Sbeitla   el Aouareb
Bekkaria                     Pass           Hadjeb el Aioun
          Bou Chebka           Kasserine    Faid

                                        EASTERN
                                    Faid
          Thelepte                  Pass
                   Feriana

ALGERIA                              Sfax
TUNISIA                  Maknassy
                    Sened         Gulf
                Gafsa                of
                    El Guettar      Gabes

                         Gabes

TUNISIA
1943
          Mined area
0          30          60  Miles
0     30      60  Kilometers

MAP 4

sensitive rear areas could be disastrous. The engineers were to convert the trail leading west to Sbiba into a road the 34th Infantry Division could use by noon the next day.

Promptly at noon on the seventeenth the last large fill necessary to make the rough trail passable was in place, and two hours later the first divisional vehicle passed over it. Traffic stretched half the length of the road when rain made the fresh grades treacherous. By dark congestion was mounting. At trouble spots all along the road small parties of engineers waited with tractors, half-tracks, and winch-trucks, and throughout the night they pulled and shoved vehicles. Finally, about daybreak, the division reached new defensive positions near Sbiba, where the tired, drenched engineers found many other pressing jobs waiting for them: digging gun emplacements, laying mines, erecting wire, building supply and access roads, and freeing stuck vehicles.[20]

At Kasserine, the 1,200 men of the 19th Engineer Combat Regiment formed the nucleus of a force defending a road leading northwest to Tebessa. The force included an infantry battalion, three artillery batteries, and a tank destroyer battalion—about 2,000 men. The 1st Battalion, 26th Infantry, defended the road leading north to Thala.

Since their arrival in Tunisia on 6 January, the 19th Engineers had worked almost exclusively on improving and maintaining corps supply roads into divisional areas. When the German attack began, one company was still in the Gafsa area with Task Force Raff,

paratroopers with whom they had been operating for several weeks. Another company tunneled bombproof shelters for II Corps headquarters into a hillside near Bekkaria. The rest of the regiment, bivouacked near Bou Chebka, maintained II Corps roads leading out of Tebessa toward the front.

On 16 February, well before dawn, the 19th Engineers began a 3 1/2-hour move into Kasserine Pass. Fog and rain slowed the column, but at 0530 the regiment reached an assembly point one mile west of the pass, where the regimental commander selected defensive positions. The men spent that day and the next digging in and laying mines across their front, interrupting work long enough on the seventeenth to cover the withdrawal of 1st Armored Division units. Fog and intermittent rains that had enveloped the battlefield for several days continued.

On the evening of 17 February, Lt. Edwin C. Dryden of the 19th Engineers received orders to supervise the installation of a minefield in front of an infantry battalion's position. Along with two noncoms, he loaded a truck with mines and proceeded to Headquarters, Company C, 26th Infantry, arriving after midnight. At the infantry command post the engineers found no work detail ready to emplace the mines, nor anyone who knew where the mines were to go or what part they were to play in the defense. In the end, the engineer lieutenant, who had never seen the terrain in daylight, had to select the site and instruct a makeshift work party in laying and arming the mines. Work began after 0330. The light entrenching tools of the infantry proved useless in the rocky ground, and in order to finish by daylight the work

_____
[20] Hist 109th Engr Bn, 2 Jan–15 May 43.

party had to leave the mines unburied, strung across the road from a hill on one side to an embankment on the other.

Enemy artillery fire started to fall on the American positions at Kasserine on 18 February. Engineers from Company A, 19th Engineers, had begun to grade a lateral road across the rear of the defenses, but the enemy took the bulldozer under fire and the grading had to be abandoned. That evening the II Corps commander, Maj. Gen. Lloyd R. Fredendall, instructed Col. Alexander N. Stark, Jr., commander of the 26th Infantry, to "Go to Kasserine right away and pull a Stonewall Jackson. Take over up there." Colonel Stark assumed command of a provisional force (Task Force Stark) early on 19 February, about the time the first German probe entered the pass. This initial thrust turned back, and the rest of the morning passed while the enemy reinforced. During the early afternoon several more companies of American infantry and a few tanks arrived in Kasserine, some of them before the Germans renewed their attack in midafternoon.

About 1600 the enemy's third attack of the day drove Company D, 19th Engineers, from its positions. A counterattack failed to dislodge the enemy troops, and the day ended with the engineer positions seriously weakened but still holding. A French 75-mm. battery was in position to support the engineers, but no heavier American 105s.

The Germans attacked again before dawn, falling mainly on the 26th Infantry. When the infantry positions collapsed, the engineers used reserves gathered for a counterattack to protect an exposed left flank, but the leverage exerted on the 19th Engineer's exposed flank soon proved too great. German infantry, infiltrating behind well-directed artillery fire, took over the rest of the Company D positions and then drove back Company E. The regimental command post had to move, but the Germans brought the new position under machine-gun fire and the defenses quickly crumbled. Company F managed to keep control of its platoons until late afternoon, but the rest of the engineers made their way to the rear as best they could as platoons, squads, and individuals. When the regiment assembled again, it counted its losses in the three-day battle at 11 killed, 28 wounded, and 88 missing.

As the members of the provisional force, beaten and bloodied, found their way to the rear, few probably knew what they had accomplished. Field Marshal Erwin Rommel was operating on a tight time schedule, for Montgomery would soon fall on German positions in southern Tunisia. The rebuff at Sbiba and the delay at Kasserine gave II Corps time to assemble the strength to stop the *German-Italian Panzer Army* a few miles north along the road to Thala.

Analyzing the preparation and conduct of the defense at Kasserine, Col. Anderson T. W. Moore, commanding the 19th Engineers, pointed out serious defects. Foxholes and gun emplacements had not been dug deep enough; few alternate positions had been prepared; barbed wire was delivered late and used little; and leadership and control left much to be desired. But the engineers had performed creditably for a partially trained unit. The 19th Engineers had not even completed rifle training before going overseas, and only one man in the regiment was known to have been in combat before. Their experience at Kasserine underscored a lesson taught repeatedly in Tunisia: engineer units sent to meet German veterans in combat required hard, realistic training.[21]

One of the most persistent irritations for engineer officers was the use of their troops in other than engineer capacities. Standard doctrine permitted the use of engineers as fighting men under certain conditions, but in North Africa the procedure and the criteria for attaching engineer units to fighting units were hardly consistent or uniformly applied. Engineer units frequently undertook nonessential jobs simply because they were at hand. As a result, essential engineer tasks went undone. Furthermore, attachment sometimes tied up valuable pieces of engineer equipment where they were not needed. The II Corps engineer, Col. William A. Carter, Jr., carried on his arguments against using engineers without weighing the disadvantages in taking them away from support duties, especially in offensive operations. By the end of the campaign, only one of the four American divisions resorted to attaching engineer troops.[22]

After the Germans retired from Kasserine, many of the roads in the II Corps sector were virtually impassable. The clay surfaces, softened by frequent rains, had deteriorated rapidly under the heavy military traffic. The enemy had little or no hope of regaining this area and left behind scattered mines, cratered roads, and demolished bridges. Fortunately, there was little of value to destroy. New roads could be built easily across the central Tunisian plateau, and ruined bridges could be bypassed by fords or culverted fills, for there were not perennial rivers to cross. The rains had done more damage than the enemy.

Engineer road work on a considerable scale was necessary before II Corps could launch its attack through Gafsa. To move the 1st Infantry Division and the 1st Armored Division in this offensive, ninety-five miles of trail had to be made into two-way dirt roads. Grading these roads was no great problem. Using two D–7 bulldozers, two R–4 bulldozers, and two graders, Company C, 19th Engineers, with one platoon of Company B attached, in three days improved a rough fifteen-mile road to the last infantry outpost east of Thelepte and graded twenty-four miles of new road from there joining the Sbeitla-Gafsa road. Other units made similar progress. The main problem was keeping existing roads open in the heavy rains.

During the attack through Gafsa (17 March–10 April) corps engineers had 341 miles of other road to keep open, including a 140-mile bituminous macadam route from Ain Beida to Gafsa

---

[21] Hist Record of the 19th Engr Rgt, 20 Oct 42–1 Oct 43; Hist 19th Engr Rgt, pt. A, Prior to Arrival in Italy, 1944–45; Memorandum of Combat Operations of Engineer Troops Under Second U.S. Army Corps, prepared by Lt Col Carter, Corps Engr, and given to Gen Noce during recent trip to Africa, dated 24 Mar 43, African Campaign, EAC files; Eisenhower Dispatch, pp. 24–36; Erwin Rommel, *The Rommel Papers*, ed., B. H. Liddell Hart (London: Collins, 1953), pp. 400, 404; Opns Rpts, 26th Inf Rgt, 11 Nov 42–14 Apr 43.

[22] Brig Gen D. O. Elliott to CofEngrs, Washington, D.C., 19 Jul 43, Rpt on U.S. Engrs in the Tunisian Campaign, Doc 1547, hereafter cited as Elliott Rpt, 19 Jul 43; Annex 16, Lt Col H. C. Rowland, 20 Apr 43, in AAR, 1st Engr C Bn, 8 Nov 42–14 Mar 43; 5th Ind, HQ, NATOUSA, 30 Oct 45 to AAR, 16th Armd

Engr Bn, 3 Sep 43; Memo, Lt Col W. A. Carter, II Corps Engr, for Engr, AFHQ, 23 May 43.

and five dirt roads that required constant maintenance. As divisional combat engineers became involved in mine work, they had little time left for road maintenance, and that task fell to the corps engineers. At this time the 20th Engineer Combat Regiment made the long trip from French Morocco to aid the 19th Engineers. The 175th General Service Regiment was also sent into the II Corps area to help.[23]

Again, during II Corps' attack on Bizerte in late April and early May, road work was vitally important, although once the rainy season was past, maintenance was less a factor. The corps roadnet consisted of about 100 miles of rough, water-bound macadam and about 260 miles of dirt roads, some little more than cart tracks. Offsetting the advantage of dry weather was the hilly terrain. Here, enemy mines and demolitions were more effective because the avenues of approach ran through the narrow valleys, and the bridges in these valleys could not be so easily bypassed. The attack in the north avoided the valleys when possible and generally followed the high ground. Some seventy-six miles of new roads were built from the main supply route to pack mule trails to reach infantry positions on the hills. Bypasses around demolished bridges accounted for some of this mileage.[24]

While no major, radical changes in engineer TBA resulted from experience in Tunisia, some additions appeared eminently desirable. For example, a definite need developed that each combat engineer battalion have at least one of the large D–7 bulldozers. More road graders and dump trucks would have proved useful in certain situations, but it was debatable whether this was a matter of changing the Table of Basic Allowances or of providing more Class IV equipment. One of the most needed Class IV items was the power shovel, for there was little point in providing a combat engineer regiment fifty-four dump trucks to haul road fill unless the means existed for providing crushed rock and for loading it on the trucks. Road maintenance took up a disproportionate share of the combat engineers' time in Tunisia because mechanical means for loading fill were lacking. The only exception was a civilian-owned steam shovel the 19th Engineer Combat Regiment put into service. In the final days of the campaign the 20th Engineer Combat Regiment also made good use of a shovel— probably the same one. If so, only one shovel was available to the combat engineers in all Tunisia.[25]

Central and southern Tunisia had wet-weather wadis aplenty but no permanent streams. Except after very heavy rains, combat unit vehicles could cross wet-weather streams as soon as engineers bulldozed dry fords or built bypasses around demolished bridges. In northern Tunisia, on the other hand, there were permanent streams, and bridge building was an important engi-

---

[23] Rpt of Engr Opns, Carter, II Corps, 15 Mar–10 Apr, dated 1 May 43; File, ENGP–19–0.3 (23568) Master Historical Record–19th Engr C Gp, Oct 42– Jan 44, HRS, DRB, AGO; File, 301–Eng–0.3 (22313) AAR, 1st Engr C Bn, 8 Nov 42–14 Mar 43, HRS, DRB, AGO; Rpt, HQ, II Corps (Patton) to AG, USA, Washington, D.C. thru 18 Army Gp, 15 Mar–10 Apr 43, dated 10 Apr 43, Bx 49768 KCRC; Capt George E. Horn, The Twentieth Engineers, 1 Jul 43.

[24] Rpt, Lt Col W. A. Carter, II Corps Engr, 28 May 43, sub: Rpt of Engr Opns II Corps, 22 Apr–8 May.

[25] Ibid.; Elliott Rpt, 19 Jul 43; AAR, 16th Armd Engr Bn, 3 Sep 43.

neer activity. During this campaign the British Bailey bridge first proved its tactical value to Americans.

During the closing days of the campaign, the 9th Infantry Division employed a compromise plan that proved satisfactory. Under this plan the regimental combat teams (RCTs) had the support of one company of combat engineers each, with each company supporting its combat team in three echelons. In the vanguard, a small group of reconnaissance engineers accompanied forward infantry elements. Not far behind, a platoon of combat engineers cleared mines and prepared paths over which mules carried rations and ammunition to the front. The rest of the engineer company helped the artillery to displace forward; built roads, and cleared minefields. The 3d Regimental Combat Team had only one platoon of combat engineers attached; being in reserve, this team moved less than the others. The rest of the engineer battalion remained under division control, to be used where most needed.[26]

Engineer combat battalion manpower increased from 634 to 745 in the years before 1942. In 1943 Army Ground Forces redesigned the American infantry division, reducing its organic engineer support to a battalion of 647 men, and cut the armored engineer battalion by 40 percent. North African experience argued for substracting the bridge company formerly assigned to engineer battalions, especially in armored divisions. Though highly enthusiastic about its Bailey bridge sets, the 16th Armored Engineer Battalion car-

ried the equipment for three months in central Tunisia before putting it to hard use in the closing weeks of the campaign. The NATOUSA engineer also found that he rarely had enough reconnaissance forces either at corps level or below. The new organization gave each combat battalion a 22-man reconnaissance section equipped with three SCR-511 portable radios, binoculars, and compasses.[27]

## Mine Clearing

As the Germans withdrew through the Kasserine Pass and Sbeitla to the Eastern Dorsal, clear skies enabled Allied planes to harry their retreat. On the ground American pressure bogged down, partly because at Kasserine American troops encountered "mines and demolitions on such a scale as to suggest a new weapon in warfare." Behind a covering screen of thousands of mines, the enemy broke contact and withdrew unmolested by ground troops.[28]

The engineers were as ill prepared as the infantry for mine warfare, although they had responsibility for mine laying and mine clearing. One engineer combat company commander, who "had never seen a German mine, picture, or model before entering combat in Tunisia" had to rely on one noncom, who had attended a British mine school in the theater, to train company officers and key men only a few days before his unit encountered its first live minefield.[29]

[26] Lt. Col. Frederick A. Henney, "Combat Engineers in North Africa, Pt. II, Operations in Tunisia," The Military Engineer, XXXVI, no. 220 (February 1944), 40–42.

[27] Greenfield, Palmer, and Wiley, The Organization of Ground Combat Troops, pp. 309, 331, 374, 446; Elliott Rpt, 19 Jul 43; AAR, 16th Armd Engr Bn, 3 Sep 43; Ltr, Brig Gen D. O. Elliott to AGF Board (G–3 Training) AFHQ, 8 Jul 43, sub: G–4 Engr Questions for AGF Observers, 071.01 AGF file, Jul 43–Dec 44.
[28] Eisenhower Dispatch, p. 36.
[29] Ltr, Lt Col Webb (190th Engr C Bn), 23 Apr 56; Ltr, Lt Col Wallace (15th Engr C Bn), 17 Jan 56.

Antitank mines were customarily placed in staggered rows, checkerboard fashion, spaced far enough apart to avoid sympathetic detonation. They were laid according to specific pattern for two reasons: an enemy tank or other vehicle missing mines in the first row would stand a good chance of coming to grief on the second, third, or fourth row; and, when necessary, friendly troops could more easily locate and lift mines laid in a pattern. This second consideration was important, for armed mines played no favorites. Minefields had to be charted and marked with care.

During their retreat in Tunisia the Germans were hardly concerned with having to relocate mines, so they scattered them indiscriminately anywhere Allied troops and vehicles were likely to travel. Since Allied trucks and motorized equipment were confined mainly to roads or to occasional stretches off the road, the Germans mined shoulders, particularly where the roads narrowed; they also mined road junctions, likely turnouts, probable bivouac areas, and wadi crossings. The Germans used many tricks to deceive and slow down mine detection teams: they booby-trapped some mines and buried others two and three deep; around some they scattered bits of metal that Allied mine detector operators had to mark for investigation. One of the enemy's most effective tricks was to bury mines too deep to be detected. In this way scores of trucks could pass safely over a road and then, when ruts became deep enough, a mine would explode. Such methods had a heavy psychological effect on attacking troops and delayed the advance more effectively than pattern mining could have. In such circumstances, even though

only a few mines might have been laid in some areas, many miles of roadway had to be swept. All antitank mines had to be handled as if booby-trapped, even though only a small percentage actually were. And no matter how slowly or methodically mine clearance teams worked, they could never guarantee a clear route.[30]

The land mines that the engineers had to deal with fell into two categories, antitank (AT) and antipersonnel (AP). AT mines were generally pressure-activated—a man's weight would not detonate them, but that of any military vehicle would. They contained several pounds of explosives which could demolish a jeep or immobilize a tank by breaking a track and damaging bogie-wheels. AP mines were smaller charges of explosives set for the unwary. Activated by sensitive push-pull, pressure, or pressure-release devices, they required much more delicate handling then AT mines. Varieties of these two types, and the subterfuges with which they could be employed, were endless.

The antitank Teller mine ("plate" in German) was the mine the Germans used most in Tunisia, although they also employed others of Italian, French, and Hungarian manufacture as well as captured British and American mines. Four different models of the Teller mine found in North Africa had the same general characteristics: disc

---

[30] II Corps Intel Info Summary 2, 18 Jan 43; Ltr, Lt Col Ellsworth I. Davis to XO, The Engr Bd, 26 Apr 43, sub: Report of Trip to UK and NA with Ref to AT Mines, Demolitions and Airborne Engrs; Ltr, Lt Ralph M. Ingersoll to CG, Engr Amphib Cmd, 14 Apr 43, sub: Memorandum on Opns with AT & AP Mines in the Tunisian Campaign, African Campaign file, EAC; Military Attache Rpt 59181, MID WDGS, sub: Battle of Tunisia, 22 July 1943, AFHQ Engr Intel Summaries beginning Jan 43.

GERMAN S-MINE. *The activated canister burst from the earth and fired over 300 steel pellets in all directions.*

shaped, about a foot in diameter, three to four inches thick with a zinc or steel jacket encasing eleven pounds of TNT, and a total weight of about twenty pounds. Teller mines had three igniter wells, one on top for a shear-pin type pressure igniter and others on the side and bottom for more sensitive and more varied booby-trap igniters. These extra wells, and the igniters to fit them, gave the mines a built-in antilifting feature that no American mines could match. American engineers had to assume that every Teller mine was booby-trapped.

The German antipersonnel "S" mine was a particularly clever innovation. Nicknamed "Bouncing Betty" by British troops, the mine's activation detonated a small black powder charge, throwing a grapeshot canister out of the earth. Exploding at waist or chest level, the canister discharged a murderous hail of steel ball bearings in all directions.

The Germans made widespread use of booby traps with blocks of explosives rigged to houses, equipment, or even bodies—anything curious or unwary troops were likely to touch, move, or walk on. AFHQ engineer intelligence bulletins promptly circulated information on various types of reported booby traps, sometimes before they could be confirmed. For example, reports of a water bottle that exploded when the cork was withdrawn, a German whistle that exploded when blown, and a booby-

ITALIAN BAR MINES. *The opened casing shows the simple pressure detonating device.*

trapped cake of soap were published throughout the command; how many others—real and unreal—circulated by word of mouth can only be conjectured.[31]

In Tunisia a large part of the combat engineers' time was given to laying, lifting, and clearing mines, often to the neglect of other work such as road maintenance. The 16th Armored Engineer Battalion, for example, spent virtually half its time on mine work, as did combat engineers with infantry divisions. To compensate, corps-level engineers had to push their road maintenance and minefield clearance work well forward into divisional areas. Although the engineers were better prepared to deal with mines than was the infantry, engineer training in the subject left much to be desired.[32]

While the engineers often had to use the slow and tedious method of probing with bayonets for mines, they generally relied on the magnetic mine detector (SCR−625) for speed on long stretches of roads, in bivouac areas, and on airfield sites. The detector was a 7 1/2-pound instrument consisting of a set of earphones and a search plate

[31] AFHQ Engr Intel Summaries 1, Jan 43, to 14, May 43.

[32] Ltr, Ingersoll, 14 Apr 43, sub: Memo on Opns with AT & AP Mines; AAR, 16th Armd Engr Bn, 3 Sep 43; U.S. Engrs in Tunisian Campaign, Engr Sect, AFHQ, 19 Jul 43; Rpt, Maj Gen W. H. Walker to CG, AGF, 12 Jun 43, sub: Report of Visit to North African Theater of Opns, 319.1/84, AGF file (F.O.), binder 1, Observer Rpts, 1 Jan−20 Jul 43.

mounted on a wooden disc at the end of a six-foot handle. Dry cell batteries induced a magnetic field around the search plate and produced a low hum in the operator's earphones. The soldier "swept" a wide arc before him with the instrument. In the presence of metal buried less than a foot deep, the hum in the operator's ears continually increased in pitch until it became a near-shriek when the detector was directly above a mine. Engineers in the mine-clearing party marked the spot, and other engineers, following behind, unearthed and deactivated the mines. They dug out but did not deactivate mines unfamiliar or suspected of being booby-trapped. They sometimes placed a block of explosive beside these mines and relied on sympathetic detonation; more often they attached a length of wire and pulled the mines out of their holes from a safe distance.[33]

The SCR–625 was a valuable piece of equipment when it worked but had two serious shortcomings: it was not waterproof and was quite fragile. The instrument shorted out in wet weather and required such careful handling and delicate tuning that normally about 20 percent were broken or out of adjustment. In spite of these drawbacks, after Kasserine Pass the magnetic detector became one of the most sought-after pieces of equipment in the Army. The 16th Armored Engineer Battalion urged that the allocation be increased from

THE SCR–625 MINE DETECTOR *in action on a Tunisian road.*

eighteen to seventy-one. Experience in Tunisia prompted most engineer units to ask that one detector be provided per squad, with some provision for a battalion reserve.[34]

Experiments conducted in the Mediterranean theater as well as in the United States sought to find a faster way of detecting or eliminating mines, particularly under fire. The demand arose for larger magnetic detectors, mounted on vehicles, that could sweep long sections

---

[33] Ltr, Ingersoll, 14 Apr 43, sub: Memo on Opns with AT & AP Mines. For background on the development of this detector, see Coll, Keith, and Rosenthal, *The Corps of Engineers: Troops and Equipment,* pp. 54–55. Rpt of Engr Opns, Carter, II Corps, 15 Mar–10 Apr, dated 1 May 43; Rpt, Maj Gen C. P. Hall to CG, AGF, 24 Apr 43, sub: Report of Visit to NATO, 319.1/84, AGF file (F.O), binder 1, Observer Rpts, 1 Jan–20 Jul 43.

[34] Ltr, Ingersoll, 14 Apr 43, sub: Memo on Opns with AT & AP Mines; AAR, 16th Armd Engr Bn, 3 Sep 43; U.S. Engrs in Tunisian Campaign, Engr Sect, AFHQ, 19 Jul 43.

of road rapidly. Engineers of I Armored Corps in French Morocco experimented with mechanical means, explosives, and fire to make gaps in pattern minefields. They found that tanks could push long sections of explosive-filled pipe across a minefield and that when detonated these "snakes" cleared a path wide enough for a tank to pass through. Bangalore torpedoes and nets made of primacord also tested well. But mine-clearing explosions alerted the enemy, and bulky devices occupied a great deal of shipping space. Nearby concussions also made more sensitive the unexploded mines which the snakes left alongside their path. Engineer units carried snakes in Tunisia but did not use them to blow gaps in minefields.[35]

Two mechanical means of detection and detonation offered some promise. The British Eighth Army developed the Scorpion—lengths of chain attached to a revolving axle suspended well in front of a tank. As the tank moved forward, the chain flailed the ground. The Scorpion exerted enough ground pressure to explode mines and could absorb at least the initial concussions; however, it also created clouds of dust and destroyed the chain flails quickly. The machine moved about one thousand yards into an active minefield before the blasts took so many links from the ends of the chains that they no longer struck the ground. The enemy could counteract the flails with wire entanglements, and the whirling chains often activated delayed-action mines that destroyed following vehicles. In the end, the only antimine innovation that American engi-

neers employed in Tunisia was a "pilot vehicle" the 16th Armored Engineer Battalion and 1st Armored Division ordnance personnel developed, an M−3 tank with concrete-filled, spiked steel drums mounted in front. Its purpose was to find the forward edge of a minefield without needless searching. Used twice during the last days of the campaign, the vehicle revealed a serious defect—the mines demolished the roller. The first time the engineers employed the vehicle they replaced the roller under fire, but the second time they had to withdraw.[36]

American engineer officers in March and April 1943 studied British minefield clearing techniques and other mine warfare methods. Training teams from the British Eighth Army, made up of men with two years of experience in mine warfare, provided valuable aid. Before the major attack during the third week of April, about forty American officers and more than a hundred noncoms attended a mine school that the British First Army conducted with instructors brought to Tunisia from the British Eighth Army. Other mine schools sprang up. Experienced engineers taught the less experienced, and they trained instructors from infantry, artillery, and other units. Fifth Army established a Mine Warfare School at Ain Fritissa that drew a few instructors from the British Eighth Army.

---

[35] Data from I Armd Corps, 26 Jun 43, Engr Sch Lib, 7641; see Coll, Keith, and Rosenthal, *The Corps of Engineers: Troops and Equipment,* pp. 476ff, for efforts in the United States to develop mine-clearing devices.

[36] AFHQ Engr Intel Summary 14, May 43; Rpt, Carter, 28 May 43, sub: Rpt of Engr Opns II Corps, 22 Apr−8 May; Address by Col Edwin P. Lock, Staff and Faculty, Engr Sch, Ft. Belvoir, Va., 31 May 43, "Reduction of Obstacles and Fortifications," ETOUSA MAS file, Assault Trng Ctr Conf. For efforts of the Ordnance Department to develop a satisfactory mine exploder, see Constance M. Green, Harry C. Thomson, and Peter C. Roots, *The Ordnance Department: Planning Munitions for War,* United States Army in World War II (Washington, 1955), pp. 387−94.

SCORPION TANK CREW LOADING BANGALORE TORPEDOES

One of the prime difficulties in conducting mine training was obtaining deactivated enemy mines. Although thousands of German and Italian mines were deactivated in the combat zone, they were scarce in the rear areas. There were exceptions. Some mines were sent to England for training purposes, and Lt. Gen. Mark W. Clark's private plane ferried some from the front to the Fifth Army mine school. But most mine training had to be carried out without enemy mines. The main reason was the danger involved, which the theater command believed outweighed the advantages. Besides the normal hazards of handling unfamiliar varieties of live explosives, explosive sensitivity increased with age. In one incident on 30 March 1943, a 109th Engineer Combat Battalion truck loaded with 450 neutralized mines exploded, killing an entire twelve-man squad.[37]

German patterns of mining continued superior to American in most respects, as did the German system of charting and recording minefields. Where American units kept sketchy records or none at all in local unit files, German engineers carefully plotted each mine barrier and sent records to a central office in Germany.

[37] Ltr, Ingersoll, 14 Apr 43, sub: Memo on Opns with AT & AP Mines; Ltr, Lt Col E. I. Davis, 26 Apr 43, Rpt of Trip to UK and NA; Ltr, Lt Col John A. Chambers, 5 Apr 56; Hist 109th Engr C Bn Tunisian Campaign, 2 Jan–15 May 43.

The SCR−625's noncollapsible handle forced the operator to stand upright, often in sight of an enemy covering the minefield with small-arms fire. Whatever reliability the detector promised for the future, it was useless in finding the German nonmetallic Schu mines, encased in wooden boxes, that appeared in small numbers in North Africa and would become more plentiful on the Continent. Out of their experience the engineers also demanded a new anti-tank mine that would do real damage to enemy armor; the German Teller, with twice the explosives of the American models, usually destroyed the hull and undercarriage of any tank striking it, while the American mine would only damage a track, leaving a salvageable vehicle.[38]

The magnetic mine detector, the bayonet, and a sharp, suspicious eye were the antimine measures that engineers relied upon most in Tunisia. From late February, when the Germans fell back to the Eastern Dorsal, until 13 April, American engineers found over 39,000 mines. In the area from Thala and Bekkaria through Kasserine to Sbeitla and along the road from Thelepte to Gafsa mine detection parties removed 10,750 enemy mines, and in the Gafsa area they found 8,700 more. Around E1 Guettar they lifted 12,450 and found 7,300 more in the Maknassy-Sened area.[39]

*Water Supply*

Because reliable sources were scarce, the provision of water came next to road work and mine clearing in importance to combat engineers in Tunisia. Water supply involved three principal jobs: locating sources, testing and purifying, and distributing water to the troops. The engineers were concerned primarily with the first two; the arms and services usually provided their own trucks to haul water from engineer water points.

Each combat engineer battalion carried equipment to establish four water points and normally set up two forward and one or two back. As the divisions moved forward the rear water points leapfrogged over the forward ones. Combat engineer regiments provided similar service to corps units, as did general service regiments for units in areas to which they were assigned, although in rear areas much of the work was done by engineer units specifically organized and equipped for water supply. When II Corps' offensive through Gafsa was impending, the 518th Engineer Water Supply Company moved forward to supplement the work combat engineers had done to establish water points, for the approaching end of the rainy season promised to make the job more difficult.[40]

The first step in activating a water point was to locate a stream, well, pond, or spring. In Tunisia most of the sources were wells, which were marked in the

[38] WD Pub, "Lessons Learned from the Tunisian Campaign," 15 Oct 43; AAR, 16th Armd Engr Bn, 3 Sep 43; I Armd Corps, Data file, 26 Jun 43; AFHQ Engr Intel Summary 7, Mar 43; Coll, Keith, and Rosenthal, *The Corps of Engineers: Troops and Equipment,* pp. 479−80; AFHQ Engr Intel Summary 10, Apr 43; Herchal Ottinger, Engineer Agency for Resources Inventories, "Landmine and Countermine Warfare," *North Africa, 1940−1943* (Washington: Corps of Engineers, 1972), pp. 255−62.

[39] Rpt of Engr Opns, Carter, II Corps, 15 Mar−10

Apr, dated 1 May 43; Rpt, Carter, 28 May 43, sub: Rpt of Engr Opns II Corps, 22 Apr−8 May.

[40] Hist 109th Engr C Bn, Tunisian Campaign; Rpt of Engr Opns, Carter, II Corps, 15 Mar−10 Apr, dated 1 May 43; Henney, "Combat Engineers in North Africa, Pt. II," pp. 40−42.

central and southern parts of the country by clusters of trees. The next step was to test the water for potability, turbidity, and poison. An engineer technician carried a kit of test tubes and chemicals for this purpose. If he approved a particular source, a squad brought in a truck loaded with a motorized pump, a sand filter, a chlorinator, and a collapsible 3,000-gallon canvas tank which when erected stood about four feet high. Within about thirty minutes the squad had water pumping through the filters. The engineers used chemical disinfectants, principally chlorine gas or sodium hypochlorite. The purification equipment proved entirely adequate, even for water that was highly turbid and contaminated.[41]

During the Tunisian campaign the engineers continually put in and took out water points. Some sources had to be abandoned because pumps sucked them dry, others because the units they supplied had moved. During II Corps' offensive through Gafsa between 17 March and 11 April, the 518th Engineer Water Supply Company had tanker trucks haul over three million gallons of water to forward distribution points called dry points. Trucks from the arms and services came to these dry points, as they would to any other water source, to fill five-gallon cans for their units. During the offensive the 518th also repaired a generator and a diesel well pump, which the Germans had damaged, to put the Gafsa and Station de Sened water systems back into operation.

In mountainous northern Tunisia during the final phase of the campaign, hauling water was less a problem since sources were more numerous. Combat engineers were able to operate several points in their own areas, while the 518th operated sources for corps troops and hospitals. The large number of enemy troops captured in the closing days of the campaign precipitated something of a water crisis, and all available tankers were needed again to haul water to prisoner of war enclosures. On its peak day during this period the 518th distributed 72,840 gallons of water.[42]

### Camouflage

Engineer performance in camouflage was less successful than in water supply. Before the invasion AFHQ had specified that each army, corps, and major air force headquarters would have a qualified camouflage officer and that each unit down to the battalion and separate company level should name a unit camouflage officer. These officers became so burdened with additional duties during the campaign that unit camouflage suffered. To remedy this situation II Corps obtained Company B, 601st Engineer Camouflage Battalion, and for three weeks before the Gafsa attack had instruction teams teach corps units camouflage techniques. But, in the combat zone, more than teaching was essential, for camouflage was probably better understood than enforced.[43]

[41] Capt. Ralph Ingersoll, *The Battle Is the Payoff* (New York: Harcourt, Brace & Co., 1943), pp. 48–49; Lt. William J. Diamond, "Water Supply in North Africa," *The Military Engineer*, XXXV, no. 217 (November 1943), 565–66.

[42] Rpt of Engr Opns, Carter, II Corps, 15 Mar–10 Apr, dated 1 May 43; Rpt, Carter, 28 May 43, sub: Rpt of Engr Opns II Corps, 22 Apr–8 May; Henney, "Combat Engineers in North Africa, Pt. II."

[43] AFHQ Opns Memo 20, Camouflage Policy, 17 Oct 42; Memo, Maj Fred K. Shirk, U.S. Camouflage Officer, Engr Sect, AFHQ, Comments on Camouflage Operations During the North African Campaign (8

Camouflage was a command responsibility, and many commanders tried to enforce it. Covered windshields did not glint, and dusty, muddy vehicles blended with the terrain. Some units draped camouflage nets over their vehicles, some used the nets for bedding, and some did not use them at all. Units seldom attempted camouflaging vehicle tracks, for the barren North African landscape made it virtually impossible to conceal the army's bulky motorized equipment, particularly when it was in motion. The best hope was to mask equipment identity. Toward the end of the campaign, as the Allies gained superiority in the air, camouflage discipline relaxed almost completely.[44]

### Maps

The II Corps engineer was responsible for distributing maps to American units in Tunisia, with British First Army providing the maps according to stock levels set for the corps. The system worked well. Five men of the 62d Engineer Topographic Company issued all maps, using a 2 1/2-ton, 6-by-6 that the 470th Engineer Maintenance Company converted into a mobile map depot.

Old French maps provided the base for the maps II Corps used in Tunisia;

the corps' engineer topographic company overprinted more recent information. The maps often proved inaccurate on important points. Scales varied from the 1:10,000 town plan of Bizerte (useful during mine clearing and reconstruction work) to 1:200,000 road maps. Those most in use were 1:200,000 for southern Tunisia and 1:100,000 for northern Tunisia. These scales were satisfactory for regimental and higher headquarters but not for lower level units and artillery. Two days before the attack got under way in the north, British First Army furnished II Corps 1,000 copies of a 1:25,000 edition and a few days later 2,000 more copies containing revised intelligence data. This large-scale map proved valuable, as did a 1:50,000 operational series.[45]

Aerial photographs could have done much to correct and supplement the maps, but those available in Tunisia were wholly inadequate. Enlarged small-scale maps were poor substitutes for large-scale tactical maps. Good aerial photography was needed for intelligence and high altitude photomapping for map substitutions. The British First Army furnished some aerial photographs, but II Corps was never able to get enough. Wide-angle, high-altitude photomapping was not available at all.[46]

Nov 42–8 May 45); Rpt, 601st Engr Camouflage Bn to CG, II Corps, 26 May 43, sub: Resume of Opns; all in file Camouflage, 2 Jul 43, Intnl AFHQ, A–1434, Engr Sch Lib. Rpt, Engr Sect, AFHQ to CofEngrs, WD, 19 Jul 43, U.S. Engrs in the Tunisian Campaign.

[44] AFHQ Opn Memo 20, Camouflage Policy, 17 Oct 42; Ltr, Lt Col E. I. Davis, 26 Apr 43; Rpt, Hall to CG, AGF, 24 Apr 43, sub: Rpt of Visit to NATO; Bradley, A Solider's Story, pp. 37, 40; Rpt, Lt Col G. E. Lynch, Observer from HQ AGF, for Period 30 Dec 42–6 Feb 43, ca. 5 Mar 43, 319.1/84, AGF file (F.O.), binder 1, Observer Rpts, 1 Jan–20 Jul 43.

[45] Rpt, Carter, 28 May 43, sub: Rpt of Engr Opns II Corps, 22 Apr–8 May; 26th Inf Rpt, Lessons Learned in the Gafsa–El Guettar Opns, 13 Apr 43; Memo, Col Michael Buckley, Jr., for CG, AGF, 17 May 43, sub: Observer Rpt, II Corps, Tunisia, 21–26 Apr 43; Rpt, Maj Gen William H. Simpson to CG, AGF, 7 May 43, sub: Rpt on Visit to North African Theater (hereafter cited as Simpson Rpt); both in 319.1/84, AGF file (F.O.), binder 1, Observer Rpts, 1 Jan–20 Jul 43.

[46] Rpt, Carter, 28 May 43, sub: Rpt of Engr Opns II Corps, 22 Apr–8 May; Rpt, Maj Gen Walker to CG, AGF, 12 Jun 43, sub: Rpt of Visit to North African Theater; Simpson Rpt.

*Command Reorganizations*

With the Allies moving on an increasingly isolated but still dangerous enemy in Tunisia, the chief abiding difficulty in engineer supply in North Africa, apart from expected delays in shipments from the United States, was the tangled command structure that evolved in the area. In the attempts to resolve the awkward relationships between AFHQ and the ETOUSA headquarters in London, the War Department pushed for and General Eisenhower accepted the idea of a theater command in North Africa. A reorganization on 30 December 1942 centralized control of the Atlantic and Mediterranean Base Sections directly under AFHQ, relieving Western Task Force and II Corps of port and supply line operation. On 4 February 1943, taking advantage of the momentary lull in the Tunisian campaign, the War Department directed the establishment of the North African Theater of Operations, U.S. Army (NATOUSA), to consolidate and administer all American affairs in North Africa. General Eisenhower headed AFHQ and the new theater but acted on all theater administrative detail through his deputy commander, Brig. Gen. Everett S. Hughes. General Hughes, attempting to clarify his position for American forces, requested that he be designated commanding general of the Communications Zone, NATOUSA (COMZ, NATOUSA), since no American doctrine specified the office of deputy theater commander that Eisenhower had conferred upon him. Formally instituted on 9 February 1943, COMZ, NATOUSA, existed as a graft onto AFHQ, with senior American AFHQ officers doing triple duty as the staff for the COMZ command, for the NATOUSA headquarters, and for AFHQ.

Further complicating the structure after 14 February 1943 was the SOS, NATOUSA, command, established over arguments against maintaining a headquarters G–4, a communications zone command, and a separate services of supply organization in the same theater. Under the command of Brig. Gen. Thomas B. Larkin, former head of the Mediterranean Base Section, SOS, NATOUSA, was another level of command between the theater headquarters and the base sections; however, while the directive establishing his command assigned to Larkin all U.S. Army logistical functions except high-level planning and policy making, it failed to give him adequate control of the base sections. Already an anomaly under the current field service regulations, since American doctrine did not envisage a communications zone and a services of supply in the same theater, Larkin's command entered into informal agreements with the base section commanders that placed overall control of supply, construction, maintenance, and transportation with SOS, NATOUSA. But COMZ, NATOUSA, did not confirm this arrangement; the agreements existed only as policy guidelines, which base section commanders could circumvent. Since SOS, NATOUSA, had to issue all directives to the base sections through COMZ, NATOUSA, General Larkin's plans were altered or delayed in accord with other plans and priorities. Though the theater command tried to untangle the channels of command, the end of the Tunisian campaign found the lines of responsibility between COMZ, NATO-

USA, and SOS, NATOUSA, and between SOS, NATOUSA, and AFHQ's G–4 still unclear. The AFHQ G–4, acting as planner for the inter-Allied staff and also in his NATOUSA capacity, frequently operated in the field of supply and dealt with the base sections directly where SOS authority should have prevailed. This command chain persisted for another year until the dissolution of COMZ, NATOUSA, and the consolidation of logistical operations under SOS, NATOUSA, on 20 February 1944. Within that chain, Brig. Gen. Donald A. Davison, as AFHQ engineer, also acted as chief engineer to the NATOUSA and the COMZ, NATOUSA, commands. As with other American staff officers similarly situated, he had to remember in which capacity he was acting in any given matter.

Other complications continued to plague the U.S. Army logistical system in North Africa. The chiefs of U.S. Army technical services remained at AFHQ/NATOUSA instead of transferring to SOS, NATOUSA, as might have been expected. This arrangement further circumscribed Larkin's span of control and authority. Finally, SOS, NATOUSA, had to set up its headquarters at Oran, the principal American supply base in North Africa, although AFHQ/NATOUSA headquarters installations lay at Algiers, over 200 miles to the east. Communications over this distance often slowed logistical reaction time.

The establishment of SOS, NATOUSA, created a new set of personnel problems for the engineers. The Engineer Section of SOS, NATOUSA, informally came into being in February with six officers and seven enlisted men borrowed from the 1st Engineer Amphibian Brigade. Not until April did the section receive an allotment of five officers and fourteen enlisted men and return the borrowed personnel to the brigade. Initially, the principal function of the small SOS, NATOUSA, Engineer Section was to control and edit requisitions for engineer supplies that the base section engineers drew on the United States or the United Kingdom. In turn, the main tasks of the base section engineers during the Tunisian campaign were to construct and maintain supply routes and to operate engineer supply depots.[47]

### Atlantic Base Section

All along the long line of communications from Casablanca east, preparations went forward with all possible speed for the decisive battles in Tunisia. Engineer supplies and equipment came into Atlantic Base Section (ABS) at Casablanca at the rate of 2,000 tons per convoy, and ABS issued large amounts of engineer supplies to units staging for Tunisia. The depot responsibilities taxed the ABS engineer supply personnel (built around the 451st Engineer Depot Company) to the limit, and local labor could not meet the emergency. In April the arrival of an engineer general service company eased the problem at the ABS engineer depot.

---

[47] Leo J. Meyer, The Strategy and Logistical History: MTO, chs. VI–VII, MS in CMH; History of Allied Force Headquarters, pt. I, Aug–Dec 42, pp. 61–62; and pt. II, sec. 1, p. 200; G–4 Staff, MTOUSA, *Logistical History of NATOUSA-MTOUSA* (Naples: G. Montanio, 1945), p. 24; Memo, Lt Col O. B. Beasley, XO, Engr Sect, AFHQ, for CG, NATOUSA, 27 Mar 43, sub: Orgn of the Engr Sect, AFHQ/NATOUSA, NATOUSA Engr Sect, 320.2 (2); WD, Field Service Regulations, Administration, FM 100–10, 9 Dec 40, pp. 20–23.

Unit demands for many items in excess of Table of Basic Allowances, together with a growing need for vastly more material for housing, hospitals, and sanitary facilities than originally planned, placed most items in ABS engineer dumps in the "critical" category. Construction supplies from the United States lagged far behind requisitions and procuring locally such items as cement, lumber, and electrical and plumbing equipment was difficult. A major drop in imports since the outbreak of war in Europe in 1939 had created a serious shortage of construction supplies of all types throughout French Morocco, and local merchants and manufacturers tended to hold back materials that might later bring higher prices; however, centralized purchasing for engineer supply items largely overcame the local procurement problem.

By mid-May, at the end of the Tunisian campaign, ABS engineers had virtually completed their own construction program and had issued tons of locally procured construction material. At the same time, less than half the construction supplies ABS engineers had requisitioned from the United States had reached Casablanca. Much of the missing materiel that began to arrive during succeeding weeks was no longer needed. By late June ABS engineer dumps contained 10 million board feet of unwanted lumber.[48]

*Mediterranean Base Section*

At Oran, the site of both Mediterranean Base Section (MBS) and SOS,

NATOUSA, personnel problems were much the same as those at ABS. Four engineer supply depots were in the Oran area by late December 1942, but only the 450th Engineer Depot Company (less one platoon) was available to operate them. As early as December an engineer dump truck company and two companies of the 1st Engineer Amphibian Brigade had to be diverted to depot operations, and the depots also employed about 800 local laborers. In midwinter the understrength (1 officer and 80 enlisted men) 715th Engineer Depot Company joined the force. By March, when the 460th Engineer Depot Company reached Oran from the Zone of the Interior (ZI), the MBS engineer depots were employing approximately 1,500 local laborers. In April the 462d Engineer Depot Company arrived from the ZI. Nevertheless, the MBS engineer constantly had to add nonsupply engineer detachments to the depot force. These detachments generally had no supply training and had to learn on the job to unload, handle, store, and account for engineer supplies.[49]

Shortages of equipment, especially vehicles, also plagued engineer supply operations within MBS. As of February 1943 the 450th Engineer Depot Company, the first such unit in the Oran area, was 30 percent short of its TBA vehicles, the 715th Engineer Depot Company 60 percent short, and other engineer units assigned to depot operations an average of 31.5 percent

[48] History of the Atlantic Base Section to June 1, 1943, vol. I, pp. 29–32.

[49] Memo, Col George D. Pence, G–1, MBS, for CG, MBS, 24 Jan 43, sub: Status, Shipments of U.S. Units and Casual Personnel; Rpt, Col Morris W. Gilland, Dep Engr, MBS to CG, MBS, 27 Dec 42, sub: Lessons from Operation TORCH, HQ, MBS; Rpt, Lt Col R. W. Colglazier, Jr., Asst XO, Engr Sect, to CG, MBS, 24 Jan 43, sub: Current Status Rpt, Engr Serv, MBS.

short. The most serious need was dump trucks, and the MBS engineer constantly tried to obtain more of them. In late January 1943 he requested the highest shipping priority for dump trucks, pointing out that they represented a very small percentage of engineer tonnage.[50] The Tunisian campaign ended, however, before the problem was solved.

During January 1943 MBS engineer depots shipped an average of 250 tons of engineer supplies per day eastward to support operations in Tunisia. The figure rose to 400 tons in February, 500 tons in March, and 900 tons in April; however, the end of the Tunisian campaign in mid-May brought that month's average down to 450. While the MBS engineers were issuing supplies, they also had to handle increasingly large receipts. In February, for example, MBS engineer depots received an average of 600 tons of supplies and equipment per day, and at the end of the month engineer depot stocks approximated 35,000 tons. The receipt average for March was about 700 tons a day, for April approximately 1,400 tons, and for May 1,375 tons. At the end of May, MBS engineer depots held more than 100,000 tons of engineer supplies and equipment.[51]

### Eastern Base Section

NATOUSA established the Eastern Base Section (EBS) on 13 February

1943 to support II Corps in Tunisia. The commander was Col. Arthur W. Pence, and the chief of the Engineer Section was Col. Donald B. Adams. The command organized and undertook planning at Oran, and on 23 February began moving eastward to Constantine, in Algeria, about 100 miles short of the Tunisian border. The organization of EBS nearly coincided with significant changes in tactical command within Allied forces in North Africa. On 7 March Lt. Gen. George S. Patton, Jr., took over command of II Corps from Maj. Gen. Lloyd R. Fredendall, and II Corps passed from the control of the British First Army to that of 18 Army Group, General Sir Harold R. L. G. Alexander commanding. The British First and Eighth Armies constituted the other major components of 18 Army Group.

The principal problems EBS engineers faced were receiving, storing, and issuing materiel; repairing and maintaining supply roads; building adequate depot facilities and shops; and rehabilitating ports at Philippeville and Bone, on the Mediterranean coast north from Constantine. The necessity of quick reaction to changes in the progress of the ground campaign differentiated EBS from ABS and MBS.

In March the principal EBS engineer depot lay at Tebessa, close to the Tunisian border, about 110 miles southeast of Constantine and within relatively easy supporting distance of II Corps. When II Corps suddenly moved to northern Tunisia in April, EBS engineers followed suit. They concentrated at a partially constructed EBS general depot at Mondovi, about twenty-five miles south of Bone, and rapidly set up advance engineer dumps at La Calle

---

[50] Rpt, Colglazier to CG, MBS, 24 Jan 43, sub: Current Status Rpt; Portfolio entitled Nov 42–Jan 43, MBS.

[51] Monthly Rpts, Engr Serv, MBS, Mar, Apr, May, and Jun 43, 314.7 Hist, 1942–44, North African Service Comd file; History of the Mediterranean Base Section, Sep 42–May 44, in CMH.

and Tabarka, on the coast east from Bone. Employing eight-ton and sixteen-ton trailers, among other vehicles, engineers rushed forward engineer supplies and equipment not only from Tebessa and Mondovi but also from EBS depots at St.-Charles and Ouled Rahmoun. The rapid, 24-hour-a-day engineer displacement played a large part in making II Corps' swift advance toward Bizerte possible.[52]

For all the engineer units involved,

one of the greatest practical drawbacks in applying the experience of North Africa was the short period in which to determine required changes in doctrine, organization, and practice. Though much of this knowledge was cumulative and was absorbed from the first in the theater, the process of learning was uneven. Some units, the engineer amphibian brigade in particular, were shunted into duty in rear areas where they could not gain experience in a unique mission. Nevertheless, the lessons of past shortcomings were applied to the planning for the invasion of Sicily, scheduled for mid-July 1943, only seven weeks after the close of the Tunisian battles that ended German and Italian military influence in Africa.

---

[52] History of the Eastern Base Section, Feb–1 Jun 43, in CMH; Rpt, Engr, EBS, to CofEngrs, WD, Activities of the Engr Serv, EBS, 2 Nov 43; Rpt, Lt Col Robert B. Gear, AFHQ Engr Sect, to Chf Engr, AFHQ, Rpt of Supply Inspection Trip to Tunisia, 333, Rpts on Visits and Inspections, NATOUSA Engr file.

# CHAPTER VI

# Sicily: The Beachhead

The British and American Combined Chiefs of Staff (CCS) agreed at Casablanca in January 1943 that Sicily would be the next major Allied target in the Mediterranean after Tunisia.[1] Soon afterward AFHQ named several officers to Allied planning staffs for HUSKY, the code name of the Sicilian venture. They met on 10 February 1943 in Room 141 of the St. George Hotel in Algiers and took the cover name Force 141. The group operated as a subsection of G–3, AFHQ, until 15 May, when it merged with the deactivated headquarters of 15th Army Group to become an independent operational and planning headquarters. On D-day of HUSKY, the merged organization became Headquarters, 15th Army Group, General Sir Harold R. L. G. Alexander commanding. Force 141 prepared a general plan, and separate American (Force 343) and British (Force 545) task forces worked out details. Force 343 evolved into Headquarters, Seventh U.S. Army, under General Patton, and Force 545 into Headquarters, British Eighth Army, under General Montgomery.

The engineer adviser to Force 141 during the early planning months was Lt. Col. Charles H. Bonesteel III, who later became deputy chief engineer (U.S.) at Headquarters, 15th Army Group. Despite the limited Force 141 planning, the force engineers and the Engineer Section at AFHQ from the first sought to line up the engineer units, equipment, and supplies that would be required once detailed preparations got under way. The engineer planners also compiled supply lists for the elements of Forces 343 and 545 that would be mounted in North Africa and gave them to SOS, NATOUSA, and the British Engineer Stores for procurement.

Supplies not available in the theater had to come from the United States, a process that would take ninety days for many items. Anticipating a mid-July target date for HUSKY, SOS, NATOUSA, asked that requisitions be in by 18 April. Since this date was well before detailed plans for the assault were completed, the requisitions Force 141 and AFHQ prepared were aimed at providing a general reserve from which the task forces could draw later. The original supply lists were predicated on the assumption that the port of Palermo would be in use about D plus 8, but

---

[1] The general sources for this chapter are: Lt. Col. Albert N. Garland and Howard McGaw Smyth, *Sicily and the Surrender of Italy*, United States Army in World War II (Washington, 1965); History of Allied Force Headquarters, pt. II, Dec 42–Dec 43, sec. 1; HQ, Force 141, Planning Instr 1, in Rpt of Opns, Seventh U.S. Army in the Sicilian Campaign, 10 Jul–17 Aug 43 (hereafter cited as Seventh Army Rpt Sicily).

in May tactical planners changed the location of assault. Earlier planning had to be revised completely, and, for the most part, supply requirements had to be increased. The result was oversupply of some items and shortages of others. Supply planners made up the shortages by drawing from units that would temporarily remain in North Africa.[2]

Force 141 and the AFHQ Engineer Section also drew up a troop list in an effort to assure that the necessary troops reached the theater. Engineer planners were able to get approval for an engineer allocation of about 15 percent of the total HUSKY ground forces. They asked for several special engineer organizations, including a headquarters and headquarters company of a port construction and repair group, an equipment company, a utilities company, and two "Scorpion" companies.[3]

In the meantime engineers labored under two major unknowns—the time and the place of the assault. Not until 13 April did the Combined Chiefs of Staff approve a target date of 10 July, and the decision on where to land on Sicily came even later. Messina, only three miles from the Italian mainland, was the final objective, but was considered too strong for direct assault. The Americans and British would have to land elsewhere and move overland against Messina. Ground forces would need ports to ensure their supply lines, and airfields close enough to provide fighter cover.

The chief ports and airfields on Sicily clustered at opposite ends of the island. In the northwest lay Palermo, the largest port, and nearby were several airfields, while another group of airfields lay along the southeastern coast. The assumption that Palermo had to be seized early shaped HUSKY planning for months, but General Montgomery, commanding the British Eighth Army, insisted that the landings be concentrated at the southeast corner of the island, and on 3 May General Eisenhower approved Montgomery's plan.

The new plan called for the simultaneous landing of eight divisions along a 100-mile front between Licata and Syracuse. The British Eighth Army, landing on the east, was to seize Syracuse and other moderate-sized ports nearby. The American Seventh Army, under General Patton, was to land along the shores of the Gulf of Gela, far from any port of consequence. Seventh Army would depend upon supply over the beach for as much as thirty days, a prospect that would have been considered impossible only a few weeks earlier.

During the latter part of 1942 the production of landing ships and craft accelerated, reaching a peak in February 1943. Force 141 had ordered all of these vessels it could get, and when they became available in some numbers supply over the southern beaches began to

[2] Seventh Army Engr Rpt Sicily; Col Garrison H. Davidson, Preliminary Rpt of Seventh Army Engr on the Sicilian Opn, 23 Aug 43; Ltr, Brig Gen D. O. Elliott to AFHQ, 21 Sep 43, sub: Administrative Lessons Learned from Opns in Sicily from the Engr Viewpoint; latter two in 370.212 Sicily, Rpts of Opns, Aug 43 to Oct 43, AFHQ files. Ltr, Lt Col Bonesteel to Brig Gen C. R. Moore, Chf Engr, ETOUSA, 22 Jul 43, 321 Engr Units 42–43, AFHQ files.
[3] Ltr, Bonesteel to Moore, 22 Jul 43. During the campaign engineer troops, including aviation engineers, made up 10.5 percent of Seventh Army strength in Sicily. See Chf Engr, 15th Army Gp, Notes on Engr Opns in Italy, no. 6, 1 Jan 44.

PONTON CAUSEWAY EXTENDING FROM AN LST TO SHORE

seem feasible.[4] The new amphibious equipment included DUKWs, naval pontons, and new types of landing craft. The DUKW was a 2 1/2-ton amphibious truck that could make five knots at sea and normal truck speeds on land. It offered great promise, for it could bridge the critical gap between the ships offshore and the supply dumps behind the beach.

New types of shallow-draft landing craft featured hinged bows and ramps forward. Flat-bottomed, without projecting keels, they were difficult to

maneuver in a high cross wind or surf but could come close enough to shore to put men and vehicles in shallow water. The 36-foot LCVP, which could carry thirty-six combat-equipped infantrymen or four tons of cargo, swung into the water off an invasion beach from a larger vessel in a ship-to-shore operation. Newer LSTs (Landing Ship, Tank), coming into production in December 1942, were designed for shore-to-shore amphibious assaults. The American model was 328 feet long, had a 50-foot beam, and on ocean voyages accommodated up to 1,900 tons of cargo or 20 medium tanks; 163 combat-ready troops could find adequate, if sparse, berthing aboard. British-built versions were slightly larger and drew more water at the stern

[4] Richard M. Leighton, "Planning for Sicily," U.S. Naval Institute Proceedings, LXXXVIII, no. 5 (May 1962), 90–101; Seventh Army Rpt Sicily, pp. A–5 to A–8; Col A. H. Head, Notes on the Planning, Training, and Execution of Operation HUSKY, Misc Papers NEPTUNE, HQ, ETOUSA, files.

than at the bow and so tended to ground on the gradually sloping shelves and shifting sandbars in front of the Mediterranean beaches. Navy steel pontons running from the ship's bow to shore would serve as causeways to dry land for cargo and vehicles aboard the LSTs. Two intermediate-size landing craft that served as lighters for the LSTs and for larger attack transports and auxiliaries were the 50-foot LCM (Landing Craft, Mechanized) and the 150-foot LCT (Landing Craft, Tank). Both had a speed of ten knots and drew little more than three feet of water fully loaded. The LCM took on 1 medium tank, 30 tons of cargo, or 120 troops. The invaluable LCT could transport five thirty-ton tanks or a comparable load of cargo or troops.[5]

### Plans and Preparations

Eisenhower selected Headquarters, I Armored Corps, at Rabat as the headquarters for Force 343, and the I Armored Corps engineer, Col. Garrison H. Davidson, was named the Force 343 engineer. On 25 March he began planning for HUSKY, but unlike Force 545 (the British task force), I Armored Corps still had some operational duties in North Africa. Not until 13 June did Force 343 issue a complete engineer plan outlining boundaries and setting general policies. Each subtask force

commander, who was to control his assault area for the first few days, worked out his own detailed assault and engineer plans.[6]

Planning for HUSKY was difficult. The time and place of the assault were fixed late. AFHQ's preoccupation with the Tunisian campaign meant that the list of major combat units to be used in HUSKY could be determined only after Axis forces in North Africa capitulated early in May. Also, AFHQ wrapped heavy security around the coming operation. Engineer unit commanders were briefed on HUSKY only after embarking for Sicily, too late for realistic preinvasion training. Even in the higher engineer echelons, essential information was slow in coming. Though Headquarters, I Armored Corps, was named the task force headquarters for the invasion in early March, no one told the corps engineer of his new assignment for another three weeks. On 19 March Colonel Davidson also belatedly learned of the decision to redirect the assault to the southeastern beaches of Sicily instead of the town of Palermo on the north shore.[7]

Another impediment to planning was the great distances that separated the several staffs. The Force 141 (15th Army Group) plan called for assault landings by three American divisions, with a strong armored and infantry reserve to be held close offshore on the left flank of the American sector. Four subtask forces were set up: the three reinforced assault divisions, JOSS (3d

[5] Fifth Army Training Center History; ONI 226, 7 Apr 44, Allied Landing Craft and Ships, and Supplement 1 to ONI 226; Robert W. Coakley and Richard M. Leighton, *Global Logistics and Strategy, 1943–1945*, United States Army in World War II (Washington, 1968), apps. B–1, B–2, pp. 827–29; Samuel E. Morison, "History of United States Naval Operations in World War II," vol. IX, *Sicily-Salerno-Anzio, January 1943–June 1944* (Boston: Little, Brown Company, 1957), pp. 30–32.

[6] Ltr, AFHQ to Fifth Army, 5 Mar 43, sub: Orgn of Western Task Force, 320.2 Orgn and Tactical Units (1942–43), AFHQ files; Rpt of Seventh Army Engr Sicily.
[7] Rpt of Seventh Army Engr Sicily; Ltr, Brig Gen Dabney O. Elliott, AFHQ Engr, to AFHQ, 21 Sep 43.

Infantry Division), DIME (1st Infantry Division), and CENT (45th Infantry Division) and, a reserve force, KOOL (2d Armored Division less Combat Command A, plus the 1st Division's 18th Regimental Combat Team). SHARK (Headquarters, II Corps) was to coordinate DIME and CENT. During the planning stage, these and higher headquarters were scattered across the breadth of North Africa. AFHQ was at Algiers, the British task force headquarters (Force 545) at Cairo, and Force 343 at Rabat in Morocco until the latter part of April when it moved to Mostaganem in Algeria. JOSS headquarters was at Jemmapes, SHARK at Relizane, and DIME at Oran. Western Naval Task Force headquarters remained at Algiers, which seemed to Army authorities too far from Force 343, but the two services cooperated well.[8]

According to the instructions Force 141 issued in April, U.S. engineers were responsible for breaching beach obstacles, clearing and laying minefields, supplying water and bulk petroleum products, repairing ports and airfields, and rebuilding railways. The instructions emphasized the importance of repairing airfields as soon as possible. The Transportation Corps was to determine requirements for railway reconstruction and request the engineers to do the work, but the Seventh Army engineer staff worked with G−4 of Force 141 in actual preparations. Troop accommodations were to be an "abso-

lute minimum," and hospitals were to use existing buildings or tents. Engineers were to provide light, water, and latrines.[9]

While all the subtask forces had common engineer missions, each also had special missions. SHARK engineers were to prepare a landing strip at Biscari as soon as possible after the assault, have runways ready at Comiso and Ponte Olivo Airfields by D plus 8, repair a jetty at Gela, and build bulk storage and pipelines to the airfields. By D plus 4 the 2602d Engineer Petroleum Distribution Company was to be ashore at DIME beaches and ready to handle over 1,000 tons of gasoline per day. JOSS engineers were to repair the small port of Licata and a landing strip at a nearby airfield. KOOL engineers were to be ready to rehabilitate Porto Empedocle, a small harbor thirty miles west of the JOSS beaches.

The engineers were to rely largely on local materials for repairing railway and electrical installations and building troop barracks. Lumber was to be provided for hospital flooring and for twenty woodframe tarpaulin-covered warehouses. All civilian labor was to be hired and paid by the using arm or service. Until D plus 3 real estate was to be obtained either by "immediate occupancy" or by informal written agreements between unit purchasing and contracting officers and owners. An important engineer responsibility was providing water, known to be scarce in Sicily during the summer. The minimum water requirement was set at one U.S. gallon per man per day. Water enough for five days was to be carried

[8] II Corps Bull Y/1, Notes on the Planning and Assault Phases of the Sicilian Campaign, by a Military Observer, Oct 43, 1st ESB files; Seventh Army Rpt Sicily, p. A−2; Rpt, Vice Adm H. K. Hewitt, WNTF in Sicilian Campaign; Bradley, *A Soldier's Story*, p. 108; Hist 1st Engr C Bn Rpt, Sicilian Campaign, 10 Jul–Dec 43.

[9] HQ, Force 141, Planning Instr 11, Engr Requirements for HUSKY, 12 Apr 43.

in five-gallon cans on the D-day convoy or in Navy bulk storage.[10]

In accordance with the Loper-Hotine Agreement, the Geographical Section, General Staff, British War Office, was responsible for revising maps for HUSKY, but AFHQ was responsible for reproduction. The Engineer Section, AFHQ, established a large field map service organization, the Survey Directorate, in a suburb of Algiers. The directorate furnished general tactical maps for all HUSKY forces except CENT, which, staging in the United States, obtained its maps through OCE in Washington.

In February the 66th Engineer Topographic Company, formerly with I Armored Corps, joined HUSKY. While preparing some tactical maps, the 66th concentrated on such secret materials as visual aids, naval charts, loading plans, photo mosaics, city plans, harbor layouts, and convoy disposition charts. The bulk of the company remained in North Africa under the Survey Directorate throughout the Sicily campaign, with only its survey platoon, essentially a field unit, going to Sicily for survey and control work.

In addition to tactical and strategic maps, the topographic engineers produced a number of special issues: town plans, an air map, and defense and water supply overprints. Combat units got valuable information from the defense overprints, particularly those marking enemy positions covering the beaches and issued to the subtask forces before the invasion began, as did engineers from the water supply overprints, which pinpointed probable sources of

fresh water. The HUSKY maps were considerably better than those for the Tunisian campaign.

HUSKY saw continued progress in solving map-handling and distribution problems that had been so vexing in Tunisia. Two new thirteen-man units, the 2657th and 2658th Engineer Map Depot Detachments, were responsible for storing maps and for distributing them in bulk at division, corps, and army levels. The two units set up a map depot at Constantine on 5 June and immediately began to receive large stocks. Security considerations, the scattered deployment of assault units across North Africa, the drastic change in the basic HUSKY plan, and the tardy arrival of maps from England hampered distribution. AFHQ and Force 141 had to help the depot detachments sort map stocks, and truck convoys loaded with maps had to be given priority along North African roads to get the maps out in time. Final deliveries to ships and staging areas began on D minus 11 and were completed to assault units on D minus 8, but last minute distribution continued aboard ship until D minus 1.[11]

## Training

The subtask forces had decentralized responsibility for training their own troops for the assault. The Seventh Army (Force 343) Engineer Section inspected the training of engineer units assigned to the subtask forces, gener-

---

[10] Seventh Army Engr Plan, Sicilian Opns, Joss Task Force (8–12 Jul).

[11] Ltr, Bonesteel to Moore, 22 Jul 43; II Corps Engr Rpt, 10 Jul–18 Aug 43, particularly an. 3, Map Supply and Distribution; II Corps Bull Y/1, Notes on the Planning and Assault Phases of the Sicilian Campaign, Oct 43; HQ, Force 141, Planning Instr 15, Maps and Charts.

ally supervised that of shore regiments, and guided that of SOS, NATOUSA, engineer units scheduled to join the task force later. The troops underwent refresher and special amphibious training. Refresher training emphasized physical conditioning, mines, marksmanship, and other combat techniques. Experience in Tunisia had demonstrated that nearly all engineer units needed such training; but, with the exception of mines, little of it could be geared directly to the coming operation. There was not much time to train units for HUSKY, nor could what time there was be used to best advantage. In the main, engineers in the subtask forces, other than shore engineers, had to get by with general engineer instruction.[12]

Early in March AFHQ decided to use the 1st Engineer Amphibian Brigade in the invasion of Sicily. The early HUSKY plan had given the brigade a vital role; the final plan made it even greater. The new plan called for the brigade to support three assault divisions and the floating reserve. It also called for the supply of all Seventh Army forces in Sicily for as long as thirty days over the beaches and through such tiny ports as Licata and Gela. The brigade itself was to function as the sole American base section in Sicily and handle all supplies for the first month on the island.[13]

It was quite apparent that the techniques employed during the TORCH operation would not suffice against the determined opposition expected on

Sicily. New techniques, with new equipment especially designed for amphibious operations, would be necessary. Army and Navy efforts had to be coordinated, and such problems as offshore sandbars and man-made underwater obstacles had to be overcome. The 1st Engineer Amphibian Brigade had much to do to prepare for its role on Sicily, a role on which the entire undertaking could well depend. But AFHQ remained preoccupied with the Tunisian campaign.

Brigade participation in planning for HUSKY began on 23 April when Brig. Gen. H. C. Wolfe, then commander of the headquarters unit known as the 1st Engineer Amphibian Brigade, attended a conference of unit commanders at Rabat.[14] At the time the brigade consisted of less than a hundred officers and enlisted men, for it had all but passed out of existence after TORCH, its units spread out in support roles in North Africa. In February one battalion of the 531st Engineer Shore Regiment and another of the 591st Engineer Boat Regiment assumed identities as provisional trucking units and operated in support of II Corps until the end of the Tunisian campaign. The 36th and 540th Engineer Combat Regiments, which had participated in the TORCH landings, had construction and labor assignments in Morocco through April. Only the 2d Battalion of the 531st, attached to the Fifth Army's Invasion Training Center at Port-aux-Poules in Algeria, remained associated with amphibious warfare in the early months of 1943. An entirely new orga-

---

[12] Ltr, Bonesteel to Moore, 22 Jul 43; Seventh Army Engr Rpt Sicily.

[13] 1st ESB Rpt of Action Against the Enemy, 10–13 Jul 43, Sicily; Rpt, Shore Engineers in Sicily, 1st ESB files; Hist 1st ESB, Jun 42–Sep 45.

---

[14] On 25 May 1943 General Wolfe became deputy G–3, NATOUSA, and Col Eugene Caffey became the brigade commander.

nization had to be formed to carry out Army responsibilities in support of the HUSKY landings.[15]

In the Pacific, engineer brigades followed the pattern conceived for them at the Engineer Amphibian Command. They operated landing craft as well as handling their duties on the beaches. These brigades had a unity of command not enjoyed by those in the Mediterranean and European theaters, for on the Atlantic side landing craft belonged to the Navy. Thus, naval responsibility in amphibious operations extended to the shoreline, whereas Army engineer responsibility began at the waterline and extended inland. Both services accepted this line of demarcation in principle, but many specific questions remained. Army and Navy representatives tried to spell out answers in detail during HUSKY planning, but neither in North Africa nor in later amphibious operations were they completely successful. The definition of Army-Navy amphibious responsibilities continued to be a source of friction throughout the war in Europe.[16]

In the end, U.S. Army engineers developed a new type of engineer amphibian brigade for HUSKY. With no assignment in the assault waves, the newly designated 1st Engineer Special Brigade consisted of four shore groups: one for each of the three infantry divisions making the assault and the fourth held offshore as part of the reserve force (KOOL). An engineer regiment formed the backbone of each task-organized shore group, and each group's other assigned or attached units included such organizations as a medical battalion, a quartermaster DUKW battalion, a naval beach battalion, a signal company, and an ordnance maintenance company. A number of smaller units, such as dump-operating details from each of the several technical services, were attached according to anticipated need. Still other attachments operated local facilities such as railways, furnished specialized services such as water supply and camouflage, or reinforced the brigade in some area such as trucking.[17]

The organization of the new brigade started toward the end of April, when two engineer combat regiments (36th and 540th) and an engineer shore regiment (531st) assembled at Port-aux-Poules, twelve miles east of Arzew. The fourth shore group, built around the 40th Engineer Combat Regiment, received amphibious training in the United States and arrived at Oran with the 45th Infantry Division on 22 June.[18]

---

[15] Hist 1st ESB, Jun 42–Sep 45.

[16] RG 110 A48–139, Notes on War Council, CofS files 1941–42; AFHQ Incoming Msg, Marshall to Eisenhower and Andrews, 5 Mar 43; Rpt, ACofS G–4, EAC, to CG, EAC, Rpt on Opn and Maint of Landing Craft in North Africa and European Theaters, 13 Apr 43; A Memorandum of Agreement between the Chief of Staff, U.S. Army, the Commander in Chief, U.S. Fleet, and Chief of Naval Operations, dated 22 March 1943, defined the primary responsibilities of the Army and the Navy for amphibious training. For background on the development of amphibious doctrine, see Coll, Keith, and Rosenthal, *The Corps of Engineers: Troops and Equipment,* ch. XVI. For a full account of amphibious operations in the Southwest Pacific, see "Engineers of the Southwest Pacific 1941–45," vol. IV, *Amphibian Engineer Operations* (Washington, 1959).

[17] The 1st Engineer Amphibian Brigade was redesignated 1st Engineer Special Brigade on 10 May 1943 and reorganized under TOE 2–510–S, 21 April 1943. 1st ESB Rpt of Action Against the Enemy, 10–13 Jul 43, Sicily; Memo, HQ, 1st ESB, 31 May 43, sub: Beach Group Organization and Functions.

[18] Hist 1st ESB, Jun 42–Sep 45. The 591st Engineer Boat Regiment, which had no boats, became surplus to the needs of the 1st Engineer Special Brigade (ESB), and during the remainder of its stay in the

The 36th Engineer Shore Group was the largest of the four and when finally assembled for the invasion totaled 4,744 officers and enlisted men. Its nucleus was the 2,088-man 36th Engineer Combat Regiment, plus the 2d Battalion, 540th Engineer Combat Regiment (623 men). A naval beach battalion (413 men) was attached to make hydrographic surveys, maintain shore-to-ship communications, and coordinate the beaching of landing craft and LSTs. A 322-man quartermaster battalion (amphibious), to operate trucks and DUKWs, and the 56th Medical Battalion (505 men) were added, as were a number of smaller units. These last included a signal company to provide radio and wire networks on the beach, a military police company to control motor traffic and guard prisoners, a four-man engineer map depot detachment to handle reserve map stocks, and a detachment from an ordnance maintenance company to repair ordnance equipment. An ordnance ammunition company, detachments from two quartermaster units, and an engineer depot company were included to operate beach dumps. The 531st Engineers' shore group consisted of 3,803 troops, its composition similar to that formed around the 36th; the 40th Engineers' group had approximately 4,465 officers and men. The smallest shore group, from the 540th, was with KOOL Force and had a strength of about 2,815. The total strength of the four shore groups was approximately 15,825, including 1,270 naval personnel with three naval beach battalions.

U.S. Army engineer troops represented about 52 percent of the 1st Engineer Special Brigade as organized for the assault. Later accretions on Sicily would bring the brigade's strength to nearly 20,000.[19]

Some differences existed between the 531st Engineer Shore Regiment and the engineer combat regiment that formed the nucleus of the other three shore groups. Although the total strength of the shore regiment was about the same as that of a combat regiment, the former had more officers, more specialists, and more specialized engineering equipment. The shore engineers knew all that combat engineers did, even for combat operations inland, but not vice versa. The combat engineers had more organic transportation, but they also had much organizational equipment not needed for beach operations. If they left the equipment behind, they also had to leave men to guard and maintain it, thus weakening the combat regiment.[20]

In accordance with an AFHQ directive, Fifth U.S. Army trained Force 141 units in amphibious operations at its training center at Port-aux-Poules.[21] When the 1st Engineer Special Brigade came together there, less than 2 1/2 months were left until D-day. The shore

Mediterranean worked primarily in port operations. The unit was disbanded at Naples on 1 November 1944.

[19] Rpt, Col Eugene Caffey, Shore Engineers in Sicily, app. A. This and a number of other valuable reports on HUSKY are contained in Rpt, HQ, ETOUSA, to FUSAG and others, 3 Dec 43, sub: Notes on the Sicilian Campaign and Extracts from Reports on Operation HUSKY, (cited hereafter as Notes and Extracts, HUSKY); Chf Engr, 15th Army Gp, Notes on Engr Opns in Sicily, no. 3, 10 Sep 43, and Notes on Working of Sicilian Beaches, 10 Jul 43; Rpt of Seventh Army Engr Sicily, apps. to an. 12.
[20] Rpt, Shore Engineers in Sicily, 1st ESB files.
[21] Ltr, Lt Col Bonesteel to Brig Gen D. O. Elliott, Chf Engr, AFHQ, 17 Jul 43, 353–A Training Policy, AFHQ files.

groups had to be organized, equipped, and trained. Experiments had to determine how to deal with a number of problems, such as breaching obstacles on the beaches. Troops had to become familiar with DUKWs and with the new types of landing craft. Combat troops and naval units had to train together and rehearse landings.[22]

The 1st Engineer Special Brigade carried out extensive experiments to learn the characteristics of landing craft just being introduced into the theater and to establish procedures for landing supplies across the beaches. All through May regular training took a backseat to tests and experiments, those with landing craft and others geared to such problems as offshore sandbars.[23]

The discovery of sandbars off many of the beaches on Sicily raised serious doubts about the whole HUSKY undertaking. The typical sandbar lay about 150 feet offshore under two or three feet of water; only the most shallow-draft landing craft could ride over them. Water often deepened to ten feet shoreward of the bars, and naval ponton causeways were to get troops and vehicles aboard LSTs across this gap. Another problem, water supply for the beaches, was solved by equipping twenty LSTs to carry 10,000 gallons of water each. Shore parties equipped with canvas storage tanks and hoses were to pump this water ashore.[24]

On 3 June Col. Eugene M. Caffey, commanding officer of the 1st Engineer Special Brigade, became responsible for organizing, equipping, and training the shore units, and, by the fifteenth, engineer regimental shore groups were attached to the subtask forces for combined training and rehearsals. As during TORCH, the brigade had to train with other Army organizations and with the Navy before it could prepare its own units adequately.[25]

Rehearsal landings took place between 22 June and 4 July, for JOSS in the Bizerte-Tunis area and for DIME and KOOL in the Arzew area. CENT Force, which came from the United States, rehearsed near Oran. To Admiral Hewitt, whose Western Naval Task Force was to land the Seventh Army, these hurriedly conceived exercises were at best a dry run on a reduced scale. They had some value for assault troops but virtually none for the engineer shore groups. The CENT rehearsals, for instance, ended before any shore party equipment had been landed or any supplies put across the beach.[26]

Limited time and opportunity made the training of many other engineer units just as meager, while security prevented specific training for HUSKY. The Fifth Army mine school and the British Eighth Army mine school at

[22] Davidson, Preliminary Rpt of Seventh Army Engr on the Sicilian Opn, 23 Aug 43; Rpt of Seventh Army Engr Sicily.

[23] Rpt of Seventh Army Engr Sicily; Seventh Army Rpt Sicily, pp. C–2 and D–3; Ltr, Col Eugene M. Caffey, CO, 1st ESB, to CG, First U.S. Army, 16 Jan 44, 310.2 Opns, 1st ESB files; Rpt, Shore Engineers in Sicily, 1st ESB files; Hist 1st ESB, Jun 42–Sep 45; Ltr, Bonesteel to Moore, 22 Jul 43.

[24] Col A. H. Head, Notes on the Planning, Training, and Execution of Operation HUSKY, 25 Jul 43.

NEPTUNE, HQ, ETOUSA, files; *Building the Navy's Bases in World War II*, 2 vols. (Washington, 1947), vol. II, p. 86; Rpt of Seventh Army Engr Sicily; Brief of Engr Plan, Incl 1 to Rpt of Seventh Army Engr Sicily; Interv, Maj Gen Charles H. Bonesteel III, 10 Feb 60.

[25] Rpt, Shore Engineers in Sicily, 1st ESB files; Rpt of Seventh Army Engr Sicily; Ltr, Caffey to CG, FUSA, 16 Jan 44; Hist 1st ESB.

[26] Hewitt Rpt, WNTF in Sicilian Campaign, p. 31; Rpt, Shore Engineers in Sicily, 1st ESB files; Ltr, Caffey to CG, FUSA, 16 Jan 44; 40th Engr C Rgt, Rpt of Engr Opns, 10 Jul–18 Aug 43.

Tripoli trained instructors who could return to their units and pass on their knowledge, but most such training was without the benefit of enemy mines. Warnings from the U.S. chief ordnance officer at AFHQ that aging explosives could become dangerously sensitive proved justified in a British attempt to ship enemy mines to the United States; while the mines were being loaded aboard a small coaster at Algiers the entire lot blew up, sinking the coaster and firing an ammunition ship at the next berth.[27]

On the whole, the troops scheduled for HUSKY were far better prepared to deal with mines than were those in Tunisia. Concern arose in some quarters lest overemphasis on mine warfare damage troop morale, but engineers were convinced that thorough instruction was the best answer. Nor did they concur in the decision to restrict the use of live enemy mines in training. Colonel Davidson believed that "realism in training [was] essential regardless of the risk to personnel and equipment," a view with which 15th Army Group agreed and which AFHQ accepted.[28]

Toward the end of June assault units began moving into their embarkation areas: CENT Force (45th Infantry Division) at Oran, DIME (1st Infantry Division) at Algiers, and JOSS (3d Infantry Division) at Bizerte. The initial assault—Seventh Army would have 82,502 men ashore in Sicily by the end of D-day—included approximately 11,000 engineers scheduled to land with the subtask forces, plus nearly 1,200 more in the floating reserve. Engineers with DIME Force numbered nearly 3,200. Another 4,300, plus Company A of the 17th Armored Engineer Battalion, were with JOSS Force and 3,500 with CENT Force. About 1,350 engineer vehicles accompanied these troops on D-day. Additional engineer troops and vehicles were to reach the JOSS and DIME areas with the D plus 4 and D plus 8 convoys. In North Africa 22 engineer units totaling 7,388 men stood by, ready to be called forward as required.[29]

The convoy carrying CENT Force sailed from Oran harbor on 5 July, and as it moved along the North African coast DIME and JOSS Force convoys joined. The faster ships feinted south along Cape Bon peninsula, while the slower vessels proceeded by more direct routes to a rendezvous area off the island of Gozo. On the ninth a steady wind began to blow out of the north and increased during the afternoon, piling up a heavy sea and raising serious doubts that the invasion could proceed. Then, during the night, the wind dropped. As H-hour approached the seas begain to settle and prospects for a successful landing brightened.[30]

### D-day

Before dawn on 10 July 1943, the

---

[27] Rpt of Seventh Army Engr Sicily; Seventh Army Rpt Sicily, p. A–4.

[28] Seventh Army Rpt Sicily, p. C–4; Davidson, Preliminary Rpt of Seventh Army Engr on the Sicilian Opn, 23 Aug 43, and 1st Ind, HQ, 15th Army Gp, 6 Sep 43; Ltr, AFHQ to AG, WD, 2 Oct 43, sub: Preliminary Rpt of Seventh Army Engr on the Sicilian Opn, 370.212 Sicily, Rpts on Opns, Aug 43 to Oct 43, AFHQ files.

[29] Seventh Army strength on Sicily on 23 August totaled 165,230 men, exclusive of 11,900 USAAF troops also on the island. Ltr, HQ, Seventh Army, to CG, NATOUSA, 22 Nov 43, sub: Date for Logistical Planning; Final Engr Troop List, Seventh Army, by Convoys, Engr Units Only, 28 Jun 43, G–3 Misc Papers, 1st ESB files.

[30] Morison, Sicily-Salerno-Anzio, pp. 62–63, 65, 67–68.

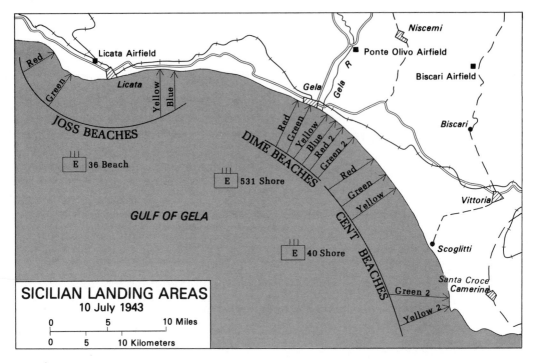

MAP 5

assault waves of three American infantry divisions landed along a forty-mile stretch of Sicilian beach. *(Map 5)* On the west the 3d Infantry Division (JOSS Force) straddled the small port of Licata, landing on five separate beaches. In the center, about seventeen miles east of Licata, the 1st Infantry Division (DIME Force) went in over six beaches just east of Gela, and on the division's left a Ranger force landed directly at Gela. The 45th Infantry Division (CENT Force) beached at eight points extending from Scoglitti halfway to Gela. Farther east, the British made simultaneous landings along another stretch of the Sicilian coast extending from Cape Passero almost to Syracuse. DIME Force went in on time at 0245, but weather slowed the other two forces. The wind had dropped to about fifteen miles an hour,

but a 2 1/2-foot surf still ran along most beaches and a considerably higher one at Scoglitti. The initial landings on some beaches in the JOSS and CENT areas came just as dawn was breaking at 0550.[31]

Enemy strength on Sicily consisted of about ten divisions. The equivalent of about five were disposed in or near coastal defenses, and five were in mobile reserve. Most of the troops were dispirited Italians; only two divisions, both in reserve, were German.[32]

---

[31] Seventh Army Rpt Sicily, p. 6–4; Morison, *Sicily-Salerno-Anzio*, p. 78; Combined Operations (Br), Digest of Some Notes and Reports from Opn HUSKY, reproduced Oct 43 by Information Sect, Intel Div, OCE, SOS ETOUSA.

[32] Brig Gen A. C. Wedemeyer, Extracts from Rpt on Opn HUSKY, 28 Dec 43, Notes and Extracts, HUSKY.

American assault troops swept through enemy shore defenses with little trouble. A few strands of barbed wire stretched across most of the beaches, and on some a few bands of antitank mines, but there were no man-made underwater obstacles and few antipersonnel mines or booby traps. Many concrete pillboxes, cleverly camouflaged, well supplied, and well provided with communication trenches, existed, some so new that wooden forms still encased them. None proved very troublesome, mainly because the Italians manning them had little disposition to fight.

Here and there infantrymen skirmished briefly along the shoreline before pushing inland, and at a number of points shore engineers joined in to clean out scattered pockets of resistance.[33] At some points the enemy had sections of beach under small-arms fire as the shore engineers came in, but for the most part only intermittent artillery fire and sporadic enemy air action harassed the beaches. No enemy strongpoint held out stubbornly, and shore engineers were soon free to go about organizing their beaches. By nightfall all three subtask forces had beachheads that stretched two to four miles inland, and they had taken 4,265 prisoners. The cost had been relatively small: 58 killed, 199 wounded, and 700 missing.[34]

_____

[33] On CENT beaches, two officers and two enlisted men, 1st Lt. Keith E. Miller, 2d Lt. George S. Spohn, T/5 Robert L. Beall, and Sgt. Warren W. Beanish of the 40th Engineers won Distinguished Service Crosses for their part in taking pillboxes that had the beach under fire.

[34] Seventh Army GO 3, 25 Jan 44; 1st ESB GO 8, 27 Aug 43; USMA study, Opns in Sicily and Italy—Invasion of Sicily.

## Joss Beaches

From west to east JOSS beaches were named Red, Green, Yellow, and Blue. The first two lay west of Licata, the other two east of it, and all were the responsibility of the 36th Engineer Shore Group. Along the 4,500-yard length of Red Beach ran a sandbar, and between the sandbar and beach was a runnel 100 to 300 feet wide and, in many places, more than 6 feet deep.

About 0440, nearly two hours after the first wave of infantrymen had splashed ashore from LCVPs, shore searchlights that had been playing over the water off Red Beach winked out. At 0510 heavy fire broke out along the beach and a destroyer began shelling shore positions. An LCT carrying engineers of the 36th Engineer Shore Group joined five others carrying medium tanks to make the run in to the beach, covered by two destroyers coursing along the shoreline belching out a smoke screen as dawn broke. The six LCTs grounded successfully, the tanks lumbered off into 3 1/2 feet of water and waded ashore. The engineers discovered that the beach, in places only twenty feet wide, consisted of soft sand strewn with large boulders. Behind it rose cliffs fifteen to sixty feet high, with only one exit road usable for wheeled vehicles, a steep, sandy wagon track that led through vineyards and fields of ripening tomatoes and melons to the coastal highway some three miles away. The first six LCTs did better than craft of successive waves. Some stuck on the offshore bar and discharged trucks into water that drowned them out—thirty-two of the sixty-five vehicles that disembarked for Red Beach from nine LCTs failed to bridge the water gap.

Ashore, congestion and confusion mounted. Tractors had to drag vehicles over the sandy beach exit road while recovery of stalled vehicles was slow and unorganized, for no definite preparations for this work had been made. Some sections of beach became choked off completely. T−2 recovery units, tanks, and DUKWs tried to unravel the problem; D−7 dozers, well suited to the task, were inland working on beach exit roads, but the smaller R−4s proved ineffective in the soft sand. Vehicles stalled or awaiting better exit routes soon jammed the beaches with supplies. As congestion increased and more landing craft broached, many men stood idle, uncertain what to do.

Offshore an LST tried to unload its ponton floats, but the surf was too rough and the floats washed ashore. The craft then tried to get nearer the beach to discharge without the causeway but grounded fifty to sixty feet out in about four feet of water. The first truck off stalled ten feet from the LST's ramp. Two DUKWs recovered the truck, but a motor crane stalled in about the same place. When DUKWs could not move the crane, the LST pulled offshore for the night. Next morning two D−7 tractors spent some five hours pulling the crane ashore and then succeeded in moving the naval ponton causeway into position.

Here, as at other beaches, the causeways proved of great value once they were in use. Vehicles were driven ashore over them, and an LST could unload in about two hours. But the causeways did not always hold head on against the shore. As one LST pulled off, the causeways tended to broach before another LST could come up. After forty-eight hours broached craft and

stalled vehicles still choked Red Beach, and on D plus 3 it was abandoned. The only enemy opposition had been Messerschmitt 109s, each carrying a single bomb, that made eight bombing and strafing raids during D-day. The aircraft had caused delays but no casualties.

Halfway between Red Beach and Licata lay Green Beach, also difficult but selected because it could take assault units within close striking distance of the port of Licata. Green consisted of two half-moon beaches, each about 1,000 feet long, separated by a point of land jutting out from the shore. The coastal highway was about 1 1/2 miles away. Offshore bars were no problem but exits were, for behind the beaches towered abrupt bluffs more than 100 feet high. One platoon of Company C, 36th Engineers, along with a naval beach detachment and some medical personnel, supported the landing of the 2d Battalion, 15th Infantry, and the 3d Ranger Battalion. As expected, exit difficulties ruled out Green Beach for supply operations, and twelve hours after the initial landings the beach was closed. The small engineer shore party there rejoined the 1st Battalion, 36th Engineers, on Red Beach, taking along twenty-six captured Italian soldiers. But Green Beach paid off, for the men landed, took Licata, a small port that offered facilities for handling five LSTs simultaneously, and by 1600 on D-day an LST was unloading.

At Yellow and Blue beaches things went much better. Yellow Beach, centering about six miles east of Licata, was probably the best American beach. The sand there had no troublesome boulders, and the main coastal highway lay only some 400 yards away across slightly rising sandy loam planted in grapes and tomatoes. Blue Beach, beginning about a mile farther east, was almost as good. After the initial assault most of JOSS Force landed over these two beaches, and those elements of the 36th Engineer Shore Group that supported landings on the other JOSS beaches soon moved to Yellow and Blue. Some LSTs sent vehicles ashore over a naval ponton causeway, but most stood one-half to three-quarters of a mile out and unloaded on the LCTs or DUKWs. DUKWs were the workhorses on the beach, invaluable because they could eliminate much of the man-handling of supplies. Nearly all carried more than their rated 2 1/2 tons, and some went in with so little freeboard that the wake of a passing landing craft could have swamped them. At least one, overloaded with 105-mm. shells, sank as soon as it drove off a ramp.

The 36th Engineer Shore Group headquarters landed at 0714 on D-day and established itself on a hill overlooking both Blue and Yellow beaches. By noon the shore group had consolidated battalion beach dumps into regimental dumps behind the two beaches. Shore engineers worked throughout the night and into D plus 1 with only temporary halts during enemy bombing raids. During the afternoon of D-day, the 2d Battalion, 540th Engineers, landed along with two platoons of the 2d Naval Beach Battalion, and before noon on 11 July units of the 382d Port Battalion (TC) entered Licata port to clear LST berthings. As order emerged and supplies began to move smoothly, it became evident that Seventh Army could be supplied across the beaches so long as the seas remained calm. During the first three days 20,470 men, 6,614 tons of supplies, and 3,752 vehicles landed at

Licata or across the JOSS beaches. In the same period, more than 200 wounded and over 500 POWs were evacuated to North Africa.[35]

## Dime Beaches

Seventeen miles east of Licata a wave of Rangers went in at Gela at H-hour (0245), a second wave following within a few minutes. One-half hour later two waves of the 39th Engineer Combat Regiment were ashore preparing to clear away beach obstacles and demolish pillboxes. Some mortar men, providing support for the Rangers, comprised the fifth wave, which went in about H plus 1, while shore engineers from the 1st Battalion, 531st Engineers, landed in the sixth wave. By dawn (0515) Rangers and the 39th Engineers were digging in on their objective on the north edge of Gela, and shore engineers were preparing the beaches for an influx of cargo.[36]

Just to the east the 16th and 26th Regimental Combat Teams, 1st Infantry Division, landed simultaneously with the Rangers, while the 18th Regimental Combat Team and elements of the 2d Armored Division lay offshore in floating reserve. In these landings divisional engineers, attached by platoons to infantry battalions, went in with the assault waves. The 1st and 2d Platoons, Company A, 1st Engineer Combat Battalion, landed with the 16th Regimen-

[35] Opns Rpt, 36th Engr C Gp, 10–18 Jul 43, 1 Aug 43; Notes and Extracts, HUSKY; Maj Roy C. Conner, First Partial Rpt, Observations, in HUSKY—Joss Task Force (8–12 Jul)—Rpt of Observations, EUCOM Engr files; Hist 1st ESB, Jun 42–Sep 45; Hewitt Rpt, WNTF in Sicilian Campaign; Seventh Army Rpt Sicily, pp. 6–10.

[36] Hist 39th Engr C Rgt; Hist 1st Bn, 531st Engr Shore Rgt.

tal Combat Team; the 1st and 2d Platoons, Company C, were with the 26th Regimental Combat Team. These engineers were to clear enemy obstructions, but they found little wire, few antipersonnel mines, and no artificial underwater obstacles. Enemy resistance was light, and combat engineers soon disappeared inland with the infantry. Some of them removed demolition charges on bridges leading into Gela.[37]

DIME beaches were much like Yellow and Blue beaches in the JOSS sector except in one important respect—the main coastal highway was nearly two miles away. Enemy defenses in the area were somewhat more developed than at other points on the southern shore, but pillboxes gave little trouble to infantry-engineer assault teams, and the only underwater obstacles were offshore sandbars.

Mines proved somewhat troublesome, largely for want of SCR−625s. Mine detectors belonging to the 39th Engineers were on trucks or other vehicles that did not land until D plus 1, while the 531st Engineers carried a number of detectors ashore only to find that salt spray had short-circuited many of them. Most of the mines lay in regular patterns and were not booby-trapped, but some were buried as deep as five feet. On one Gela beach, engineers found six rows of Teller mines spaced three yards apart; five Navy bulldozers were lost in this mine belt. Mines also destroyed a number of trucks and DUKWs—some because operators ignored the warning tapes the engineers had put down. No antipersonnel mines

were found on the beaches themselves, where, said one observer, they would have been "horribly effective," but some in the dunes and cover just back of the beaches caused casualties.[38]

While the 1st Battalion, 531st Engineers, landed at Gela in support of the Rangers, the 2d and 3d Battalions followed the assault waves of the 16th and 26th Regimental Combat Teams ashore. The infantry moved inland as rapidly as possible, while the shore engineers remained behind to organize the beaches. The shore engineers landed before dawn, but not until midmorning could landing craft stop ferrying men ashore and start bringing in cargo. In the interim shore engineers cut exit roads, cleared away mines and other obstacles, set up beach markers to guide landing craft, established beach communications systems and traffic control measures, and organized work parties.[39]

As at JOSS, mishaps caused craft to broach and vehicles to stall in the water off DIME Beach, but the primary disruption was an enemy counterattack through most of D plus 1.[40] During the

---

[37] Hist 531st Engr Shore Rgt, 11 Jun−16 Jul 43; Maj. T. T. Crowley and Capt. G. C. Burch, *Eight Stars to Victory, Operations of 1st Engineer Combat Battalion in World War II*, pp. 45, 47.

[38] Chf Engr, Combined Opns (Br), Lessons Learned from HUSKY, 25 Aug 43, app. B, Description of Certain Beaches, G−3 Misc Papers, 1st ESB files. The foregoing is the primary source for all beach descriptions in this chapter. Hist 1st Bn, 531st Engr Shore Rgt; Ltr, Bonesteel to Moore, 22 Jul 43; Davidson, Preliminary Rpt of Seventh Army Engr on the Sicilian Opn, 23 Aug 43; Hist 39th Engr C Rgt, 10 Jul−18 Aug 43; HQ, Seventh Army, Lessons Learned in Sicilian Campaign; Hewitt Rpt, WNTF in Sicilian Campaign, p. 56.

[39] Brig Gen N. D. Cota, Landing Data, DIME Beach, app. 5 to Observation of Opn HUSKY, 4−31 Jul 43, G−3 Misc Papers, 1st ESB files; Hist 531st Engr Shore Rgt, 11 Jun−16 Jul 43; Hist 1st Bn, 531st Engr Shore Rgt.

[40] Seventh Army Rpt Sicily, p. 6−4; Crowley and Burch, *Eight Stars to Victory*, pp. 47−48; Hist 531st Engr Shore Rgt; Morison, *Sicily-Salerno-Anzio*, pp. 99, 103ff; Comments on HUSKY—JOSS Task Force (8−12 Jul)—Rpt of Observations.

early hours of D-day Italian guns laid intermittent artillery fire on the beaches, destroying a pier at Gela that planners had counted on for unloading LSTs. Then at 0830 enemy armor started moving south out of Niscemi toward Gela. One column drove to within a mile or two of the coastal highway before paratroopers, elements of the 16th Infantry, and the guns of the cruiser *Boise* and the destroyer *Jeffers* stopped it. In the meantime, a second column of about twenty-five light Italian tanks approached Gela from Ponte Olivo. The destroyer *Shubrick* knocked out three but others came on, and the defense section of the 1st Battalion, 531st Engineers, moved forward to reinforce the Rangers and the 39th Engineers. In the ensuing fight the shore engineers scored several hits with bazookas, and when nine or ten Italian tanks drove into Gela, the Rangers drove them off.

With enemy armor in the vicinity, the greatest need ashore was for tanks and artillery, most of which were still aboard LSTs. Early on D-day LST–338 ran a ponton causeway ashore. The causeway's crew rigged it amid falling shells, and by 1030 the LST had unloaded and pulled away. But before another LST could take its place the causeway began to drift, and repositioning it cost valuable time. The lack of adequate anchors for the seaward ends of the ponton causeways was especially felt on DIME beaches, where plans for using the Gela pier had limited the number of causeways to three. Artillery pieces had to be ferried ashore by DUKWs while tanks, too heavy for DUKWs, came in on LCTs and LCMs. As the afternoon wore on, the surf became littered with abandoned vehicles and broached land-

ing craft and the beach clogged with stalled vehicles and piles of materiel.

Late in the afternoon of D-day General Patton ordered ashore KOOL Force, the floating reserve consisting of the 18th Regimental Combat Team and two combat commands of the 2d Armored Division. The movement did not get under way until about 1800; by 0200 on 11 July men on the beach, exhausted after working around the clock, began to drop off to sleep, stalling KOOL landings until daylight. In the meantime the enemy, now reinforced by larger German tanks of the *Hermann Goering Division,* prepared to launch a new attack on Gela.

Few antitank guns or 2d Armored Division tanks were ashore when the enemy struck on the morning of D plus 1, and the only American tanks engaged were five Shermans an LCT had brought ashore about 1030. The German tanks fanned out across the Gela plain, overran American infantry guarding the beachhead perimeter, and rolled on toward the beaches, some lobbing shells into the mass of vehicles, materiel, and men assembled there. Divisional artillery, an infantry cannon company, the five Sherman tanks, and fire from cruisers and destroyers halted the Germans. At 1130 two causeways were operating and tanks rolled ashore over them. The enemy attack faltered shortly after noon, but sporadic fighting continued into the night.

On the beaches conditions had already begun to improve, and by 1600 on D plus 2 the D-day convoy had completely unloaded. By D plus 3 order prevailed, and, with the arrival of the 540th Engineer Combat Regiment (less one battalion), the shore engineers of the 531st were able to concentrate on keeping the beaches clear. Casualties in the 531st were somewhat higher than in any other shore regiment during the landings: as of 16 July the regiment had losses of 22 men killed, 68 wounded, and 2 missing.[41]

The 540th Engineers took over responsibility for road work, mine removal, beach dump operations, and other jobs inland from the beaches. It also operated the tiny port of Gela, where U.S. Navy engineers had anchored two ponton causeway sections alongside the damaged pier for unloading LCTs and LSTs.

The 531st Engineers' beach operations settled down to routine: clearing the beaches, operating dumps, guarding POWs, removing waterproofing from vehicles, and protecting the beach area. One of the most efficient means of moving supplies across the beaches was cargo nets which enabled DUKWs to be unloaded with one sweep of a crane. DUKWs equipped with A-frames, a nonstandard item manufactured and installed in the theater, proved particularly valuable.[42]

After 11 July enemy strafing and bombing attacks subsided, and, favored by ideal weather, supply across JOSS and DIME beaches could have continued indefinitely except for very heavy equipment. But Palermo fell on 22 July, and the beaches lost their importance rapidly. They continued to function during the first week in August, but DIME averaged less than a hundred tons a day. On 7 August DIME beaches closed down in favor of JOSS beaches and captured ports on the north coast.[43]

## Cent Beaches

Two groups of beaches ten miles apart provided the landing sites for the 45th Infantry Division in the CENT area. One group of beaches (Red, Green, and Yellow) north of Scoglitti had been chosen for proximity to Biscari Airfield, about eight miles inland; the group south of Scoglitti (Green 2, Yellow 2), for proximity to Comiso Airfield, some fourteen miles away.

The 120th Engineer Combat Battalion, attached by platoons to infantry battalions, began landing on the northern beaches at 0345, H-hour having been set back sixty minutes in this sector because of heavy seas. The engineers hastily cleared sections of the beaches, reconnoitered for exit routes, and knocked out enemy pillboxes. By noon two companies of the 19th Engineer Combat Regiment had come ashore. Though earmarked to repair inland airfields, they helped on the beaches until the airfields were taken. The men of the 19th Engineers were doubly welcome because of their three rare D−7 bulldozers and three road graders, but most of this equipment could not land until the following day because of high seas and trouble with causeways.[44]

The landings on CENT beaches were the most difficult in Sicily. One trouble

---

[41] Cota, Landing Data, DIME Beach; Hist 531st Engr C Rgt.

[42] Rpt, Shore Engineers in Sicily, 1st ESB files; Hist 531st Engr C Rgt; Information from Capt Napp, S−3, 540th Engr Shore Rgt, contained in HUSKY—JOSS Task Force (8−12 Jul)—Rpt of Observations; Rpt of Seventh Army Engr Sicily; Seventh Army Rpt Sicily, pp. 6−10.

[43] Rate of Discharge in Long Tons from Ports and Beaches in Sicily, app. D to Seventh Army Adm Sitrep, 10 Jul 43−18 Aug 43; Rpt, Shore Engineers in Sicily, 1st ESB files; Hist 531st Engr C Rgt.

[44] Hist 19th Engr C Gp, Oct 42−Jan 44.

was the loading plan, which followed the U.S. amphibious standing operating procedure, calling for assault battalions to be unit-loaded aboard a single ship. This plan did not apply to the 120th Engineer Combat Battalion, which sailed aboard nineteen different ships, but it did apply to the assault units to which the combat engineers were attached.[45] The system had obvious theoretical tactical advantages, but at Sicily practical disadvantages tended to outweigh them. No single ship carried enough landing craft to put a full assault wave in the water. As a result, landing craft from one ship had to grope about in the predawn darkness seeking other ships or the landing craft that formed the rest of the assault wave.

Waves and surf higher and rougher than in the JOSS and DIME areas made offshore rendezvous at the CENT beaches more difficult. Well-trained landing craft crews might have been equal to the offshore problems, but at least half the 45th Infantry Division's coxswains had been replaced just as the division left the United States. The high surf took a fearful toll of landing craft. By noon on D plus 1, in one sector 109 LCVPs and LCMs out of an original 175 were damaged, stranded, sunk, or missing. Along one stretch of beach one craft was stranded an average of every twenty-five yards.[46]

Many of the landing craft that reached shore missed their mark because of heavy surf, too few landmarks, and a strong southeast current; part of one regimental combat team (including the commander) landed six miles northwest of its assigned beach. The 40th Engineers' shore group, mounted in the United States, had not instructed its components to develop whatever beach they landed on. When men of the 40th found themselves on the wrong beaches, many searched along the shoreline for the right ones. But even those who stayed where they landed and set to work on exit routes could not build roads fast enough to handle the cargo coming ashore. Exits had to cross a belt of sand dunes up to a thousand yards wide, and the main coastal highway was several miles away.

The CENT beaches soon became heavily congested, and many shore engineer units shifted their location—some several times—to find better exit routes. Each move cost the shore groups time, control over their organization, discipline, and equipment. Naval beach battalions, for instance, had heavy equipment that could not be shifted about easily.[47]

D−7 angledozers had to build most exit roads at the beaches, for the smaller R−4s again proved too weak for either road construction or vehicle salvage. The engineer regiments working the beaches had two D−7s per lettered engineer company and could easily have used a third. Cyclone wire and

[45] Opns Rpt, 120th Engr C Bn, 1 May−31 Oct 43.
[46] HQ, Combined Operations (Br), Bull 4/1, Notes on the Planning and Assault Phases of the Sicilian Campaign; Morison, *Sicily-Salerno-Anzio*, pp. 127−28, 138, 140; Hist 40th Engr C Rgt, 1 Apr 42−11 Feb 44; AFHQ, Notes on HUSKY Landings, 23 Jul 43, G−3 Misc Papers, 1st ESB files; Hewitt Rpt, WNTF in Sicilian Campaign, pp. 39, 48.

[47] AFHQ, Notes on HUSKY Landings, 23 Jul 43; Memo, Brig Gen A. C. Wedemeyer, Chf, Strategy and Policy Gp, WDGS, for CofS, 24 Aug 43, sub: Observer's Rpt, 319.1, binder, AGF files; Hewitt Rpt, WNTF in Sicilian Campaign, p. 59; Hist 40th Engr C Rgt, 10 Jul−18 Aug 43; Memo, HQ, 1st ESB, for Unit Commanders, 2 Jun 43, sub: Remarks on Landing Opns.

LANDING HEAVY EQUIPMENT OVER THE CAUSEWAY AT SCOGLITTI

Sommerfeld mat that came ashore on sleds were used to surface sandy roads. Engineers also cut and laid cane to make sandy roads passable.

DUKWs carried most supplies inland. Bleeding the tires to ten pounds of pressure enabled the craft to cross the sandy beaches but cut tire life to about 3,500 miles. Other supplies had to be manhandled, mostly by POW volunteers, and dragged to the dumps on sleds hauled by bulldozers. Not much went into the beach dumps on D-day, and before D plus 1 ended CENT beaches were hopelessly jammed. That night and the next day the original Green, Red, and Yellow beaches were abandoned, and unloading moved some three miles to the southeast, where the inland roadnet was more accessible.

Operations continued at new beaches in the Scoglitti area for another week before events inland and farther west along the coast closed the CENT beaches permanently.[48]

During the first three days of the invasion 66,235 men, 17,766 dead-weight tons of cargo, and 7,416 vehicles went ashore over Seventh Army beaches, while 666 U.S. Army troops and 614 POWs were evacuated. By the end of July the 1st Engineer Special Brigade had put ashore 111,824 men,

---

[48] Hist 40th Engr C Rgt, 10 Jul–18 Aug 43; Cota, Landing Data, DIME Beach; AFHQ, Notes on HUSKY Landings, 23 Jul 43; Information from Capt Kennedy, CO, 361st QM Co (DUKW), in HUSKY—Joss Task Force (8–12 Jul)—Rpt of Observations; Info Sect, Intel Div, OCE, SOS ETOUSA, Answers to Engrs Questionnaire, 15 Sep 43, North African Opns.

104,734 tons of cargo, and 21,512 vehicles, and had shipped out to North Africa 1,772 wounded and 27,939 POWs. The performance quieted fears that the beaches would be unable to support the Seventh Army.[49] Around 17 July the 1st Engineer Special Brigade, on orders from General Patton, began to gather all Seventh Army supply activities and many service units under its command, taking over all unloading and supply at DIME, CENT, and JOSS beaches. The brigade's beach operations on Sicily demonstrated that Allied planners would not have to be so closely bound by requirements for ports in pre-

paring for future moves against the Continent.

Despite the generally favorable conditions for amphibious operations in Sicily, the engineers still suffered from their own inexperience. The frequent inability to adapt existing plans and procedures to new conditions in the midst of a developing situation led to continued delays in supply movement off the beaches. The haste of preparations and the curtain of security for the Sicilian landings also brought many engineers their first glimpse of new types of equipment on the busy beaches. They soon would have to apply what they learned in new thrusts onto the Italian mainland against a still determined German enemy.

---

[49] Rpt, Shore Engineers in Sicily, app. B, 1st ESB files; Seventh Army Rpt Sicily, p. E–12.

# CHAPTER VII

# Sicily: The Drive to Messina

By 15 July the Allies held a beachhead stretching from Syracuse to Licata, and Seventh Army, strengthened by the D plus 4 convoy, was preparing to break out of its beachhead. General Patton created the Provisional Corps, consisting of the 3d Infantry Division, the 3d Ranger Battalion, the 5th Armored Field Artillery Group, and elements of the 2d Armored and 82d Airborne Divisions, to sweep around the western coast of Sicily and to move against Palermo from the south and southwest. The II Corps, initially consisting of the 1st and 45th Infantry Divisions, was to strike across central Sicily to the north coast east of Palermo. The attacks began on 17 July.[1]

During Provisional Corps' drive on Palermo, which met little opposition, combat engineers speedily bypassed several destroyed bridges and removed explosives from others captured intact. Divisional engineer bulldozers and mine detectors paced the corps' advance, for a time without corps engineer support, because Provisional Corps originally had no corps engineer organization. On 20 July the 20th Engineer Combat Regiment joined Provisional Corps; one

battalion supported 3d Division engineers, the other 2d Armored Division engineers.[2]

Palermo fell on 22 July. Allied bombs had left the port with only 30 percent of its normal capacity. Forty-four vessels—ships, barges, and small craft—lay sunk in the harbor, and bomb craters pitted quays and railway tracks. On 23 July the 20th Engineer Combat Regiment set about providing berths for thirty-six LSTs and fourteen Liberty ships, and naval personnel began salvage work in the roadstead and ship channels. At the port engineers bulldozed debris from pier areas and exit routes, filled bomb craters, and cut steps into the masonry piers to accommodate LST ramps; they also cleared city streets of debris, leveled badly damaged buildings, and laid water lines to the piers. They cut away superstructures of some ships sunk alongside the quays and built timber ramps across the scuttled hulks. Eventually Liberty ships moored alongside the derelicts and unloaded.[3]

---

[1] In addition to Garland and Smyth, *Sicily and the Surrender of Italy,* the general sources for this chapter are: Seventh Army Rpt Sicily; Rpt of Seventh Army Engr Sicily; II Corps Engr Rpt, 10 Jul–18 Aug 43.

[2] Rpts, 20th Engr C Rgt to CG, 3d Div, 18, 22, and 28 Jul 43, sub: Action of 20th Engineer Combat Regiment, 10–17 Jul 43, 3d Inf Div files; Hist Rcds, Prov Corps, Seventh Army, 15 Jul–20 Aug 43.

[3] Hist 20th Engr C Bn, 17 May–17 Jun 45. (Organized in August 1942, the 20th Engineer Combat Regiment was broken up on 15 January 1944, with the regiment's 1st Battalion being redesignated the 20th Engineer Combat Battalion.) Chf Engr, 15th Army

On the morning of 23 July, the day after Provisional Corps captured Palermo, elements of II Corps reached the north coast of Sicily. A regimental combat team of the 45th Infantry Division entered the town of Termini Imerese, thirty-one miles east of Palermo on Highway 113, the coastal road between Palermo and Messina. The 1st Division reached Petralia on Highway 120, an inland road about twenty miles south of Highway 113.

That same day, General Alexander changed the direction of American forces. He had originally ordered Patton's Seventh Army to Palermo and the north coast to protect the left flank of Montgomery's British Eighth Army drive on Messina. On 23 July, becoming aware that Montgomery's forces were not strong enough to overrun the Germans in front of Eighth Army, Alexander directed Patton to turn his army to the east and advance on Messina along the axis of Highways 113 and 120. Patton lost no time. The two divisions of Lt. Gen. Omar N. Bradley's II Corps, already in position athwart the two highways and soon to be bolstered by units of the Provisional Corps, were in motion before nightfall.

### Supply Over the Beaches

At the outset supplies for the American drive on Messina had to come from dumps at small ports and beaches on the south coast—Porto Empedocle, Licata, and Gela—because the first coasters did not reach Palermo until 28 July. The agency responsible for logistical support was still the 1st Engineer Special Brigade, acting as SOS, Seventh Army, under the general supervision of the army's G–4.[4]

Once the attack out of the beachhead began, the most critical supply problem was not unloading supplies but moving them forward to the using troops, a problem compounded by prearranged shipments that did not reflect reality. The 1st Engineer Special Brigade soon was burdened with unneeded materiel.

Trained and equipped to unload supplies across the beaches and through the small ports on Sicily's southern shore, the 1st Engineer Special Brigade performed efficiently after overcoming earlier problems at the beaches. But the brigade also had to stock and operate Seventh Army depots inland at points convenient to the combat forces, and there were never enough trucks on Sicily.[5]

Railroads became important in moving supplies inland to support the rapid advance. Lines from Porto Empedocle and Licata converged not far from Caltanissetta, a town near the center of the island and about thirty miles inland. Seventh Army captured the lines intact, and Transportation Corps railway troops had supplies rolling over them from the beaches immediately. The dumps were opened at Caltanissetta on 19 July. Beyond this point German demolitions limited the use of railways, and supplies had to be trucked to forward corps dumps.

The using services, even the engi-

---

Gp, Notes on Engr Opns in Sicily, no. 3, 10 Sep 43; Brig Gen C. R. Moore, Rpt of Observations in North Africa and Sicily, 9 Sep 43.

[4] HQ, Force 343, FO 1, 18 Jun 43, Engr Annex; Rpt, Caffey, Shore Engineers in Sicily; Moore, Rpt of Observations, 9 Sep 43.
[5] Ltr, HQ, Seventh Army, to CG, NATOUSA, 22 Nov 43, sub: Data for Logistical Planning; Bradley, *A Soldier's Story*, p. 145.

neers, were critical of the 1st Engineer Special Brigade's inland dumps, complaining that they could not find needed items. The 1st Engineer Combat Battalion, supporting the 1st Infantry Division, reported sending its trucks back to the beaches for needed materiel no less than four times. Ordnance officers complained that forward dumps were overstocked with small-arms ammunition (which the brigade moved first because it was easiest to handle), while they urgently needed artillery ammunition.[6]

Whatever the deficiencies, the beaches, especially at Porto Empedocle and Licata, carried a heavy supply responsibility throughout the Sicilian campaign, mainly because the campaign was short and the rehabilitation of Palermo slow. An early and important activity at the beaches was supplying aviation gasoline to the Ponte Olivo and Comiso Airfields. The chief engineer, 15th Army Group, termed the work of the 696th Engineer Petroleum Distribution Company in building fuel pipelines and tanks at Gela "the outstanding new engineer feature of the campaign."[7]

A small reconnaissance party of petroleum engineers landed on DIME beaches on D-day, and by 18 July all the men and equipment of the 696th were ashore. Engineers used the damaged Gela pier to berth shallow-draft tankers in about seventeen feet of water. The company laid discharge lines along the pier, erected two 5,000-barrel bolted-steel storage tanks on shore, and by 21 July completed a four-inch pipeline to Ponte Olivo Airfield, about seven miles away. The first tanker, originally scheduled to arrive off Gela on 18 July, did not actually begin to discharge until 24 July. Two days later a 22-mile pipeline to Comiso Airfield was also completed. About the same time a detachment from the 696th erected facilities for receiving, storing, and canning gasoline at Porto Empedocle.

The petroleum engineers had wanted their equipment shipped in two equal parts on two coasters, each accompanied by some of their experts, but the equipment arrived in seven different ships at several different beaches—some as far afield as the British port of Syracuse. Workers at the beach dumps were unfamiliar with the POL equipment and had so much difficulty gathering it that the 696th had to send men to search for items along the beaches. As late as 21 July the company had found only 60 percent of its materiel and had to improvise elbows and other fittings to complete the pipelines.[8]

Bailey bridges had proven their worth in the final days of the Tunisian campaign. Seventh Army brought several sets to Sicily, though some arrived with vital parts missing. The main advantage of the Bailey—one of the most valued pieces of equipment in World War II—was its adaptability. It was made of welded lattice panels, each ten feet

[6] Seventh Army Rpt Sicily, p. E−7; Hist 1st Engr C Bn, Sicilian Campaign, 10 Jul−Dec 43; Lida Mayo, *The Ordnance Department: On Beachhead and Battlefront,* United States Army in World War II (Washington, 1968), p. 167.

[7] Chf Engr, 15th Army Gp, Notes on Engr Opns in Sicily, no. 3, Sep 43.

[8] Rpt, Capt M. D. Altgelt to Lt Col S. A. Potter, Jr., Chf, C&Q Planning, 5 Oct 43, sub: Report Covering Trip to North Africa (POL Inspection) with extracts from six important documents pertaining to HUSKY POL; Hist 696th Engr Pet Dist Co, 1 Sep 42−30 Apr 44.

long, joined together with steel pins to form girders of varying length and strength. The girders could be up to three panels wide and high. The Bailey could accommodate a great variety of loads and spans; it could be erected to carry twenty-eight tons over a 170-foot span, or as much as seventy-eight tons over a 120-foot span. The bridges were designated according to the number of parallel panels and stories in each girder. A double-single (DS) Bailey was two panels wide and one story high, a triple-double (TD) three panels wide and two stories high. Engineers could assemble and launch these bridges entirely from the near shore. A light falsework of paneling served as a launching nose and the bridge itself as a counterweight.[9]

The Bailey was especially valuable in Sicily because of the terrain. Along the coast from Palermo to Messina ran a narrow littoral flanked by the sea on one side and by steep, rocky mountains on the other. Here and there, where the mountains crowded all the way to the sea, Highway 113 was no more than a winding, shoulderless road chipped into headlands. For the most part vehicles—and sometimes even foot troops—were roadbound. The Germans had demolished bridges and culverts across the numerous ravines. To the south and inland, Highway 120 ran through rugged mountain ranges nearly due east from Petralia through Nicosia, Troina, and Randazzo to the east coast. Since maneuvering off this road was difficult at best, blown bridges could stop forward movement. After II Corps engineers established their dump in Nicosia, Baileys accounted for over 90

percent of the 298 tons of fortifications material, bridging, and road maintenance supplies the dump issued during the campaign.[10]

On 29 July II Corps engineers established a bridge dump at Nicosia and organized a provisional Bailey bridge train. The 19th Engineer Combat Regiment outfitted one of its platoons with nine trucks and seven four-wheeled German trailers. Each of the cargo trucks carried all the components for a ten-foot, double-single bay of Bailey bridging. The bridge train carried 100 feet of double-single Bailey plus material for a seventy-foot launching nose, and the bridge unit had enough extra parts for two eighty-foot Class 40 bridges.[11]

### Corps and Army Support of Combat Engineers

At the time II Corps began slicing across Sicily to the north coast on 17 July, German forces were falling back to stronger defensive positions, using a covering screen of mines, booby traps, and demolitions to delay pursuit. Except for brief stands at Caltanissetta and Enna to gain time to consolidate new defenses to the east, the enemy abandoned western Sicily. But by 23 July, when the 45th Division reached the

---

[9] Coll, Keith, and Rosenthal, *The Corps of Engineers: Troops and Equipment*, p. 51.

[10] II Corps Engr Rpt, 10 Jul–18 Aug 43.

[11] Davidson, Preliminary Rpt of Seventh Army Engr on the Sicilian Opn, 23 Aug 43; II Corps Engr Rpt, 18 Aug 43, ans. 5 and 7; Ltr, Elliott to AFHQ, 21 Sep 43, sub: Administrative Lessons Learned from Opns in Sicily from the Engr Viewpoint; Hist 19th Engr C Gp, Oct 42–Jan 44. (The 19th Engineer Combat Regiment was broken up on 1 March 1945; Headquarters and Headquarters Company became Headquarters and Headquarters Company, 19th Engineer Combat Group; the 1st Battalion became the 401st Engineer Combat Battalion; the 2d Battalion became the 402d Engineer Combat Battalion.)

north coast, evidence was mounting that the enemy would soon make a stand. The 1st Division, on the right and inland, ran into sharp fighting and increasing numbers of mines and demolitions near Alimena, northwest of Enna. To the east the British Eighth Army stalled before powerful German defenses south and southwest of Mt. Etna. (*Map 6*)

Up to this point the work load for divisional engineer battalions had not been heavy. Their main tasks during the establishment of the beachhead had been to help build exit roads and to help the infantry take and destroy pillboxes. There had been mines to search out and a few roadblocks to clear, but for the most part divisional engineer formations had organized and occupied defensive positions alongside the infantry units to which they were attached. During the subsequent advances across Sicily, divisional engineers spent most of their time probing for mines and bypassing blown bridges by cutting roads down banks and across dry streambeds.

The 120th Engineer Combat Battalion opened the way for the 45th Division along Highway 113, the 1st Engineer Combat Battalion for the 1st Division along Highway 120, where mines and demolitions were somewhat denser. By the end of July the 1st Engineer Battalion had repaired or bypassed twenty-three bridges, nineteen large craters, and several bomb or shell holes. They also had cleared away wrecked vehicles, rubble, and roadblocks and had swept the route for mines.[12]

Backing up the divisional engineers

in II Corps was the 39th Engineer Combat Regiment, one battalion behind the 120th and another behind the 1st. Corps engineers in close support improved bypasses and, where bypasses were impractical, erected Bailey bridges. They also cleared more mines, reduced grades, and eliminated traffic bottlenecks. A battalion of the 19th Engineers joined II Corps to handle work the 39th Engineers could not do because much of the regiment's equipment and many of its vehicles had not yet arrived. This battalion had been working on Comiso Airfield and had with it several road graders, bulldozers, six-ton trucks, and sixteen-ton trailers.[13]

Behind II Corps, the 20th Engineer Combat Regiment on Highway 113 and the 343d Engineer General Service Regiment on Highway 120 shared road maintenance responsibility within the army area. Most main roads were in excellent condition: surfaced with black top or water-bound macadam, wide enough for two-way traffic, and moderately graded and curved. Towns, with their sharp turns and narrow streets, were the principal bottlenecks. Second-class roads were usually in fair condition but were narrow with sharp curves and steep grades; Seventh Army made good use of them by making them one-way and by controlling traffic. Dry weather made the engineers' job easier. Road repair machinery such as rollers and portable rock crushers were captured in many localities, while stockpiles of crushed stone and asphalt enough for initial repairs were found along all main roads.

By the time army engineers took over

---

[12] Hist 120th Engr C Bn, May 44; Hist 1st Engr C Bn, Sicilian Campaign, 10 Jul–Dec 43.

[13] II Corps Engr Rpt, Sicilian Campaign; Hists, 39th Engr C Rgt, 10 Jul–18 Aug 43, and 19th Engr C Gp, Oct 42–Jan 44.

main supply routes from corps engineers, they generally found the roads in excellent condition. After removing roadblocks, widening bottlenecks, and improving some bypasses, they built culverts, paved the slopes of fills, and built wooden trestle bridges. The 20th Engineers improved eighteen bypasses on Highway 113 between Palermo and Cape Orlando, and the 343d Engineers did similar work on twenty-one bypasses on roads from Cape Orlando to Messina and Randazzo. The two regiments also cleared minefields and rebuilt six railroad bridges.[14]

Between Highways 113 and 120 lay the rugged Madonie-Nebrodi ranges, with peaks over 6,000 feet high. Few roads crossed these mountains, and lateral roads connecting 113 with 120 were some fifteen miles apart. At the end of July traffic between the 1st and 45th Divisions had to make a long trip around to the rear. Engineers of the 45th Division began reopening Highway 117, running south out of Santo Stefano. As soon as Santo Stefano fell into American hands, Company B, 120th Engineer Battalion, went to work at a demolished bridge two miles north of Mistretta. Engineers grading a bypass there lost two bulldozers to enemy mines, although the site had been checked. Afterward, engineers spent more time on mine clearance work and paid particular attention to areas around demolitions, for the Germans, impressed by the speed with which American bulldozers cut bypasses, were bent on making the most likely bypass routes the deadliest ones.[15]

After II Corps turned east, enemy mining became more plentiful and more deliberate. The Germans planted mines in potholes and covered them with hot asphalt to resemble patches. They also booby-trapped antitank mines, as many as 90 percent of them in places. Before roads and trails could be opened, divisional engineers had to sweep traffic lanes and shoulders thoroughly. For this job they needed many more SCR–625 mine detectors than the fifteen allocated to each of the engineer combat regiments, divisional engineers, separate combat battalions, and armored engineer battalions. The 19th Engineers carried forty-two detectors, and after the campaign both Seventh Army and AFHQ recommended that the number provided as organic equipment for infantry and armored divisional engineer battalions be raised to forty-two and fifty-four, respectively.[16]

SCR–625s proved as valuable in Sicily as in Tunisia—and less troublesome. Since rain fell only once in the II Corps area, the only trouble with moisture shorting out the detectors came from sea spray during the initial landings. The detectors were fragile, however, and seldom were more than 75 percent working. Sweeping with the SCR–625 was slow and tedious, but neither so slow nor so tedious as probing. Engineers relied heavily on the SCR–625s, but doubt was growing as to how long they could continue to do so. In Sicily the Germans used two types of mines that SCR–625s could not detect under more than an inch of soil. One was a

[14] Rpt of Seventh Army Engr Sicily.
[15] Hist 120th Engr C Bn in Sicilian Campaign, May 44.

[16] Opns Rpt and S–2 Jnl, 120th Engr C Bn, 10 Jul–31 Oct 43, in Hist 120th Engr C Bn, 31 May–Nov 43; Ltr, Engr Sect, AFHQ, to CofEngrs, 28 Nov 43, sub: Changes in T/E, 370.212 Sicily, Rpts on Opns, Aug 43 to Oct 43, AFHQ files.

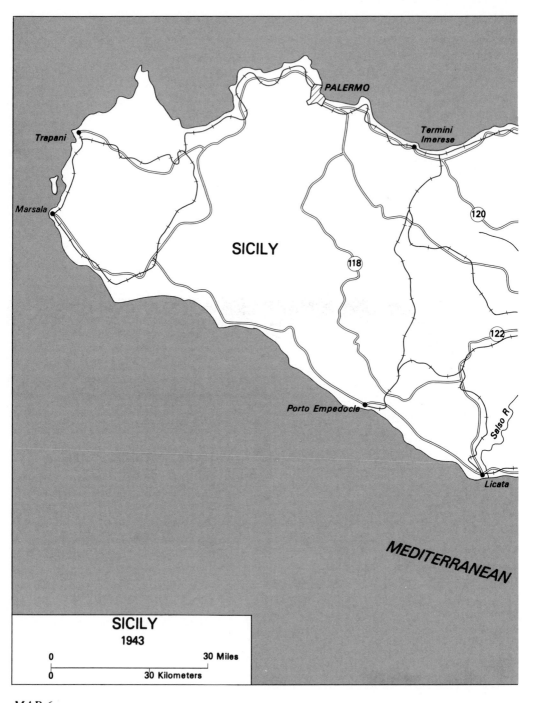

SICILY
1943

0                                    30 Miles
0                              30 Kilometers

*MAP 6*

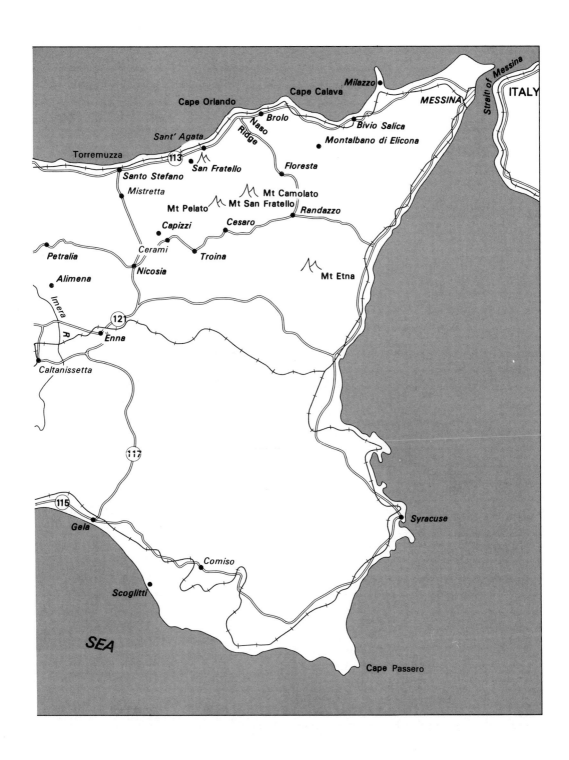

German wooden box mine that had a metal detonator, the other an improvised mine made of plastic explosive wrapped in paper or cloth and equipped with a bakelite detonator. Around Randazzo, where enemy mines were found in great numbers, the high metallic content of the soil made SCR−625s useless. The less sensitive British mine detector was of some use, but the only sure way to find mines there was by probing for them with a bayonet.[17]

Before the invasion the 17th Armored Engineer Battalion obtained four Scorpion mine exploders mounted on M−4 tanks for clearing lanes through minefields protected by enemy fire. They landed at Licata on 14 July. Because no trailers or prime movers were available for transporting the often trouble-prone tanks, they had to be walked into position over mountainous roads, and after twenty miles their bogeys wore out. They were never used in the heavily mined fields along the north coast between Cape Orlando and Milazzo on Highway 113 toward the close of the campaign because when they finally arrived after their long road march, all needed major repairs.[18]

The arrival in early August of the 39th Engineers' vehicles and heavy equipment, as well as missing elements of the 19th Engineers, made it possible for a full engineer combat regiment to support each attacking division. The II Corps engineers also received sixteen greatly needed D−7 and D−8 heavy bulldozers from southern beaches; the 19th Engineer Combat Regiment got five to go with its three organic D−7s, and two divisional engineer combat battalions got two each.

Only three sixteen-ton trailers were available to move heavy bulldozers, and they were too light, breaking down so often that most of the time bulldozers had to be driven from one construction site to another. The larger bulldozers proved invaluable, however, for the three R−4s allotted divisional engineers were too light for many jobs. For the engineers' requirements on Sicily, wrote one engineer battalion commander, his unit needed six R−4s, three D−7s, a prime mover, and a twenty-ton trailer. After the campaign Seventh Army recommended that divisional engineer battalions be issued one D−7 as organizational equipment and engineer combat regiments three. D−7s no longer exceeded the "division load" limitation, but production was a problem. In July 1943 engineer regiments appeared to be at least nine to twelve months away from getting more heavy bulldozers.[19]

*Maps and Camouflage*

The map used most in Sicily was a

---

[17] II Corps Engr Rpt, 10 Jul−18 Aug 43; Seventh Army Rpt Sicily, pp. I−3 and C−42; Hist 1st Engr C Bn, Sicilian Campaign. (This unit reported that the American detector could, with accurate tuning, locate the new German wooden box mines.) Hist 19th Engr C Rgt, 20 Oct 42−1 Oct 43; Comments collected by Capt Alden Colvocoresses, 24 Aug 43, in HUSKY—Joss Task Force (8−12 Jul)—Rpt of Observations.

[18] Rpt of Seventh Army Engr Sicily; Opns of CCA, 2d Armd Div, 21 Apr−25 Jul 43; Hist 17th Armd Engr Bn.

[19] Rpt of Seventh Army Engr Sicily; II Corps Engr Rpt, 10 Jul−18 Aug 43; Ltr, Lt Col L. L. Bingham, CO, 10th Engr C Bn, to CG, 3d Div, 29 Jul 43, sub: Engr Recommendations and Lessons Learned from Sicilian Campaign, 10th Engr C Bn files; Hist 19th Engr C Gp; Davidson, Preliminary Rpt of Seventh Army Engr on the Sicilian Opn, 23 Aug 43, and indorsements by HQ, 15th Army Gp, 6 Sep 43, and AFHQ, 2 Oct 43; Incl to Ltr, Col Robert H. Burrag, Actg Chf Opns and Trng Br, Troops Div, OCE, WD, to Col Donald P. Adams, HQ, EBS, 9 Jul 43; Hist 10th Engr C Bn in Sicilian Opn, 31 Jul−18 Aug 43.

multicolored one in the 1:100,000 series which in twenty-six sheets offered complete coverage of the island. Such coverage was not available in the tactical 1:50,000 and 1:25,000 series, but the 1:50,000 maps were accurate, and artillery used them with good results when no 1:25,000 sheets were to be had. The 1:10,000 beach mosaic was of some use during the initial landings, but its quality was poor and its coverage inadequate. Photomaps on a scale of 1:25,000, the product of air sorties before and during the campaign, were of little use because many areas were blank and detail and contrast were frequently lacking.

More overprints were needed during the latter stages of the campaign when enemy resistance stiffened. Two photo interpreters from the 62d Engineer Topographic Company came to Ponte Olivo Airfield to copy information on enemy defenses in the northeastern areas from aerial photographs. They were able to spot routes of advance, pick bypass routes, evaluate enemy demolitions, and even estimate lengths of bridging that would be needed at certain places. The aerial information was printed on base maps prepared in advance, and copies went to every interested division as well as to army headquarters, corps headquarters, corps artillery, and the Naval Operations Board. The value of this work for frontline units in Sicily was limited, however, because they moved so rapidly that ground reconnaissance often was possible before the photo-interpreters' reports reached them.[20]

The only camouflage units in the Sicilian campaign were Company B, 601st Engineer Camouflage Battalion, and a platoon of the 904th Engineer Air Force Headquarters Company. Company B of the 601st reached Sicily late in July and was attached by platoons to the assault divisions. Its only assignments during the campaign involved camouflaging the Seventh Army command post and building a dummy railhead. However, the campaign ended before the railhead task could be finished. The 904th Company's platoon for a time painted deceptive patterns on planes and trucks but later relied on dispersal to reduce losses at airfields.

Apart from the work of these two units the engineers' part in camouflage was chiefly supplying materials and giving instruction in their use. Before HUSKY got under way, engineers furnished reversible nets for each TBA vehicle scheduled to go to Sicily and additional oversize nets to build up a reserve of 250 on each of the three beachheads. One side of each net was sand-colored to blend with barren landscape; the other side was green-toned for verdant areas. The nets were put to good use, notably in concealing artillery from *Luftwaffe* attacks during the battle for Troina.[21]

### Highway 120: The Road to Randazzo

Late in July the 39th Infantry, 9th Division, which was to replace the 1st Infantry Division along Highway 120, arrived at Nicosia. Maj. Gen. Terry de la Mesa Allen, commanding the 1st

---

[20] II Corps Engr Rpt, 10 Jul–18 Aug 43, an. 3, Map Supply and Distribution; HQ, Force 141, Planning Instr 15, Maps and Charts.

[21] Hist 601st Engr Camouflage Bn, 1943; Hist, The Aviation Engineers in the MTO, Hist Sect, AAF Engr Cmd, MTO (P), 12 Jun 46, p. 183, Maxwell AFB.

Division, expected relief with the fall of Troina, the next main objective. Leading the advance, the 39th Infantry took Cerami on 31 July, but the following day heavy German fire stopped the regiment about four miles short of Troina.

Though the Germans were withdrawing, they had determined to delay pursuit at Troina, which was ideal for their purpose. The highest town in Sicily, Troina perched atop a 3,600-foot mountain dominating the countryside, a natural strongpoint and "a demolition engineer's dream" because approaches could be blocked by blown bridges and mines.[22] On 2 August General Allen committed his 26th Infantry, but its attack proved fruitless. Another push by the reinforced 16th Infantry, 1st Division, also made little progress.

On 4 August, the fifth day of the battle for Troina, the 9th Division's 60th Infantry arrived on the scene and began deploying to outflank German defenses well north of Troina. Farther south, the 39th Infantry, 9th Division, and the 26th Infantry, 1st Division, were to continue efforts to encircle Troina from the northwest and north; the 16th Infantry, 1st Division, was to drive eastward on the town across virtually trackless hills; the 18th Infantry, 1st Division, was to outflank it on the south. Company A, 1st Engineer Combat Battalion, had the mission of bulldozing a road along the 16th Infantry's axis of advance, while the 9th Division's 15th Engineer Combat Battalion had a similar mission in support of the 60th Infantry.

Maj. Gen. Manton S. Eddy, commanding the 9th Division, intended that

the 60th Infantry push generally east from Capizzi across Monte Pelato and Camolato and then, striking from the north, drive toward Cesaro, on Highway 120 east of Troina, in an attempt to cut off German forces withdrawing from the Troina sector. The attack began on the morning of 5 August, with three light R–4 angledozers of the 15th Engineer Battalion soon struggling to build a new road along the infantry's axis of advance. In the afternoon two D–7 heavy bulldozers arrived from corps; one broke down almost immediately, but the other did yeoman work.

During the night of 5–6 August the Germans abandoned Troina and fell back behind a cover of mines and demolitions. The next day the 9th Division replaced the 1st along Highway 120, and the 15th Engineer Combat Battalion took over from the 1st Engineer Combat Battalion. Some of the heaviest German mining and demolitions were along Highway 120 between Troina and Randazzo, the next main objective. Nowhere during the campaign was mine clearance and bypass construction more important, because Randazzo lay high on the slopes of Mt. Etna. Just as important was building new roads through the mountains.[23]

On 8 August Company B, 15th Engineer Battalion, withdrew from the new road to Mt. Camolato to support the 47th Infantry on Highway 120 east of Troina. By this time the new road was open to Colle Basso, perhaps two-thirds of the way to Mt. Camolato, but the

---

[22] Garland and Smyth, *Sicily and the Surrender of Italy,* p. 329.

[23] This account is drawn from: Hists of the 15th Engr C Bn, Sicilian Campaign, 23 Aug 43, and the 1st Engr C Bn, Sicilian Campaign, 10 Jul–Dec 43; Seventh Army Rpt Sicily, pp. 6–17; ETOUSA Engr Observers Rpt 3, 18 Feb 44, 319.1, binder 1, 1944, AFHQ files.

15th faced difficult problems. Company A's R−4 broke down, and mist and rain began to hinder the work. Company C pushed the road to completion at 1700 on 9 August. Earlier that day Company A moved off to repair the Mt. Camolato−Cesaro road and to build a north-south bypass around Cesaro, using a D−8 bulldozer that had just arrived from corps.

After joining the 47th Infantry on 8 August, Company B cleared mines to within a mile of Cesaro, where enemy shell fire halted the work. Next morning the company used a repaired D−7 to build a four-mile-long east-west bypass, which for 1 1/2 miles followed the Troina River bed and detoured around both Cesaro and three demolished bridges east of Troina. Company C ultimately extended to forty miles the 60th Infantry's road through the mountains north of Troina and Cesaro.

Slowed by mines, the 9th Division did not enter Randazzo until the morning of 13 August; shortly thereafter the British 78th Division entered from the south. The 1st Infantry Division came back into the line at Randazzo, and the 9th Division swung north and north-east toward the north coast. In anticipation of this shift, engineers had already scouted a narrow road that ran north from Highway 120 at a point a few miles west of Randazzo, and Company B, 15th Engineer Battalion, began opening the road on 13 August. Two demolished bridges and two road craters caused little trouble, but a quarter mile of abatis was heavily strewn with S-mines and Teller mines, one of which claimed a D−8 bulldozer. Nevertheless, Company B opened the road to one-way traffic shortly after noon. Elements of the battalion then moved to Floresta,

and the next day Company A opened a one-way road as far as Montalbano. At this point all 9th Division engineer work halted—with the campaign almost over, the 9th Division came out of the line.

The 15th Engineer Battalion had been in action fifteen days. During that time the battalion built 45 miles of new supply roads through mountains, repaired 14 miles of existing roads, bypassed 15 demolished bridges, filled 4 major craters, cleared a quarter mile of abatis, and searched 30 miles of road for mines. The unit's water points supplied over 1,500,000 gallons of purified water. There had been twelve casualties, ten (including two deaths) caused by two S-mines near Cesaro on 11 August.

On 13 August the 1st Engineer Combat Battalion came back into action with the rest of the 1st Division. Company B and a platoon of Company A worked throughout the night improving the road through and east of Randazzo for the 18th Infantry to use the next morning. The engineers found nine bridges destroyed within a few miles and worked continuously until 15 August bypassing them. At one site a forty-foot bank rose on the near side—a perfect spot for Bailey bridging, but none was available. During its thirty-one days in the line, the 1st Engineer Combat Battalion bypassed thirty-nine bridges, filled twenty-eight road craters, and searched out hundreds of mines. The battalion suffered 30 casualties: 4 killed, 3 missing, and 23 wounded.

*Highway 113: The Road to Messina*

After fighting its way into the north coastal town of Santo Stefano on 31 July, the 45th Division went into reserve and the 3d Infantry Division took over on Highway 113. As the 3d Division advanced east along the north coast, it was confined to a single road even more than was the 9th Division along Highway 120. On the left was the sea, on the right mountainous terrain fit only for mules and men on foot. Maj. Gen. Lucian K. Truscott, Jr., commanding the division, sent one element forward astride Highway 113 to clear spurs overlooking the road and to protect the engineers who were making a path through demolitions and minefields so that artillery and vehicles could move forward. He sent other elements with pack animals (he was to use more than 400 mules and 100 horses) over mountain trails on the right and inland to strike the enemy's flank and rear.[24]

An advantage Highway 113 had over Highway 120 was the possibility of landing men and supplies by sea. Supplies came ashore from LSTs at Torremuzza beach near Santo Stefano at an unloading point the 2d Battalion, 540th Engineer Combat Regiment, opened on 3 August. This same battalion also furnished a platoon and a D−7 to clear mines and wire from a beach at Sant' Agata when Truscott attempted a small amphibious operation to outflank the San Fratello position, the first major German strongpoint east of Santo Stefano.[25]

At Monte San Fratello, a 2,200-foot peak about fifteen miles east of Santo Stefano, the 3d Division was stopped from 3 to 8 August, as effectively as the 1st Division had been at Troina and for the same reason—the Germans were

buying time for their withdrawal. When heavy fire and dense minefields halted the 15th Infantry, two battalions of the 30th and the entire 7th had to be committed before any progress could be made, and that progress was made partly because the Germans were thinning out their defenses. A battalion leapfrogged behind the San Fratello position at Sant' Agata in an amphibious landing before dawn on 8 August, the battalion landing team including a platoon of the 3d Division's 10th Engineer Combat Battalion and a platoon of the 540th Engineer Combat Regiment. The operation failed to cut off the Germans but did hasten their withdrawal.

Resuming the advance, which heavy mining and considerable demolition work slowed, the 3d Division encountered a second strong line at Naso ridge near Cape Orlando on 11 August. A second end run, attempted early on the twelfth near Brolo, twelve miles behind the enemy's lines, almost proved disastrous. The enemy boxed in the landing force and inflicted heavy casualties before relief arrived by land. Two engineers of the 10th Engineer Combat Battalion were killed and two were wounded; two engineers of the 540th platoon were killed and three were wounded.[26]

Five or six miles beyond Brolo along the coastal highway, the 30th Infantry, leading, halted on 12 August before the most formidable roadblock German demolition engineers had yet put up. Overcoming it was to be "a landmark of American engineer support in Sicily."[27]

[24] Lt. Gen. L. K. Truscott, Jr., *Command Missions* (New York: Dutton, 1954), pp. 230–31.

[25] HQ, Seventh Army, Adm Sitreps, Jul and Aug 43, app. D; Interv, Capt Napp, S−3, 540th Engr C Rgt; Hist 540th Engr C Rgt, 1942–45.

[26] Hist 10th Engr C Bn in Sicilian Opn, 26 Aug 43; Rpt of Seventh Army Engr Sicily; Bradley, *A Soldier's Story*, pp. 158–59; Hist 540th Engr C Rgt, 1942–45.

[27] Garland and Smyth, *Sicily and the Surrender of Italy*, p. 406.

About fifty feet beyond a tunnel at Cape Calava the Germans had blown out 150 feet of the road that ran along a shelf carved out of a sheer rock cliff rising abruptly from the sea. Infantrymen could pick their way one by one across the steep rock face, and guns and supplies could be ferried by sea. But the division's supply trucks and heavy guns had to use the road, for landing craft were in short supply. Grading could close two-thirds of the gap, but any fill dumped into the center would roll down to the sea, 200 feet below. This section had to be bridged, but no Bailey bridging was available. With captured timbers, the 10th Engineer Combat Battalion "hung a bridge in the sky"—and did it in twenty-four hours.[28]

Shortly after noon on 13 August, several engineer officers halted their jeep at a roadblock on Highway 113 four miles west of Cape Calava and hiked to the break in the road. They computed what would be needed to do the job, ordered up the necessary men and equipment, and estimated they could bridge the gap by noon the next day. Within an hour or two, men from Company A, 10th Engineer Battalion, were on hand, breaking rock with jackhammers. Trucks and trailers loaded with heavy timber beams and flanks began to move forward. In the meantime a bulldozer was needed on other demolitions farther east. To get one forward, engineers built a raft on two fishing smacks, loaded a bulldozer aboard, and used an amphibious jeep to tow the makeshift ferry five miles around Cape Calava.[29]

At the constricted bridge site, Company A could put only one platoon at a time on the job. All night the unit labored to meet the deadline. At dawn the gaping hole remained, but the foundations for a bridge had been laid. Engineers swung a heavy timber into the gap and set it upright on a seat cut into the cliff. They laid another beam from the top of this upright to another seat chipped out of the rock and pinned the two timbers together to form a bent. Then they looped a steel cable around the upright and anchored it to pins set in the cliff. The cable prevented the bent from sliding downhill when heavy, spliced-timber girders were worked into place. Twenty-man teams picked up the girders one by one and slid them into position.

A rickety bridge began to take shape. As the last floor plank was spiked down and the final touches added to the approaches, General Truscott climbed aboard his jeep. Promptly at noon on 14 August men of Company A stepped back and watched the division commander test the newly completed span. Other light vehicles loaded with ammunition and weapons for frontline troops were waiting to follow. After they crossed, the bridge was closed so that engineers could strengthen it to take 2 1/2-ton trucks. At 1700 the bridge was reopened and cargo trucks—even a bulldozer—began to cross.

Beyond Cape Calava the 3d Division's 7th Regimental Combat Team advanced so rapidly that an amphibious landing by the 157th Regimental Combat Team,

---

[28] This account of the Cape Calava bridge is drawn from Ernie Pyle, *Brave Men* (New York: Henry Holt, 1944), pp. 65–71, and Hist 10th Engr C Bn in Sicilian Opn, 26 Aug 43.

[29] Merrill Mueller, NBC War Correspondent Overseas, Letter to the Editor, *Look Magazine*, March 20, 1944.

CONSTRUCTION BEGINS AT CAPE CALAVA *to close gap blown by retreating Germans.*

45th Division, during the night of 15–16 August at Bivio Salica fell miles short of the advance infantry elements. Darkness found the 7th Regimental Combat Team pushing strong patrols into Messina. By dawn, organized resistance in Sicily had ended and American artillery was dueling with enemy guns across the Strait of Messina.

A measure of the German demolitions in the mountains rising from the sea was the time it took Truscott's forces to traverse the coastal road. The 3d Division took sixteen laborious days to reach Messina; on the morning of 20 August General Truscott made the return journey from Messina to Palermo in just three hours.[30]

In the drive along the coast the 10th Engineer Combat Battalion took casualties of four men killed and twenty-three wounded; most of the casualties were from mines. Lt. Col. Leonard L. Bingham, commanding the battalion, thought the unit had been used improperly in the later stages of the campaign. At the outset, on 1 August, its three line companies were strung out along Highway 113, all working under division engineer control. Two companies leapfrogged each other from demolition site to demolition site, while the third company provided mine removal parties for divisional units. Headquarters, Headquarters and Service Company, maintained the division engineer supply dump, established water points, serviced engineer vehicles, and operated

---

[30] Truscott, *Command Missions,* p. 244.

GENERAL TRUSCOTT TESTS THE TEMPORARY SPAN AT CAPE CALAVA

the battalion aid station. But this arrangement did not last, and soon many units of the 10th Engineer Battalion—frequently whole companies—were attached to infantry units. This procedure had officers who were not engineers directing the platoons and companies and cost the engineers their cohesiveness within the division.[31]

### Palermo

After the capture of Palermo on 22 July, Seventh Army had no sooner

---

[31] Hist 10th Engr C Bn in Sicilian Opn, 26 Aug 43; Seventh Army Rpt Sicily, pp. 6–20 and E–2; Ltr, Bingham to CG, 3d Div, 29 Jul 43, sub: Engr Recommendations and Lessons Learned from Sicilian Campaign.

established headquarters and main supply dumps when requests for work began to pour in to Col. Garrison H. Davidson, the army engineer. No formal construction program was established, and army engineer troops handled mine sweeping, road clearing, and construction requests as they came in. Space was urgently needed for offices, billets, storehouses, laundries, bakeries, and maintenance shops, while hospitals set up in unoccupied buildings had to have window screens and more water and sewage facilities. The municipal water and sewage systems needed repairs, and generating plants at Palermo and Porto Empedocle had been bombed out of operation.

Several engineer units had a part in rehabilitating Palermo. The 20th Engineer Combat Regiment began work there on 23 July but left a week later to extend the railroad line to Santo Stefano. On this job the regiment rebuilt four bridges and repaired one tunnel and a considerable amount of track. For one bridge the 20th Engineers used prefabricated trestling found in the Palermo shipyards; for another, Bailey highway bridging was used, with planking between the rails so trucks as well as trains could use the bridge, and for others, captured timbers were used. On 9 August the railroad was open to a forward railhead at the junction of Highways 117 and 120 near Santo Stefano. In the first five miles beyond this railhead were four demolished bridges; therefore, the engineers made no attempt to extend rail service east of Santo Stefano.[32]

The 540th Engineer Combat Regiment (less one battalion) worked briefly at Palermo, then moved on to operate beaches at Termini Imerese. The 343d Engineer General Service Regiment, whose responsibility for Palermo was also brief, replaced the 540th on 30 July. The 1051st Engineer Port Construction and Repair Group, organized especially for such work, took over the assignment on 11 August. The group's equipment did not arrive for some time, and in the interim it had to use whatever captured equipment it could find.

Italian POWs did most of the work under the 1051st's supervision.[33]

The 1090th Engineer Utilities Company, which arrived in Palermo on 7 August, handled most of the repairs on utilities. The principal project was steam power plants. The unit employed an average of 120 POWs and 100 civilians and used borrowed tools and captured equipment, including two 5,000-kilowatt turbines. A new type of engineer unit, the 1090th had been hastily activated for HUSKY. The company was in Sicily a month before its organizational equipment arrived, and one-third of its men never caught up with the parent unit there.[34]

After its surrender, Sicily became part of the British line of communications in the Mediterranean. The U.S. 6625th Base Area Group (Provisional) handled American interests until Seventh Army units could be shipped out and American installations closed. On 1 September 1943 the 6625th Base Area Group was redesignated Island Base Section (IBS). Operating directly under NATOUSA, IBS supervised the steadily diminishing American activities on the island. The principal engineer task after the campaign ended was replacing bypasses with bridges and culverts in preparation for the fall rains.[35]

___

[32] Seventh Army Rpt Sicily, p. E–15; 1st ESB Rpt of Action Against the Enemy, 10–13 Jul 43; Hist 20th Engr C Bn, 17 May–17 Jun 45.

[33] HQ, Seventh Army, Adm Sitreps 22, 1 Aug 43; 23, 3 Aug 43; and 25, 5 Aug 43; Hist 343d Engr GS Rgt, 1942–45; Interv, Col Dickerson, XO, 1051st Engr PC&R Gp, and Capt Napp, S–3, 540th Engr Shore Rgt, HUSKY—Joss Task Force (8–12 Jul) —Rpt of Observations.
[34] Hist 1090th Engr Utilities Co, 7 Aug–6 Oct 43.
[35] History of Island Base Section, in CMH.

# CHAPTER VIII

# From Salerno to the Volturno

At the TRIDENT Conference in Washington in May 1943, the British and Americans agreed that after Sicily they should undertake further operations in the Mediterranean "calculated to eliminate Italy from the war and to contain maximum German forces."[1] That statement glossed over disagreements between British and Americans about the relative emphasis to be given the Mediterranean, the British insisting that resources should be concentrated there in 1943 while the Americans wanted to prepare for a cross-Channel attack in 1944. As the Allies swept through Sicily, however, growing signs of Italian collapse produced agreement on an immediate invasion of Italy to follow up on the victory in Sicily. On 16 August General Eisenhower decided to move British Eighth Army forces across the Strait of Messina at the earliest opportunity and to launch Lt. Gen. Mark W. Clark's Fifth Army (with a British corps attached) on a major invasion of the Italian mainland on 9 September.

Engineer preparation for the invasion began with the establishment of Fifth Army headquarters on 5 January

1943 at Oujda, French Morocco. The army engineer, Col. Frank O. Bowman, had organized his section on paper a month earlier, but his staff, drawn largely from the American II Corps engineers, was hardly versed in engineer planning at the army level. Bowman provided what direction he could from his experience as the AFHQ engineer in England and in North Africa, but his temporary reassignment from April to August 1943 as SOS, NATO-USA, engineer left the section to Col. Mark M. Boatner, Jr., who presided over the interim work on other proposed invasions in the Mediterranean.

Fifth Army headquarters considered a number of proposals, and the engineers contributed map plans, supply schemes, and terrain studies to nearly all of them. An inherited plan, Operation BACKBONE, called for a foray into Spanish Morocco should Spain change its nominally neutral stance in the war. In the summer of 1943 the engineer staff entered the planning for BRIMSTONE, the invasion and occupation of Sardinia. Several plans involved a thrust into Italy itself, and many of the accumulated concepts coalesced into the final assault plan. BARRACUDA aimed directly at the harbor of Naples, GANG-

---

[1] CCS 242/6, 25 May 43, sub: Final Rpt to President and Prime Minister.

WAY at the beaches immediately north of the city. MUSKET would have brought Fifth Army into Taranto and required a much longer overland campaign to the Italian capital. Operation BAY-TOWN was the British move across the Strait of Messina to Reggio di Calabria. The Combined Chiefs of Staff ruled out BRIMSTONE on 20 July, and after the twenty-seventh the main features of BARRACUDA and GANGWAY were combined into planning for AVA-LANCHE. Through August the Fifth Army staff wrestled with choosing a target for the invasion. General Clark favored the Naples operation for the leverage it would provide in landing slightly farther north and cutting off German forces in southern Italy. With the cooperation of British engineers from 10 Corps, scheduled to make the landing as part of Fifth Army, and with reliance upon American terrain analyses and British Inter-Service Information Series (ISIS) reports, Colonel Bowman formulated his own recommendations, leaving room for the attack near either Naples or Salerno, 150 miles southwest of Rome on the Italian coast. Since Naples lay just outside the extreme range of Allied fighters operating from Sicilian airfields, the beaches at Salerno, just within range, became the primary choice for the assault.[2]

The Salerno beaches had advantages and disadvantages for the invaders. (Map 7) Slightly steeper than those in the Gulf of Naples, they afforded transport craft closer access to the shore. Sand dunes at Salerno were low and narrow and tended to run easily into beach-exit routes. The topography be-

hind the beaches was suited for dispersed supply dumps, and a roadnet close to shore could support forward troop and supply movement. Though there were no clearly organized defensive positions in the area, the mountains behind the beaches formed a natural amphitheater facing the sea. Enemy observation posts would detect any movement below, and artillery fire from the high ground could reach the attacking forces easily. Once ashore, troops would find the way to Naples obstructed by the rugged Sorrento ridge, which sloped out into the sea on the northern arm of the Gulf of Salerno. The actual landing zone was split almost exactly in two by the mouth of the Sele River, which would hinder communication between the two halves of the beachhead until the engineers could bridge the stream.

Enemy strength in the area was considerable. Under the command of *Tenth Army,* German forces were withdrawing from the southern tier of the Italian boot throughout the latter part of August in accordance with rough plans to concentrate a strong defense just south of Rome. The movement accelerated after the British jump into Italy early in September, with the *XIV Panzer Corps,* composed of the reconstituted *Hermann Goering Division,* the *16th Panzer Division,* and the *15th Panzer Grenadier Division,* strung along the Italian west coast from Salerno north to Gaeta.

Recognizing that the Salerno beaches were suitable for an Allied incursion, the *16th Panzer Division's* engineers in the area emplaced mines and beach obstacles along the dunes from Salerno to Agropoli, at the southern extent of the bay—but not so extensively as might

---

[2] *Engineer History, Mediterranean,* pp. 3–4.

ITALY INVASION PLANS

Planned

Planned & executed

0    75    150 Miles

0    75    150 Kilometers

CORSICA

Rome

ITALY

Gaeta

Naples

Ischia    Salerno

SARDINIA    Capri    Agropoli

GANGWAY
BARRACUDA

AVALANCHE
5TH ARMY

Bari

Brindisi

Taranto

Crotone

Pizzo

BRIMSTONE
(BRITISH)

Messina

MUSKET
5TH ARMY

Palermo    Reggio di
Calabria

SICILY    BAYTOWN
(BRITISH)

Bizerte    Syracuse

Cassibile

TUNISIA    Tunis

MAP 7

have been expected. The Germans, regarding the Italian will to fight as negligible amid rumors of imminent defection, took over the coastal defenses of the Salerno area, executing the protesting commander of an Italian division in the process. They supplemented local batteries with their own heavy pieces in the mountains behind the beaches, especially on the imposing 3,566-foot Monte Soprana. They also emplaced a series of strongpoints in the foothills fronting the sea, with a particularly heavy concentration back of the southern complex of beaches in the area eventually chosen for the VI Corps attack. Panzer forces were expected to support these points with mobile counterassaults and supplementary fire. An Italian minefield offshore completed the defenses of the beaches.[3]

[3] Martin Blumenson, *Salerno to Cassino*, United States Army in World War II (Washington, 1969), p. 67; Morison, *Sicily-Salerno-Anzio*, p. 260.

Unit assignments for the invasion force continued all summer. In the final operation plan of 26 August, the American VI Corps, with five divisions, was to seize the right-hand half of the landing zone south of the Sele River around the Roman ruin of Paestum while the British 10 Corps assaulted the northern half of the beachhead closer to the town of Salerno. All veterans of the theater, the 3d, 34th, 36th, and 45th Infantry Divisions would accompany the 1st Armored and 82d Airborne Divisions. Apart from the support provided for the invasion, each division had its assigned organic engineer battalion, the 10th Engineer Battalion with the 3d Division, the 109th with the 34th Division, the 111th with the 36th, and the 120th with the 45th; the 1st Armored Division had the services of the 16th Armored Engineer Battalion, and the airborne division had the 307th Airborne Engineer Battalion. As one of the most practiced units in amphibious attacks, the 36th Infantry Division was assigned the actual beach assault. The division's 141st Infantry Regiment was on the extreme right, landing on Yellow and Blue beaches, where a medieval stone tower at Paestum afforded a good point of reference for incoming boats. The 142d Infantry, to land on Red and Green beaches to the left of the 141st, covered the area north to an artificial waterway, the Fiumarello Canal; the two regiments were assaulting an expanse of 3,740 yards of contiguous beach front.

A Navy beachmaster was to maintain all communications with the ships and control all the operational landings. A port headquarters, consisting of two Transportation Corps port battalions, was to coordinate all unloading into small craft offshore, but the pivot of beach supply operations was the 531st Engineer Shore Regiment and the 540th Engineer Combat Regiment, the former assuming responsibility during the assault phase. The 531st, a component of the 1st Engineer Special Brigade for the invasion, replaced the 343d Engineer General Service Regiment, which was trained in beach support operations but had neither the experience nor the equipment to carry out this function. Alerted in Sicily only two weeks before the invasion, the 531st traveled to Oran, the staging area for part of the invasion force, while the 540th reported to the assembly area of the 45th Infantry Division around Palermo. Neither regiment participated in the planning for the invasion, nor did their officers see the maps for the operation or the stowage plans for the vessels to be unloaded off the beaches; for the most part, they saw the troops they were supporting for the first time on the sand under German fire.[4]

In other respects engineer preparations for the Salerno invasion were more thorough. Fifth Army and NATOUSA engineers requisitioned supplies, trained engineer troops, analyzed terrain, and produced detailed maps. After the final selection of the Salerno site the engineer mapping subsection, Fifth Army, studied in detail the terrain of the region, its ridge and drainage systems, communications, water supply, ports, and beaches. These studies gave the engineers vital information for annotating maps.

---

[4] *Engineer History, Mediterranean*, p. 5; Hist 531st Engr Shore Rgt, 29 Nov 42–Apr 45; AGF Bd Rpts, NATOUSA, 15 Nov 43; Interv, Brig Gen George W. Gardes, 5 Nov 59.

Planning for engineer supply at Salerno rested ultimately with the engineer of SOS, NATOUSA. On 25 July Maj. Irving W. Finberg, chief of the Fifth Army Engineer Supply Section, reported to the SOS engineer as Fifth Army liaison officer to prepare requisitions covering the estimated needs of Fifth Army engineers. Within two weeks Finberg submitted the basic requirements. Wherever possible, his listing became the basis for freeze orders on SOS, NATOUSA, stocks in North Africa, which eventually reserved 10,545 long tons of engineer supply for the invasion. Base section depots reported items not available in the theater pipeline, and units in the theater not scheduled for the forthcoming operation gave supplies and equipment to units going into the assault. The SOS, NATOUSA, command made up shortages by ordering critical items directly from the New York Port of Embarkation, requisitions amounting to 3,638 long tons. Confusion still reigned in some quarters, especially since engineer, quartermaster, and ordnance supply was intermixed in theater stocks, and inadequate inventory procedures frequently led to ordering materiel already on hand but unidentified.[5]

As the supply planning and acquisition proceeded, Fifth Army operated eight training schools. At Port-aux-Poules, near Arzew in Algeria, Brig. Gen. John W. O'Daniel opened the Fifth Army Invasion Training Center on 14 January 1943. Relieved of its function in Sicily late in the summer, the 1st Engineer Special Brigade practiced combined operations with naval units and coordinated air cover over beach areas serving the center. The 17th Armored Engineer Battalion, the 334th Engineer Combat Battalion, the 540th and 39th Engineer Combat Regiments, and two separate engineer battalions, the 378th and the 384th, took part in training exercises with live fire, the object being to make men battle-wise in the shortest possible time. Outside the center, elements of the 16th Armored Engineer Battalion, the 109th Engineer Combat Battalion, and the 1st Engineer Special Brigade headquarters had joint and combined training in beach operations which included mine-clearing work. The 16th Armored Engineer Battalion also ran two mine schools at Ste.-Barbe-du-Tlelat for the men of the 1st Armored Division and organized its own refreshers in infantry tactics, bridging, and field fortifications.

A separate engineer training center opened on 12 March 1943, near Ain Fritissa in French Morocco at an abandoned French Foreign Legion fort. Under Lt. Col. Aaron A. Wyatt, Jr., the school concentrated on practical work under simulated battle conditions. British Eighth Army instructors taught mine and countermine warfare. The final problem, usually undertaken at night, split the students into two groups, one of which planted mines for the second to unearth. Though the mines employed were training devices with only igniter fuses attached, several live and armed standard charges were interspersed with the dummies. As the engineer students struggled in the darkness, assembled tanks and infantry fired 37-mm. shells and automatic and small-arms rounds overhead, and instructors stationed in towers detonated buried artillery shells on the field. By the time

---

[5] *Logistical History of NATOUSA-MTOUSA*, p. 58.

of the invasion over a thousand officers and noncoms had completed the courses at the engineer center, with twenty-seven casualties and one fatality during the exercises.

An adjunct to the center was a research and development staff that investigated and tested new mechanical mine-clearing devices such as the Scorpion flail as it became available from British sources. As soon as they appeared in the theater, the German Schu mines were also the object of the staff's attention. Though the center operated with unqualified success, it labored constantly under the disadvantages of being an ad hoc organization with no standard organization tables. Originally blessed with one armored engineer company and four combat engineer companies as demonstration units, Colonel Wyatt could rarely keep on hand enough veteran technicians in mine warfare and never had enough transportation.

The engineers produced maps and charts by the thousands for the American invasion force. Originally relying on existing small-scale charts on hand, some of foreign manufacture, the mapmakers found their enlargements poor. Urgent requisitions for new maps scaled at the standard 1:25,000, 1:50,000, 1:100,000, and 1:250,000 soon supplied adequate coverage for nearly the whole of the south-central Italian peninsula from the latitude of Salerno to that of Anzio. Larger scale maps, 1:500,000 and 1:1,000,000, covered the area north of Rome. Finally the engineers obtained detailed road maps of the Naples area and beach defense overlays for Salerno which gave annotated legends for points of concealment, lines of communications, water supply, and

ridge lines in the immediate area of assault. A single map unit, the 2699th Engineer Map Depot Detachment (Provisional), attached to the 531st Engineer Shore Regiment for the operation, spent most of the time before the invasion virtually imprisoned in a large garage in Oran while it packed 1:50,000 and 1:1,000,000 maps, fifty to the sealed roll. The map depot detachment carried enough maps into the invasion to resupply each combat unit with 100 percent of its original issue.

Amphibious exercises in the two weeks before the invasion suffered from too little realism. In COW-PUNCHER, run from 26 to 29 August, the 36th Infantry Division acted as attacker at Port-aux-Poules and Arzew against the defending 34th Infantry Division. Loath to expose vessels to enemy submarine attacks during the exercise, the Navy could not support the rehearsal in detail, and only a token unloading of vehicles, supply, and munitions over the beaches was possible. On 29 August Company I, 531st Engineer Shore Regiment, demonstrated beach organization procedure to 1,000 sailors; three days later Company H participated in a simulated beach exercise with the Navy, but no small boats were used. On Sicily, the 45th Infantry Division staged one rehearsal for the coming landing.

*The Invasion*

On 3 September the British Eighth Army struck across the Strait of Messina, and the long and bitter Italian campaign was under way. On 5 September the first of the invasion convoys for AVALANCHE left Oran and Mers-el-Kebir, and at precisely scheduled intervals thereafter, convoys moved out of other ports in North Africa and Sicily. They came together north of Palermo and converged on the Gulf of Salerno during the evening of 8 September. Aboard were the U.S. VI Corps' 36th Division, the British 10 Corps' 46th and 56th Divisions, three battalions of American Rangers and two of British commandos, and a floating reserve, the American 45th Division less one regimental combat team. The 141st had the southern Yellow and Blue beaches as assault targets; the 142d was to take the northern Red and Green beaches on the left, closer to the Fiumarello Canal. *(Map 8)*

Fortune seemed to favor the landings. As the convoys approached the mainland under air cover, the ships' radios picked up the voice of General Eisenhower declaring that "hostilities between the United Nations and Italy have terminated, effective at once." When the assault began shortly before 0330 on 9 September, the weather was good, the sea was calm, and the moon had set. As the first wave of LCVPs carrying VI Corps' troops grounded south of the Sele River, the men saw flashes of gunfire to the north where the British were landing, but their own beaches were dark and silent. Then, as they were leaving their craft and making their way ashore through the shallows, flares suddenly illuminated the shoreline, machine-gun and mortar fire erupted from the dunes, and from the arc of hills enclosing the coastal plain artillery shells rained down.

The heaviest concentration of German fire fell on the southernmost beaches, Yellow and Blue. The 3d Battalion of the 531st Engineer Shore Regiment, coming in on the second wave in support of the 141st Infantry, was unable to land on Yellow and had to turn to Blue, where things were not much better. No boats could land on Blue after daybreak, and for most of the day the engineer battalion's Company I was pinned down. At one time the company's command post was only 300 yards from a point where the infantry was fending off a German attack.

The regiment's 2d Battalion, supporting the 142d Infantry, was able to land on Red and Green beaches. The unit suffered several casualties but reported at 0530 that Red Beach was ready for traffic. Landing craft and DUKWs floundering offshore converged on Red, but the concentration drew heavy artillery fire that knocked many of them out. The disruption made it impossible to open any of the beaches for several hours; much of the engineers' equipment was scattered or sunk, and the mine-clearing and construction crews could not land as units. The delay in opening the beaches, as well as enemy fire on boat lanes, prevented VI Corps from landing tanks and artillery before daylight, as had been planned.

At daylight another menace appeared. A German tank came down to the shore between Yellow and Blue beaches and fired on each landing craft that approached. More enemy tanks began firing from the main road behind the dunes. The landing parties, without tanks and heavy artillery, had to repel the Germans with 40-mm. antiaircraft guns, 105-mm. howitzers, and bazookas, an effort in which the engineers of the 531st played an important part. When five Mark IV tanks tried to break through to Blue Beach, seven engineers of Company I helped to repel them with bazookas. At Yellow Beach, where

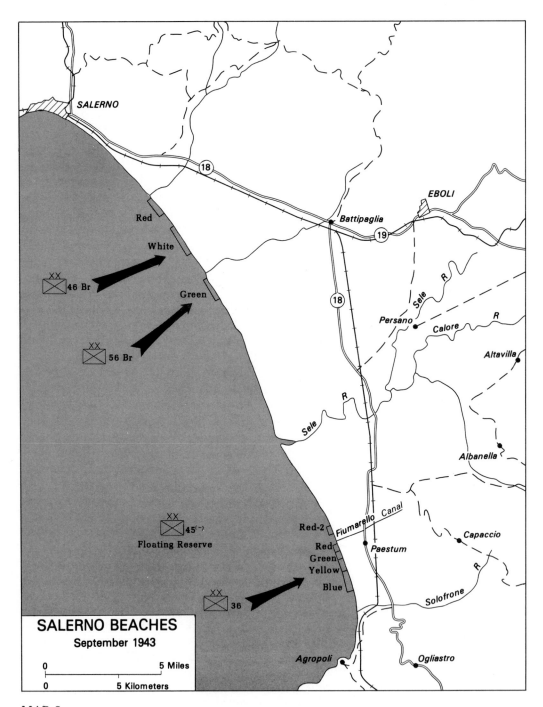

SALERNO BEACHES
September 1943

SALERNO

18

EBOLI

Red

White

46 Br

Green

56 Br

Battipaglia

19

18

Persano

Sele R.

Calore R.

Altavilla

45 (–)
Floating Reserve

Albanella

Red-2

Red
Green
Yellow

36

Blue

Fiumarello Canal

Paestum

Sele R.

Capaccio

Solofrone R.

Agropoli

Ogliastro

0      5 Miles
0      5 Kilometers

*MAP 8*

DUKWS HEAD FOR THE SALERNO BEACHES

40-mm. antiaircraft guns and 105-mm. howitzers had been hastily set up at the water's edge, a bulldozer operator of Company H, T/5 Charles E. Harris, pulled the guns into position in the dune line. He was wounded by machine-gun fire from a German tank but continued to operate his bulldozer until it went out of action. On all the beaches the big bulldozers were easy targets, their operators working under constant fire.

The first beaches open were Red and Green. Not until shortly after noon were landing craft discharging at Yellow, while Blue remained closed most of the afternoon. By nightfall all were in operation, and tanks, tank destroyers, and heavy artillery were landing and moving out of the beachhead. The engineers cut through wire obstructions, laid steel matting, and improved exit roads, while the 36th Division's infantry regiments advanced inland. That night two companies of the 36th Engineer Combat Regiment, landing on D-day as part of 36th Division's infantry reserve, served as a screen against armor along the Sele River.[6]

Next morning German planes came over Red Beach and dropped a bomb squarely on the command post of the 531st Engineers' 2d Battalion, killing

---

[6] Hist 531st Engr Shore Rgt, 29 Nov 42–Apr 45; 2d Bn, 20 Aug–30 Sep 43; 3d Bn, 20 Aug–30 Sep 43; Comments of Brig Gen George W. Gardes, Incl to Ltr, Gardes to Jesse A. Remington, 8 Dec 59.

LSTs and Auxiliary Ships Unload Men and Supply at Salerno

two officers and seriously wounding two others. Artillery shells also fell on the beachhead, but there was no ground fighting in the American sector near Paestum on 10 or 11 September. The Germans were concentrating their forces in the north against the British 10 Corps.

General Clark became concerned about a group of American Rangers that had landed on the west flank of 10 Corps on the Sorrento peninsula between the tiny ports of Amalfi and Maiori to help the British secure the mountain passes leading to Naples. On Clark's orders a task force built around an infantry battalion moved by sea from the VI Corps' beaches to support the Rangers. Aboard the eighteen landing craft that started north on 11 September were two companies of engineers, one from the 36th Engineer Combat Regiment and the other from the 540th Engineer Combat Regiment, the latter having landed with the 45th Division on D plus 1.[7]

The bulk of the 540th pitched in to aid the 531st in organizing the beaches. Goods of all description crowded the shoreline, barracks bags accumulated on the narrow beachhead, and the congestion finally forced the closing of Red and Green beaches. Unsorted stacks of ammunition, gas, food, water, and

---

[7] Gardes comments, 8 Dec 59; Hist 540th Engr C Rgt, 11 Sep 42–15 Feb 45.

equipment extended seaward into several feet of water, while ships offshore could not unload. This situation improved somewhat after a new beach, Red 2, opened to the left of Red Beach and north of the Fiumarello Canal.[8]

Naval officers criticized engineer operation of the beaches and attributed traffic jams to poor beach exits and the failure of some engineers to make adequate arrangements to transfer supplies from the beaches to dispersal areas farther inland. A major Navy complaint was that Navy boat crews had to do most of the unloading with little assistance from the engineers, whose responsibility it was. The Navy beachmaster estimated that during the assault phase Navy crews unloaded or beached 90 percent of the supplies and equipment.[9]

In fact, the beach engineers could not possibly have handled all the tonnage that came to the beaches during the assault phase. Combat units and equipment grew out of all proportion to service troops. The 531st went ashore on the morning of D-day more than 200 men understrength and soon was weakened further by casualties. To assist the 531st in unloading, setting up dumps, maintaining roads, and clearing minefields, a battalion of the 337th Engineer General Service Regiment, a Fifth Army unit, landed on Red Beach at 1630 but could accomplish little because its equipment did not come in for several days. Both the 531st and the 540th Engineer Regiments arrived short of

equipment, notably mine detectors and trucks. Few engineer supplies began arriving before D plus 1, and most of what came in was not what was most wanted. The first engineer supply item ashore was a forty-gallon fire extinguisher, while other items landed early were sandbags, lumber, and tools. Later, a few cranes came in. Once ashore, the two regiments felt they did not get enough information from the Navy beachmaster as to what LSTs or cargoes were arriving and where they would land. As in TORCH and HUSKY, the line between Army and Navy responsibility remained vague.[10]

The Fifth Army engineer, Colonel Bowman, came ashore on D plus 1 and set out in a jeep to find a suitable place for the army command post. He turned north from the congested beachhead, and near the juncture of the Sele and Calore Rivers, not far from the boundary between VI Corps and 10 Corps, he found the house of Baron Roberto Ricciardi, set in a lovely Italian garden.

In the next three days, the sound of artillery fire in the north, where the Germans were concentrating against 10 Corps, came close; and it was in this sector between the two corps that engineer troops first manned frontline positions. On a warning from General Clark that a German counterattack might hit the north flank, the VI Corps commander, Maj. Gen. Ernest J. Dawley, reinforced two regiments of the 45th Division with the 3d Battalion of the 36th Engineer Combat Regiment. The

---

[8] VI Corps Hist Record, Sep 43; WNTF Action Rpt of Salerno Landing, Sep–Oct 43, p. 152; AGF Bd Rpt 279, MTO, 24 Jan 45.
[9] WNTF Action Rpt of Salerno Landings, pp. 151–52; Morison, *Sicily-Salerno-Anzio*, pp. 264, 269.

[10] Rpt of SOS Observer of Opn AVALANCHE, 9–21 Sep 43, SOS NATOUSA; Rpt, HQ, 1st ESB, to CG, NATOUSA, 29 Oct 43, sub: Operation of Shore Engineers, Italy; *Engineer History, Mediterranean*, pp. 18, 19.

engineers moved into the line a few miles north of the Sele River shortly after midnight on 12 September, along with a battery of 105-mm. howitzers; by dawn they were in contact with British 10 Corps patrols. At 1000 the division launched an attack. The Germans counterattacked with tanks and artillery, killing two engineer officers, and by dusk had infiltrated and cut off a forward body of engineers that included the battalion commander. The engineer regimental commander, Lt. Col. George W. Gardes, took over the battalion. Before daybreak on 13 September the battalion attained its objective, which turned out to have been one of the strongpoints of the German defense system.[11]

During 12 September German fire increased in the American sector and an enemy attack dislodged a 36th Division battalion from its position on hills near Altavilla, south of the Calore River. The increased German pressure resulted from the reinforcement of the *16th Panzer Division*, which had borne the full force of the invasion, by the *29th Panzer Division*, moving up from Calabria. Not only divisional engineers of the 111th Engineer Combat Battalion but also corps and even army engineers bolstered 36th Division defenses. On 13 September two battalions of the 531st Engineer Shore Regiment were called off beach work for combat. One went inland to act as reserve, the other took up defensive positions on high ground south and southeast of the beachhead.[12]

The situation worsened during the day, indicating that the Germans were

trying to break through to the beachhead, and the 36th Engineer Combat Regiment had to furnish another battalion to act as infantry. Moving out at midnight, the regiment's 2d Battalion occupied high ground along the south bank of the Calore River astride a road leading into the beachhead from Altavilla. This position came under heavy artillery fire throughout 14 and 15 September, and tank and infantry attacks also menaced it. On the afternoon of 14 September German tanks clanked over a stone bridge spanning the Calore and began to move up a narrow, one-way road winding toward the engineers' position. The engineers were ready for them. From a quarry recessed into the hillside, they fired a 37-mm. cannon and a .50-caliber machine gun point-blank at the lead tank, knocking it out to form a roadblock in front of the following tanks, which then withdrew under American artillery fire. The next afternoon the engineers saw German infantrymen getting off trucks on the north side of the river, apparently readying for an attack. The engineers brought the German infantry under fire, inflicting observed losses.

In the 45th Division sector north of the Sele River, a tank-infantry attack hit the 3d Battalion, 36th Engineers, on 14 September. German tanks overran part of one company's position, but the engineers stayed in their foxholes and stopped the following infantry while U.S. tank destroyers engaged the tanks. Another company of the 3d Battalion stopped a Mark IV tank with bazookas and that night captured a German scout car and took three prisoners. During the day the battalion was reinforced by part of the 45th Division's 120th Engineer Combat Battalion, all

[11] Gardes comments, 8 Dec 59.
[12] Hist 531st Engr Shore Rgt, 29 Nov 42–Apr 45.

of which had operated as infantry since 13 September.[13]

General Clark, who had hastily moved Colonel Bowman's command post to the rear, was so concerned about a German breakthrough to the beachhead that at one point on 13 September he contemplated a withdrawal to the 10 Corps' zone. But the lines held long enough for reinforcements to come from Sicily. Parachute troops of the 82d Airborne Division, dropped on the beachhead in the early hours of 14 September and trucked to the southern flank, turned the tide. When the 3d Infantry Division began landing from LSTs on the morning of 18 September the enemy was withdrawing.[14]

Plans for the advance beyond Salerno were determined at a conference General Clark called on 18 September. Naples on the west coast, one of the two prime objectives, was to be the target of Fifth Army; the other objective, the airfields around Foggia near the east coast, was to be the target of General Montgomery's Eighth Army, which by 18 September was in a position·to move abreast of Fifth Army up the Italian peninsula. In the Fifth Army effort, 10 Corps was to move north along the coast to capture Naples and drive to the Volturno River twenty-five miles beyond while VI Corps made a wide flanking movement through the mountains to protect the 10 Corps advance.

## A Campaign of Bridges

In addition to active German resis-

tance, terrain was a principal obstacle in the flank march that opened on 20 September. Maj. Gen. John P. Lucas took over the VI Corps advance just as it started, arraying the 3d Division on the left and the 45th on the right, but found his troops entirely roadbound. Italian terrain was far worse for military maneuver than that in Sicily; cross-country movement was next to impossible, not only over mountain heights but even in the valleys, where vehicles were likely to be stopped by stone walls, irrigation ditches, or German mines. The enemy had blown all the bridges carrying roadbeds over the numerous gullies, ravines, and streams. Forward movement in Italy became for the engineers a campaign of bridges.

According to policies Colonel Bowman laid down, divisional engineers were to get the troops across streams any way they could: bypasses when possible, fills when culverts had been blown, or Bailey bridging. Corps engineers were to follow up, replacing the small fills with culverts and the bypasses with Bailey bridges. Army engineers were to replace the larger culverts and the Baileys with fixed pile bridges. All bridges were to be two-way, Class 40 structures.

Even veteran units had rough going. The 10th Engineer Combat Battalion, supporting the 3d Division in the advance to the Volturno, was the battalion that had built the "bridge in the sky" in Sicily. The divisional engineers of the 45th Division, the 120th Engineer Combat Battalion, had also had hard service in the mountains during the Sicily campaign. The corps engineers behind them came from the 36th Engineer Combat Regiment, which had distinguished itself in the defense of

---

[13] Gardes comments, 8 Dec 59; *Engineer History, Mediterranean,* pp. 20, 22.

[14] Donald G. Taggart, ed., *History of the Third Infantry Division in World War II* (Washington: Infantry Journal Press, 1947), p. 80.

the beachhead. Yet it took these experienced, battle-hardened engineers ten days to get the troops sixty miles over the mountains to the first major VI Corps objective, Avellino, a town about twenty-five miles east of Naples on the Naples-Foggia road.

The Germans had blown nearly every bridge and culvert, made abatis of tree trunks, sown mines, and emplaced booby traps. Demolitions, shelling, and bombing had cratered road surfaces. In the towns, rubble from destroyed stone buildings blocked traffic. But the weather was still good, so engineers could bulldoze bypasses around obstructions. "There was no weapon more valuable than the engineer bulldozer," General Truscott attested, "no soldiers more effective than the engineers who moved us forward." Bypasses around blown bridges saved the time required to bring up bridging. In the advance to the Volturno the 10th Engineer Combat Battalion constructed sixty-nine bypasses but only a few timber and Bailey bridges.[15]

The Bailey seemed made for the steep-banked, swiftly flowing rivers and the narrow gorges of the Italian countryside. It could be launched from one side or bank without intermediate supports. In the early phase of the Italian campaign the Germans did not comprehend its potential, so they were satisfied with destroying only parts of long bridges instead of all the spans and piers. The engineers quickly used those parts left standing to throw a Bailey over a stream or ravine.[16]

The Bailey became all the more essential when the engineers discovered that timber for wooden bridges was scarce, at times as much as seventy-five miles distant. Yet the supply of Baileys was woefully inadequate. The 36th Engineer Combat Regiment built more than eighty bridges and sizable culverts between the breakout at Salerno and the end of December but during that time received only three Baileys.[17] In the first month after the landings, the Fifth Army engineers had only five sets of the much sought after 120-foot double-double Baileys.

One major reason for the shortage of bridging in this early stage of the Italian campaign was a faulty estimate by planners at AFHQ. They had foreseen that highway destruction would be tremendous, had assumed that the enemy would demolish all bridges, and had figured that an average of thirty feet of bridging per mile of main road would be required. But the estimate did not take into account the secondary roads that had to be used to support the offensive.[18]

A shortage of bridge-building material and heavy equipment also hampered the work of engineers building a bridge over the Sele River to carry Highway 18 traffic northward from the beachhead to Avellino. This bridge was crucial because the beaches continued to be the main source of supplies for Fifth Army for a considerable time after Naples fell.

A company of the 16th Armored Engineer Battalion put in the first bridge over the Sele, a floating treadway, on 10 September. It was replaced the fol-

[15] *Engineer History, Mediterranean,* p. 25; Truscott, *Command Missions,* p. 259.

[16] VI Corps Hist Record, Sep 43, The Mounting of AVALANCHE, p. 14; Chf Engr, 15th Army Gp, Notes on Engr Opns in Italy, no. 6, 1 Jan 44.

[17] Gardes comments, 8 Dec 59.

[18] *Engineer History, Mediterranean,* p. 10.

lowing day by a 120-foot trestle tread-way to carry forty-ton loads. During 12 and 13 September a battalion of the 36th Engineer Combat Regiment emplaced two more floating bridges, and on 22 September the 337th Engineer General Service Regiment began building the first fixed bridge the U.S. Army constructed in Italy over the Sele. It was of trestle bent construction, 16 spans, and 240 feet long. In spite of the equipment shortage, the job was completed by 28 September.[19]

However, the bridge was undermined by the shifting sands of the river bottom and from the start required constant maintenance. When heavy rains fell early in October, making a rushing torrent of the normally sluggish Sele, the bridge went out. The 531st Engineer Shore Regiment altered the railroad bridge over the Sele to take trucks so that the vital supply line would not be interrupted. Then they repaired the road bridge by driving piling through the floor and jacking the bridge up and onto the new pile bents. After this experience, engineers abandoned trestle construction in favor of pile bridges. In the construction of a 100-foot pilebent bridge about halfway between Salerno and Avellino, near Fisciano, the engineers of the 531st improvised a pile driver, using the barrel of a German 155-mm. gun and a D-4 tractor.[20]

## Naples

When Naples fell on 1 October 1943,

Fifth Army's supply situation was deteriorating rapidly. Truck hauls from the Salerno beaches were becoming longer and more difficult. Unloadings over the Salerno beaches were at the mercy of the elements, and the elements had just struck a blow for the enemy. A violent storm that blew up on 28 September halted unloading for 2 1/2 days and wrecked a large number of landing craft and ponton ramps. Supplies dwindled. On 6 October the army had only three days' supply of gasoline, and during the first half of October issues of Class I and Class III supplies from army dumps outstripped receipts. The early reconstruction of Naples and of transportation lines was of prime importance.[21]

Naples, with a natural deepwater harbor, was the second ranking port in Italy and had a normal discharge capacity of 8,000 tons per day.[22] The water alongside most of its piers and quays was thirty feet deep or more, enough to accommodate fully loaded Liberty ships. There was virtually no tide; the water level varied only a foot or two, a result of wind swell as much as tidal action.

Naples was the most damaged port U.S. Army engineers had yet encountered during the war. Allied aerial bombardment had probably caused one-third to one-half the destruction in the port area and more than half that in the POL tank farm and refinery areas. Carefully planned German demolition had been effective. Damage to the quays

---

[19] Ibid., pp. 12, 13, 20, 22; Hist of Activities of the 337th GS Rgt with the Fifth Army in Italy, 9 Sep 43–1 Nov 44.
[20] Interv, Shotwell with Brig Gen Frank O. Bowman, 19 Jan 51; Hist 531st Engr Shore Rgt, 29 Nov 42–Apr 45.

[21] *Fifth Army History*, vol. I, p. 66.
[22] Except as otherwise noted, this section on Naples is based on Rpt on Rehabilitation of Naples and Other Captured Ports, by Col Percival A. Wakeman et al., 28 Nov 43.

and piers was slight, for they were built of huge blocks of masonry and not easily demolished. Most of the damage to them came incidentally from demolitions that destroyed pier cranes and other port-operating equipment. The Germans had directed their destruction toward cargo-handling equipment, and they blocked the waters with every piece of once-floating equipment available. When Fifth Army troops entered the city, thirty-two large ships and several hundred smaller craft lay sunk in Naples harbor, blocking fifty-eight of the sixty-one berths available and cutting the normal capacity of the port by 90 percent.[23]

On the land side, a wall of debris isolated the dock area from the rest of the city; Allied bombing and German demolitions had destroyed most of the buildings near the docks. Only steel reinforced buildings stood, and most of them were badly damaged and littered with debris. The enemy destroyed all of some 300 cranes in the port area; in many cases the demolition charges were placed so as to tip the structure into the waters alongside the quays. Tons of rubble from nearby buildings were also blown into the water to block access to the quays.[24]

Despite the widespread destruction, engineer and survey parties had reasons for optimism. Sea mines were found only in the outer harbor. Also, the enemy had sunk ships adjacent to the quays or randomly about the harbor, not in the entrance channels where

they could have denied the Allies use of the port for weeks, perhaps months.

Within the city debris blocked several streets. Rails and bridges on the main lines had been systematically destroyed. Ties and ballast, on the other hand, were generally undisturbed in Naples itself. Most of the large public buildings were either demolished or gutted by fire, and others were mined with time-delay charges. Large industrial buildings and manufacturing plants generally were prepared for demolitions, but most charges had not been fired. No booby traps were found in the harbor area and not a great many throughout the city.

Public utilities—electricity, water, sewage—were all disrupted. With the great Serino aqueducts cut in several places, the city had been without water for several days, for most of the wells within the city had long since been condemned and plugged. The only electricity immediately available came from generators Allied units brought in. Local generating stations were damaged, and transmission lines from the principal source of power, a hydroelectric plant fifty miles south of Naples, were down. The distribution system within the city was also damaged, and demolitions had blocked much of the sewer system.

Fifth Army engineer units entering the city from the land side started clearing debris from the port. Detachments of the 111th Engineer Combat Battalion (divisional engineers of the 36th Division) went to work clearing a road around the harbor. The 540th Engineer Combat Regiment, bivouacking in a city park overlooking the Bay of Naples, had the job of clearing the harbor. With dynamite, bulldozer, torch, crane,

---

[23] PBS, Public Relations Sect, *Tools of War: An Illustrated History of the Peninsular Base Section* (Leghorn, Italy, 1946); *Fifth Army History*, vol. II, p. 66.

[24] History of Restoration of Port of Naples, 1051st Engr Port Construction and Repair Gp, 10 Dec 43, Engr Sch Lib.

and shovel, the men of the 540th filled craters, hacked roads through debris, cleared docks, and leveled buildings. Within twenty-four hours the harbor was receiving LSTs and LCTs, and exit roads were making it possible for DUKWs to bring cargoes inland from Liberty ships in the bay.[25] The 1051st Engineer Port Construction and Repair Group, attached to the Fifth Army Base Section, arrived on 2 October but could do little more than survey the chaos until base engineer troops came on the scene.

The engineers working on the docks undertook their tasks in three phases. The first, based on quick estimates, was the clearing of debris to provide access to those berths not blocked by sunken ships. The second involved expedient construction, and this the engineers undertook after a reasonably comprehensive survey made it feasible to plan for future activities. The third phase, reconstruction, involved more time-consuming projects that started only after the possibilities of providing facilities by expedient construction had been exhausted.

The first phase, which occurred from 3 to 5 October, was the most critical one. Since demands for berthing and unloading space were urgent, there was no time for deliberate, planned activity. All available army and base section engineers and equipment had to be committed against obstacles blocking the initial unloading points. Navy salvage units, equipped with small naval salvage vessels and aided by Royal Navy salvage units with heavy lifting equipment, entered the harbor on 4 October to locate ships and craft that obstructed berthing space. Coordinating with the naval units, the 1051st Engineer Port Construction and Repair Group surveyed landward obstructions.

Although only 3 1/2 Liberty berths were available on 7 October, berthing space grew rapidly with the expedient construction. On 16 October, 6,236 tons of cargo came ashore, a figure that included 263 vehicles. By the end of the month 13 1/2 Liberty berths and 6 coaster berths were available for use (the goal set early in October was 15 Liberty berths and 5 coaster berths by 1 November). The most urgent requirements had been met, and supplies in the dumps amounted to 3,049 tons.

Ramps of standard naval pontons, laid two units wide, were built far enough out into the harbor to accommodate Liberty ships. These ramps were easy to build and feasible enough in tideless waters, but they were too narrow for cargo and were used only for unloading vehicles. More widely used were steel and timber ramps which engineers were able to construct across the decks of sunken ships alongside the piers. These ramps became the trademark of the engineers in the rehabilitation of Naples.

All but two of the large ships blocking the piers were too badly damaged to patch and float aside immediately; but most of them lay alongside the quays, with their decks above or just below the surface of the water. When engineers cleared away the superstructures and built timber and steel ramps across the decks, Liberty ships could tie up alongside the sunken hulks and unload directly onto trucks on the ramps. As a rule T-shaped ramps ten to fifteen feet wide were built at each berth and spaced

---

[25] Hist 540th Engr C Rgt, 11 Sep 42–15 Feb 45.

DECKING PLACED OVER SUNKEN VESSELS *to enable loading in Naples harbor.*

to correspond with the five hatches of a Liberty ship. The head of the T was twenty to twenty-five feet long, allowing room on the ramp for temporary cargo storage and for variations in the spacing of hatches on individual ships. At first these ramps went out only over ships sunk on an even keel; later they were built on ships that lay on their sides or at an angle to the quay. Eventually engineers filled the spaces between the ramps with decking to provide more working room.

Another improvisation made the larger of two dry docks into a Liberty berth. The caisson-type gates had been damaged and two ships lay inside the dock. Leaks in the gate were sealed with tremie concrete, which cures under water, and the ships were braced to the sides of the dock. The basin was then emptied so the ships could be patched. Since the walls of the docks were not perpendicular, steel scaffolding had to be built out over the stepped masonry walls and covered with timber decking. After the ships were refloated and pulled away, both sides of a Liberty ship could be unloaded at the same time in the dry dock. The smaller dry dock was used for ship repairs once a sunken destroyer had been patched and floated out.

At the foot of one pier a cargo vessel lay sunk with one side extending eight to ten feet above water. The vessel was flat bottomed, so a Liberty ship could come in close alongside. Engineers built a working platform on the ship with a bridge connecting to the pier. At another pier, where a large hospital ship lay sunk with its masts and funnels resting against the quays, walkways and steps leading across the hulk and down to the pier made a berth for discharging personnel.

Clearing away underwater debris also released berthing space. Floating and land-based cranes removed debris along the piers and quays, while port construction and repair group divers went down to cut loose sunken cranes and other steel equipment.

### Peninsular Base

With the arrival of more service troops from North Africa, the Fifth Army Base Section assumed more responsibility for supply in the army's rear. Through summer 1943, Fifth Army's support organization was only a skeleton, designated 6665th Base Area Group (Provisional) and modeled after the NATOUSA Atlantic Base Section. It changed its provisional character and its name to the full-fledged Fifth Army Base Section on 28 August. Under Brig. Gen. Arthur W. Pence, an advance echelon accompanied Fifth Army headquarters to Italy, landing at Salerno on D plus 2. General Pence established his headquarters at Naples the day after the city was captured, and on 25 October his command became the Peninsular Base Section, with its Engineer Service under Col. Donald S. Burns.[26]

By 10 October the first full-sized con-

GENERAL PENCE

voy brought the 345th Engineer General Service Regiment to the base section. The Base Section Engineer Service also had at its disposal the 540th Engineer Combat Regiment, two engineer general service regiments (the 345th and 94th), the 386th Engineer Battalion (Separate), one company of a water supply battalion (attached from Fifth Army), an engineer port construction and repair group, an engineer maintenance company, a depot company, and a map depot detachment—in all, about 6,000 engineers.[27]

Colonel Burns ran all engineer functions in the base section area, was re-

---

[26] History of the Peninsular Base Section, North African Theater of Operations, 9 Jul 43–1 May 44, vol. I, pp. 6–8.

[27] Ltr, Pence to Truesdell, 26 Nov 43, sub: Organization of PBS; Hist PBS, 28 May 44; Hist of the PBS, Phases II and III, 28 Aug 43–3 Jan 44; PBS Engr Hist, pt. I, 1943–45, sec. I, Chronological Summary; Col. Joseph S. Gorlinski, "Naples: Case History in Invasion," *The Military Engineer*, XXXVI (April 1944), 109–14.

sponsible for building and operating bulk petroleum installations, and was also responsible for new railroad construction without regard to the army rear boundary. When the army's advance was slow, base section engineers were able to carry both pipeline and railroad work well into the army area. As for air force construction, the Engineer Service was responsible not only for bulk POL systems in the vicinity of airfields, but it also was to provide common engineer supplies to aviation engineers operating in the area. All engineer units assigned to the base area, except for fire-fighting detachments (under the base section provost marshal), were under the command of the base section engineer.[28]

The Engineer Service had six branches: administration, operations, construction, supply, real estate, and petroleum. An important function of the administrative branch involved negotiating with the Allied Military Government Labor Office (AMGLO) and with the labor administration office of the base purchasing agent for civilians to work with engineer units and for office personnel to work at engineer headquarters. By the end of 1943 3,126 civilians worked directly for engineer units or on contracts the base section engineers supervised. Workers employed by individual engineer units were paid semi-monthly by specially appointed agent finance officers at wages the AMGLO established.

The operations branch was responsible for issuing administrative instructions to engineer units, coordinating engineer troop movements, and keeping strength, disposition, and status reports of personnel and equipment. It also issued orders to engineer units for minefield clearance.

The construction branch, heart of the Engineer Service organization, applied the Engineer Service's resources against the mass of requests for construction that poured in. It provided technical assistance to engineer units, allocated priorities among jobs, and established and enforced standards of construction. The number of jobs was staggering: reconstructing the Naples port area; restoring public utility services in Naples and removing public dangers such as time bombs and building skeletons; reopening lines of communications; providing troop facilities such as hospitals, rest camps, replacement camps, quarters, stockades and POW enclosures, laundries, and bakeries; building supply depots and maintenance shops; and helping local industries get back into production.[29]

The supply branch received material requirements estimates from the Fifth Army engineer, the III Air Service Area Command, the petroleum branch, and, later, from the various branches of the Engineer Service, Peninsular Base Section. It consolidated these requisitions for submission to the engineer, SOS, NATOUSA, through the base section supply office (G–4). Fifth Army had requisitioned supplies for a thirty-day maintenance period and had forecast its needs through November. Thereafter, responsibility for requisitioning engineer supplies rested with

[28] Extracts from Report on Peninsular Base Section, NATOUSA, 10 Feb 44, sec. VIII, Engr Service, 381 NATOUSA, EUCOM Engr files.

[29] PBS Engr Hist, pt. I; Hist of the PBS, Phases II and III.

the base section engineer. Except for emergency orders, engineer requisitions were submitted monthly and were filled from depots in North Africa; items not available there were requisitioned from the New York POE. The supply branch also coordinated local procurement.

Responsibility for requisitioning real estate for all military purposes in connection with U.S. base section forces also rested with the engineer. Ultimately, a separate real estate branch was established.

The designation of a petroleum branch underscored the importance of this new engineer mission. POL products represented nearly half the gross tonnage of supplies shipped into Italy, and engineer pipelines were the principal means for moving motor and aviation gasoline once it was discharged from tankers at Italian ports.[30]

### Petroleum, Oil, and Lubricants

Petroleum facilities in Naples were heavily damaged. Allied bombers had hit the tank farms as early as July 1942, and many tanks and connecting pipelines had been pierced by bomb fragments; others had buckled or had been severed by concussion. German demolitionists had added some finishing touches at important pipe connections, discharge lines, and tanker berths. However, existing petroleum installations in Naples were large and much could be salvaged.[31]

Sixteen men from the 696th Engineer Petroleum Distribution Company entered Naples on 2 October. This advance party surveyed existing installations, recruited civilian petroleum workers, and began clearing away debris and salvaging materials. The 345th Engineers furnished teams of mine sweepers. After the main body of the 696th arrived two weeks later, the connecting pipelines in the terminal area were traced, patched, cleaned, and tested, and new threaded pipe was laid. One after another the huge steel storage tanks were patched and cleaned. This work often involved cutting a door in the bottom of a tank, shoveling out accumulated sludge, and scrubbing the walls with a mixture of diesel oil and kerosene.

Some of this early work proved wasteful. It began before any master plan for the POL terminal was available. Engineers repaired some tanks with floating roofs before they discovered that the tanks were warped. The 696th had no training or experience in such work, and plates welded over small holes cracked when they cooled until the company learned how to correct the problem. Other practices, such as the best method for scrubbing down tanks, had to come from trial and error.[32]

Not until 24 October did the 696th company have the terminal ready to receive gasoline, and the first tanker, the *Empire Emerald*, did not actually dis-

---

[30] PBS Engr Hist, pt. 10, sec. 1.

[31] Extracts from Rpt on PBS, NATOUSA, 10 Feb 44, sec. VIII. Engr Service; PBS Engr Hist, West Italy Pipelines, pt. I, sec. IV, 1943–45.

[32] Extracts from Rpt on PBS, NATOUSA, 10 Feb 44, sec. VIII, Engr Service; Observers Rpt on the Engr Service, SOS NATOUSA, Lt Col William F. Powers (ca. Mar 44), 370.2 (MTO-NA), EUCOM Engr files; Ltr, Col C. Kittrell, SOS NATOUSA Engr, to Chf Engr, AFHQ, 10 Aug 44, sub: Cleaning of Storage Tanks, and 1st Incl by Engr, PBS, 9 Jun 44 to Ltr, HQ, SOS NATOUSA, 8 May, same sub, 679.11, Oil Pipelines, MTOUSA files.

ENGINEER OFFICER READS PRESSURE GAUGES *at pumping station, Foggia, Italy.*

charge its cargo until five days later. In the meantime engineers set up dispensing and refueling stations in the terminal area, and once the *Empire Emerald* discharged, Fifth Army and base section units were able to draw some of their fuel supply from the bulk installations. The petroleum engineers did not limit their operations to providing facilities for ground force units. The 696th company·readied separate lines and storage tanks to receive 100-octane aviation fuel, as well as storage tanks, discharge lines, and fueling facilities for naval forces.

The engineer work to make possible the discharge of POL and other supplies at Naples became increasingly urgent as October advanced. By the end of the first week in October advance elements of Fifth Army were at the Volturno River, and a week later the crossings began.

### The Volturno Crossings

To the engineers involved in getting the troops across the river, where all bridges were down, the most important feature of the Volturno was that it was shallow. From 150 to 220 feet wide, the river was normally only 3 to 5 feet deep; even after the rains of early October began, spots existed on the VI Corps front where men could wade across and tanks could ford. The VI Corps crossings were to be made by the 3d and 34th Divisions abreast between

Triflisco (the boundary with British 10 Corps on the west) and Amorosi, where the Volturno, flowing down from the northwest, joins the Calore and turns west toward the sea. The corps' 45th Division was east of Amorosi in a sector adjoining British Eighth Army and would not be involved in the Volturno crossings.

By 6 October the 3d Division was at the river, but for days rains and stiffening German resistance made it impossible to bring up the 34th Division, as well as 10 Corps, which was to cross simultaneously with VI Corps. Flooded swamplands and enemy demolitions held the British back; and in the path of the 34th Division the fields were so deep in mud that cross-country movement was impossible. Punishing military traffic deepened the mud on the few roads and continually ground down and destroyed surfaces already cratered from heavy shelling. Enormous quantities of gravel and rock had to be used, even timber for corduroy cut from the banks of the Volturno.[33]

The 3d Division made good use of the week's delay. Reconnoitering the banks, patrols found wheel tracks where the Germans had crossed. At night patrols waded or swam the Volturno and marked fording spots. The troops were to cross in assault boats or wade, in either case holding on to guide ropes anchored to trees on the opposite bank. Heavy weapons were to be carried in assault boats. The 3d Division's 10th Engineer Combat Battalion rounded up five miles of guide rope and found some life jackets in a Naples warehouse. Some assault boats had to be impro-

vised. Naval officers in Naples provided some life rafts; other rafts were manufactured and floated by oil or water drums; and rubber pontons from treadway bridges came in handy.

At the place where waterproofed tanks were to ford, the engineers built a road to the riverbank. Bridges would be required for vehicles unable to ford. A railway yard in the neighborhood yielded material for a prefabricated cableway and some narrow-gauge railroad track which, overlaid with Sommerfeld matting and supported by floats, made a usable bridge for jeeps.[34]

Waiting on the mountain heights beyond the now racing, swollen Volturno, the Germans were prepared to repel the crossings. They had emplaced heavy artillery, laid mines, dug gun pits, and sighted machine guns to cover the riverbanks with interlocking fields of fire. They killed many men probing for crossing sites, but still did not know where the attack would come. General Truscott misled them into thinking the main crossing would be made on the American left at Triflisco Gap, then crossed the river in the center, spearheading the advance with the 7th Infantry of his 3d Division.

At 0200 on 13 October, after a heavy preliminary bombardment of German positions, troops of the 7th Infantry entered the river under a smoke screen, one battalion in rafts and assault boats,

---

[33] *Fifth Army History*, vol. II, 7 Oct–15 Nov 43, pp. 15–16, 49.

[34] Taggart, *History of the Third Infantry Division in World War II*, pp. 88–89; Nathan William White, War Department, Military Intel Div, *From Fedala to Berchtesgaden*, (Brockton, Mass.: Keystone Print, Inc., 1947), pp. 51–52. Details of the crossings are taken from these two sources as well as Blumenson, *Salerno to Cassino*, pp. 196–206; and War Department, Military Intel Div, *From the Volturno to the Winter Line (6 October–15 November 1943)*, American Forces in Action Series (Washington, 1944), pp. 27–54.

two battalions wading the icy waters and holding their rifles above their heads. The men in the boats had the worst of it; many of the trees anchoring the guide ropes tore away from sodden banks; rafts broke up in the swift current; and the rubber boats tended to drift downstream and were held back only with great difficulty by a party from the 39th Engineer Combat Regiment. Despite the struggle against the river, daylight found all the combat troops of the initial waves on the far bank picking their way through the minefields.

By 0530 General Truscott had word that all of the 7th Infantry was over the river and that two battalions of the 15th Infantry had crossed in the same manner and with much the same problems. On the right of the 3d Division two battalions of the 34th Division had crossed the Volturno with relative ease.

Truscott's main worry was a delay in getting the tanks across. At the ford in the 7th Infantry sector, bulldozer operators at first light had begun trying to break down the riverbank so the tanks could get to the water's edge without tipping over; but the bulldozers were unarmored, and enemy shelling caused so many casualties among the operators that the work stopped. Around 1000, Truscott learned from the commanding officer of the 7th Infantry, Col. Harry B. Sherman, that German tanks were advancing toward the riflemen on the far bank and that the enemy was probably about to launch a counterattack.

Leaving Sherman's command post, Truscott encountered a platoon of engineers from Company A of the 111th Engineer Combat Battalion on their way to the site where work was starting

on the division bridge. "In a few brief words," Truscott later recalled, "I painted for them the urgent need for courageous engineers who could level off the river bank even under fire so that tanks could cross and prevent our infantry battalions being overrun by the enemy. Their response was immediate and inspiring. I left them double-timing toward the river half a mile away to level off the bank with picks and shovels—which they did, while tanks and tank destroyers neutralized enemy fire from the opposite bank."[35] By 1240 fifteen tanks and three tank destroyers had reached the opposite bank and were moving to the aid of the riflemen.

By that time the jeep bridge in the 7th Infantry area, being built by Company A of the 10th Engineer Combat Battalion, was almost finished. But work the battalion's Company B was doing on the division bridge in the 15th Infantry area to the east had been stopped by German artillery fire, which caused casualties among the engineers, punctured pontons, and damaged trucks. General Truscott hurried to the site and told the engineers they would have to disregard the shelling and finish the bridge. The company "returned to work as nonchalantly as though on some engineer demonstration" and completed the bridge that afternoon, although shelling continued to cause casualties.[36]

Sites for the division bridge and for a thirty-ton bridge to carry tanks, corps artillery, and heavy engineer equipment had been selected entirely from aerial photographs. Later, ground re-

---

[35] Truscott, *Command Missions*, pp. 271–72.
[36] Ibid., p. 43; War Dept, Mil Intel Div, *From the Volturno to the Winter Line*, pp. 31, 40.

connaissance justified this method of selection.[37]

The thirty-ton corps bridge went in near Capua about 500 yards from a blown bridge that had carried Highway 87 across the river at Triflisco. Aware that this site was the only one suitable for a heavy bridge, the Germans stubbornly dominated the heights all through the day on 13 October, and not until the next day could work begin. To build the 270-foot-long treadway VI Corps had to call on the 16th Armored Engineer Battalion, which had treadway equipment and experienced men. Engineers from the 10th Engineer Combat Battalion and the 39th Engineer Combat Regiment prepared the approaches across muddy fields connecting the bridge with Highway 87. Construction began under a blanket of smoke which seemed to draw artillery fire. In spite of casualties and damaged pontons the engineers finished the treadway early in the afternoon, in only six hours. Later that same afternoon General Clark changed the boundary between VI Corps and British 10·Corps, giving the British responsibility for the 3d Division's objective on the left flank. This change gave the bridge to the British. In its first five days the treadway carried 7,200 vehicles across the Volturno.[38]

In the 34th Division's zone to the east, south of Caiazzo, the task of building a division bridge over the Volturno fell to Company A of VI Corps' 36th Engineer Combat Regiment, the regiment

that had helped repel German counterattacks after the Salerno landing and had contributed its Company H to the Rangers at Amalfi. Company H had marched into Naples with the Rangers to clear mines and booby traps. At the Italian barracks where the company was billeted, a German delayed-action demolition charge exploded on 10 October, killing twenty-three men and wounding thirteen.[39]

Misfortune also dogged the efforts of Company A to build the division bridge over the Volturno at Annunziata. According to plan, infantrymen on the far bank were to have taken a first phase line, including heights where German artillery was emplaced, before the engineers moved forward to the river from their assembly area three miles to the rear. On orders, the engineer convoy got under way at 0700 on 13 October, with trucks carrying floats already inflated to save time. But the high ground had not yet been taken, and no one had informed the engineers.

At Annunziata an enemy barrage began, and by the time the first three floats were launched the German fire had become so accurate that all were destroyed. During the day engineer casualties amounted to 3 men killed, 8 wounded, and 2 missing. Not until well after dark did the infantrymen take the first phase line. By that time the engineers had found another site upstream. Working under a smoke screen that (as at Triflisco) attracted enemy fire, they were able to finish the bridge by midmorning on 14 October. That afternoon a company of the 16th Armored

---

[37] Chf Engr, 15th Army Gp, Notes on Engr Opns in Italy, no. 8, 1 Feb 44, app. A−1, p. 4; Hist 1554th Engr Heavy Ponton Bn, 1 Jan 45−8 May 45.

[38] Truscott, *Command Missions*, pp. 268, 274; *Engineer History, Mediterranean*, p. 33.

[39] *Engineer History, Mediterranean*, p. 40.

WRECKED M2 FLOATING TREADWAY ON THE VOLTURNO

Engineer Battalion began building near Caiazzo a 255-foot, 30-ton treadway bridge and finished it before midnight. Next morning, although German planes made several passes at it, the bridge was carrying the 34th Division's heavy vehicles over the Volturno.[40]

From the time troops crossed the lower Volturno at Capua and Caiazzo to the time they crossed the upper Volturno a few weeks later at Venafro and Colli, the engineers were so short of bridging material that they had to resort to low-level bridges, sometimes constructed of any material they could scrounge from the countryside. They speedily slapped temporary bridges (largely treadways) across the river. Flash floods in November and December washed them out. On one occasion when the Volturno rose eighteen feet in ten hours, all the bridges but one were out for some time. Alternate routes—long, difficult, and circuitous—slowed supplies and added to traffic congestion. The one bridge sturdy enough to resist the torrent was a semipermanent structure the 343d Engineer General Service Regiment built at Capua between 16 October and 9 November. This pile bridge was for six months thereafter a major link in the

[40] Hist 36th Engr C Rgt, 1 Jun 41–23 Jun 44, including Ltr, 1st Lt Thomas F. Farrell, Jr., to CO, 36th Engr C Rgt, 28 Oct 43, sub: Volturno River Crossing; Hist 109th Engr C Bn, 10 Feb 41–8 May 45, app. I, pt. III; *Engineer History, Mediterranean*, pp. 32, 33, 40; Gardes comments in Ltr, 5 Nov 59.

Fifth Army lifeline. It was 32 feet high, some 370 feet long, and was classified as a two-way Class 40, one-way Class 70 bridge. In the first twenty-four hours after the bridge opened to traffic, 10,000 vehicles crossed; during the campaign, a million.[41]

In spite of this experience at the Volturno the engineers built a number of temporary bridges too low to withstand the swift currents of Italian streams and lost several more to flash floods. Any floating bridge was built at the existing level of the river or stream. As the rivers rose or fell, floating or fixed spans had to be added or removed. When Italian streams rose rapidly the engineers could not always extend the bridge fast enough to save it. The height of the bridge also depended upon the availability of construction materials, hard to come by in Italy. As the supply of Baileys improved, longer and higher structures were built.[42]

During the early part of November the enemy reinforced his units in front of the Fifth Army in an attempt to establish and hold the "Winter Line," increasing their strength from three to five divisions. By 15 November the British 10 Corps was stopped on a front approximately sixteen miles from the sea to Caspoli, while VI Corps was stalled on a front extending through the Mignano Gap past Venafro and north to the Eighth Army's left wing near Castel San Vincenzo. General Alexander called a halt and General Clark set about regrouping Fifth Army. Allowing the 34th and 45th Divisions time to rest and refit, he sent the 36th Division into the line and withdrew the 3d Division, which, slated for Anzio, came to the end (as General Truscott remarked) of "fifty-nine days of mountains and mud."[43]

---

[41] Gardes comments in Ltr, 5 Nov 59; *Engineer History, Mediterranean*, p. 51.

[42] Comments, Brig Gen D. O. Elliott, in Ltr to Dr. Jesse A. Remington, 18 Mar 60.

[43] Truscott, *Command Missions*, p. 285.

# CHAPTER IX

# The Winter Line and the Anzio Beachhead

The region of Fifth Army operations during the winter of 1943–44 was admirably suited for stubborn defense. Its topography included the narrow valleys of rivers rising in the Apennines and emptying into the Tyrrhenian Sea, irregular mountain and hill systems, and a narrow coastal plain. The divide between the Volturno-Calore and the Garigliano-Rapido valleys consisted of mountains extending from the crest of the Apennines southward about forty miles, averaging some 3,000 feet above sea level and traversed by few roads or trails. The slopes rising from the river valleys were often precipitous and forested, and all the rivers were swollen by winter rains and melting snow. In these mountains and valleys north and west of the Volturno, German delaying tactics slowed and finally halted Fifth Army's progress. The engineers had to fight enemy mines and demolitions as well as mountains and flooded streams.

Before the Allies launched an attack on the Winter Line on 1 December 1943, the U.S. II Corps took its place in the Fifth Army center near Mignano. The British 10 Corps and U.S. VI Corps occupied the left and right flanks, respectively. Early in January VI Corps withdrew from the Fifth Army front to prepare for the Anzio operation, and the French Expeditionary Corps (FEC), initially consisting of two divisions from North Africa, took its place. A number of Italian units, including engineers, also joined Fifth Army. But these additions did not assure rapid progress. The army pushed slowly and painfully through the mountains until it came to a halt in mid-January at the enemy's next prepared defenses, the Gustav Line, which followed the courses of the Rapido and Garigliano Rivers for most of its length. Opposing Fifth Army and the British Eighth Army was the German *Tenth Army*.[1]

In January Fifth Army attacked on two fronts. VI Corps' surprise flank attack in the Anzio landing (SHINGLE) of 22 January penetrated inland an average of ten miles, but then the German *Fourteenth Army* contained the beachhead, and for the remainder of the winter VI Corps was on the defensive. In the mountains to the south Fifth Army could gain little ground. When an attack began on 17 January, II Corps held the Fifth Army center along the Rapido and tried repeatedly to smash through the Gustav Line. By the thirty-first II Corps had penetrated some German lines but failed to capture Cassino, key to enemy defenses. The opening of the second front at Anzio had reduced the

---

[1] For terrain and tactical details, see Blumenson, *Salerno to Cassino*, chs. XIII–XV, and *Fifth Army History*, vol. II, pp. 2–3; vol. III, p. 2 and an. 5; vol. IV, pp. 2, 4, 187–88.

length of the inland front Fifth Army could hold; hence, in February three divisions moved from Eighth Army to take over the Cassino-Rapido front while Fifth Army units concentrated in the southern half of the line, along the Garigliano. Despite heavy casualties, the gains in the winter campaign were negligible, and a stalemate existed until the offensive resumed in the spring.

### Minefields in the Mountains

Approaching the Volturno, the Allies had run into increasingly dense and systematic minefields which included unfamiliar varieties of mines and booby traps. The German mine arsenal in Italy contained the "S" (or "Bouncing Betty") and Teller plus many new types including the Schu and the Stock, mines with detonations delayed up to twenty-one days, and mines with improvised charges. Nonmetallic materials such as wood and concrete in many of the newer mines made detection more difficult and more dangerous.

Allied troops dreaded the Schu mine especially. Approximately 6-by-4-by-2 inches, this mine consisted of a 1/2- to 2-pound block of explosive and a simple detonating device enclosed in lightweight pressed board or impregnated plywood. It could be carried by any foot soldier and planted easily in great numbers; it was most effective placed flush with the ground and covered with a light layer of dirt, grass, and leaves. The Schu did not kill, but as little as five pounds of pressure would set it off to shatter foot, ankle, and shin bones.

At the Volturno the enemy had recovered from the confusion of retreat, and to the end of the Italian campaign each successive German fortified line had its elaborate mine defenses. The Germans frequently sowed mines without pattern and used many confusing methods. Distances, depths, and types varied. A mine might be planted above another of the same or different type in case a mine-lifting party cleared only the top layer.

The scale of antipersonnel mining increased as the campaign progressed. Booby traps were planted in bunches of grapes, in fruit and olive trees, in haystacks, at roadblocks, among felled trees, along hedges and walls, in ravines, valleys, hillsides, and terraces, along the beds and banks of streams, in tire or cart tracks along any likely avenue of approach, in possible bivouac areas, in buildings that troops might be expected to enter, and in shell or bomb craters where soldiers might take refuge. The Germans placed mines in ballast under railroad tracks, in tunnels, at fords, on bridges, on road shoulders, in pits, in repaired pot holes, and in debris. Field glasses, Luger pistols, wallets, and pencils were booby-trapped, as were chocolate bars, soap, windows, doors, furniture, toilets, demolished German equipment, even bodies of Allied and German civilians and soldiers.[2]

In areas sown with S-mines bulldozer operators wore body armor, and each combat battalion had four "flak" suits. More than fifty bulldozers struck mines during the campaign. In many cases the operators were thrown from their seats, but none was killed. Some had broken legs, but had they been in cabs with roofs many would have had their necks broken or skulls fractured.[3]

---

[2] *Engineer History, Mediterranean*, pp. 34, 36, 42; Bowman notes, 31 Mar 44, Fifth Army Engr files.

[3] Hist 10th Engr C Bn, 1944; Hist 313th Engr C Bn, 1944–45; Interv, Col John D. Cole, Jr., CO, 310th Engr C Bn, 1959.

Although detecting and clearing mines was not exclusively an engineer function, the engineers were primarily responsible. But they were not adequately trained. As late as September 1944 engineers in the field complained that no organization or procedure had been established for collecting enemy mines for training.[4]

Infantrymen retained the dread of mines that had been so marked in North Africa. To ease that dread and to pass on proper procedures for lifting mines, the engineers emphasized that mines were one of the normal risks of war; only one man should deal with a mine; skilled help should be called in when needed; ground should be checked carefully in a mined area; all roads and shoulders should be cleared and accurate records made of such work, with roads and lanes not cleared being blocked off and so reported; and large minefields should not be cleared except on direct orders.[5]

The engineers often found that infantrymen did not comprehend the time required to check an area. Checking and clearing mines were slow and careful processes, requiring many men and involving great risks even when there was no enemy fire. For example, the 10th Engineer Combat Battalion in the Formia-Gaeta area, north of Naples, suffered fifty-seven casualties, including fifteen deaths, in clearing 20,000 mines of all types during a period of sixteen days. Often a large area contained only a few mines, but the number found bore little relation to the time that had to be spent checking and clearing. Furthermore, much of the work

had to be done under artillery, machine gun, and mortar fire. Ordinarily the infantry attacked with engineers in support to clear mine paths, and engineer casualties were inevitable.[6]

New problems in mine detection arose during the Italian campaign. With the increasing number of nonmetallic enemy mines, the SCR-625 detector became less dependable and the prod more important. Italian soil contained heavy mineral deposits and large concentrations of artifacts buried over the ages.[7] A detector valuable in one spot might be useless a mile away, where the metallic content of the soil itself produced in the instrument a hum indistinguishable from that caused by mines. Shell fragments and other scraps of metal scattered in many areas caused the same confusion.

The wooden Schu mine was difficult for the SCR-625 to spot. Since the fuse was the only metal in the mine, the detector had to be carefully tuned and the operator particularly alert. The prod was a surer instrument than the detector in this work, but it had to be held carefully at a thirty-degree angle to avoid activating the mine. The Schu charges were too small to damage bulldozers seriously, but ordinarily the Germans placed these mines in areas inaccessible to bulldozers. However, Schu mines in open fields or along paths were often interspersed with S-mines, which could be costly to bulldozers and operators. One solution was to send sheep or goats into the minefield to hit trip wires and detonate the mines.[8]

---

[4] AGF Bd Rpt, Lessons Learned in the Battle from Garigliano to North of Rome, 21 Sep 44.
[5] *Fifth Army History*, vol. VIII, p. 91.

[6] Hist 126th Engr C Bn, 1944-45; Hist 10th Engr C Bn, 1944.
[7] Comments, Warren E. Graban, geologist, Waterways Experimental Station, Vicksburg, Miss., 30 Apr 59.
[8] 36th Div Opns Rpt, Jan 44, an. 14; Hist 111th Engr C Bn.

The fact that the SCR−625s were not waterproof continued to limit their usefulness. They had difficulty finding mines buried in snow, and any lengthy rain usually rendered them useless. However, covering the detector with a gas cape protected it somewhat against rain and snow. The 10th Engineer Combat Battalion (3d Division) had as many as ninety detectors on hand at one time, but at times most were unserviceable. Its use was limited near the front, because the enemy often could hear the detector's hum, especially at night when much of the work was done and when the front lines were comparatively quiet.[9]

The engineers tried out new types of detectors at various times. The Fifth Army received the AN/PRS−1 (Dinah) detector in August 1944. It was less sensitive than the SCR−625 and in a seven-day test proved not worthwhile. A vehicular detector, the AN/VRS−1, mounted in a jeep, was also tested and rejected as undependable.

Of numerous other countermine devices and procedures tried, a few proved useful. The best of these were primacord ropes and cables. The 48th Engineer Combat Battalion developed a simple device for clearing antipersonnel mines—a rifle grenade that propelled a length of primacord across a minefield. The exploded primacord left a well-defined path about eighteen inches wide, cutting nearly all taut trip wires and sometimes detonating Schu mines. In all cases the engineers cleared the ground of any growth or underbrush to reveal mines or trip wires.

On the Cisterna front, fifteen miles northeast of Anzio, the 16th Armored Engineer Battalion used six Snakes to advantage when the Allies broke out of their perimeter. Segments of explosive-filled pipe that could be assembled into lengths up to 400 feet, the Snakes threw the enemy into momentary panic and permitted Combat Command A (CCA), 1st Armored Division to advance; Combat Command B, which did not use the devices lost a number of tanks in its breakout. In practice, the Snakes were effective only over flat, heavily mined ground. They were susceptible to rain and mud, slow to build, difficult to transport and vulnerable to artillery fire and mine detonations.[10]

Other devices and methods for finding and removing mines in Italy included aerial detection—especially valuable along the Garigliano River and at Anzio—D−7 bulldozers with rollers, bazooka shells, bangalore torpedoes, and grappling hooks that activated antipersonnel mine trip wires.[11]

*Bridge Building and Road Work*

In the winter campaign, the steel treadway and the Bailey (fixed and floating) were the tactical bridges the engineers used most, and the Bailey proved the more valuable. In the opinion of the Fifth Army engineer, it was "the most useful all-purpose fixed bridge in existence." Its capacity and length could be increased speedily by adding trusses and piers. It could be used where other bridges could not, particularly over mountain streams where flash floods quickly washed out other temporary bridges. There were never enough

---

[9] Hist 120th Engr C Bn, 31 May−Nov 43; Hist 10th Engr C Bn, 1944.

[10] Hist 48th Engr C Bn, 1944−45; Hist 16th Armd Engr Bn, May 44.
[11] Hist 337th Engr C Bn; Hist 111th Engr C Bn, an. 14 to II Corps Rpt, Rapido Crossing, Jan−Feb 44.

Baileys. An early attempt to supplement the British supply with Baileys manufactured in America failed. The engineering gauges sent from England to American factories were improperly calibrated, and the sections that came to Italy from the United States were incompatible with the British-manufactured parts in use; bridges assembled from American parts would not slide as well as the British bridges. Upon discovering the discrepancies, General Bowman outlawed the American bridge sets in the Fifth Army area.[12] Treadways, both floating and trestle, were almost as well suited to Italian conditions as Baileys, but the constant shortage of Brockway trucks needed to haul them limited their usefulness. The treadways were too narrow to accommodate large equipment carriers such as tank transporters and heavy tanks.[13]

The engineers of Fifth Army erected many timber bridges, usually as replacements for Baileys or treadways. The timber structures could carry loads of over seventy tons. Made not to standard dimensions but to the needs of the moment, they consisted ordinarily of a series of steel or timber stringer spans with piers of single or double pile bents. The acquisition of the Ilva Steel Works at Bagnoli, after Naples fell, increased the use of steel stringers. Timber floor beams or steel channels rested on the stringers and supported wood decking of two layers, the upper laid diagonally to decrease wear. From the Ilva steel mill also came a light, steel-riveted lattice-type girder, suitable for semipermanent bridges, which became standard equipment.[14]

When Fifth Army engineers had to build abutments, they usually spiked logs together to make hollow cribs and then filled the cribs with stone. They had learned through experience that a dirt-fill abutment that extended into the channel restricted normal stream flow, which, in turn, scoured the abutment. Abutments needed to be well cribbed, and timber was the best expedient.

During the winter campaign the engineers devised new methods and new uses for equipment in bridge building. The 16th Armored Engineer Battalion claimed credit for first putting cranes on the fronts of tanks or tank-recovery vehicles to get various types of treadway bridges across small streams or dry creek beds; the cranes enabled engineers to install bridges under heavy enemy fire. When a treadway across the Volturno at Dragoni almost washed away in November 1943, a company of the 36th Engineer Combat Regiment anchored it with half-track winches. On the night of 15 November the 48th Engineer Combat Battalion used the winches of Brockway trucks as holdfasts to save another bridge at Dragoni. Engineers saved time by building Baileys with raised ramps on each end to put the bridge roadway two to three feet above the normal elevation. They could then build a more permanent bridge directly under the Bailey without closing the bridge to traffic and could quickly lay the flooring and wearing surface of the new bridge after they removed the Bailey.[15]

[12] Coll, Keith, and Rosenthal, *The Corps of Engineers: Troops and Equipment*, pp. 549, 551.

[13] Fifth Army History, Mediterranean, app. J; Hist 1108th Engr C Gp, 1944–45; Hist 317th Engr C Bn, Oct–Dec 44.

[14] Hist 175th Engr GS Rgt, Feb 42–Oct 45; AGF Bd Rpt, NATOUSA, Second Orientation Conf at HQ, Fifth Army, 15 Nov 43.

[15] *Engineer History, Mediterranean*, p. 41; Comments, Col K. S. Anderson in Ltr, 8 Jun 59.

Bridge companies were in short supply throughout the Italian campaign, and for a time the treadway company of the 16th Armored Engineer Battalion was the only bridge company in Fifth Army. The companies were needed not only to construct, maintain, and dismantle bridges but also to carry bridge components. The treadway company of the 16th served as a bridge train from the first but could not meet the demand. As a stop-gap measure two companies of the 175th Engineer General Service Regiment were equipped with enough trucks (2 1/2-ton and Brockway) to form bridge trains, and later two more bridge train companies were organized from the disbanded bridge train of the 16th Armored Engineer Battalion. In addition, Fifth Army from time to time employed bridge companies of 10 Corps for bridge trains. Elements of the 1554th Engineer Heavy Ponton Battalion and Companies A and C of the 387th Engineer Battalion (Separate) also served as bridge train units. The main problem all units converting to bridge trains faced was to find experienced, reliable drivers for their trucks.

Such was not the case for the 85th Engineer Heavy Ponton Battalion, which could unload its ponton equipment and, by carefully reloading, handle Bailey bridge components. One company of the 85th could carry two standard Baileys, and the ponton trailers also hauled piling and steel beams to engineer units replacing temporary bridging. One problem remained—the large, ungainly trailers could not traverse many Italian roads.

Since the speed with which wrecked bridges were rebuilt or replaced often determined the Fifth Army's rate of advance, much of the bridge equipment had to be kept on wheels. Some equipment, such as Brockway trucks, was always in short supply. In the latter part of October 1943 the 85th Engineer Heavy Ponton Battalion established a bridge depot near Triflisco, operating directly under the Fifth Army engineer and sending bridging to the corps on bridge trains. It was a tactical depot, with stocks kept to a minimum for quick movement. The depot stocked fixed and floating Baileys, steel treadways, infantry support and heavy ponton bridges, and other stream-crossing equipment. Tactical Bailey and treadway bridges replaced with fixed bridges were returned to the army bridge depot, where they were reconditioned and put back in stock.[16]

In reconnoitering for bridge sites, an important engineer function, experienced photo interpreters, studying aerial photographs of the front lines, were able to save much time. During the stalemate before Cassino, Lt. Col. John G. Todd, chief of the Mapping and Intelligence Section; Col. Harry O. Paxson, deputy Fifth Army engineer; and Capt. A. Colvocoresses worked out a plan to use aerial photos for engineer reconnaissance. One officer and one enlisted man specially trained in photo interpretation remained at the airfield where the photos were processed, and they could obtain copies of all aerial photos taken in front of the American lines. Those covering the front to a depth of ten miles went forward immediately to the Engineer Section, Fifth Army, and there Captain Colvocoresses recorded on a map everything that might help or hinder Fifth Army's ad-

---

[16] Hist 85th Engr Heavy Ponton Bn, Dec 44.

vance: locations, characteristics, and dimensions of all bridges; possible bridge or crossing sites; places along roads where enemy demolitions could cause serious delays; locations of enemy dumps; and marshy ground that could prohibit tanks. This information Colvocoresses sent to the army G–3 and the army engineer's operations and supply sections. Meanwhile, the officer and the enlisted man at the airfield did the same type of work for the area beyond the ten miles in front of the lines, though in much less detail. As another result of the photo-interpretation process, Colonel Paxson represented the Fifth Army engineer on the target selection board for heavy artillery.

Aerial photographs helped planners to estimate the material, equipment, and troops needed for bridge work. Information on blown bridges went back to the engineer supply section at army headquarters and forward to the frontline troops, who could prepare for necessary repairs. Engineers could then have the bridging on hand when an attack went forward. Aerial photographs were especially important where enemy fire forestalled close ground reconnaissance.

Building bridges under fire was difficult at best—sometimes impossible. But engineers did build bridges under withering fire. In December 1943 Company H, 36th Engineer Combat Regiment, put a Bailey across a tributary of the Volturno, a few miles to the west of Colli al Volturno, and in February 1944 the 109th Engineer Combat Battalion bridged the Rapido in two hours.

Some engineers built bridges at night to escape enemy fire. Insofar as possible they put material together some-

what to the rear and brought forward partially prefabricated bridges in the dark. Others, trusting to Allied air superiority, preferred to build bridges by daylight under the protection of counterbattery fire that aerial reconnaissance directed. Another protective device was a dummy bridge to draw fire away from the real site.[17]

Winds and floods caused havoc. On 30 December a company of the 344th Engineer General Service Regiment was building a Bailey across the Volturno near Raviscanina. While the engineers were putting concrete caps on the stone piers of the demolished span, a high wall of water plunged down the river, quickly washing away concrete and equipment. On the thirty-first high winds and subfreezing temperatures ended all work for several days. The gale ripped down company tents and blew away, buried, or destroyed personal equipment.[18]

During the winter campaign divisional engineers worked rapidly to clear rubble-clogged village streets, remove roadblocks and abatis, and fill cratered roadways to take one-way traffic. Sometimes they built roads over demolitions instead of clearing them. On several occasions they used railbeds cleared of ties and rails as emergency roads. In December 1943 the 48th Engineer Combat Battalion built one such road at the Cassino front under artillery fire. The battalion suffered many casualties while extending the road for six miles from Mignano to the flank of Monte Lungo and on to a point 200 yards in advance of infantry outposts.[19]

[17] Hist 334th Engr C Bn, 21 Sep–31 Oct 43; Hist 109th Engr C Bn, 21 Sep–31 Oct 43.
[18] Hist 344th Engr GS Rgt, 1942–45.
[19] Hists, 344th Engr GS Rgt and 1108th Engr C Gp, 1944–45.

Corps engineers normally followed divisional engineers to widen one-lane roads and bypasses for a freer flow of traffic, finish clearing rubble, remove debris from road shoulders, eliminate one-way bottlenecks, check each side of the road for mines, post caution and directional signs, and open lateral roads. Fifth Army engineers finished filling craters and resurfaced and widened roads to take two-way traffic.

The policy was for divisional engineers to concentrate on the immediate front; they could ask corps engineers to take over any other necessary work in the division area. Similarly, as corps engineers took over work in the divisional areas they could ask army engineers to take over work in the corps areas. These requests were never turned down, although there were some complaints of work unfinished in the army area. The system worked better than retaining specified boundaries and continually shifting engineer units among division, corps, and army as the work load varied.

Much road repair and construction—especially that undertaken by division and corps engineers—was done under heavy enemy artillery, mortar, and small-arms fire. At times, engineer troops had to slow or even stop work because of enemy fire or had to abandon one route for another. Such experiences gave rise to engineer complaints of lack of infantry support, and frequently the engineers provided their own protection, especially for dozer operators. Avoiding enemy fire by working at night had serious drawbacks, especially in the mountains. Only the most skilled graders and dozer operators could feel their way in the dark. Also, the noise of the equipment often drew enemy fire,

even through the smoke screens that provided protection. The engineers set smoke screens for themselves, with varying success, and on numerous occasions Chemical Warfare Service units furnished excellent screens.

The engineers had to contend not only with the enemy but also with heavy snows, mountain streams that rains turned into raging torrents, water pouring into drainage ditches from innumerable gullies and gorges, and tons of mud clogging ditches and covering road surfaces. At times, engineers worked waist deep in mud. Army vehicles hauled huge quantities from side roads and bivouacs. The only answer was "rock, plenty of rock."[20]

For proper drainage crushed rock or gravel, or both, had to cover the whole surface of a road, and the crown had to be maintained. When engineer units assumed responsibility for a new area one of the first things they did was to find a ready and reliable source of rock and gravel. In most parts of Italy supplies were plentiful. Rubble from demolished stone houses—even Carrara marble quarried from the mountainsides—supplemented rock.

Quarries sometimes operated day and night. In December 1943 a 235th Engineer Combat Battalion quarry on Highway 6 east of Cassino worked twenty-two hours a day, lit at night by giant torches "after the fashion of a Roman festival in Caesar's time," though "the torches attracted a not inconsiderable amount of attention from German planes and artillery."[21] The engineers dumped and roughly spread rock; then Italian laborers used sledges or small

---

[20] *Engineer History, Mediterranean,* p. 43.
[21] Ibid.

portable rock crushers to break up the larger stones.[22]

Engineers drained water from the wide shoulders along secondary roads by digging ditches across the shoulders at intervals or by using various types of culverts. Steel pipe culverts of twelve-inch diameter worked effectively, and the engineers had little difficulty finding local pipe for them. Curved sheets of corrugated iron made excellent forms for masonry culverts. During the fighting at the Winter Line, Lt. Col. Frank J. Polich of the 235th Engineer Combat Battalion designed a prefabricated hexagonal culvert. Sixteen feet long with two-foot sides and steel reinforcements, it was intended for emergency jobs but proved so successful that Fifth Army adopted it as a standard engineer item. The culvert could be thrown into gaps in the road at the site of a blown bridge, over a bomb crater, or at assault stream crossings to make a passable one-way road. The culvert sustained the weight of 32-ton medium tanks without any earth covering yet could be loaded and transported comparatively easily; it weighed two to three thousand pounds depending upon the kind of wood used in its construction. Other engineer units built similar culverts of varying lengths.[23]

Of the roads leading forward to the area of the Winter Line campaign, only three were first-class: Highways 7, 6, and 85. As a result, Fifth Army had to depend on unsurfaced secondary roads and on tracks and trails. While the engineers' main problem during this period was maintenance (the VI Corps engineer, for instance, reported that the 36th and 39th Engineer Combat Regiments devoted almost all their time in December to revetments and drainage control), they built numerous jeep and foot trails through the mountains to supplement the inadequate road system.[24]

A very large part of VI Corps' traffic passed through Venafro, a bottleneck through which an average of 4,000 vehicles moved every day during December 1943. To lighten the load on Highway 85 and a narrow road to Pozzilli, the 120th Engineer Combat Battalion, 45th Division, built two additional roads from Venafro to Pozzilli. The engineers eventually extended these roads beyond Pozzilli well into the mountains, where mules or men with packboards had to take over.[25]

### Engineers in Combat

In the midst of helping combat troops move over difficult terrain in winter weather, engineers sometimes fought as infantry during the drive on Rome. Perhaps the most spectacular instance was the commitment of II Corps' 48th Engineer Combat Battalion at Monte Porchia during the first week of January 1944.

Although Monte Porchia was not a primary objective for II Corps, it was needed to protect 10 Corps' right flank in a projected operation to cross the Garigliano. A small elevation compared with the mountainous terrain generally typical of central Italy, Monte Porchia's isolated position commanded low ground lying between the Monte Maggiore—Camino hill mass to the south

---

[22] Ltr, Col William P. Jones, Jr., 1 Jun 59.
[23] HQ, 34th Inf Div, Lessons Learned in Combat, 1944.
[24] *Fifth Army History*, vol. III, p. 4.
[25] Hist 120th Engr C Bn, 31 May–Nov 43.

ENGINEER ROCK QUARRY NEAR MIGNANO

and Monte Trocchio to the northwest. From this observation point the enemy could survey the Allied line along the Garigliano. The British 10 Corps held the Allied left, while the U.S. 34th Division was in the mountains to the right. In the center, astride the only two roads into Cassino, the U.S. 1st Armored Division had massed Task Force Allen and its attached units. Enemy observation posts on Monte Porchia were able to direct punishing fire on all Allied installations in the valley. It was vitally important to take this hill, and at 1930 on 4 January the attack began.

The weather was cold, wet, and windy. The 6th Armored Infantry Regiment led off, but German mortar and artillery fire was so concentrated that by daylight the 2d Battalion of the 6th Armored was back at its starting point. More wind-driven snow fell on 5 January as the 48th Engineer Combat Battalion was attached to Task Force Allen, placed in reserve, and told to be ready to go into the line. During 7–9 January, in three days and two nights, when a gap developed on the left flank of the task force, Companies A, B, and C of the 48th went forward. They helped secure the flank and drive the enemy off. For its work in this action the 48th received a Presidential Unit Citation, as did the 235th Engineer Combat Battalion, which also took part in the engagement. Individual awards to men of the 48th included 3 Distinguished Service Crosses, 21 Silver Stars, and 2 Bronze Stars. The highest award, the Congressional Medal of Honor, was awarded posthumously to Sgt. Joseph C. Specker, Company C, for his bravery on 7 January in wiping out an enemy machine-gun nest single handedly despite severe wounds.[26]

The 235th Battalion was to open and maintain axial supply routes for Task Force Allen. The work of the battalion, often under heavy fire, enabled armor to move forward in support of the infantry. The 235th also fought as infantry, twice driving the enemy from strongly fortified positions to clear routes for the armor.[27]

### At Cassino: 20-29 January 1944

In mid-January Fifth Army reached the enemy's Rapido-Garigliano defenses. The removal of VI Corps from the Allied line left II Corps as the only U.S. Army corps on this front. For the assault against the Gustav Line, II Corps was in the center, opposite the Germans' strong position at Cassino. Plans for the attack called first for the 36th Division to cross the Rapido south of Cassino.

The 36th began the operation late on 20 January. The enemy's defenses were formidable and his position very strong. Along that part of its course in the division's sector the Rapido was a narrow stream flowing swiftly between steep banks, in places no more than twenty-five feet wide and elsewhere about fifty. The Sant' Angelo bluff or promontory, from which the enemy could survey the immediate area, rose

forty feet above the river's west bank, but there were no comparable vantage points east of the river. Between 20 and 22 January the 36th Division made two attempts to establish a bridgehead but suffered a costly defeat. The 36th then went on the defensive while the 34th Division between 26 and 29 January pushed across the Rapido north of Cassino and made a slight but important breach in the Gustav Line.[28]

During these attacks engineers were to clear mines at crossing sites, build and maintain bridges and bridge approaches, and find and maintain tank routes. They also were to maintain roads and clear mines in seized bridgeheads. The 36th Division's 143d Infantry was to attack south of Sant' Angelo, and its 141st was to cross north of the bluff. The 111th Engineer Combat Battalion, reinforced by two companies of the 16th Armored Engineer Battalion, was to clear enemy mines before the crossings. During the night of 19 January the 1st and 2d Battalions of the 19th Engineer Combat Regiment, a II Corps unit, were to spot footbridge equipment and assault boats for the attack. The 1st Battalion, during the night of 20 January, was to build an eight-ton infantry support bridge in the area of the 143d and the 2d Battalion a similar structure in the attack zone of the 141st.[29]

The Gustav Line was heavily mined, with box mines notably more numerous. At the Rapido the Fifth Army encountered a mine belt a mile in length, chiefly of the S, Teller, and wooden box types. German patrols interrupted mine clearing, and they crossed the

---

[26] History of II Corps; Hist 48th Engr C Bn, 7 Ap 43-Jun 44; Hist 1108th Engr C Gp, 1944-45.

[27] Hist 235th Engr C Bn, Jan-Dec 44.

[28] *Fifth Army History*, vol. IV, pp. 39-48, 57; Ltr, Jones, 1 Jun 59.

[29] II Corps Rapido Crossing, Jan-Feb 44.

river and emplaced more mines so that markers indicating the safe passage meant little. Poor reconnaissance resulted partly from the position of the infantry which was 500 yards from the river. When the 141st began to advance, the lanes were difficult or impossible to follow because of heavy fog or because much of the white tape had been destroyed, some by German fire.[30]

The enemy met the several attempted crossings with intense and continuous artillery, mortar, and machine-gun fire, which destroyed assault boats and frustrated the engineers in their attempts to build floating footbridges. The engineers had no standard floating bridge equipment and had to improvise all footbridges over the Rapido. In the 141st Infantry zone artillery fire tore to shreds several footbridges made from sections of catwalk placed over pneumatic boats, while floating mines destroyed another. Most of Companies A and B of the 141st got across on one intact footbridge that the 19th Engineers had managed to put together from the remnants of others. This bridge, although almost totally submerged, remained usable for a time because the engineers strung four ropes across the Rapido to form a suspension cable that supported the punctured boats.[31]

Dense fog hampered the whole operation, but the 1st Battalion, 19th Engineers, was able to guide troops of the 1st Battalion of the 143d Infantry through the minefields. By 0500 on 21 January, the 19th Engineers had installed two footbridges in the 143d's area south of Sant' Angelo, but one was

soon destroyed and the other damaged. The infantry battalion nevertheless crossed in boats or over the bridges but suffered heavy casualties, and its remnants had to return to the east bank to escape annihilation. Fog confused troops of the 19th Engineers who led the boat group of the 3d Battalion of the 143d Infantry. The engineers and infantry stumbled into a minefield, where their rubber boats were destroyed. Enemy fire completed the disorganization of the infantry battalion and defeated its attempt to make a crossing.

During the 36th Division's second attempt to break through the enemy line the 19th Engineers succeeded in installing several footbridges, but the 16th Armored Engineer Battalion, in the face of artillery and mortar fire, could make no headway with the installation of a Bailey. The action ended in defeat.[32]

Reviewing the failure to build the Rapido bridges as planned, Colonel Bowman pointed out that the near shore of the river was never entirely under Fifth Army control, so reconnaissance, mine clearance, and approach preparation were incomplete. He concluded that the attempt to build and use a Bailey as an assault bridge was unjustified. Some engineer officers on the scene blamed a shortage in bridge equipment, bad timing, and one infantry regiment's lack of training with the engineers supporting it. Others claimed that the terrible raking fire from well-placed artillery and small arms directly on the sites made bridge construction all but impossible.

The success of the 34th Division's Rapido crossing north of Cassino de-

[30] Interv, Col J. O. Killian, CO, 19th Engr C Rgt, and Ltr, Jones, 1 Jun 59.
[31] Ltr, Jones, 1 Jun 59; *Engineer History, Mediterranean*, p. 39.

[32] *Fifth Army History*, vol. IV, p. 45; Killian interv.

pended greatly on getting tanks over narrow muddy roads and then across the river. The crossing itself was less a problem than that to the south because terrain and other factors were more favorable. The Germans had diverted the Rapido and flooded the small valley; now the American engineers prepared the dry riverbed for a tank crossing. On the morning of 27 January, after artillery preparation, tanks of the 756th Tank Battalion led the attack. Some of them slipped off the flooded trail and others stuck in the mud, but a few got across the river.[33]

Engineers of the 1108th Engineer Combat Group and two companies of the 16th Armored Engineer Battalion started building a corduroy route south of the tank trail. On that day and the twenty-eighth the infantry was able to hold some ground west of the Rapido. Meanwhile, the engineers worked to improve the tank routes. The attack against enemy strongpoints resumed on the morning of the twenty-ninth. By that time the engineers had tank routes ready for the advance, and the infantry, aided by armor, captured two strongpoints on 30 January. Next day the infantrymen took Cairo village, headquarters of an enemy regiment. After the 34th Division had broken through the enemy's outpost line and occupied a hill mass north of Cassino, the 109th Engineer Combat Battalion improved a main supply route by constructing two one-way roads that led across the Rapido from San Pietro to Cairo.[34]

### Anzio

To the north, the landing at Anzio

(SHINGLE) was under way. Planning and training were compressed into little more than two months. In mid-November 1943 a planning group with three engineer representatives assembled at Fifth Army headquarters in Caserta. Here Colonel Bowman, having reviewed the findings of engineer aerial photo interpreters and having studied harbors from Gaeta to Civitavecchia, recommended Anzio for the projected landing of an Allied flanking force. Col. Harry O. Paxson, the Fifth Army Engineer Section's expert on evaluating topographic intelligence, also had a part in choosing Anzio. As General Eisenhower's topographic intelligence officer at AFHQ in 1942 he had learned from the British a method of analyzing offshore terrain that enabled him and others to find an opening in the submerged sandbars off the coast at Anzio.

AFHQ based the final decision to land at Anzio on the existence of suitable beach exits and good roads leading twenty miles to the Alban Hills, a mountain mass rising across the approaches from the south to Rome and affording access to the upper end of the Liri valley. Here was a possibility of cutting off German forces concentrated on the Cassino front. At the very least, AFHQ hoped that a flanking operation at this point, as part of a great pincer movement, would force an enemy withdrawal northward and that Rome would fall quickly into Allied hands.[35]

Beginning on 4 January near Naples, VI Corps underwent intensive amphibious training which culminated in a practice landing below Salerno. Early on 21 January over 250 ships carrying nearly 50,000 men moved out of Naples.

---

[33] *Engineer History, Mediterranean*, p. 45.
[34] Ibid, pp. 45–46.

[35] Interv, Col Harry O. Paxson, May 59; *Fifth Army History*, vol. IV, pp. 21, 85.

To keep the enemy from suspecting its destination and to avoid minefields, the convoy veered to the south on a wide sweep around Capri. After dark it turned toward Anzio and dropped anchor just past midnight. The enemy was caught almost completely off guard, and the Allies met only token coast defenses. The Germans had been aware of Anzio's possibilities as a landing beach but had weakened defenses there in order to hold the Cassino front.[36]

Good weather and a calm sea favored the operation. The landings began promptly at H-hour, 0200, 22 January, and went rapidly and efficiently. (*Map 9*) U.S. troops (X-Ray Force) went ashore over beaches south of Nettuno, a few miles southeast of Anzio, and over Yellow Beach, near Anzio. The port fell quickly. Meanwhile, the British (Peter Force) landed six miles north of Anzio. The smoothness and dispatch that marked the U.S. 3d Division landing and the rapid organization of the beaches was helped by the 540th Engineer Combat Regiment's experience in beach operations. By daylight the beaches were ready to receive vehicles. In addition to the 540th, beach troops included the 1st Naval Beach Battalion, the 36th Engineer Combat Regiment at the port, and the British 3d Beach Group on the Peter beaches. All were under Col. William N. Thomas, Jr., VI Corps engineer.[37]

All assault troops from LCVPs and LCIs debarked on the beaches on schedule. The port of Anzio was taken almost intact, and by early afternoon the 36th Engineers had cleared it sufficiently to receive landing craft. Except for a brief period on D-day, the beaches were never congested. Excellent 1:10,000 scale beach maps, distributed at the beachhead by the 1710th Engineer Map Depot Detachment, helped avoid confusion. Beach crews with attached service units reported directly to assigned areas and began organizing their respective dumps. After midafternoon American supplies could move on 2 1/2-ton trucks or DUKWs directly to corps dumps, which were accessible to the gravel-surfaced roads inland. All beach dumps except ammunition were "sold out" or moved to corps dumps inland. On D plus 1 the 540th found the two best beaching channels and favorable exit roads and consolidated unloading at two American beaches. The regiment eliminated the British Peter beaches by D plus 3, and British supply rolled in over the American beaches as well.[38]

One obstacle to hasty unloading was shallow water, which made it necessary to anchor the Liberty ships two miles offshore. Cargoes therefore came in on LCTs or DUKWs. The average load of all LCTs was 151 long tons; of DUKWs, three tons. Cargo from Liberty ships began to reach the beaches on the afternoon of D plus 1, and the VI Corps dumps (one mile beyond the beach) opened at 2300 the same day. All the D-day convoys of LCTs and LSTs were completely unloaded by 0800 on 24 January, D plus 2. But even their rapid discharge could not obviate the fact that the scarce LSTs supplying the Anzio beachhead had to remain on the scene until spring, long past the time allotted. Their continued stay in the Mediterranean to serve shallow-water ports denied

[36] *Fifth Army History*, vol. IV, pp. 59–62; Paxson interv.

[37] *Engineer History, Mediterranean*, pp. 85–86.

[38] Hist 36th Engr C Rgt, 1 Jun 41–23 Jun 44; *Engineer History, Mediterranean*, p. 100; Hist 540th Engr C Rgt, 1942–45; Paxson interv.

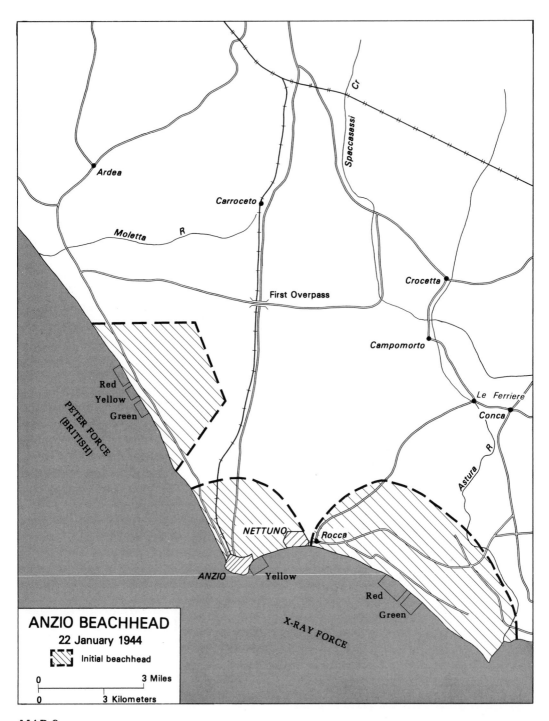

Ardea

Carroceto

Moletta    R

First Overpass

Crocetta

Campomorto

Red
Yellow
Green

Le Ferriere

Conca

PETER FORCE
(BRITISH)

Spaccasassi    Cr

Astura    R

NETTUNO

Rocca

ANZIO    Yellow

Red

Green

X-RAY FORCE

ANZIO BEACHHEAD
22 January 1944

Initial beachhead

0                                  3 Miles

0                      3 Kilometers

*MAP 9*

them to the BOLERO planners in England, who were bent on accumulating at least half the assault shipping required for the invasion of the Continent by the beginning of 1944.[39]

The 540th owed its performance at Anzio to several factors. The men of the unit had been able to plan for SHINGLE at Caserta with the 3d Division, and they had practiced landings with the division and its attached units. During 17–19 January the final exercise, WEBFOOT, involved the 3d U.S. and 1st British Divisions, a Ranger force, and attached supply troops. The rehearsal was not full scale; LSTs did not carry vehicles and LCTs were only token loaded, but the assault units did get some training in passing beach obstacles, unloading personnel and equipment, combat firing, and general orientation.[40]

The 540th had been able to obtain extra 1/4- and 3/4-ton trucks, D–7 angledozers, sixteen- and six-ton prime movers, cranes, mine detectors, beach markers, and lights. The D–7s proved especially valuable on D plus 1 in pulling out 100 vehicles mired down in the dewaterproofing area. Compared with previous landings, the 540th Engineers had a better system of recording the numbers of vehicles and personnel and quantities of supplies by class. These advantages helped to nullify mistakes in planning and deficiencies in training. Not until the 540th was about to leave Naples for Anzio did its attached units

report—after loading plans were complete. Since the 540th had to plan for the embarkation on the basis of TOEs rather than actual unit strengths, it was difficult to load units properly. The loading plan was faulty in that beach groups went aboard by units instead of by teams.[41]

Supplies landed late at the port of Anzio on D-day, when LSTs did not enter from the outer harbor until eight hours after naval units had signaled that the harbor had been swept for mines. The Navy beachmaster would not take the responsibility of acting on the signal, and the deadlock was broken only when two Army officers appealed personally to Admiral Hewitt.

Officers of the 540th Engineers sometimes found working with the British easier than working with the U.S. Navy, possibly because there were more opportunities for friction with the U.S. Navy. Its responsibility for unloading extended to the beaches, whereas the Royal Navy's jurisdiction ended when the craft hit the beaches. Teamwork was often poor between floating and shore U.S. Navy echelons. Furthermore, the commanding officers of the naval beach battalion had been reluctant to train and live with the Army. The naval beach group did not have enough bulldozers and needed Army help for salvage work. The Navy also needed bulldozer spare parts, but these the Army could not provide because the Navy used Allis-Chalmers bulldozers, which the Army did not have.[42]

At the beach the principal engineer work was to improve exit roads over soft, boggy clay soil. Engineers had to

[39] Joseph Bykofsky and Harold Larson, *The Transportation Corps: Operations Overseas*, United States Army in World War II (Washington, 1957), p. 58; Coakley and Leighton, *Global Logistics and Strategy, 1943–45*, p. 233.

[40] Mark W. Clark, *Calculated Risk* (New York: Harper and Brothers, 1950), pp. 268–69.

[41] Hist 540th Engr C Rgt, 1942–45.

[42] Rpt, Col D. A. Newcomer, 28 Jun 44, in AGF Bd Rpt 162, NATOUSA.

36TH ENGINEER COMBAT REGIMENT TROOPS REMOVE GERMAN CHARGES *from buildings in Anzio.*

use corduroy because they did not have enough rock, even after taking as much as possible from the rubble-strewn towns of Anzio and Nettuno. They used Sommerfeld matting, which the 540th Engineers modified for beach roads, to some extent. They made the rolls lighter and the footing better by removing four out of every five lateral rods and using the extra rods as pickets to hold down the matting. The engineers tried brush on the roads, but corduroy proved the best substitute for rock.[43]

On 7 February the enemy began a series of assaults that threatened to split the bridgehead within a fortnight. Engineers went into the line as infantry, holding down both extreme flanks of the Anzio enclave, the 39th Engineer Combat Regiment on the right and the 36th Engineer Combat Regiment, a corps unit, taking over the British 56th Infantry Division's responsibility in a sector about nine miles northwest of Anzio on the extreme left. In the line for forty-five days through February and March, the 36th held 5,600 yards of front along the Moletta River with 2,150 men, its reserve almost constantly employed. The engineers spent 1 1/2 days training mortar men and consider-

---

[43] Notes on Landings in Operation SHINGLE, 8 Feb 44, in Hist 1st ESB, Jan–Dec 44; Maj Gilbert T. Phelps, Observations in Amphibious Landing, Anzio, in AGF Bd Rpt 120, NATOUSA; Hist 540th Engr C Rgt.

able time afterward gathering necessary sniper rifles, automatic weapons, and 37- and 57-mm. antitank guns.[44]

Though the 39th performed well, the hard-pressed 36th quickly showed its inadequate infantry training. Conspicuous was its failure to seize prisoners during night patrolling in the early commitment to the line. Upon a corps order to send out one patrol each night from each battalion on the front, the engineers blackened their faces and reversed their clothing to camouflage themselves and left their helmets behind to avoid making noise in the shrubbery. When they sallied out into the darkness, however, they lost two men to the Germans and captured no prisoners in return. One observer remembered that the men were not "prepared to kill" and seemed afraid to fire their rifles in fear of drawing the attention of the whole German Army to themselves. The regiment's inexperience also showed in casualty figures, which reached 16 percent. Seventy-four men were killed in action, 336 wounded, and 277 hospitalized.[45]

During the fighting at Anzio destroying bridges was more important to the engineers than building them. A bridge VI Corps engineers blew up at Carroceto on the afternoon of 8 February kept twelve German tanks from breaking through to the sea. On the tenth the engineers staved off a possible German breakthrough by destroying a bridge over Spaccasassi Creek.[46]

When the Allies were forced on the defensive at Anzio the engineers laid extensive minefields for the first time in the Italian campaign. They planted mines haphazardly and made inaccurate and incomplete records. They laid many mines, both antipersonnel and antitank, at night in places with no distinct natural features. Some of this haste and inefficiency was attributed to insufficiently trained men, including some who were not engineers and who were not qualified for mine-sowing. Troops disregarded instructions 15th Army Group issued early in the campaign on recording friendly minefields. The result was a marked increase in casualties.

As the Anzio beachhead stabilized, haphazard methods became more deliberate and careful. Fields were marked and recorded before mines were actually laid. After 10 February VI Corps insisted that antipersonnel mines be placed in front of protective wire and that antitank mines be laid behind the final protective line, both in order to guard against night-lifting by the enemy. At regular intervals the VI Corps engineers issued a map overlay numbering and locating each antipersonnel and antitank minefield on the beachhead.[47]

No standard method of planting mines existed, but the system developed by the 109th Engineer Combat Battalion was representative. The battalion used four men to a row, with teams made up of a pacer who measured the distance, a driver who placed the mines, and two armers who activated the mines. At Anzio in April 1944 a platoon of the 109th in one day devoted 240 manhours to planting 2,444 antitank mines

---

[44] Hist 36th Engr C Rgt, 1 Jun 41–23 Jun 44.
[45] Ibid.; Rpt, Newcomer, 28 Jun 44, in AGF Bd Rpt 162, NATOUSA.
[46] Dept of the Army, Historical Div, *Anzio Beachhead, (22 January –25 May 1944),* American Forces in Action Series (Washington, 1947), pp. 83–84, 97.

[47] AGF Bd Rpt 465, MTO, 9 Jun 45; Rpt, Newcomer, 28 Jun 44, in AGF Bd Rpt 162, NATOUSA.

SOLDIER FROM THE 39TH ENGINEER COMBAT REGIMENT ASSEMBLES M1A1 ANTITANK MINES AT ANZIO

and 199 antipersonnel mines. A separate squad took ninety-six man-hours to mark these minefields.

One of the most serious mistakes in planting mines was laying them too close together. For example, the 39th Engineer Combat Regiment laid a large minefield that a single mortar shell detonated. The experience of many units proved that a density of 1 1/2 antitank mines per yard of front was the optimum for regularly laid out fields to avoid sympathetic detonation. The engineers obtained this density by laying several staggered rows of mines, an approximation of the German pattern. The AFHQ engineer specified wider spacing for antipersonnel mines, a rule

of thumb that established one mine per three to five yards of front, assuming the use of trip wires.[48]

Once the Germans stopped trying to eliminate VI Corps' beachhead, the Anzio front settled down into stalemate. The 39th Engineers, with assistance from the 540th, then had an opportunity to improve all roads within the beachhead. Good macadam roads ran through the area in wagon-spoke style, and a few smaller gravel roads branched off. Engineers bulldozed additional dirt roads across the open fields, but trucks using them had to drop into very low

[48] Hist 109th Engr C Bn, 1943–45; AFHQ Engr Technical Bull 15, 10 Feb 44.

gear to plow through the mud. The engineers maintained only about thirty-one miles of road at the beachhead, but constant enemy bombing and shelling compelled continuous inspections and surface repair. Engineers built a considerable number of bridges in the beachhead area; the 10th Engineer Combat Battalion, for instance, built 2 Baileys, 9 treadways, and 19 footbridges.[49]

During the breakout from the Anzio beachhead, the 34th Division's 109th Engineer Combat Battalion had the task of opening and maintaining roads to the front lines, clearing lanes through Allied minefields up to the front, and opening gaps in Allied wire on the front to ensure the safe and uninterrupted passage of another infantry division, the 1st Armored Division, and the 1st Special Service Force through the 34th Division's sector. Work started during the night of 14 May; enemy observation forced the engineer units to work only after dark. Many of the minefields had been under heavy enemy fire from small arms, machine guns, and artillery. The mines became extremely sensitive and were likely to detonate under the slightest pressure. The engineers completed most of the mine clearing during the night of 20 May, but they had to wait to remove wire and to mark gaps which would disclose the direction of the corps attack. On the night of 22 May the engineers removed the wire

from the gaps and marked each lane with tracing tape and luminous markers. The breakout was a complete success.[50]

On 31 May Peninsular Base Section took over the Anzio port after four months and twenty-five days of operation by the 540th Engineer Combat Regiment. Supply had been slow through much of February and March because of bad weather and enemy air raids. The shallow offshore gradients and the small beaches hampered the use of regular cargo ships and coasters. Such vessels were excellent targets for German aircraft, so shallow-draft craft were used as much as possible. The whole process of delivering supplies speeded up in March with the use of preloaded trucks, which discharged from the LSTs and other vessels directly onto Anzio harbor's seawalls and pier and moved directly to the dumps. Liberty ships carrying supplies unloaded onto LCTs or DUKWs. In turn, the LCTs unloaded onto DUKWs offshore or directly onto wharves in Anzio harbor; the DUKWs went directly to the dumps. Between 6 and 29 February, 73,251 tons were discharged at Anzio; between 1 and 31 March, 158,274 tons. The 7,828 tons that came in on 29 March made Anzio port the "fourth largest in the world."[51]

---

[49] Hist 39th Engr C Rgt, Jan–Dec 44; Hist 10th Engr C Bn, 1944.

[50] Hist 109th Engr C Bn, 1943–45.

[51] *Engineer History, Mediterranean*, p. 86; Bykofsky and Larson, *The Transportation Corps: Operations Overseas*, pp. 223–24.

# CHAPTER X

# The Advance to the Alps

By the time the Allied armies collided with the German Winter Line defenses in late 1943, the American theater command had changed considerably. In the aftermath of the North African invasion the need to reorganize had been clear; the issue of new command arrangements was a lively one at the American headquarters, but the demands of combat kept it pending until the downfall of Axis forces in Tunisia and Sicily.

The chief defect still lay in the overlapping and sometimes contradictory authorities in the administrative and supply chain. A new theater engineer, Brig. Gen. Dabney O. Elliott, continued to exercise his advisory and staff functions in three separate commands—AFHQ; NATOUSA; and COMZ, NATOUSA—an arrangement that bypassed the Services of Supply command. No formal controls of the engineering function existed between SOS, NATOUSA, and the chief engineer of the theater as they did in General Lee's SOS, ETOUSA, jurisdiction in the United Kingdom. Maj. Gen. Thomas B. Larkin as chief of the SOS, NATOUSA, command had only nominal control over the base sections then existing in the theater and virtually no say in the flow of supply once materiel moved out of the bases for the front lines. Larkin's relationship with the AFHQ G–4 was unclear and in many ways duplicative through the period of operations in North Africa; it improved only after his concerted efforts to revise the command situation met with some success.[1]

## Reorganization

In March 1943, one month after the formation of the theater, General Larkin began a campaign to eliminate the anomalies and duplications that weakened or destroyed his effectiveness as supposed chief of all American supply operations in the theater. He made small headway against the resistance of the staff officers at NATOUSA and AFHQ who insisted upon retaining their acquired authority, citing in their own behalf the dangers of repeating the bitter disputes over the SOS, ETO-USA, empire under General Lee. In hopes of reducing the manpower drains in theater-level headquarters, the War Department sent an Inspector General's survey team to North Africa and to England in late spring 1943. The team's report, in effect, recommended a 50 percent reduction in the number of overhead personnel in the theater staffs in NATOUSA, a solid impetus for reorganization and economy in manpower.

---

[1] See ch. V. This section is based upon Meyer, The Strategy and Logistical History: MTO, ch. VII, except as otherwise noted. General Elliott was succeeded as theater engineer on 1 September 1944 by Maj. Gen. David J. McCoach, Jr.

Various plans originating at AFHQ and NATOUSA undertook to eliminate the command discrepancies and to reduce the manpower surpluses in headquarters' staffs. Their authors usually proceeded on the assumption that vast changes were necessary in any staff element but their own. After a summer and fall of conflicting suggestions in 1943, the SOS, NATOUSA, command had no increased authority to deal with its increased responsibilities, which now spanned the Mediterranean and extended to a new base section in Italy. Headquarters, NATOUSA, insisted upon the continued control of personnel in the base sections, denying to Larkin efficient use of manpower and timely use of specialty units when he needed them.

The arrival of a new theater commander broke the impasse and presaged the decline of Headquarters, NATOUSA, and the disappearance of COMZ, NATOUSA, in early 1944. On 31 December 1943, Lt. Gen. Jacob L. Devers relieved General Eisenhower, who returned to ETOUSA. When Devers arrived in North Africa on 8 January 1944, the War Department had imposed a deadline of 1 March for the revision of the NATOUSA command structure. Devers' arrival also roughly coincided with another exchange between SOS, NATOUSA, and Headquarters, NATOUSA, about more men for the burgeoning supply responsibilities in the theater. Within a week in late January General Larkin received two contradictory orders from NATOUSA. The first instructed him to tap the existing base sections for manpower, a course he was reluctant to take since it would rob already shorthanded organizations in his nominal chain of command; the second canceled the authority to secure manpower from even that source and removed manpower allocations authority for base sections entirely to the NATOUSA level.

On 14 February Devers called the conference that restructured the theaters. *(Chart 2)* His NATOUSA General Order Number 12, effective 24 February, transferred all duties and responsibilities of COMZ, NATOUSA, originally set up only as a rationale to support the position of deputy theater commander, to SOS, NATOUSA. In the month after the meeting the NATOUSA staff took much of the theater reduction in manpower.[2] While the staff did not disappear altogether, its functions became almost entirely identified with the American side of AFHQ. Headquarters, NATOUSA, concerned itself with matters of broad policy at the theater level, and General Larkin formally assumed command of all base sections in the theater and the service and supply functions between them and the combat zones.

Consistent with this general transfer and with a subsequent NATOUSA staff memorandum, the AFHQ-NATOUSA engineer retained only policy and planning responsibility. He could initiate broad directives, recommend theater-wide engineer stock levels, write training directives and standards, recommend troop allocations in the communications zone, maintain technical data on Allied or enemy engineer equipment or doctrine, and provide analyses of operations plans and American engineer commitments in the theater. The

[2] NATOUSA GO 12, 20 Feb 44; History and Composition of the North African/Mediterranean Theater of Operations, 12 Sep 42–2 Dec 47, p. 67.

# CHART 2—THEATER STRUCTURE, AFHQ AND NATOUSA, 8 FEBRUARY 1944

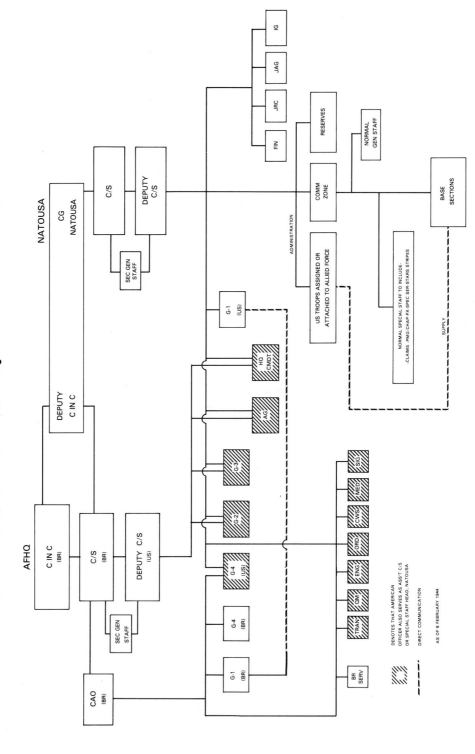

broader engineer aspects of Allied military government also fell within his purview.[3]

In General Larkin's SOS, NATO-USA, executive agency, the SOS engineer had unfettered jurisdiction over operational engineer matters in the theater COMZ. He controlled engineer units assigned to that command, governed the issue of nonstandard equipment to all American engineer troops, ruled on all requests to exceed accommodation scales, and handled all American real estate questions. He also controlled the issue of engineer supply to Allied forces, coordinating with AFHQ only on British requests. He was responsible for taking general operational directives emanating from AFHQ and preparing supply requisitions and bills of materials to support stated theater programs and policies.[4]

When the Fifth Army Base Section at Naples became the Peninsular Base Section (PBS) on 25 October 1943, it passed from Fifth Army control to the still divided American theater command in North Africa. Until February 1944 the base section in the Mediterranean came under NATOUSA headquarters for command and administration but answered to General Larkin's SOS, NATOUSA, organization for supply. General Pence's PBS command also had some responsibilities to the 15th Army Group in administrative areas, especially those affecting the Italian population.

As Fifth Army moved north, base section jurisdiction grew: the army rear boundary was always the PBS forward boundary. The base section engineer, Col. Donald S. Burns, submitted his first consolidated estimates for the supply requirements of the Fifth Army engineers, the III Air Service Area Command, and various other branches of the PBS Engineer Service and the Petroleum Branch on 15 October 1943, but the Fifth Army G–4 continued to prepare engineer requisitions until December, when the responsibility shifted entirely to PBS for Fifth Army and base section engineer supply. Requisitions then went directly from PBS to SOS, NATOUSA, and its successor command, designated Communications Zone, NATOUSA, on 1 October 1944. Exactly one month later the theater command changed from NATOUSA to Mediterranean Theater of Operations (MTOUSA). On 20 November the COMZ structure was eliminated and its functions passed to the G–4 and the special staff of the MTOUSA headquarters, which then handled engineer requisitions and other supply for the theater. (Chart 3)[5]

While the theater reorganization was bringing order to the higher echelons on the American side of AFHQ and its immediately subordinate commands, several important changes also occurred in Fifth Army's command and administration of its engineers and other service troops. Col. Frank O. Bowman, the Fifth Army engineer, promoted to brigadier general on 22 February, became convinced by early spring

[3] NATOUSA Adm Memo 2, 20 Feb 44; NATOUSA Staff Memo 14, 21 Mar 44, app. B.

[4] NATOUSA Staff Memo 14, 21 Mar 44, app. B; History of Allied Force Headquarters and Headquarters NATOUSA, pt. III, Period of the Italian Campaign from the Winter Line to Rome, sec. 4, pp. 968–73.

[5] Ltr, Brig Gen Arthur W. Pence, CG, PBS, to Maj Gen Karl Truesdell, CG, C&GSC, 26 Nov 43, sub: Organization of PBS; Periodic Rpt, SOS NATOUSA, G–4, 31 Dec 43.

CHART 3—OFFICE OF THE CHIEF ENGINEER, MTOUSA, 28 JANUARY 1945

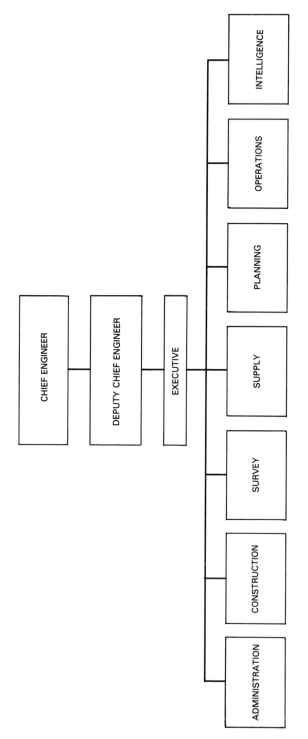

As of 28 January 1945

of 1944 of the necessity of obtaining direct command of all Fifth Army engineer troops. Other technical service staff officers shared this idea, particularly General Clark's ordnance officer, Col. Urban Niblo.[6]

On 26 March 1944, all corps and army engineer units were assigned to a new Fifth Army Engineer Command. Corps engineer units, however, remained attached to their respective corps. Accordingly, though General Bowman obtained administrative and supply control over all engineer units except those organic to divisions, he did not have operational control over those attached to corps. His headquarters, designated a major command of the Fifth Army, had an operational and administrative status similar to a general staff division, and he had the authority he considered necessary to meet his responsibilities. He could move army engineer troops from point to point on his own authority and could transfer Fifth Army engineers from American to British sectors and back.[7]

Below General Bowman in the Fifth Army engineer organization were corps engineer sections, each with a TOE calling for only six officers and fourteen enlisted men. Some attempt was made to obtain approval for corps-level engineer commands patterned after General Bowman's, but the corps commanders preferred that the corps engineer remain a staff officer only.[8]

The engineer combat regiment was the mainstay of corps-level engineer strength at the start of the Italian campaign, but in December 1942 War Department planning revised the formal and rigid structure of Army units, eliminating the "type army" and "type corps" conceptions. The redivision of forces that followed placed engineer units by functions, under Army Ground Forces control if they supported combat units or under Army Service Forces control if they had primarily service support assignments in base sections or the communications zone. Engineer units were frequently hard to classify since the nature of their assignments and training carried them across the boundaries established in Army Ground Forces Commander Lt. Gen. Lesley J. McNair's reorganization.

Further revision of the unit classification continued through 1944; at the end of the year only divisional engineers were listed as combat troops, with nondivisional engineers supporting fighting units being listed as combat support. At the same time General McNair pushed for economies in service forces and in staff overheads in field commands. He strove to separate nondivisional service regiments, including engineers, into their component battalions and to impose a group headquarters capable of handling four battalions at once in place of the formal and traditional regimental headquarters in the field.[9] The group headquarters had no units assigned organically but controlled the movements and work assignments of each battalion as an attached unit.

In the summer of 1943, McNair outlined his new organizational precepts

---

[6] Mayo, *The Ordnance Department: On Beachhead and Battlefront*, pp. 187–89, 218.

[7] *Engineer History, Mediterranean*, p. 266.

[8] Hist 1108th Engr C Gp, Feb–Oct 44; Comments, Col L. B. Gallagher, II Corps Engr, May 59.

[9] WD Memo WDGCT 320 (17 Dec 42) for CG, AGF, 24 Dec 42, sub: Reorgn of Units of the Army, 320.2/5816; Coll, Keith, and Rosenthal, *The Corps of Engineers: Troops and Equipment*, p. 222.

in a letter to all training commands under his control. He recommended that to manage troops engaged in combat the higher level headquarters divide the administrative load, making the corps solely a tactical headquarters and limiting field army headquarters to overall tactical supervision with responsibility for supply and all other administrative functions. The new program did make for marked economies in manpower, and at the end of the war the revisions had contributed to far more efficient combat units. But General McNair's innovations were not received with favor everywhere, nor were they applied consistently. The technical services, notably the engineers, had already anticipated some aspects of the reform, but as the distance from Washington increased the revision tended to become watered down or compromised with proven local practice.[10]

Resistance to the group concept began at the top of the Fifth Army Engineer Command in Italy. When the War Department authorized the establishment of group headquarters for all service units in October 1943, the rate of conversion was left to the theater command. General Bowman, with the concurrence of General Elliott, the AFHQ engineer, slowed down the adoption of groups, keeping "the correspondence about the change bouncing between Italy and Washington." Bowman believed that the group organization hurt morale because the attachment of single battalions to larger units lasted for only brief periods. Some engineer regiments continued to operate as such until 1945.[11]

Even after all the combat engineer regiments had converted, arguments continued over the value of the change. General Bowman also believed that the various group headquarters added to administrative overhead and reduced even further the amount of construction equipment available, thereby aggravating an already critical problem. The II Corps engineer, Col. Leonard B. Gallagher, held that the group operated less efficiently than the regiment. Lt. Col. William P. Jones, Jr., commander of an engineer battalion attached to II Corps' 1108th Engineer Combat Group, contended that the group wasted scarce trained engineer officers and specialists. There were, however, strong defenders of group organization who stressed the gain in flexibility and pointed out that a group headquarters could control more battalions than could a regimental headquarters. The 1108th Combat Group in 1945, for example, had under it as many as seven units at one time and for a period supported five divisions. The quality of the group or regimental commander and the experience of his men were the keys to the effectiveness of both organizations. In any case, the self-contained battalion became a workable organization.[12]

The divisional engineers had both staff and command responsibilities. Unlike the G-3, who thought mainly in terms of objectives, a division engineer was largely concerned with such matters as routes of approach, crossing sites, and covered assembly areas for

---

[10] Ltr, Lt Gen L. J. McNair to Comdding Generals, 21 Jul 43, sub: Orientation with Reference to Revised Organization, 320.2/6031 (R) (21 Jul 43), GNGCT.

[11] WD Cir 256, 16 Oct 43.
[12] Paxson comments.

equipment. Since building and maintaining roads in the division area as well as supporting three regimental combat teams were necessary, the three companies of each divisional engineer battalion had to be divided among four missions. This dispersion made the battalion less efficient and overburdened the men. Consequently, from the very beginning of the campaign, corps engineer units answered constant requests to move forward into divisional areas.[13]

General Bowman believed that those in command needed convincing that tactical boundaries between divisions and corps could not apply to engineer work. The division engineer could—and did—ask the corps engineer to take over work in division areas that the division could not do with its own forces. In fact, army engineers sometimes worked well into divisional sections. The belief was quite common that the divisional combat battalion was simply too small to do all the work required of it.

Throughout the long campaign the engineers of Fifth Army, especially those in the divisions, resisted attachment to combat teams. In the 313th Engineer Combat Battalion, 88th Division, the line companies normally supported the same infantry regiment all the time, with the engineer company commander becoming practically a member of the regimental staff. The companies never waited for the engineer battalion to direct them to perform their normal mission, so infantry regimental commanders rarely insisted on having the engineer companies attached to them. But by the end of the war attachment was rare in other divisions because the

GENERAL ELLIOTT

infantry commanders finally became convinced that engineer support would be where they wanted it when they needed it.[14]

Most engineer officers favored a daily support system in the belief that once engineer troops became attached to a forward echelon they could not easily be transferred again. They believed it impossible to forecast accurately the amount of engineer work required in the areas that lay ahead; any specific number of engineers attached would be either too large or too small. Additionally, improvised task forces and

---

[13] Comments, Col Hugh K. Burch, 16 Jun 59.

[14] Summary of Opns, 19th Engr C Rgt with II Corps, 1944–45; Bowman comments; Comments, Cole, 25 Feb 59, and Armogida, 27 Apr 59.

regimental combat teams in general did not have the staff organization to control engineer work, so lost motion and confusion became common. The engineers also maintained that subordinate commanders retained engineer units after their specific task was done.

The nature of engineer tasks often splintered engineer units—regiments, battalions, and detachments alike. Depot, camouflage, maintenance, and dump truck companies were more susceptible than others. In June 1944 the 16th Armored Engineer Battalion came together for the first time in more than four months. Such dispersion inevitably affected performance, discipline, and morale, caused duplication of effort, and made administration more difficult.[15]

### The Offensive Resumed

When the Allied offensive resumed in May 1944, the main Fifth Army line south of Anzio was to drive north up the coast to meet VI Corps troops breaking out of the static bridgehead. North of Anzio, other VI Corps units were to strike for Rome. Preparations for the renewed offensive began in March with a shift of British Eighth Army units westward to take over the Cassino and Rapido fronts, leaving in their place a garrison force on the eastern Italian coast. Thus relieved, and with replacements arriving to bring its divisions up to strength, Fifth Army consisted of the American II Corps and the French Expeditionary Corps concentrated on

a thirteen-mile front between the Italian west coast and the Liri River, with II Corps holding the left flank of the line. Two fresh but inexperienced American divisions, the 85th and the 88th, would bear the brunt of the drive along Highway 7 to effect a junction with the forces at Anzio, now reinforced to a strength of 5 1/2 divisions.[16]

A devastating artillery bombardment commencing at 2300 on 11 May sparked the offensive on the southern front, and at dawn the Mediterranean Allied Air Forces rained destruction on the enemy rear. The Anzio breakout began on 23 May, and on the twenty-fifth VI Corps was advancing toward the Alban Hills. The same day, after II Corps had driven sixty miles through the mountains, the beachhead and the Fifth Army main line were linked for the first time when men of the 48th Engineer Combat Battalion, II Corps, shook hands with the engineers of the 36th Engineer Combat Regiment, VI Corps, outside the demolished village of Borgo Grappa. The linkup was part of the campaign that smashed the German Gustav Line and the less formidable Hitler Line, which the enemy had thrown across the Liri valley and the mountain ranges flanking it.

The nature of the terrain and the scarcity of roads made the Fifth Army's offensive on the southern front largely mountain warfare, in which the experienced French corps bore a major share of the burden. The only good road available to Fifth Army, Highway 7, crossed the Garigliano near its mouth

---

[15] Comments, Armogida, Bowman, Cole, Burch, and Killian; Hists, 423d Engr Dump Truck Co, 15 Apr 42–1 Sep 45, and 16th Armd Engr Bn, Jun 44. Unit histories of separate, specialized engineer units bear out these conclusions.

[16] For tactical details see Ernest F. Fisher, Jr., *From Cassino to the Alps*, United States Army in World War II (Washington, 1977), pp. 29–38; see also Lt. Col. Chester G. Starr, *From Salerno to the Alps: A History of the Fifth Army* (Washington: Infantry Journal Press, 1948), pp. 176–77.

and followed the coast to Formia. From there it bent northwest and passed through mountains to Itri and Fondi, then along the coastal marshes to Terracina, where it turned again to the northwest, proceeding on a level and nearly straight course through the Pontine marshes to Cisterna. Beyond Cisterna the road led toward Rome by way of Velletri, skirting the Alban Hills to the south.

Highway 7 lay at the extreme left of the line of advance, but it was II Corps' sole supply route. Apart from this highway Fifth Army had the use of two or three lateral roads, a few second- and third-class mountain roads in the French corps' area, and some mountain trails. Insufficient as the roadnet was, it was spared the sort of destruction that the enemy might have been able to visit upon it in a less hasty withdrawal.

After the breakout began, the engineers labored night and day to open the roads and keep them in shape under the heavy pounding of military traffic. At first the engineers' chief concerns were to erect three additional Class 40 bridges over the Garigliano, two for the French and one for II Corps; to strengthen to Class 30 a bridge in the French Expeditionary Corps zone; and to build several assault bridges for troops and mules. Then engineers began improving trails into roads for jeeps, tanks, and 2 1/2-ton trucks, often under artillery fire. Starting about the middle of May the principal engineer work was clearing and repairing Highway 7 and a road leading across the northern slopes of the Aurunci Mountains to Pico on lateral Highway 82. (Map 10)[17]

The 313th Engineer Combat Battalion, 88th Division, undertook swift construction to outflank the Formia corridor on Highway 7. In one day the men of this battalion opened a mountain road that the Germans had spent two weeks preparing for demolition. This road connected with a trail two miles long that the 313th built in nine hours over steep hills that vehicles had never before traversed. A few men working angledozers through farmland and brick terraces and along mountain slopes did the work. A German engineer colonel, captured a few hours after the battle and evacuated over the road, was amazed, for no road had been there twenty-four hours earlier.[18]

At Itri on Highway 7 a platoon of Company A of the 310th Engineer Combat Battalion, 85th Division, built a 100-foot Bailey and turned over its maintenance to the 19th Engineer Combat Regiment. The 235th Engineer Combat Battalion, a II Corps unit that normally supported the 310th, followed up the 310th's repair and clearance work along Highway 7. The Germans had destroyed many bridges between Fondi and Terracina, and the American engineers had to build bypasses and culverts. At a narrow pass between the mountains and the sea east of Terracina, tank traps and roadblocks, covered by German fire from nearby hills, slowed the advance along the highway. When a blown bridge along this stretch halted American tanks, armored bulldozers of the 235th and 310th Engineer Battalions and the 19th Engineer Regiment, all under fire, built a bypass that made it possible to resume the advance. Lt. Col. Allen F. Clark, Jr.,

---

[17] *Engineer History, Mediterranean*, p. 82; *Fifth Army History*, vol. V, pp. 6–8, 98–99.

[18] *Engineer History, Mediterranean*, p. 113; Comments, Armogida, 27 Apr 59.

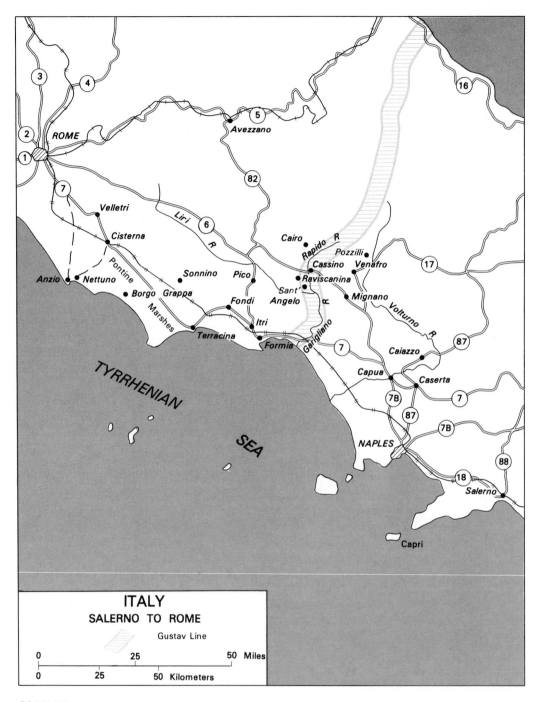

**ITALY**

SALERNO TO ROME

Gustav Line

| 0 | 25 | 50 Miles |

| 0 | 25 | 50 Kilometers |

*MAP 10*

commanding the 235th, operated one of the bulldozers.[19]

When the advance slowed at Terracina the 310th Engineer Combat Battalion immediately started on an alternate route to connect the highway with Sonnino. A road capable of carrying the traffic of an entire division had to be cut into the rocky slopes of the Ausonia Mountains. The engineers' road-building machinery had done remarkable things in the mountain chain during the drive from the Garigliano, but this job required much hand work and many demolitions, explosives for which had to be carried by hand up rugged mountain slopes. The engineers had cut six miles of the new road, with only one mile left, when a breakthrough at Terracina made it unnecessary to finish the alternate route. The work was not entirely lost, for the road reduced the need for pack-mules and made it possible to move division artillery farther forward to interdict the road junction at Sonnino.[20]

Beyond Terracina the highway ran thirty miles straight through the Pontine marshes to Cisterna. All the engineers available worked around the clock repairing and maintaining three routes through the marshy flats. The Germans had attempted to flood much of this region but were only partially successful; the water was low in the streams and canals. Nevertheless, the engineers had to do considerable filling along the main routes as well as some bypassing and bridging. When Highway 7 and the supplementary routes were open to the Anzio beachhead, troops and supplies came up from the southern front in an uninterrupted stream. Fifth Army's momentum was so great that after the capture of Rome on 4 June the advance proceeded beyond the city without pause.

### The Arno

During the summer advance to the Arno, about 150 miles, the Fifth Army front reached inland approximately 45 miles. Two main national highways ran northward in the army zone. Highway 1 ran northwest up the coast through a succession of important towns, including Civitavecchia and Leghorn, to Pisa, near the mouth of the Arno. For most of its length the highway ran along a comparatively flat coastal plain, nowhere more than ten miles wide, but between Cecina and Leghorn, Highway 1 twisted over mountains that reached down to the sea. The other main road, Highway 2, wound through hills, mountains, and river valleys along a route that led from Rome through Siena to Florence. There were five good two-way lateral roads in the area between Rome and the Arno; numerous smaller roads were, for the most part, narrow and unpaved.

During the advance to the Arno the army had to cross only two rivers of any size, the Ombrone and the Cecina, both at low water. The port of Leghorn fell to the 34th Division, II Corps, on 19 July. Beyond Leghorn lay numerous canals, but engineers quickly bridged them. Four days later the 34th Division reached Pisa. The march in the dry summer weather took place in clouds of dust that drew artillery fire and choked the troops. Soldiers wore goggles over their eyes and handkerchiefs

---

[19] *Engineer History, Mediterranean,* p. 110; Comments, Cole and Killian.
[20] Comments, Armogida, 27 Apr 59.

across their noses and mouths. Some of the roads, surfaces ground through by military traffic, were six to eight inches deep in dust. Sprinkling the roads with water was the best way to lay the dust, but water tanks were so scarce that only the most important roads could be sprinkled. Sometimes the engineers applied calcium chloride, but it was also scarce and its value questionable. Engineers had some success with used oil, but even that was in short supply.[21]

During the June and July drive to the Arno much of Fifth Army's forces departed to prepare for ANVIL, the invasion of southern France. The army lost VI Corps and the French Corps. That loss amounted to seven full divisions, and the loss of separate combat units amounted to another division. The nondivisional engineer units splitting away at that time included the 36th and 540th Engineer Combat Regiments, the 48th Engineer Combat Battalion, and the 343d and 344th Engineer General Service Regiments. On 1 June Fifth Army's assigned strength had been approximately 250,000; on 1 August it was little more than 150,000. Making up the losses were the Japanese-American 442d Regimental Combat Team (which arrived in May but left for France in late September); two new and inexperienced U.S. Army infantry divisions, the 91st and 92d; and the first elements, about a regimental combat team, of the untried Brazilian Expeditionary Force, which was to grow to the size of a division. In August General Clark gained control over the veteran

British 13 Corps consisting of four divisions.

From mid-July to mid-August Fifth Army made little forward progress; it paused to rest, to build up supplies, and to prepare for the ordeal ahead. The II and IV Corps held the 35-mile sector along the Arno, IV Corps occupying the greater part of the line while the major portion of II Corps was in the rear preparing for the coming offensive. The troops received special instruction in river crossing and mountain warfare. Engineer detachments gave instruction in handling footbridges and boats, in scaling steep banks with grappling hooks and ladders, and in detecting and clearing mines.

The Italian campaign resumed in earnest on 24 August with an Eighth Army attack on the Adriatic front. The Fifth Army crossed the Arno on 1 September, and on 9 and 10 September II Corps launched an offensive north of Florence. With 13 Corps beside it, II Corps battled through the mountains, capturing strongpoint after strongpoint, and on the eighteenth reached the Santerno valley by way of Il Giogo Pass. The 88th Division outflanked Futa Pass, key to the enemy's Gothic Line defenses, and on the twenty-second a battalion of the 91st Division secured the pass. Fifth Army had breached one of the strongest defense lines the enemy had constructed in Italy. The attack had been well timed, for the Germans had diverted part of their strength to the Adriatic front to ward off an Eighth Army blow. With Futa Pass in the hands of Fifth Army troops, the way was clear to send supplies forward by way of Highway 65 and to prepare for an attack northward to Bologna.

Rain, mud, and many miles of moun-

---

[21] Hists, 313th Engr C Bn, 387th Engr C Bn, 11th Engr C Rgt, 1108th Engr C Gp, and other unit histories.

THE RISING ARNO RIVER THREATENS A TREADWAY BRIDGE *in the 1st Armored Division area, September 1944.*

tain terrain combined to aid the enemy. Highway 65 was the only completely paved road available to II Corps, and off that highway 2 1/2-ton trucks mired deep in mud. Such conditions made a mockery of mechanized warfare. Mules and men had to carry food and ammunition to the front. Nevertheless, II Corps troops pushed steadily on and brought the front to a point two miles from Bologna by mid-October. By 23 October the forward troops were within nine miles of Highway 9 and could look down upon their objective in the Po valley. But here the fall offensive faltered. Exhaustion and heavy rains forced a halt, and II Corps dug in.

The fall rains had given the engineers an enormous task. In September the Arno west of Florence in IV Corps' zone flooded its banks and on one occasion rose six to eight feet at the rate of eighteen inches an hour. Late in the month the Serchio also overflowed its banks north of Lucca, at Lucca itself, and at Vecchiano. So much bridge equipment was lost that the IV Corps engineer had to divert engineers from bridge construction and road work to salvage operations.[22] Mountain streams that had dwindled to a trickle in the sum-

---

[22] IV Corps Engr Rpt, Sep–Oct 44; Killian comments.

BAILEY BRIDGE CONSTRUCTION *over the Arno near Florence.*

to supporting frontline troops, corps engineers had to maintain supply routes in the divisional zones.[23]

More floods came in November, and at one time or another during that month all the principal highways were blocked with high water. The 39th Engineer Combat Regiment reported fourteen major road breaks along a six-mile stretch of Highway 6 northwest of Florence, making necessary the construction of four Bailey and three timber trestle bridges. The autostrada, a four-lane superhighway that carved an arc through the Arno valley, connecting Florence with Pistoia, Lucca, and the coastal road north from Pisa, was covered for miles with water as deep as two feet. As the campaign ground to a halt, the whole Italian front settled down into mud.[24]

### The Winter Stalemate

The stalemate continued throughout the winter of 1944–45. To permit supplies to be brought forward, the engineers had to work unceasingly on the roads. On Highway 65—the direct road to Bologna from the south, the main supply route for the Fifth Army's central sector, and the only fully paved road in the II Corps zone—jeeps, trucks tanks, and prime movers rolled along almost without letup day and night. Already in bad condition and cut in places by the enemy, Highway 65 suffered serious damage from rain, snow, and the constant pounding of thousands of vehicles, many of them equipped with tire chains. Army, corps, and

mer changed in a few hours to raging torrents. Through most of October the rain continued unabated, becoming a torrential downpour by the end of the month. Cross-country movement virtually ceased, and great quantities of mud were tracked onto the main roads from secondary roads and bivouac areas. Culverts and fills washed out, fords were impassable, and roads softened until they could not withstand heavy military traffic.

Engineer vehicles and equipment deteriorated from constant hauling through deep mud over very rough roads. Breakdowns were so numerous and the supply of spare parts so low that at times some engineer units had to operate with only half of their organic equipment. Because divisional engineers had to devote all their efforts

---

[23] IV Corps Engr Rpt, Sep–Oct 44; Hist II Corps Engr Activities, 10 Sep–Nov 44; Burch comments.
[24] Hist 39th Engr C Rgt, Jun–Dec 44.

divisional engineer units had constantly to maintain the whole length of the road, especially north of Futa Pass, where the pavement virtually disappeared. The main inland supply route for IV Corps, Highway 64, running from Pistoia to Bologna, carried less traffic than Highway 65 and therefore remained in somewhat better condition.[25]

In preparation for winter, the engineers placed snow fences and stockpiled sand. They speeded clearance after snowfalls to prevent ice formation and during thaws to prevent drainage problems. Foreseeing that the greatest difficulty with snow would come in the passes leading to the Po valley, AFHQ developed a plan involving joint transportation and engineer operations to clear the roads. The plan included control posts, road patrols, and a special communications system to report conditions throughout each day. The Engineer Section, Fifth Army, prepared a map that indicated the areas where trouble could be expected, including areas the Germans held. The engineer and transportation units involved piled sand along the roads where the most snow could be expected and parked snow-removal equipment at strategic points along the roads.

The plan worked in the II Corps area, where winter conditions were the most severe. In addition to American and British troops, hundreds of Italians, both civilian and military, worked to keep the roads open. Large rotary snowplows augmented jeeps, graders, bulldozers, and wooden and conventional snowplow attachments fitted to 2 1/2- and 4-ton trucks. Some German and Italian equipment the enemy had left behind also proved useful. Unfortunately, the plan did not develop successfully all along the front. IV Corps was not able to set up a system comparable to the one II Corps employed because IV Corps did not have anything like the snow-removal equipment of II Corps. Instead, IV Corps units had to drop whatever they were doing when snow began to fall and clear the roads with whatever equipment was available. Only a few roads in IV Corps' area were seriously menaced by snow, however, and most lay in the coastal plain.[26]

During the fall and winter the engineers were able to open mountain trails. Soft banks and shoulders gave way readily before bulldozers, which widened roads, provided turnouts on one-lane sections, and improved sharp curves and turns. Huge quantities of rock were required to keep these roads open to a volume of traffic never before contemplated. The 19th Engineers used 25,000 cubic yards of rock to rebuild a 10 1/2-mile stretch of secondary road adjacent to Highway 65 in the Idice valley. Keeping the improved trails open as roads necessitated unending work, including draining, graveling, revetting soft shoulders, removing slides, and building rock retaining walls. The greatest problem was drainage maintenance, for the mountain creeks, gullies, gorges, and cascades, when not properly channeled, poured floods upon the roads. Two months of constant work by thousands of civilians and soldiers using

[25] Hist 185th Engr C Bn, 1944–45; Killian comments; Jones comments.

[26] Engr Tech Bull 28, 28 Feb 45; Chf Engr, 15th Army Gp, Notes on Engr Opns in Italy, no. 26, Mar 45; Hist 39th Engr C Rgt, 1945; Hist 175th Engr GS Rgt, Feb 42–Oct 45; Comments, Bowman and Jones.

both hand labor and machinery not only kept the roads open but improved them. In forward areas infantry units took over the maintenance of some of the lateral roads leading to their dispersed forces.[27]

The first of the units reorganized according to the new group concept began operations in December 1944. To improve control over miscellaneous engineer units operating under the Fifth Army engineer, General Bowman organized the 1168th Engineer Combat Group, with Lt. Col. Salvatore A. Armogida in command. The cadre for the new command came from an antiaircraft headquarters, and under it were such engineer units as a map detachment, dump truck companies, a heavy equipment company, a maintenance company, a fire-fighting detachment, a camouflage company, a topographic company, and a water supply company. Also attached were some Italian engineer battalions and a number of other units under an Italian engineer group.[28]

### The Final Drive

Exceptionally mild weather beginning in mid-February enabled engineers to make substantial progress in repairing and rehabilitating the roadnets and improving and extending bridges. With snow rapidly receding from the highlands, a company of the 126th Engineer Mountain Battalion, organic to the 10th Mountain Division, built a 1,700-foot aerial tramway over Monte Serrasiccia (located 18 miles northwest of Pistoia) on 19 February.

Built at an average slope of 18 to 20 degrees, the tramway was finished in ten hours despite enemy fire. Casualties could come down the mountainside in three minutes instead of six to eight hours. The tramway hauled blood plasma, barbed wire, emergency K rations, water, and ammunition up the mountain. Another timesaver the battalion contributed was a 2,100-foot cableway constructed on 10 March, when the 10th Mountain Division was attacking over rugged terrain. Supported by two A-frames and built in six hours, the cableway saved a six-mile trip for ambulances and supply trucks.[29]

Lt. Gen. Lucian K. Truscott, Jr., became commander of the Fifth Army in December when General Clark moved up to command the 15th Army Group. Before the spring offensive began, the Fifth Army received reinforcements of infantry, artillery, and reserves. Its divisions were overstrength and its morale high as the troops looked forward to a quick triumph over the sagging enemy. The British 13 Corps had returned to Eighth Army, but Fifth Army's reinforcements helped balance that loss.

In April the two Allied armies, carefully guarding the secrecy of the movement, went forward into positions from which they could strike a sudden, devastating blow against the enemy. The Fifth Army front was nearly ninety miles long, reaching from the Ligurian Sea to Monte Grande, ten miles southeast of Bologna. The IV Corps held the left of this line—indeed, the greater part of it—stretching from the sea and through the mountains as far as the Reno River, a distance of about seventy miles. The II Corps crowded

---

[27] Hists, 1108th Engr C Gp, Sep–Dec 44, and 1138th Engr C Gp, 1944–45; *Fifth Army History*, vol. VIII, pp. 21–22, 26; Bowman, Burch, and Cole comments.

[28] Bowman comments.

[29] Ltr, Col Robert P. Boyd, Jr., 8 Jun 59.

GENERAL BOWMAN

into a twenty-mile sector, and to its right the Eighth Army, with four corps, extended the line to the Adriatic.

Formidable mine defenses lay ahead. Typical was a minefield just west of Highway 65 that consisted of six to eight rows of antitank mines laid in an almost continuous band for two miles. Before the final Allied offensive could begin it was necessary—after passing through the Allies' own defensive minefields— to cut through or bypass such defenses, clearing German wooden box, Schu, and other mines that were difficult to detect, notably the Topf, with its glass-enclosed chemical igniter.[30]

The final battle of the campaigns in Italy began early in April with a 92d Division diversionary attack on the extreme left, followed by an Eighth Army blow on the extreme right. Reeling, the enemy began to fall back, and troops of the Fifth and Eighth Armies captured Bologna on 21 April. The two armies moved into the Po valley behind armored spearheads and once across the river spread out swiftly in pursuit of the disorganized enemy.

In the broad valley the roadnet was good, in some places excellent, with many paved highways connecting the cities, towns, and villages scattered over the plain, a rich and thriving region in normal times. Most of the secondary roads were graveled and well kept, affording alternate routes to almost any point. Roughly parellel main arteries ran from east to west across the valley, while others ran north and south. With such a large, spreading roadnet and with secondary routes sometimes offering shortcuts for the pursuing forces, the fleeing enemy could do little to impede the Allies' progress. As the campaign drew swiftly to its close, little road maintenance was necessary and was mostly confined to primary routes. The prinicpal engineer task was crossing the Po, and that had to be done quickly to keep up the tempo of the pursuit and cut off enemy escape routes.[31]

The Po is a rather slow stream with many bars and islands and is generally too wide for footbridges. In front of Fifth Army its bed varied in width from 330 to 1,315 yards, the actual water gap

[30] *Fifth Army History*, vol. VI, pp. 84–85; Clark, *Calculated Risk*, p. 385; Jones comments. No true plastic mines were found in the Mediterranean theater, although rumors persisted throughout the war that the Germans were using them. All enemy mines had at least a small amount of metal in them. The rumor had begun in Sicily where a single improvised mine

made of plastic explosive with a standard detonator was found. The nearest approach to the plastic mine was an Italian mine resembling the German Teller but made of bakelite.

[31] *Engineer History, Mediterranean*, pp. 231–32.

extending from 130 to 490 yards. Allied air strikes had destroyed the permanent high-level and floating highway bridges. The Germans maintained communication across the river by ferries and by floating bridges, many of which they assembled from remnants of permanent floating bridges after dark and dismantled before daylight.

The engineers knew that a huge amount of bridging would be necessary to cross the Po. Treadway bridging was in limited supply. The 25-ton pontons of the 1554th Engineer Heavy Ponton Battalion would be essential, as would many floating Baileys, which Fifth Army could borrow from the British. The width of the Po required storm boats as well as assault boats, heavy rafts, infantry-support rafts, and Quonset barges assembled from naval cubical steel pontons and powered by marine motors.

Fifth Army engineers were confident that they could build bridges on piles eighty feet deep or more despite the soft mud of considerable depth that formed the Po's bed. Such piles came from U.S. engineer forestry units working in southern Italy, and the long trailers of the 1554th Heavy Ponton Battalion brought them to the front.

On 22 September 1944, Fifth Army engineers distributed a special engineer report on the Po throughout the army. The report consolidated all available information, and revised editions came out from then until the actual crossing. The 1168th Engineer Combat Group controlled camouflage, maintenance, depot, and equipment units and provided administrative service for some engineer units not under its operational control. The 46th South African Survey Company carried its triangulation net into the Po valley, while early in

1945 the 66th Engineer Topographic Company issued 1:12,500 photo-mosaic sheets covering the area and special 1:10,000 mosaics of possible crossing sites. The 1621st Engineer Model Making Detachment produced a number of terrain models of the Po valley.[32]

Special river-crossing training concentrated mainly on II Corps engineer units, but close to the actual crossing day Fifth Army switched bridging to IV Corps.[33] The engineer units had thoroughgoing drills, and a group of II Corps' combat engineers got special instruction in all the assault and bridging equipment the army stockpiled during the winter. This group was to operate with the troops ready to make the main movement across the Po, whether of II or IV Corps. Fifth Army had estimated that a floating Bailey would be required in both II Corps and IV Corps areas; the 1338th Engineer Combat Group's 169th Engineer Combat Battalion was to build the II Corps bridge and the 1108th Engineer Combat Group's 235th Engineer Combat Battalion, the IV Corps bridge. During March and April the 169th Engineer Combat Battalion sent several of its men to the British Floating Bailey Bridge School at Capua, and in April the entire battalion moved to a site on the Arno west of Pisa for training in building the bridges. The 235th Combat Battalion got only a few days of training—and even that for only part of the battalion.[34]

Estimating that the Germans would expect II Corps to make the main attack

---

[32] Jones comments.

[33] Killian comments.

[34] Engr Hist II Corps, p. 248; Hists, 39th Engr C Rgt, Jun–Dec 44; 169th Engr C Bn, 1 Nov 44–8 May 45; and 235th Engr C Bn, Jan–May 45; Comments, Killian and Jones.

ENGINEERS BRIDGING THE WIDE BUT PLACID PO RIVER

along the axis of Highway 65, Fifth Army determined to surprise them by having IV Corps deliver the first heavy attack along Highway 64. To avoid warning the enemy General Bowman decided to keep major bridging equipment at Florence and Leghorn, approximately 125 miles from the Po, rather than establish a forward bridge dump. Moreover, no suitable areas for bridge dumps existed along the parts of Highways 64 and 65 that Fifth Army held. To make dumps would have required a great deal of earth moving in the middle of winter, would have diverted engineers from other important jobs, and might have given away the plans for the attack. Because he expected the Germans to make a stand at the Po, Bowman believed he would have plenty of time to bring bridging to a place in the valley where it would be available for either corps.[35]

The German retreat was so precipitous that much of the planning proved a handicap rather than an advantage. The three leading divisions of IV Corps were at the river on 23 April, in advance of any II Corps units. Enemy resistance had become so weak that each division tried to get across the Po as fast as possible to keep up the chase without interruption. Engineers had to work feverishly to push the troops across by all means available.[36]

[35] Bowman comments.
[36] Hist 39th Engr C Rgt, Jun–Dec 44; Comments, Bowman and Killian.

The II Corps engineers diverted to IV Corps during the crossing operation included operators for storm boats and Quonset barges, a company of the 39th Engineer Combat Group's 404th Engineer Combat Battalion to operate floating equipment, the 19th Engineer Combat Group's 401st Engineer Combat Battalion, and the 1554th Heavy Ponton Battalion.[37] During the morning of the twenty-third all II Corps' bridging that was readily available, including an M1 treadway bridge, 60 DUKWs, 4 infantry support rafts, and 24 storm boats with motors, moved in convoy to IV Corps. At Anzola fifty assault boats belonging to IV Corps joined the convoy, which went forward to the 10th Mountain Division and arrived at San Benedetto on the morning of 24 April. On the night of the twenty-second, fifty other IV Corps assault boats had also reached the 10th Mountain Division.[38]

The crossing began at noon on 23 April, when troops of the 10th Mountain Division ferried over the Po in IV Corps assault boats operated by divisional engineers of the 126th Engineer Mountain Battalion. Some of the men of the 126th made as many as twenty-three trips across that day. Starting at noon the engineers used the only equipment available to them—fifty sixteen-man wooden assault boats. By 2000 the 126th had ferried across the 86th and 87th Mountain Infantry Regiments plus

medical detachments and two battalions of divisional light artillery (75-mm. pack). Only twelve boats were left, most of the rest having been destroyed by heavy German fire. The engineers suffered twenty-four casualties, including two killed.[39]

The 85th Division followed close behind. All assault river-crossing equipment the divisional engineers (the 310th Engineer Combat Battalion) had held had been turned over to IV Corps engineers in April before the Po crossing. When the division reached the Po its engineers had only nine two-man rubber boats and had to use local materials to build four infantry support rafts and three improvised rafts. On these, with the help of the 255th Engineer Combat Battalion of the 1108th Engineer Combat Group, the 310th crossed all reconnaissance and combat units of the division except medium artillery. The crossing took forty-eight hours, but in spite of enemy artillery fire the engineers suffered no casualties.[40]

The IV Corps engineers had not expected to be in the vanguard crossing the Po and had to cope with problems for which they were not prepared. During the afternoon of 24 April the 401st Engineer Combat Battalion, a II Corps organization on loan to IV Corps, started building a treadway bridge near San Benedetto. Working all night, with the help of the 235th Engineer Combat Battalion, the 401st completed the 950-foot span at 1030.[41]

---

[37] On 1 March 1945, Headquarters and Headquarters Company (HHC), 19th Engineer Combat Regiment, became HHC, 19th Engineer Combat Group. The regiment's 1st Battalion was redesignated the 401st Engineer Combat Battalion, and the 2d Battalion became the 402d Engineer Combat Battalion.

[38] II Corps Hist, Gen Staff Confs, 23 Nov 44–5 May 45; Comments, Burch and Jones.

[39] Ltr, Col Robert P. Boyd, Jr., CO, 126th Mtn Engr Bn, 8 Jun 59; *Engineer History, Mediterranean*, p. 237.

[40] Hists, 310th Engr C Bn, 1 Nov 44–8 May 45, and 255th Engr C Bn, Apr–Jun 45; *Engineer History, Mediterranean*, p. 242; Comments, Jones, Boyd, and Burch.

[41] *Engineer History, Mediterranean*, pp. 244–45; Hist 401st Engr C Bn, Jan–Aug 45; Killian comments.

Late on the afternoon of 24 April the 1554th Heavy Ponton Battalion (II Corps) started work three miles upstream on a heavy ponton bridge even though much of the equipment did not arrive until after the bridge had been completed with improvised equipment. When finished on the afternoon of the twenty-fifth the bridge was 840 feet long and consisted of 56 pontons, 49 floats, and 4 trestles. A ferry of Navy Quonset barges, which could haul two 2 1/2-ton trucks, had operated all during the night of 24 April. Day and night, for forty-eight hours after the completion of these first two bridges over the Po, two IV Corps divisions and part of a II Corps division went over the river; within the first twenty-four hours some 3,400 vehicles crossed the bridges.[42]

Meanwhile, II Corps' engineers seriously felt the diversion of men and equipment to IV Corps, which left them with no floating bridges or assault equipment. Much equipment supposedly still available to II Corps was lost, misplaced, defective, or still in crates. During the night of the twenty-third bridging equipment began to arrive, but treadway equipage was loaded on quartermaster semitrailers instead of Brockway trucks. On the morning of the twenty-fourth the II Corps engineer, Col. Joseph O. Killian, reported to General Bowman that he had no bridging available and that he had no idea when it would be available since treadway construction depended upon Brockways with their special facilities for unloading. The Brockways had gone to IV Corps, and

Colonel Killian had to depend upon Fifth Army engineers for other equipment. Also, many motors for Quonset barges that reached the river were defective. These conditions held up operations for almost a day. The confusion appreciably reduced II Corps engineer support to division engineers and led to last-minute changes in plans and hasty improvisations. The M2 treadway and ferries remained the chief means for crossing the Po in the II Corps area until missing parts for the Quonsets arrived from Leghorn.

After the Po the hard-pressed II Corps engineers had two more major streams to cross, the Adige and the Brenta, and again bridging equipment was late getting to them. An almost intact bridge II Corps troops seized near Verona proved sufficient until other bridges could be erected. At the Brenta River bridging arrived with the advance guard of the 91st Division. One of the first elements across a temporary trestle treadway at the Brenta was a section of the bridge train moving ahead with forward elements of the 91st Division to the next crossing. In the IV Corps sector German defenders of a bridge across the Mincio at Governola held up the forward drive on the twenty-fourth only momentarily. Although damaged, the bridge proved usable, and the 37th Engineer Combat Battalion, which for more than two days and nights had been working with little or no rest, had it open for traffic in a few hours.[43]

The drive rolled on, led by the 88th Division. The 10th Mountain Division and the 85th Infantry Division pushed

---

[42] *Engineer History, Mediterranean*, p. 254; II Corps Hist, Gen Staff Conf, Apr–May 45; Hist 401st Engr C Bn, Jan–Aug 45; Jones comments.

[43] II Corps Hist, 1 Apr–2 May 45, an. 6; Comments, Bowman and Killian.

RAFT FERRIES A TANK DESTROYER ACROSS THE PO

on to Verona, and the 1st Armored Division helped to seal off all escape routes to the north with an enveloping sweep to the west. These moves, in conjunction with those of the Eighth Army, brought about the capitulation of the enemy and an end to the Italian campaign.

### The Shortage of Engineers

From the landings at Salerno to the end of the war in Italy, a shortage of personnel affected practically all engineer work in Fifth Army and Peninsular Base Section areas. Experienced men were constantly drained off as the war progressed: too few engineers were allocated to the theater at the start; War Department policies worked to the detriment of engineer strengths; units went to Seventh Army and the invasion of southern France; and the engineer contingent in Italy suffered casualties. The effect showed up not only in numbers but also in fluctuating training levels, varying proficiency in standard engineer functions, and problems of supply common to the theater. Not the least important for the engineers was the loss of experienced leaders.

In its search for skilled manpower, the War Department imposed strictures on the theaters in addition to the organizational one of the group concept. To build new engineer units around sound cadres the department often ordered experienced engineer officers home to form a reserve pool of knowledgeable men for new units but did not replace them in overseas units with men of equal ability. Replacements in Italy were usually deficient in engineer back-grounds, and some had no technical knowledge at all. Between 6 October 1943 and 11 May 1944, forty-eight offi-cers of company and field grade went back to the United States as cadre, Gen-eral Bowman agreeing that they could be replaced by first and second lieuten-ants from training schools at home. Only some 50 percent arrived during that period, and the replacement sys-tem never made up the shortage. In the fall of 1944 the War Department stopped shipping individual engineer replacements, and the engineers turned to hastily trained elements such as anti-aircraft gun crews left in rear areas, usually ports, to protect traffic there from nonexistent Axis air raids. From September 1944 to April 1945, new engineer units formed from nonengi-neer organizations included three com-bat battalions, one light equipment company, one depot company, one maintenance company, two engineer combat group headquarters, and two general service regiments. One general service regiment and two combat engi-neer regiments already existing became group organizations, and another two general service regiments were reorgan-ized under new tables of organization and equipment. But with the exception of some separate companies, none of the new units ever attained its author-ized strength. The constant rotation of officers to the United States reduced some of the existing units to 85 percent of their usual strength.

The number of engineer units drawn off by the Seventh Army in the spring of 1944 was somewhat counterbalanced by the reduction of Fifth Army's respon-sibilities when the British Eighth Army took over a major part of the front. But the units lost at the time were what remained of the best, for General Clark allowed Seventh Army to take any engi-neer unit it wanted.

Casualties also took an expected toll. Of the peak engineer strength of 27,000 in June 1944, 3,540 officers and men were lost. Of the 831 who died, 597 were killed in action, 140 died from wounds received in action, and 94 died from other causes. Of the 2,646 wound-ed in action, 786 were wounded seri-ously and 1,860 only slightly. Some thirty-six were taken prisoner, and thir-ty remained missing in action. The numbers varied from unit to unit de-pending on proximity to the front line and the type of work performed. In forty-five days of combat at Anzio, the 36th Engineer Combat Regiment lost 74 men killed and 336 wounded. On the same front, where it was difficult to distinguish front lines from rear, the 383d Battalion (Separate) in five months sustained casualties of four officers and eleven enlisted men killed and three officers and fifty-eight men wounded. Enemy artillery brought down the most engineers. For example, the 109th Com-bat Battalion between 20 September 1943 and 11 May 1944 had seventy-one battle casualties, 90 percent from artillery blasts or shell fragments, and 10 percent from mine blasts and small-arms fire. At other times the losses from artillery were fewer, as low as 61 per-cent, but artillery always remained the chief culprit.[44]

[44] Hist 185th Engr C Bn, Sep 44; Fifth Army Rpt of Army Commanders Weekly Confs, 24 Mar–14 Apr 45; *Engineer History, Mediterranean,* p. 163; Summary

## Training

To offset inexperience, the engineers concentrated on training troops coming into the North African theater. Units had no choice but to accept troops without engineer training, and they took men with only basic military training. They had to be satisfied, in fact, with only a small percentage of Class II personnel (categorized as rapid learners in induction tests), with the remainder Class III (average learners) and Class IV (slow learners). New officers were assigned to four to six weeks of duty with rear area general service engineer units before being thrust into work with combat engineers.

Each engineer unit tried to maintain a reserve of trained specialists to fill any vacancies that occurred and to keep up job training. Even so, engineer units in the Fifth Army did not have enough trained operators and mechanics, especially for heavy equipment. A good operator could do three to five times the work of a poor one.

Training in bridging, river crossing, mine techniques, heavy equipment, motor maintenance, surveying, intelligence techniques, mapping, photography, scouting and patrolling, mountain climbing, driving, marksmanship, and the use of flame throwers and grenade launchers went on throughout the campaign, most of it within the engineer groups, regiments, battalions, or companies. Many units trained at night. For example, the 19th Engineer Combat Regiment, before the spring offensive of May 1944, spent a third of its training time on night practices. One company of a battalion might perform assigned missions while the rest of the battalion trained.[45]

When the time was available, almost every unit practiced bridge construction. The 235th Engineer Combat Battalion spent five days at the Arno building floating treadways. Experienced units trained the inexperienced: the 16th Armored Engineer Battalion instructed the 36th and 39th Engineer Combat Regiments and the 10th Engineer Combat Battalion in building steel treadways, and the 1755th Treadway Bridge Company trained a number of units, including the 19th Engineer Combat Regiment. In August and September 1944 the 175th Engineer General Service Regiment conducted a school for the British in building timber bridges. In April 1944 each company of the 310th Engineer Combat Battalion, 85th Division, built and dismantled a 100-foot double-single Bailey.

As early as November 1943 Fifth Army established a school in river crossing at Limatola, near the Volturno, and here a number of units practiced for the Rapido crossing. During a fortnight in January 1944 the 16th Armored Engineer Battalion practiced assault crossings with the 6th Armored Infantry Regiment, 1st Armored Division. Four companies of the 19th Engineer Combat Regiment practiced between 10 and 15 January 1944 with elements of the 36th Division at Pietravairano, sixteen miles north of Capua, instructing the infantry in the use of river-crossing equipment during both daylight and darkness. The engineers conducted similar training in preparation for the Arno and Po crossings.

---

of Activities (Statistical) Mediterranean Theater, vol. XV, p. 18.

[45] Hist 19th Engr C Rgt, 1944. The following is based on histories of the units mentioned.

Engineers also learned by attachment. Units just arriving in the Fifth Army zone sent officers and enlisted men—or whole units—to work with, observe, and learn from engineers who were more experienced. Elements of the 310th Engineer Combat Battalion were attached to the 313th Combat Battalion, elements of the 316th Combat Battalion to the 10th and 111th Combat Battalions, and elements of the 48th Combat Battalion to the 120th Combat Battalion.

The engineers also instructed non-engineer units in a number of other skills, most notably recognizing, laying, detecting, and removing mines. Two Fifth Army engineer mine-training teams supplemented the instruction that divisional engineer battalions gave to the infantry. The 16th Armored Engineer Battalion subjected the 92d Division to rigorous drill, requiring the whole division to go through a live minefield.

Early in the campaign the British established a Bailey bridge school, open to Americans, at Capua, where some units felt the instruction was better than that provided at the American school.[46] Americans gave some supplementary instruction at the British School of Military Engineering at Capua. Most of the American schools in the theater were subordinate to the Replacement and Training Command, MTOUSA. In the summer of 1944 MTOUSA established an American Engineer Mines and Bridge School along the Volturno in the vicinity of Maddaloni. As the Fifth Army moved northward and out of touch, the school shifted its emphasis to converting American antiaircraft artillery (AAA)

troops into engineers and to training the Brazilian Expeditionary Force and the 92d Division.[47]

Lacking engineer troops, Fifth Army employed thousands of Italians. Some Italian engineer troops participated in the campaign, but most of the laborers were civilians who bolstered almost all the U.S. Army engineer units, especially those at army and corps level. Each unit recruited its own civilian force with help from Allied military government detachments. At one time the 310th Engineer Combat Battalion had more than three times its own strength in civilian laborers. The work of the Italians, while not always up to the standard desired by the American engineers, released thousands of engineers and infantrymen for other tasks. Some three thousand manual laborers worked for the engineers during the winter of 1944–45; in April 1945 army and corps engineer units had employed 4,437 Italian civilians, most of them on road work. The Italians loaded, broke, and spread rock; worked at quarries; cleared ditches and culverts for use of mule pack trains; and hand-placed rock to build up firm shoulders and form gutters. Those more skilled rebuilt retaining walls and masonry ditches along road shoulders.[48]

A specialized Italian civilian group, the *Cantonieri,* was the equivalent of U.S. county or local road workers. These

[46] Jones comments, 1 Jun 59.

[47] Engr Service, PBS, Work Accomplished, 2 Oct 43–1 Sep 44; Comments, Jones, 1 Jun 59; Fifth Army Rpt of Army Commanders Weekly Confs, 24 Mar and 14 Apr 45; *Engineer History, Mediterranean,* p. 163; Summary of Activities (Statistical) Mediterranean Theater, vol. XV, p. 18.

[48] Comments, Jones and Armogida; *Engineer History, Mediterranean,* pp. 31, 164, 267; *Fifth Army History,* vol. VIII, p. 26; Fifth Army Rpt of Army Commanders Weekly Confs, 10, 24 Feb; 3, 10, 17, 24, 31 Mar; 7, 14, 21 Apr; and 14 May 45.

workers became available as the front lines moved forward and were especially valuable in rapidly moving situations when engineer road responsibilities increased by leaps and bounds. The chief of the *Cantonieri* of a given area did the same tasks on his section of road (about twelve miles) that he had done for his government. Truckloads of crushed rock and asphalt were unloaded along the road as required, and the *Cantonieri* patched pavements and did drainage and other repair jobs.[49]

### Engineer Supply

Fifth Army was not in Italy long before defects in the engineer supply system became evident. The engineers acted rapidly on the invasion plans that called for them to make the most use possible of locally procured material. Soon after Naples fell, reconnaissance parties scoured the area for supplies, making detailed inventories of plumbing and electrical fixtures, hardware, nails, glass, and other small standard items. Italian military stocks, especially those at the Fontanelle caves, were valuable sources of needed materiel, and prefabricated Italian barracks served as hospital wards until American huts arrived. Though American engineers sequestered and classified over a hundred different types of stock and placed orders on Italian industry through the Allied military government that spurred the local economy and saved critical shipping space, control of requisition and issue of supply suffered from too few qualified men.[50]

The strain was particularly manifest closer to the combat elements. No organization existed at Fifth Army corps or division levels to allocate engineer supply, and the individual units drew directly from army engineer depots. Though the Fifth Army engineer tried to keep the dumps as far forward as possible, the using units had to send their own trucks back to collect supplies since the depots frequently did not have the transportation to make deliveries. The time needed for supply runs varied with the distances involved, the road conditions, and the frequent necessity for traveling blacked out. The average was one day, but the 313th Engineer Combat Battalion reported that trips of up to 250 miles required two days for the round trip.[51]

Many engineer units could ill afford either the time or the transportation required for frequent trips back to army dumps, so they began to maintain small dumps of their own, stocking them with supplies from army engineer dumps and with material captured or procured locally. The only condition Fifth Army imposed on these dumps was that all stocks be movable. It was common practice for each company of a divisional engineer combat battalion to set up a forward dump in the infantry regimental sector, and such dumps often leapfrogged forward as the division moved. In the 45th Division, the 120th Engineer Combat Battalion in a mobile situation always kept its dump about 1 1/2 miles behind its own command post.[52]

---

[49] Bowman comments.

[50] Engr Service, PBS, Work Accomplished, p. 275; PBS, Public Relations Sect, *Tools of War*, p. 22.

[51] Bowman comments; Hists, 39th Engr Rgt, Jun–Dec 44; 313th Engr C Bn, 1944–45; 337th Engr GS Rgt, 9 Sep 43–1 Nov 44; and 120th Engr C Bn, 9 Sep 43–1 May 44.

[52] Hists, 182d Engr C Bn, 16 Sep 44–5 May 45, and 337th Engr GS Rgt, 9–15 Sep 43; AGF Bd Rpt 162, NATOUSA, 28 Jun 44.

There were never enough depot troops to operate army engineer supply dumps. Before the breakout in May 1944 Fifth Army had only one platoon (one officer and forty enlisted men) of the 451st Engineer Depot Company, while the rest of the company remained with PBS. The platoon had to move often to stay close to the front but still managed to fill an average of seventy-five requisitions every twenty-four hours. Frequently, the platoon operated more than one depot simultaneously—three in May 1944. When the 451st concentrated at Civitavecchia in June, it took 500 trucks, enough for seven full-strength infantry regiments, to move the unit's stock and equipment north. Help in depot operations came from other engineers as well as from British, French, and Italian military units. Several companies of Italian soldiers were regularly attached to the 1st Platoon as mechanics, welders, carpenters, and laborers. Italian salvage crews repaired tools and equipment, manufactured bridge pins, and mended rubber boats.[53]

The shortage of engineer depot units made it impossible to open new engineer dumps as often or as rapidly as desirable, particularly after the May 1944 breakout. As a result the supply furnished to engineer units deteriorated, and in June one platoon of the 450th Engineer Depot Company had to be made available to Fifth Army. In August, however, the platoon reverted to Seventh Army, and for the next few months Fifth Army again had only one platoon for engineer depot support. Finally, in December 1944, MTOUSA

formed the 383d Engineer Depot Company from the 1st Platoon, 451st, and men from disbanded antiaircraft units. Through the rest of the campaign Fifth Army engineer units could count on supply support from this company, aided by Italian Army troops trained in engineer supply procedures.[54]

### Mapping and Intelligence

Planners had estimated that Fifth Army would need a full topographic battalion, plus one topographic company per corps, to reproduce and revise maps; yet there were never more than two topographical companies available at any one time. The 66th Engineer Topographic Company served for nineteen months; the 661st served only eight months, mainly with VI Corps. Both, from time to time, had to get help from South African and British survey companies.[55]

The 66th Topographic Company was the American unit on which Fifth Army placed its chief reliance. Upon arrival in Italy in early October 1943, the men of this unit went to work revising material derived chiefly from aerial photographs. Photo mosaics and detailed defense studies covering the projected attacks along the Volturno and Sacco-Liri Rivers were made and reproduced.

In November the 66th was assigned to II Corps but continued to revise and reproduce maps for the Fifth Army Engineer Section. This company consisted of four platoons: a headquarters or service platoon; a survey platoon, which as a field unit performed the sur-

[53] Rpt, Engr Fifth Army, 25 Jun 44, Engineer Lessons from the Italian Campaign; Hist 451st Engr Depot Co, May–Dec 44.

[54] Hists, 450th Engr Depot Co, May–Aug 44, and 383d Engr Depot Co, 1944–45.
[55] Bowman comments.

vey and control work; a photomapping platoon responsible for drafting as well as planning and revising maps; and a reproduction platoon responsible for the lithographic production of the printed sheet. In January 1944 the company furnished men for two provisional engineer map depot detachments, one at Anzio and the other on the main front. When the two fronts merged in May it was possible to establish forward and rear map depots, and NATOUSA formally activated the 1710th and 1712th Engineer Map Depot Detachments.

The 66th Topographic Company moved twelve times between 5 October 1943 and the fall of Rome in June 1944. Between those dates the company processed an average of a half million impressions a month. In addition to 866 different maps, the 66th printed field orders, overlays showing engineer responsibilities, road network overlays, defense overprints, German plans for Cassino defense, a monthly history of II Corps' operations, the disposition of German troops in the II Corps area, special maps for the commanding general of II Corps, special terrain studies, photomaps, and various posters and booklets. It produced a major portion of all the 1:100,000, 1:50,000, and 1:25,000 maps Fifth Army units used. In April 1945, for the Po operation, the 66th produced 4,900,000 operational maps, working around the clock and using cub planes to speed distribution to units.[56]

After the fall of Rome the 66th Topographic Company, then the only such unit with Fifth Army, could not pro-

duce the required amount of work with its authorized personnel and equipment. The company procured additional equipment and employed Italian technicians and guards, virtually becoming a topographic battalion. Using the Italian technicians, the company was able to work two shifts reproducing maps but could not get enough people for two shifts on other jobs. The company trained its men for several different specialties, but the multiple responsibilities overtaxed them.

The 1712th Detachment issued 1,331,000 maps for the drive against the Gustav Line in May 1944. For the entire Italian campaign Fifth Army handled and distributed over 29,606,000 maps. Ordinarily the corps maintained a stock of 500 each of all 1:25,000 and 1:50,000 sheets of an area and fewer 1:100,000 and smaller scale sheets. When new units arrived or large orders came in, the maps were drawn from the army map depot; such orders could normally be filled within a day. Periods of relatively static warfare in the Italian campaign called for large-scale maps. Unfortunately, not enough 1:25,000-scale maps were available to meet the need, and some of those in stock were of dubious quality. The 1:50,000-scale maps provided complete coverage, but many panels were considerably out-of-date and in some cases illegible.

The combined sections of mapping and intelligence collected data on weather, crossing sites, defense works, observation points, and fields of fire. When Lt. Col. William L. Jones joined Bowman's staff in January 1944, intelligence became divorced from mapping, and Jones became chief of the Plans, Intelligence, and Training Section. This arrangement continued until September

[56] Hist 66th Engr Topo Co, 1944–45; AGF Bd Rpt 179, NATOUSA, Notes on Mapping an Army, 16 Aug 44. Unless otherwise cited, this section is based on these two sources.

1944 when Colonel Jones left to take command of the 235th Engineer Combat Battalion; then mapping and intelligence reconsolidated under Lt. Col. John G. Ladd.[57]

Information came to the section from many sources, including the Army Map Service and other agencies in the United States and Britain. The Intelligence Branch, OCE, WD, supplied a ten-volume work on Italy's beaches and ports covering such subjects as meteorological conditions and water supply. Many studies dealing with Italy's highway bridges, railroad bridges, and tunnels originated in the Research Office, a subdivision of the Intelligence Branch. A valuable source from which the engineers derived information was a sixteen-volume Rockefeller Foundation work on malaria in Italy with specific information concerning the regions where malaria prevailed. Lessons, hints, and tips came from two series of publications issued frequently during the campaign: Fifth Army Engineer Notes and AFHQ Intelligence Summaries.[58]

Although the Fifth Army G–2 was technically the agency for collecting and disseminating topographic information, the Fifth Army staff relied on the engineer to evaluate all topographic intelligence required for planning. This system worked well, for by the nature of his work and training the engineer was best equipped to provide advice concerning terrain and communication routes. Corps and division staffs generally expected less terrain information from their engineers because no ade-

quate photo-interpretation organization existed below the army level. Engineer intelligence data seldom covered terrain more than one hundred miles in advance of the front lines. On the whole intelligence was adequate, for the rate of advance in Italy was not rapid enough to require greater coverage. The timing of engineer intelligence was important; information conveyed to the lower units too far in advance might be filed away and forgotten.[59]

Skilled interpretation of aerial photographs was an important phase of engineer intelligence. Use of such photographs, begun in the stalemate before Cassino, proved so valuable that by February 1944 a squadron of USAAF P–38s made four to ten sorties (about 350 pictures) daily. Two engineers at the photo center sent all photographs within ten miles of the front forward and kept the rest for their own study. Periodically they also sent forward reports on roads, bridges, streams, and other features.[60]

The engineers used long-range terrain reports of the AFHQ Engineer Intelligence Section to plan the forward movement of engineer bridge supplies and the deployment of engineer units. The reports were rich sources of information on roads and rivers. Road information included width, nature of surface, embankments, demolitions, and suitability for mules, jeeps, or other transportation. River information included bed width, wet gap, width measured from the tops of banks, nature and height of banks, levees, potential crossing places, approaches, needed

[57] Comments, Jones, 1 Jun 59.
[58] Coll, Keith, and Rosenthal, *The Corps of Engineers: Troops and Equipment*, pp. 457–58; II Corps Hist, an. A, G–2 Rpt 612.

[59] Comments, Jones, 1 Jun 59, and Paxson, May 59.
[60] Bowman comments; Hist 313th Engr C Bn, 1944–45; II Corps Rapido Crossing, Jan–Feb 44.

bridging equipment, fords, and practicability of bypasses. The error was seldom more than ten feet for estimated bridge lengths or 20 percent for bridge heights. Sometimes the terrain reports were useful in selecting bombing targets such as a dam in the Liri valley. They could be used not only to estimate long-range bridging requirements but also to anticipate floods, pinpoint tank obstacles and minefields, and locate potential main supply routes, airfield sites, strategic points for demolition, and possible traffic blocks. General Bowman was so impressed by the value of the reports that he tried repeatedly to have the AFHQ Engineer Photo Interpretation Section made part of his office, but AFHQ retained control of the section.[61]

### Camouflage

At no time during the entire Italian campaign were there more than two companies of the 84th Engineer Camouflage Battalion available, and after the middle of 1944 only one company remained with Fifth Army. Moreover, since in the United States camouflage troops had been considered noncombatant, the unit, responsible for camouflage supervision and inspection, consisted of limited service and older-than-average personnel. This policy impaired efficiency in view of the fact that front-line units had the greatest need for deception and disguise. In addition, the camouflage companies had neither enough training in tactical camouflage nor enough transportation to move the large amount of materials and equipment required.[62]

In spite of these handicaps engineers did some excellent work with dummies, paint, nets, and other materials. Sometimes road screens and dummies confused and diverted enemy artillery posted in the hills. For example, early in the campaign, troops of the 337th Engineer General Service Regiment erected a series of structures made from nine 30-by-30-foot nets, along a 220-foot stretch of road near the Volturno. This section had been subject to observation and shelling, but after the erection of the road screen the shelling stopped.[63]

Road screens were the main device in camouflage operations. As a rule the engineers used a double thickness of garnished net, but the best type of net for all purposes remained an unsettled question. Engineers of the 84th Battalion preferred shrimp nets to garnished twine, yet the 15th Army Group engineer concluded at the close of hostilities that the shrimp nets had not been dense enough to obscure properly. Pregarnished fish nets had the same defect. None of the nets was sufficiently durable or fire resistant. And as snow fell in December 1944, no white camouflage materials were available.[64]

The most ambitious operational camouflage programs of the Italian campaign took place during preparations to attack the Gothic Line. Engineers

---

[61] Comments, Bowman, Jones, and Armogida.

[62] Hists, 84th Engr Camouflage Bn, 14 Apr 43–Jul 44, and Co A, 84th Engr Camouflage Bn, 1944; Coll, Keith, and Rosenthal, *The Corps of Engineers: Troops and Equipment*, p. 222; Comments, Elliott, 18 Mar 60.

[63] Engr Tech Bull 19, Rpt on Volturno River Bridge at Cancello, 17 May 44; and 29, Camouflage, 5 Apr 45; IV Corps Opns Rpt, Aug 44.

[64] AGF Bd Rpt 279, MTO, 24 Jan 45; Killian comments.

made every effort to conceal the II Corps buildup in the Empoli-Florence area and to simulate strength on the left flank in IV Corps' Pontedera sector. Among the devices employed were dummy bridges over canals and streams and smoke to make the enemy believe that heavy traffic was moving over the dummy bridges. One dummy bridge at a canal southwest of Pisa drew heavy fire for two hours.[65] In October 1944 in the IV Corps area, engineers raised a screen to enable them to build a 120-foot floating treadway across the Serchio during the daytime. During the same month Company D of the 84th Camouflage Battalion erected a screen 300 feet long to conceal all movement across a ponton bridge that lay under direct enemy observation. The engineers put up a forty-foot tripod on each bank of the river, used holdfasts to secure cables, and raised the screen with a 3/4-ton weapons carrier winch and block and tackle. In November a bridge over the Reno River at Silla, also exposed to enemy observation, was screened in a similar fashion. Here the engineers used houses on the two riverbanks as holdfasts.[66]

Engineers set up dummy targets at bridge sites, river crossings, airstrips, and at various other locations, building them in such shapes as artillery pieces, tanks, bridges, and aircraft. They were used to draw enemy fire to evaluate its volume and origin. They also served to conceal weakness at certain points, to permit the withdrawal of strong ele-

ments, and to conceal buildups. When a shortage of dummy material developed in January 1945, planners looked upon it as a serious handicap to tactical operations.[67]

Dummies and disguises took many forms. Large oil storage tanks became houses. Company D used spun glass to blend corps and division artillery with surrounding snow. The engineers used painted shelter halfs and nets with bleached garlands to disguise gun positions, ammunition pits, parapets, and other emplacements. Camouflage proved valuable enough in many instances to indicate that its wider application could have resulted in lower casualties and easier troop movements.[68]

Behind Fifth Army in Italy, a massive work of reconstruction continued as divisions moved forward against a slowly retreating enemy. In the zones around the major ports on the western side of the peninsula and on the routes of supply to the army's rear area, the base section made its own contribution to the war. Suffering many of the same strictures and shortages as Fifth Army engineers, the Peninsular Base Section Engineer Service carried its own responsibilities, guaranteeing the smooth transfer of men and material from dockside to fighting front. A host of supporting functions also fell to the engineer in the base section, often taxing strength and ingenuity to the same degree as among the combat elements.

---

[65] IV Corps Opns Rpt, Aug 44; Killian comments.
[66] IV Corps Opns Rpt, Oct 44; *Engineer History, Mediterranean*, p. 211.

[67] Hist Co A, 84th Engr Camouflage Bn; Comments, Bowman and Elliott, 18 Mar 60.
[68] IV Corps Opns Rpt, Feb 45; *Engineer History, Mediterranean*, pp. 211–12.

# CHAPTER XI

# Engineers in the Peninsular Base Section

The support organization behind Fifth Army grew from an embryonic planning group before the invasion of Italy to an entity of corporate size. Its functions were more varied than those in the combat zones and as important; it had management responsibility under Brig. Gen. Arthur W. Pence, an engineer officer, for combat supply and for requisitioning or foraging materiel for its own wide-ranging projects. Specialty units abounded in the base section enclaves. Through the end of the war, engineers were the largest single segment in the Peninsular Base Section (PBS) command.[1]

The main task of the PBS engineers in late 1943 remained the rehabilitation of the port of Naples. Their work at the docks helped Naples to become one of the busiest ports in the world.

They provided depots for receiving supplies and road, railroad, and pipeline facilities for moving supplies. They improved highways serving PBS depots and Fifth Army supply dumps to handle heavy traffic, built pipelines to carry thousands of gallons of gasoline from Naples to pipeheads within range of enemy artillery, and established railheads in Fifth Army territory by reconstructing some of the worst damaged lines of the war. Behind the army boundary PBS engineers also built hospitals, rest camps, repair shops, and other facilities.

On 7 November 1943, five weeks after Naples fell, one-third of the 31,629 American troops assigned or attached to PBS were engineers. The PBS Engineer Service had at its disposal 19 engineer units: 2 combat regiments, 2 general service regiments, 2 separate battalions, and 13 units of company size or less, including the headquarters of a port construction and repair group, a petroleum distribution company, a special utilities company, a water supply company, 2 fire-fighting platoons, 2 mobile searchlight maintenance units, a 3-man engineer mobile petroleum laboratory, and a map depot detachment. By early January 1944 the PBS

---

[1] Except where otherwise noted, this chapter is based on the following: PBS Engr Hist, pt. I, 1943–45, sec. I, Chronological Summary; Meyer, Strategy and Logistical History: MTO, ch. XIX, pp. 1–44. See also: Ltr, Pence to Truesdell, 26 Nov 43, sub: Organization of PBS; Periodic Rpt, SOS NATOUSA, G–4, 31 Dec 43; Brig. C.J.C. Molony, "The Campaign in Sicily 1943 and The Campaign in Italy 3rd September 1943 to 31st March 1944," vol. V, *The Mediterranean and Middle East*, in the series "History of the Second World War" (London: HMSO, 1973), pp. 398–413.

Engineer Service alone had twenty-eight units totaling 10,464 men.[2]

When preparations for the invasion of southern France (ANVIL) got under way in early 1944, there were not enough engineer troops to support the operation. The accompanying French invasion forces would need American help. A Fifth Army breakout, expected in the spring, meant that ANVIL would take place when the demand for engineer troops in Italy was at a peak. Of eighteen engineer combat battalions required for ANVIL, the French could furnish two and the U.S. Army eight trained in shore operations. The invasion would also need eight engineer general service regiments; PBS and Fifth Army, each with five, would both have to give up two. Shortages in engineer map depot detachments also existed. The only port construction and repair group in the theater, the 1051st, would be needed at Marseille and was allocated to ANVIL; this meant PBS would have to reopen Leghorn without experienced port specialists. ANVIL would need three pipeline companies, two of which were to come from outside the theater.[3]

The loss of engineers to ANVIL forced the PBS engineer, Col. Donald S. Burns, to use more Italian troops and civilians. By early October 1944 he was employing 10,000 men from Italian military engineer units and about 5,177 civil-

ians; but these numbers dropped where new base section installations in Leghorn took shape. About 9,700 American engineers were in PBS after ANVIL, and by the end of the campaign in Italy PBS engineer strength had increased to some 10,200.[4]

When Fifth Army stalled before German defenses along the Garigliano and Rapido Rivers during the winter of 1943–44, PBS engineers were able to provide close support no longer feasible when the army broke loose in May 1944. In two months Fifth Army drove to the Arno, a distance of 250 miles, and PBS support deteriorated steadily. The Germans blew many railroad bridges and culverts as they retreated, and PBS engineers could not repair them at the pace the troops were moving. Nor were petroleum engineers able to build gasoline pipelines at the fifteen-mile-a-day pace the army sometimes achieved. Thus the main burden of supplying Fifth Army fell to motor transport, which soon began to falter under increasingly longer hauls, bottlenecks in hastily repaired roads, and breakdowns.

As Fifth Army drew up to the Arno at the end of July 1944, it was in no condition to assail the Gothic Line. Men were tired and equipment worn after the long sweep from the Rapido. The army's strength was depleted by the withdrawal of units for ANVIL, and its supply lines were stretched thin. Before it could drive for the Po valley, Fifth Army needed time to rest, to repair and

---

[2] Station List, HQ, PBS, 7 Nov 43; Rpt, HQ, PBS, to CG, SOS NATOUSA, 15 Jan 44, sub: Rpt on Disposition of Engr Units, app. VIII B to Rpt of the Engr PBS.

[3] Estimate of Engr Troop Situation, Engr Sect (U.S.) AFHQ, 14 Feb 44; Ltr, Chf Engr, PBS, to G–4, AFHQ, 3 Jun 44, sub: Engr Troop Requirements, NATOUSA; PBS Periodic G–3 Rpt 8, Jun 44; 10, Aug 44; and 11, Sep 44, 319.1 PBS files.

[4] PBS Engr Hist, pt. I, 1943–45, sec. II, app. II, showing engineer units in PBS on various dates, and their strengths. PBS Periodic G–3 Rpt 11, Sep 44; Memo, Engr Service, PBS (Col D. S. Burns), for Col Oxx, 3 Oct 44, Procurement Action Rpts, PBS files.

replenish equipment, and to establish a firm supply base in northern Italy.

The logical place was Leghorn, 300 miles north of Naples, a port with a man-made harbor that could accommodate ships drawing up to twenty-eight feet of water. The Germans (with considerable assistance from Allied bombers) had so wrecked the port that a month's work would be required before deep draft vessels could enter, but as soon as the harbor was open to shipping it became the main supply base for Fifth Army. To oversee the work there and at the same time look after American installations in the Naples area, Headquarters, PBS, divided into two groups. The one in Leghorn came to be known as PBS (Main); the other in Naples was designated Pensouth and operated as a district under the larger headquarters at Leghorn.

### Port Rehabilitation

Restoring Italian ports after November 1943 was a battle of supply and demand complicated by the fact that supply tonnages for combat units had higher priority than those for rebuilding the ports. As Naples began functioning again it imported an average of 10,700 tons per day, well above its prewar capacity, but the engineers still had to forage locally for materiel to expand facilities. At Bagnoli they located substantial stocks of steel sections, without which they could never have built ramps for the Liberty ships. Railroad track and torpedo netting also came from local sources, and combat engineers supplemented the American forestry units in cutting and milling timber at Cosenza for the quays in Naples harbor. For piling the engineers welded together locally procured ten-inch diameter pipes and filled them with concrete. Wood and prefabricated steel structural members were always in short supply.[5]

Even with the shortages of materiel, AFHQ steadily revised upward the planned port capacity goals for the city. In the beginning of January 1944 the 1051st Port Construction and Repair Group had orders to build twenty-six temporary LST berths, but the demand increased piecemeal and by month's end the unit had constructed thirty-five berths with still more to come. At that time, when accumulated unloading at Naples and the satellite ports to the north had passed the million-ton level, the revised program called for over 35 Liberty berths, 3 troopship spaces, and 4 smaller berths for coasters. Port capacity increased through the spring, and in one record day in April 33,750 tons of cargo came ashore. With the May offensive, Fifth Army was drawing on the massed stocks that had piled up in beach dumps at Anzio, particularly during the breakout offensive of 1944. (Map 11)[6]

With Fifth Army's advance, Peninsular Base Section acquired additional ports, but they were usually damaged severely. Rome fell on 4 June, Civitavecchia three days later, Piombino on 25 June, and Leghorn on 19 July. At Civitavecchia, the first seaport north of Anzio potentially useful to the Allies,

---

[5] NATOUSA Statistical Summary 8, 319.1 (MTO) OCE files; Wakeman et al., Rpt on Rehabilitation of Naples and Other Captured Ports, 28 Nov 43; Col Ewart G. Plant et al., Rpt on Peninsular Base Section, 10 Feb 44, in OCE ETOUSA Hist Rpt 2, Operational Planning.

[6] PBS, Public Relations Sect, *Tools of War*, pp. 13–23; Plant, Rpt on PBS, 10 Feb 44.

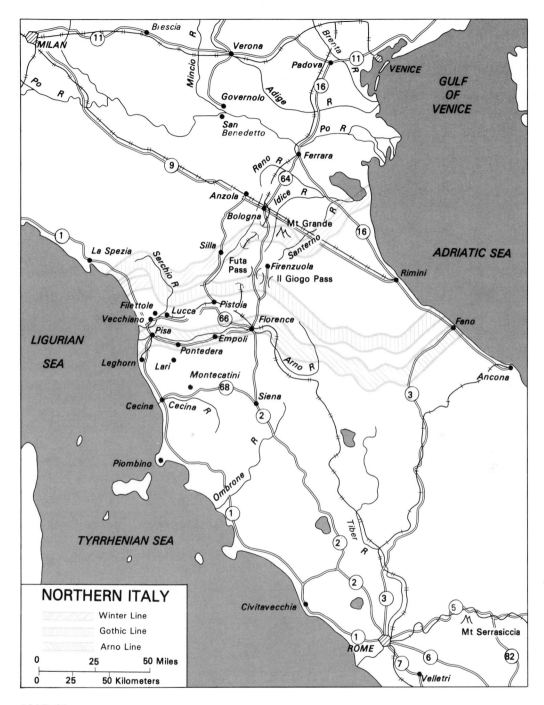

NORTHERN ITALY

*Winter Line*

*Gothic Line*

*Arno Line*

| 0 | 25 | 50 Miles |
| 0 | 25 | 50 Kilometers |

MAP 11

BLASTING OBSTACLES AT CIVITAVECCHIA, JUNE 1944

the 540th Engineer Combat Regiment forged through the heavy wreckage to open DUKW and landing craft hardstands. On 11 June the first cargo craft, an LCT, unloaded; next day an LST nosed into a berth, and ferry craft began to unload Liberty ships. Cargo was soon coming ashore at the rate of 3,000 tons a day. Later the 1051st Port Construction and Repair Group provided Liberty berths by building ramps across sunken ships as at Naples.[7]

Even while improvements were under way at Civitavecchia, a new entry

[7] PBS Engr Hist, pt. I, sec. II, app. IV; Fifth Army Engr Hist, vol. I, pp. 130, 142; War Diary, AFHQ Engr Sect, Entry 9 Aug 44; Fifth Army History, vol. VI, pp. 7, 9, 22, 115.

for Fifth Army supplies opened 100 miles farther north at Piombino, a small port on a peninsula opposite the island of Elba. Elements of both the 39th and 540th Engineer Combat Regiments reopened the port, which, like Civitavecchia, had suffered heavy bomb damage. The main pier lay under a mass of twisted steel from demolished gantry cranes and other wreckage, while destroyed buildings and railroad equipment cluttered the area. But the engineers did not find the profusion of mines and booby traps the retreating Germans usually left behind, and they were able to remove 5,000 tons of scrap steel and pig iron from the main piers during the first two days. Pier ribbing and flooring repair required considerable underwater work. After three days facilities for LCTs to dock head on were available and one alongside berth was ready to receive a coaster; within the next few days hardstands for LCTs, LSTs, and DUKWs were available; and at the end of the third week the engineers built a pier over a sunken ship to provide berths for two Liberty ships. Piombino joined Civitavecchia as a main artery of supply for Fifth Army during July and August 1944.[8]

After the summer offensive, Fifth Army needed Leghorn to support an attack against prepared defenses in the rugged northern Apennines. Early in July, when Fifth Army was still about 18 miles south of Leghorn, PBS selected the 338th Engineer General Service Regiment to rehabilitate the port. The 338th, which had been working on hospitals in Rome, had no experience in port repair but received planning aid from several specialists of the 1051st Group, representatives of the British Navy charged with clearing the waters of Leghorn harbor, and shipowners and contractors who knew the port. The reinforced engineer regiment was not only to repair ship berths but also to be PBS's engineer task force in the city. The 1528th Engineer Dump Truck Company and an Italian engineer construction battalion were attached to the task force, and PBS made preparations to provide the force with a large amount of angledozers, cranes, a derrick, and other, heavy construction equipment. Much of this equipment was to move to Leghorn aboard an LST, an LCT, and

several barges, but general cargo was to be discharged directly from Liberty ships.[9]

Early on the morning of 19 July, Leghorn fell to elements of the 34th Infantry Division. Twelve men from the 338th Engineers arrived in the city a few hours later to clear mines from predetermined routes into the port area. Leghorn was heavily mined, and for the first few days little other than mine clearing could be accomplished. As the mine-clearing teams made room, more elements of the 338th Engineers arrived, set up quarters, and began preparing a berth for the LST and the LCT carrying construction equipment. By 26 July both craft had unloaded. In the meantime, engineers repaired electrical lines and started to restore the municipal water system.

Not until 28 July were engineer and naval officers able to complete a survey of conditions in Leghorn harbor. They were soon convinced that reopening Leghorn would be a much more formidable job than Naples had been. At Naples the Germans had not blocked the harbor entrances, but in Leghorn sunken ships completely blocked entrances to all but shallow-draft craft. In each channel the hulks were so interlocked that no single ship could be floated and swung aside to make a passage. Ultimately the engineers had to spend nearly a month blasting a passage through the blockships.

The stone quays were pocked by craters, some forty feet in diameter, and not one of the eighty-two berthing spaces was untouched. Elsewhere in the

[8] *Fifth Army History*, vol. VI, pp. 53, 115–16; Hists, 540th Engr C Rgt, 1942–45, and 39th Engr C Rgt, Jun–Dec 44.

[9] This account of the rehabilitation of Leghorn is based on Hist 338th Engr GS Rgt, Sep 42–Nov 44, as well as PBS Engr Hist, pt. I, 1943–45, Chronological Summary.

port area the enemy's work was almost as devastating. Port equipment and buildings were demolished; roads, railroads, and open spaces between roads were cratered; and every important bridge leading out of the port was destroyed.

The threat of sea mines in the harbor delayed the unloading of engineer equipment and construction materials. A floating pile driver and three barges loaded with piling, timber, and decking arrived at Leghorn on 30 July but could not enter the harbor until late on 2 August. The next day engineers began rigging the floating pile driver and a 1 1/2-yard crane, also to be used as a pile driver. Port and depot traffic patterns were also developing. The Italians had handled freight directly from wharfside to rail, so few of their piers were hard surfaced. But Allied military cargo had to be moved by truck, and to provide the large quantities of rock needed for surfacing the engineers set up a rock crusher to pulverize rubble from shell-torn buildings and opened a quarry nearby. By November the 338th Engineers had eight quarries in operation.

While the 2d Battalion, 338th Engineers, worked on roads in the area, the 1st Battalion began to build berths for Liberty ships and the 696th Engineer Petroleum Distribution Company restored pipelines from a tanker berth to local tank farms. Pile-driving for the first Liberty berths started on 5 August, and four were ready by the seventeenth. Three days later, after British naval demolition teams had forced a passage into the harbor, the Liberty ship *Sedgewick* came into the port with piling that enabled the engineers to complete two additional berths. The six Liberty

berths then available gave the port a daily capacity of about 5,000 tons.

The goal for Leghorn was to reach a capacity of 12,000 tons a day by the end of September. The port achieved that goal on the twenty-fifth after a ramp the engineers built from a sunken tanker to the shore provided additional Liberty ship berths and after landing craft returned from the ANVIL operation. By that time Leghorn was the main supply port for Fifth Army, and Civitavecchia and Piombino had closed.

*Petroleum: From Tanker to Truck*

At ports along the Italian coast, PBS engineers had to devote considerable attention to unloading and distributing petroleum products, which accounted for nearly half the tonnage the Allies shipped into the Mediterranean theater. The engineers were responsible for building, and in most cases operating, not only tanker discharge facilities and port terminal storage but also pipelines that carried the POL to dispensing and refueling stations in the Fifth Army area. At the dispensing points quartermaster units operated canning installations, and they usually took over truck refueling points. In early planning for the discharge of oil tankers the PBS engineers had counted on using Civitavecchia, the first port north of Naples capable of receiving tankers. These plans were revised after the capture of San Stefano, forty miles north of Civitavecchia, where, on a spit of land connected to the mainland by a causeway, were located a tanker berth and large underground storage facilities.[10] San

[10] Ltr, Capt R. H. Wood, Supply and Construction Sect, to AFHQ Engr Sect, 9 Aug 44, sub: Rpt on Trip to Fifth Army Hqs; PBS Engr Hist, pt. I, pp. 49–50.

Stefano, along with Naples and Leghorn, became a major terminal for POL supplies. Three of the six pipeline systems built in Italy emanated from Naples, two from San Stefano, and one from Leghorn.[11]

By 18 November 1943, engineers of the 696th Petroleum Distribution Company had 574,000 barrels of storage space at Naples ready for motor and aviation gasoline and nearly 55,000 barrels for diesel oil. Another quarter of a million barrels of underground storage, found relatively undamaged at Pozzuoli, was cleaned and used to store Navy fuel oil.[12] While part of the 696th—along with as many as 550 civilian workers—was rehabilitating the Naples terminal, the rest of the unit built a four-inch gasoline pipeline into the Fifth Army area. The pipeline originated on the outskirts of Naples at a Socony refinery and followed Highway 6 northward. The twelve-mile section to Fertilia became operational on 12 November, but thereafter fall rains and gusty winds slowed construction. Since it was apparent from the beginning that one four-inch pipeline would be inadequate for Fifth Army's needs, petroleum engineers had to prepare to construct a second pipeline by putting double crossings under roads and over streams and canals. The most difficult crossing was over the Volturno River, a 400-foot gap. Petroleum engineers prepared a

suspension crossing over the Volturno, using two existing high tension electric line towers for supports, but flood waters knocked the line out soon after it was finished. Engineers repaired the break and also prepared another emergency line on an old railroad bridge 2 1/2 miles upstream.[13]

Early in December 1943 the 705th Engineer Petroleum Distribution Company joined the 696th on pipeline work in the Naples area, taking over operation of the port terminal and of pipelines as far as the Volturno. By 22 December two four-inch pipelines with a daily capacity of 260,000 gallons were in operation to Calvi Risorta, twenty-eight miles north of Naples. In January engineers extended these lines to San Felice, nearly forty-one miles from Naples, then on to San Vittore where a dispensing point was set up only 2 1/2 miles from embattled Cassino. A third four-inch pipeline followed as far as Calvi Risorta, then turned east along Highway 7 for over twelve miles. On 27 March 1944, the 696th, with the help of a French POL unit, opened a forward fueling point on this line at Sessa. Both forward fueling points were within range of enemy artillery, but engineers of the 396th Engineer Camouflage Company concealed them and they were never shelled.[14]

Before the spring offensive began in late May 1944, petroleum engineers assembled more than one hundred miles of six-inch pipe (which could

[11] Unless otherwise noted this section is based on Operational Rpt, Receipt, Storage and Distribution of Bulk Petroleum in West Italy, 3 Oct 43–15 Oct 45, prepared for PBS by 407th Engr Service, 15 Oct 45, 670.11, Pipeline History 1944–45, NATOUSA files. See also Pipeline Rpt, Petroleum Branch, Engr Service, PBS, 1 Mar 44, 670.11, Pipeline History 1944–45, NATOUSA files.

[12] See ch. VIII.

[13] PBS Engr Hist, pt. I, 1943–45, sec. IV, West Italy Pipelines; Hist 705th Engr Pet Dist Co, Apr 45.

[14] Hist 705th Engr Pet Dist Co, Apr 45; *Fifth Army History,* vol. III, pp. 69–70; Distances used are those given in Pipeline Operations Rpts, PBS, 21 Jul 44–20 Aug 44, and 21 Apr 44–20 May 44; and Operational Rpt, Pipeline Dispensing, 1944–45.

deliver as much gasoline as two four-inch pipelines) at forward points on Highways 6 and 7, to be used between Calvi Risorta and Rome. A third engineer petroleum distribution company, the 785th, arrived from the United States during April and went to work on a four-inch pipeline along Highway 7 while the 696th was laying a six-inch line along Highway 6. The 705th was to operate the pipeline system.[15]

As Fifth Army pressed forward during June and July, sometimes as much as fifteen miles a day, it left the pipeheads ever farther behind. By the time the pipeline reached Rome on 7 July, Fifth Army was nearing Leghorn and San Stefano had fallen. The 785th Engineer Petroleum Distribution Company reached San Stefano on 24 June, and five days later a tanker was discharging 80,000 barrels of motor gas at the new terminal. By 2 July the 785th had built ten miles of six-inch pipeline inland, for only fifty miles away tanks and trucks were running dry. The 785th expanded the San Stefano system to cover 143 miles, and for some time to come it was the main source of motor fuel for Fifth Army.[16]

At Leghorn, captured on 19 July, the port was so heavily damaged and German shell fire so persistent that no tanker could enter until 18 September. The 696th Engineer Petroleum Distribution Company, which set up bivouac at a Leghorn refinery, soon found that only 25 percent of the tankage in the area was repairable. At the port all tanker discharge lines were wrecked, but a tanker berth about 1 1/2 miles from the refinery was still in good condition. The 696th, recruiting about one hundred civilian workers, set about repairing storage tanks at the refinery while a French petroleum unit worked on storage facilities at a nearby tank farm. By 10 August the 696th had restored a large amount of storage and had completed a discharge line from the tanker berth. When the first tanker entered the port, storage was ready for nearly 275,000 barrels of gasoline. Eventually, the Leghorn POL terminal had facilities for 62,000 barrels of 100-octane gasoline, 307,000 barrels of 80-octane, 43,500 barrels of lower octane for civilian use, 76,100 barrels of diesel oil, and 34,500 barrels of kerosene. In all, the engineers rehabilitated thirty-two storage tanks.

Early in September Fifth Army struck north across the Arno, coordinating its attack with an Eighth Army offensive along the Adriatic coast, and by the end of the month Fifth Army troops were only fourteen miles from Bologna. October found forward units only nine miles from the Po valley, but for the next few months the army had to use nearly all its resources just to survive the northern Apennine winter. Gasoline issues to Fifth Army troops continued heavy through the winter, averaging 357,000 gallons a day between November 1944 and April 1945. Much of it went to warm troops at gasoline stoves in the mountains some ninety miles from Leghorn.

In late September the 696th left for southern France, and the 703d Engineer Petroleum Distribution Company, relieved from a Highway 2 project, took over both the operation of the Leghorn

[15] Hist 696th Engr Pet Dist Co, May–Sep 44; War Diary, AFHQ Engr Sect, Jun 44; Hist 705th Engr Pet Dist Co, Apr 45.

[16] Ltr, Wood to AFHQ Engr Sect, 9 Aug 44, sub: Rpt on Trip to Fifth Army Hqs; PBS Engr Hist, pt. I, 1943–45, sec. I, Chronological Summary, pp. 49–50.

terminal and the construction of pipelines in the wake of Fifth Army. As soon as Fifth Army began to move, the 703d pushed pipeline construction and by the end of October had a double four-inch line in operation to Sesto, thirty-six miles farther. By mid-December the 703d had carried the line to Loiano, over eighty-one miles beyond Leghorn. For the last ten miles snow, mud, and water got into the line and froze solid in low spots before the line could be tested.

In mid-December 1944 engineer petroleum companies were spread over 450 miles. The Petroleum Section of the Engineer Service, PBS, exercised direct control over the units but was finding this more and more difficult. On 25 December 1944, the section activated the 407th Engineer Service Battalion according to TOE 5–500, drawing most of the personnel from an engineer utilities detachment. The battalion was a skeleton headquarters that could supervise a number of independently operating units and coordinate operation and construction activities. All troops on POL work in western Italy (three American and one Italian engineer petroleum distribution company and two battalions of other Italian troops for security and labor work) came under the 407th. This move not only relieved the Petroleum Section but also made for better supply, planning, and maintenance support for engineer pipeline units. The battalion set up a major maintenance shop in Leghorn and, in February 1945, a smaller one in Naples for third echelon and higher maintenance and repair of POL equipment.[17]

When the spring offensive began in 1945, the 785th Petroleum Distribution Company, along with a hundred Italian troops, stood ready to lay a double line up Highway 65 from Loiano to Bologna, twenty-two miles away. The work got under way on 24 April 1945, but, plagued with traffic congestion on the highway and the multitude of mines in the area, was not finished until 7 May.

The greatest handicap to efficient pipeline operations was the telephone system. Standard issue telephones were totally inadequate; the wire was of such low conductivity that messages traveling farther than twelve miles had to be relayed, a process that caused such delays and confusion that the PBS engineer asked the PBS Signal Section to provide a communication system solely for pipelines. The system helped, but did not solve the problems. Conversation between Leghorn and Bologna was impossible, and only clear weather and shouting permitted Sesto to converse with either Leghorn or Bologna.

Deliberate sabotage of pipelines was negligible, but civilian theft of petroleum products was a constant problem. In one thirty-day period, pipeline losses near Rome averaged three hundred barrels a day. Usually thieves loosened couplings, though in some cases they knocked holes into pipe. Breaks on long downhill stretches, where leaks could not be detected by a drop in pressure, were especially costly. One such break occurred a few miles south of Bologna, at the bottom of a 32-mile grade. Someone carelessly lighted a cigarette near the spilled gas. Eight civilians died in

---

[17] AMO (Lt Col Beddow) 1945, Work Sheets of Engr AMO Survey Team, 10 May 45; Ltr, Lt Col E. P. Streck, Actg Engr Ofcr, PBS, to all Branch Chfs, Engr Service, Pensouth, 10 Mar 45, sub: Deputy Theater Commanders' Conf (6 Mar 45), NATOUSA file, Conf, Deputy Theater Commander.

the ensuing holocaust, which also broke two other lines. An estimated 12,000 gallons of gasoline were lost. Leaks caused by tension failures on couplings that thieves had loosened kept repair crews busy. Patrolling Italian soldiers and even horse-mounted GIs did not stop the tampering. Italian courts treated the few thieves who were caught quite leniently, and American authorities sometimes had to pressure the Italians to prosecute such cases.[18]

### Tasks of Base Section Engineers

Base section engineers drew a multitude of assignments. (*Map 12*) Many of them were calls for a few men to sweep mines, clear away debris, or repair plumbing. Others' tasks were larger. The ninety-five work orders the 345th Engineer General Service Regiment handled in August 1944 ranged from repairing a water faucet at Villa Maria (the General Officers Rest Camp in Naples) to installing 225 pieces of equipment for a huge quartermaster laundry and dry cleaning plant at Bagnoli. This unit was the first base section engineer construction organization in Naples. Its early assignments included setting up an engineer and a quartermaster depot, repairing railroads, building POW camps, and working on the Serino aqueduct. The 345th was also responsible for all street and sewer repair in Naples, although civilians did the actual work.[19]

Railway repair was an unexpected task. In AVALANCHE planning the Transportation Corps' Military Railway Service (MRS), with help from the Italians, was expected to handle railroad rehabilitation and engineers were to be responsible only for new rail construction—mainly spurs into dumps and depots.[20] But the rail net was so badly damaged and the Italian railroad agencies so disorganized that MRS had to ask the engineers for help. Most of the work fell to the 94th Engineer General Service Regiment, which arrived in Naples the second week of October 1943 and started rehabilitating lines to the Aversa railhead even before their vehicles and equipment were ashore.[21]

Supplies for track reconstruction had to be cannibalized. For example, to repair one lane of double-track lines the engineers used rails, ties, and fish plates from the other track. They also gathered material, as well as frogs and switches, from railway yards and unessential spur lines. Sometimes engineers could stockpile items, but because the Germans had destroyed many of the frogs and switches they were scarce. Luckily, a large stock of unused rails turned up in Naples. For bridging the engineers used steel salvaged from destroyed spans and from a steel mill at Bagnoli. However, they also needed timber. Railroad bridging supplies remained short, and in many instances

[18] Ltrs, HQ, 705th Engr Pet Dist Co, to Engr, Engr Service, Pensouth, various dates, sub: Loss of Gasoline on the Naples-Rome, Italy, Pipeline, PBS file, Loss of Gas on Naples-Rome PPL 1944–45; NATO-USA Statistical Summary 10, 1 Jan 44, 319.1 (MTO), OCE file.

[19] Unless otherwise cited this section is based on Engr Service, PBS, Work Accomplished, and the histories of the units mentioned.

[20] Wakeman et al., Rpt on Rehabilitation of Naples and other Captured Ports, 28 Nov 43; Extracts from Rpt on Peninsular Base Section, NATOUSA, 10 Feb 44, sec. VIII, Engr Service.

[21] Hist of PBS, Phases II and III, 28 Aug 43–3 Jan 44; Rpt, Functions of the Base Engr, prepared by PBS Engr, 25 Oct 43, 381 NATOUSA file; Extracts from Rpt on PBS, NATOUSA, 10 Feb 44, sec. VIII, Engr Service.

ADRIATIC SEA

*Modena*

*Bologna*

*Loiano*

*Sesto*

*Pisa*

*Florence*

*Leghorn*

*Volterra*

I T A L Y

*Cecina*

*Piombino*

*San Stefano*

TYRRHENIAN SEA

*Civitavecchia*

ROME

*Cisterna
Station*

*San
Biagio*          *Cassino*

*Mignano*    *San Vittore*

Mt Orso Tunnel    *Fondi*    *Sessa*    *San Felice*

*Terracina*          *Calvi Risorta*

*Sparanise*    *Capua*

*Fertilia*

*Bagnoli*    *Naples*

*Pozzuoli*

## PENINSULAR BASE SECTION

- - - - - -  Approximate pipeline route

+—+—+—+  Major rail repairs

★  Repaired ports

| 0 | 50 | 100 Miles |
|---|---|---|
| 0 | 50 | 100 Kilometers |

*MAP 12*

the engineers had to resort to culverts topped by huge earth fills.[22]

By the end of November 1943 the rail reached Capua and before the spring offensive stretched to Mignano, less than ten miles south of Cassino. The closest yet built to combat lines, the railhead was within range of German 270-mm. artillery. Early in June 1944 the 94th Engineers began the largest single railroad repair assignment in Italy, reopening a 32-mile stretch from Monte San Biagio station to Cisterna station on the main coastal line to Rome. The main block was the 4 1/2-mile Monte Orso tunnel, blown in three places, a few miles out of San Biagio. The south portal was blocked partially and the north portal completely, but the main obstruction was deep inside the mountain. These engineers worked with air hammers and explosives, cutting a passage by breaking up large rocks and carting off the debris on a small industrial railway installed for the purpose. The work was slow at best, but toward the end of June a front-end loader mounted on a D–4 tractor more than doubled the removal capacity.

The engineers relied on a natural draft to carry off fumes from generator engines that supplied power for lighting and for air compressors, but when the draft occasionally reversed, dangerous fumes soon fouled the air. Large exhaust fans did not solve the problem, and ultimately the generators had to be moved outside the tunnel. The engineers then installed a four-

inch pipeline to carry compressed air to a pressure tank near the main block, whence two smaller lines carried the compressed air to the work forces.

The main problem was to cut a passage through the mass of debris without bringing down more rock and dirt. The engineers first built a broad-base masonry wall atop the debris on each side of the passage to support the roof. Then they removed the material between the two walls, tamped crevices and cracks exposed in the debris supporting the walls with mortar, and filled undermined sections with stone masonry. The engineers had another major difficulty at track level, where the debris was composed of fine material that had filtered down through the larger rocks. This material tended to run out from under the new walls, and, once started, was hard to stop. In one instance the fine material undermined a forty-foot section of new wall and delayed work for four days. Only by making undermined sections shorter could the engineers alleviate the problem. This process slowed all work on the tunnel, and the rail line to Cisterna did not open until 20 July.

North of the Monte Orso tunnel the Germans had blown overpasses and bridges, removed whole sections of rail to help build defensive works, and prepared culverts for demolition but had actually blown few. The main job north of Monte Orso was bridging the Mussolini Canal, where two of three concrete-arch spans were down. The 94th Engineers restored this crossing by using a 68-foot steel girder to span the center section of the bridge and an earth fill to replace the northern span.

On this and other jobs along the section of railroad north of Monte Orso a

[22] Ltr, HQ, AGF, to CG, Second Army et al., sub: Observer's Notes on the Italian Campaign, 4 Oct 43–29 Mar 44, 319.1, AGF file, Binder 1, Jan–Jun 44; PBS Engr Hist, pt. I, 1943–45, sec. I, Chronological Summary, p. 31; Engr Service, PBS, Work Accomplished, 2 Oct 43–1 Sep 44, pp. 142–46.

major problem was getting supplies. Engineer equipment and construction material had to be trucked 80 to 115 miles from the Naples area; cement and bridge steel came 40 to 70 miles from the Minturno railhead; some lumber came 50 miles from Anzio (but most of it by truck from Naples); and sand came from beaches 5 to 15 miles from the railroad. Until it closed, the Fifth Army fuel point at Fondi supplied gasoline. Later, gas and oil had to be hauled sixty to ninety miles from Sparanise.

Once Fifth Army reached Leghorn on 20 July, almost all rehabilitation was centered on lines well north of Rome. In PBS (Main), rehabilitation included forty-eight miles of mainline track, nine major bridges, and six railheads. Much of this work was in the immediate vicinity of Leghorn, but the largest single assignment was a twelve-mile stretch of track between Pisa and Florence, where five demolished bridges had to be rebuilt. By V−E Day 3,000 miles of rail lines were in use in western Italy.

Work on roads accounted for nearly one-third of base section construction man-hours from July 1944 to mid-March 1945. In northern Italy, Italian soldiers and contractors working under engineer supervision accounted for over 75 percent of the man-hours that went into road maintenance and repair. But many assignments—particularly building and maintaining roads in base section depots—were either too difficult or too urgent for local authorities to handle, and these fell to American engineer units.

One of the main occupations of base section engineers was general hospital construction, which consisted mostly of expanding existing buildings and facilities. In the Naples area, the unfinished exhibition buildings at Bagnoli fairgrounds housed six hospitals, a medical laboratory, and a medical supply depot. The Army took over modern civilian hospitals in the city and used schools and other public buildings to house nine more hospitals. A general hospital operated in an apartment building near Pomigliano Airfield, and an unfinished apartment building at Fuorigrotta, near the Bagnoli fairgrounds, was home to the 37th General Hospital. Much of the engineer work went into increasing the water, electric, and sanitary systems. At most hospitals engineers had to black out windows, clear away debris, put up or take out partitions, install equipment, and erect prefabricated barracks where more space was needed.

Using existing buildings had great advantages over putting up standard buildings, but from the engineer standpoint it also had certain disadvantages. Since the scale of allowances NATOUSA established was barely applicable, each potential site had different construction and alteration requirements. As each site was selected, the Engineer Service and the surgeon's office determined what work would be required. In most cases engineers were able to move hospital personnel in within a few days and then continue their work.

By mid-March 1944, twenty-three general and station hospitals were open in the vicinity of Naples. Five more were started before the end of May, but finding large buildings to convert was becoming increasingly difficult. After the spring offensive began only one more was built south of Anzio, and it consisted mainly of 20-by-48-foot prefabricated barracks. The offensive opened up a new supply of barracks, schools, and other public buildings adaptable to hospitals. In June hospitals started operating in Rome and in smaller towns to the north. During the latter months of the campaign, hospital construction centered in the Leghorn-Florence area; of the twenty-three hospitals built north of Anzio by mid-March 1945, five were in Rome, six in Leghorn, and four in Florence.

For a long time the largest general construction assignment was hospitals, but toward the close of 1944, with the end of the war in sight, another program loomed for PBS engineers: preparing training and staging areas for redeploying troops and building enclosures for prisoners of war. By mid-February 1945 tentative redeployment plans called for eight 25,000-man training areas, two 5,000-man training areas, and two 20,000-man staging areas. Also in prospect was a major construction program to accommodate liberated Russians and another for Nazi prisoners of war. The two 20,000-man staging areas were then well toward completion, but MTOUSA and the War Department delayed the POW enclosures. Repeated changes in instructions for the Florence redeployment training area also made it difficult for the Engineer Service to allocate construction equipment, personnel, and material. By mid-April construction had started on four POW camps: one at Aversa for 10,000 men, another at Florence for 13,000, and two at Leghorn for 60,000. Construction for redeployment and for POWs continued beyond V−E Day. When Germany surrendered, 20,000-man redeployment training areas at Francolise, Montecatini, and Florence, as well as three 30,000-man POW camps, were still under construction.

On nearly every PBS engineer job, mine clearing had first priority—even in areas once held by Fifth Army troops. To remove mines in areas into which Allied troops moved, PBS relied on base section engineers, British as well as American, who got some help from attached Italian engineer troops and at the end of the war from volunteer Italian prisoners of war. Mine clearing took considerable time; for example, in June 1944 at Scauri the 345th Engineers spent 22,405 man-hours during an eighteen-day period searching a building to be used by the 49th Quartermaster Group. At a hospital site north of Naples the same unit found 230 Teller mines and 47 other mines and booby traps. At Leghorn, one of the most heavily mined areas in Italy, base section engineers, with the help of two British bomb disposal units, removed 25,000 mines. Other mine removal was a responsibility of the Allied Military Government Labor Office, which recruited and trained civilian volunteers for the work. By mid-April these volunteers had found 69,000 mines, bombs, and projectiles in and around Florence alone.

In addition to the large body of PBS engineers working on construction— the general service regiments, combat battalions and regiments, port construction companies, separate battalions, construction battalions, and petroleum distribution companies, which built ports, roads, bridges, railroads, camps, hospitals, stockades, depots, and other installations—were a number of the small special units such as water supply and mapping. In August 1943 the War Department abolished water supply battalions in favor of separate companies and left reorganizing the battalions to the theaters' discretion. Fifth Army chose not to reorganize its 405th Engineer Water Supply Battalion until after V—E Day. PBS had to reorganize the 401st Engineer Water Supply Battalion in August 1944 to furnish units for ANVIL and redesignated Companies A and B the 1513th and the 1514th Engineer Supply Companies, respectively. The former took over water supply work in PBS, and the 1514th went to southern France.

The 405th Water Supply Battalion provided 74 percent of the 454,765,000 gallons of water the army drew through the campaign.[23] When the rear section of Company C entered Naples from the land side on 1 October, the city had been without fresh water for more than a week, for the retreating Germans had destroyed the 53-mile-long aqueduct bringing spring water from Serino. Sewer lines were clogged and overflowing, and the danger of a typhoid or typhus epidemic threatened a half million people. At first the rear section could accomplish little, for all purification equipment was out in the harbor aboard ship with the main section; but the following morning the rear section discovered within a hundred yards of the headquarters they had established in the Poggioreale area, the undamaged Bolla aqueduct, which brought industrial water to the city. With meager equipment the section pumped this water into tankers, purified it, and set up four water points in the city. Crowds

of civilians with containers gathered, the press so great that armed guards had to keep order. By curfew the same day, 60,000 gallons of water had been distributed. After the arrival of the main section of the company and eleven days and nights of work, fresh water reached Naples by 13 October.

Company C of the 405th remained in the Naples area until the 401st Water Supply Battalion arrived in mid-November 1943 to handle water supply in the PBS area. Thereafter the 405th employed a company for supplying army installations, particularly hospitals. During the winter of 1943–44 not all of the 401st was needed in the PBS area, and at least one company was generally available for well drilling, water hauling, and general construction.

In the north at Leghorn the main source of water was a series of wells at Filettole pump station, some fifteen miles north of Pisa. When Leghorn fell these wells were still in German hands, but engineers were able to furnish water from other sources. When the Filettole station was captured, engineers found that the Germans had destroyed all the pumps, and restoring the facility appeared hopeless. Closer inspection, however, showed that new pumps could make the station operational. This job was undertaken by Company F of the 338th Engineer General Service Regiment, aided by civilian workers. Also required to reopen the line to Leghorn were repairs to a twenty-mile-long, sixteen-inch cast-iron pipeline that had been broken in many places, the worst at the 550-foot Arno River crossing, the 300-foot Serchio River crossing, and a 100-foot canal crossing.

The most difficult repair job was at the Arno River crossing. In September

---

[23] Capt. William J. Diamond, "Water Supply in Italy," *The Military Engineer*, XXXIX (August 1947), 332; Rpt, Functions of the Base Engr, prepared by PBS Engr, 25 Oct 43; Extracts from Rpt on Peninsular Base Section, NATOUSA, 10 Feb 44, sec. VIII, Engr Service; PBS Engr Hist, pt. I, 1943–45, sec. I, Chronological Summary, pp. 27–30; *Engineer History, Mediterranean*, app. K.

Company F tried to put a pipe across the Arno on bents built on the trusses of a demolished bridge, but flood waters washed it out before it was finished. Company F then tried to put a welded pipe across the river bottom, but the pipe broke on 23 October. In the meantime a new Serchio River crossing had to be raised six feet to get it above flood stage. In November a third attempt to get a line across the Arno succeeded, and water began to flow through to Leghorn. Many leaks showed up in the pipeline, and repairs and improvements continued well into 1945. Over 96,000 man-hours, divided about equally between several engineer units and Italian civilians, ultimately went into the restoration.

At both Naples and Leghorn, as well as in other cities, the municipal water systems were badly damaged, but not destroyed. The Germans had needed to use municipal water supplies until the last minute, and civilians had frustrated some destruction.[24] Engineers were able not only to restore water for public use in a remarkably short time but also to provide railroad engineers with water for locomotives and to send tank trucks to engineer fire-fighting platoons.[25]

The War Department first authorized fire-fighting units for the Corps of Engineers in August 1942, and by the end of 1943 six platoons of thirty-eight men each were in Peninsular Base Section. Several more were formed in June 1944 from the 6487th Engineer Construction Battalion, and five Italian fire-fighting units were organized and equipped; just before ANVIL, PBS had nineteen fire-fighting platoons. The new platoons trained at a fire-fighting school in Aversa, each equipped and organized to operate in four sections. The main job was not to fight fires but to prevent them by inspecting for fire hazards and by keeping fire extinguishers filled and in good working order. Despite such precautions a number of fires broke out. One fire-fighting platoon assigned to Fifth Army averaged three fire calls a week for several months, and at the Anzio ammunition depot fifty fires broke out during April 1944 alone. Tankdozers and armored bulldozers, used to scatter burning ammunition boxes and then smother them with dirt, were effective against dangerous ammunition dump fires.[26]

A less familiar task in Italy was real estate operations. In the AVALANCHE plans the responsibility for procuring properties for American agencies went to the engineers. The Real Estate Branch of the PBS Engineer Service processed all requests by American units for property in the base section area. It also took control of real estate records for property that Fifth Army released to Peninsular Base Section. In the combat area when Fifth Army troops damaged property they occupied (and their occupancy was a matter of record) the owner was entitled to compensation. Damage that occurred before occupancy was charged to "fortunes-of-war," for which no compensation was paid. Careful records had to be kept to separate the two categories. For these purposes photographic records showing the condition

[24] Chf Engr, 15th Army Gp, Notes on Engr Opns in Italy, no. 8, 1 Feb 44.
[25] Diamond, "Water Supply in Italy," p. 332.

[26] Fred K. Shirk, "Engineer Fire Fighters in the March on Rome," *The Military Engineer*, XXXVII (April 1945), 147–48.

of properties, particularly when removal of damaged portions was necessary, proved valuable, as did detailed inventories of small, movable furnishings and fixtures. When the war ended, the Real Estate Branch held active files on more than 3,900 properties ranging from open fields to beautiful villas. Hundreds more had been requisitioned, used, and returned to private owners.

Before the invasion of Italy the engineers had made few preparations to handle real estate work. The field was fairly new, and few officers were experienced. For the most part, forms and procedures had to be worked out by trial and error in Italy. Under the terms of the armistice the Italian government undertook to make all required facilities, installations, equipment, and supplies available to the Allies and to make all payments in connection with them. Allied military agencies made only emergency payments required to keep financially alive individual workers and contractors employed by the Allies.[27]

Procuring real estate for military use and keeping the necessary records were nevertheless considerable tasks. One of the biggest stumbling blocks for the Real Estate Branch was the lack of a central agency in Fifth Army to handle real estate; thus, records the army turned over to PBS were often confused. The establishment of a real estate section in the Fifth Army engineer command, after nearly a year in Italy, helped matters considerably. Thereafter this section, together with G–4, Fifth Army, was able to plan in advance for real estate needed for dumps, bivouac areas, and other installations.[28]

Engineers in PBS were to handle, store, and issue maps. Under the Supply Branch of the PBS Engineer Service, two thirteen-man engineer depot detachments operated a map depot and made bulk issues to both Fifth and Eighth Armies. Peninsular Base Section had no topographic units for survey, drafting, or reproduction. The map depot detachments had reproduction sections but limited their operations to copying construction drawings and preparing administrative directives and reports for the PBS engineer and engineer units.

Soon after Naples fell the 2634th Engineer Map Depot Detachment set up a map library at the Engineer Service headquarters and a base map depot at Miano. The map library filled small orders while the Miano depot made bulk issues to Fifth and Eighth Armies. A second map depot detachment arrived in the base section in November 1943 and a third in April 1944. NATOUSA activated other map depot detachments for ANVIL, and, of the final total of six, three went to southern France.

In preparation for the 1944 offensives to and past Rome, PBS engineers took over some twenty tons of maps from Fifth Army depots at Paestum, but these sheets covered only the area south of the Volturno. Additional maps covering the area north to Leghorn arrived later, and before the end of 1943 some 700 tons of maps had reached the Miano depot. The PBS map depots stocked ground maps of Italy in four scales (1:25,000, 1:50,000, 1:100,000, and 1:250,000) as well as air maps, small-scale coverages of Europe,

---

[27] Garland and Smyth, *Sicily and the Surrender of Italy,* pp. 559–64.

[28] Extracts from Rpt on Peninsular Base Section,

NATOUSA, 10 Feb 44, sec. VIII, Engr Service; PBS Engr Hist, pt. I, 1943–45, sec. I, Chronological Summary.

town plans, and road maps. The number of map sheets ran into the millions.[29]

For the first time in the European war, engineer lumber operations in Italy assumed importance. Engineer training was based largely on the use of locally procured lumber for all aspects of construction, but in the United Kingdom, North Africa, and Sicily the supply had been so short that the engineers had come to rely on substitutes.

Italy offered the first real opportunity overseas to obtain large quantities of lumber from local sources. In two years, PBS forestry operations in Italy produced lumber amounting to 370,885 ship tons, more than the total tonnage of engineer supplies recovered through Italian ports during the first year of the campaign. The lumbering operations also saved money; Italian lumber cost an estimated $25.00 per 1,000 board feet delivered to the using unit; the price in the United States at the time was $40.00 per 1,000 board feet at the mill.[30]

At about the time of the Salerno landing, engineers crossed the Strait of Messina to investigate timber reserves and lumbering facilities in Cosenza Province and found approximately nine million board feet of milled lumber, a large stockpile of unsawed logs, extensive timber tracts, and scores of existing sawmills. With the capture of Naples, lumber quickly became a critical item. The engineers needed piles for port rehabilitation, bridging, and power line poles; timbers and heavy planking for building and decking; ties for railroads;

and lumber for boxing, building, and dunnage. The only American forestry unit in the theater, the 800th Engineer Forestry Company, was then operating a sawmill in Tunisia, but this unit had a relatively low shipping priority and could not be moved promptly to Italy. Therefore, during the latter part of November PBS sent a detachment of about fifty men from the 40th Engineer Combat Regiment to the Cosenza area to ship stockpiled lumber.[31]

Soon after the 800th Engineer Forestry Company reached Naples in mid-December 1943, it split into three detachments. Twenty men went to Cosenza to give the 40th Engineers experienced mill men and lumber checkers, while a smaller group remained in Naples to search out lumber stocks. The rest of the company moved into a timber stand at Montesano, about 120 miles southeast of Naples, and on Christmas Day began milling operations. With its portable sawmill the company produced over 75,000 board feet of lumber at Montesano and then, on 21 January 1944, moved to Cosenza. There it took over lumber production from the 40th Engineers and by June 1944 had forty-three civilian sawmills operating in the area, producing about a quarter of a million board feet per day.

The 800th, operating over a wide area 250 miles from Headquarters, PBS, virtually took over operation of the Cosenza-Camigliatello narrow-gauge railroad relay track after washouts and landslides and cleared away deep snow drifts during the winter. The company also performed its own road construction and maintenance, including build-

---

[29] AGF Bd Rpt 179, NATOUSA, Notes on Mapping an Army, 16 Aug 44; PBS Engr Hist, pt. I, 1943–45, sec. 1, Chronological Summary.

[30] PBS Engr Hist, pt. I, 1943–45, sec. II, app. V and app. VI; Hist 800th Engr Forestry Co, 13 Dec 43–30 Jun 44.

[31] Interv with Col Smullen; Engr Service, PBS, Work Accomplished, p. 275.

ing culverts and bridges. The unit operated a motor pool that expanded from an original fifteen vehicles to a fleet of seventy-seven trucks and performed its own maintenance. It operated a depot where civilian laborers loaded an average of thirty-five cars of lumber piling a day; it employed 400 civilians directly and supervised nearly 3,000 others employed at civilian sawmills.

During its first year at Cosenza the 800th's sawmill, working two shifts a day seven days a week, produced approximately 7,956,290 board feet of lumber. Peak production came during October 1944, when the mill produced an average of 37,245 board feet a day. Total lumber shipments from the Cosenza area during the twelve months ending January 1945 amounted to 63,987,350 board feet.[32]

Producing the lumber was one thing; delivering it was another. At times breaks in the rail lines, heavy snowfalls in the mountains, and shortages of railroad cars cut sharply into shipments from Cosenza. At such times the engineers had to pile the lumber in the Cosenza railroad yards, and on one occasion these stockpiles contained approximately 1,750,000 board feet of lumber. For seven weeks, from February to April 1944, and again the following January, blizzards in the mountains curtailed shipments by 300,000 to 400,000 board feet a week. Mt. Vesuvius erupted on 18 March 1944, burying several miles of railroad track under six to eight inches of cinders and tying up nearly seven hundred railroad cars for several days.[33]

In September 1944 four members of the 800th went to Leghorn to teach men of the 338th Engineer General Service Regiment and Italian troops how to operate sawmills. This reduced the amount of lumber that had to be shipped to Leghorn from Cosenza, 650 miles away. By February 1945 two mills in northern Italy were producing 40,000 board feet a day. Though many logs and trees in timber stands in northern Italy were worthless for military operations because of imbedded shrapnel, lumber production in the area nevertheless increased. On one day early in May 1945 four mills there achieved a peak production of 108,639 board feet.[34]

### PBS Supply and Maintenance

The Peninsular Base Section supply and maintenance units came under a provisional base depot group headquarters command in Naples as soon as PBS became operational. Depot companies directed operations and supervised Italian laborers in the supply outlets; maintenance companies handled construction equipment pools and third, fourth, and fifth echelon maintenance of heavy equipment; and a heavy shop company made tools and spare parts for the maintenance units and did some repairs.[35]

Engineer depot companies operated two main depots in western Italy. One, near Naples, was located at an Italian Army barracks, and the other at an Italian movie studio at Tirrenia, a few miles

---

[32] Hist 800th Engr Forestry Co, Monthly Rpts, 13 Dec 43 – May 45, Personal files, M/Sgt Robert Kaufman.

[33] Hist 727th Engr Railway Operating Bn, Transportation Corps, p. 60.

[34] Hist 800th Engr Forestry Co, Mthly Rpts, 13 Dec 43 – May 45, with annexes.

[35] Engr Service, PBS, Work Accomplished, pp. 273 – 74. Unless otherwise indicated this section is based on this source and the histories of the units mentioned.

north of Leghorn. In the Naples area special engineer depots were also set up for POL construction supplies, stream-crossing equipment, and maps. PBS engineers also took over Fifth Army engineer depots at Anzio, Civitavecchia, Piombino, and other points as the army moved forward. These army depots either operated where they were until their stocks were exhausted, or they closed forthwith to move stocks to more central locations.

Initially the 458th Engineer Depot Company handled all administrative duties at all PBS engineer depots, while the 386th Engineer Battalion (Separate), aided by several hundred civilian workers, received, stored, and issued supplies. The 386th also kept several men on duty day and night in the port of Naples to identify engineer supplies and to see that they went to the proper depots. The 473d Engineer Maintenance Company received and issued heavy equipment at the depots and maintained equipment in the depots and in engineer units. A second engineer depot company, the 462d, arrived in Naples toward the end of November 1943 and ultimately took over the engineer depots Fifth Army left behind in its drive north during June and July 1944.

With the opening of the engineer depot near Leghorn, those at Civitavecchia and Piombino were closed as rapidly as transportation permitted, and elements of the 462d moved up to operate the Leghorn depot. There, two Italian engineer companies joined the American unit as a labor force, and civilians from as far off as Pisa and Lari were hired to help. As many as a thousand civilians a day—a number limited only by the amount of transportation available—worked at the Leghorn depot. During December 1944 a total of 23,959 tons of engineer supplies reached the depot, which issued 20,907 tons. With Leghorn the focal point for engineer supply in the PBS forward area, the Supply Section of the PBS (Main) Engineer Service took up quarters there and kept stock records of all engineer depots in the PBS forward area.

Two types of engineer units, light equipment and base equipment companies, could service, issue, and when necessary, operate Class IV equipment—extra and special equipment such as bulldozers issued temporarily or for specific jobs. In July 1944 the 688th Engineer Base Equipment Company reached Naples to assemble equipment coming into engineer depots, service it, transport it to requisitioning units, and provide instructors for receiving units. But in mid-September the 688th passed to Seventh Army control, and thereafter PBS engineer maintenance companies had to do the 688th's work as well as their own.

In August 1944 Brig. Gen. Dabney O. Elliott, NATOUSA engineer, put theater requirements for maintenance companies at eleven and estimated that the theater also needed at least one heavy shop and three maintenance companies to support Army Air Forces units properly. At the time only three engineer maintenance companies and two engineer heavy shop companies were available in the theater.[36]

The 469th Engineer Maintenance Company went to Italy with Fifth Army, and the 473d, a PBS unit, reached

---

[36] Elliott comments, 18 Mar 60; G-3 Section, HQ, 15th Army Group, *A Military Encyclopedia*, pp. 322-23.

Naples on 10 October 1943. The 473d took in equipment for second, third, fourth, and even fifth echelon repairs and also functioned as a base equipment company, hauling heavy engineer equipment from the port and uncrating, assembling, and servicing it for both PBS and Fifth Army units. Roads in the shop area deteriorated badly during the fall, and in January the unit had to move to a new hard-surfaced area near the port, ten miles from the engineer depot. In mid-April, with the coming of dry weather, the company returned to Naples. Both moves cost the unit heavily, for it took eleven days and help from other units to move the 5,200 tons of heavy engineer equipment back to the depot.

Engineer maintenance forces in PBS had been strengthened in February 1944 by the arrival of the 496th Engineer Heavy Shop Company, but a month passed before all of the 496th's equipment reached Italy. In the meantime the unit established itself at a civilian steel jobbing concern in Naples. There it set up and operated a series of separate shops for engine rebuilding, carburetor and injection repair, electrical repair, salvage and reclamation work, forging, welding, and patternmaking.

An important function was manufacturing spare parts that could not be obtained through normal supply channels: piston rings and cylinder sleeves for internal combustion engines, air compressors, and reciprocating pumps. The 496th also salvaged and reconditioned usable parts from scrapped equipment, did fourth and fifth echelon engineer maintenance, and took on third echelon maintenance until a third engineer maintenance company, the 470th, arrived in Italy during May 1944.

ANVIL laid a heavy hand on engineer maintenance resources in Italy. Fifth Army gave up its 469th Engineer Maintenance Company; PBS lost the 470th Engineer Maintenance Company and the 688th Engineer Base Equipment Company. Italy was left with one maintenance company (split among the Army Air Forces, Fifth Army, and PBS), one heavy shop company, and one base shop company. PBS had to turn more and more to Italian sources. The 1st Engineer Maintenance Company (Italian) was activated in July 1944 and attached to the 473d Engineer Maintenance Company at the Naples engineer depot; the 2d Engineer Maintenance Company (Italian) came into being in mid-August and worked with the 496th Engineer Heavy Shop Company until ready to function independently. Although handicapped in personnel and equipment, both units were soon doing good work. Machinists, blacksmiths, welders, and carpenters were easy enough to find among Italian soldiers and civilians, but skilled mechanics, patternmakers, and foundry workers were not. Moreover, securing adequate maintenance equipment for the Italian units was difficult. U.S. Army tables of basic allowances did not provide for equipping either unauthorized or expanded units, so the two Italian companies never had more than half the equipment allotted their American counterparts.

During the summer of 1944 the maintenance of engineer equipment became critical; in June, when daily advances were great, the 19th Engineer Combat Regiment had to haul its dozers long distances for minor repairs. During the next month and into September as much as 50 percent of the unit's heavy equipment was under repair, and over the last half of 1944 the 19th Engineers had an average of fifty pieces of equipment in its "waiting line." The shortage of engineer maintenance units was the main reason, but there were others: poor preventive maintenance, particularly during the rapid advances of July and August; equipment that had worn out after two or more years of use; replacement of some trained mechanics with untrained limited-service men; and a shortage of certain critical spare parts. Another important factor was extra wear and tear that equipment suffered at the hands of unskilled operators. Multiple shifts and heavy use of Class IV equipment required several times the number of operators provided by unit TOEs.

Toward the end of 1944, MTOUSA was able to achieve a better balance of engineer forces, largely with men from deactivated antiaircraft units. The engineers used some of these men to activate two new engineer maintenance companies. In Pensouth the 5th Engineer Maintenance Company was activated on 10 November with a cadre of a few men from both the 473d and 496th Engineer Companies. In Fifth Army the 40th Engineer Maintenance Company came into being on 1 December with a cadre from the 473d Engineer Company. Neither of the new engineer maintenance companies came up to full strength until the end of December 1944, and many of the men had had no experience in maintenance. Already a heavy backlog of deadlined equipment had built up, while hard winter usage and age kept broken machines flowing to repair shops. Gradually, greater attention to first and second echelon maintenance reduced

breakdowns, and in March five inspection teams, made up of men from the maintenance and heavy shop companies, began to make frequent trips among units. In April Fifth Army reported the fewest equipment breakdowns in six months.

Probably the most challenging supply job the engineers had was handling spare parts—between eighty and ninety thousand different items. By early 1944 fast-moving parts were noticeably lacking throughout the engineer shops in the theater, whereas slow-moving items were overstocked. In August 1944, inspection teams from the United States found that about one-fourth of the 10,000 tons of spare parts in MTOUSA was excess that had accumulated as a result of the automatic supply policy. Some of the heavy parts in third echelon maintenance sets had been stocked, unused, for two years, while allowances for certain other parts needed to be doubled, tripled, or increased even tenfold.

Efficient handling of available parts required men thoroughly familiar with engineer equipment, with nomenclature and cataloging, with interchangeable parts, and with the repair history of parts and equipment. The 754th Engineer Parts Supply Company, the only such unit in MTOUSA, furnished cadres for spare parts platoons in engineer depot companies and, during the latter part of 1944, also lost men for retraining as infantry. By early 1945, 60 percent of the company was newcomers, few of whom had any qualifications for their assignments.

Italian theater shortages came from sacrifices for the more decisive theater in northern Europe. Beginning in early 1944, Fifth Army gave up support and combat units of all types to the ETOUSA command and to the invasion of southern France. In losing some of the best of its engineer units, the theater, in small measure, replenished some of what was borrowed in 1942 for commitment to Operation TORCH. The focus of the war shifted again to the Continent opposite England.

# CHAPTER XII

# Reviving BOLERO in the United Kingdom

The decisions at the TRIDENT Conference in May 1943—to undertake a strategic bombing campaign leading up to a cross-Channel invasion with a target date of 1 May 1944 while continuing operations in the Mediterranean—rescued BOLERO from the doldrums into which it had fallen as a result of the diversions to North Africa. To be sure, the drain of the continuing campaigns in the Mediterranean and the British seeming reluctance to sacrifice those campaigns to a cross-Channel operation left some doubt in American minds that the operations would be executed in a timely manner. Accordingly, for some months after TRIDENT the buildup proceeded haltingly and under relatively low priority. The appearance in July of an outline plan for the operation, now designated OVERLORD, and the acceptance of that plan at the Quebec Conference (QUADRANT) in August produced new momentum in the fall of 1943. But only the final resolution of all doubts at the meetings at Cairo-Tehran (SEXTANT) at the very end of the year gave BOLERO the top priority that would reawaken the buildup in the United Kingdom.[1]

ETOUSA engineers were essential to the buildup. They had to construct depots and camps to house the flood of incoming men and supplies, build the airfields from which preinvasion air strikes would be launched, and prepare plans and stockpile supplies for the engineer role in the invasion itself.[2]

The bases for planning the construction program during 1943 remained the BOLERO Key Plans, and they changed as the OVERLORD concept developed. Engineer planning late in 1942 was based on the third BOLERO Key Plan, which held preparations for a full-scale invasion in abeyance although it prescribed a vague goal of 1,049,000 men in England with no firm target date. As early as January 1943 Col. Cecil R. Moore, the ETOUSA chief engineer, directed base section engineers to return to the second BOLERO Key Plan as a guide and to use its troop basis of 1,118,000 men with a completion date of 31 December 1943.[3] The TRIDENT decisions produced firmer data to work

---

Except where otherwise indicated the account that follows is based on this volume.

[2] On this aspect of the engineer effort in the United Kingdom and for other engineer support to the AAF see Craven and Cate, *Europe: TORCH to POINT-BLANK*, pp. 599–664.

[3] Colonel Moore was promoted to brigadier general on 26 April 1943 and to major general on 1 March

---

[1] See Ruppenthal, *Logistical Support of the Armies, Volume I*, pp. 114–71, 231–68 for a detailed account.

with, and on 12 July 1943, a fourth BOLERO Key Plan set the troop basis at 1,340,000 men to be in Britain by 1 May 1944. On the basis of decisions at the Quebec Conference in August the British War Office (with the advice of the American staff) on 30 October 1943 issued an amended version of the fourth plan, setting the goal at 1,446,000 U.S. officers and enlisted men to be in the United Kingdom by 30 April 1944. This was the last of the key plans within which the engineer supply and construction programs proceeded.

## The Continuing Problem of Organization

The organizational framework within which the engineers operated—specifically the division of function between the theater headquarters and the SOS—continued to cause problems during 1943. As Commanding General, SOS, Maj. Gen. John C. H. Lee continued the drive he had begun in 1942 to bring all supply and administration in the theater under his control. He continued to meet determined resistance from those who insisted that the theater staff must remain responsible for theater-wide policy and planning for future operations and that the chiefs of services in particular must serve the theater commander directly in these areas even if their services were part of the SOS. Until the very end of the year compromise arrangements prevailed, but none of them were entirely satisfactory for the performance of engineer functions.

The duplication of functions created by moving SOS headquarters to Cheltenham in May 1942 persisted after Lt.

Gen. Frank M. Andrews replaced General Eisenhower as theater commander on 6 February 1943, and to a lesser degree after Lt. Gen. Jacob L. Devers replaced Andrews, who died in a plane crash on 3 May 1943.[4] In early March of that year Lee proposed to Andrews that he, Lee, be designated deputy theater commander for supply and administration as well as commanding general, SOS, with the theater G–4 and all the chiefs of the technical and administrative services serving under him in his dual capacity. The solution was not unlike that adopted eventually, but at the time Andrews rejected the scheme. He insisted that planning for future operations, a function of the theater headquarters, should remain separate from administration and supply of troops in the British Isles, a function of the SOS. Although he granted Lee more control over the chiefs of services, he also specified that they be ready to serve the theater commander immediately if needed. At the same time, he moved the whole SOS headquarters back to London close to ETOUSA.[5] While SOS planning came to be centered in London, an SOS deputy commander handled operations at Cheltenham. The operating echelons of the technical services remained at Cheltenham, and chiefs still had to spend some time there.

General Devers lent a more willing ear to Lee's arguments and vested the commanding general, SOS, with the office of the G–4 on the theater staff. An ETOUSA order of 27 May 1943 gave Lee in this dual role jurisdiction over all supply concerns of the theater and divided his SOS command between

---

1944. See ch. II; Memo, Moore for Lee, 11 Jan 43, 325.21 Policies and Plans, EUCOM Engr files.

[4] See ch. II.
[5] ETOUSA GO 16, 21 Mar 43.

two equal chiefs of theater service functions, one for administration and one for services. The seven technical services, including the engineers, lumped together with a purchasing service and a new theater area petroleum service, then had a chain of access to the theater commander running through Col. Royal B. Lord as chief of services, SOS, and General Lee himself as surrogate theater G−4.[6] Except for the limited consolidation involved in the G−4 position, ETOUSA and SOS staffs continued as separate entities, and the chiefs of services continued in dual roles in the two headquarters. Even this limited consolidation suffered a setback when the G−4 position on the ETOUSA staff was removed from the SOS commander and given to Maj. Gen. Robert W. Crawford between 8 October and 1 December 1943.[7]

On 1 December General Crawford moved to the Chief of Staff to the Supreme Allied Commander (COSSAC), a provisional Allied staff planning the invasion pending the establishment of a command for that purpose. General Lee then assumed the position of G−4, ETOUSA, again. Another month brought the realization of his proposals of early 1943. The expansion of the COSSAC role in England and the establishment of active field, army, and army group commands in England reduced the ETOUSA administrative and long-range planning function to little more than that of the SOS, ETOUSA, command. In effect, the two separate headquarters existed for the same reason and shared the same special staff, which included the engineers. When General

Eisenhower resumed command of the American theater and of the new Supreme Headquarters, Allied Expeditionary Force (SHAEF), which succeeded COSSAC on 15 January 1944, the ETOUSA and SOS staffs were consolidated. At the same time, General Lee assumed the formal title of deputy theater commander, in which capacity he was to act for General Eisenhower in all theater administrative and service matters.[8]

The consolidation reduced the duplication and inconsistencies and relieved the confusion that had characterized supply and administrative channels in 1943. It provided the basis for organizing an American Communications Zone command for operations on the Continent. But the organizational picture was still complicated and command relationships confusing. Theoretically General Lee's ETOUSA-COMZ staff served General Eisenhower in his role as American theater commander while his Allied staff served him in his role as supreme commander, Allied Expeditionary Force. Senior American field commanders tended to regard Lee's headquarters as strictly an SOS or Communications Zone headquarters, equal to but not above their own headquarters and equally subject to Eisenhower's directions as supreme Allied commander. They never accepted Lee's role as deputy theater commander and succeeded in having it abolished in August 1944.

In a sense the ETOUSA-SOS relationship with the Allied SHAEF command created some of the same problems that had characterized the relationship of SOS and ETOUSA because

---

[6] ETOUSA GO 33, 27 May 43.

[7] SOS ETOUSA GO 79, 19 Aug 43; ETOUSA GO 71, 8 Oct 43; ETOUSA GO 90, 1 Dec 43.

[8] ETOUSA GO 5, 17 Jan 44.

GENERAL MOORE *(Photograph taken in 1945.)*

Eisenhower sometimes used the American component of the SHAEF staff as an American theater staff. General Moore's misgivings about the command on the eve of the invasion were common among his fellow technical service chiefs. The continued assignment of the Engineer Service under the SOS made the other elements in the theater regard the chief engineer as part of a "co-ordinate command and not one that had authority or supervision over their commands."[9]

The command arrangements in the theater thus remained unsatisfactory to the Engineer Service throughout the buildup and preparation for the invasion. In manpower problems alone, Moore's headaches in bidding against other services for skilled men and in allocating work forces increased since he could not always exercise the weight and the rank of a theater commander's name in his own behalf. Equally difficult was engineer supply in the theater.

*New Supply Procedures*

When the buildup in England was expressed in terms of troop ceilings in the high-level international conferences of spring and summer 1943, the figures automatically implied demands for increased shipments of engineer supply and equipment. General Moore's SOS Engineer Service would have to plan not only for accommodations for the incoming men but also for protection and depot warehousing for both current operating supply and invasion materiel. The early part of 1943 saw the influx of comparatively small numbers of troops, primarily Air Corps reinforcements for the stepped-up aerial offensive. Later arrivals would require coordination of construction and supply functions, but the OCE Construction and Quartering Division had moved back to London in General Andrews' separation of planning and operating staffs in March 1943, leaving the Supply Division at SOS headquarters, ninety miles away. The division nevertheless contributed to some attempts at improving the supply flow to the United Kingdom, among them a program of preshipping unit equipment and new methods of marking shipments for destinations in England.

Until the summer of 1943, engineer

---

[9] Interv, Lt Col Shelby A. McMillion, Chf, Liaison Sect, OCE, with Maj Gen Moore, 10 May 44, sub: Overall Theater Problems in the United Kingdom, app. 17 to OCE ETOUSA Hist Rpt 1, Organization, Administration, and Personnel. (Hereafter cited as Moore Interv.)

units arriving from the United States brought their organic equipment with them. After 1 July they turned in all their equipment except necessary housekeeping supplies at their port of embarkation and upon reaching the United Kingdom drew new equipment, including supplemental maintenance supplies, from stocks previously shipped from the United States. The preshipment program took into account the probability that larger numbers of troops would arrive in England in late 1943 and early 1944 and sought to avoid overtaxing British port capacity and inland transportation nets with both troops and cargo by shipping the cargo beforehand. It also would permit British and American dock crews to take advantage of the long summer days for unloading.

But the limitations of the preshipment program immediately made themselves felt. Interpretations of the supply flow differed from the start. The European theater command perceived the system as a guarantee that bulk stocks would arrive before using troops docked in Great Britain, where they would immediately pick up TBA material and draw other needed supply, but not necessarily the same items they surrendered before leaving the United States. War Department interpretations relied at first on force-marking, under which units were to recover the same equipment they had turned in at home. Begun under constraints arising from little excess supply in American inventories and training schedules that prevented units from giving up equipment until just before they sailed, preshipment from May to August 1943 was primarily a vain struggle to fill available shipping space.

The priority system established for supplying Army Ground Forces in England also hobbled the program, with ETO supply occupying eighth place in the order of shipping importance in the United States. Until after SEXTANT the War Department was reluctant to change the priority for a theater that had no clear-cut and overriding strategic precedence. By the time Army Service Forces arguments produced a higher priority in November 1943, troop sailings rivaled those of preshipped cargo and shipping space went to troops and their personal gear.

The advance flow of heavier equipment for engineer work suffered from the uncertain supply policy in effect throughout 1943.[10] During July and August of that year General Moore complained that bulk-shipped TBA items arrived in the United Kingdom long after engineer units. In that period 75,000 engineer troops reached the theater to find that only 5 percent of their organizational equipment was waiting for them. As a result, most of the units could not contribute to the general construction program or even train effectively.[11] Receipt of bulk TBA equipment improved enough in September 1943 to take care of the units arriving that month but was not sufficient to replenish reserve stocks depleted during the two previous months. Eventually, engineer troops received standard equipment within seven to ten days after they arrived instead of the sixty to ninety days common under the old system.[12]

---

[10] Ruppenthal, *Logistical Support of the Armies, Volume I*, pp. 133–39; Leighton and Coakley, *Global Logistics and Strategy, 1943–45*, pp. 51–52.
[11] OCE ETOUSA Hist Rpt 4, Troops.
[12] Interv, Maj. J. H. Thetford, OCE Supply Div, 22 Sep 44, OCE.

Many engineer items shipped from the United States were poorly marked; some even lacked service identification marks. Of 3,920 items of prefabricated hutting more than 300 could not be used, largely because so many parts had been mixed together.[13] Supply processes improved for the engineers—and for other troops in the ETO—when SOS changed the UGLY marking system evolved in 1942. Under that system the first element in cargo identification, the code word UGLY, indicated the ETO; the second element indicated the supply service making the shipment; and the third indicated the class of supplies. Thus, engineer Class II supplied going to the ETO were marked UGLY-ENGRSII.

Early in 1943, SOS and the British refined this system with the aim of eliminating long rail hauls from the ports. They divided the United Kingdom into three zones: Zone I, Northern England, identified by the code word SOXO; Zone II, Bristol and London, called GLUE; and Zone III, Northern Ireland, called BANG. Thereafter, most cargo bore the shipping destination SOXO, GLUE, or BANG; UGLY indicated cargo not intended for any particular port in the United Kingdom. This system cut down reshipment from port to port, brought supplies to the correct depot sooner, relieved pressure on the already overloaded British rail system, and enabled supplies to be moved out of ports sooner—a necessity with German air raids an ever present danger. Manifests also improved, and the new ISS (Identification of Separate Shipments to Overseas Destinations) forms completely identified, in the third element of the UGLY address, separate shipments made against particular requisitions.

No amount of new markings could revise the shortages in large items of engineer equipment throughout 1943. One of the most important items was the dump truck; at late as September the engineers had 1,000 fewer than the standard tables of allocations called for. Heavy construction equipment, general-purpose vehicles, and cranes were in critically short supply well into 1944. Augers, semi-trailers, graders, shop equipment, tractors with angledozers, generators, various hand tools, asphalt paving equipment, and spare parts of all types fell into this category. On 30 April 1943, the backlog of engineer supply alone due in from the United States stood at 79,832 ship tons; by the end of August, it had increased to 124,224 tons.[14]

*Construction*

At the beginning of 1943 American engineers in the United Kingdom could not look back on an impressive construction record. They had built no hospitals, and although they had undertaken fourteen camp projects they had not completed any. They had worked on twelve airfields but none was more than 25 percent complete, and they had begun ten depots but none was finished. In one respect, however, the engineers had made considerable progress—they had learned, of necessity, how to work closely with the British.

---

[13] Shipment of Supplies, 400.22, EUCOM Engr files; OCE ETOUSA Monthly Rpt 8, Nov 43.

[14] Moore interv; OCE ETOUSA Monthly Rpts, Apr 43–Jun 44; Notes on Command and Staff Conf, 3, 10 Jan 44, Adm 457, ETOUSA Hist Sect; Rpt, Lt Col John H. Hassinger, Chf, Tractor and Crane Sect, OCE WD, to Moore, Nov 43, 319.1 Rpts (General), EUCOM

Because all facilities would ultimately go back to the British, many plans and specifications the engineers used were British, and the British had to approve deviations. British materials also had to be used. Influencing construction standards and specifications were the small area available for military use; a shortage of lumber and a consequent reliance on steel, cement, and brick; and wet weather that produced continuous mud. Plans and procedures were affected by differences in diction, custom, and nomenclature; slow delivery of supplies; red tape and British centralization; and heavy reliance on civilians.[15]

Every project the engineers worked on had to be approved in the War Office by the Directorate of Quartering, the Directorate of Fortifications and Works, and by Works Finance which was made up entirely of civilians. The Construction Division, OCE, ETOUSA, had a liaison officer from the Directorate of Fortifications and Works; another, for a time, from the Directorate of Quartering; and a third from the Air Ministry Works Directorate. In turn, the division kept a liaison officer on duty with the Directorate of Fortifications and Works in the War Office.[16]

Getting standards for quarters and airfields approved was a problem, for in many cases American standards were higher than British. The increased cost per capita for U.S. forces was incomprehensible to the British Works Finance. Many projects were delayed fifteen to forty-five days while the British investigated the need for the work.

Another cause for delay was failure to receive British supplies promptly. That tardiness and shortages, the engineers estimated, cut the effectiveness of American troop labor by 30 percent. Fortunately, matters improved in the later stages of the buildup.[17]

When General Moore directed the base section engineers to go back to the second Key Plan in February 1943, the BOLERO construction program was 29 percent complete. Priorities were air projects and depots, shops, and special projects, to be finished by 1 August 1943; accommodations previously planned, to be finished by 15 October 1943; and the hospital program, to be finished by 1 November 1943. Any additional accommodations were to be completed by the end of the year.[18]

The more rapid buildup under the fourth BOLERO Key Plan in July 1943 and its amendment in October stepped up all types of construction in the United Kingdom. New troop ceilings set at the international conferences raised the demand for construction far above that established for the 1,118,000-man limit in the second Key Plan without changing the basic construction priorities favoring airfields. The QUADRANT decisions, in anticipating OVERLORD, moved the staging areas for much of the invasion force from southern to southwestern England. Compared with the earlier construction demands, the work described in the fourth Key Plan expanded upon all previous work loads.

---

Engr files; Ltr, Moore to Col Joseph S. Gorlinski, 3 May 43, 321 Gen, Apr–Dec 43, EUCOM Engr files.
[15] Moore interv; see chs. II and III.
[16] Interv, McMillion with Col Paul D. Berrigan, 8 May 44.

[17] Interv, Col C. J. Barker, Chf, Ground Proj Sect, C&Q Div, OCE, 12 May 44; Intervs, Moore and Berrigan.
[18] Ltr, OCE ETOUSA to Base Sect Engrs, 10 Feb 43, sub: BOLERO Construction Program, 600.1, EUCOM Engr files; For the earlier BOLERO Key Plans, see ch. I.

The July version of the plan specified 970,000 accommodations for incoming ground troops; the revised plan of October considered 1,060,000. Closed or covered storage and workshop space expanded from 15 million square feet in the third Key Plan to 18 million in the fourth plan and then to over 18 million in the amended fourth plan. Open storage, set at 26 million square feet in the third plan, rose to 34 million in the fourth but declined to 29,736,000 in the amended version. Petroleum products requirements rose from 130,000 tons in July to 234,000 tons in October; ammunition from 244,000 tons to 432,000 tons and then to 452,000 tons in the amended fourth plan, all requiring special handling and storage.[19]

To meet deadlines under the new programs, the engineers had to limit construction to the bare necessities. Safety factors were at the minimum for the importance of the structure, while durability, cost, and appearance became minor considerations.[20] The new construction largely ignored camouflage. Camps frequently went up in parade ground style, in open spaces and straight lines, adjacent to prominent landmarks. Bulldozer tracks and construction materials, supplies, and equipment left in open fields attracted German bombers.[21]

The English winter created its own set of construction problems. There were only eight hours of light each day, and using searchlights at night risked drawing German aircraft. Many men were stricken with colds, respiratory diseases, and other ailments in the damp weather. Every site had to be well drained, or the engineers and their equipment soon bogged down in mud.[22]

Determining when a construction project was finished became perplexing. Two interpretations were possible—when the contract was fulfilled or when the using service declared the job complete. The first criterion was complicated by extras that might or might not affect the usefulness of the particular facility. Some items such as work ramps, added after an original contract, upset completion schedules yet did not materially delay when a facility could be used. At the insistence of the chief engineer, progress reports reflected physical completion, including extra work authorized during construction, rather than availability of facilities.[23]

By the end of May 1944 the construction program was 97.5 percent complete except for hospitals and continuous maintenance (especially at airfields). Depots were 99.6 percent complete; accommodations, 98 percent; and hospitals, 93.9 percent. The estimated value of installations provided by American forces in the United Kingdom as of 31 May was $991,441,000. New British construction cost an estimated $668,000,000. Of this total

---

[19] The Adm and Log Hist of the ETO, vol. III, "Troop and Supply Buildup in the UK Prior to D-Day," pp. 57–73.

[20] OCE ETOUSA Monthly Rpt 5, 14 Sep 43, p. 10.

[21] Ltr, WBS Engr to CO, 368th GS Rgt, 11 Jan 44, sub: Camouflage Instructions, and Ltr, OCE, SOS ETOUSA, to SOS, WBS, EBS, and NIBS, 30 Nov 43, sub: Camouflage of . . . Installations, 384.6, EUCOM Engr files.

[22] Ltr, OCE, EBS, to SOS ETOUSA, 5 Feb 44, sub: Project Study, OCE; Ltr, SOS ETOUSA to CG, ASF, 14 Jan 45, sub: Rpt on Overseas Construction, AG 600.1, ASF files.

[23] Ltr, OCE, SBS, to Chf Engr, 13 Aug 43, and Ltr, P. D. Berrigan to Engr, SBS, 20 Aug 43, sub: Construction Progress Rpts, both in 600 Rpts, EUCOM Engr files.

PETROLEUM, OIL, AND LUBRICANTS DEPOT, LANCASHIRE

$502,000,000 ($262,000,000 acquired, $240,000,000 constructed) involved air forces installations; $166,800,000 involved hospitals ($151,200,000 for new construction and $15,600,000 for acquired). Some $41,174,000 went to depots, all but $4,374,000 to new construction. The entire construction program encompassed 150,000 buildings and 50,000 tents.[24]

*Depots*

In November and December 1942 and January 1943 the chief engineer had cut back the depot program in ETOUSA and deferred work on some depots and shops. In February 1943, after the Casablanca Conference, General Moore called upon the base section engineers to produce firm building plans. The fourth Key Plan called for the completion of the depot program by 31 March 1944, and its 18 million square feet of covered storage space was 20 percent more than in the second Key Plan.[25] By the time the fourth plan was announced in July

---

[24] OCE ETOUSA Monthly Rpt 14, May 44; OCE ETOUSA Hist Rpt 7, Field and Service Force Construction, p. 115; Berrigan interv, 8 May 44.

[25] OCE ETOUSA Hist Rpt 7, Field and Service Force Construction, pp. 128, 135, 190; Ltr, OCE ETOUSA to Base Section Engrs, 13 Jan 43, sub: Modifying Plan for BOLERO Construction Program, 600.1, EUCOM Engr files.

1943, 13,398,000 square feet were ready. Open storage, which was to total 34 million square feet, then amounted to 27 million. In addition, space was to be provided for 432,000 long tons of ammunition and 215,000 long tons of POL.

Until well into 1943, the various services requiring depot space changed their requests from day to day. The British might move out of a selected depot site only to have the asking service turn down the site after all. In some such instances British civilian concerns had been put out of business in order to make facilities available.[26] But much of the work and storage space the British provided was hard to adapt to modern American methods. Many of the depots were too low and doors too narrow; many multistoried buildings had either very small elevators or none at all. Some of the depots were far inland and had only tenuous access to the ports from which the OVERLORD operation was to be mounted. To make requisitions coming from other technical services more orderly and consistent, Colonel Lord required them to designate liaison officers to the engineers managing the depot construction and acquisition program, but requirements continued to change and some difficulties with site selection persisted.[27]

As one answer to the time, labor, and construction materials problems, the chief engineer planned to use open fields for storage space whenever practicable. In most cases roads and rail lines had to be brought to the site and the ground conditioned to provide rapid drainage. The damp English climate was hard on the poorly packed supplies coming from the United States. These factors and difficulties in using British facilities made it necessary to raise estimates for covered storage.

The depot program was not finished by the end of 1943. However, by 1 May 1944, only 29,673 square feet of covered storage in Southern Base Section (SBS) and 1,200,000 square feet of open storage in Western Base Section (WBS) were lacking. At the end of that month all but 7 percent of the work had been completed.[28]

Within the depots the American forces used several types of buildings. One of the first they tried was the Iris, a 35-foot-wide Nissen hut. The Nissen, a British development, was an igloo-like half cylinder made of steel. More successful was the Romney hut, similar to the Nissen but with a heavier frame. With special bolting the Romney proved to be an exceptionally tight structure. The Romney huts often had set-in windows, twelve on each side. The end walls were of brick, concrete, or, preferably, sheeting, which permitted the use of sliding doors as well as a small access door. The foundation was continuous plain concrete footing, with an eight-inch brick foundation extending a minimum of four inches aboveground. The floor was five inches of concrete on four inches of gravel fill. The concrete apron that joined the building to a railroad siding was customarily six inches thick.

The largest warehouses were of Marston shedding which could provide rectangular buildings as large as 45-by-

---

[26] OCE ETOUSA Hist Rpt 7, Field and Service Force Construction, apps. 8 and 9.

[27] Memo, Col Lord for Liaison Officers of Quartermaster Ordnance et al., 10 Feb 43, 600.1, EUCOM Engr files.

[28] OCE ETOUSA Hist Rpt 7, Field and Service Force Construction, p. 128.

250 feet. These consisted of structural steel frames, corrugated iron roofs, corrugated asbestos siding, and six-inch concrete floors. Large sliding doors were at each end. The higher ceiling in the Marstons made it possible to install two ten-ton overhead cranes. A railroad spur ran into one end of the buildings. Sometimes made of wood from packing boxes and composite board panels, the Marston structures were ordinarily 60 feet long with an 18 1/2-foot span. The wooden buildings were cheap and easy to knock down and transport but were so light that they had to be repaired frequently. To save steel and wood, structures of curved asbestos and corrugated cement sheets with end walls of brick were also built. Some attempts were made to use precast concrete.[29]

About twenty-nine depots (each with an average of one hundred buildings) constituted the U.S. Army depot program in the United Kingdom. The construction of new covered storage and the expansion of existing facilities accounted for about one-fourth of the total space, while about one-half of the open storage and hardstandings was derived from new facilities and expansion. The estimated value of acquired depots was $4,374,000; that of new depots $36,800,000. Of covered storage and shop space the British turned over 67 percent and constructed 20 percent; American engineers built 13 percent. Of open storage and hardstandings the British turned over 51 percent and built 13 percent while U.S. Army engineers provided 36 percent. For storing ammunition the British turned over facilities to handle 33 percent of the job and constructed 27 percent; American engineers constructed 40 percent. Providing depot space for POL was largely an engineer job, with the British contributing only 5 percent (3 percent in space turned over and 2 percent in new construction).[30]

*Accommodations*

The first Key Plan did not provide for camp construction, for the British were to make available the necessary 845,200 winterized accommodations. The second Key Plan did not break down the number of hut and tent camps that would have to be erected but mentioned a total of 845,000. In January 1943 ETOUSA announced that all small camp expansions that were 50 percent or more complete could be finished; work on all others was to stop, at least temporarily.[31] At the end of January some 65,000 spaces of the 137,000 to be provided by camp expansions and new hutted camps were ready for use. More than 543,000 spaces already were available, for a total of slightly more than 600,000. The following month ETOUSA directed that accommodations be completed by 15 October 1943, and any needed thereafter by 1 December 1943.[32]

In January 1943 the British and Americans designated G–3, ETOUSA, to supervise the preparation of a monthly priority list showing the units

---

[29] Waldo G. Bowman, "Engineers Overseas," *Engineering News-Record*, 26–27.

[30] Adm 119, Engr Construction, ETOUSA Hist Sect.
[31] EUCOM Engr file 600.1.
[32] Unless otherwise cited this section on camp construction is based on OCE ETOUSA Hist Rpt 8, Quartering; Staff Conf Notes 1943, Adm 454 and 455, ETOUSA Hist Sect.

to arrive in the ETO within the next month or within a longer period if such data were available. Called long-term forecast, the lists were derived from information the War Department provided and from a convoy program the British quartermaster general prepared. At the same time the Allies agreed that each British military command would provide holding areas for American units whose final locations had not been determined and for units that arrived unexpectedly. The Air Forces did not have to determine destinations for units in these long-term forecasts but coordinated its needs with the Air Ministry, not with the American base sections or the War Office.

Early in February 1943 the Construction and Quartering Division of the theater engineer's office drew up plans for quartering U.S. troops expected in the United Kingdom by the end of the year. These forces would be located with a view to their future operational roles and available facilities and training areas. They would be quartered in tents between 15 March and 15 October.

The quartering program did not make great strides in early 1943. Though the engineers were using overall estimates of 1,118,000 arrivals listed in the second Key Plan, they were still working against the total of 427,000 men established in the third Key Plan of November 1942 as a basis for calculating accommodations. Even this figure caused no sense of urgency; troops other than Air Forces were not arriving in any great numbers. Of the 5,244 men for whom quarters were found in April 1943, 4,873 were air personnel. Southern Base Section had at that time 380,000 covered accommodations. Army engineers constructed space for 60,000 and expanded existing struc-

tures to take 60,000 more. In July 1943 they widened the program to provide 82,000 spaces: 52,000 for air forces personnel, 27,000 for SOS troops, and 2,435 for ground forces increments. As of March 1943, no troops were housed under canvas.

The first of a series of joint monthly forecasts concerning the arrival of American troops in the United Kingdom appeared on 14 July 1943. From these engineers received word on units alerted in the United States for shipment to Europe but not always on sizes of convoys or timing of movements. News of a unit's scheduled arrival sometimes reached England while the unit was at sea. As late as September General Moore could not get accurate information on unit destinations. In mid-October, when the amended fourth Key Plan had raised estimates for accommodations to 1,060,000, Moore finally could announce that he had a construction program for the phased arrival of the growing swell of ground force units.

By April 1944 the camp construction program had provided 1,296,890 accommodations in huts, tents, or billets. Of this figure, the British had turned over 40 percent and constructed for American use another 30 percent, leaving the remainder for American military construction crews. At the end of May 1944 the camps were 99.5 percent finished. A heavy concentration of tent cities, all in Southern Base Section, included 123,664 permanent tent accommodations and 49,302 temporary.[33]

Essential to providing quarters was determining living standards, which dictated space requirements. At first,

---

[33] OCE ETOUSA Hist Rpt 7, Field and Service Force Construction, pp. 115, 159, 193.

the U.S. Army accepted for its ground and air forces the respective British standards. This practice made for two scales, with the USAAF's the higher.[34] The accommodations provided officers under both standards were about the same, but the British provided thirty square feet per enlisted man and seventy-five per sergeant while the Americans provided thirty-five square feet per enlisted man regardless of grade. Taking over facilities from the British and making them meet U.S. Army standards usually involved renovations and minor alterations. In July 1943 Lt. Gen. Jacob L. Devers, ETOUSA commander, concluded that the scale of accommodations for U.S. forces could be reduced to the British scale or its equivalent. The chief engineer and chief surgeon agreed that the best scheme was sixteen men per hut, or thirty-five square feet per noncom or enlisted man, and seventy-two square feet per officer. This "austerity scale" lay between the British and American standards.

The Construction and Quartering Division, OCE, ETOUSA, had a number of problems in carrying out its assignment. Frequently, units were unwilling to accept facilities the British offered, preferring newly constructed accommodations. Occasionally the services failed to turn in complete plans for quartering requirements, tending instead to submit their needs bit by bit. In addition, each time the staff of the using service changed, revised requirements arose, for each new section chief had his own ideas on the subject.[35]

American officers added to the confusion by not following prescribed channels in requesting facilities.

Two varieties of billets were common outside the camps: furnished lodgings, which included the use of toilet facilities, water, and lighting; and furnished lodgings in which the U.S. Army provided beds and the British water and lights. Although a British law required civilian householders to provide shelter for troops at a fixed rate, private billeting was on an entirely voluntary basis until the end of 1943. With the fourth Key Plan billeting became systematized, and some forced billeting occurred.

*Hospitals*

In early 1942 the American forces used British and Canadian hospital services and operated a few British hospitals themselves. Members of the British Directorate of Fortifications and Works, the Ministry of Works and Planning, the U.S. Medical Department, and the Engineer Service drew up plans for new construction as well as for alterations to existing buildings. To speed matters the engineers, the Medical Department, and the British agreed on certain standard designs for new hospitals and for converting existing facilities, subject to changes on advice of the chief surgeon. He frequently made adjustments because of location, terrain, and special needs.[36]

Hospital floors gave the engineers trouble. Because concrete floors created considerable dust, they were covered with pitch mastic, but the black cover-

[34] Moore interv.

[35] Interv, Col C. J. Barker, Chf, Ground Projects, C&Q Div, 12 May 44, Adm 122, ETOUSA Hist Sect.

[36] EUCOM Engr file 600 H Gen, 1 Jul–31 Dec 43; OCE ETOUSA Hist Rpt 7, Field and Service Force Construction, p. 192.

ing showed dust and always looked dirty. A covering of oil and wax solved the problem in the wards but not in the psychiatric and operating wings, where static electricity could cause anesthetic gases to explode. Finally, a cement finish treated with sodium silicate was substituted for pitch mastic in operating rooms.[37]

All through 1943 and early 1944, hospital construction lagged considerably. Because arable land was at a premium, the British Ministry of Agriculture refused to approve many suggested sites, and locations became limited mostly to parks and estates of the "landed gentry." Inadequate transportation to haul materials to the sites also slowed work. Since labor and materials came through different agencies, one or the other often was not available when needed. Labor shortages held up all construction, especially for the hospital program.[38] The lag in hospital construction was not too serious, for the full capacity of hospitals would not be needed until casualties started coming back from the Continent. On 31 May 1944, just one week before the invasion, the hospital program was 94 percent complete.

### The Manpower Shortage

Personnel became General Moore's most abiding concern in 1943. As the year began, only 21,601 U.S. Army engineers were in the United Kingdom, with just 9,727 allotted to the Services of Supply. Many SOS engineer troops

were still in the labor pool that manned depots supporting the North African invasion. General Moore explored all avenues to solve manpower problems. Some aid came from tactical units, including USAAF organizations, and, on the hospital program, from Medical Department personnel and even convalescent patients. Considerable reliance also had to be placed on British civilian labor.[39]

### British Labor

Civilian labor was an important aspect of Reverse Lend-Lease. In December 1942 British and U.S. Army officials established procedures for employing British civilians. Pooling their limited civilian labor force, the British allocated civilians according to priorities the War Cabinet set, while contracts and contractual changes were made to fit existing priorities. For ground projects the order of priority was depots, camps, and hospitals.[40]

In April 1943 approximately half of the 120,000 British civilians assigned to the BOLERO program were working on American engineer projects—30,000 on air force and 28,000 on ground force projects. Complaining that the shortage of British labor was delaying completion of BOLERO, engineers at SOS, ETOUSA, constantly demanded more civilian help. The British government did what it could, but the supply was limited; indeed, the British had to cut the civilian work force in the spring and summer of 1943 to meet domestic demands for agriculture and industry.

---

[37] Rpt of Inspection Trip of CG, SOS, and Party to Dep Chf Engr, ETOUSA, 18 Nov 43; Adm 119, Engr Construction, ETOUSA Hist Sect.

[38] Interv, Col C. J. Barker, Chf, Ground Projects, C&Q Div, 12 May 44, Adm 122.

[39] OCE ETOUSA Monthly Rpt, Sep 43 dated 15 Oct 43, p. 16; Moore, *Final Report*, p. 247.

[40] OCE ETOUSA Hist Rpt 6, Air Force Construction, p. 21; Moore, *Final Report*, p. 247.

By 1 September 1943, more American engineers than British civilians were working on U.S. Army projects, and the differential grew larger as more American engineer troops arrived in the United Kingdom.[41]

The British civilian labor force was the product of a nation already drained by three years of war. Consisting of older men and boys below draft age, the work crews were neither well trained nor effective without close supervision. They worked an average of seven hours a day, less than troop labor. British habit dictated a 28-day work month, with alternate Sundays off; frequent holidays cut into the work schedules. British workers also had many absences due to colds and influenza.

British insistence on semipermanent rather than temporary structures slowed the construction program. The Ministry of Works continued to justify more sturdy buildings since they were to be used after the war. There was an eight-month difference in the time needed to complete contracted airfield construction jobs. U.S. Army engineers took 13 1/2 months to construct a heavy bomber base while British civilian contractors needed two years to finish the same type of project with their limited work force and lighter equipment.[42] On the other hand, not all American engi-

neer units coming into England lived up to expectations.

### Field Force Units on Construction Jobs

Engineer combat battalions were available for construction work from late July until 11 December 1943, when they were to be released for invasion training. By the end of July the number of field force engineers on construction tasks had risen to 11,233—more than twice the number available in June.[43]

Although SOS, ETOUSA, which for months had been calling for the highest shipping priority for its units, had succeeded in obtaining a very high priority for engineer construction units in November 1943, the buildup of SOS engineer units was slow, complicated by uncertainty over the ultimate size of the invasion forces and changes in the troop basis. The shipment of service units began to improve in September 1943, but not enough to meet the deadline for the release of field force engineers. In October engineer combat battalions were extended on construction jobs until 31 January 1944. Combat group headquarters as well as light equipment, maintenance, and dump truck companies were also pressed into service. At the end of the year the deadline date was extended again; some units were assigned to construction indefinitely. In the spring of 1944 several engineer camouflage battalions were added to the construction force.[44]

---

[41] Ltr, OCE to G–4, 27 Apr 43, 381, BOLERO, USFET Key Plan H 1942–43; Ltr, Moore to G–4, 24 Apr 43, sub: Labor Requirements for U.S. Construction Program, 231.4, Labor, 30 Oct 42–31 Oct 44, EUCOM Engr files.

[42] Interv, Col C. J. Barker, Chf, Ground Projects, C&Q Div, 12 May 44, Adm 122; OCE ETOUSA Hist Rpt 6, Air Force Construction, p. 21; Ltr, OCE, EBS, to SOS ETOUSA, 5 Feb 44, sub: Project Study, 601 P&Q Gen, Apr–Aug 43, EUCOM Engr files; OCE ETOUSA Hist Rpt 7, Field and Service Force Construction, p. 87; Hist 359th Engr GS Rgt.

[43] Ltr, OCE ETOUSA to the Engrs, SBS, EBS, WBS, etc., 25 Jul 43, sub: Proposed Allocation of Ground Construction Units, 600 Gen; EUCOM Engr files; OCE ETOUSA Hist Rpt 7, Field and Service Force Construction, p. 85.

[44] Staff Conf Notes, 11 Oct 43, Adm 454, ETOUSA Hist Sect; AGF Bd Rpt 162, NATOUSA.

In December 1943 five of eight non-divisional engineer combat battalions, one combat regiment, and one light equipment company—all from the field forces—were still attached to SOS for construction. Two months later nine combat battalions, a maintenance company, and a light equipment company were still assigned to construction tasks. In late March the numbers dropped sharply. Only a few field force engineers remained on construction jobs, and most ground force engineer units turned to training for the invasion.[45]

U.S. Army engineers on construction jobs numbered 40,436 on 1 September 1943; 49,000 at the end of October (28,000 on ground projects, 21,000 on air force projects); 55,027 at the end of the following month; and 56,000 at the close of the year. Peak strength came in March 1944 with 61,000 engineers working on construction projects (35,500 men on ground and 25,500 on air force jobs). At the end of May, a week before the invasion, 13,794 engineers were still engaged in construction.[46]

The effectiveness of field force, SOS, and aviation engineers on construction jobs decreased—and motor maintenance increased—because units were split to work on widely scattered jobs. The 1323d Engineer General Service Regiment at one time was scattered over an area 200 miles long and 80 miles wide. Elements of the 346th Engineer General Service Regiment were separated for nineteen months, assembling as a complete unit only in April 1944. The 342d Engineer General Service Regiment had no unit larger than a battalion in the same area between 12 July 1942 and 31 December 1943.[47]

The quality of engineer units working at construction jobs ranged from very good to marginally effective. The absence of planning by officers and noncoms caused inefficiency. Some engineer units on construction jobs lacked specialists in steel, brick, and electrical work, and men had to be trained in these skills. Many officers lacked either administrative ability or technical knowledge.[48]

The shortage of officers with construction and engineering experience persisted throughout the war in almost every type of unit. In the summer of 1943 a civilian consultant from the United States found a greater need for training among officers than enlisted men. "Civilian experience of the officers," he remarked, "in many cases does not exist."[49] General Moore felt that, considering the large number of people who had engineering education, "a very poor job was done" in getting the proper personnel into the engineers.[50]

### Engineers at the Depots

In January 1943 ETOUSA had only one engineer depot company split among three depots to process engineer supplies for units in the United Kingdom and for TORCH organiza-

[45] OCE ETOUSA Monthly Rpt 11, Feb 44, dated 15 Mar 44.
[46] Ibid.; 12, Mar 44; and 14, May 44.

[47] OCE ETOUSA Hist Rpt 7, Field and Service Force Construction, pp. 86–87; Hist 1323d Engr GS Rgt, Mar 44; Hist 342d Engr GS Rgt.
[48] Operation of GS Rgts, Dec 43, Incl to Ltr, Engr School to Chf Engr, 28 Dec 43, OCE; OCE ETOUSA Hist Rpt 1, Organization, Administration, and Personnel, p. 46.
[49] Rpt, Paul M. King, Engr Training Mission in England, 26 May–24 Aug 43, OCE 413.8 (ETO).
[50] Moore interv.

tions. Three companies of an engineer aviation battalion, the 347th Engineer General Service Regiment, and several separate engineer battalions provided temporary help at the depots.[51] As the number and size of depots grew, decentralization became necessary. In February 1943 operational control of the depots passed from the Supply Division, OCE, ETOUSA, to the base sections.

Depot operations improved markedly as the base sections assumed more control over supply. By August 1943 the base sections were exercising internal management of all previously exempted depot activities and were free of the limitations of Class II and IV supply levels imposed on their counterparts in the United States. The new authority made the engineer representatives in the United Kingdom base sections responsible to their base section commanders rather than to General Moore, though he still retained limited technical supervision.[52]

The engineers stocked their supplies in three types of depots. (*Map 13*) Reserve depots stocked an assortment of items, in large enough quantities for overseas use, that were issued to units in the United Kingdom only when the British could not provide them. Key depots stored and issued selected items for specific purposes. Distribution depots stored and issued all types of supplies and equipment. By 1944 twelve engineer depots, both solely engineer and engineer subdepots at general depots, had been set up—one in Northern Ireland Base Section, three in Eastern Base Section, and four each in Southern Base Section and Western Base Section. By 31 March 1944, these twelve had provided a total of 17,143,914 square feet of storage space, of which 1,161,452 was covered storage space, 15,909,694 square feet was open, and 72,768 square feet was shop space.[53]

The number and type of units performing engineer supply operations varied from depot to depot. The largest engineer section was at Newbury in Southern Base Section. With little covered storage, the section handled mainly heavy and bulky stores. The engineer section at Ashchurch handled a variety of heavy and bulky supplies, small parts, tools, and spare parts. Another depot held Class IV supply, most of it reserved for Continental operations, in open storage. This practice involved considerable risk, especially in winter, since iron and steel items with machined or unpainted surfaces left in the open rusted.[54]

The troops at engineer depots fell into two categories, engineer depot operating units—companies and group headquarters—and quartermaster labor, referred to as "touch labor." In July 1943, with only two depot companies and two base depot companies on hand,

[51] Memo, Col R. B. Lord for G–1, 22 Jan 43, 600–A–Gen (1 Jan–28 Feb 43), EUCOM Engr files; Draft, Talk on C&Q Div based on second and third Key BOLERO Plans, 325.51, Policies & Plans, EUCOM Engr files.

[52] Status Rpts, 30 Nov 42–3 Jul 43, 319.1, EUCOM Engr files; OCE ETOUSA Hist Rpt 3, Supply.

[53] OCE ETOUSA Monthly Rpt 5, Aug 43, and 10, Jan 44; MS, T/4 Russell M. Viets, Construction in the United Kingdom, Oct 44, p. 29.

[54] Corresp between Quartermaster Gen and Chf Engr, ETOUSA, 8 Aug 43, 320.3, Jun 42–Jan 44, EUCOM Engr files; Ltr, Lt Col J. H. Pengilly, Chf, Engr Service, NYPOE, to Overseas Supply Officer, NYPOE, 23 Apr 44, sub: Rpt of Liaison Mission to ETO, 519.1 (ETO), OCE (hereafter cited as Pengilly Rpt); Progress Rpt XCIX, 12 Jun 44, Statistics Sect, Sec Gen Staff, HQ, ETOUSA; Cir 18, 7 Nov 43, sub: Rust Prevention at Engr Depots, Adm 124, ETOUSA Hist Sect.

MAP 13

the shortage of depot personnel was critical. By mid-September the U.S. engineers were running seven depots (soon to be eight) with five depot and base depot companies. Three of these units had been in the theater less than eighty days and were of limited value— a depot company needed ninety days of experience in the United Kingdom before it could be expected to carry its full share of work. Neither officers nor enlisted men had had much practical experience before going overseas because civilians ran U.S. depots. For many of the engineers, training in the United States consisted of only six weeks in the field or on maneuvers, during which time the depot units had only one or two transactions to handle. Approximately 30 percent of the engineer supplies handled in the United Kingdom were of British manufacture, and their nomenclature could be learned only in the United Kingdom.[55]

Since only a small portion of engineer supplies could be manhandled, a large number of crane operators and riggers was needed. Men with such skills were not often available in the small quartermaster labor force or in the engineer depot companies. The 445th Engineer Base Depot Company, as an example, arrived in August 1943 and immediately began operating the engineer section of a major depot at Sudbury. The men often spent eigh-teen to twenty hours at a stretch trying to learn their tasks. The unit was constantly short of labor and equipment, especially of material-handling equipment, which had to be overworked and ultimately broke down completely.[56]

The engineers employed various expedients to overcome the personnel shortage. The few well-trained depot companies (such as the 397th) were split, usually three ways, and dispersed so that all engineer depots would have at least some trained personnel. Depots used men from dump truck, heavy equipment, and general service organizations, a last-ditch expedient since identification of various items of engineer equipment and supplies was a difficult job requiring alertness and training.

The number of engineers at depots increased slowly to 5,400 at the end of January 1944, 6,200 by the end of February, 6,500 the next month, and 7,500 by the end of April. Then nondivisional engineer field units had to be called in to help.[57] The shortage of depot personnel, especially crane operators, riggers, and trained clerical help, hindered engineer depot work all through 1943 and well into 1944. Trained crane operators were as scarce as cranes, and the fumbling efforts of untrained operators added to spare part and repair problems.[58]

*Equipment Maintenance*

Engineers in the United Kingdom

[55] OCE ETOUSA Monthly Rpt 7, Oct 43; and 8, Nov 43; Ltr, Ofc CW to Dep Engr, 17 Sep 43, sub: Depot Personnel, 322, Depots, EUCOM Engr files; Rpt, 1st Lt Eugene N. Nelson, sub: Spare Parts for Engr Equip in ETO, 475, Engr Equipment, Dec 42–Dec 43, EUCOM Engr files (hereafter cited as Nelson Rpt); Rpt, Lt Col John H. Hassinger for the Chf, Tractor and Crane Sect, OCE WD, to Gen Moore, Chf Engr, ETOUSA, sub: A Rpt of Trip to ETO, 10 Oct–10 Nov 43, 319.1, Rpts (Gen), EUCOM Engr files.

[56] Hist 445th Engr Base Depot Co.
[57] Nelson Rpt; OCE ETOUSA Hist Rpt 3, Supply; OCE ETOUSA Monthly Rpts 10–14, Jan–Jun 44.
[58] IRS, Capt Dunbar to SD, 30 Dec 43, sub: Rpt on G–4 Inspection, 29 Dec 43, 681, Depots General, EUCOM Engr files; OCE ETOUSA Monthly Rpt 4, Jul 43; 7, Oct 43; and 8, Nov 43; Mins Depot Mtg, 25 Oct 43, 319.1, Materiel Rpts, EUCOM Engr files.

sorely needed more third echelon maintenance companies equipped with mobile shop trailers to make field repairs and replace major unit assemblies at construction sites, depots, or wherever the engineers needed more extensive equipment maintenance than they could accomplish with their own second echelon tools and parts. In his first monthly report to the United States in April 1943 General Moore emphasized this shortage. In May 10 percent of all engineer equipment was deadlined for third echelon maintenance repairs with an additional 5 percent deadlined for fourth echelon repairs. Fourth and fifth echelon maintenance repair was the responsibility of heavy shop companies which provided base shop facilities and, when necessary, manufactured equipment either at mobile heavy duty shops or at large, centrally located fixed shops. Mobile shops provided emergency and general-purpose repair and welding service.[59]

The absence of heavy shop companies at some base sections placed an additional burden on third echelon companies, and their efforts to undertake major repairs for which they were not equipped often resulted in delay or unsatisfactory work. To improve matters General Moore assigned special maintenance officers to each base section to coordinate the work of the maintenance and heavy shop companies and the spare parts depots. But the shortage of maintenance companies persisted, and at the end of November 1943 there were only seven such units

in the European Theater of Operations. At that time the Supply Division, OCE, WD, felt that maintenance in the United Kingdom was not more than 75 percent adequate.[60]

When preventive maintenance such as lubrication and cleaning by equipment operators was inadequate, the maintenance companies' work load increased. Often the equipment operator received neither proper tools nor supervision, nor were sufficient periodic inspections made. Careless handling of equipment by inexperienced operators added to the problem. Frequently, equipment was turned into the engineer maintenance companies for third and higher echelon repair in a "partially dismantled condition," short many parts.[61]

*Spare Parts*

Obtaining first echelon spare parts such as spark plugs, fan belts, bolts, nuts, cotter pins, and lock washers and second echelon carburetors, fuel oil and water pumps, distributors, gaskets, and various clutch, brake, and chassis parts was a constant problem, partly because of poor procurement procedures—too few short-lived parts and too many long-lived ones. The engineers' problem was aggravated by the large number of nonstandard pieces of equip-

[59] OCE ETOUSA Monthly Rpt, Apr 43; MS, Echelon System of Engr Maintenance; Plan for SOS ETOUSA, vol. II, Supply, Installations, Transportation, Maintenance, 1 Jan 44, Adm 375, ETOUSA Hist Sect.

[60] Ltr, Moore to Chf of Adm, 30 Nov 43, app. 15 to OCE ETOUSA Hist Rpt 1, Organization, Administration, and Personnel; Ltr, OCE ETOUSA to SBS, WBS, and EBS Engrs, 15 May 43, sub: Maintenance of Engr Equipment, 475, Engr Equipment, Dec 42–Dec 43, EUCOM Engr files; Coll, Keith, and Rosenthal, *The Corps of Engineers: Troops and Equipment,* p. 571.

[61] Ltr, Chf Engr, SOS ETOUSA, to CG, CBS et al., 2 Feb 44, sub: Maintenance of Engr Equipment, Engr Maint Co, 1942–43, EUCOM Engr files; Staff Conf Notes, 12 Apr 43, Adm 455, ETOUSA Hist Sect.

ment—British-made or U.S. items made to British specifications—for which parts were often unavailable.[62]

The first engineer spare parts depot began operating at Ashchurch in the spring of 1943. In June the first of the specialized spare parts companies to arrive in the theater, the 752d Engineer Parts Supply Company, took over the depot. Several similar companies arrived from the United States during the summer and fall, enabling the theater engineer to set up spare parts subdepots at Conington, Sudbury, and Histon and to establish an effective daily courier system between the subdepots and the general depot at Ashchurch.[63]

The spare parts companies did excellent work, constructing most of their own bins and, despite the handicap imposed by a lack of training and proper equipment, reducing substantially the large backlog. In conjunction with the engineer heavy shop companies, the parts supply units salvaged or reclaimed many parts that might otherwise have been lost. In early 1944, as the days grew longer, the companies worked two and even three shifts. Despite these efforts the shortage of spare parts, particularly such vital items as cranes, continued to be a serious concern to engineer planners as preparations accelerated for the invasion of Europe.[64]

The Continent assumed an ever-larger share of the attention of the Allied and theater planning staffs in England in the latter part of 1943. Across the Channel lay a host of engineering problems associated with the projected invasion of German-occupied territory and the maintenance of armies there for the final phases of the war.

---

[62] MS, Echelon System of Engr Maintenance; Ltr, Moore to CG, NYPOE, 24 Apr 44, sub: Expeditious Shipment of Spare Parts for Engr Equipment, ETO 400, OCE; Hist 482d Engr Maint Co.

[63] Hists, 491st Engr Equip Co and 752d, 751st, 756th Engr Parts Supply Cos; Memo for Capt Austen, 16 Nov 43, file J.A.T. S-Miscel.

[64] Hist 756th Engr Parts Supply Co; Wkly Rpts, Supply Div, OCE ETOUSA, 12 May 43 and 24 Aug 43; Pengilly Rpt.

# CHAPTER XIII

# Looking Ahead to the Continent

Detailed engineer planning for a Continental invasion continued in 1943 with the addition of a forecasting technique imposed upon theater planners by ASF headquarters in Washington. To involve theater staffs around the world in procurement planning for major operations Army Service Forces had devised a system of so-called operational or keyed projects. Theater planners were to compile lists of Class IV and Class II items (in excess of regular TOE and TBA allotments) and to key the requested items to specific and foreseeable tasks such as the reconstruction of an individual port.

On 4 June 1943, the War Department directed ETOUSA to begin studying what equipment would be needed for an invasion of the Continent. These studies were known in England as Projects for Continental Operations, or PROCO. Their objective was to allow ASF ample time to procure from American industry major items of machinery and specialized equipment and have them on hand in the New York Port of Embarkation for shipping as theater users requested them. The forecasting system required detailed information on numbers of items needed, intended use, tonnage estimates, and operational justification. Not intended as requisitions in themselves, the project requirement statements went directly to the War Department for action. The PROCO system produced some successes but in many ways ran afoul of realities and practices in the theater.[1]

## Engineer PROCO Projects

Engineer PROCO studies began with some confusion. When the technical services involved in PROCO planning began their work, formal Allied agreement to the OVERLORD concept was still three months away. Upon receiving word of the War Department's requirements, General Moore protested that he needed basic data on eight separate aspects of the forthcoming operation in order to proceed with operational or keyed planning. Specifically, his engineer staff needed to know the maximum size of the assault force, the approximate size of forces expected to be employed on the Continent on D plus 90, maximum forces to be employed in active operations, the number of lines of communications, the number of ports to be built or rebuilt, the number of airfields required in each calendar quarter through the end of 1944, the state

[1] Ruppenthal, *Logistical Support of the Armies, Volume I*, pp. 260–68; Coakley and Leighton, *Global Logistics and Strategy, 1943–45*, pp. 129–30, 166–68; *Annual Report of the Army Service Forces for the Fiscal Year 1944* (Washington, 1944), pp. 11–12.

of repair of facilities in France, and an evaluation of areas to be occupied on the Continent as of the end of 1944. While American engineer members of COSSAC gathered some of the data, General Lee provided the basis of engineer supply planning for the majority of PROCO projects on 24 June.[2]

In a letter of instruction to his subordinate SOS elements Lee listed the objectives for what he described as a ROUNDUP-type operation. American forces ashore in France by D plus 30 would number 480,000; 985,000 were expected by D plus 90. To support this strength, two one hundred-mile-long lines of communications were to be operating by D plus 90, and by D plus 240, or the end of 1944, the lines were expected to be two hundred miles long. On D plus 90 two additional lines of communications were to open to receive supplies shipped directly from the United States to the European mainland. The overall plan called for four major and eight minor ports to be fully operational by D plus 240. On these assumptions the engineers worked all summer, with each division of the theater engineer's office responsible for its assigned portion of the thirty categories of engineer functions represented in the PROCO statements. They divided delivery schedules according to the planning timetable General Lee had described, earmarking materiel for shipment in the first ninety days after the invasion or for D plus 91 to D plus 240. With D-day later set tentatively for 1 May 1944, the engineers wanted to have 75 percent of the equipment and supply for the first ninety-day phase on hand in the United Kingdom by 1 Janu-

ary 1944. Materiel for the second period was to be in the theater ninety days before it was needed. By late September, they had sent to Washington twenty-eight studies with tonnage estimates totaling 1,136,713 long tons.[3]

Differing views on the purpose of PROCO and on the proper content of PROCO studies also fueled lively correspondence between the theater and the War Department through the summer. In late June 1943 General Lee asserted that requisitions for the material listed in the theater PROCO studies would be appended to those studies. Though this was not the original scheme for the keyed projects, the War Department acquiesced in the procedure on 25 July. In September the War Department complained about the content of some of the submitted studies, citing especially quartermaster PROCO submissions for medals and decorations, breadsacks, and standard two-inch plugs for gasoline cans. The engineers' submissions conformed to the letter and the spirit of the ASF program, but engineer planners often neglected to identify those items that could be procured in England through reverse lend-lease. Though these items were to be included in the studies, the PROCO procedures called for flagging them with asterisks in the material lists. Once the British had supplied the items, the theater would notify the War Department to cancel them in the PROCO studies.[4]

In Washington, engineer PROCO projects followed a tortuous path. From

---

[2] OCE ETOUSA Hist Rpt 3, Supply, p. 29.

[3] Ltr, CG, SOS, 24 Jun 43, sub: Projects for a Continental Operation, as cited in Ibid., p. 31.
[4] OCE ETOUSA Hist Rpt 3, Supply, app. 21, PROCO Procedures; ETO Gen Bd Rpt 128, Logistical Build-up in the British Isles, p. 20.

the War Department adjutant general they went to the director of plans and operations, ASF, who was responsible for control until the projects were approved. The director of plans, ASF, sent the studies to the Logistics Group, Operations Division, War Department General Staff, which determined whether the projects were necessary. The director of plans, ASF, next forwarded the studies to OCE, WD. OCE decided whether each project was necessary and adequate, from both technical and tactical standpoints. OCE then edited the bill of materials based on availability and corrected all nomenclature and catalogue numbers. The director of plans, ASF, then sent the projects to the director of the Requirements Division, ASF, who determined whether the requirements fitted into worldwide plans for each item or whether the Army Supply Program would have to be changed. The projects again went through the director of plans, ASF, to the Logistics Branch, OPD, for approval and finally to G–4, War Department General Staff, for concurrence. The approved projects then became the basis upon which the engineers in the United Kingdom requisitioned Class IV items from the United States.[5]

Confusion existed for a time at the New York Port of Embarkation because ETOUSA included in PROCO tonnage figures all of the Class IV operational needs estimated before PROCO began. NYPOE, on the other hand, had accounted only for tonnages submitted as PROCO projects. Wide discrepancies in the records of shipments ASF,

NYPOE, and ETOUSA maintained added to the confusion. For example, ASF figures included items released for shipment to the United Kingdom. ASF considered them delivered, but these figures were meaningless to the engineers in the United Kingdom because some time elapsed between the date items were released in the United States and their arrival in theater. As late as March 1944 the OCE Supply Division estimated that 120 days were required for delivery of supplies from the United States after requisitions had been placed, assuming the supplies were actually available in U.S. Army depots. Therefore the division felt it was necessary to provide the United States with estimates of Class IV supplies required for the next fifteen months.[6]

By the end of April 1944, shipments of engineer supplies from the United States, particularly materials requested under PROCO, were seriously behind schedule—a backlog of 320,278 long tons existed. The situation improved only somewhat during May, with 246,521 long tons still overdue. Meanwhile, engineer projects had been placed in a common pool with all others. Supplies and equipment were issued based on established priorities to organizations having approved projects whether or not the specific supplies had arrived. Along with other services and commands the engineers were given a credit and a priority on the central pool based on their project submissions or their project supply allocation. This system

---

[5] Rpt, Maj John A. Thetford to CE, 20 Dec 43, sub: Rpt on Trip to United States, 333, Inspections, EUCOM Engr files; Ltr, Francis H. Oxx to Engr, Third Army, 28 Mar 44, sub: Engr Supply, file 381 PROCO.

[6] Ltr, Lt Col J. H. Pengilly, Chf, Engr Service, NYPOE, to Overseas Supply Ofc, NYPOE, 23 Apr 44, sub: Rpt of Liaison Mission to ETO, file 519.1 (ETO), OCE; Ltr, Oxx to Engr, First Army et al., 12 Mar 44, sub: Time Factor in Engr Supply, 381 Supply, EUCOM Engr files.

BULLDOZERS AT THE ENGINEER DEPOT AT THATCHAM BEFORE THE INVASION

enabled using units to check equipment issued in the United Kingdom for completeness and workability before they departed for the Continent.[7]

*Planning for Construction on the Continent*

When PROCO projects began the ETOUSA engineers were already well aware of the problems involved in estimating materials and troop labor that would be needed for heavy construction on the Continent. Such activities normally fell into seven broad categories: ports, railways, roads, pipelines, inland waterways, utility systems, and general construction such as hospitals, shops, depots, and troop housing.[8]

Lacking firm plans for specific operations, engineer planners at COSSAC drew up a comprehensive list of all the engineer Class IV supplies that would be needed for a large overseas operation. The planners considered every activity that would need engineer Class IV items and set up units of supply corresponding to each activity. The set of staff tables they developed could be used to compute supplies for regular engineer operations and for the PROCO studies. The tables also proved useful to plan-

---

[7] OCE ETOUSA Monthly Rpt 13, Apr 44, and 14, May 44; Pengilly Rpt.

[8] Lt. Col. S. A. Potter, "Engineer Construction Planning for Operation OVERLORD," *Military Review*, XXX (December 1950), 3. Unless otherwise noted, this section on construction is based on this source.

ENGINEER CRANE STACKS LUMBER AT THATCHAM, APRIL 1944

ners of other services who wanted quick estimates of engineer work. The estimates varied greatly in kind—from requirements for a mile of railroad track to complete details for building and equipping a 1,000-bed hospital.

Even after more definite information on OVERLORD became available in July 1943, engineer planners were hampered—more than the other services—because the demand for the utmost secrecy deprived them of information on specific terrain. At the insistence of the chief engineer security was relaxed, and the details of OVERLORD were revealed in the late summer of 1943. Theoretically, planners could then study the specific ports, rail lines, and highways involved, but the need for long-

range procurement action and for time to activate and train engineer units made only changing estimates possible.

Ports that could serve the Allied invaders came under close scrutiny in a series of PROCO studies. Prompted by the belief, later confirmed at Naples, that the Germans would destroy any suitable harbors to thwart Allied efforts to seize them, the engineers tried to forecast the reconstruction job expected in each port covered in PROCO planning. They continued the work of a port committee established early in 1943 under a British officer to chart the capacities of ports from the Netherlands to the Spanish border. Eventually planners included for consideration only eighteen ports in the Brittany and

Normandy peninsulas. On 12 August 1943, the ASF received an exhaustive PROCO study covering Class II and Class IV construction material and special equipment deemed necessary to reopen Cherbourg, an important objective in the final OVERLORD plan.[9]

When planning for specific ports proved virtually impossible without knowledge of port conditions and facilities, the engineers turned to more generalized methods of construction planning. They first correlated the planning demands to a fixed length of quay. Then, taking the OVERLORD phased tonnage requirements for the invasion, they tied the phased capacity to the figures they had derived for the fixed pier length. One ton of cargo per linear foot of pier per day became the standard engineer planning yardstick for port reconstruction. These data were combined with others to produce master lists and general requirements requisitions for the Continent.

French harbors had silted up during the enforced inactivity under German occupation, and it would take extensive dredging to clear them for the sort of supply operations envisioned in the invasion plan. The Germans were also likely to sink blockships and other obstacles in the harbor channels and alongside berthing areas. The engineers took into account the amounts of explosives or specialized equipment needed to remove the blockages. They also requested specially designed shallow-draft port repair ships, to remain under Army control, that would provide floating machine shops to maintain construction equipment in use or to make re-

placement parts for damaged lock gates and power plants.

The engineers attempted to develop standard repair methods and bills of materials for the lines of communications and supply leading out of the port areas. They tabulated the labor and material needed to repair a mile of railroad track or of oil or gasoline pipeline and to provide 1,000 square feet of general-purpose shop or depot space. There were some forty-one contingency plans for dealing with unpredictable Channel tides and weather, which could make repairs necessary under other than normal water levels.

Realizing that ports would not be available for at least ninety days after the invasion, COSSAC allocated authority for beach operations among the Navy, the Army's Transportation Corps, and the Corps of Engineers, which carried the heaviest load. At this stage the main problem in planning beach supply operations was selection. Beaches had to be wide and sheltered from high winds and heavy surf. Terrain and beach outlets were of prime importance in the early days of the invasion, and the engineers tried to locate supply beaches near ports that would serve as supply arteries once beach operations closed down. Plans also included optimum sites for beach air strip construction, for inland movement and communication, for protection by Allied air power, and for limited enemy opposition.

## Lines of Communications

Influenced by the widespread rail and road demolition they had met in Italy, ETOUSA engineer planners at first estimated that destruction of traf-

[9] *Annual Report of the ASF, 1944*, p. 12.

fic nets on the Continent would reach 75 percent. Since such an estimate called for staggering tonnages of railroad equipment, it was cut to 25 percent for main line tracks and to 35 to 50 percent for yards and sidings. U.S. Army engineer and British planners provided the following revised estimates of expected damage: railroads in the port area, 75 percent; railroads up to thirty miles inland, 50 percent; those beyond that distance, 25 percent. Railway bridges in ports and up to thirty miles away would be damaged 100 percent; those beyond, 50 percent. In fact, the engineers overestimated the amount of new rail and wooden ties that would be needed in northern France. Though the destruction in major centers was severe, the trackage in open countryside escaped extensive damage, often more affected by Allied air attacks than enemy action, and cancellation orders stopped much of the continued movement of rails to Europe later in the year.

Thousands of aerial photographs helped engineer planners estimate the amount of railroad bridging that would be required on the Continent. The engineers studied track maintenance, railroad grades, the number and length of sidetracks needed, the carrying capacity of various lines, bridge capacities, water and commercial facilities, and available materials.[10]

The engineers' chief concern in road

planning lay with maintenance rather than new construction. They generally confined estimates to maintenance of one mile of various types of roads for one month. By studying typical roadnets in other theaters, planners could obtain an average road density per square mile of territory occupied, and by computing the total area under occupation from the phase lines marked out for OVERLORD, they could calculate total road mileage during successive periods. The engineers doubted that the Germans would systematically destroy road surfaces. In the Mediterranean the Germans had limited deliberate destruction to roads in difficult terrain where repairs would constitute a major problem, and little such terrain existed in northern France.[11]

Tactical and highway bridging occupied much of the planners' attention. A tactical bridge policy developed in ETOUSA in April 1943 remained the basis for planning, though it changed with tactical planning. The engineers computed their requirements for highway bridges by using aerial photographs, expecting to use standard 35-ton capacity steel treadway to bridge the thirty- to sixty-foot gaps anticipated on the Continent. In the theater, the engineers used Bailey bridging for everything from tactical floating spans to lines of communications bridges for army and division use. But ongoing theater planning coincided with a search for new models of tactical bridging in the United States necessitated by new, wider replacements for the M-4 Sherman tank and by Army Ground Forces demands on

[10] Engr Planning Data for Operations in Northwest Europe, Railway Reconstruction, Mar 44, OCE; Rpt of Communications Sect. "Railroad and POL Projects—Channel Base," *Estimates for Railroad Reconstruction*, C&Q Div, OCE, Mar 44: Daily Jnl, ETOUSA G–4 Opns, 3 Apr 44, Adm 475, ETOUSA Hist Sect; OCE ETOUSA Hist Rpt 12, Railroad Reconstruction and Bridging (United Kingdom), 1946, Liaison Sect, Intel Div, ETOUSA Adm file 547.

[11] OCE ETOUSA Hist Rpt 14, Road Maintenance and Highway Bridging (United Kingdom), 1946, p. 17, Liaison Sect, Intel Div, ETOUSA Adm file 547.

the Engineer Board for a complete revision in floating bridge equipage. Testing of new prototypes and of new Bailey bridging applications continued into early 1944. Thus, as late as January 1944, many engineers in the United States were still considering the Bailey strictly as a line of communications bridge while engineers in the ETO, remembering the Italian campaign, favored its use in any tactical situation to which it could be adapted.[12]

Initial estimates on the consumption of gasoline in the ETO were indefinite; only late in the planning stage were engineer planners able to make fairly accurate calculations. Except for bulk storage installations, which were usually in the vicinity of ports, existing POL facilities generally lay underground and were not well suited to military needs. Pipelines had to be laid along existing roads to minimize the problems of transporting and distributing construction materials. The terrain along selected routes was an important factor, for it had a direct bearing on the number and spacing of pumping stations. The tactical plan and the location of large supply depots generally would determine both the location and capacity of bulk storage installations. Thus, with every major change in the tactical plan (or with any other material change in plans) a new pipeline distribution system had to be designed.

Ship-to-shore pipelines also posed a difficult problem. Assurance was needed that pipeline distribution of liquid fuels could be undertaken before a port was available. A method had to be devised to permit tankers anchored one-half to one mile off the beaches to discharge their contents directly into a shore-based distribution system. After experimenting, American and British forces adopted a simple British solution. A small vessel with powerful winches such as a submarine-net tender could pull successive lengths of rigid pipe seaward from a beach. A flexible buoyed hose attached to the seaward end of the pipe would permit direct discharge of tankers into the system.[13]

The engineers could not estimate in advance requirements for the reconstruction of the inland waterways of northeast France and Belgium, which the Germans were using extensively, for there was no standardization in their dimensions or in their equipment. Many were the product of centuries of development of internal communications. Except for lock structures, reconstruction would be largely an earthmoving job requiring the type of equipment organic to engineer construction units. The repair of locks and lockgates, the engineers believed, could be accomplished by improvisation using local materials.[14]

The major problem the engineers faced with utilities systems on the Continent was determining civilian needs—military requirements were to be met by self-contained utilities provided for all new camps and hospitals. Planners gathered population statistics and per capita figures on water consumption and electric power. They established

---

[12] Coll, Keith, and Rosenthal, *The Corps of Engineers: Troops and Equipment*, pp. 490–97; Dossier of Tactical Bridging, 18 Jan 44, Supply G–4 Directives; Rpt on Observations Made During Visit to the ETO, 16 Jun–17 Sep 43.

[13] "Railroad and POL Projects—Channel Base," in booklet, *Estimates for Railroad Reconstruction*, C&Q Div, OCE, Mar 44.

[14] OCE ETOUSA Monthly Rpt 12, Mar 44, and 13, Apr 44.

minimum standards for civilian use and studied existing utilities systems and anticipated damage.

In the end the engineers regarded the PROCO system as problematic, either as a means for estimating necessary theater stocks accurately or as a supply system. Though PROCO studies were an obvious method of drawing up broad estimates and planning requirements for construction on the Continent, there was no possibility of pinpointing engineer requirements under PROCO or any other system. While their objectives were still in enemy hands the engineers could only guess at the type and amount of materials they would need. They also had a problem in estimating the requirements of major field commands that had not yet arrived in England. First Army headquarters came only in October 1943, and the engineer planners had to calculate the field army's necessities anew. Nor did PROCO reduce the time it took for material to move through the supply pipeline to the theater. In the opinion of the theater engineer, the projects "proved to be a poor device for obtaining supply action."[15]

## Responsibility for Civilian Labor

By early 1944 theater planners had tentative outlines for tapping the wealth of civilian labor on the Continent. SHAEF established a Combined Military Procurement Control as an executive agent for General Eisenhower in matters of local supply procurement and civilian hiring for both British and American forces. Overall American theater-level planning for employing civilians abroad was the job of the theater general purchasing agent, who delegated his authority among various levels of the projected Communications Zone command that General Lee would head on the Continent. On 19 April 1944, Lee formally gave responsibility for managing the procurement of civilian labor in the field to the engineers since they would be the first to need workers for beach dumps, ports, storage areas, and roadnets. Maj. Gen. Cecil R. Moore's staff had no plans for this eventuality, few qualified officers or enlisted men to run a personnel clearinghouse, and no understanding of the problems of pay levels, housing, and welfare of civilian workers. Despite repeated effort to get engineer officers who could handle the job, the civilian labor responsibility fell to the theater engineer's administrative division. Actually, the engineer-spawned Civilian Labor Procurement Service had assigned members of other technical services who could screen prospective employees for specialized work. The general purchasing agent, privy to the highest counsels of the Allied command on the subject of civilian workers in the Combined Military Procurement Control, coordinated activities from the theater command level. SHAEF retained the final say in matters of pay and set wage tables keyed to prewar salary levels in given geographic areas.[16]

---

[15] Ltr, Col J. S. Seybold, Chf, Supply Div, OCE ETOUSA, to Overseas Supply Div, NYPOE, 5 Jul 44, sub: Req PROCO Projects, file 381 PROCO; Memo, J.R.H. [Col John R. Hardin] for Chf, Opns, OCE, 20 Sep 43, sub: Questions of Policy Affecting Engr Planning, Key BOLERO Plans folder; Moore, *Findl Report*, p. 49.

[16] Henry G. Elliott, The Administrative and Logistical History of the European Theater of Operations, vol. X, "Local Procurement of Labor and Supplies, United Kingdom and Continental," pp. 74–80, in CMH.

The engineers set broad classifications to delineate conditions of employment and skill levels for workers. Two general categories aligned prospective employees by their willingness to work in mobile or static detachments. Static laborers usually worked in a single location, lived nearby, and were responsible for their own quarters and food. Mobile workers, who received their sustenance and housing from the Allied command employing them, usually performed as part of a transient labor company organized on military lines. Both static and mobile workers served under contract and were considered unskilled until they proved otherwise. Their wages would then change accordingly.

The foundation for regional and local management of labor offices also came into being before the invasion. Each base section was to have a procurement office, and in each French region there would be a representative in a centrally located major city. The first organization was scheduled for the immediate invasion area, and plans called for offices in Ste. Mere-Eglise, Longueville, Carentan, Bricquebec, Cherbourg, Isigny, and UTAH Beach.[17]

### Refinements in Overlord's Operation

Tactical command for the invasion consisted of a three-phased allotment of responsibilities to the higher headquarters arriving in Normandy to control the incoming combat and support units. In the assault phase, the U.S. First Army and the British Second Army operated separately to consolidate the beaches under the remote command of the British 21 Army Group. Phase II would begin when 21 Army Group came ashore and assumed tactical control of both field armies. Until the second stage was concluded First Army and all the incoming service troops attached to it were under 21 Army Group control. The last invasion phase foresaw the introduction of another American field army, the Third, and of the American 1st Army Group headquarters. General Sir Bernard L. Montgomery, commanding the 21 Army Group, was responsible for SHAEF tactical planning, but he relied heavily on American contributions to the NEPTUNE plan which referred to actual operations under the OVERLORD invasion plan. Though the 1st Army Group headquarters was involved in this process, Montgomery also delegated the planning for the actual assaults to the First Army staff.[18]

Detailed planning for supply and for rehabilitation of Continental ports and rail and roadnets fell to two new organizational echelons established to smooth the transfer of supply and administrative functions across the English Channel. Fifth Army in Italy had briefly but successfully experimented with an advance supply section at Naples to eliminate the long and uncontrollable supply lines that had become necessary in North Africa. In December 1943 COSSAC established a similar section to relieve First Army of supply responsibilities immediately behind its area of operations in the first days of the invasion. Formally in existence after 7 February 1944, Headquarters, Advance Section, or ADSEC, was under the com-

---

[17] Ibid., p. 87.

[18] First U.S. Army, *Report of Operations, 20 October 1943–1 August 1944*, p. 25; 12th Army Group, *Report of Operations*, vol. XII, p. 51.

mand of Col. Ewart G. Plank, an engineer officer who had commanded Eastern Base Section. The ADSEC engineer was Col. Emerson C. Itschner. The section was to remain attached to First Army in the American chain of command and be responsible for supply installations behind it until the arrival on the Continent of a second, higher command, Forward Echelon, Communications Zone. Forward Echelon, also in existence under ETOUSA since 7 February, was formally established by SHAEF directive two days later. Designed as an extension of General Lee's SOS organization and equipped to run the communications zone in France until the entire SOS moved across the Channel, the command, known as FECOMZ, would become ADSEC's parent as soon as General Bradley drew a rear boundary for First Army. Planning proceeded under Col. Frank M. Albrecht, General Moore's former plans officer, as chief of staff. On 14 March 1944, Brig. Gen. Harry B. Vaughan, former commander of Western Base Section, took over FECOMZ.[19]

First Army was to estimate the tonnage and supply needs from D-day to D plus 15 (Phase I) for all U.S. forces, including air and naval forces in the assault, and have ETOUSA fill the requisitions. In Phase II, D plus 16 to D plus 40, 1st U.S. Army Group was to compile the required tonnage figures but would have ETOUSA fill the requirements through ADSEC. FECOMZ was to arrange for the buildup to COMZ and to introduce base sections at the same time that 1st Army Group was strengthening the combat zone with additional armies. Between D plus 41 and D plus 90 (Phase III), 1st Army Group would continue to assemble the overall tonnage requirements, but they would be implemented through FECOMZ, which would assume active control when a second base section arrived on the Continent and ADSEC moved forward with the armies. Not until D plus 90 was COMZ to reach the Continent and take over from FECOMZ.

Whereas First Army issued its plans in February 1944, the FECOMZ plan was not complete until 30 April 1944. The detail involved in some aspects of the planning was enormous, and the ADSEC engineer plan literally outweighed that of all the other technical services combined. Two thick volumes of data on the Normandy ports included an analysis of each port's facilities, a schedule of reconstruction, and a catalogue of equipment and materials required.

Planning for post-OVERLORD operations (D plus 90 to D plus 120) forced Moore, along with other technical service chiefs, to furnish an estimate—by month and class—of the tonnages he would need for the entire period from D plus 90 to D plus 360. Planning for this period continued under the PROCO system according to ETOUSA SOS Series H directives. Two directives before D-day established progressive phase lines and troop counts to D plus 360 and required engineer statements on which material was to be stored in the United Kingdom and which would go directly to the Continent.

A British officer, Maj. Gen. H. B. W. Hughes, headed the SHAEF engineer division, but he had an American dep-

---

[19] Ruppenthal, *Logistical Support of the Armies, Volume I*, pp. 204–13; ETO Gen Bd Rpt 127, Organization and Functions of the Communications Zone, ch. 4, pp. 32–38.

uty, Brig. Gen. Beverly C. Dunn, and the four branches under Hughes were also headed by Americans. The division's chief task was to coordinate the work of the army group engineers and to provide terrain and engineer intelligence studies; recommendations on new techniques, equipment, and tactics; and engineer estimates of the situation. Perhaps the most important feature of this high-level assistance was anticipating what engineer supplies the army groups would need and helping to obtain them from Allied supply organizations.[20]

### Joint Stockpiling With the British

Because OVERLORD was an Allied undertaking, a system of combined supply or joint stockage was desirable to prevent overprocurement of interchangeable items; to ensure sufficient supply where procurement was difficult and it was unclear which force would employ the item; and to provide items that would, in fact, serve British and American forces simultaneously. Joint stockpile items included Bailey bridges and railroad and port construction equipment. Some parts of such items were manufactured in the United Kingdom, others in the United States. The British were responsible for procurement of some items, turning over to American forces their share; others the Americans procured and divided with the British.[21]

Planning for the joint stockpiling of railroad items began in the summer of 1942 when the Transportation, Plant, and Personnel (TPP) Section of SOS, ETOUSA, was formed with both U.S. and British members under a central planning staff. This group included a representative from the Corps of Engineers. At the time railway planning started no standard U.S. military railroad bridge had been developed, and it became necessary to adopt those the British had. Since the British were unable to produce enough bridges for both armies, the TPP Section arranged for production of the same types in the United States and ensured that they were interchangable with those manufactured in Britain. Later agreements provided that stockpiles would be divided equally between American and British forces and that any reallocation would be the responsibility of an Allied headquarters.[22]

During the summer of 1943 the British repeatedly tried to broaden the base for joint stock items, which had been limited to items for joint use or for provision of a joint service. U.S. engineers objected strenuously to these efforts and, after long discussion, won their point. The British had argued that most engineer requirements should be calculated jointly and the supplies handled in joint stockpile. Some British agencies even proposed that they handle procurement of all such items, whether they came from the United States or the United Kingdom. These proposals were hardly advantageous to the U.S.

---

[20] Rpts, Feb–Jun 44 in file Weekly Rpts, CE, SHAEF, Dec 43–Dec 45.

[21] History of the Office of the General Purchasing Agent, May 42–Oct 45, pp. 57–59, Adm 556, ETOUSA Hist Sect; Ltr, Oxx to the Engr, ETOUSA, 10 Dec 43, sub: Procedure for Supply and Allocation of Joint U.S.-British Requirements for Operation in

Western Europe, 381, Planning Northwest Europe 1944–45, EUCOM Engr files.

[22] OCE ETOUSA Hist Rpt 12, Railroad Reconstruction and Bridging.

Army, for if pooling American and British resources meant absorbing American personnel into British operations, American engineers would be deprived of much-needed experience in doing their job independently according to their own procedures.[23]

With the establishment of COSSAC, joint policies and procedures were defined. A COSSAC circular issued on 25 June 1943 required written provisions for joint stockpiles and COSSAC approval for talks between American and British counterparts. SOS, ETOUSA, further clarified the issues in August, September, and November 1943. Allied commands could jointly stockpile items only if definite economies would result during the period when forces on the Continent would be supplied principally from the United Kingdom. Later, American policy required that, except for agreements already made, joint stockpiling with the British would be discontinued; no further agreements were to be made after 21 November 1943. This decision came almost simultaneously with a PROCO pronouncement calling for firm plans for PROCO supplies for the first 240 days after the invasion. Since the PROCO items were in addition to the U.S. share of joint requirements, the Americans had to order them independently.[24]

## Training

Most engineer units arriving in the theater in 1943 and early 1944 needed considerable training. Camouflage units arriving in the United Kingdom were unfamiliar with the most important equipment they were to use on the Continent. General service regiments needed to learn about mines and booby traps and the uses of Bailey bridges. Engineer combat battalions lacked training in recording minefields and repairing roads. Drivers and mechanics of dump truck companies had trained with non-TOE vehicles. Port construction and repair units had trained in the United States with different types of equipment than those they received in the United Kingdom. The one notable exception was the topographic organizations, which arrived well trained for their work on the Continent.[25]

Training SOS engineers in the United Kingdom was the responsibility of Troops Division, OCE, ETOUSA, which had a London branch planning for future operations and a Cheltenham branch providing training aids to SOS troops and supervising SOS engineer schools. The base section supervised training. Theoretically one hour a day or one day a week was given over to training for future operations, but construction priorities often made it impossible to follow any training schedule. Troops might be working on day and night shifts, or bad weather would intervene and training would have to be canceled. In any case, the alloted one hour a day was of little use, for it often took that long to reach a training area.

---

[23] Ltr, CE, ETO, to CofEngrs, Washington, D.C., 2 Jul 43, sub: Engr Supply in ETO, 400, General Supplies, EUCOM Engr files.

[24] History of the Office of GPA, p. 57; OCE ETOUSA Hist Rpt 12, Railroad Reconstruction and Bridging, p. 8; Memo, OCE for Chf, Opns, 17 Sep 43, 400, Col Hardin—Supplies and Equipment Procurement of 1943–44, EUCOM Engr files.

[25] 1st Ind to Ltr, Brig Gen L. D. Wersham, 26 May 44, Construction Div files, OCE; Moore interv; AGF Bd Rpt 599, Training, 1 Feb 45. For training problems in the United States, see Coll, Keith, and Rosenthal, *The Corps of Engineers: Troops and Equipment*, pp. 241–59.

MODELS OF BELGIAN GATES, *patterned after German obstacles on Normandy beaches.*

Limiting the training time to an hour also meant that a subject had to treated completely in that time, for it often proved impossible to continue a subject during the next training period. When longer lapses occurred between sessions, men forgot subject matter and continuity was destroyed. *(Map 14)*[26]

In March 1944 when extensive training opportunities became possible, Troops Division, OCE, ETOUSA, suggested one to two months for many units. Full-time training was frequently more arduous than construction work. Often the day's schedule was extended from 10 hours to 12–15 hours so that the troops could practice techniques used in night operations. Considerable time also had to be devoted to basic subjects that had been forgotten or only infrequently put to use.[27]

Virtually every type of military subject was available. The American section of the British School of Military Engineering included courses in mines, booby traps, demolitions, Bailey

[26] Albrecht interv, Adm 122, ETOUSA Hist Sect; HQ, USFET Engr Sect, 353 Training Gen (Current) 1944; History of Western Base Section, Jul 43; Hist 833d Engr Avn Bn, 10 Jul 42–25 Sep 45, Maxwell AFB; Incl to Ltr, Engr School to CofEngrs, 28 Dec 43, sub: Opn of GS Rgts, OCE; OCE ETOUSA Hist Rpt 6, Air Force Construction.

[27] Hists, 341st, 346th, 355th, and 95th Engr GS Rgts.

WIRE ENTANGLEMENTS AND DRAGON'S TEETH *at the Assault Training Center, Woolacombe.*

bridging, camouflage, waterproofing, and airfield engineering and reconnaissance. A port construction and repair training center in Wales specialized in construction of V-type trestles, Baileys, wooden trestle bridges, Sommerfeld mats, and tubular scaffolding. On the Isle of Wight the engineers conducted marine pipeline training. A five- to seven-week course at the Transportation Training Center trained general service regiments for railroad work, especially railroad bridging.[28]

ETOUSA conducted courses in mess management, fire fighting, cooking, motor transport, enemy personnel and equipment identification, basic radio operation, gas warfare, and waterproofing. At the engineer section of the American School Center, run by G-3, ETOUSA, the primary objective was developing physical stamina and endurance necessary for combat while providing three months of basic technical and tactical training. Officers and enlisted men attended a two-week course in logistical planning at the British Air Ministry's Joint British and American School. Engineers could attend schools offering instruction in quartermaster transport, bomb reconnaissance, field

[28] USFET Engr files, 353 Training (General), 1943; Specialist Course Theater Engr Trng Ctr, Ofc of Theater Chf Engr, ETOUSA, Aug 46; OCE ETOUSA Monthly Rpt, Apr–May 44.

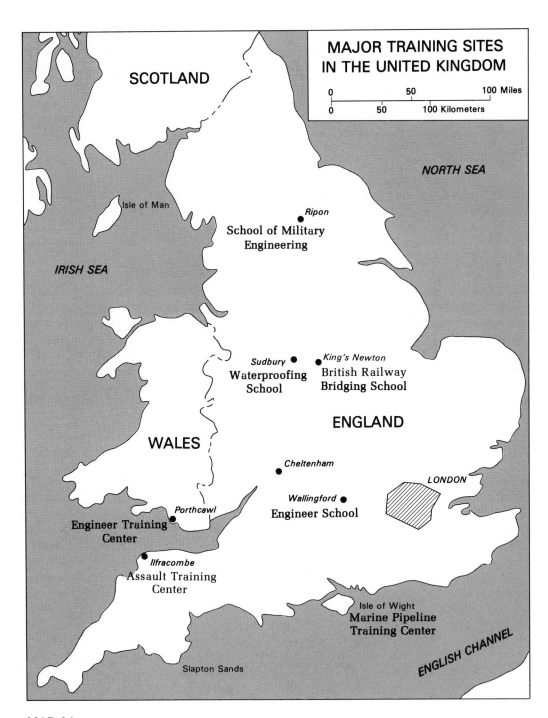

MAP 14

artillery (for antiaircraft fire), landing craft loading, bituminous paving and road construction, troop leadership, enemy document evaluation, and order of battle.[29]

Engineers took a leading part in the well-known Assault Training Center. Col. Paul W. Thompson, an engineer officer, commanded the school from 2 April 1943 until early March 1944. Thompson and his staff spent April and May 1943 studying the French coastline. They calculated that at no place along the coast of northwest France could the Germans use more than one platoon per 2,000–2,500 yards to protect beach fortifications. They deduced that Germans would have extremely strong field defenses with concrete pillboxes, emplacements, and shelters, and thinly spread defenders providing considerable automatic fire. The Assault Training Center prepared units to deal with such a defensive strategy. Set up on the northwest coast of Devonshire at Ilfracombe, the center was completed in March 1944, allowing over two months before the invasion for unit training and a series of full-scale exercises. Engineer units constructed and placed beach and underwater obstacles (modeled after those on the beaches of northern France) and gave lectures on a number of subjects connected with an assault landing.[30]

The British contributed in many ways to training, opening their schools to American engineers and offering ideas and equipment. British and American units exchanged parties, usually composed of one officer and ten enlisted men, for fifteen days. Each group learned the characteristics, methods, weapons, tools, nomenclature, problems, and tactics of the other. The practice also increased understanding and comradeship between Allies.[31]

First Army's training emphasized bridge building, road maintenance and construction, mine placement, and enemy mine detection and removal. First Army also recommended that all company grade engineer officers receive instruction in adjusting artillery fire by using forward observation methods. Engineer units used schools, lectures, and demonstrations to train their own men and sent enlisted men and officers to schools in higher British or American echelons.[32]

American corps and divisions trained units for special missions in the assault. Engineers practiced the rapid construction of plywood treadway bridges mounted on pneumatic floats for crossing flooded areas and absorbed whatever they could on terrain problems to be expected on the Continent.[33]

*Maps for the Invasion*

U.S. and British military forces could

---

[29] Hist Trng Div, OCE ETOUSA, 1 Apr 43–1 Apr 45; Ltr; Maj H. E. Webster to Chf, Troop Div, OCE, SOS ETOUSA, 7 Apr 43, sub: Rpt on Visit to American School Center, 319.1, EUCOM Engr files; Hist 51st Engr Bn.

[30] Specialist Course Theater Engr Trng Ctr, OCE ETOUSA, Aug 46; First U.S. Army, *Report of Operations, 20 Oct 43–1 Aug 44*, vol. I, p. 19; 1st. Lt. G. W. Favalion, 1st. Lt. Alex M. Marsh, and Maj. E. R. Kline, eds., *Potholes and Bullets* (Highland Park, Illinois: Singer Printing and Pub. Co, 1946), a pictorial account of the 5th Engineer Combat Battalion in World War II. Hists, 112th and 204th Engr C Bns.

[31] USFET Engr files, 353 Training (General) 1943; First U.S. Army, *Report of Operations, 20 Oct 43–1 Aug 44*, vol. I, p. 22.

[32] First U.S. Army, *Report of Operations, 20 Oct 43–1 Aug 44*, vol. I, p. 18, and vol. V, p. 209.

[33] Ibid.; HQ, ETOUSA, WD Observer Bd, 22 Apr 44, sub: Quarterly Rpt Engr Section, 451.3, OCE.

ENGINEER MAPMAKER USES A MULTIPLEX *to establish accurate contours on invasion maps.*

be proud of the maps they prepared jointly for operations on the Continent. In 1939 the British had had to start almost literally from scratch. Only for eastern France were World War I maps available on a scale as large as 1:25,000; few of them had been revised to show roads, bridges, or railroads built since that time or changes in fields and woods. For western France the only military maps were based on those Napoleon had used. They had been edited and enlarged to a scale of 1:50,000 but had not been made more accurate. Few maps had had any terrain corrections since 1900.

Shortly after the evacuation of Dunkirk in 1940 the British Army inaugurated the Benson project, named for an airfield in Oxfordshire. From this airfield Royal Air Force (RAF) planes took off to map the French coast from Cherbourg to Calais and an area extending inland approximately sixty miles; the British succeeded in producing 1:25,000 scale maps.[34] Early in 1942, in accordance with the terms of the Loper-Hotine Agreement, the British assumed general mapping responsibility for most of western Europe. Americans helped in taking aerial photographs for mapmaking and reproducing maps for use by U.S. forces.[35]

---

[34] OCE ETOUSA Hist Rpt 5, Intelligence and Topography, pp. 6–7.
[35] See ch. III.

General mapping (as distinguished from "intelligence" mapping of individual spots) began with aerial photographs showing roads, streams, railroads, bridges, buildings, fields, woods, and flood areas. Using the aerial photograph, mapmakers drew with instruments a topographic contour, or "topo map," divided into small military grid squares that enabled the user to locate areas exactly. When manpower or time did not permit making topo maps, the original photograph could be made to serve as a map by the application of grid lines, contours, place names, and indications of scale and direction. The poor quality of many photomaps prejudiced the users against them, but the chief engineer saw their value in alleviating the burden on mapmakers and aerial photographers and planned to use photomaps in the preinvasion period.[36]

Topo maps of 1:25,000 scale were produced from aerial photographs taken with a six-inch metrogen lens with high-speed multiplex equipment which registered both horizontal and vertical dimensions of terrain features. Production of these maps was the primary mission of the base topographic battalion, the most important element in the ETO topographic service. Each base topographic battalion contained a photomapping company that had a complete set of multiplex equipment including approximately one hundred projectors, enough to put fifty operators to work after the aerial triangulation and control extensions were finished. A photomapping company, working with good quality aerial photography, could map approximately one hundred square miles a day.[37]

Until the summer of 1943 the greatest hindrance to mapmaking in the European theater was the difficulty of obtaining good aerial photographs to work with—a responsibility of the Army Air Forces. After four special B–17E photographic aircraft sent to the ETO in the fall of 1942 were diverted to North Africa, the British gave an RAF reconnaissance squadron the job of filling U.S. photographic mapping needs. By May 1943 this squadron had photographed some 22,000 square miles of the first-priority area. But because the RAF used a type of camera not suited to American equipment, fewer than 10,000 square miles of large-scale topo maps had been produced. The U.S. Army Air Forces had not helped, mainly because the AAF's Director of Photography, Lt. Col. Minton W. Kaye, then in the ETO, felt that the hazards and costs of securing wide-angle vertical photography over heavily defended areas were too great. He advocated a system of aerial photography known as trimetrogen photography. Developed for small-scale aeronautical charts, the system used wide-angle cameras that tilted in divergent directions to produce one vertical and two high oblique photographs which made a composite picture of an area from horizon to horizon. The engineers objected to trimetrogen pictures because oblique photography multiplied the difficulties of making enlargements and produced

---

[36] Engrs file 121, General, Adm 212, ETOUSA Hist Sect.

[37] OCE ETOUSA Hist Rpt 5, Intelligence and Topography, p. 83; Speech (no signature), 27 Jan 45, sub: Aerial Photographic Mapping, H–4 061 General, EUCOM Engr files.

distortions that no known instrument could correct.[38]

In June 1943, General Moore, Col. Herbert Milwit, head of Moore's intelligence division, and Maj. Gen. Ira C. Eaker, commanding officer of the Eighth Air Force, discussed the problem. General Eaker said he would help the engineers get more accurate photos. Beginning on 22 June 1943, the 13th Photo Squadron, using K17 cameras in F−4 and F−5 aircraft—reconnaissance versions of the P−38 Lightning—took wide-angle photographs covering more than 10,000 square miles without any loss from enemy action. The success of this project promoted greater Air Force−engineer cooperation, and there was no serious shortage of aerial photography during the invasion and for several months thereafter.

U.S. support of the Benson project began early in 1944. Using aerial photography sent from England, the U.S. Geological Survey and the Tennessee Valley Authority, on assignment from OCE, prepared 200 sheets at the 1:25,000 scale covering 16,000 square miles of northern France. To enable the mapmakers to meet deadlines for the Normandy landings, the OCE Intelligence Division permitted the omission of much fine detail such as hedgerows but backed up each battle map with a photomap of the same area.[39]

In assuming responsibility for providing engineer intelligence as well as topographic service, General Moore was treading on new ground. No background of intelligence experience existed in the Corps of Engineers equivalent to that acquired in construction engineering on rivers and harbors duty. Few officers were competent to handle the expanded duties in engineer intelligence and topography, nor was any precedent available upon which to base an effective organization or plan. By agreement with a succession of theater G−2s, General Moore gave the Intelligence Division, OCE, ETOUSA, responsibility for all problems pertaining to the topographical service, including map policy, theater map library operation, and planning for map production, reproduction, supply, and distribution.

In planning map production the Intelligence Division had to consider what map series should be completed, which maps the forces involved would need, how much time was available, and which cartographic and reproduction facilities could be used in the field. Planners soon realized that the required maps could not be produced with the available facilities in the time remaining. They decided to put first priority on 1:25,000 maps and photomaps of France north of the Loire and west of the longitude of Paris, with all new maps of the same design; second priority on 1:50,000 maps of the coastal regions in the invasion area; third priority on 1:100,000 series covering the entire operational area; and fourth priority on a 1:200,000 road map. A more satisfactory 1:250,000 map suitable for both ground and air use was also required; the 1:1,000,000 series needed considerable revision; and many town plans—several thousand sheets—had to be produced.

The expectation that the British War

---

[38] Maps and Mapping, May 42−Apr 45, L−6 060, EUCOM Engr files. Coll, Keith, and Rosenthal, *The Corps of Engineers: Troops and Equipment*, pp. 446−54.

[39] Coll, Keith, and Rosenthal, *The Corps of Engineers: Troops and Equipment*, pp. 457−58; OCE ETOUSA Hist Rpt 5, Intelligence and Topography, pp. 28−30, 49.

Office's Directorate of Military Survey could provide most of the maps that U.S. forces in Europe would need soon had to be abandoned. Computations in 1943 indicated that the four U.S. armies planned for European operations would need 7 million maps a month, more than base and field topographic units and local civilian facilities could provide. To produce that many maps, 35 million impressions would have to be made, one for each of the five colors needed for the average map. As this was beyond British capability, in mid-December 1943 Col. Herbert B. Loper of OCE, WD, arranged for the United States to assume a large share of supplying American forces. For security reasons British and American facilities located in England would provide maps needed from D-day to D plus 90. After D plus 90 all maps for U.S. forces would be produced in the United States except those required for special, unanticipated, or highly classified projects. Army Map Service (AMS) received the first monthly requisition in April 1944 and was ready with the first shipment in July. Eventually, out of every ten maps used in the theater Army Map Service and private contractors in the United States printed four; the British, the overseas topographic units, and the French National Geographic Institute, six.[40]

November 1943 plans for map service in support of the tactical forces provided one topographic battalion for each army group and each army and one company for each corps and air force. Realizing the need to strengthen staff control of these units, General Moore recommended adding topo-

graphic sections to the engineer headquarters of army groups and armies. His proposal could not be put into effect because of the time it took to obtain theater approval; therefore, he provided each of the four armies planned for European operations with an engineer survey liaison detachment of five officers and ten enlisted men to handle the topographic service. This improvisation worked well and in his opinion "probably meant the difference between outstanding success . . . and a rather dismal failure." He later came to feel that a topographic officer should also be added to the corps engineer staff.[41]

The topographic battalions and companies were well organized and well equipped, except for map distribution, a problem that the War Department and ETOUSA had neglected. Experience showed that maps could not be handled in the same way as other Class IV items, for they were too closely related to tactical operations. Distribution had to respond immediately to changes in tactical plans, and a constant flow had to be maintained. Maps were so bulky that stocks to cover any contingency for a ten-day period would weigh at least sixty pounds—too much for an officer to carry on his person. Moreover, the transportation of stocks between depots and from depots to troops was to cause more trouble than any other aspect of map distribution on the Continent.[42]

Security of maps was all important in the OVERLORD planning stage. The maps were sealed in coded bundles from which individual maps could be

[40] Coll, Keith, and Rosenthal, *The Corps of Engineers: Troops and Equipment*, p. 458.

[41] Moore, *Final Report*, pp. 107–08.
[42] AGF Bd Rpt 552, Map Distribution, 7 Jan 45.

drawn without revealing much about the general plan for any given area. On 1 September 1943, the British Directorate of Military Survey and General Moore's Intelligence Division agreed to establish four special simnel depots, named for the code system applied to the map bundles. The depots, located at Aldershot, Oxford, Reading, and Towchester, had identical stocks, the code keys for the maps being kept by a minimum number of officers. In late 1943, only the Oxford simnel depot had American personnel, but as the American invasion forces outnumbered the British in May 1944 the U.S. Army took over a second facility at Lockerley.

The United States also had a depot at Witney, set up in March 1944 with bulk stocks for the Continent; one at Reading, opened in January 1944 with reserves for the Air Force; another at Cheltenham, organized in September 1942 to store maps for use in the United Kingdom; and a fourth at Swindon, established in January 1943 with bulk stocks of United Kingdom and Air Force maps. From Cheltenham and Oxford the maps went to the marshaling area mapping depots, then to camp commanders who undertook detailed distribution. Maps for troops in the marshaling areas were under guard at all times before they were issued to individual troop units and during movement from depots to camps had a guard detail of an officer and several armed enlisted men. When any coded rolls (packages of twenty and fifty maps) were opened in a depot, all persons handling the maps were locked into the storage buildings under strict security control.[43]

In mid-1943 as forces massed in the United Kingdom to prepare for the invasion of France, attention also turned to specific landing places for the assault force. The engineering problems associated with getting the troops across the mined and defended beaches were in themselves immense; organized and rapid supply movement across the same terrain was essential to the success of the operation. It was clear that engineers would be in plentiful evidence on the D-day beaches.

---

[43] OCE ETOUSA Hist Rpt 5, Intelligence and Topography, pp. 41, 49, 60, 65, and app. 26.

# CHAPTER XIV

# Preparing for D-day Landings

By early spring 1944 tactical planning for the most ambitious amphibious operation ever attempted was well under way. OVERLORD represented the fruits of two years of strategic thought, argument, experiment, and improvisation and included compromises reflecting American and British aims. The beaches at Normandy offered the best combination of advantages as a foothold from which the Allies could direct a blow at the Third Reich from the West.

After 1 February 1944, the general concept of an invasion of the Continent in 1944 went by the name OVERLORD. (The increasingly detailed American field army planning—proceeding under tight security at First U.S. Army headquarters—was code named NEPTUNE.) In its final form OVERLORD called for landing two field armies abreast in the Bay of the Seine west of the Orne River, a water barrier that was a suitable anchor for the left flank of the operation. While the British Second Army occupied the easternmost of the chosen landing areas on the left and took the key town of Caen, two corps of the American First Army under Lt. Gen. Omar N. Bradley were simultaneously to assault two beaches west of the town of Port-en-Bessin. Once ashore the American forces were to swing west and north to clear the Cotentin penin-

sula by D plus 15, gaining the prize of Cherbourg with its harbor for invasion supply.[1]

*The American Beaches*

Invasion planners studied carefully the size, location, gradients, and terrain features of the American OMAHA and UTAH beaches. Within easy reach of the tactical fighter airfields in England, they lay separated from each other by the mouths of the Vire and the Douve rivers. The current in the river delta area where the two streams emptied into the sea deposited silt to form reefs offshore, making landings in the immediate neighborhood infeasible. Protected from westerly Channel swells by the Cotentin peninsula, the waters off OMAHA and UTAH normally had waves up to three feet in the late spring. The six-fathom line ran close enough to shore to allow deep-draft attack transports to unload reasonably near the beaches and naval vessels to bring their guns closer to their targets. Both beaches had a very shallow gradient and tides that receded so rapidly

---

[1] Unless otherwise noted, detail for this chapter is derived from Harrison, *Cross-Channel Attack,* and from Samuel E. Morison, "History of United States Naval Operations in World War II," vol. XI, *The Invasion of France and Germany* (Boston: Little, Brown and Co., 1957).

that a boat beached for even a few moments at ebb stuck fast until the next incoming water. The tidal range of eighteen feet uncovered a 300-yard flat at low tide. An invasion attempt at low tide would thus force the infantry to walk 300 yards under enemy fire across the undulating tidal flat, crisscrossed with runnels and ponds two to four feet deep. (*Map 15*)

The assault objective of V Corps' 1st and 29th Infantry Divisions was the smaller OMAHA Beach, a gentle, 7,000-yard curve of sand. An eight-foot bank of coarse shingle marked the seaward edge of the western part of the beach. The shingle offered some meager cover to an infantryman but barred passage to wheeled vehicles. Back of the beach, and some two hundred yards from the shingle line at the center, a line of grass-covered bluffs rose dramatically 100 to 170 feet. At either end the bluffs ran down to merge with the rocky headlands that enclosed OMAHA and made the flanking coastline impractical for amphibious landings of any consequence. A bathing resort before the war, the area was not thickly populated, but four farming settlements were nestled 500 to 1,000 yards inland on the bluffs above the beaches. A single main road, part of a predominantly east-west network, roughly paralleled the coast from Vierville-sur-Mer at the western reaches of OMAHA through St. Laurent-sur-Mer, Colleville-sur-Mer, and finally Ste. Honorine-des-Pertes before passing into the British Second Army sector behind the beaches to the east. Access to the beaches from the farming communities was through four large and several smaller gullies or draws. Through one of these, dropping from Vierville to the water, a gravel second-

ary road ran to the beach and turned to the east. It continued beside a six- to twelve-foot timber and masonry seawall to Les Moulins, a small village directly on the sea in the draw in front of St. Laurent. From there back to St. Laurent and in the draw from Colleville to the water, roads were no more than cart tracks or sandy paths. A line of bathing cabanas and summer cottages had nestled beneath the bluffs west of Les Moulins in an area known as Hamel-au-Pretre, but the Germans had razed most of them as they erected their beach defenses and cleared fields of fire. There were few signs of habitation east of Les Moulins, and the foot paths at that end of the beach ran out altogether in the marsh grass sand.[2]

The NEPTUNE planners divided OMAHA Beach into eight contiguous landing zones. From its far western end to the draw before Vierville, Charlie Beach was the target of a provisional Ranger force. Next were the main assault areas, Dog and Easy beaches. Dog Green, 970 yards long, Dog White, 700 yards, and Dog Red, 480 yards, stretched from the Vierville draw to the one at Les Moulins. Easy Green began there, running 830 yards east. Easy Red, 1,850 yards, straddled the draw going up to Colleville, and Fox Red, 3,015 yards at the far left of the beach, had a smaller draw on its right-hand boundary. The five draws, vital beach exits, were simply named: the Vierville exit became D−1, the one at Les Moulins leading to St. Laurent, D−3; E−1 lay in the middle of Easy Red leading up between St. Laurent and Colleville; the Colleville draw off

---

[2] War Department, Historical Div, *Omaha Beachhead, 6 June–13 June 1944*, American Forces in Action Series (Washington, 1945) pp. 8–16.

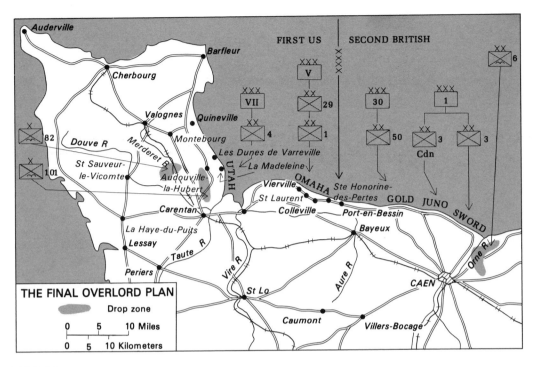

MAP 15

Fox Green became E—3, and the smaller one leading off Fox Red, F—1. .

After a 45-minute air and naval bombardment on D-day, the reinforced 116th Regimental Combat Team, assigned to the 29th Infantry Division (but attached to the 1st Division for the assault), was to land on Dog Green, Dog White, Dog Red, and Easy Green, preceded moments earlier by four companies of the 741st Tank Battalion serving as assault artillery. The 16th Regimental Combat Team, 1st Infantry Division, was to touch down on Easy Red and Fox Green, with a battalion landing team on each beach. The assault units were to push through the German defense along the beaches, especially in the draws leading inland, by the time the landing was three hours old. Reinforced with additional forces coming ashore, V Corps would then consolidate an area of hedgerow country bounded on the south by the line of the Aure River by the end of D-day.

German defenses in the area from Caen west, taking in the Cotentin and Brittany peninsulas, fell under the German *Seventh Army*. In the OMAHA area the counterinvasion force on the coast consisted of two divisions, the *716th*, a static or defense division having no equivalent in the American Army, and the *352d*, a conventional infantry division capable of counterattack and rapid movement. In general the Germans concentrated on emplacing a coastal shield, following Field Marshal Erwin Rommel's strategy of defeating an invasion at the water's edge. The demands of the war in the east denied the vaunted German Atlantic Wall the concrete, the mines, and the trained men Rommel wanted, but the beach defenses, though incomplete, were formidable enough for any assault force.[3]

Since the Germans considered a low-tide landing impossible because of the exposed area in front of their guns, they littered the tidal flat with obstacles to catch landing craft coming ashore at high tide. About 250 yards from the shingle line stood a row of complicated structures called Element C, nicknamed Belgian gates because they resembled the ornamental ironwork of a European chateau. Festooned with waterproofed mines, they covered either end of the beach but not its center. Behind them were irregular rows of single upright or slightly canted steel stakes, V-shaped channeled rails that could tear out the bottom of a landing craft; roughly every third one had a Teller mine fixed atop it. The Germans had emplaced and mined logs and built shallow, mined ramps with one upright wooden pole supported by two longer trailing legs. Closest to the high-water mark was a row of hedgehogs, constructed by bolting or welding together three or more channeled rails at their centers so as to project impaling spokes in three directions. The tidal flat contained no buried mines, since the sea water rapidly made them ineffective.[4]

On shore, twelve fixed gun emplacements of the German coastal defense net between the Vire River and Port-en-Bessin could fire directly on the beach. The defenders concentrated their pillboxes at the all-important beach exits and supplemented the artillery pieces with automatic-weapons and small-arms firing pits. They dug anti-tank ditches ten feet deep and thirty feet wide across the mouths of the draws. One pillbox, set in the embankment of the Vierville draw, D−1, could enfilade the beach eastward as far as Les Moulins. On the landward side of the shingle bank and along the seawall they erected concertina barbed wire and laced the sand with their standard Schu and Teller mines. From the trench system on the bluffs above they could also activate an assortment of explosive devices, using old French naval shells and stone fougasses (TNT charges that blew out rock fragments) against any attackers scaling the heights.

In January 1944 the COSSAC staff decided to strengthen the American attempt to seize Cherbourg by revising OVERLORD to bring another corps ashore closer to that port. Because of the river lines and the marshy terrain to the west of OMAHA, V Corps ran the risk of being stopped around the town of Carentan before wheeling into the Cotentin peninsula. The revised plan assigned the VII Corps, with the 4th Infantry Division in the assault, to the second American D-day beach.

A straight 9,000-yard stretch of rather characterless coastline, UTAH lay on a north-south axis west of the mouth of the Douve and to the east of the town of Ste. Mere-Eglise. A masonry seawall eight feet high ran the length of the beach, protecting the dunes behind it from storms. At intermittent points along this barrier sand had piled up to make ramps as high as the wall itself; only a wire fence atop the wall marked its presence. German defenders had

[3] Ibid., pp. 20−28.
[4] Operation Rpt NEPTUNE, OMAHA Beach, 26 February−26 June 1944, 30 Sep 44, pp. 62−66.

flooded the low-lying pastureland between the beach and Ste. Mere-Eglise to a depth of four feet. A series of east-west causeways carried small roads across the flood; each ended at a break in the seawall which normally gave access to the beach, but which the Germans had also blocked to contain an assault force from the sea.

The beach assault area lay between two hamlets, La Madeleine on the south and Les Dunes de Varreville on the north. The southerly Uncle Red Beach, 1,000 yards long, straddled a causeway road named Exit No. 3; it led directly to the village of Audouville-la-Hubert, due east of Ste. Mere-Eglise and three miles behind the beach. Tare Green Beach, occupying the 1,000 yards to the right of Uncle Red, had few distinguishing natural features. At UTAH, the 8th Infantry Regiment, 4th Infantry Division, was to go ashore two battalion landing teams abreast, closely followed by the 70th Tank Battalion as artillery support.[5]

NEPTUNE also called for a parachute and glider assault into the area behind UTAH. To cut the Cotentin peninsula at its base, COSSAC planners originally scheduled airdrops south and east of Ste. Mere-Eglise and farther west in the vicinity of St. Sauveur-le-Vicomte. But when the *91st Infantry Division* reinforced the peninsula in May, the First Army staff had to consider a less ambitious airborne undertaking. The 82d Airborne Division would be dropped astride the Merderet River, a tributary of the Douve running two miles west of Ste. Mere-Eglise, and the 101st Airborne Division in the area south of the

town early on D-day before the 4th Infantry Division landed at UTAH. Glider trains would bring in reinforcements and heavier weapons to consolidate a perimeter enclosing a section of the Carentan-Cherbourg highway and at least the inland portions of the causeways that would serve as beach exits.[6]

A lack of high ground made the German defenses at UTAH somewhat less imposing than at OMAHA. The defenders relied heavily on the inundated lowlands behind the beach to channel an attack and on a series of small infantry strongpoints to pin down a larger force trying to leave the beach over the causeways. Consistent with their strategic conception, the German works were well forward. Two German divisions, the *709th Infantry*, manned with eastern Europeans, mainly Georgians, and the *243d Infantry*, had constructed numerous resistance points along the high-water mark. On the tidal flat they had placed the obstacles encountered at OMAHA and another antitank device called a tetrahedron, a small pyramid of steel or concrete. Barbed-wire entanglements and minefields, covered by rifle, automatic, and mortar fire from the infantry trenches, began at the water's edge. Concrete pillboxes, some with tank turrets set into them, swept the beaches with arcs of fire. The villages at the edges of UTAH were converted into fortified areas commanding both the beach and sectors of the inundated land to the rear. Just right of center on Tare Green, the Germans dug a deep antitank ditch to hinder vehicles and tanks coming in from the sea. At UTAH the enemy also introduced the Goliath, a miniature, radio-controlled tank loaded with explosives

---

[5] Dept of the Army, Historical Div, *Utah Beach to Cherbourg, 6 June–27 June 1944*, American Forces in Action Series (Washington, 1947), pp. 4–7.

[6] Ibid., p. 9.

and designed to engage incoming landing craft and armor. The arrival in late May of the *91st Division,* with a battalion of tanks, gave considerable depth to the defense between Carentan and Valognes, but the defenders of the beaches themselves could hardly maneuver, since their own flooding confined them to positions in the narrow coastal strip where there was little room for regrouping and counterattack.

Despite the serious German aggregation of firepower along the coastline, NEPTUNE planners in the months before the invasion worried most about obstacles. In early 1944 as aerial photographs of the German-held coastal areas showed a proliferation of obstacles on the invasion beaches, the Allies grew more and more alarmed. A month before D-day, General Eisenhower listed the devices as among the "worst problems of these days."[7]

### Beach Obstacle Teams

In deriving plans and stratagems to overcome the obstacle problem the Allies drew on their experience, though the new situation exceeded in size and complexity anything they had previously encountered. In the ill-fated Dieppe raid of August 1942, British and Canadian forces had met concrete walls and blocks set with steel spikes designed to impale landing craft. The British had then established an Underwater Obstacle Training Center, but its elaborate training courses were chiefly geared for Mediterranean beach landings. The British experience prompted the chief of engineers to propose a similar Army center in the United States, but in the

spring of 1943 the Navy took over all amphibious training. The engineers then selected a site for a beach obstacle course close to the Navy's Amphibious Training Base at Fort Pierce, Florida.

The course began in July 1943, and throughout the fall a company of combat engineers conducted experiments in coordination with the Navy. The tests indicated that the obstacles that remained after a thorough bombing of the beaches could probably be blown to bits by such devices as the "Apex," a remote-controlled drone boat, and the "Reddy Fox," an explosive-laden pipe that could be towed into the area and sunk. The engineers could also destroy obstacles with rocket fire, preferably from rocket launchers mounted on a tank; at low tide heavy mechanized equipment such as the tankdozer could push most obstacles out of the way.[8]

Although the engineers were testing these methods, ETOUSA planners hoped that such removal work would prove unnecessary, for during 1943 reconnaissance had uncovered no obstacles along the Normandy coast. Indeed, an early engineer plan assumed that there would be no obstacles or that, if the Germans attempted to install any at the last minute, naval gunfire and aerial bombardment would take care of them. As a last resort, alternative beaches might be chosen.[9]

This optimism waned in late January 1944, when aerial reconnaissance disclosed hedgehogs on the beach at Quineville, just north of the UTAH section of

[7] Ltr, Eisenhower to Marshall, 6 May 44, Eisenhower personal files.

[8] Coll, Keith, and Rosenthal, *The Corps of Engineers: Troops and Equipment,* pp. 472–76; Ltr, Senior Member, Joint Army-Navy Experiment and Testing Board, to CinC, U.S. Fleet, 18 Dec 43.

[9] Col E. G. Paules, Notes on Breaching Under-Water and Shore Obstacles and Land Mine Fields, Mar–Apr 44, Incl 1.

the Cotentin coast. Disturbed at this turn of events, General Eisenhower sent Lt. Col. Arthur H. Davidson, Jr., of General Moore's staff and Lt. Col. John T. O'Neill, commander of V Corps' 112th Engineer Combat Battalion, to attend an obstacle demonstration at Fort Pierce in Florida between 9 and 11 February.[10]

Returning to the theater about two weeks later, Davidson and O'Neill found D-day planners studying aerial photographs that showed the Germans were planting obstacles on the tidal flats below the high-water mark—a great hazard to landing craft. Subsequent photographs revealed that obstacles, usually planted in three rows, were multiplying rapidly not only in the UTAH area but also, beginning late in March, at OMAHA. Planners assumed that they were all strengthened with barbed wire and mines. That assumption proved correct on 23 April when an Allied bomb intended for a coastal battery fell on the beach, producing fourteen secondary explosions. Aerial photographs showed the obstacles proliferating on all beaches right up to D-day.[11]

Detailed planning for breaching the obstacles on D-day began in the United Kingdom in mid-March 1944 when General Bradley directed V and VII Corps to submit clearing plans for OMAHA and UTAH beaches by 1 April. Because time was short, Bradley told planners to depend on only the troops,

materials, equipment, and techniques then available in the theater.

Available troops included the corps' combat engineers, engineer special brigades, and sixteen naval combat demolition units (NCDUs). Each NCDU consisted of five enlisted men and an officer—the capacity of the black rubber boats NCDUs used in their work. They had been trained to paddle to shallow water and then go overboard, wading to shore and dragging the explosive-filled boat behind them. The first unit, members of the earliest Fort Pierce graduating class, arrived in the theater at the end of October 1943. By March 1944 all sixteen units had arrived and had been assigned to naval beach battalions training at Salcombe, Swansea, and Fowey. The demolition units had little idea of precisely what their role on D-day would be. They had no training aids other than those they could improvise, nor were they told until mid-April (because of strict security regulations) the type of obstacles being discovered along the Normandy beaches.[12]

On 1 April 1944, V Corps submitted to First Army a plan for breaching obstacles, prepared jointly with the XI Amphibious Force, U.S. Navy. The plan recommended that an engineer group consisting of two engineer combat battalions and twenty NCDUs be organized and specially trained for the OMAHA assault; VII Corps submitted a similar smaller scale plan for UTAH.[13]

[10] Engineer Operations by the VII Corps in the European Theater, vol. II, "Normandy," p. 2; Rpt, Lt Col J. T. O'Neill, Summary of Activities of the Provisional Engr Gp, 8 Jul 44 (hereafter cited as O'Neill Rpt), in AGF Bd Rpt 253, ETO, Engr Rpt on Landings in Normandy, 5 Oct 44.

[11] O'Neill Rpt; AAR, OMAHA Beach Provisional Engr Spec Bde Gp, Operation Rpt NEPTUNE, pp. 62–66; Engr Opns VII Corps, vol. II, "Normandy," p. 3.

[12] Cdr. Francis Douglas Fane, USNR, and Don Moore, *The Naked Warriors* (New York: Appleton, Century, and Crofts, 1956), p. 21; Rpt on the Work of U.S. Naval Combat Demolitions Units, Naval and Air Support folder, Adm 493, ETOUSA Hist Sect. Unless otherwise cited the section on underwater obstacles is based on these two sources and on O'Neill Rpt and Engr Opns VII Corps, vol. II, "Normandy."

[13] HQ, V Corps, Prefacing Plan, Underwater and Beach Obstacles, OMAHA Beach, in Engineer Special

The V Corps commander, Maj. Gen. Leonard T. Gerow, was disturbed to learn on 9 April that First Army still had adopted no definite obstacle plan and that training had barely started. That same day First Army asked V Corps to send two engineer companies and a tank company with tankdozers to the Assault Training Center at Woolacombe. The 299th Engineer Combat Battalion, with personnel specially trained at Fort Pierce, was to arrive in the United Kingdom on 16 April, but only about one-third of the battalion had been trained in the removal of underwater obstacles. Another cause for worry was a scarcity of tankdozer blades. To speed the adoption of a specific plan and undertake vital training, Gerow enlisted the support of Brig. Gen. William B. Kean, First Army chief of staff. Kean had to admit that "this whole subject had been worked out far too late." Gerow sent two engineer companies with four tankdozers and six NCDUs to begin training at Woolacombe on 12 April.[14]

Army and Navy representatives formulated detailed plans beginning 15 April, when for the first time demolition men obtained precise information on the tidal-flat obstacles they could expect to encounter. Because of the number and density of the obstacles, the conferees decided to attack them "dry shod," ahead of the incoming tide.

This decision helped fix the invasion date—only on 5, 6, or 7 June would the engineers have enough daylight after H-hour to destroy the obstacles before the onrushing Channel tide covered them. The decision to attack dry shod also obviated the need for Apex boats—luckily, for the freighters bringing them from the United States did not arrive in England until mid-May, too late to prepare the boats for use. The first Reddy Foxes, which might have helped, came in the same shipment and had to be put in storage along with the Apexes because there was no time to train men in their use. Under such circumstances, the most practicable method of breaching the obstacles seemed that of placing explosive charges by hand, although NCDU officers continued to warn that this course would be possible only if enemy fire could be neutralized.[15]

On OMAHA, gaps fifty yards wide were to be blown through the obstacles, two in each beach subsector. The broader Easy Red would be breached in six places. Combined Army-Navy boat teams of thirty-five to forty men carried in LCMs were to undertake the task. The sailors were to destroy the seaward obstacles, the soldiers to handle those landward and to clear mines from the tidal flat. First on the scene would be the assault gapping team (one to each gap), composed of twenty-seven men from an Army engineer combat battalion (including one officer and one medic) and an NCDU augmented to thirteen men by the attachment of five Army engineers to help with demolitions and two seamen to handle the explosives and tend the rubber boats.

The assault teams were to be followed by eight support teams, one to every

---

Brigades on OMAHA Beach, Notes and Data Used in Connection with Operation NEPTUNE, OMAHA Beach, Prov Engr Spec Bde Gp (hereafter cited as Notes and Data NEPTUNE).

[14] Ltrs, Gerow to Kean, 10 Apr 44, and Kean to Gerow, 13 Apr 44, copies in Notes and Data NEPTUNE; O'Neill participated in the planning for OMAHA along with Colonel McDonough, commanding officer of the 112th Engineer Combat Group, and Lt. Col. Patillo, V Corps representative at the Obstacle Training Center to study British methods and techniques. O'Neill Rpt.

[15] Bradley, *A Soldier's Story,* pp. 260–61.

two assault teams, of about the same composition. Two command boats completed the flotilla. Command was to be an Army responsibility because the obstacles would presumably be dry at the time of clearing operations. Each assault team was to be supported by a tankdozer to clear obstacles. All boats were to carry some 1,000 pounds of explosives, demolition accessories, mine detectors, and mine gap markers. The command boats were to carry a ton of extra explosive.[16]

At UTAH Beach eight fifty-yard gaps were planned, four in each of the two landing sectors. Boat teams were to be employed in a somewhat different manner. Twelve NCDUs, each consisting of an officer and fifteen men (including five Army engineers) carried in twelve LCVPs, were to attack the seaward band of obstacles. Simultaneously, eight Army demolition teams, each consisting of an officer and twenty-five enlisted men carried in eight LCMs, were to attack the landward obstacles. Four Army reserve teams of the same size, also in LCMs, were to follow the eight leading Army teams shoreward. As at OMAHA, the attackers would rely heavily on standard engineer explosives and tankdozers, and the Army would have command responsibility for obstacle-clearing operations.

On 30 April, V Corps organized the V Corps Provisional Engineer Group for the OMAHA assault. Under Colonel O'Neill, formerly commander of the 112th Engineer Combat Battalion, the provisional group consisted of the 146th Engineer Combat Battalion, the 299th Engineer Combat Battalion (less one company), and twenty-one NCDUs.

Ultimately, 150 demolition-trained men of the 2d Infantry Division joined the provisional group to bring its strength to 1,050. Upon its attachment to the 1st Infantry Division for the assault, the provisional group was redesignated the Special Engineer Task Force.

For UTAH obstacle-clearing operations VII Corps organized the Beach Obstacle Demolition Party under Maj. Herschel E. Linn, commander of the 237th Engineer Combat Battalion. Smaller than the OMAHA organization, the UTAH group consisted mainly of one company of the 237th Engineer Combat Battalion, another from the 299th Engineer Combat Battalion, and twelve NCDUs. To supply the remaining naval support to the UTAH and OMAHA forces, additional NCDUs arrived from the United States on 6 May.[17]

On 27 April, when direction of training for OMAHA passed from First Army to V Corps control, two engineer combat battalions (less one company) and twenty-one NCDUs went to Woolacombe for training, but not until 1 May were aerial photographs of OMAHA available for study. Obstacles of the kind shown in detail in low-level photographs were then erected at Woolacombe, and though training aids were lacking the troops practiced debarking from landing craft with explosives and equipment and experimented with waterproofing methods, tankdozer employment, barbed-wire breaching, and other techniques.[18]

An NCDU officer, Lt. (jg.) Carl P. Hagensen, developed a method for flattening the big Belgian gate obstacles

---

[16] Hist 146th Engr C Bn, Jun–Dec 44; FO 1, 299th Engr C Bn, 28 May 44, in Notes and Data NEPTUNE.

[17] Hist 1106th Engr C Gp, Jun–Dec 44.
[18] Rpt, T/5 Royce L. Thompson, Sep 44, in folder, U.S. Training Center, Adm 533, ETOUSA Hist Sect.

with the least danger to troops and landing craft from steel fragments and shards. Tests indicated that sixteen "Hagensen packs"—small sausage-like waterproof canvas bags filled with two pounds of a new plastic explosive, Composition C−2, and fitted with a hook at one end and a cord at the other—could be quickly attached to the gates' steel girders. When a connecting "ring main" of primacord exploded the packs simultaneously, the gate fell over.

Ten thousand Hagensen packs—with canvas bags sewn by sailmakers in lofts throughout England—were produced during an eleventh-hour roundup of gear and equipment that began when the brief training period ended in mid-May. Some improvisation of supplies proved possible. For example, mortar ammunition bags could hold waterproof fuses and the twenty Hagensen packs each demolition man would carry. Nevertheless, procurement problems were considerable. The OMAHA obstacle teams alone required twenty-eight tons of explosives and seventy-five miles of primacord. Tankdozers, D−8 armored dozers, special minefield gap markers, special towing cables, and a multitude of miscellaneous engineer items also had to be procured. The materiel was found and assembled in a remarkably short ten days.

There was also little time for training the demolition teams. Joint training for most of the Army-Navy teams started late and for many units lasted no more than two weeks. On 15 May the NCDUs moved to Salcombe, a Navy amphibious training center, and spent their time preparing Hagensen packs and obtaining final items of gear. Not until the end of May did they rejoin the Army demolition teams, which since

mid-May had been waiting for D-day in their marshaling areas farther east.[19]

In addition to the obstacle problem there remained a second engineer responsibility, equally central to the success of the operation: the organization of the supply moving on an unprecedented scale across a complex of invasion beaches. First Army planners turned to the proven engineer special brigades, but then devised new command arrangements to accommodate the sheer mass of the invasion traffic.

### The Engineer Special Brigades

At this stage of the war, the engineer special brigades in the European theater were exclusively shore units since the Navy had taken their watercraft. The brigades now had additional service units to accomplish the enormous cargo transfers necessary for assault operations. Basic units included three engineer combat battalions, a medical battalion, a joint assault signal company, a military police (MP) company, a DUKW battalion, an ordnance battalion, and various quartermaster troops. Extra equipment included power cranes, angledozers, motorized road graders, tractors, and six-ton Athey trailers.[20]

---

[19] For criticism by officers of the 299th Engineer Combat Battalion demolition teams on the inadequacy of the Navy briefings, as well as the length of time spent in marshaling areas with "nothing to do," see interviews with Capt. William J. Bunting and Maj. Milton Jewett, in Notes and Data NEPTUNE.

[20] Lt Clifford L. Jones, The Administrative and Logistical History of the European Theater of Operations, vol. VI, "Neptune: Training for Mounting the Operation, and Artificial Ports," March 1946, in CMH. Unless otherwise noted, the rest of this chapter is based on this source and on Heavey, *Down Ramp! The Story of the Army Amphibian Engineers*. For the assumption by the Navy early in 1943 of landing craft operation and amphibious training, see Coll, Keith, and Rosenthal, *The Corps of Engineers: Troops and Equipment*, pp. 385–90.

The 1st Engineer Special Brigade, which had reached a strength of some 20,000 men in Sicily, moved to England in December 1943 with only a nucleus of its old organization—3,346 men, including a medical battalion, a quartermaster DUKW battalion, a signal company, and some ordnance troops. Unlike the other two engineer brigades to be employed in NEPTUNE, the 1st Engineer Special Brigade had an experienced unit in the 531st Engineer Shore Regiment, which had served in the Northwest Africa, Sicily, and Salerno landings. The 1st Engineer Special Brigade expanded in England to some 15,000 troops by D-day.[21]

The 5th Engineer Special Brigade was organized in the United Kingdom on 12 November 1943 from the 1119th Engineer Combat Group with three attached engineer combat battalions (the 37th, 336th, and 348th). The 6th Engineer Special Brigade was formed in January 1944 from the 1116th Engineer Combat Group (147th, 149th, and 203d Engineer Combat Battalions). The staff of the 1116th brought with it a plan, conceived during training in the United States, to employ battalion beach groups, each composed of an engineer combat battalion with attached troops. This concept was similar to that the 1st Engineer Special Brigade had developed in the Mediterranean.

The 6th Engineer Special Brigade planned to deploy two battalion beach groups on the beach, with another engineer combat battalion assuming responsibility for most of the work inland. The beach groups were to unload cargo from ships and move it to dumps. They were also responsible for roads, mine

clearance, and similar engineer work; reinforced quartermaster and ordnance battalions would operate the dumps. In the assault phase all operations of the 6th Engineer Special Brigade were to be controlled by the reinforced 149th Engineer Combat Battalion Beach Group. As operations progressed into the beach maintenance phase, the various battalions were to regain control of their elements initially attached to the 149th and to assume responsibility for their operations.[22]

The 5th Engineer Special Brigade divided itself into three battalion beach groups. Each consisted of an engineer combat battalion, a naval beach company, a quartermaster service company, a DUKW company, a medical collection company, a quartermaster railhead company, a platoon of a quartermaster gasoline supply company, a platoon of an ordnance ammunition company, a platoon of an ordnance medium automotive maintenance company, military police, chemical decontamination and joint assault signal platoons, and two auxiliary surgical teams.[23]

Headquarters, First Army, the American tactical planning agency, outlined the responsibilities of the engineer special brigades in an operations memorandum on 13 February 1944. Each engineer battalion beach group would support the assault of a regimental combat team and each engineer company groupment the assault landing of an infantry battalion landing team. First Army also authorized the grouping of

[21] Hist 1st ESB, Jun 42–Sep 45.

[22] Rpt, HQ, 6th ESB, to TAG, thru CO, OMAHA Beach Cmd, 20 Jul 44, sub: Operation Rpt NEPTUNE (hereafter cited 6th ESB NEPTUNE Rpt).

[23] Col Doswell Gullatt, Operation Rpt NEPTUNE, 6–26 Jun 44, inclusive, HQ, 5th Engr Spec Bde, 20 Jul 44 (hereafter cited as 5th ESB Gullatt Rpt NEPTUNE).

the 5th and 6th Engineer Special Brigades under a headquarters known as the Provisional Engineer Special Brigade Group. It soon became evident that the two brigades would not be sufficient to handle the OMAHA operation, which, besides the beaches, included an artificial port and the minor ports of Grandcamp-les-Bains and Isigny. The 11th Port (TC), which had been operating the Bristol Channel ports, then augmented the engineer group with four port battalions, five DUKW companies, three quartermaster service companies, three quartermaster truck companies, an ordnance medium automotive maintenance company, and a utility detachment—more than 8,000 men in all. Earmarked to operate the pierheads and minor ports, the 11th Port required no training in beach operations.

### Assault Training and Rehearsals

The combat battalions of both the 5th and 6th Engineer Special Brigades had had amphibious training on the Atlantic coast at Fort Pierce, Florida, the U.S. Navy's Amphibious Training Base. But some units, notably quartermaster units, had had no amphibious training before joining the brigades, and the training the 5th Engineer Special Brigade's combat battalions received in the United States proved "elementary" in the light of the heavy demands soon to be placed upon the units. Brigade units received further training in mine work, Bailey bridge construction, road maintenance, and demolitions upon arrival at Swansea on the south coast of Wales early in November; by early January 1944 they were receiving training in landing operations at nearby Oxwich Beach. The 6th Engineer Special Brigade, stationed

at Paignton in Devon, conducted similar exercises at neighboring Goodrington Sands during February.[24]

The first of a series of major exercises involving assault troops and shore engineers began in early January 1944 at Slapton Sands on the southern coast of England, an area from which some 6,000 persons had been evacuated from eight villages and eighty farms. The exercise, called DUCK I, involved 10,000 troops. The assault forces consisted of the inexperienced 29th Infantry Division of V Corps. To give the division some training with shore engineers, the V Corps commander called on Col. Eugene M. Caffey, commanding officer of the 1st Engineer Special Brigade (stationed at Truro in Cornwall), for support. The brigade had arrived in England from the Mediterranean understrength and with no equipment, but, by scouring England for equipment and borrowing officers and units, Colonel Caffey was able to furnish elements of his brigade for the exercise.

Succeeding exercises, DUCK II and III, were held in February to train elements of the 29th Division and the 1st Engineer Special Brigade that had not participated in DUCK I. The beach at Slapton Sands was ideal for training, since it approximated conditions later found at UTAH. But one purpose of the combined exercise—accustoming assault forces to the beach organization tasks that would face them on D-day—could not be realized because OVERLORD tactical plans were not firm until late in February. After the 1st Engineer Special Brigade learned it would not be with the 29th Division but with

---

[24] 6th ESB NEPTUNE Rpt; 5th ESB Gullatt Rpt NEPTUNE; De Arman, Hist 5th ESB; Hist 6th ESB, 1944.

INFANTRY TROOPS LEAVE LST DURING EXERCISE FABIUS *at Slapton Sands, April 1944.*

the 4th, the brigade participated in a series of seven exercises with elements of the 4th Division during the last two weeks of March. The first four practice sessions involved engineer detachments supporting battalion landing teams; the next two involved regimental combat teams. VII Corps conducted the last exercise on a scale approaching DUCK I. Two regimental combat teams trained with a large beach party from the 1st Engineer Special Brigade and extra engineers, parachute troops, and air forces elements.[25]

Exercise FOX, involving 17,000 troops

scheduled to land at OMAHA, took place at Slapton Sands 9–10 March. The 37th Engineer Combat Battalion Beach Group of the 5th Engineer Special Brigade supported the 16th Regimental Combat Team, and the 149th Engineer Battalion Beach Group of the 6th Engineer Special Brigade supported the 116th Regimental Combat Team. This exercise had been delayed so that it could parallel final tactical planning for OVERLORD, and it suffered to some extent from late and hurried preparations as well as the inexperience of the units participating. Neither the mounting nor the beach operations went as well as hoped, but both the engineers and the assault troops learned better

---

[25] T/4 Clifford L. Jones, Notes on UTAH Beach and 1st ESB, Feb 45.

use of DUKWs and more efficient water-proofing of vehicles.[26]

The major exercises led to the two great rehearsals for the invasion: TIGER and FABIUS. TIGER, the rehearsal for the UTAH landings, came first. Some 25,000 men including the 4th Infantry Division, airborne troops, and the 1st Engineer Special Brigade participated under the direction of VII Corps. TIGER lasted nine days (22–30 April) with the first six given over to marshaling. Landings in the Slapton Sands area were to begin at 0630 on 28 April.

At 0130 eight LSTs, proceeding westward toward the assault area with the 1st Engineer Special Brigade, troops of the 4th Division, and VII Corps headquarters aboard, were attacked off Portland by enemy craft, presumably German E-boats. Torpedoes sank two LSTs and damaged a third so badly that it had to be towed back to Dartmouth. The German craft machine-gunned the decks of the LSTs and men in the water. LST–531, with 1,026 soldiers and sailors aboard, had only 290 survivors; total U.S. Army casualties were 749 killed and more than 300 wounded. The 1st Engineer Special Brigade, with 413 dead and 16 wounded, suffered heavily in the action. Its 3206th Quartermaster Service Company was virtually wiped out, and the 557th Quartermaster Railhead Company also sustained heavy losses. Both had to be replaced for the invasion.[27]

Shattered by the disaster, which reduced it to little more than its assault-phase elements, the 1st Engineer Special Brigade made a poor showing in

TIGER. Observing the landings from an LCI offshore, General Bradley was disturbed. For some "unexplained reason" a full report on the loss of the LSTs, which he came later to consider "one of the major tragedies of the European war," did not reach him, and from the sketchy report he received he concluded that the damage had been slight. Attributing the poor performance of the brigade to a breakdown in command, he suggested to Maj. Gen. J. Lawton Collins, commanding VII Corps, that a new commander be assigned. Collins gave the job to Brig. Gen. James E. Wharton. Thus by a combination of misfortune and misunderstanding, Col. Eugene M. Caffey, who had led the 1st Engineer Special Brigade in the Sicily landings, was not to lead it on D-day in Normandy.[28]

FABIUS consisted of six exercises carried out under the direction of 21 Army Group. FABIUS I was the rehearsal for Force O, the 1st Division units that were to assault OMAHA Beach. Approximately 25,000 troops participated in FABIUS I, including three regimental combat teams and various attached service troops. FABIUS II, III, IV, and V were British rehearsals carried out at the same time. FABIUS VI was a marshaling exercise for follow-up Force B (the 29th Division) and the British forces in the buildup. It ran from 3 April to 7 May, with a simulated D-day on 3 May.

Every effort was made to deploy regimental combat teams from the 1st and 29th Divisions plus two Ranger and two tank battalions supported by three engineer combat battalions on the second tide on D-day and 300 tons of supply

---

[26] Ruppenthal, *Logistical Support of the Armies, Volume I*, pp. 348–49.
[27] Hist 1st ESB, 6 Dec 43–1 Nov 44; 1st ESB (UTAH), pp. 22–24.

[28] Bradley, *A Soldier's Story*, pp. 247–49.

on D plus 1—including treadway bridging, Sommerfeld track, coir matting, and other material for building and improving beach roads. A number of faults showed up in beach operations, but since D-day was only a month away no drastic revisions could be undertaken. The most important result of the exercise was a change in the landing schedules; elements of the military police company, the brigade headquarters, and the signal company were to land considerably earlier than originally planned. After FABIUS was over, most of the units that had participated went directly to their marshaling areas.

### Marshaling the Invasion Force

The primary responsibilities for marshaling engineer personnel, vehicles, and supplies for shipment to Normandy fell to the engineers of Western Base Section (WBS) and especially Southern Base Section (SBS), which had a larger number of marshaling areas. U.S. forces in the initial assault were to embark from points in England west of Poole, and early reinforcements were to load at ports in the Bristol Channel in advance of the operation. Later reinforcements were to move through Southampton, Portland, and Plymouth.

Of the nine major marshaling and embarkation areas in SBS, the British operated one. The British and Americans jointly ran two areas around Southampton; the Americans operated the other six areas. Each marshaling area was to be used to 75 percent of its capacity, with the remaining 25 percent kept in reserve to accommodate troops and vehicles that might not be able to move out because of enemy action, adverse weather, or other circumstance.

COLONEL CAFFEY *(Photograph taken in 1952.)*

SBS made available many engineer troops, including general service regiments, camouflage companies, water supply companies, fire-fighting platoons, and various smaller detachments to help operate the marshaling areas.[29]

In the marshaling areas the first step was to construct necessary additional installations. Because the ports did not have the capacity to load the huge invasion fleet at one time, base section engineers had to build, either within the ports or along riverbanks, concrete

---

[29] OCE ETOUSA Hist Rpt 9, Marshalling for OVERLORD (United Kingdom), 1946, pp. 10–18, and fig. 1, Marshalling Areas for OVERLORD, Liaison Sect, Intel Div, ETOUSA Adm file 547.

aprons from existing roads to the water's edge. Known as "hards" (for hard-standings), the aprons had to extend out into the water. They consisted of precast concrete units, called "chocolate bars" because of their scored checkerboard surfaces. Averaging ten inches in thickness, each section measured about 2-by-3-feet, which, laid end to end, formed a rough road. Both sides of the slabs were scored—the top surface to prevent vehicles from slipping, the bottom surface to bite into the beach. The landing craft or landing ships anchored at the foot of the hard or apron, let down their ramps, and took on vehicles and personnel dry shod; no piers or docks were necessary. Because landing craft were of shallow draft, flat-bottomed, and most unstable in rough seas and because the south coast of England was generally unprotected, windswept, and subject to tides that greatly changed water depths, careful reconnaissance and British advice were necessary to locate loading sites or embarkation points in sheltered sections, generally in a port or a river mouth.[30]

Next came the selection of temporary camp sites near embarkation points. The capacity for out-loading from a certain group of hards determined the size and number of camps located nearby. Each marshaling area had railheads for storing all classes of supplies, and every camp was supposed to maintain a stock of food, along with fast-moving items.

The marshaling areas were of two patterns, large camps that might accommodate as many as 9,000 men and sausage-style camps—fourteen small camps, each with a capacity of 230 men, ranged along five to ten miles of roadway. These small camps provided better dispersal and the possibility of good camouflage, for tentage followed hedgerows. But they required more personnel for efficient operation because some degree of control was lost. Good camouflage practices were not always followed.[31]

Most of the camps consisted of quarters for 200 enlisted men (often in pyramidal tents), officers' quarters, orderly rooms, supply rooms, cooks' quarters, kitchen, mess halls, and latrines. Special briefing tents with sand tables were also available. Where necessary, engineers erected flattops over open areas used for mess lines.[32] In both the Southern and Western Base Sections they also constructed security enclosures and special facilities. Engineers had to maintain and waterproof engineer task force vehicles. Each marshaling camp had either a concrete tank or a dammed stream for testing waterproofing. Roads, railroads, bridges, and dock and port facilities were primarily British responsibilities, and American engineers performed maintenance in these areas only on request or in case of emergency.[33]

The Western Base Section's task was easier than Southern Base Section's for little new construction was required. Existing troop camps were big enough and close enough to the ports. Camp capacities were increased by billeting eighteen instead of sixteen men in each

---

[30] Southern Base Section History, Aug 43–Aug 44 p. 4, Adm 601, ETOUSA Hist Sect.

[31] Hist 604th Engr Camouflage Bn.

[32] Hist 1306th Engr GS Rgt.

[33] Col Fenton S. Jacobs, Western Base Section, vol. II, p. 349, Adm 603D, ETOUSA Hist Sect. The account of WBS activities is based on this source.

16-by-36-foot hut and by adding an extra man to each seven-man 16-by-16-foot pyramidal tent. Additional tents were also erected with construction materials the Royal Engineers contributed.

Providing the needed accommodations in both Western and Southern Base Sections entailed much more than acquiring buildings and erecting tents. An acute shortage of base section engineer operating personnel which arose in the spring of 1944 promised to become worse once the invasion-mounting machinery went into full swing. SOS, ETOUSA, officials recognized the problem as early as February 1944 and saw the need to use field forces to help out. General Lee estimated that at least 15,000 field force troops would be required, along with 46,000 SOS troops who would have to be taken off other work. As a result, ETOUSA permitted an entire armored division to be cannibalized to provide some of the troops needed for housekeeping in the marshaling areas. Of the total, 4,500 were assigned as cooks, but many of these men were not qualified. General Moore thought the shortage in mess personnel was frequently the weakest part of the engineer phase of marshaling.[34]

Briefings began in the marshaling areas on 22 May 1944. The Provisional Engineer Special Brigade Group's commander, Brig. Gen. William M. Hoge, issued a simple but effective order: "It is my desire that every individual soldier in this command, destined for the far shore, be thoroughly instructed as to the general mission and plan of his unit, and *what he is to do.*" The men received instruction in briefing tents containing models of the Normandy beaches, maps, overprints, charts, aerial photographs, and mosaics.[35]

Battalion beach groups formed from the 5th and 6th Engineer Brigade Groups, the latter initially under the 5th Engineer Special Brigade, were to support the V Corps landings on the 7,000-yard stretch of beach fronting the Vierville-Colleville area. The 5th Engineer Special Brigade was to operate all shore installations in sectors Easy, Fox, and George to the left of the common brigade boundary. The 6th Engineer Special Brigade was to operate those in sectors Charlie, Dog, and Easy to the right of the brigade boundary. Headquarters, Provisional Engineer Special Brigade Group, was to assume control of the two brigades as soon as its command post was established ashore. The 1st Division (less the 26th Regimental Combat Team), with the 29th Division's 116th Regimental Combat Team and other troops attached, made up Force O, the initial assault force. The 29th Division, less the 116th Regimental Combat Team but with the 26th Regimental Combat Team and other troops attached, constituted the immediate follow-up force, Force B.[36]

Upon landing, engineer special brigade engineers were to relieve divisional engineers on the beaches. Then they were to develop and expand the roadway system and open additional exits and roads within the established beach maintenance area, with the goal

---

[34] Bradley, *A Soldier's Story*, p. 247; OCE ETOUSA Hist Rpt 9, Marshalling for OVERLORD, p. 58.

[35] Hist 5th ESB, p. 60, Adm 120, ETOUSA Hist Sect.

[36] De Arman, Hist 5th ESB. Unless otherwise noted, this account of the 5th Engineer Special Brigade plans is taken from this source.

of having that area fully developed by D plus 3. Initially beach dumps were to be set up about a thousand yards inland; later the brigade group was to consolidate these dumps up to five miles inland. Separate areas were to be set aside for USAAF dumps, troop transit areas, and vehicle transit areas.

The 5th Engineer Special Brigade undertook a number of tasks, some in support of or in coordination with the Navy. The men marked naval hazards near the beach, determined the best landing areas, and then marked the beach limits and debarkation points. They helped remove beach obstacles and developed and operated assault landing beaches. They controlled boat traffic near the beach and directed the landing, retraction, and salvage of craft as well as unloading all craft beaching within their sector. Brigade members also developed beach exits to permit the flow of 120 vehicles an hour by H plus 3, organized and operated initial beach dumps, directed traffic, and maintained a naval ponton causeway. They operated personnel and vehicle transit areas, set up and operated a POW stockade, kept track of organizations and supplies that landed, and established initial ship-to-shore communications. Finally, they gave first aid to beach casualties before evacuating them to ships.

The general plan called for progressive development of the OMAHA beachhead in three phases. The assault phase would be under company control, the initial dump phase under battalion beach group control, and the beach maintenance dump phase under brigade control. During the first two phases at OMAHA Beach, groups of the 5th and 6th Engineer Special Brigades were to support the landings of the 1st Division.

The 37th Engineer Battalion Beach Group (of the 5th Engineer Special Brigade) was to support the 16th Regimental Combat Team; the 149th Beach Group, with the 147th Beach Group attached (both from the 6th Engineer Special Brigade), was to support the 116th Regimental Combat Team; and the 348th Beach Group (of the 5th Engineer Special Brigade) was to support the 18th Regimental Combat Team. The 29th Division's lead regimental combat team, the 26th, was to be supported by the 336th Engineer Combat Battalion Beach Group of the 5th Engineer Special Brigade.

The duties of the 1st Engineer Special Brigade, supporting the assault landings of the 4th Infantry Division of VII Corps on UTAH Beach, were similar to those of the 5th Engineer Special Brigade on OMAHA. Uncle Red Beach on the left and Tare Green Beach on the right were each to be operated by a battalion beach group of the brigade's 531st Engineer Shore Regiment; as soon as a third beach group could land, a third beach, Sugar Red, was to be opened at the right of Tare Green.[37]

In the briefings before D-day, the engineer special brigades received intelligence information concerning enemy forces, the progressive development of enemy defenses, detailed geographic and hydrographic studies, reports on local resources, and a model of the beach and adjacent areas. Defense overprints provided detailed information about gun positions, minefields, beach obstacles, roadblocks, and antitank

---

[37] FO 1, HQ, 1st ESB, 10 May 44, Adm 493, ETOUSA Hist Sect.

ditches. An Admiralty Tide Chart prepared at scale 1:7,920 was valuable, as was a 1:5,000 chart-map that the Information Section, Intelligence Division, OCE, published. However, the overprints of land defenses and underwater obstacles provided with these charts arrived too late to be of maximum benefit to the troops: the land defense overprint for the Admiralty Tide Chart was distributed after D-day. In addition, enemy defense information was not as recent as it might have been.[38]

### Embarkation

After the briefings and final waterproofing of their vehicles to withstand 4½-foot depths, the troops split into vessel loads and moved to their embarkation points or hards. The 5th Engineer Special Brigade embarked at Portland, Weymouth, and Falmouth between 31 May and 3 June. Elements of the brigade scheduled for the first two tides with Force O loaded aboard troop transports (APs and LSIs), landing ships and craft (LSTs, LCTs, and LCIs), cargo freighters, and motor transport ships.

Like other components of the assault force, the engineers were to go ashore in varied craft to reduce the risk of losing an entire unit in the sinking of a single vessel. Each unit of the brigade had an assigned number of personnel and vehicle spaces, and the total was considerable—4,188 men and 327 vehicles, including attached nonengineer units. Force B, scheduled to land on the third tide with 1,376 men and 277 vehicles, loaded on a single wave for better control on the assumption that the risk of losing vessels would be much

less by the time of its landing.[39] The 1st Engineer Special Brigade units in Force U loaded at Plymouth, Dartmouth, Torquay, and Brixham beginning on 30 May. The assembly of Force U was somewhat more difficult than that of Force O because its loading points were more widely scattered.[40]

Most assault demolition teams were jammed aboard 100-foot LCTs, each already carrying two tanks, a tankdozer, gear, and packs of explosives in addition to its own crew. When they arrived at the transport area, the teams were to transfer to fifty-foot LCMs to make the run to the beach. Because insufficient lift was available to carry the LCMs in the customary manner, such as on davits, LCTs towed them to the transport area.[41]

Before midnight of 3 June the engineers were aboard their ships and on their way to their rendezvous points beyond the harbors. D-day was to be 5 June. The slow landing ships and craft of Force U got under way during the afternoon of 3 June because they had the greatest distance to go; those of Force O sortied later in the evening. The night was clear but the wind was rising and the water was becoming choppy. At dawn, after a rough night at sea, the vessels were ordered to turn back. D-day had been postponed. Sunday, 4 June, was a miserable day for the men jammed aboard the landing ships and craft under a lashing rain.

At dawn next morning the order went out from the supreme commander that D-day would be Tuesday,

---

[38] 5th ESB Gullatt Rpt NEPTUNE; Jones, Notes on UTAH Beach.

[39] De Arman, Hist 5th ESB.

[40] 1st ESB, Boat Assignment Table, an. 2 to FO 1, Adm 493, ETOUSA Hist Sect; Ruppenthal, *Logistical Support of the Armies, Volume I*, pp. 372–73.

[41] Fane and Moore, *The Naked Warriors*, p. 51; O'Neill Rpt; Engr Opns VII Corps, vol. II, "Normandy," p. 9.

6 June. The word came to many of the engineers as it did to those of the 147th Engineer Combat Battalion aboard LCI-92:

Suddenly a hush spread above the din and clamor of the men. . . . And then, as if coinciding with silence, a clear, strong voice extending from bow to stern, and reaching every far corner of the ship, announced the Order of the Day issued by the Supreme Commander. The men strained to catch every word, "you are about to embark on the Great Crusade. . . . Good Luck! And let us all beseech the blessing of Almighty God upon this great and noble undertaking." For the next few moments, heads were bowed as if in silent prayer. This was the word. Tomorrow was D-day.[42]

_____

[42] Hist 147th Engr C Bn, 29 Jan 43–4 Mar 46.

# CHAPTER XV

# The Landings on OMAHA and UTAH

Darkness over the English Channel on the night of 5 June 1944 concealed five thousand ships, spread over twenty miles of sea, plowing the choppy waters toward Normandy. Two American and three British task forces traveled their separate mine-swept lanes to the mid-point of the Channel. Each lane divided there into two sublanes, one for the naval fire support vessels and the faster transports, the other for slower craft jammed with tanks, field pieces, and wheeled vehicles.

Force O, destined for OMAHA, and Force U, headed for UTAH, arrived in designated transport areas ten miles off the French coast after midnight, and the larger ships began disgorging men and equipment into the assault LCVPs swinging down from the transports' davits and hovering alongside. Smaller landing craft churned around the larger ships with their own loads of infantry, equipment, and armor for the assault. LCTs carried the duplex-drive amphibious Sherman tanks that would play a vital part in the first moments of the invasion. The spearhead of the assault on OMAHA, the tanks were to enter the water 6,000 yards offshore, swim to the waterline at Dog White and Dog Green, and engage the heavier German emplacements on the beaches five minutes ahead of the first wave of infantry.

At H-hour, 0630, with the tide just starting to rise from its low point, another wave of Shermans and tank-dozers was to land on Easy Green and Dog Red, followed a minute later by the assault infantry in LCVPs and British-designed armored landing craft called LCAs. At 0633 the sixteen assault gapping teams were due on OMAHA, and their support craft were to follow them during the next five minutes. The demolition teams, with the help of the tankdozers, had just under half an hour to open gaps in the exposed obstacle belts before the main body of the infantry hit the beaches. The later waves also had combat engineers to blow additional gaps, clear beach exits, aid assault troops in moving inland, and help organize the beaches. Off UTAH a similar scene unfolded, with the duplex-drive tanks scheduled to go in on the heels of the first wave of the 8th Infantry assault, followed in five minutes by the Army-Navy assault gapping teams and detachments from two combat engineer battalions.[1]

### Engineers on Omaha

The eight demolition support teams

---

[1] War Dept, Hist Div, *Omaha Beachhead*, pp. 38–42; Dept of the Army, Hist Div, *Utah Beach to Cherbourg*, pp. 43–44; Operation Rpt NEPTUNE, p. 80.

for OMAHA and the three command teams aboard a British transport had had a chance to get some sleep during the night. But the gapping teams, crowded aboard LCTs and towed LCMs, were miserable. One of the LCTs had broken down early in the voyage, and several swamped in the Channel swell. Their drenched and seasick passengers transferred to the bucking LCMs in the blackness, no small feat considering the amount of equipment involved. *(Map 16)*

The engineers were overburdened for their trip to shore. Each man carried a forty-pound bag of Hagensen packs, wire cutters, a gas mask, cartridges, an inflatable life belt, a canteen, rations, and a first aid packet. They had either carbines or Garand rifles and bangalore torpedoes to tear apart the barbed wire on the beach. Some had mine detectors, others heavy wire reels wound with 800 feet of primacord, and some carried bags of fuse assemblies. Over their uniforms all wore coveralls impregnated against gas, and over them a fur-lined jacket. Each LCM held two rubber boats, each containing about 500 pounds of explosives, extra bangalores, mine detectors, gap markers, buoys, and from 75 to 100 cans of gasoline.[2]

Almost from the beginning, things began to go wrong for the sixteen gapping teams. They managed to transfer from the LCTs to the LCMs on schedule, around 0300. At 0450, twenty minutes after the amphibious tanks and the first infantry assault wave started for shore, the demolition teams were on their way to the line of departure, some two miles

offshore. Behind them, their support teams were delayed when their LCMs failed to arrive on time, and they encountered difficulties getting into smaller craft from the attack transports. Unable to load completely until 0500, the support elements finally got under way at 0600, far too late to reach the tidal flat in time to help the gapping teams. The precisely timed schedules, conceived for fair weather and calm seas, were breaking down even before the engineers reached the shore.[3]

The assault gapping teams headed landward heartened by the rain of metal descending on enemy positions. The eight assault teams assigned to the eastern sector of OMAHA with the 16th Regimental Combat Team reached the line of departure at first light; Navy control boats herded them into their correct lanes for Easy Red and Fox Green beaches. As they headed for shore, heavy shells of the naval bombardment whistled over their heads, and at 0600 bombers arrived with the first of some 1,300 tons of bombs dropped on the invasion area on D-day. The sight made the drenched, shivering men in the boats momentarily forget their misery. They were cheered in their certainty that the Air Forces would saturate the beaches, and when a British rocket ship loosed the first of a barrage of 9,000 missiles at the German positions, hope mounted that the German artillery and machine-gun nests would be silent when the LCMs came in. Optimists recalled a statement from a briefing aboard one of the transports: "There will be nothing alive on the

---

[2] Fane and Moore, *The Naked Warriors*, pp. 51–52; Interv, Capt William J. Bunting, Jnl, and FO 1, 299th Engr C Bn, in Notes and Data, NEPTUNE.

[3] Interv, Maj Milton Jewett, CO, 299th Engr C Bn, in Notes and Data, NEPTUNE; Hist 146th Engr C Bn; O'Neill Rpt.

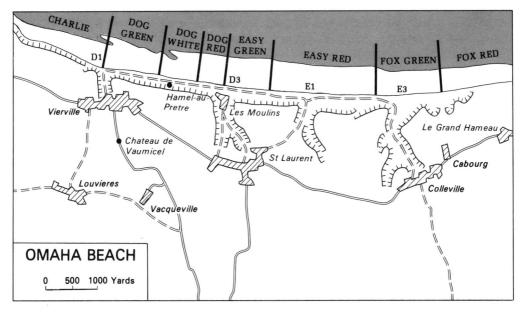

*MAP 16*

beach when you land."[4]

The illusion did not sustain them long, for the bombers had flown through cloud cover that forced their crews to rely on imperfect blind bombing techniques. Only two sticks of bombs fell within four miles of the shore defenses, though the area behind the beaches took a thorough pounding. The British rockets made a fine display, but disappeared over the cliffs to dig up the landscape behind the German coastal works. The naval barrage beginning at H minus 45 minutes was also more effective inland, contributing to the disruption of German communications. The combined power of the air and naval bombardment did much to isolate the battle area. But the German shore batteries on OMAHA, located in bunkers and enfilading the beach so

that they could fire no more than a few hundred yards out to sea, remained mute during the opening moments of the action. Offering no muzzle flashes to give away their positions to the Navy gunners and invite their own destruction, they were largely intact when the first wave of engineers, tanks, and infantry hit the tidal flat.[5]

For the first troops in, OMAHA was "an epic human tragedy which in the early hours bordered on total disaster."[6] The morning mists and the smoke raised in the bombardment concealed landmarks in some sectors, and a strong tidal crosscurrent carried the boats as

[4] Fane and Moore, *The Naked Warriors*, p. 50; Intervs, Bunting and Jewett, Notes and Data, NEPTUNE.

[5] The Adm and Log Hist of the ETO, vol. VI, "Neptune: Training for Mounting the Operation, and Artificial Ports," pp. 14–15; Operation Rpt NEPTUNE, p. 82; Col. Paul W. Thompson, "D-day on Omaha Beach," *Infantry Journal*, LVI (June 1945), 40.

[6] S. L. A. Marshall, "First Wave at Omaha Beach," in *Battle at Best* (New York: William Morrow and Co., 1963), p. 52.

TANKS AND VEHICLES STALLED AT THE SHINGLE LINE ON OMAHA BEACH

much as two thousand yards east of their intended landfalls. The 741st Tank Battalion launched twenty-nine of its thirty-two duplex-drive tanks offshore and immediately lost twenty-seven when they foundered or plunged directly to the bottom of the Channel upon leaving their LCTs. Two swam ashore, and the remaining three landed from beached LCTs, only to fall prey at the waterline to German gunners. Machine-gun fire whipped among the engineer and infantry landing craft, intermingled now, and followed them to the beach. As the ramps dropped, a storm of artillery and mortar rounds joined the automatic and small-arms fire, ripping apart the first wave. Dead men dotted the flat; the wounded lay

in the path of the onrushing tide, and many drowned as the surf engulfed them. An infantry line formed at the shingle bank and, swelled by fearful, dispirited, and often leaderless men, kept up a weak volume of fire as yet inadequate to protect the engineers. In the carnage, the gapping teams, suffering their own losses, fought to blow the obstacles.

On the left of Easy Red, one team led the entire invasion by at least five minutes. The commander of Team 14, 2d Lt. Phill C. Wood, Jr., was under the impression that H-hour was 0620 instead of 0630. Under his entreaties, the Navy coxswain brought the LCM in at 0625, the boat's gun crew unsuccessfully trying to destroy Teller mines on the upright stakes. Wood and his team dragged their explosive-laden rubber boat into waist-deep water under a hail of machine-gun fire. No one was on the beach. The lieutenant charged toward a row of obstacles, glancing backward as he ran. In that moment he saw an artillery shell land squarely in the center of the craft he had just left, detonating the contents of the second rubber boat and killing most of the Navy contingent of his team. The LCM burned fiercely. Wood's crew dropped bangalore torpedoes and mine detectors and abandoned their load of explosives. Dodging among the rows, they managed to wire a line of obstacles to produce a gap, but here the infantry landing behind them frustrated their attempt to complete the job. Troops, wounded or hale, huddled among the obstacles, using them for cover, and Wood finally gave up trying to chase them out of range of his charges. Leaving the obstacles as they were, he and his team, now only about half of its original strength, rushed forward and took up firing positions with the infantry concentrated at the shingle.[7]

Other teams had little more success. Team 13's naval detachment also fell when an artillery shell struck its boatload of explosives just after it landed on Easy Red. The Army contingent lost only one man but found the infantry discharging from the landing craft seeking cover among the obstacles, thus preventing the team from setting off charges. Team 12 left its two rubber boats aboard the LCM, yet managed to clear a thirty-yard gap on Easy Red,

but at a fearful cost. A German mortar shell struck a line of primacord, prematurely setting off the charges strung about one series of obstacles, killing six Army and four Navy demolitions men and wounding nine other members of the team and a number of infantrymen in the vicinity. Team 11, arriving on the far left flank of Easy Red ahead of the infantry, lost over half its men. A faulty fuse prevented the remainder from blowing a passage through the beach impediments.

Only two teams, 9 and 10, accomplished their missions on the eastern sector of OMAHA. Team 9, landing in the middle of Easy Red well ahead of the infantry waves, managed to open a fifty-yard path for the main assault. Team 10's performance was encouraging in comparison with that of the others. Clearing the infantry aside within twenty minutes of hitting the beach, the men demolished enough obstacles in spite of heavy casualties to create two gaps, one fifty yards wide and a second a hundred yards across. They were the only gaps blown on the eastern half of the assault beaches.

The remaining teams assigned to that area had much the same dismal experience as Lieutenant Wood's team, and the failure of the assault gapping effort became evident. At Fox Green, Teams 15 and 16 came in later than those on Easy Red but met the same heavy artillery and automatic fire. At 0633 Team 16 plunged off its LCM, leaving its rubber boats adrift when it became apparent that they drew German attention. Here too the men gave up trying to blow gaps when the infantry would not leave the protection of the German devices. Team 15 touched down at 0640, just as the tide began rising rap-

---

[7] Interv, Lt Wood, in Notes and Data, NEPTUNE; Hist 146th Engr C Bn; Fane and Moore, *The Naked Warriors*, p. 53–64.

idly, and lost several men to machine-gun fire before they left the LCM. In a now common occurrence, they sustained more casualties when a shell found the rubber boat with its volatile load. The survivors nevertheless attacked the Belgian gates farthest from shore and fixed charges to several. The fusillade from shore cut away fuses as rapidly as the engineers could rig them. One burst of fragments carried away a fuseman's carefully set mechanism—and all of his fingers. With no choice but to make for shore, they ran, only four of their original forty uninjured, to the low shingle bank on Fox Green, where they collapsed, "soaking wet, unable to move, and suffering from cramps. It was cold and there was no sun."[8]

Seven teams bound for the 116th Infantry's beaches on the western half of OMAHA—Dog Green, Dog White, Dog Red, and Easy Green—were on schedule, most of them, in fact, coming in ahead of the infantry companies in the first waves. The eighth team landed more than an hour later; its LCT had foundered and sunk shortly after leaving England, and the team transferred to other craft. When it finally landed at 0745, the team found the obstacles covered with water. The duplex-drive tank crews on the western half of the beach came in all the way on their landing craft rather than attempting the swim ashore, but their presence was only briefly felt. German fire disabled many tanks at the shingle line where they had halted, unable to move farther, and those remaining could not silence the heavier enemy guns. The men of Team

8, landing a little to the left of Dog Green, saw no Americans on the beach but confronted a German party working on the obstacles. The Germans fled, and the team was able to blow one fifty-yard gap before the American infantry arrived. Teams 3 and 4, badly shot up, achieved little, and Teams 5 and 7 could do no blasting after the incoming infantry took cover among the beach obstructions. The only positive results came when Teams 1 and 6 each opened a fifty-yard gap, one on Dog White and one on Dog Red. Command Boat 1, on the beach flat at 0645, unloaded a crew that made an equally wide hole in the obstacles on Easy Green. Where the engineers successfully blew lanes open, they had first to cajole, threaten, and even kick the infantry out of the way. Gapping team members later recalled that the teams had more success if they came in without firing the machine guns on the LCMs, since their distinctive muzzle flashes gave their range to the enemy.

The tardy support teams appeared off the eastern beaches, all carried off course and landing between 0640 and 0745 on or around Fox Red. The German artillerymen at the eastern reaches of OMAHA met them with fearsomely accurate fire. One 88-mm. piece put two rounds into Team F's LCM, killing and wounding fifteen men; only four men of the original team got to shore. Team D got a partial gap opened, making a narrow, thirty-yard lane, but the other teams could do little. The men arriving later found the German fire just as heavy, and the incoming tide forced them to shore before they could deploy among the obstacles. They joined the earlier elements that had found

[8] Interv, S/Sgt James M. Redmond, Team 15, Notes and Data, NEPTUNE.

shelter under the cliffs at the eastern end of the beach.[9]

Their strength reduced to a single machine, engineer tankdozers could offer little help. Only six of the sixteen M–4s equipped with bulldozer blades got ashore, and the enemy picked off five of them. The remaining one provided the engineers an alternative to blowing up the obstacles, an increasingly hazardous undertaking as more troops and vehicles crowded onto the beaches. Instead of using demolitions, which sent shards of metal from the obstacles careening around the area, the teams set about removing the mines from stakes, ramps, hedgehogs, and Belgian gates, and let the tankdozers, joined later in the day by several armored bulldozers, shove the obstacles out of the way as long as the tide permitted. Pushed ashore after 0800 by the inrushing water, the gapping teams helped move wounded men off the tidal flat and consolidated equipment and the supply of explosives to await the next ebb.

In the meantime the Navy had discovered that the obstacles did not pose the expected problem once they were stripped of their mines. Shortly after 1000, several destroyers moved to within a thousand yards of the beach. Engaging the German emplacements with devastating 5-inch gunfire, they began to accomplish what the tanks in the first assault could not. Using the covering fire, two landing craft, LCT–30 and LCI–554, simply rammed through the obstacles off Fox Green, battering a path to shore with all automatic weap-ons blazing. Though LCT–30 was lost to fire from the bluffs, the other vessel retracted from the beach without loss, and dozens of other craft hovering offshore repeated the maneuver with the same result.[10]

When the first morning tide interrupted the work of the gapping teams, they had opened just five holes, and only one of these, Team 10's 100-yard-wide lane on Easy Red, was usable. Their ranks virtually decimated in their first half-hour ashore, the teams' members were often bitter when they discussed their experience later. Most of the equipment the LCMs carried had been useless or worse; the rubber boats with their explosives had drawn heavy fire, and the engineers had abandoned them as quickly as possible. The mine detectors were useless since the enemy had buried no mines in the flat, and German snipers made special targets of men carrying them. With no barbed wire strung among the obstacles, the bangalore torpedoes the engineers brought in were only an extra burden. Overloaded and dressed in impregnated coveralls, the engineers found their movement impeded, and wounded and uninjured men alike drowned under the weight of their packs as they left the landing craft. The survivors also criticized the close timing of the invasion waves that left them only a half hour to clear lanes. The confusion produced when the engineers landed simultaneously with or even ahead of the infantry led to the opinion that there also should have been at least a half hour between the first infantry assault

[9] Cornelius Ryan, *The Longest Day, June 6, 1944* (New York: Simon and Schuster, 1959), pp. 190–91; Operation Rpt NEPTUNE, p. 85; O'Neill Rpt.

[10] Morison, *The Invasion of France and Germany*, p. 141.

and the arrival of the gapping teams. In future actions, support teams should go in with the groups they were backing up rather than behind them in the invasion sequence. Lastly, as a tactical measure, the gapping team veterans recommended that the first concern should be to strip the mines from any obstacles encountered so as to render them safe for tankdozers or landing craft to ram.[11]

The human cost of the engineers' heroism on OMAHA was enormous. When the Army elements of the gapping teams reverted on D plus 5 to control of the 146th and 299th Engineer Combat Battalions, then attached to V Corps, they had each lost between 34 and 41 percent of their original strength. The units had not yet accounted for all their members, and the Navy set losses among the naval contingents of the teams at 52 percent. Fifteen Distinguished Service Crosses went to Army members of the team; Navy demolitions men received seven Navy Crosses. Each of the companies of the 146th and 299th Engineer Combat Battalions involved and the naval demolition unit received unit citations for the action on D-day.[12]

The end of the first half hour on D-day saw approximately 3,000 American assault troops on OMAHA, scattered in small clumps along the sand. Isolated from each other and firing sporadically at the enemy, they sought to advance up the small defiles leading to the flanks and rear of German positions, but no forward motion was yet evident. On the right, or western, flank of the beach in front of Vierville in the 116th Infantry's zone, the Germans had taken the heaviest toll among the incoming men, and the assault of Company A, 116th Infantry, crumbled under the withering fire. Reinforcements were slow, often carried off course to the east in the tidal current. A thousand yards east, straddling Dog Red and Easy Green, lay elements of two more companies from the 116th, confused by their surroundings but less punished by German fire since the defensive positions above were wrapped in a heavy smoke from grass fires that obscured vision seaward. Sections of four different companies from both assault regiments landed on the Fox beaches and, huddled with engineers from the gapping teams, fired at opportune targets or contemplated their next moves. Only in the stretch between the Colleville and St. Laurent draws, Exits E−1 and E−3, was there relative safety. The German posts in the bluffs here seemed unmanned through the whole invasion, which also permitted the more successful performance of the gapping teams on Easy Red. But the success of the invasion on OMAHA now depended upon getting the troops and vehicles off the beaches and through the German coastal defensive shell.[13]

*Opening the Exits*

While the ordeal of the gapping teams was still in progress, a second phase of

[11] Operation Rpt NEPTUNE, p. 92; Cdr. Kenneth Edwards, RN, *Operation Neptune* (London: Collins, 1946), p. 149; Intervs, Bunting and Jewett, Notes and Data, NEPTUNE.

[12] O'Neill Rpt; War Dept, Hist Div, *Omaha Beachhead*, pp. 43, 165−66; Fane and Moore, *The Naked Warriors*, pp. 65−66.

[13] Col. Paul W. Thompson, "D-day on Omaha Beach," *Infantry Journal*, LXI, no. 6 (June 1945), 34−48; Harrison, *Cross-Channel Attack*, p. 315; War Dept, Hist Div, *Omaha Beachhead*, pp. 45−47.

engineer operations on OMAHA began with the arrival of the first elements of the 5th Engineer Special Brigade. These units were charged with bringing some order out of the chaos of the invasion beaches. For the purpose some engineer combat battalions became the core units for beach groups, which included a DUKW company, quartermaster units for gasoline and other supply, a medical detachment, ordnance ammunition, maintenance, and bomb disposal units, and an assortment of signal, chemical, and military police companies. A company from a naval beach battalion completed the organization to assist in structuring the beaches for supply operations. Four groups had assignments on OMAHA for D-day. The 37th Engineer Battalion Beach Group supported the 16th Regimental Combat Team, 1st Division, and the 149th was behind the 116th Infantry. The 348th was to facilitate the landing of the 18th Infantry, following the 16th on the eastern end of the beach. The 336th Engineer Battalion Beach Group was scheduled to arrive in the afternoon to organize Fox Red. All the groups were under 5th Engineer Special Brigade control until the assault phase was over; the 149th Engineer Battalion Beach Group would then revert to the 6th Brigade.[14]

The earliest elements stepped into the same fire that cut up the gapping teams. First in was a reconnaissance party from Company A, 37th Engineer Combat Battalion, led by the company commander; it landed at 0700, ten minutes ahead of schedule, opposite the E−3 draw on Fox Green. Sections of the remainder of Company A and a

platoon of Company C, accompanying a headquarters group, arrived over the next several minutes, but the entire complement of the battalion's men wound up hugging the shingle bank and helping to build up the fire line. Another engineer section, this one from Company C, 149th Engineer Combat Battalion, scheduled for landing on Dog Red, landed on Easy Green. They set to work there, and a small detachment began digging a path through the dune line to the road paralleling the shore. A second detail wormed its way through gaps cut in the barbed wire and approached the base of the cliffs, only to be halted by an antitank ditch. Enemy fire forced the group back to the shingle line. Two companies from the 147th Engineer Combat Battalion suffered forty-five men lost to artillery fire even before their LCT set them down off Dog White at 0710. In the five-foot surf they lost or jettisoned their equipment and found shelter after a harrowing run for the shingle.[15] An LCI put Company B, 37th Engineer Combat Battalion, ashore safely at 0730 at Exit E−1, leading to St. Laurent, which the battalion was supposed to open for the 2d Battalion of the 16th Infantry. Company A was to open Exit E−3 for the 3d Battalion but did not arrive until 0930. Landing near E−1, Company A had to make its way through the wreckage on the beach to E−3, where the unit ran into such withering artillery, mortar, and small-arms fire that it could accomplish little all day. Unluckiest of all was Company C, which was to push inland and set up transit areas. A direct hit to its LCI on landing at Exit E−1 killed many men. In the same area one

---

[14] Operation Rpt NEPTUNE, p. 37.

[15] Ibid., p. 87.

of two LCIs carrying the battalion staff broached on a stake; the men had to drop off into neck-deep water and wade ashore under machine-gun fire.[16] Coming in with the fifth wave, they had expected to find OMAHA free of small-arms fire. Instead, the beach was crowded with the men of the first waves crouching behind the shingle. Deadly accurate artillery fire was still hitting the landing craft, tanks, and half-tracks lining the water's edge; one mortar shell killed the commander of the 37th Engineer Combat Battalion, Lt. Col. Lionel F. Smith, and two members of his staff, Capts. Paul F. Harkleroad and Allen H. Cox, Jr., as soon as they landed. Badly shaken, the engineers joined the infantrymen behind the shingle bank.

By 0930, infantry penetrations of the German positions above the beach were beginning to have some effect, though only a few men were scaling the heights. Rangers and elements of the 116th Infantry got astride the high ground between Exits D−1 and D−3 around 0800 and slowly eliminated some of the automatic weapons trained on American troops below. Between St. Laurent and Colleville, companies from both regiments got men on the heights. One company raked the German trenches in the E−1 draw, capturing twenty-one Germans before moving farther inland. In the F−1 draw back of Fox Red, most coordinated resistance ended by 0900, but isolated nests of Germans remained. The movement continued all morning, and the engineers either joined attempts to scale the bluffs or made it possible for others to climb.

Beyond the shingle on Easy Green and Easy Red were a double-apron barbed-wire fence and minefields covering the sands to the bluffs. As the infantry advances began to take a toll of the German defenders on the bluffs, Sgt. Zolton Simon, a squad leader in Company C, 37th Engineer Combat Battalion, gathered his five-man mine-detector crew, cut a gap in the wire, and led his men into the minefield. Disregarding the fire, they methodically opened and marked a narrow path across the mined area, into a small defile, and up the hill. Simon was wounded once while helping to sweep mines and again when he reached the hilltop, this time so seriously that he was out of action. By now, infantry was on the trail behind him, urged into the gap by 1st Lt. Charles Peckham of Company B, who stood exposed to enemy fire directing men across the mine-swept corridor.[17]

The task remained of getting the tanks inland. A platoon of the 20th Engineer Combat Battalion, landing in support of the 1st Battalion, 16th Infantry, began blowing a larger gap through the minefield with bangalore torpedoes. Mine-detector crews of Company C of the 37th Engineer Battalion followed to widen the lanes to accommodate vehicles. But the tanks could not get past the shingle, where they could get no traction. Behind the shingle lay a deep antitank ditch. Pvt. Vinton Dove, a bulldozer operator of Company C, made the first efforts to overcome these obstacles, assisted by his relief operator, Pvt. William J. Shoemaker, who alternated with him in driving and guiding the bulldozer. Dove cleared a

[16] Hist 37th Engr C Bn, Mar 43−Aug 44.

[17] Ibid. Simon received the Silver Star, Peckham the Bronze Star.

ENGINEERS ANCHOR REINFORCED TRACK *for vehicles coming ashore at Omaha.*

road through the shingle, pulled out roadblocks at Exit E−1, and began working on the antitank ditch, which was soon filled with the help of dozer operators from Company B and a company of the 149th Engineer Combat Battalion that had landed near E−1 by mistake. The pioneer efforts of Dove and Shoemaker in the face of severe enemy fire, which singled out the bulldozer as a prime target, won for both men the Distinguished Service Cross.[18]

Company C's 1st Lt. Robert P. Ross won the third of the three Distinguished Service Crosses awarded to men of the

37th on D-day for his contribution to silencing the heavy fire coming from a hill overlooking Exit E−1. Assuming command of a leaderless infantry company, Ross took the infantrymen, along with his own engineer platoon, up the slopes to the crest, where the troops engaged the enemy, killed forty Germans, and forced the surrender of two machine-gun emplacements.[19] Cleared fairly early, the E−1 exit became the principal egress from OMAHA Beach on D-day, largely due to the exertions of the 37th Engineer Combat Battalion. The unit suffered the heaviest casualties among the components of the 5th

---

[18] Hist 20th Engr C Bn, Jun 44; Operation Rpt NEPTUNE, pp. 87, 92; Recommendations for Awards, 5th ESB, Aug−Oct 44.

[19] Hist 37th Engr C Bn.

Engineer Special Brigade—twenty-four men killed, including the battalion commander.

Exit E−3 yielded only slowly to the persistence of the engineer troops in the area, including Company A, 37th Engineer Combat Battalion. Still under accurate if intermittent artillery fire around 1630, the beach remained unmarked for incoming boat traffic, as the shelling tore down the signposts as soon as they were erected. By 1700 the 348th Engineer Combat Battalion had cleared the lateral road along the beach of mines, and the members of both battalions moved to the base of the uplands to begin work in the draw, already choked with wrecked American tanks and half-tracks. Night drew on as the men opened the road leading up from the beach. A particularly troublesome 88-mm. gun interfered with their work until dark, and Capt. Louis J. Drnovich, commanding Company A, 37th Engineers, determined that he "would get that gun or else." Taking only his carbine and a few grenades, he set off up the hill. His body was found three days later a short distance from where he had started. The exit carried its first tank traffic over the hill to Colleville at 0100 on D plus 1, but trucks could not negotiate the road until morning.[20]

By that time, tanks were moving to Colleville through Exit F−1, easternmost in the 16th Infantry's sector and close to bluffs dominating Fox Red. This was the sector where many troops of the first assault waves, including some of the 116th Regimental Combat Team, had landed as a result of the easterly tidal current. The task of opening Exit F−1 belonged to the 336th Engineer Battalion Beach Group, which was scheduled to land after 1200 on D-day at Easy Red near E−3 and then march east to Fox Red. Some of the advance elements went ashore on E−3 at 1315 and made their way toward their objective through wreckage on the beach, falling flat when enemy fire came in and running during the lulls.[21]

Heavy enemy fire drove away two LCTs carrying three platoons of Company C, and the platoons landed at the end of OMAHA farthest from the Fox beaches. An artillery shell hit one LCT; the other struck a sandbar. Both finally grounded off the Dog beaches between Les Moulins and Vierville—the most strongly fortified part of OMAHA, where stone-walled summer villas afforded protection to German machine gunners and snipers and the cliffs at the westward end at Pointe de la Percee provided excellent observation points for artillery positions behind the two resorts. This was the area of the 116th Regimental Combat Team, whose engineer combat battalions—the 112th, 121st, and 147th—suffered severely during the landings.

Survivors of the first sections of the 147th Engineer Combat Battalion to come in on Dog White at 0710 joined infantrymen in the fight for Vierville or climbed the cliffs with the Rangers. At midmorning the battalion commander, concerned about a growing congestion of tanks and vehicles on Dog Green, ordered all his units to concentrate on blowing open Exit D−1, blocked by a concrete revetment. They set to work, collecting explosives from dead bodies and wrecked vessels, and with

---

[20] Operation Rpt NEPTUNE, p. 101; De Arman, Hist 5th ESB. Drnovich was awarded the Silver Star posthumously.

[21] Hist 336th Engr C Bn, 25 Jul 42–31 Aug 44.

the help of men of the 121st Engineer Combat Battalion, who had mislanded on Easy Green and had made their way to Dog Green, were able to open the exit, but it was not fully usable until 2100. At Exit D−3, the Les Moulins draw between Dog Red and Easy Green, the 112th Engineer Combat Battalion commander was killed early on D-day, and the men were pinned down by enemy fire behind a seawall. Even with the assistance of a platoon of the 147th, which came in with most of its equipment during the day, the 112th Battalion was not able to open Exit D−3 until 2000.[22]

Wading ashore at Dog Green about 1500, troops of the 336th Engineer Combat Battalion assembled at the shingle bank and began a hazardous march toward Fox Red, more than two miles away. The unit moved in a long irregular column, followed by a D−7 tractor that towed an Athey trailer loaded with explosives. As the battalion made its way around bodies and wreckage through smoke and gunfire, it witnessed the awful panorama of D-day on OMAHA. Artillery fire had decreased at Exit D−1 after destroyers knocked out a strongpoint on Pointe de la Percee about noon. It grew heavier as engineers approached Exit D−3, several times narrowly missing the explosive-laden trailer. At E−1 the fire let up, but congestion on the beach increased. Bulldozers were clearing a road through the shingle embankment, and the beach flat was jammed with vehicles waiting to join a line moving up the hill toward St. Laurent. DUKWs with 105-mm. howitzers were beginning to come in;

the first (and only) artillery mission of the day from the beach was fired at 1615 against a machine-gun nest near Colleville.

The worst spot they encountered on the beach was at Exit E−3, still under fire as they passed. There the 336th Battalion's column ran into such heavy machine-gun fire and artillery shelling that the unit had to halt. The commander sent the men forward two at a time; when about half had gone through the area, a shell hit a bulldozer working at the shingle bank. The dozer began to burn, sending up clouds of smoke that covered the gap and enabled the rest of the men to dash across. As the troops proceeded down the beach, they saw a tank nose over the dune line and fire about twenty-five rounds at a German machine-gun emplacement, knocking it out; but artillery barrages continued hitting the beach in front of E−3 every fifteen or twenty minutes.

At the end of its "memorable and terrible" march across OMAHA, during which two men were killed by shell fragments and twenty-seven were injured, the engineer column reached the comparative safety of the F−1 area at 1700. The surrounding hills had been cleared of machine-gun nests, and although enemy artillery was able to reach the tidal flat, it could not hit the beach. The first job was mine clearance: the area was still so heavily mined that several tanks, one of them equipped with a dozer blade, could not get off the beach. The men had only one mine detector but were able to assemble several more from damaged detectors the infantry had left on the beach. More were salvaged when the last elements of the battalion came in from Dog Green around 1730. After they had cleared the fields

[22] Hists, 147th Engr C Bn, 29 Jan 43−4 Mar 46; 121st, 1 Jun−31 Aug 44; and 112th, 1944.

near the beach of mines and a tank-dozer had filled in an antitank ditch, the teams began to work up a hill with a tractor following, opening the F−1 exit. Tanks began climbing the hill at 2000; two struck mines, halting the movement for about an hour, but by 2230 fifteen tanks had passed through the exit to the Colleville area to help the infantry clear the town.[23]

Brig. Gen. William M. Hoge, commanding general of the Provisional Engineer Special Brigade Group, had landed at Exit E−1 shortly after 1500 and had set up a command post in a concrete pillbox just west of the exit; from there he assumed engineer command responsibility from the 5th Engineer Special Brigade commander, Col. Doswell Gullatt. As units of the 6th Engineer Special Brigade reverted to that unit, additional infantry units were landing to support the 116th and the 16th Infantry. The 115th, ahead of schedule and also carried eastward, landed in the middle of the 18th Infantry, east of the St. Laurent draw. This produced some confusion, but the new strength swelled the advance moving slowly off the beaches by evening. In the morning of D plus 1 vehicular traffic, infantry, and engineers alike were moving through the exits, off the beaches, and over the hills. By that time the 4th Infantry Division of Force U had penetrated the German defenses some ten miles to the west at UTAH Beach.[24]

*Utah*

As the first assault elements transfer-red into landing craft a dozen miles off UTAH, alarmed German local commanders were trying to fathom the intentions and to gauge the strength of the paratroopers that had dropped into their midst around 0130. Separated in the cloud cover over the Cotentin peninsula while evading German antiaircraft fire, the transport aircraft headed for partially marked drop zones astride the Merderet River and the area between Ste. Mere-Eglise and UTAH itself. Scattered widely in the drop, the troopers of the 82d and 101st Airborne Divisions struggled to concentrate their strength and find their objectives. The 82d had one regiment fairly consolidated from the start east of the Merderet. The division took the town of Ste. Mere-Eglise with mixed contingents, some troops from the 101st working with the 82d even as glider-borne reinforcements came in shortly before dawn. The 101st Airborne Division, equally dispersed, managed to mass enough of its own men and troopers of the 82d who fell into its area of responsibility to secure the western edges of the inundated land behind UTAH and the all-important causeway entrances on that side of the German beach defenses. With German strength threatening the landing zone from across the Douve River to the south, the paratroopers could not muster enough men to control or destroy all the bridges across the river. Engineers of Company C, 326th Airborne Engineer Battalion, rigged some for destruction, and small groups held out nearly all of D-day in the face of German units south of the stream, awaiting relief by other airborne units or by the main body of the invasion. Their losses and their disorganization notwithstanding, the paratroops had thoroughly confused the

[23] Hist 336th Engr C Bn, 25 Jul 42–31 Aug 44; Operation Rpt NEPTUNE, pp. 98–100; War Dept, Hist Div, *Omaha Beachhead,* pp. 101–06.

[24] Operation Rpt NEPTUNE, pp. 96, 102–03.

German defenders and engaged their reserves, especially the veterans of the *91st Division,* far from the beaches.[25]

Compared with OMAHA, UTAH was practically a walkover. Owing to the smoke of the prelanding bombardment and the loss of two small Navy control vessels marking the line of departure off the beach, the entire first wave of the 8th Infantry's assault grounded 2,000 yards south of its intended landfall. The operation of UTAH shifted to the left of the original beaches, fortuitously striking a shoreline far less heavily defended and with much sparser obstacle belts than expected. (*Map 17*)

Engineer demolitions were to begin at 0635, five minutes after the infantry landing. The teams involved were under an ad hoc Beach Obstacle Demolition Party commanded by Maj. Herschel E. Linn, also the commanding officer of the 237th Engineer Combat Battalion. Underwater obstacles above the low tide line were the targets of the first demolition units, eight sixteen-man naval teams, each including five Army engineers. Eight of the twelve available 26-man Army demolition teams were to land ten minutes later, directly behind eight LCTs carrying the dozer tanks to be used on the beach. Navy and Army teams were to clear eight fifty-yard gaps through the beach obstructions for the subsequent waves, and the fourth and fifth waves of the assault would bring in the remainder of the engineers to help clear the area as necessary. Linn and his executive officer, Capt. Robert P. Tabb, Jr., planned to supervise the beach operations from their M−29 Weasels, small tracked

cargo vehicles capable of negotiating sand and surf.[26]

The plan came apart immediately. Army and Navy teams landed almost simultaneously between 0635 and 0645. On the run to the beach, Major Linn's craft was sunk off Uncle Red; he did not arrive ashore until the following day. Captain Tabb, now in command, drove his Weasel off the LCT on Tare Green and felt it sink beneath him. He salvaged the radio after getting the crew out and made for the beach, where he encountered Brig. Gen. Theodore Roosevelt, Jr., assistant commander of the 4th Infantry Division, walking up and down the seawall back of UTAH and directing operations. At the time enemy fire was so much lighter than expected that the landing seemed to Tabb almost an anticlimax. Except for six Army engineers, who were killed when a shell hit their LCM just as the ramp dropped, all the demolition men got ashore safely and immediately began to blast gaps in the obstacles. About half were steel and concrete stakes, some with mines attached to the top; the rest were mostly hedgehogs and steel tetrahedrons, with only a few Belgian gates.[27]

The four Army gapping support teams landed on the northern part of Tare Green Beach at 0645 after a harrowing trip from the transport area. They had been aboard an attack transport with the commanding officer of the 1106th Engineer Combat Group, Col. Thomas DeF. Rogers. Rogers discovered at the last minute that no provi-

---

[25] Dept of the Army, Hist Div, *Utah Beach to Cherbourg,* pp. 14−42; Chester Wilmot, *The Struggle for Europe* (New York: Harper, 1952), p. 245.

[26] Dept of the Army, Hist Div, *Utah Beach to Cherbourg,* p. 47; Engr Opns VII Corps, vol. II, "Normandy," pp. 9−10; Hist 1106th Engr C Gp, Jun−Dec 44; Jnl, 237th Engr C Bn, Jun 44; Interv, Capt Roland G. Ruppenthal with Maj Robert P. Tabb, Jr., 6 Sep 44, ML 1032, ETOUSA Hist Sect.

[27] Interv, Tabb, 6 Sep 44.

sion had been made for getting the reserve teams ashore, and he arranged with the ship's commander to load the whole party of ninety-three men, with explosives, into a single LCM. Rogers went along in the dangerously over-loaded craft, proceeding shoreward at full speed. Landing in an area where no gap had been blown, he got the men to work and then walked southward down the beach to inspect the work the leading teams were doing. The Army and Navy teams had partly blown fifty-yard gaps, which Rogers instructed them to widen to accommodate the landing craft bunching up offshore. He saw two tankdozers in use but observed that gaps were cleared mainly by hand-placed charges connected with prima-cord.

The work went on under artillery fire that increased at both the southern and northern gaps after H-hour. Rogers and others were deeply impressed by the heroism of the men, but casualties were light compared to those on OMA-HA. The Army teams had 6 men killed, 39 wounded; the Navy teams, 4 killed and 11 wounded. The initial gaps were cleared by 0715. Then the demolition-ists worked northward, widening cleared areas and helping demolish a seawall. By 0930 UTAH Beach was free of all obstacles. The Navy teams went out on the flat with the second ebb tide and worked until nightfall on the flanks of the beaches, while by noon the Army teams were ready to assist the assault engineers in opening exit roads.[28]

While the demolitionists were blow-ing the obstacles, Companies A and C of the 237th Engineer Combat Battal-ion, which had landed with the 8th Infantry at H-hour, were blowing gaps in the seawall, removing wire, and clear-ing paths through sand dunes beyond. For these tasks the two companies had bangalore torpedoes, mine detectors, explosives, pioneer tools, and markers. Later in the morning they received equipment to bulldoze roads across the dunes.[29]

Beyond the dunes was the water bar-rier, running a mile or so inland from Quineville on the north to Pouppeville on the south, which the Germans had created by reversing the action of the locks that the French had constructed to convert salt marshes into pasture-land. Seven causeways crossed the wet area in the region of the UTAH landings to connect the beach with a north-south inland road. Not all the causeways were usable on D-day. Most were under water; the northernmost, although dry, was too close to German artillery. The best exits were at or near the area where the troops had landed—another stroke of good fortune. Exit T−5, just north of Tare Green Beach, was flooded but had a hard surface and was used dur-ing the night of D-day. Exit U−5 at Uncle Red was above water for its entire length and became the first route in-land, leading to the village of Ste. Marie-du-Mont. South of U−5, some distance down the coast near Pouppe-ville and the Douve River, lay the third road used on D-day, Exit V−1. Al-though in poor condition, the road was almost completely dry.[30]

[28] Ltr, Col Thomas DeF. Rogers to Engr, VII Corps, 23 Jun 44, sub: Report on Demolition of UTAH Beach Obstacles, 237th Engr C Bn Jnl, 1944; Commo. James E. Arnold, "NOIC UTAH," *United States Naval Institute Proceedings*, LXXIII (June 1947), 675; Hist 1st ESB (UTAH), sec. VII, p. 67; Interv, Tabb, 6 Sep 44.

[29] Interv, Tabb, 6 Sep 44.
[30] Engr Opns VII Corps, vol. II, "Normandy," p. 12; 1st ESB (UTAH), p. 52.

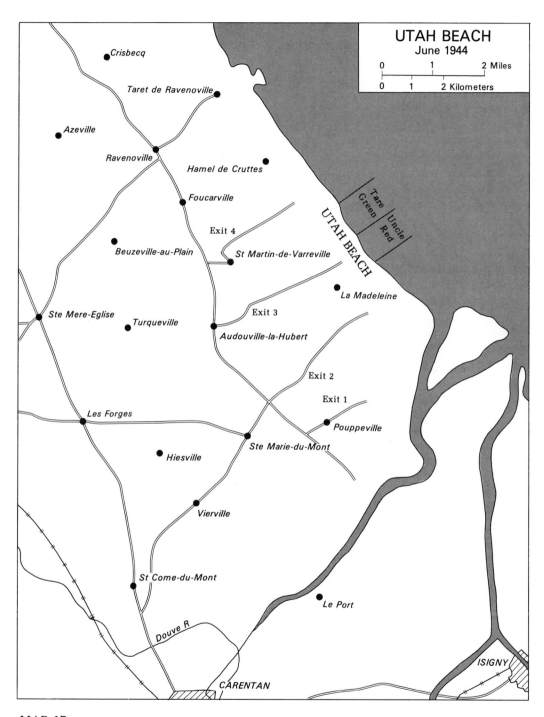

UTAH BEACH
June 1944

0      1      2 Miles
0    1    2 Kilometers

Crisbecq

Taret de Ravenoville

Azeville

Ravenoville

Hamel de Cruttes

Foucarville

Exit 4

Beuzeville-au-Plain

St Martin-de-Varreville

Tare | Uncle
Green | Red

UTAH BEACH

La Madeleine

Exit 3

Ste Mere-Eglise

Turqueville

Audouville-la-Hubert

Exit 2

Exit 1

Les Forges

Pouppeville

Ste Marie-du-Mont

Hiesville

Vierville

St Come-du-Mont

Le Port

Douve R

ISIGNY

CARENTAN

*MAP 17*

TELLER MINE ATOP A STAKE *emplaced to impale landing craft on Utah Beach.*

At the entrance to Exit U−5 the Germans had emplaced two Belgian gates. Company A, 237th Engineer Combat Battalion, blew them and also picked up several prisoners from pillboxes along the seawall. Then the engineers accompanied the 3d Battalion, 8th Infantry, inland along Exit U−5. Halfway across the causeway they found that the Germans had blown a concrete culvert over a small stream. The column forded the stream and proceeded, leaving Captain Tabb to deal with the culvert. He brought up a bridge truck and a platoon of Company B to begin constructing a thirty-foot treadway bridge—the first bridge built in the

UTAH bridgehead. Men of the 238th Engineer Combat Battalion, who had landed around 1000 with the main body of the 1106th Engineer Combat Group, helped. By 1435, Exit U−5 was open to traffic.[31]

Two companies of the 49th Engineer Combat Battalion, also landing with the 1106th in midmorning, accompanied the 2d Battalion, 8th Infantry, on its march south to Pouppeville. The engineers were to work on Exit V−1 leading from the beach through Pouppeville to the north-south inland road, while infantry was to make contact with the 101st Airborne Division, protecting the southern flank of VII Corps. Company G of the 8th Infantry also had the mission of capturing the sluice gates or locks southeast of Pouppeville that the Germans had manipulated to flood the pastureland behind Tare Green and Uncle Red beaches. An enemy strongpoint still farther south at Le Grand Vey protected the locks.[32]

While Company E of the 8th Infantry moved down the road along the eastern edge of the inundations, Company G hugged the seawall. All the way down the coast the two companies encountered continuous small-arms fire, and Company G met artillery fire from a strongpoint on the seaward side about halfway down. At a road junction northeast of Pouppeville, the infantry battalion assembled and advanced to the village, where shortly after noon occurred the first meeting of seaborne and airborne troops on D-day.

---

[31] Interv, Tabb, 6 Sep 44; Hists, 238th and 237th Engr C Bns and 1106th Engr C Gp.
[32] Hist 1106th Engr C Gp, Jun–Dec 44; 1st ESB (UTAH), p. 65; Dept of the Army, Hist Div, *Utah Beach to Cherbourg,* map 8.

During the probe to Pouppeville the infantrymen bypassed the sluice gates. But Company A of the 49th Engineer Combat Battalion moved south, secured the locks, took twenty-eight prisoners, and dug in to protect the locks from recapture. Next day the company overcame the German strongpoint at Le Grand Vey, capturing fifty-nine prisoners, seventeen tons of ammunition, large quantities of small arms, and three artillery pieces, which the engineers used to reinforce their defenses. During the next few days, with the aid of a platoon of Company B, Company A continued to hold its position, protecting the south flank of the beachhead and operating the locks to drain the water barrier.[33]

Except for the 49th Engineer Combat Battalion, which bivouacked near Pouppeville, all elements of the 1106th Engineer Combat Group including the beach obstacle demolitionists went into bivouac on the night of D-day at Pont-Hebert, a village on the north-south inland road about halfway between causeways U−5 and V−1. Total D-day casualties for the group had been seven men killed and fifty-four wounded. For a few days work on the exits continued, but the next major task for the group was to help the 101st Airborne Division cross the Douve River. Improving the causeways, clearing and developing Tare Green and Uncle Red, and opening new beaches then became the responsibility of the 1st Engineer Special Brigade.[34]

When Brig. Gen. James E. Wharton, commanding the 1st Engineer Special Brigade, landed on UTAH at 0730 on D-day he found his deputy, Col. Eugene M. Caffey, already on the beach. Not scheduled to land until 0900, Caffey had smuggled himself, with no equipment except an empty rifle, aboard an 8th Infantry landing craft. En route he managed to load his rifle by taking up a collection of one bullet each from eight infantrymen. He arrived ashore very early in the assault and found General Roosevelt in a huddle with infantry battalion commanders, debating whether to bring later waves in on the actual place of landing or to divert them to the beaches originally planned. Men of the 8th Infantry were already moving inland on Exit U−5. The decision was made. "I'm going ahead with the troops," Roosevelt told Caffey. "You get word to the Navy to bring them in. We're going to start the war from here."[35]

The first elements of the 1st Engineer Special Brigade to land were men of the 1st and 2d Battalions, 531st Engineer Shore Regiment, who came in about the same time as Wharton. They set to work widening gaps the combat engineers had blown in the seawall, searching out mines, improving exits, and undertaking reconnaissance. Because one of the main tasks of the engineer regiment was to open Sugar Red, a new beach to the north of Tare Green, the officers reconnoitered the area, and elements of the 2d Battalion partially cleared it in preparation for its complete clearance and operation by the 3d Battalion, scheduled to arrive on the second tide. The brigade headquarters

---

[33] Hists, 49th Engr C Bn, Jun, Jul, Dec 44, and 1106th Engr C Gp, Jun−Dec 44; Dept of the Army, Hist Div, *Utah Beach to Cherbourg*, p. 53.

[34] Hist 1106th Engr C Gp, Jun−Dec 44.

[35] 1st ESB (UTAH), p. 63; Ryan, *The Longest Day*, pp. 205, 233. Ryan based his account on an interview with Caffey.

ROADS LEADING OFF THE BEACHES *opened by engineers, 8 June 1944.*

was ashore by noon, and at 1400 Wharton established his command post in a German pillbox at La Grande Dune, a small settlement just beyond the dune line and near the entrance to Exit U−5.

Less than half of the road-building equipment the engineers counted on reached shore on D-day. Twelve LCTs were expected, but only five landed safely, all on the second tide. German shells hit three of the remainder, and the other four were delayed until D plus 1. Many engineer vehicles drowned out when they dropped into water too deep; hauling out such vehicles of all services was one of the heaviest engineer tasks on D-day, and a good deal of the work had to be done under artillery fire.

Artillery accounted for most of the D-day casualties in the brigade—twenty-one killed and ninety-six wounded; strafing by enemy planes, which came over in the evening, caused most of the rest.

By nightfall of D-day the brigade engineers had opened Sugar Red, and had made the road leading inland from it (Exit T−5) passable for vehicles. They had cleared beaches of wrecked vehicles and mines, had improved the existing lateral beach road with chespaling (wood and wire matting), and had set up markers. The brigade's military police were helping traffic move inland. The engineers had also estab·lished dumps for ammunition and medi·

cal supplies and had found sites for other dumps behind the beaches.[36]

Despite the doubts and fears of the early hours on OMAHA, the invasion was successful. To be sure, the troops were nearly everywhere behind schedule and nowhere near their objectives behind OMAHA, but at UTAH the entire 4th Division got ashore within fifteen hours after H-hour with 20,000 men and 1,700 vehicles. In the UTAH area, the fighting remained largely concentrated in battalion-size actions and scattered across the segments of French terrain tenuously held by American airborne units. Nevertheless, the Allied forces had a strong grip on a beachhead on the Continent, and German counterattacks were feeble at best. The job of the next few days was to consolidate the flow of supply across the beaches and through the artificial port complex that the invasion force had brought with it across the Channel. Despite the tragic losses among the gapping teams and the collapse of their efforts on D-day, the Provisional Engineer Special Brigade Group by D plus 1 had provided the early basis for the supply organization on the beaches that would operate until the end of the year. Backlogs of invasion shipping fed by factors beyond the engineers' control developed immediately off both beaches, and the limited numbers of trucks and DUKWs available affected supply movement just behind the shore. But on balance, the engineers' contribution in ingenuity and blood in the Normandy assault was immeasurable.

[36] 1st ESB (UTAH), pp. 63–69; Hist 531st Engr Shore Rgt, 6–17 Jun 44.

# CHAPTER XVI

# Developing Beaches and Reconstructing Ports

Once the invasion force was ashore the engineers of the Provisional Engineer Special Brigade Group entered upon a three-phased schedule for organizing beach supply operations. The first two phases were tied directly to the tactical situation since they involved setting up dumps on the beaches and later moving the dumps to protected sites as much as four miles inland. The last phase would begin with the completion of the MULBERRY, an artificial harbor to be made of sunken blockships and concrete caissons offshore, providing more efficient discharge of cargoes and men directly from pierhead structures to the beaches at OMAHA via floating roadways. UTAH, with more limited constructed facilities serving it, would continue to receive heavy traffic in men and materiel from lighters, the various landing craft, makeshift Rhino ferries, and barges plying between larger vessels and the beach. Gradually, as captured ports came into service, the logistic load would shift there, and the MULBERRY complex would close down before the autumnal storms interfered with the operation.[1] No clear-cut dividing line

separated these activities, and, in fact, they tended to overlap each other as shore engineers developed the supply system. While the engineers organized the beaches into administrative subdivisions, providing roads to the water's edge and laying out supply areas just inland, Transportation Corps troops would help unload cargo, move supplies to depots or using units, and control traffic on and behind the beaches. The Transportation Corps would also operate smaller captured ports in the area once the engineers had cleared obstacles and mines and restored dockside equipment and storage space.

The initial dump phase demanded a clear marking scheme for all the beaches in both landing areas. The Provisional Engineer Special Brigade Group followed the so-called British World Wide System, extending the military alphabet and color codes already in use on the invasion beaches. By 1600 on 8 June the engineers had subdivided the original Easy Red and Fox Red beaches on OMAHA into two more beaches, Easy White and Fox White. Each sector was marked with large, color-coded wooden panels. For night identification the OMAHA beaches first had lights blinking the Morse code for Dog, Easy, or Fox. When this system caused confusion,

---

[1] Unless otherwise noted the following is based chiefly on Ruppenthal, *Logistical Support of the Armies, Volume I*, pp. 389–426; Operation Rpt NEPTUNE; and Morison, *The Invasion of France and Germany*, p. 162.

TETRAHEDRONS AT OMAHA BEACH

the brigades erected signboards with nine-foot-high lettering outlined in colored lights matching the beach names. On UTAH, the 1st Brigade resorted to hanging barrage balloons directly over the beaches, painting them to correspond to the coding of Uncle Red and Tare Green. They added a second red balloon above Sugar Red, opened to the right of Tare Green by the 531st Engineer Shore Regiment.[2]

During the week after D-day the engineers also cleared the OMAHA beaches and improved the roads running the length of the beach and up through the draws. The men could only cut paths through the debris in some spots. The gapping team survivors from the 149th and the 299th Engineer Combat Battalions joined the group engineers in clearing junk and salvaging vehicles. Bulldozer crews either assisted in this work or leveled the shingle bank, using the stones and wreckage to fill in antitank ditches. At UTAH other German forces withdrawing up the Cotentin peninsula toward Cherbourg kept the beaches under artillery fire for a week after the landings, but the main difficulty in managing supply was the lack of dump space in the low fields behind the beach. Though drainage operations began on D-day in the Pouppeville area when 1106th Engineer Combat Group

[2] The Adm and Log Hist of the ETO, vol. VI, "Neptune: Training for Mounting the Operation, and Artificial Ports," pp. 68–71.

units reset the locks there to draw off the flood behind the southern end of the beach, the terrain was still too marshy to support the weight of large amounts of supplies and the vehicles necessary to move them.

Confusion offshore and unbending adherence to the NEPTUNE plan added to the delay in unloading. Until D plus 4 First Army plans called for the discharge of items according to a rigid priority system. But shipping manifests identifying priority cargoes and vessels did not reach the proper hands among Transportation Corps crews or the Navy officer in charge of beach operations. Engineer brigade officers at first joined naval officers and transportation troops in small launches in time-consuming searches for specific ships but later simply took the nearest vessels ready for discharge. The Navy refused to beach LSTs for fear of German artillery fire at UTAH and in the belief that they would break their keels as they settled onto the uneven tidal flats. Once the latter worry proved unfounded, LSTs after D plus 2 "dried out" regularly—the vessels would ground just after high tide, discharge their cargo onto the dry flat after the water receded, and pull off again with the next tide. This method slowed the shipping shuttle between the beaches and the mounting out ports in southern England because it took twelve hours to refloat the craft. Nevertheless, it did more than any other single expedient to reduce the shipping backlog off Normandy and to boost the lagging discharge rates of troops, supply, and vehicles before segments of the MULBERRY harbor came into full service.

The arrival at UTAH on 10 June of the 38th Engineer General Service Regiment, an Advance Section (ADSEC)

unit attached to the 1st Engineer Special Brigade, heralded the beginning of the beach maintenance phase of engineer operations. The regiment was to work behind the beaches, removing mines, improving roads and bridges, and draining flooded areas. One battalion had the task of opening a fourth beach, Roger White, to the north of Sugar Red. Blasting holes in the seawall and clearing beach obstacles from the tidal flat, the battalion had the new sector ready for operation two days later on 12 June, but shellfire from German batteries to the north postponed the opening of Roger White. The enemy opposition there also stopped work on the northernmost sluice gates behind UTAH until mid-June, though the southernmost gates, in the area where most of the landings were made, were already functioning when the 38th arrived. On 13 June the regiment could report that all roads in its area were open and passable.[3]

Beach maintenance dumps of the 5th and 6th Engineer Special Brigades, located along the Isigny-Bayeux road, were ready for operation on 13 and 14 June. By then the fields were clear of mines and, after the capture of Trevieres on 10 June, of enemy resistance except for scattered sniper fire. The dumps were located in a series of relatively small fields divided by hedgerows, small trees, and drainage ditches. The engineers filled the trenches and cut gaps through the hedgerows to allow trucks to move from field to field and to relieve congestion on narrow roads.

As combat troops inland eliminated the last direct German fire on OMAHA on D plus 4, the buildup on shore took

---

[3] Hist 38th Engr GS Rgt, 1944.

TWISTED SECTIONS OF LOBNITZ PIERS AT OMAHA BEACH

impetus from the gradual completion of artificial harbor installations and their protective breakwaters—a line of sunken ships known as a GOOSEBERRY. Naval construction elements opened two 2,450-foot causeways on each of the major invasion beaches by 10 June, the spans at OMAHA coming in at Exits E−1 and F−1. Two days later, when General Bradley stood on OMAHA, the sight of the massive construction off the beaches convinced him that the invasion area had become the major port of Europe.

On 12 June the influx of men and supply still lagged behind the planned figures: just over 17,000 troops landed with 22,869 called for; only 9,896 long tons of supply arrived ashore compared to the 12,700 tons planned; and 2,645 of the more than 4,000 vehicles scheduled for the day arrived. With VII Corps ready to begin cutting off the Cotentin peninsula and isolating Cherbourg, an ammunition shortage, especially in artillery shells, was already developing. Cumulative totals among the various categories of discharge were 88 percent of the planned troops, 73 percent of the supply tonnage, and 66 percent of the vehicles. But on 16 June hopes rose for meeting unloading schedules as the first LST nosed up to the Lobnitz pierhead off OMAHA and discharged its load of vehicles directly to shore via a 3,000-foot "whale," or floating roadway, in just under two hours. Not the least elated was Col. Richard

Whitcomb, whose 11th Port organization was manning the pierheads while attached to the Provisional Engineer Special Brigade Group. But the optimism died on the eighteenth, as nature began reducing the American MULBERRY to ruins.[4]

Unloading slowed to a crawl from 19 to 22 June while a howling Channel storm tore the harbor apart, driving smaller vessels into causeways, pierheads, and whale structures and casting the wreckage ashore in tangled heaps of caissons, coasters, and landing craft. The engineers managed to get a total of 2,557 long tons of cargo out of beached craft during the four days. In several cases, as with the coaster *Highware,* the men resorted to cutting holes in ships' sides to get at the holds. The more fortunate British MULBERRY, farther east, rode out the storm without extensive damage. The debris at UTAH was not heavy, but the engineer brigades at OMAHA faced the same beach clearance problem on 22 June that they had on the seventh.

Clearance and salvage now vied with the rush to unload necessary men and supply in the days after the storm. All LSTs dried out on the Fox beaches at OMAHA, where there was less wreckage. By using every available LCT, LCM, and DUKW to ferry material from ship to shore, the brigades began to realize a potential for moving supply and troops across an open beach that the planners apparently had not recognized. DUKWs, which had all escaped the storm's effect by hastening ashore to wait out the weather, were invaluable at both beaches. Tonnage figures exceeded the

planned daily tables consistently between 24 and 30 June although the discharge rate never caught up with cumulative figures expected. By the end of the month the troop buildup had reached 452,460, roughly 78 percent of the estimated 579,000 that should have been ashore on that date. Supplies amounted to 80 percent of the 360,000 long tons scheduled, and the 70,910 vehicles unloaded were only 65 percent of the 111,000 First Army expected by D plus 24. Despite the lag, the engineers had recovered remarkably well from the devastation of the storm and had sustained operations on the beaches as the fighting moved toward Cherbourg and, south of the beaches, into the hedgerow country of Normandy. In the meantime some measure of help in supplementing the over-the-beach supply operations came with the rehabilitation of several minor ports in the area.

### Small Ports Near the Beaches

OVERLORD planning had taken into consideration six minor ports: Grandcamp-les-Bains and Isigny just west of OMAHA; St. Vaast-la-Hougue and Barfleur north of UTAH; Granville on the west coast of the Cotentin peninsula; and St. Malo in Brittany. All these ports were tidal, drying out at low water; even at high tide they could accommodate only small vessels. Therefore, their capacity was not expected to be great, and they were to be developed only as a stop-gap measure to provide some additional discharge facilities until the full potential of larger ports could be realized. All minor ports were to be open by 6 July. *(Map 18)*

According to the plan of the ADSEC engineer, Colonel Itschner, who was

---

[4] Bradley, *A Soldier's Story,* p. 289; Operation Rpt NEPTUNE, pp. 12, 144; Alfred Stanford, *Force Mulberry* (New York: William Morrow, 1951), pp. 139, 171.

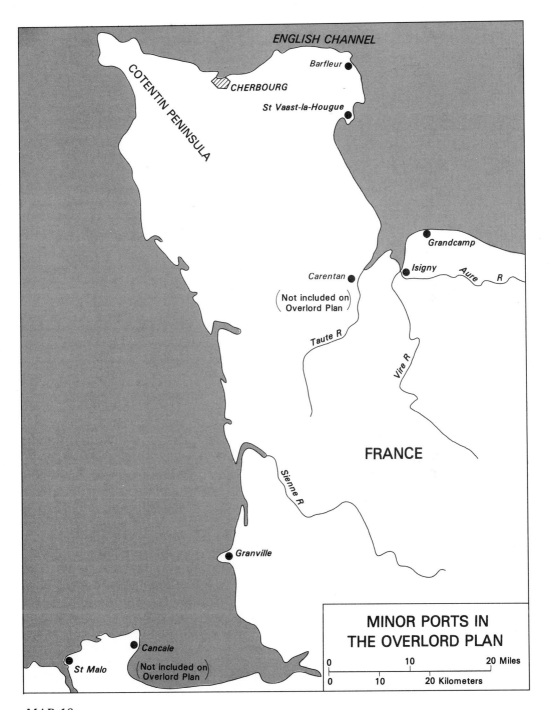

ENGLISH CHANNEL

*Barfleur*

CHERBOURG

COTENTIN PENINSULA

*St Vaast-la-Hougue*

*Grandcamp*

*Isigny*  *Aure*  R

*Carentan*

(Not included on
Overlord Plan)

*Taute R*

*Vire R*

*Sienne R*

FRANCE

*Granville*

MINOR PORTS IN
THE OVERLORD PLAN

0          10          20 Miles

0    10    20 Kilometers

*Cancale*

(Not included on
Overlord Plan)

*St Malo*

*MAP 18*

responsible for opening the ports, the headquarters of the 1055th Port Construction and Repair Group and advance elements of the group's 342d Engineer General Service Regiment were to tackle the repair of the ports in turn, beginning with Grandcamp and Isigny. After rehabilitation, operation of these two small ports near OMAHA would be the responsibility of the 11th Port (TC), attached to the Provisional Engineer Special Brigade Group. The 11th Port was also to furnish a detachment to the 1st Engineer Special Brigade to operate St. Vaast, while the 4th Port (TC) was to supervise operations at Barfleur, Granville, and St. Malo.[5]

Access to Grandcamp, a small fishing port and summer resort about five miles west of OMAHA, was through a fifty-foot-wide channel between two jetties. The jetties extended from the beach for about 350 feet to the port proper, a rectangular artificial basin with a concrete wharf and one quay. From the information available, planners had estimated the minimum high-tide depth of channel and basin at eight feet, making it possible to bring in LCTs and small coasters. Because the little port was so vulnerable to enemy demolitions the engineers were not sure that it could be used at all, but they hoped it could be opened by 20 June, with a goal of 500 tons of cargo daily thereafter. A TC port company, a quartermaster truck platoon, and an administration detachment from Headquarters, 11th Port, were to operate Grandcamp port.

Grandcamp fell on 9 June. Next morning, while the port was still under sniper fire, Capt. Andrew F. Klase of 11th Port headquarters arrived to survey conditions and was agreeably surprised to find that the Germans had done no damage beyond sinking two hulks across the channel. Five wrecks lay in the basin, probably victims of Allied aircraft. Less agreeable was the discovery that the water in the basin and channel was only 4 1/2 feet deep. The estimate of eight feet, based on old charts, proved wrong because the port had not been dredged in six years. Nevertheless, Captain Klase began the task of rehabilitation, calling in units of the 358th Engineer General Service Regiment, which floated and beached two of the wrecks and blasted apart and hauled away the pieces of the other five. With help from men of the 342d Engineer General Service Regiment, who cleared the port of mines, underwater obstructions, and barbed-wire entanglements, Grandcamp was ready to operate on 17 June. At the time the only men available to operate the port consisted of an administrative staff of four officers and thirty-seven enlisted men from 11th Port.[6]

On 23 June the small Dutch coaster *June* entered the basin—the first Allied ship to berth in a French port in the American sector. Ordered to Isigny, she had entered Grandcamp harbor by mistake, somehow managing without a pilot to navigate the shallow water and treacherous channel and tie up at the quay. As no labor troops had yet reported at Grandcamp, the 11th Port

[5] Unless otherwise cited, this section on the small ports is based on: Ruppenthal, *Logistical Support of the Armies, Volume I*, pp. 62, 288–90, 310, 463–65, and *Volume II*, pp. 61–62; Operation Rpt NEPTUNE, pp. 159–62, 166–69.

[6] Interv, Capt Andrew F. Klase, 1 Jul 44, Adm 493 B, Minor Ports, ETOUSA Hist Sect; Hists, 342d Engr GS Rgt, 15 Apr 42–31 Dec 45 and 358th Engr GS Rgt, 6 Jan 43–30 Jun 45.

men left their typewriters and pitched in to unload her, aided by civilians. By the end of the day the ad hoc labor force had put 158 tons of cargo aboard trucks for movement to inland dumps. Despite the successful berthing of the *June,* coasters could not be handled efficiently at Grandcamp, and only landing craft could be used. Because the basin was too small to permit LCTs to turn around, the best choice was the LBV, a fifty-ton, self-propelled barge able to carry vehicles and supplies. The first came in on 24 June, bringing cargo from vessels anchored off OMAHA. That day the 4145th Quartermaster Service Company arrived to take over unloading, with some continued civilian help. In its eighty-eight days of operations, from 23 June to 19 September (it was the first of the small ports to close), Grandcamp took in 58,382 tons of cargo for an average daily discharge rate of 675 tons, considerably more than the 500 tons expected.[7]

Isigny, a somewhat more prepossessing port, was a small dairying town on the Aure River near where the river flowed into the Vire about ten miles west-southwest of OMAHA. To reach the port from the sea, ships entered the mouth of the Vire and after about three miles turned left into the narrow Aure, which for three-quarters of a mile formed the port channel. Lined on the right almost continuously with stone quays terminating in a small turning basin, the channel contained two or three feet of water at mean low tide and about thirteen feet at high tide, a depth adequate for coaster operations. American forces took Isigny on 10 June, and the next day four officers

from the 11th Port and ADSEC examined the port. They found that the Germans had done no damage but that Allied bombs had sunk a German flak ship and a barge in the channel, blown part of a quay wall, and put the quayside railroad out of commission. The 358th and 342d Engineer General Service Regiments quickly made necessary repairs, and the first coaster arrived on 24 June with 486 tons of cargo, mostly gasoline unloaded by two quartermaster service companies. In its 114 days of operation, until 15 October, Isigny's average daily discharge was 740 tons.[8]

On the east shoulder of the Cotentin peninsula the ports of St. Vaast and Barfleur, left undefended as German forces withdrew toward Cherbourg, were in American hands by 21 June. The more productive was St. Vaast, which had an inner and an outer harbor. While the inner harbor dried out at mean low tide, the outer one could be used at all tides and boasted a breakwater that provided an excellent berthing area for coasters and lighters. The Germans had placed mines across the harbor entrance and had sunk fifteen ships in the harbor. ADSEC engineers removed the major obstacles, and the port began operations on 9 July. Between that date and the closing of the port on 16 October St. Vaast averaged 1,172 tons a day—by far the best record acheived by any minor port. Barfleur was found virtually undamaged, with the only major job that of removing mines across the harbor entrance. In three days the engineers had Barfleur

_____

[7] Klase interv.

_____

[8] Interv. Capt Howard E. Bierkan, HQ, 11th Port, 1 Jul 44, Adm 493 B, Minor Ports, ETOUSA Hist Sect; Hists, 342d Engr GS Rgt, 15 Apr 42–31 Dec 45, and 358th Engr GS Rgt, 6 Jan 43–30 Jun 45.

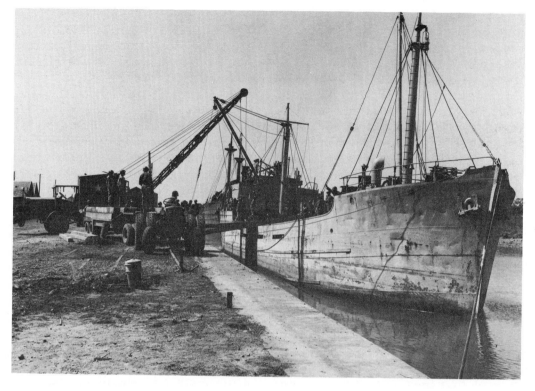

COASTER WITH A CARGO OF GASOLINE UNLOADS AT ISIGNY

ready for operation; the port opened on 26 July.[9]

In late July delays in the rehabilitation of Cherbourg, which was not able to receive cargo until 16 July, brought about renewed interest in all the minor ports. At the time, two of the six ports included in the OVERLORD planning—Granville and St. Malo—were still in enemy hands. ADSEC, therefore, concentrated on improving Grandcamp, Isigny, and St. Vaast and on opening not only Barfleur but also Carentan, which had not been included in OVERLORD planning. ADSEC planners ex-

pected to obtain from the five ports a total discharge of at least 12,000 tons of cargo a day and hoped for 17,000 tons after the ports expanded to their full capacity.[10]

At each port troops of the 2d Battalion, 358th Engineer General Service Regiment, went to work dredging, resurfacing, and improving quays and repairing roads and railroad facilities in the port area. Of these efforts the most important was dredging, and for it the engineers used a French bucket

[9] History of the ADSEC Engineer Section, 7 Sep 44–30 Jun 45, pp. 46–47; Bykofsky and Larson, *The Transportation Corps: Operations Overseas*, p. 238.

[10] Ltr, HQ, ASCZ, to CG, ASCZ, 17 Jul 44, sub: Recommendations for Minor Ports; Ltr, IRS, ADSG, to ADSEC, 26 Jul 44; Condition Rpts, Project P–4 St. Vaast, 27 Sep 44, and 2d Project P–3 Barfleur; all in ADSEC Engr Sect, file Port Hist St. Vaast.

dredge discovered in the British-controlled port of Courseulles. After repairs, the dredge was put to work at Isigny, Grandcamp, and St. Vaast. At Barfleur, a rocky bottom forestalled dredging and restricted the harbor to craft drawing no more than ten feet. Nevertheless, Barfleur did well in its eighty-four days of operation, averaging 803 tons a day. Carentan was disappointing. A small-craft harbor on the Taute River with a passageway to the sea about three times longer than that at Isigny, Carentan opened on 25 July. But after a series of mishaps, including the sinking or grounding of three vessels in the channel, Carentan closed on 31 July having averaged not more than 300 tons a day.[11]

At no time did the small ports, combined, approach the 12,000 tons of cargo per day the logisticians had hoped for. Such a total might have been achieved had the ports been developed more fully, but this step was not necessary. OMAHA and UTAH beaches proved surprisingly successful in delivering cargo, and by early October, when autumn storms showed the need for phasing out beach operations, the engineer port reconstruction effort had concentrated at Cherbourg. There, during most of the autumn of 1944, was to be discharged the bulk of the supplies required to support American forces. By 16 October 1944, Grandcamp, Isigny, St. Vaast, and Barfleur had closed down; on 9 November they reverted to French control. By this time a rear area system of base sections was in place under the COMZ command of General Lee, who took over active control of the rehabilitation efforts at the theater level.

## COMZ on the Continent

No sooner had operations on the Continent begun than the prospect of a breakout from the Allied lodgment and an ensuing war of maneuver raised the issue of control of the communications zone behind First Army. The eventual command structure governing that area would also affect the ETOUSA chief engineer. Invasion plans provided for the introduction of two interim commands prior to the transfer to France of General Lee's SOS, ETOUSA, renamed COMZ as of D-day. On 16 June the first of these, Brig. Gen. Ewart G. Plank's ADSEC organization, went into operation as planned, running supply affairs for First Army under General Bradley's direct control. At the same time ADSEC's parent command, Forward Echelon, Communications Zone, or FECOMZ, began phasing its advance parties into two chateaus near Valognes, twenty miles southwest of Cherbourg. Here Col. Frank M. Albrecht formally announced the existence of the command on 15 July and awaited Bradley's delineation of First Army's rear boundary, the event that would fully activate FECOMZ.[12]

Bradley's announcement was not forthcoming. Under NEPTUNE, he was to establish the army rear boundary around

---

[11] Hist 358th Engr GS Rgt, 6 Jan 43–30 Jun 45; Completion Rpt, Engr Sect, ASCZ, Project P–3 Barfleur, ADSEC Engr Sect, file Port Hist St. Vaast; History of the ADSEC Engineer Section, p. 47.

[12] See ch. XIII; Robert W. Coakley, The Administrative and Logistical History of the European Theater of Operations, vol. II, "Organization and Command in the European Theater of Operations," p. 139, in CMH. General Vaughan, the former commander of FECOMZ, had been reassigned commander of the United Kingdom Base Section on 26 June 1944.

D plus 20, 26 June. The introduction of the Third U.S. Army, scheduled for D plus 41, or 17 July, would necessitate the activation of the U.S. 1st Army Group headquarters on the Continent. On the same day FECOMZ would take over the communications zone from ADSEC, allowing it to advance behind 1st Army Group as the service command immediately to its rear. Dissatisfied over aspects of army supply on D-day and the tactical situation—First Army was entangled in the hedgerows and wetlands of Normandy—Bradley resolved to retain direct control of ADSEC as long as possible. On 20 June, under pressure from the COMZ headquarters still in London, he resorted to a legalism in which he drew a *forward* boundary for ADSEC instead of a *rear* boundary for the army. When COMZ took its case to General Eisenhower for resolution, SHAEF decreed the separation of ADSEC from First Army control on 14 July but did nothing about the rear army boundary, leaving the final say in troop and supply matters to General Bradley.[13]

FECOMZ in the event died aborning. It never fulfilled its role of advance headquarters for Lee's COMZ. It caused considerable confusion during its existence and actually interfered with efficient supply planning although its staff left extensive drafts on the continental system of base sections for future use. Its demise came with the arrival of the entire COMZ at Valognes on 7 August, exactly a month ahead of schedule; Colonel Albrecht's short-lived command simply melded into General Lee's head-

quarters even as the Allied breakout from the invasion lodgment reached full stride. General Lee rapidly took over 560,000 square feet of engineer-built office space and tent quarters for 11,000 individuals in the temporary headquarters at Valognes. But General Bradley surrendered his control of supply and the allocation of service troops among the field armies, ADSEC, and Lee's burgeoning Communications Zone command only when SHAEF arrived on the Continent on 1 September. Bradley, now the commander of the 12th Army Group with the First and Third Armies attached, thereupon became the coequal of General Lee in the theater organization under General Eisenhower. Though Lee dropped his earlier designation of deputy theater commander, the same command problems that had prevailed for the theater chief engineer in England during BOLERO obtained on the Continent. General Moore's access to the theater commander still ran through General Lee, and commanders of the fighting armies tended to regard Moore as less than a key member of the theater special staff though all engineer work proceeded under his technical supervision.[14]

The theater engineer's office consisted for the duration of the war of seven divisions under the chief engineer and his deputy. The Administration and Control Divisions performed internal housekeeping functions, coordinating planning, data collection, and personnel affairs. Intelligence Division compiled necessary engineer intelligence on all lines of communications,

[13] Bradley, *A Soldier's Story*, p. 305; The Adm and Log Hist of the ETO, vol. II, "Organization and Command in the European Theater of Operations," pp. 4–46.

[14] Ruppenthal, *Logistical Support of the Armies, Volume I*, pp. 434–36; ETO Gen Bd Rpt 127, Organization and Functions of the Communications Zone, ch. 4, pp. 32–38; Moore, *Final Report*, p. 326.

ports, and inland waterways and handled all mapping problems, including liaison on maps with Allied forces. The division also kept current on enemy engineering methods, mine warfare, and field works that combat engineers were likely to encounter. The Real Estate and Labor Division dealt with the acquisition of property for military use and hired civilian labor. Theater policies on engineer troop strengths, the distribution of engineers within the theater, and revisions to standard tables of organization fell within the jurisdiction of the Troops Division. It also handled training and the general technical supervision of bridge building, demolitions, camouflage, water supply, and fire fighting. The Supply Division saw to the engineer logistical line of communications on the Continent and the management of the entire theater depot system and the inventory and stock levels in it. The Construction Division set engineer construction standards and supervised the rehabilitation or building of roads, installations of all kinds, pipelines, power systems, and waterways.[15] The chief engineer's technical control extended, therefore, to the base sections on the Continent and in the United Kingdom, where all of the former base sections were consolidated into a single United Kingdom Base with subordinate districts.

The base sections that composed the COMZ empire in France began taking shape in July, and new headquarters opened as the need arose in the liberated territory. As ADSEC began the rehabilitation of Cherbourg, on 21 July General Plank established in the city the Cherbourg Command with all the prerogatives of a base section. On 16 August it became the Normandy Base Section, encompassing the Cotentin peninsula. Though the command's existence disrupted the OVERLORD plan to phase into the city one of the existing base section commands held in readiness in England, those staffs were later assigned to other section commands. Brittany Base opened on 16 August to oversee the smaller ports of that peninsula, and a short-lived Loire Base existed from 5 September until Brittany Base absorbed it on 1 December. The capture of Paris triggered the installation of the Seine Base Section in the city, where Headquarters, COMZ, also moved in early September amid considerable controversy since it occupied some of the best hotel accommodations in the city. After some administrative confusion over their missions, the last two sections evolved as Oise Base Section on 3 September and Channel Base Section a week later. Oise Base was responsible for territory east of Paris and up to the rear boundary of ADSEC as it moved forward with the field armies. Channel Base concerned itself with the Channel ports from the D-day beaches eastward but centered its attention on Antwerp once that city was wrested from German control.[16]

Essentially complete by the end of October, the base section organization nevertheless underwent boundary and organizational modifications and major shifts in emphasis through the end of the war. Another base section arrived in southern France with Operation DRAGOON to handle the Rhone valley main supply route.[17] As the war drew

---

[15] Moore, *Final Report*, app. I–K–I.

[16] Ruppenthal, *Logistical Support of the Armies, Volume II*, pp. 26–38.

[17] See ch. XX.

to a close, Normandy Base Section had progressively absorbed Brittany Base and taken over the Channel coast from Brest to the 21 Army Group boundary. Channel Base remained responsible for American supply and administration in what was a British rear area, where British forces retained a small enclave in Normandy Base Section incorporating their original D-day beaches. The port of Cherbourg in the meantime had developed into one of the principal points of entry for American forces and supply.

### Cherbourg

Combat troops fought their way into Cherbourg on 26 June. Next day, Col. James B. Cress of ADSEC and commanding officer of the 1056th Engineer Port Construction and Repair Group set off with Navy and Transportation Corps officers to inspect the city's crescent-shaped harbor. It was divided by a breakwater into an outer harbor, or Grande Rade, and an inner harbor, or Petite Rade. At the center of the inner harbor lay the Quai de France, jutting out into the roadstead beside the Darse Transatlantique, the famous deepwater basin the Germans had built between 1923 and 1935 as a World War I reparation. Here, in peacetime, the largest ocean liners docked. On the Quai de France was a huge railway station with a great vaulted roof, the Gare Maritime, which provided transatlantic passengers with speedy rail service to Paris. (Few travelers lingered in Cherbourg, for it was primarily a naval base of little interest to tourists.)

A naval installation occupied most of the western side of the inner harbor. Between the naval base and the Quai

de France the ADSEC officers saw a small seaplane base, a bathing beach (the Nouvelle Plage), and a narrow channel leading inland to two basins in the center of the city, the Avant Port de Commerce and the Bassin a Flot, where in peacetime most of the cargo handled at Cherbourg came ashore. The eastern side of the harbor, beyond the Darse Transatlantique, was the least developed. It consisted merely of open areas known as the Reclamation and the Terre Plein, bounded by a long sloping seawall where the water was quite shallow at low tide.

Although the advance party found no demolition in the Terre Plein and Reclamation areas, the great transatlantic dock area was a shambles—the most spectacular evidence of the "exemplary destruction of the harbor of Cherbourg" for which the German commander received the Knight's Cross of the Iron Cross from Adolf Hitler. The Gare Maritime was badly damaged, the two quays lay in ruins, and two sunken ships blocked the entrance to the Darse. The reconnaissance party also found widespread destruction at the naval base, some of it from Allied air attacks. Sunken ships and barges blocked the entrances to the three basins, which were filled with sunken barges, tugs, trawlers, and coasters. In the base area two tremendous craters severed the western breakwater of the Petite Rade, the Digue du Homet, a 3,300-foot-long, 70-foot-wide mole quayed on the south side and carrying three railroad tracks and several oil pipelines. The Quai du Homet, a berth for coal coasters at right angles to the Digue on its south side, was damaged in nine places.[18]

---

[18] Port of Cherbourg, Rpt, 1056th Engr Port Construction and Repair Gp; Rpt, Cherbourg Port Reconstruction, OCE ETOUSA, 1944, p. 13; Maj. Gen.

The destruction of Cherbourg, while acknowledged to be "a masterful job," was no greater than the ADSEC engineer had expected.[19] The engineers were to work first on those areas where the quickest results could be expected, so that construction machinery and equipment waiting off UTAH Beach could land as soon as possible. These areas were designated in a four-point program established by naval, engineer, and transportation officers on 28 June: first, the Nouvelle Plage bathing beach for DUKWs; second, the Bassin a Flot in the commercial port for barges; third, the Reclamation and Terre Plein area for LSTs; and, fourth, the Digue du Homet for Liberty ships and vessels carrying locomotives and boxcars.

The 332d and 342d Engineer General Service and the 333d Engineer Special Service Regiments were assigned to the 1056th Port Construction and Repair Group to begin the reconstruction of Cherbourg. Details entered the port with the advance parties to clear debris, remove mines, and scour the territory for construction materials, and by the first week in July all three regiments had numbers of men on the scene. They found huge stores of German construction materials and equipment, some at a buzz-bomb launching platform west of Cherbourg. French civilian mechanics helped get the equip-

ment in working order. By 8 July ADSEC engineers were making optimistic estimates of the daily tonnage that Cherbourg could receive—a port that in peacetime averaged less than 900 tons a day. Exclusive of POL, vehicles, and railroad rolling stock, the engineers estimated that after rehabilitation Cherbourg would have a capacity of 17,900 tons daily.[20]

At Nouvelle Plage the engineers blew gaps in the seawall, swept away barbed-wire entanglements, graded the beach, and built three concrete exit roads for DUKWs. Work started early on ramps and hards for vehicle-carrying LCTs and LSTs at the seaplane base and the north side of the Reclamation area. The engineers quickly constructed timber wharves for unloading barges and coasters along the Terre Plein and at the Bassin a Flot, which had seventeen feet of water controlled by locks at the inner end of the Avant Port de Commerce. A swing bridge over these locks, which carried traffic from one side of the city to the other, was down; the engineers replaced it with an ingenious retractable drawbridge—a movable Bailey resting on dollies that ran on old streetcar rails.

Nouvelle Plage was ready to receive DUKWs on 6 July, but none could come in for ten days because of German underwater mines. Minesweepers entered the Petite Rade on 8 July, and not until the fourteenth were the western ends of the Grande and Petite Rades free of mines. Ships waiting off the Normandy beaches now came forward. The first four Liberties steaming up the Cotentin coast arrived around

---

James B. Cress, "Reconstruction of Cherbourg," *The Military Engineer*, XLIV, no. 300 (July–August 1952), 248. Unless otherwise noted, this section is based on these three sources, and on MS, Cherbourg—Gateway to France: Rehabilitation and Operation of the First Major Port, Hist Sect, ETOUSA, 1945. See also: Ruppenthal, *Logistical Support of the Armies, Volume II*, pp. 62–89, and the histories of the units mentioned.

[19] Ltr, Col E. C. Itschner, Engr, ASCZ, to CE, ETOUSA, 5 Jul 44, sub: Port and Port Area Rehabilitation Plan: CHERBOURG, Notes on Port of Cherbourg.

[20] Ibid., Incl 6, sub: Cherbourg, Estimated Port Capacity Based on Reconstruction Plan, 8 Jul 44.

noon on 16 July and anchored safely in the Grande Rade. By 1738 a load of signal corps wire had been placed into a waiting DUKW; forty-five minutes later, it was on its way by truck to a signal corps dump five miles south of Cherbourg. Port operations had begun.

The first cargo was not typical, for DUKWs normally handled only small packages and in later operations were used almost exclusively for subsistence. Sixty-three percent of all supplies and equipment that came into the port before the end of July bore the castle marking of the Corps of Engineers, and much of that cargo consisted of construction materials for rebuilding the port. Barges had to bring in heavy engineer equipment such as girders, rail lengths, and bulldozers. Thirty 18-by-16-foot wooden barges arrived shortly after the first Liberties, loaded at once, and the next day, 17 July, discharged in the Bassin a Flot, the wet dock at the commercial port.

Meanwhile, work on the high-priority Digue du Homet, begun the week after Cherbourg's capture, was well along. The 332d Engineer General Service Regiment and other engineers filled a crater isolating the Digue from the naval base, repaired road and railroad tracks on the Digue, and constructed five pile-and-timber finger piers for Liberty ships because the quay wall had an underwater shelf. At the shore end of the Digue the engineers provided two berths for Twickenham ferries, British vessels specially built to carry locomotives and rolling stock. On 29 July a Twickenham made its first delivery—several 65-ton diesel electric locomotives and other rolling stock. The first Liberty ship docked at one of the Digue's finger piers on 9 August.

After 13 August, when the 332d Engineer General Service Regiment moved to Mayenne to undertake railroad repair in support of First Army's Falaise Gap operations, the 342d and 398th Engineer General Service Regiments took over the work at the Quai du Homet and Digue du Homet. Efforts to provide more deepwater berths increased when it became obvious that the lighterage operations—discharged into DUKWs or barges from ships anchored out in the roadstead—were too costly in labor, equipment, and time. DUKWs had a limited capacity; barges could be towed into basins only during a few hours at high tide and otherwise had to be moored to stake boats in the harbor. Moreover, all lighters were at the mercy of the weather, and storms frequently prevented them from venturing out into the harbor.

The first area to benefit from the efforts to speed ship-to-shore operations was the naval base, which could accommodate Liberty ships. The 342d Engineer General Service Regiment, aided by men from the 398th, began construction in mid-August, replacing demolished bridges and building timber wharves to provide a continuous surface along the top of the quays, which boat slips and entrance channels to dry docks indented at frequent intervals. A bridge the 342d Engineers built across a passage at the north end of Bassin Charles X illustrates the ingenious use of local and captured materials. For girders the engineers used the main beams of an old German submarine-lifting craft (turned over to the French with other reparations after 1918), which the Navy had found blocking the entrance to the Avant Port. The floor channels for the bridge came from captured special railroad cars. Eventually the naval base provided berths for eleven Liberty ships and five coasters.

The last area to benefit from the program to provide more deepwater berths was potentially the most valuable and therefore the most thoroughly subjected to German demolitions—the great Darse Transatlantique. Early in July the 333d Engineer Special Service Regiment began clearing debris from the shattered docks. In the wreckage of the Gare Maritime the engineers discovered twenty-four freight cars loaded with unexploded sea mines, rendered extremely sensitive by tons of debris that had fallen on them. The ticklish task of removing the debris and then deactivating the mines fell to the mine and booby-trap team of the 333d Engineer Special Service Regiment, which undertook most of the mine deactivation on the land side of the harbor. The team found unexploded charges, which the Germans had apparently not had time to detonate, in underground passages, sewers, bridges, and buildings throughout the port area.[21]

After the debris and mines were removed from the quays at the Darse Transatlantique, the 333d Engineer Special Service Regiment began construction. Operating two ten-hour shifts and employing hundreds of French civilians and POWs, the regiment first built finger piers at intervals to match the hatches of Liberty ships; later they filled the spaces between the piers, using timber wharfing to provide continuous berthing along the Quai de France. But construction in the Darse

was a long-term project. Not until 21 August, when the Navy declared the waters free of mines, could a survey of underwater debris be made. An access channel was not open until 18 September, and the first Liberty did not berth in the Darse until 8 October.

On 10 August the engineers working on the Cherbourg quays saw a new kind of ship steaming into the harbor. She was the *Junior N. Van Noy,* the first engineer port repair ship sent overseas. A converted Great Lakes steamer displacing only 3,000 tons, the ship had machine shops, storage bins, and heavy salvage equipment aboard. Her decks bristled with derricks and booms for lifting sunken ships and other debris. Manning the ship was the sixty-member 1071st Engineer Port Repair Ship Crew.[22]

The day after her arrival at Cherbourg the ship went under the control of the 1056th Engineer Port Construction and Repair Group but in a few days passed to the control of the 1055th Engineer Port Construction and Repair Group, which had come up from Granville to work on the vital Liberty berths along the Digue du Homet. The repair ship could not enter the wrecked inner basins because she drew twenty feet, but out in the harbor the vessel accomplished valuable work. Her divers, welders, and mechanics patched and raised several hulks. Divers with electric torches broke up a dry dock that was beyond repair. Another important

---

[21] 1st Lt S. T. Holden, Asst S–3, Pertinent Information on the 333d Mine & Booby Trap Team, 20 Sep 44, in booklet, Port of Cherbourg, Rpt of Demolition and Reconstruction, 333d Engr SS Rgt.

[22] For the conversion and equipping of such ships sent to the ETO, and crew recruitment and training, see Coll, Keith, and Rosenthal, *The Corps of Engineers: Troops and Equipment,* pp. 339–411. The ship was named in honor of an enlisted man whose heroic action at Finschhafen, Southwest Pacific Area, had earned him posthumously, the first Medal of Honor awarded an Army engineer during World War II.

task was repair of a large rock crusher found in a quarry just outside Cherbourg, equipment badly needed for road building. On 3 October 1944, the *Junior N. Van Noy* left Cherbourg, bound for Le Havre with the 1055th Port Construction and Repair Group.[23]

In the OVERLORD plan Cherbourg originally had a scheduled daily discharge capacity of 8,000 to 9,000 tons—Brest and Quiberon Bay were to become the major ports of entry for Allied forces and supplies entering the Continent. But as the bitter German defense of some Brittany ports increased Cherbourg's importance, G–4 planners raised the port's projected intake capacity to 15,000 tons daily in July. Brig. Gen. Royal B. Lord, ETOUSA G–4, expected a 20,000-ton capacity in the city by September, but in the middle of that month only 12,000 tons per day were moving through the port, then about 75 percent rehabilitated. The vital berths that could handle Liberty ships still lay in the inoperable 25 percent of the harbor, and their repair continued even as the utility of Cherbourg declined later in the year.

*Railway Rehabilitation*

By mid-August, Liberties at deepwater quays in Cherbourg were unloading onto barges because a shortage of trucks and rail cars had crowded the quays and the marginal wharves at Terre Plein with supplies and equipment awaiting transportation inland. Only about 3,000 tons of cargo a day were moving out by rail at the end of August, and a backlog of nearly 72,000 tons awaited clearance in the port area.[24]

Efforts to expedite rail service had started before the fall of Cherbourg, when the 1056th Engineer Port Construction and Repair Group began to repair demolished railway bridges over the Vire, Taute, Madeleine, and Jourdan Rivers. By 7 July the two main line tracks from Paris to Cherbourg were open. One company of the 347th Engineer General Service Regiment had cleared a demolished tunnel just south of Cherbourg, and three other companies had repaired blown frogs and switches on the tracks into the city's railway station, the Gare de l'Etat. Fortunately damage was light on a mile-long spur from the Gare de l'Etat to the Digue du Homet, and less than five of the fifteen miles of track within the city needed extensive repairs. Most of the damage had resulted from Allied bombs and artillery fire.

Railway rehabilitation, carried on under the supervision of the Transportation Corps' 2d Military Railway Service, accelerated considerably after the late July decision to increase Cherbourg's tonnage target to 20,000 tons by mid-September, with the railroads carrying the main burden of transportation inland. New spurs were needed as well as new storage and marshaling yards to ensure that a constant supply of railway cars could be fed to the docks. Primarily a passenger port, Cherbourg had storage yards for only

---

[23] Cherbourg Port Reconstruction, p. 42. A similar engineer port repair ship came into Cherbourg on 20 August and remained there under the 1056th Port Construction and Repair Group.

[24] OCE ETOUSA Monthy Rpt 17, Aug 44, dated 15 Sep 44; OCE ETOUSA Hist Rpt 11, Port Reconstruction and Repair (United Kingdom), 1946, Liaison Sect, Intel Div, ETOUSA Adm file 547.

350 cars and marshaling yards for only 400. The plan to move 20,000 tons daily through Cherbourg required 2,000 railway cars a day, and since a two-day supply of empty cars had to be on hand at all times, storage for 4,000 cars as well as marshaling yard capacity for the daily 2,000 was mandatory.

The first major railway reconstruction took place in the Terre Plein area, where an existing yard consisted of three tracks with a capacity of only 165 cars and a spur running into the Amiot Aircraft Plant. The 347th Engineer General Service Regiment repaired the tracks, which Allied bombing and shellfire had badly damaged, cleared away dragon's teeth and pillboxes from the area behind the Terre Plein, and laid 6 1/2 miles of new track to provide a marshaling yard for 714 cars. Unfortunately, the unit was inexperienced in railroad work and laid the track without ballast on filled-in land. As the track sank into the soft ground the rails spread, causing a number of derailments before the engineers stabilized the area by placing crushed rock ballast under the tracks.[25]

The same problem occurred in the construction of new yards at Couville and Sottevast, which together constituted one of the most ambitious construction projects undertaken on the Cotentin. Work at Couville began on 2 August, but heavy rains turned the area into a sea of mud. The engineers had to open a rock quarry and haul hundreds of carloads of rock to ballast the tracks. The first yard at Couville opened on 18 September, and expansion continued until 3 November, when the

yard had sixteen miles of track with a capacity of 1,740 cars. Construction of the Sottevast yard, begun on 15 August, also was plagued by heavy rains that at one time had portions of the area under eighteen inches of water. Nevertheless, some of the facilities were ready by mid-October, and when construction stopped in mid-December the yard had eighteen miles of track with a capacity of 2,280 cars.

*POL Storage*

On 24 July the tanker *Empire Traveller* discharged the first gasoline at Cherbourg, unloading at the long breakwater in the outer harbor—the Digue de Querqueville. The French and later the Germans had discharged gasoline and other POL supplies through a nine-inch pipeline running along the Digue to two nearby tank farms at the large Depot Cotier du Petrole and the somewhat smaller one at Sunic. In the same neighborhood was a tank farm at Hainneville, which the French Navy had used to store diesel fuel. The fourth farm the Americans discovered was underground, so cleverly concealed that even few Frenchmen knew of its existence. The French had built the installation, Les Couplets, in 1938 at the time of the Maginot Line construction. Double garage doors of an innocent-looking two story house facing the Rue de la Paix, which skirted the harbor between Cherbourg and Querqueville, opened on a 600-yard tunnel leading to four huge storage tanks located in a hollow carved out of a small mountain; thirty-eight feet of solid granite overhead made the tanks impervious to air attacks.

The engineers' major construction

---

[25] ETO Gen Bd Rpt 123, Military Railway Service, p. 27.

GASOLINE BEING PUMPED ASHORE
*at Cherbourg.*

effort was at the tank farm at the Depot
Cotier du Petrole, where the Germans
had demolished four huge tanks, leaving one small tank more or less intact.
The engineers built three new tanks
among the ruins left from the German
demolitions and welded patches over
holes in the one tank that had escaped
demolition. The nine-inch pipeline
from the Digue de Querqueville proved
to be corroded beyond repair. Decid-
ing to scrap it, the engineers installed
seven six-inch lines that carried diesel,
motor transport, and aviation fuel simultaneously. Aviation gasoline went to
the Sunic tank farm, diesel fuel to Les
Couplets.[26]

---

[26] OCE ETOUSA Hist Rpt 13, Petroleum, Oil, and
Lubricants (United Kingdom), 1946, pp. 67–80 and
fig. 2, Liaison Sect, Intel Div, ETOUSA Adm file 547.

On 4 November 1944, Cherbourg
discharged a peak 19,955 tons of cargo;
the daily average for that month was
14,300 tons. Thereafter, the port's discharge rate declined rapidly as personnel, equipment, and railroad cars transferred to Antwerp. A few days after
supply ships entered Antwerp on 26
November, Cherbourg's tonnage target
dropped to 12,000 tons a day; two
weeks later it went down to 7,000 tons.
Cherbourg's role as the mainstay of the
American port system in France was
over.

### Granville and the Minor Brittany Ports

OVERLORD planners concentrated
their attentions on the Brittany ports
because they expected the peninsula to
serve as the entryway for Allied forces
and materiel before any other development on the Continent. The scheduled
thrust from Normandy into Brittany
after D-day was to be the prelude to
the construction of a sturdy logistical
base to support attacks to the Seine that
would come after 1 November. Brest,
Lorient, Quiberon Bay, and St. Malo
in Brittany were expected to provide
16,240 tons of daily port capacity by D
plus 90; with the opening of Nantes,
the Brittany ports were to receive more
than 27,000 tons a day by that date.
After the breakout at St. Lo in late July,
G–4, COMZ, was planning to increase
the Brittany capacity to provide more
than half of the port discharge requirements as of D plus 90. But the major
Brittany ports held out stubbornly, and
by late August only St. Malo was in
American hands. On 25 August G–4,
COMZ, called for the speedy development of St. Malo and three small Brittany ports that had not figured in OVER-

LORD planning—Morlaix, St. Brieuc, and Cancale—as well as the small fishing port of Granville on the west coast of Normandy. At the time COMZ made this decision supplies were coming in on the Brittany coast only across a beach at St. Michel-en-Greve, where LSTs were bringing in ammunition for the siege of Brest. Morlaix, St. Brieuc, and Cancale were to be ready to handle a total of 9,500 tons a day by 5 September, St. Malo, 2,400 tons by 1 October.[27]

The goals set for the Brittany ports were never realized and at most of them the engineer effort was considered "utterly wasted."[28] Despite the heavy emphasis on those ports in July, the breakout from the bridgehead and the headlong drive across northern France moved the action far from Brittany by September. This development caused logistical planners at SHAEF to regard Antwerp as the major prize; engineers nevertheless expended considerable effort in Brittany before the tactical situation changed so drastically. The 1053d Port Construction and Repair Group and the 360th Engineer General Service Regiment worked on St. Malo, Cancale, and St. Brieuc before moving into captured Brest. The St. Malo project halted just as it neared completion, primarily because the task of reopening waterways south and inland from St. Malo did not appear worth the effort required. Some port-operating personnel went to Cancale, but tidal conditions there proved so difficult that the port was never used. St. Brieuc opened in mid-September but operated for only a month, averaging 317 tons a day, mostly coal for local generating plants and railroads. St. Michel-en-Greve did somewhat better, averaging 745 tons a day; but it closed down on 1 September, never contributing more than a small amount of port capacity and reverting to French control in mid-December. The only ports in Brittany that delivered more than token tonnages were Granville and Morlaix.[29]

Granville, captured on 3 July, was the first port taken after the breakout. The 1055th Engineer Port Construction and Repair Group, which ADSEC immediately dispatched there, found that the Germans had undertaken extensive demolition work similar to that at Cherbourg—quays cratered, cranes tipped into the water, and blockships sunk. Worst of all, they had destroyed lock gates between the outer and inner basins so that, at each change of the tide, water raced into the inner, main basin. By minesweeping, clearing debris, and removing sunken craft, the engineers opened the outer basin to coasters able to dry out alongside the jetties. When the tonnage target rose on 25 August, the 1058th Engineer Port Construction and Repair Group, originally destined for Lorient, went to Granville to prepare additional coaster berths. Operated entirely as a coaling port, Granville averaged 1,244 tons a day between

[27] Ruppenthal, *Logistical Support of the Armies, Volume II*, pp. 89–93; T/5 Robert L. Davis, The Administrative and Logistical History of the European Theater of Operations, vol. VII, "Opening and Operating Continental Ports," pp. 66–67, in CMH; Maj Charles K. McDerot and 1st Lt Adolph P. Gratiot, Bringing Supplies into the Theater, vol. I, p. 40, Hist G–4, COMZ, ETOUSA, in CMH. Histories of the units mentioned. Unless otherwise cited, this section is taken from these sources.

[28] Ltr, Col John R. Hardin to Maj Gen R. W. Crawford, 10 Oct 47, Incl to Ltr, Maj Gen R. W. Crawford to Maj R. G. Ruppenthal, 31 Oct 47, sub: Questions on the Logistics of the War in the European Theater.

[29] OCE ETOUSA Hist Rpt 11, Port Reconstruction and Repair; OCE ETOUSA Monthly Rpt 19, Sep 44, and 21, Dec 44.

its opening on 15 September 1944 and its closing on 21 April 1945. Its prosaic activities were violently interrupted shortly after midnight on 9 March 1945, when a German task force of about 150 men from their isolated garrison on the Channel Islands raided the little port, causing about eighty casualties and damaging coasters and port facilities.

Morlaix (situated about twelve miles up the Dossen River estuary) and the small neighboring port of Roscoff were the westernmost of the Brittany ports. Consistently linked in all plans, they were operated by one headquarters and were referred to as one port, Morlaix-Roscoff. Though Roscoff was tidal, Morlaix, like Granville, had outer and inner basins. Neither port was badly damaged, and the 1057th Engineer Port Construction and Repair Group quickly restored them. The two provided anchorage for six Liberty ships that discharged into lighters. Between the opening day, 5 September, and the closing date of 14 December 1944, Morlaix-Roscoff turned in the best performance of any of the Brittany group of ports—2,105 tons a day.

### The Seine Ports: Le Havre and Rouen

Although Rouen, lying seventy-five miles up the Seine River, fell on 30 August 1944, it was unusable until Le Havre, at the mouth of the Seine, was in Allied hands. The Germans held out at Le Havre until 12 September, causing the big port—the second largest in France—to be subjected to intensive Allied sea, air, and land bombardment that destroyed almost two-thirds of the city. The Germans had also damaged port facilities as at Cherbourg and Granville. All lock gates were out, an espe-cially serious matter because most of the port's activities had centered around numerous wet basins and every deep-water berth had been destroyed. Tre-mendous engineer resources would be needed to restore deepwater berths. Moreover, port clearance problems would increase at Le Havre because all American traffic inland would have to cross British lines of communications. For these reasons, and bolstered by the expectation that Antwerp (captured on 4 September) would provide plenty of port capacity closer to the front, COMZ decided against undertaking a major reconstruction effort at Le Havre.[30]

An engineer task force under Col. Frank F. Bell, commanding officer of the 373d Engineer General Service Regiment, undertook limited rehabilita-tion of both Le Havre and Rouen. In addition to his own regiment, Colonel Bell ultimately had control of the 1055th and 1061st Engineer Port Construction and Repair Groups, the 392d Engineer General Service Regiment, the 1071st Engineer Port Repair Ship Crew, the 1044th Engineer Gas Generating Unit, the 971st Engineer Maintenance Com-pany, and the 577th Engineer Dump Truck Company. He also had under his operational control two Royal Navy parties, each equivalent to a U.S. Army engineer port construction and repair group.

The 373d Engineers, moving by mo-tor convoy from the outskirts of Brest,

---

[30] Ruppenthal, *Logistical Support of the Armies, Volume II*, pp. 96–103, 167; The Adm and Log Hist of the ETO, vol. VII, "Opening and Operating Conti-nental Ports," pp. 34–36, 88–97; History of the Chan-nel Base Section, Aug 44–Jun 45, vol. I, Adm 588, ETOUSA Hist Sect; Hist Rpt, Transportation Corps in the European Theater of Operations, Oct–Dec 44, vol. V, pt. 1, Adm 582, ETOUSA Hist Sect. Histo-ries of units mentioned.

BLAST REMOVES BLOCKAGE FROM THE MOUTH OF THE LOCKS AT ST. MALO

arrived in Le Havre on 19 September. Road and mine clearance work started the next day while, offshore, naval salvage crews began clearing an entrance into the harbor. As at other ports the engineers first worked to provide the earliest possible discharge of cargo, making space on the beaches for landing craft, clearing storage areas, and preparing exits through rubble-filled streets.

The engineers built no timber pile wharves but instead installed a number of artificial piers to provide berths for deep-draft ships. One was a floating ponton pier the Navy built; the Army engineers provided the connection with the shore—Bailey bridges 130 feet long

that moved up and down with the tide.[31] Two of the artificial piers used four Phoenixes originally designed for the MULBERRY project. Another ingenious use of existing materials was the employment of Phion ferries, left over from operations on the D-day beaches, to construct floating piers in the port's wet basins.

Damage to tidal lock gates seriously affected the wet basins at Le Havre. As the tides rushed in and out, changes in hydrostatic pressure soon began to dam-

---

[31] Ltr, Maj Gen C. R. Moore to Brig Gen L. D. Worsham, 18 Apr 45, Incl 2, Project Description of Bailey Bridge Connection Floating Wharf to Shore, Le Havre, Nov 44, 312 Gen Moore, EUCOM Engr files.

age quay walls. To stop this deterioration and to make the basins usable at all stages of the tide, the 1055th Engineer Port Construction and Repair Group repaired the Rochemont lock gates, one of the outstanding engineering achievements at Le Havre. Failing in several attempts to repair the huge gates where they hung, the engineers removed them and repaired them in dry dock. The rehanging was completed on 30 November 1944, and thereafter the tidal range within the wet basins fell by nearly twenty feet. Later repairs along the Tancarville Canal, which connected with the Seine, increased the stabilization.

The first vessels entered Le Havre on 2 October, but mines in the harbor limited the arrivals to LCTs and coasters until 13 October, when the first Liberties came forward. The port never developed the number of alongside Liberty berths that logisticians had planned; consequently, lighters and DUKWs had to bring ashore a large percentage of the tonnage. Nevertheless, Le Havre's cargo capacity continued to rise gratifyingly. By the end of December more than 9,500 tons were being discharged per day, considerably exceeding expectations. By that time, the port was also making another important contribution to the American effort in Europe. Beginning in November 1944, when COMZ shifted personnel staging from the Cotentin peninsula to the Seine, Le Havre developed into the principal troop debarkation point in the European theater.[32]

Rouen, the third major port American forces reconstructed in Europe, was not as badly damaged as Le Havre.

Although the Germans had demolished cargo-handling facilities and blocked the river channel by sinking a number of ships, the quays were in good condition—some 14,000 feet were usable. On the land side, the marshaling yards adjacent to the port had suffered heavy bomb damage. This presented no particular problem because other marshaling yards twelve miles away were easily accessible over a four-lane highway.

In peacetime, two-thirds of the traffic between Rouen and Paris moved by inland waterways along an eight-foot-deep channel in the Seine that could handle barges up to twenty-one feet wide.[33] The largest task of rehabilitation at Rouen—the removal of mines, sunken cranes, ships, barges, and tugs from this river channel—fell mainly to the U.S. Navy, aided by French authorities. The engineers removed debris and filled in bomb craters. Elements of the engineer task force in Le Havre, consisting of the 1061st Engineer Port Construction and Repair Group, a Royal Navy party, and a platoon of the 37th Engineer Combat Battalion, undertook these tasks.

On 15 October the first ships, coasters with POL from England, berthed at Rouen. Because the channel between Le Havre and Rouen was shallow, coasters were the mainstay of supply operations at Rouen. They were so successful, discharging an average of more than 4,000 tons daily the first week in November, that COMZ ordered all coasters except those carrying coal to discharge at Rouen. Barge operations inland, undertaken to meet civilian needs, began on 22 November.[34]

---

[32] Bykofsky and Larson, *The Transportation Corps: Operations Overseas*, p. 318.

[33] Moore, *Final Report*, p. 275.

[34] Bykofsky and Larson, *The Transportation Corps: Operations Overseas*, p. 318.

Liberty ships could come into Rouen only after they had been partially unloaded at Le Havre. Before neap tide they had to be trimmed to as little as 16 1/2 feet of draft, for otherwise the ships would block the channel for ten days until a spring tide came in. The engineers dredged channels to facilitate the passage of deep-draft ships through the shoal water. In England the U.S. Army engineers held four seagoing, light hopper dredges, originally dispatched to the ETO to support canceled logistical operations along the Loire River. Only one, which the 1077th Engineer Dredge Crew operated, had a draft shallow enough to be employable along the Seine. Although not ideally suited for the purpose, the 1077th's dredge helped facilitate Liberty ship passage to Rouen. By the spring of 1945 the port had fifteen Liberty berths as compared to twenty-six for coasters.[35]

### Antwerp and Ghent

A visit to captured Antwerp, according to a British engineer who had viewed the battered ruins of other harbors, was "a startling experience."[36] The great port, ranking with New York, Hamburg, and Rotterdam, was in miraculously good condition, thanks to the speed of the British advance and Belgian success in forestalling German attempts at demolition.

Situated on the Schelde River estuary fifty-five miles from the sea, Antwerp provided fine deepwater quayage, 75 percent of it along a complex of eighteen wet basins, ample for the dis-

charge of supplies for both the British and American forces. During October representatives of the two forces worked out an agreement, known as the "Treaty of Antwerp," by which the Americans were to use the basins north of a line drawn through the Bassin Albert, the British those to the south. River berths were to be allocated based on need. The expected tonnage capacity was 40,000 tons a day excluding POL—22,500 for the Americans and 17,500 for the British. Command of the port was the responsibility of the British 21 Army Group; American operations were under Col. Doswell Gullatt, who had commanded the 5th Engineer Special Brigade at OMAHA. At Antwerp Gullatt commanded the 13th Port (TC), which had reached the Continent from England in October. The largest single engineer element of the 13th Port was the 358th Engineer General Service Regiment; other engineer support included two depot and two petroleum distribution companies and two of the five engineer port repair ships in the ETO. By early December Gullatt also had under his control the 5th Port (TC), sent forward to Antwerp from Morlaix-Roscoff in Brittany.[37]

Rehabilitation of the port was under British control, with as much American assistance as necessary to meet the target opening date of 15 November. The first major task was repair of a

---

[35] Ltr, Moore to Worsham, 4 May 45; Moore, *Final Report*, pp. 272, 404–05.

[36] OCE ETOUSA Hist Rpt 11, Port Reconstruction and Repair, app. 22.

[37] Ruppenthal, *Logistical Support of the Armies, Volume II*, pp. 105–10; The Adm and Log Hist of the ETO, vol. VII, "Opening and Operating Continental Ports," p. 169; Hist Rpt, Transportation Corps in the European Theater of Operations, vols. V and VI, Adm 582, ETOUSA Hist Sect; OCE ETOUSA Hist Rpt 11, Port Reconstruction and Repair, pp. 48–49, 83–90, and apps. 24, 28. Histories of the units mentioned. Unless otherwise cited, this section is based on these sources.

lock controlling the Kruisschans sluice, the longest of four sluices connecting the wet basins with the river and the only one leading into the American area. A German mine had damaged one of the gates. The 358th Engineer General Service Regiment began work on the vital sluice on 6 November in cooperation with the British. The fact that the sluice had both flood and ebb gates made repair possible in plenty of time for the first American Liberty ship to enter on 28 November.[38] American engineers also removed sand, rubble, and damaged cranes from the quays, improved quays and roads, constructed hardstandings and trackage, and rebuilt dockside warehouses.

The V–1 and V–2 rockets that the Germans sent over Antwerp beginning in mid-October 1944 inflicted surprisingly little damage at first, but in mid-December, at the start of the Battle of the Ardennes, rocket attacks on the city intensified. Between 11 and 29 December thirty men of the 358th Engineer General Service Regiment were wounded by V-bomb attacks, twenty-nine seriously; one died of wounds. On Saturday afternoon, 16 December, a V–2 bomb scored a direct hit on the Rex movie theater, killing 567 soldiers and civilians and seriously injuring 291. The 358th Engineers took over rescue and demolition operations and persevered until the last body was recovered on 22 December. For this extraordinary effort, the men of the 358th, their commander, Col. Chester L. Landaker, and the commander of the regiment's 2d Battalion, Maj. Roy S. Kelley, were

warmly thanked by the British brigadier in charge of the area, who expressed his "highest admiration for the manner in which they worked under such distressing circumstances."[39]

Antwerp provided three means of port clearance—rail, truck, and inland waterway. Damage to tracks was minor; the limiting factor for railroad supply movements was a shortage of rolling stock. Truck transport began very early, and a network of roads to the principal American depots at Liege-Namur was operational before the end of October. The major British-American engineer effort was devoted to helping Belgian agencies open the Albert Canal, which ran eighty miles from Antwerp to Liege. The British were responsible for clearing the western portion of the canal—the thirty miles from Antwerp to Kwaadmechelen, and the Americans the remaining fifty miles to Liege. The work primarily involved repairing locks and removing demolished bridges and sunken barges. The headquarters element of the 1056th Engineer Port Construction and Repair Group supervised clearing operations in the American sector, with the 332d and 355th Engineer General Service Regiments and Belgian civilian contractors undertaking most of the actual work. Although twenty-one blown bridges, including five railroad bridges, blocked the American sector, the engineers cleared that stretch for 600-ton barges by the target date of 15 December and for 2,000-ton barges by 9 March 1945. During the winter ice and flooding hampered operations, and the German counteroffensive for a time forced an embargo on barge traffic. Eventually 50 percent of

[38] Ltr, Lt Col Floyd E. Gidinsky to CG, COMZ, ETOUSA, 11 Nov 44, sub: Status Report—Port of Antwerp, and 1st Ind. 800 Antwerp, EUCOM Engr files.

[39] Hist 358th Engr GS Rgt, 1944.

all U.S. military tonnage discharged at Antwerp moved inland along the Albert Canal.[40]

After buzz-bomb and rocket attacks and German successes in the Ardennes raised the possibility that Antwerp might be wholly or partially denied to the Allies, British and American planners decided in mid-January to open the port of Ghent as a standby, making much the same sort of agreement on joint use as at Antwerp. The American allocation was 7,500 tons a day, to be cleared primarily over inland waterways and railroads; the British quota was set at 5,000 tons.

Accessible from the sea via a canal running twenty miles south of Terneuzen on the Schelde estuary west of Antwerp, Ghent was in peacetime the second port of Belgium, although its traffic was restricted to barges, coasters, and small freighters. The war had destroyed locks at Terneuzen and bridges across the canal, and many small craft were sunk in the canal. The Germans had used Ghent only for barges, mainly bringing in material used in the construction of the Atlantic Wall, and had dismantled, removed, or neglected cranes on quays along Ghent's basin. The quays were piled high with sand, gravel, scrap iron, and rubbish; some of the loading berths, undredged for five years, had become silted.[41]

On 18 December 1944, the British began repair of the Terneuzen locks and removal of bridges and sunken vessels from the canal. American assistance in rehabilitation did not begin until

after the arrival of the main body of the 17th Port (TC) in mid-January; their immediate task was the removal of approximately 450,000 tons of sand and other aggregate from the quays. Most of this material the 17th Port loaded as ballast into outgoing deep-sea vessels; the rest went to Antwerp to be used on roads and other facilities. The American forces also built roads, repaired cranes, lifted wrecks, and dredged loading berths at the Grand Bassin, the principal dock. The U.S. Army hopper dredge *W. L. Marshall*, with the 1080th Engineer Dredge Crew aboard, undertook the dredging early in April. Arriving at Antwerp in late January to replace a disabled Army dredge, the *W. L. Marshall* had spent more than two months dredging along the Schelde despite near misses by $V-1$ and $V-2$ bombs, which blew off several doors and caused "some consternation" among the crew.[42]

The first U.S. vessel to pass the Terneuzen locks and enter the port of Ghent was the *Hannis Taylor*, a Liberty ship that berthed on 23 January 1945. She was the first ship of her size to enter Ghent, and her passage through the locks, which Belgian and Dutch naval authorities considered impassable for ships of such beam, was a triumph. After the *Hannis Taylor's* entry, Liberties went through regularly, with a clearance of only one foot on either side. In line with the chief of transportation's policy to keep Ghent free of cargo so that the port would be available in case the Allies had to abandon Antwerp, unloadings were limited to 2,500 tons a day during the first month

[40] Moore, *Final Report*, p. 278.

[41] Ltr, Lt Col Carl H. Irwin to CO, Channel Base Sect, COMZ, 3 Dec 44, sub: Report of Reconnaissance, Port of Ghent; OCE ETOUSA Hist Rpt 11, Port Reconstruction and Repair, app. 28.

[42] Hist 1080th Engr Dredge Crew, 22 Nov 43–25 Nov 45.

of operations. This rate more than doubled in March, and in the final month before V−E Day an average of 9,500 tons a day was discharging at Ghent.

For all their accomplishments in port reconstruction in Europe following D-day, the engineers were never really able to keep up with the demands of harbor improvement until well into the spring of 1945. Statistics on discharges of ships showed continual increase, but the shortages of berthing capacity for vessels on the Continent and the inadequate depot system for bulk supply in the theater contributed heavily to the supply crises during the latter part of the year. Basing estimates on combat requirements instead of on port capacities, General Lee's COMZ headquarters consistently overstated the number of ships the logistical structure in the ports could handle in a single month. The excess shipments created a bottleneck at that point in the supply chain. Without unloading capacity, the ships piled up offshore, remaining idle as floating warehouses instead of returning to more efficient use in the shipping pool on the high seas. Only with the capture and the eventual development of Antwerp and Ghent did the backlog clear up and the port capacity grow to a size large enough to support the last drive into Germany.

# CHAPTER XVII

# Combat Engineers in the Breakout and Pursuit

While engineers at Cherbourg were beginning the task of port reconstruction late in June, others on the plain south of Carentan were preparing to help First Army combat troops advance to a point from which they could break through German defenses and sweep south toward Brittany and east toward the Seine. The advance was to follow three main roads, one leading through La Haye-du-Puits down the west coast of the Cotentin to Coutances, another from Carentan southwest to Periers, and the third south from Carentan to St. Lo. The VIII Corps, which had become operational on the Continent on 15 June, was to advance on Coutances; VII Corps, which had swiftly turned around after the capture of Cherbourg, was to head for Periers; and part of XIX Corps was to drive toward St. Lo. The VIII Corps, on the west or right flank, was to lead off on 3 July.[1]

At the neck of the Cotentin peninsula the Germans had a powerful ally in the terrain. About half of the Carentan plain was so marshy that passage by foot was difficult, by vehicle impossible. The other half consisted of small fields separated by hedgerows—thick parapets of dirt from three to twelve feet high topped by hedges of trees and vines that grew as tall as fifteen feet in some places. Because of the height of the hedgerows, the wagon trails that wound among them seemed to be sunken roads. The advantage of such terrain to the defender was obvious. Providing concealment for riflemen, machine gunners, and artillery, hedgerows were, in effect, miniature fortified lines. Combat forces required close engineer support to open gaps through which tanks could advance, delivering machine-gun and point-blank artillery fire. Ordnance units developed a hedgerow cutter by welding prongs to the front of a tank, enabling it to slice through hedgerows without exposing its vulnerable underbelly and thus to cut an opening through which other tanks could follow. Where hedgerows were so thick that cutter tanks could not break through, the engineers had first to blow a breach with a heavy satchel charge.

---

[1] Martin Blumenson, *Breakout and Pursuit*, United States Army in World War II (Washington, 1961), p. 40. Unless otherwise cited, tactical information in this chapter is based on this source. Information on engineering activities is based on OCE ETOUSA Hist Rpt 10, Combat Engineering (United Kingdom), 1946, Liaison Sect, Intel Div, ETOUSA Adm file 547, and histories of the engineer units mentioned.

*The Road to Coutances*

In the VIII Corps sector the Germans had another terrain advantage, a horse-shoe-shaped ring of hills around La Haye-du-Puits. So commanding were these hills that from their crests the Germans could watch the shipping off the Allied beaches. Enemy artillery denied to VIII Corps the main roads leading to the town, forcing the corps' units to use lateral one-way roads and heavily mined lanes. Engineers supporting the three divisions moving out abreast in a drenching rain early on 3 July had to clear the narrow roads of mines and then to widen them for two-way traffic.[2]

Each division, the 82d Airborne in the center, the 79th on the west (right), and the 90th on the east (left), had its organic engineer combat battalion. In addition, on 17 June First Army attached to VIII Corps the 1110th Engineer Combat Group, which had supported VII Corps during the advance to Cherbourg. The group commander placed the 300th Engineer Combat Battalion behind the 79th Division, the 148th behind the 82d Airborne Division, and the 207th behind the 90th Division. The group also had a light ponton company and a treadway bridge company, which, split into platoons, could provide support to the divisions as needed.

The VIII Corps advanced to La Haye-du-Puits in a flying wedge formation with the 82d Airborne Division at the apex. Squads of the division's 307th Airborne Engineer Battalion accompanied battalions of parachute infantry, clearing roads of mines to enable supporting tanks to advance. The mine detectors and tanks drew enemy small-arms and artillery fire that caused heavy

losses among mine detector crews. Nevertheless, the crack airborne engineers who had dropped with the 82d Airborne Division in the early hours of D-day boasted that "the enemy pioneer obstacles had no effect on the tactical situation. The whole thing resolved itself into a sort of game between the pioneers and the engineers."[3]

The 82d Airborne Division met the weakest resistance during the VIII Corps' advance, encountering mainly Poles and Georgians whose morale was poor and who seemed happy to surrender. From these prisoners the engineers gained considerable information about the Germans' use of land mines. They employed the flat, antitank Teller mine with considerable ingenuity—sometimes burying them three deep in such a way that the two bottom mines were not visible even when the top one was removed; sometimes equipping the mines with a second fuse at the bottom, timed to go off after the demolitionists had unscrewed the top fuse; sometimes burying mines upside down with a push igniter that converted the Teller into an antipersonnel mine. The familiar antipersonnel S-mine was now equipped with a wire that would set off a block of TNT when the mine was lifted. The engineers also discovered a new type of antipersonnel mine called a "Mustard Pot," which consisted of a 50-mm. mortar shell equipped with a chemical igniter.[4]

---

[2] Hist 315th Engr C Bn, 7 Mar 44–May 45.

[3] Hist 307th Abn Engr Bn, Normandy Campaign, 6 Jun–15 Jul 44.
[4] Hist 148th Engr C Bn, Jun 44, Oct 44, and Dec 44; Hist 207th Engr C Bn, Nov 43–Dec 44. At the end of June the paratroopers had discovered a German artillery shell that contained, instead of explosives, notes in Polish encouraging the Allies. William G. Lord III, *History of the 508th Parachute Infantry* (Washington: Infantry Journal Press, 1948), p. 32; 315th Engr C

By daybreak on 7 July the 82d Airborne Division had gained its objective, and its troops, longest in combat on the Continent, were "lying in rain-filled slit trenches" beginning "to sweat out the much-rumored trip to England."[5] On the right the 79th held the heights west of La Haye-du-Puits but had been unable to take the town. This division, which had participated in the conquest of Cherbourg, had encountered enemy troops of better caliber, including a battalion of *Waffen SS* troops. Ingenious mines and booby traps also slowed the 79th. When an infantry battalion attempted a reconnaissance-in-force of La Haye-du-Puits during the afternoon of 7 July, the troops ran into "mine-studded fields strung with checkerboard patterns of piano wire about a foot off the ground and the booby traps set to blow off a leg any time you tripped the strands."[6]

On the east, or left, flank of the V-shaped advance, the inexperienced 90th Division had hard going from the moment it jumped off on 3 July. By 7 July the division's foothold on a ridge east of La Haye-du-Puits known as Mont Castre was so precarious that it had to call on its organic engineer combat battalion, the 315th, for combat support at the highest point of the ridge line, Hill 122. Companies A, B, and C, which had been doing mine sweeping, road clearing, and other engineer tasks in support of the 357th, 358th, and 359th Regimental Combat Teams, were alerted shortly before midnight on the

seventh to move out as infantry, attached to the 358th Regimental Combat Team. Late in June the battalion had trained in firing bazookas and heavy machine guns, and on 3 July it had contributed a bazooka team to help rescue men trapped under German self-propelled artillery fire. Moreover, the battalion had a mortar section made up of one squad from each line company, each squad being armed with two captured German 80-mm. trench mortars.

The mortar section occupied a position near the base of Hill 122, protecting the right flank of the 90th Division. The lettered companies went into action on the hill at dawn on 8 July. Battalion headquarters and the battalion aid station set up in a gravel quarry behind the lines. Between 8 and 11 July the battalion sustained ten casualties from enemy artillery, which reached even headquarters company's position, normally out of range, destroying the kitchen truck.

After 11 July the situation on VIII Corps' front began to improve. That day the 358th Infantry was able to descend the south slope of Hill 122, and the division commander returned the engineers to their normal tasks. By noon on 9 July, the 79th Division had taken La Haye-du-Puits and turned it over to the 8th Division, which had come foward to replace the 82d Airborne Division, soon to return to England. Five days later the 8th and 79th Divisions were occupying the north bank of the Ay River and reconnoitering for crossing sites to Lessay, still in German hands. The 90th Division was at the Seves River near Periers.

Between the 3 July jump-off and 14 July, VIII Corps had advanced only

Bn, Mine and Booby Trap Bull 3, Mine Helpers, 20 Jul 44, in Opns Rpt, 315th Engr C Bn, 90th Inf Div, Jul 44.

[5] Lord, *Hist of the 508th Parachute Infantry*, p. 37.

[6] Warren A. Robinson, *Through Combat: 314th Infantry Regiment* (Salt Lake City: Lorraine Press, 1948), pp. 21–22.

some seven miles through the hedge-rows—about one-third of the distance to Coutances—but had suffered more than 10,000 casualties. Lt. Gen. Omar N. Bradley, commanding First Army, changed tactics, planning the breakout not across the Coutances—St. Lo road, Route 172, but across Route 800 from Lessay through Periers to St. Lo. The operation, called COBRA, was to begin on 21 July. In the interim, the VIII Corps' divisional combat engineer teams provided demonstrations to infantry troops on clearing mines and blowing hedgerows and benefited from a general program of reequipping and rehabilitation. The 1110th Engineer Combat Group provided hot showers for the badly crippled 90th Division.

### The Road to Periers

There was little room to maneuver. For the attack south from Carentan to Periers, VII Corps had the 4th and 9th Infantry Divisions, which had participated in the capture of Cherbourg, and the 83d Division, which had arrived in Normandy late in June to relieve the 101st Airborne Division. To reach its objective the corps had to pass down a corridor resembling an isthmus two to three miles wide, with marshes on either side. This restricted the advance at the outset to two divisions; the 83d was to lead off on 4 July, followed by the 4th. The 9th was not to be committed until the leading divisions had taken objectives on the Periers—St. Lo road.

In addition to their organic engineer combat battalions, the divisions had the support of two engineer combat groups: the 1106th, with engineer combat battalions behind the 83d and 9th Divisions, and the 1120th, supporting the

4th Division and corps troops. The commander of the 1106th Engineer Combat Group, Col. Thomas DeF. Rogers, first had to undo previous engineer efforts—drain the Douve marshes that had been flooded to protect VII Corps' rear on its march to Cherbourg and clear a huge minefield that American forces had planted below Carentan to protect the 101st Airborne Division from a frontal attack. Two companies of the 238th Engineer Combat Battalion had the task of lifting the mines. Although enemy artillery and small-arms fire slowed the work, they removed 12,000 mines in two days. Meanwhile, battalions from both engineer combat groups drained marshes and maintained and guarded bridges over the Douve River.

When the 83d Division jumped off on the Fourth of July behind a ten-minute artillery preparation—"plenty of fireworks, but of a deadlier kind than those back home"—its 308th Engineer Combat Battalion, backed by the 238th Engineer Combat Battalion, built hasty bridges, maintained defensive positions at night, and blew hedgerows so that tanks could advance.[7] The Germans, protected behind the hedgerows, reacted strongly with artillery and machine-gun fire. The advance down the narrow isthmus went so slowly that after two days the VII Corps commander turned the 83d Division east toward the Taute River to make room to commit the 4th Division. That division, with engineer support from its organic 4th Engineer Combat Battalion and the 1102d Combat Group's 298th Engineer

---

[7] *Thunderbolt Across Europe: A History of the 83d Infantry Division 1942–1945* (Munich: F. Bruckmann, 1945), p. 29.

Combat Battalion, also had hard going. Six miles northeast of Periers the narrow neck of high land descended into a rain-swollen bog. Leading elements reached this point on 8 July. A week later, still four miles south of Periers, the 4th Division halted and went into reserve. In ten days of fighting it had sustained 2,500 casualties.

Thus, by mid-July the advance to Periers along the narrow isthmus from Carentan had come to a standstill. First Army reorganized the whole front. The 83d Division (less its 330th Infantry), badly crippled by 5,000 casualties in twelve days of combat and stalled at the western bank of the Taute River, began to relieve the 4th Division and passed to the control of VIII Corps. The main VII Corps effort then focused on high ground near St. Lo.

### The Road to St. Lo

Two infantry divisions were to spearhead the XIX Corps' advance toward St. Lo, the 30th down the west bank of the Vire and the 29th down the east bank. The 30th Division deployed in an arc extending from the north bank of the Vire and Taute Canal (which ran southeast from a point near Carentan on the Taute to a point just north of Airel on the Vire) to the east bank of the Vire near Airel. The division had to put its 120th Infantry across the canal and its 117th and 119th over the river. After the troops assembled near St. Jean-de-Daye, a crossroads village about three miles from the canal and from the river, they had to push through hedgerow country for nine miles to reach their objective on the highway leading west from St. Lo to Coutances. The 29th Division would presumably

have easier going down the high ground east of the Vire to its objective, St. Lo. Therefore, the 30th Division was to lead off on 7 July, with the 29th not committed until the 30th was about halfway to its objective. A third XIX Corps infantry division, the 35th, was then arriving in France and was to be committed either east or west of the Vire as circumstances dictated. The XIX Corps also might receive an armored division for use west of the Vire, but this was not certain when the 30th Division jumped off on 7 July.

The 30th Division had the support of its organic 105th Engineer Combat Battalion, backed by the 1104th Engineer Combat Group, which supplied the 247th Engineer Combat Battalion at the Vire River crossing and the 246th Battalion at the canal. Both were to have the aid of platoons of the group's 992d Engineer Treadway Bridge Company and 503d Engineer Light Ponton Company. Since mid-June the 105th Battalion's companies had been reconnoitering for crossing sites, readying equipment, and making practice crossings near the mouth of the Vire River.

### The Vire Crossings at Airel

Before dawn on 7 July, in drizzling rain and fog, Company A of the 105th Engineer Combat Battalion met the 117th Infantry at the site selected for the first Vire River crossing, just north of Airel. There the river was about sixty feet wide and from nine to fourteen feet deep. Because the river had steep banks, at least six feet high, the engineers and infantrymen carried scaling ladders with grappling hooks in addition to twelve-man rubber assault boats. To the comforting sound of a heavy artillery preparation that began at 0330, the first wave of thirty-two boats got under way at 0420, the men of the weapons platoons dumping their mortars and machine guns into the boats and swimming alongside to avoid swamping the frail craft. The 117th Infantry was experienced, having demonstrated river crossing at the Infantry School, Fort Benning, Georgia. In ten minutes the men were scrambling up the scaling ladders on the far shore.

Enemy artillery opened up just as the engineer boats were returning to the near shore, and the second and third boat waves crossed under heavy shelling. The worst victim of German fire was a platoon of Company B, 105th Engineer Combat Battalion, which was attempting to build a footbridge. The platoon had six bays in the water when direct artillery hits destroyed them. Another concentration killed four men and wounded four more. Still under fire, the engineers had scarcely finished a second bridge when enemy artillery tore the span loose from its moorings and wounded several men. Some of the engineers swam into the river and secured the bridge, and by 0530 the troops had a footbridge. The engineer platoon, which had lost half its men, was awarded a Distinguished Unit Citation for its heroic action.[8]

While the infantry was streaming over the footbridge, combat engineers began getting the division's vehicles and tanks across the Vire. A seven-arch stone bridge spanned the river at Airel, but it was badly cratered. The 247th Engineer Combat Battalion began work on the bridge at 0700, finding on it a truck that a German shell had hit a few days before. At the steering wheel was the body of the driver and behind the truck two other bodies. Removing the corpses and winching away the truck, the engineers first cleared mines from the bridge and then set to work, under concentrated artillery fire, to cover holes and gaps. With the aid of a platoon of the 992d Bridge Company, the 247th brought up a 108-foot floating treadway bridge on Brockway trucks, which had hydraulic booms to lift the heavy steel treadways and emplace them over the craters. In the process both engineer units suffered heavy casualties, mostly burns from white phosphorus shells, but the stone bridge was usable by 0900. After a bulldozer had passed over the treadway and cleared Airel of rubble, and after a battalion of the 119th Infantry had crossed to protect the bridgehead, tanks and tank destroyers began rolling over the bridge around noon.[9]

By this time the engineers had constructed additional vehicular bridges near Airel. One was an 84-foot infantry support bridge, which the 503d Engineer Light Ponton Company began at 0730 and finished in less than an hour. The other was a floating treadway just south of the stone bridge, built under heavy artillery and machine-gun fire that cost Company A of the 247th Engineer Combat Battalion four men killed and seven wounded. The bridge was in by 1130. Thus, at noon on 7 July, the 30th Division had the three bridges initially planned, the stone bridge and the treadway for one-way

[8] Robert L. Hewitt, *Work Horse of the Western Front: The Story of the 30th Infantry Division* (Washington: Infantry Journal Press, 1946), pp. 25–27.

[9] Jnl, Engr Sect, XIX Corps, 1–31 Jul 44, in XIX Corps G–4 AAR, ans. A–G.

traffic east and the infantry support bridge for casualties and traffic moving west.

Before the day was over events placed additional burdens on the group engineers. Early in the afternoon the infantry support bridge, weakened from shelling, was put out of action when a half-track and trailer crashed through it, fouling the ponton structure. The bridge had not yet been repaired when Combat Command B of the 3d Armored Division, ordered to cross the Vire at Airel on the evening of 7 July, arrived. This formidable convoy created a traffic jam at the stone bridge. On 8 and 9 July group engineers repaired the infantry support bridge, widened the stone bridge to take two-way traffic including armor, and built a ninety-foot triple-single Bailey to supplement it.[10]

### The Crossing of the Vire and Taute Canal

The 120th Infantry was to cross the twenty-foot-wide Vire and Taute Canal at the point where Route 174, the highway from Carentan to St. Lo, crossed the canal, but the bridge there was down. Because the canal was quite shallow, the plan was for most of the infantrymen to wade over. For troops of the heavy weapons companies and for the litter bearers evacuating casualties, Company C of the 105th Engineer Combat Battalion fabricated duckboards in ten-foot sections.

The crossing was to begin at 1330 on 7 July. At midmorning the XIX Corps engineer received a message from the corps G−3 that the water in the canal was deeper than expected, presumably

because the Germans had opened locks that controlled the tidal stream. The corps engineer ordered the 1104th Engineer Combat Group to close the locks, but the unit could not do so in time to ease the crossing. Finding the canal deeper and wider than they had expected, the infantrymen hesitated to start wading, and the engineers found their duckboards inadequate. After some confusion and a fifteen-minute delay, the lead troops of the 120th Infantry finally plunged into the canal, and the men of the 105th Engineer Combat Battalion erected a footbridge in thirty-five minutes. Heavy enemy artillery, mortar, and small-arms fire cost the engineers five men killed and twenty-six wounded.[11]

Continuous German artillery fire at the site of the destroyed Route 174 bridge delayed for several hours the emplacement of a bridge that could accommodate the tanks of the 113th Cavalry Group, Mechanized. In a rear area, Company A of the 1104th Engineer Combat Group's 246th Engineer Combat Battalion had constructed thirty-six feet of treadway bridge, loaded it on Brockway trucks, and was waiting only for some halt in the artillery fire to emplace the treadway. On an order at 1615 from the commanding general of the 30th Division to disregard enemy fire and erect the bridge, the engineers arranged with divisional artillery to lay down a smoke barrage. The emplacement required split-second timing. As the first smoke shells landed, men of the 246th Engineer Combat Battalion,

[10] Ibid.; Hist XIX Corps Engrs, p. 6, ML 2220, ETOUSA Hist Sect.

[11] Jnl, Engr Sect. XIX Corps, 1−31 Jul 44: War Department, Historical Div, *St. Lo, (7 July−19 July 1944)*, American Forces in Action Series (Washington, 1944), p. 15.

aided by the 992d Treadway Bridge Company, brought the Brockways up to the site; they had the treadways in place in less than twenty minutes, just as the smoke screen lifted. Traffic started flowing across immediately. The 120th Infantry commended Company A of the 246th Engineer Combat Battalion for a "fine job."[12]

### The VII Corps in the Vire-Taute Area

To protect XIX Corps' right flank and to help VII Corps outflank German resistance on the Carentan-Periers corridor, General Bradley decided to commit VII Corps' 9th Division in the area between the Taute and Vire Rivers. The division crossed the Vire and Taute Canal on 9 July and next day attacked west toward the Taute River. In addition to its own 15th Engineer Combat Battalion, the 9th Division had the direct support of the 237th Engineer Combat Battalion, 1106th Engineer Combat Group, a battalion that had distinguished itself in the D-day landings at UTAH Beach. The group commander explained the meaning of "direct support" to the engineer battalion and company commanders at a conference on the evening before the canal crossing. He defined it as doing "anything within reason to assist the attacking divisions."[13]

This the engineers did. While the 15th Engineer Combat Battalion concentrated on furnishing hedgerow-blasting teams and performing road work and mine clearance, the 237th made a

major contribution in bridging, building bypasses, widening and patching roads, and clearing mines. During minefield clearance northwest of St. Jean-de-Daye, the engineers discovered a new type of German mine—the "bottle mine"—made from a quart wine bottle, the lower half filled with earth, the upper half with a yellow crystalline explosive mixed with copper wire, nails, and tin, and corked with an igniter. The engineers worked often under artillery fire and in the face of several strong German counterattacks.

### Vire Crossings from Airel to St. Lo

While the 30th Division battered its way down the high ridge west of the Vire, XIX Corps' 35th and 29th Divisions advanced down the east bank. The 35th, nearer the river, had the support of the 234th Engineer Combat Battalion, attached to the 1115th Engineer Combat Group.

The next bridge was to be erected near Cavigny, about halfway between Airel and Pont-Hebert, about four miles to the south. In planning, the commanding officer of the 1115th Group used aerial photographs and maps, but according to group policy the final decision on the type of bridge to be used, treadway or Bailey (both types were available), depended on reconnaissance at the site. To get exact measurements the site selection party sometimes had to wade and swim the river under heavy enemy artillery, mortar, and small-arms fire. Although the Germans had good observation of the bridge site at Cavigny, the 247th Engineer Combat Battalion was able to install a 110-foot triple-single Bailey bridge there on 12 July.

Next day the group received orders

---

[12] Hist XIX Corps Engrs, p. 6, ML 2220, ETOUSA Hist Sect; *History of the 120th Infantry Regiment* (Washington: Infantry Journal Press, 1947), p. 18.
[13] Hist 1106th Engr C Gp, Jun–Dec 44.

to build a bridge over the Vire a mile or so farther south, at La Meauffe. Moving on the heels of the infantry, the 234th Engineer Combat Battalion reached the work site on 16 July almost before the last German had left. By midnight the men had erected a Bailey similar to that at Cavigny, a treadway bridge, and a bypass to route heavy traffic away from the railroad overpass, which artillery fire had seriously weakened. The 503d Engineer Light Ponton Company, attached to the 1115th Group on 15 July, brought up the Bailey bridging. Following a pattern established at the Vire and other rivers in Normandy, the engineers replaced Bailey bridges as soon as possible with timber bridges and took the Baileys forward for use in later crossings. Likewise, whenever possible—as at the stone bridge at Airel—they removed treadway so as to make it available for subsequent temporary bridging.

Information the 1115th Engineer Combat Group obtained from a French citizen who had been the government engineer for roads and bridges in the St. Lo area considerably eased planning for an important bridge at Pont-Hebert, where Route 174 from Carentan to St. Lo crossed the Vire. Of particular value was the civilian engineer's advice on manipulating the locks on the tidal Vire River at Airel and La Meauffe. This information enabled American engineers to lower the water level when a crossing was desired and to raise it, as necessary, to protect the 35th Division's flanks. After reconnaissance discovered an underwater bridge the Germans had built at Rampan, a town at a bend of the river about halfway between Pont-Hebert and St. Lo, the engineers suddenly closed the lock at La Meauffe one night, raising the level of the water at Rampan more than seven feet. This tactic denied the bridge to the enemy and drowned some Germans leading horse-drawn artillery across.[14]

One question the French engineer could not answer was whether a railroad overpass immediately east of Pont-Hebert was intact. Here, help came from artillery observation plane crews who bivouacked in the same hedgerow fields as the group engineers. The pilots reported several times daily not only on the condition of the overpass (which the Germans never demolished) but also on the bridge itself. The task of constructing the two bridges, a treadway and a Bailey, went to the 234th Engineer Combat Battalion, largely as a result of its excellent work at Cavigny and La Meauffe. The unit began work late on 18 July, and with the help of two officers from the 992d Treadway Bridge Company had a 156-foot floating treadway bridge in place by 0630. At 1100 the 503d Ponton Company brought up a 130-foot double-double Bailey bridge, which was ready for traffic by 1800.

Several hours before the engineers began bridge operations at Pont-Hebert on 18 July, a 29th Division task force captured the battered, bombed-out city of St. Lo. With the task force came a platoon of Company C of the 29th's organic 121st Engineer Combat Battalion to clear the streets of rubble. A sergeant of the engineer platoon claimed to be the first American to enter St. Lo.[15]

---

[14] Hist XIX Corps Engrs, pp. 9–10, and MS, The XIX Corps History, p. 8. Both in ML 2220, ETOUSA Hist Sect.

[15] Joseph H. Ewing, *29 Let's Go!: A History of the 29th Infantry Division in World War II* (Washington:

## VII Corps Engineers in the Cobra Breakthrough

While XIX Corps was assuming engineer responsibility for the construction and maintenance of bridges and roads, it was also preparing its part in Operation COBRA. The operation called for troops to break out of the bocage and through the German lines to the south, then to liberate more ports in Brittany. To open the offensive, air forces were to deluge a well-defined area south of the St. Lo–Periers road with light antipersonnel bombs designed to destroy enemy troop concentrations without tearing up the terrain to the detriment of attacking American armor and infantry. The corps' mission was to seize and hold a line from Coutances to Marigny, about eight miles to the northeast, in order to cut off and destroy the enemy facing VIII Corps in the Lessay-Periers area and to prevent German reinforcements' approach from the south and east. Armor to support the thrust was to pass through gaps the 9th and 30th Infantry Divisions opened. The VII Corps engineers devoted their efforts to opening and maintaining main supply routes (MSRs) to support the advance.[16]

The 1106th Engineer Combat Group was to support the 30th Infantry Division, advancing along high ground on the Vire's west bank with the 2d Armored Division following. The area had two main supply routes. One MSR (D–77), a two-way road for Class 40 traffic, was the responsibility of the group's 49th Engineer Combat Battalion; the other (D–446), a one-way Class 40 road, the 237th Engineer Combat Battalion was to open and maintain. A third engineer combat battalion, the 238th, would support the 2d Armored Division. On VII Corps' right flank the 1120th Engineer Combat Group was to support the 1st and 9th Infantry Divisions and the 3d Armored Division. The 1120th's 294th and 297th Engineer Combat Battalions were responsible for maintaining the two main supply routes—from Tribehou to Marigny—on the right flank, while the 298th Engineer Combat Battalion was to support the 3d Armored Division. Army engineer support in the VII Corps area was the responsibility of the 1111th Engineer Combat Group. About a week before COBRA, Maj. Gen. Manton S. Eddy, commanding the 9th Division, complained that the front assigned his division was too wide. General Bradley then gave VII Corps the 4th Infantry Division to attack down the center of the breakthrough area. The 1106th and 1120th Groups divided the engineer support mission for the 4th Division.[17]

According to the VII Corps plan, the 9th, 4th, and 30th Divisions were to be near the St. Lo–Periers road on 20 July, ready to break through as soon as possible after a massive air bombardment. But pouring rain and cloudy skies forced postponement of the bombardment until the morning of 25 July. By 17 July the engineers were at work on the main supply routes down which the tanks were to roll, sweeping the roads from shoulder to shoulder for mines, repairing craters and potholes, and clearing away rubble. For the diffi-

---

Infantry Journal Press, 1948), p. 102; Hists, 121st Engr C Bn, 1 Jun–31 Aug 44, and 1115th Engr C Gp, 29 Mar 43–Dec 44.

[16] VII Corps Engr FO 3, 19 Jul 44.

[17] Ibid.; Bradley, *A Soldier's Story,* p. 332.

cult problem of removing abandoned heavy German tanks, the 1106th Engineer Combat Group supplied heavy block and tackle of about fifty-ton capacity, threaded with 7/8-inch cable and operated by a four-ton wrecker. The 49th Engineer Combat Battalion tested the equipment successfully on a Tiger tank. Later the battalion used a simpler method for one more or less intact tank—the battalion's S–3 removed booby traps from the tank and drove it off the road under its own power. For "rush crossings" of bomb craters the 1106th Engineer Combat Group supplied the 2d Armored Division with sections of treadway bridging.[18]

"It's raining very hard," noted the 1106th Group's journal on 21 July; next day it was "still pouring." Mud made the construction of bypasses for infantry troops difficult, and gravel had to be brought up and stockpiled at strategic points to keep the four main supply routes firm enough for tanks. The work went on under increasingly heavy enemy artilley fire. For example, on the evening of 21 July at an engineer bivouac near Tribehou, German shells exploded a demolition dump, killing two men of the 298th Engineer Combat Battalion and wounding fourteen. On 23 July the weather began to clear, and on the morning of the twenty-fifth the engineers maintaining the roads in the VII Corps area saw the sky blackened with Allied planes. The COBRA breakthrough had begun. As the infantry divisions broke across the Coutances-St. Lo highway between Marigny and St. Gilles, the engineers, working night and day, had roads ready for the tanks.[19]

### VIII Corps Engineers Aid the War of Movement

For VIII Corps, the "direct pressure force" in the breakthrough, H-hour was 0530 on 26 July. The commander, Maj. Gen. Troy H. Middleton, had four divisions that he planned to move abreast in a fifteen-mile zone between the west coast of the Cotentin peninsula and the Taute River: the 79th Division facing the Ay River near Lessay on the extreme west, the 8th Division facing hedgerow country, the 90th Division along the Seves River, and the 83d Division on the extreme left along the Taute. (*Map 19*) Two armored divisions, the 4th and the 6th, were to roll through gaps on the Lessay-Periers road. Because both the 79th and the 90th Divisions faced flooded regions that offered the Germans excellent fields of fire, the 8th was chosen to spearhead the attack, opening a gap. The 79th was to follow through the gap, turn west, outflank the enemy south of the Ay, and seize Lessay. Engineer support of the advance was the responsibility of the 1110th Engineer Combat Group, with its 207th Engineer Combat Battalion directly behind the 8th Division and its 148th Battalion behind the 79th Division.

In preparing for the advance the group engineers repaired roads and cleared minefields. By midafternoon, 26 July, the 28th Infantry had reached

---

[18] Map, Operation COBRA VII Corps Plan, in Blumenson, *Breakout and Pursuit*, map 10, p. 216.

[19] Hist 1106th Engr C Gp, Jun–Dec 44; Engineer Operations by the VII Corps in the European Theater of Operations, vol. III, "Northern France and Belgium," pp. 1–2.

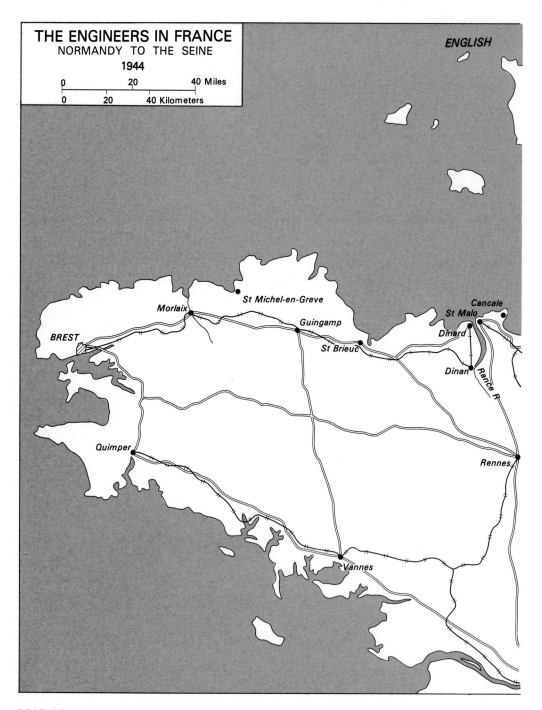

**THE ENGINEERS IN FRANCE**
NORMANDY TO THE SEINE
1944

0  20  40 Miles
0  20  40 Kilometers

ENGLISH

St Michel-en-Greve

Cancale

Morlaix

St Malo

Guingamp

Dinard

BREST

St Brieuc

Dinan

Rance R.

Quimper

Rennes

Vannes

*MAP 19*

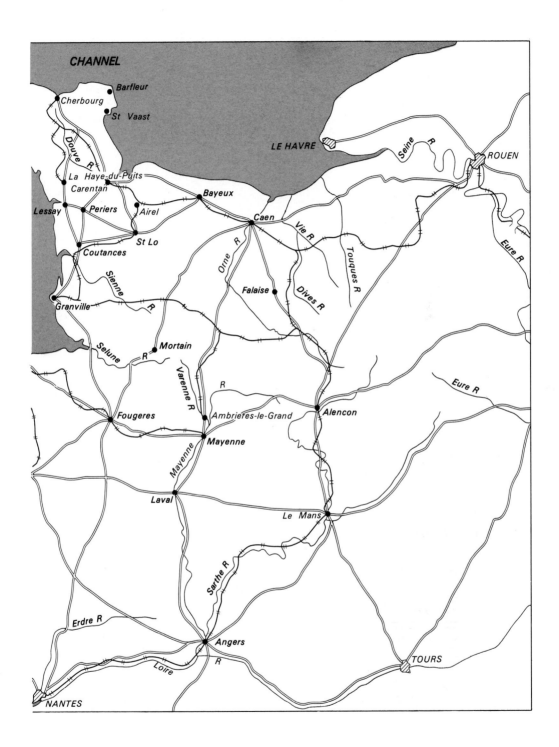

ENGINEERS ASSEMBLE AN EXPLOSIVE-LADEN "SNAKE" *to clear a path in a minefield.*

the Lessay-Periers road and had made untenable the entire enemy position along the VIII Corps front; by the evening of 28 July, the Germans were in retreat, leaving behind some of the most extensive minefields encountered on the Continent. The same evening the VIII Corps engineer, Col. William R. Winslow, ordered the engineer technical intelligence team (ETIT) attached to VIII Corps, bolstered by hastily organized teams from engineer combat battalions, to instruct the tankers of the 4th and 6th Armored Divisions in mine removal. The teams worked throughout the night giving demonstrations to the armored troops with actual mustard pot, Schu, and Bouncing Betty mines. Next morning, when the armor

rolled across a treadway bridge over the Ay River near Lessay (completed on the morning of 28 July by the 4th Armored Division's 24th Armored Engineer Battalion), the commander of the ETIT, 1st Lt. James Ball, could report that he saw "men from 4th Armored taking out mines they had never heard of before like veterans." The villages were also booby-trapped. In Lessay, a village of only 2,000, VIII Corps engineer units removed more than 300 booby traps during the afternoon of 29 July.[20]

Engineers of the 24th and the 25th Armored Engineer Battalions, organic to the 4th and 6th Armored Divisions,

---

[20] OCE ETOUSA Hist Rpt 10, Combat Engineering, p. 35.

respectively, also removed roadblocks and constructed bridges as they passed through Avranches and advanced into Brittany. Their experience illustrates operating differences between the armored engineer battalions and those in support of infantry. The armored engineer battalion was broken up into platoons, each assigned to an armored task force and operating under the command of the task force commander; the engineer battalion commander and the division engineer could thus exercise only the remotest degree of control. This situation became apparent during the speedy armored advance in the last days of July and led the 24th Armored Engineer Battalion's commanding officer to recommend placing the "utmost emphasis" on the training of platoon and company commanders.[21]

Speed in reducing obstacles—whether roadblock, minefield, blown bridge, or crater—was the essence of armored engineer operations. The engineers usually employed demolitions to reduce roadblocks and tankdozers to push away rubble. Mines were lifted by hand. While corps engineers generally bridged larger streams, the armored engineer platoon or battalion (to which a bridge company was attached) performed bridging whenever possible. Engineers of the 24th Armored Engineer Battalion considered the short, unsupported span treadway their most important bridge because it was the quickest to emplace when crossing antitank obstacles. On the night of 28 July, a platoon of Company B used a 24-foot fixed-span treadway to move 4th Armored Division tanks over a road crater; the engineers completed the operation,

including mine clearance, in twenty-five minutes.

On 1 August 1944, when Third Army became operational on the Continent, VIII Corps passed to its control. The army headquarters placed the 1102d and 1107th Engineer Combat Groups in support of the corps; the 1110th Engineer Combat Group reverted to First Army. The VIII Corps also had the support of the 1117th Engineer Combat Group until 7 August, when XV Corps became operational and took over the 1117th. Because trained engineer combat battalions were in short supply, Third Army obtained two engineer general service regiments. One of them, the 1303d, the army attached to VIII Corps.[22]

*Siege Operations in Brittany*

In the dash toward Brest—the first priority in early August because of the need for a large port—the 6th Armored Division bypassed St. Malo on the north shore of Brittany. Maj. Gen. Troy H. Middleton, the VIII Corps commander, gave the task of taking St. Malo to the 83d Division, reinforced by the 121st Infantry of the 8th Division, a medium tank company, and corps artillery. The mission included the reduction of Dinard, directly across the mile-wide Rance River estuary from St. Malo. At Dinard (in peacetime a popular bathing resort for the British), the Germans had emplaced artillery targeted on St. Malo.

The first task for the 83d Division's organic 308th Engineer Combat Battalion was to move the 121st Regimental Combat Team across the Rance River

[21] Hist 24th Armd Engr Bn, Jul–Dec 44.

[22] AAR of Third U.S. Army, 1 Aug 44–9 May 45 (hereafter cited as TUSA Rpt), vol. II, p. Eng–3.

for the advance on Dinard. Upriver near Dinan, about twelve miles south of Dinard, was a stone-arch bridge that the Germans had destroyed. There, Company A of the 308th began building two bridges on the afternoon of 5 August. The first completed was a Class 9 expedient floating bridge designed to move reconnaissance elements across the river. Company A had some difficulty with the second bridge, a 140-foot Class 40 double-double Bailey built across two spans of the stone bridge. Most of the work had to be done at night and because the roadway was about two hundred feet above the water, placing the intermediate and far-shore rocking rollers was extremely hazardous. Nevertheless, the bridge was ready for traffic by 0645 on 6 August. Before midnight, Company C had constructed a sixty-foot double-single Bailey bridge and three footbridges under such intense small-arms and mortar fire that only small parties could work at one time. Next day Company B made an assault river crossing for two infantry companies near La Vicomte-sur-Rance, four miles northeast of Dinan, against small-arms fire from Germans who held commanding ground on the far shore.

Thereafter, at Dinard and St. Malo, the engineers supporting the 121st Regimental Combat Team and the 83d Division played an important part in preliminary siege operations—destroying barricades, demolishing pillboxes to prevent the enemy from returning to them, gapping minefields, and removing booby traps. On several occasions engineers joined the infantry in flame-throwing teams. By 9 August the troops of the 83d Division had fought their way through the suburbs of St. Malo and, after bitter street fighting, reached the old part of the city near the harbor. The Citadel de St. Servan, a concrete and natural rock fortress with walls up to fifty-five feet thick, dominated the harbor. German shells were still crashing down from Dinard as well as from the tiny offshore island of Cezembre. Sending a combat team across the Rance to assist the 121st Regimental Combat Team in reducing Dinard, the main body of the 83d Division turned to battering down the last defenses of St. Malo.

Colonel Winslow, the VIII Corps engineer, maintained close personal liaison with the division engineers during the efforts between 9 and 12 August to breach the Citadel. On the afternoon of the tenth he led a party to explore St. Malo's sewerage system, hoping to locate a conduit under the Citadel where a major demolition charge might be placed; he found none. Nor did the 308th Engineer Combat Battalion have any luck aboveground. After dark on each night between the ninth and the twelfth the engineers climbed over the fortifications, dropping pole charges through the Citadel's vents and ports. Neither these nor demolitions placed under the battlements had any effect. As soon as the engineers' explosives began going off, German artillery from Cezembre Island would come in so heavily that the engineers would have to withdraw. The siege of the Citadel continued until 17 August, when the Americans forced surrender with direct 8-inch fire, using white phosphorus shells on vents and ports.

The VIII Corps then concentrated all its efforts on taking Brest. By mid-August a swift-moving task force, composed principally of cavalry and tank-destroyer units with the 159th Engineer

Combat Battalion in support, opened a supply line to the vicinity of Brest, an essential preliminary to capturing the city. The main mission was to secure vital bridges on a double-track railway running from Rennes to Brest before the Germans could demolish them. During the operation the engineers played a vital role, often taking the place of the infantry that the task force had fruitlessly requested.

The first railway bridges seized lay at St. Brieuc, on the coast about thirty-three miles west of Dinard. The task force captured the spans intact on 7 August; Company B of the 159th Engineer Battalion remained behind to guard them and set up a cage for prisoners of war. The most important bridge on the line was at the port of Morlaix, nearly fifty miles west of St. Brieuc. A stone-arch structure about a thousand feet long and two hundred feet high, the Morlaix bridge was the largest railway viaduct in France. Minefields and anti-tank obstacles temporarily slowed part of the task force, but Company B of the 159th Engineer Battalion kept going with the leading tanks and helped take Morlaix, which later became the principal port of entry for supplies used at Brest. The task force captured the bridge intact, and Company B stayed behind to guard it.

The rest of the battalion then received a new mission—to remove mines and obstacles from the beaches at St. Michel-en-Greve, some twenty-five miles northeast of Morlaix on the north coast of Brittany. Supplies for Brest came ashore there from LSTs; the first beaching was on 12 August.[23]

---

[23] Capt. William W. Baltz et al., *The 159th Engineer Combat Battalion* (Antwerp: De Vos Van Kleef, Ltd., 1945), pp. 11–15. For the events at Morlaix-Roscoff, see ch. XVI.

At 0300 on 25 August the attack on Brest began, with three infantry divisions side by side: the 8th in the center, the 29th on the right (west), and the 2d on the left. The city, France's second port and a great naval base, was fortified in depth. Ten miles out into the countryside the Germans had set up roadblocks, dug antitank ditches, planted huge minefields protected by machine-gun nests, and built concrete pillboxes. These provided a defensive position as strong as any American troops encountered on the Continent.

On the morning the siege began the commander of the 8th Division's 12th Engineer Combat Battalion, Lt. Col. E. M. Fry, Jr., was captured when he left his jeep to reconnoiter a bridge; three men of his party were killed. The battalion, aided by a company of the 202d Engineer Combat Battalion of VIII Corps' 1107th Engineer Combat Group, kept busy on road work, which enemy fire slowed, until 1 September. Then the 8th Division, having just reached the city limits, stopped in front of ramparts up to seventy feet thick and thirty feet high, on which the Germans had emplaced 88-mm. artillery and machine guns. Because of this formidable obstacle the task of taking Brest was turned over to the flank divisions, the 29th and the 2d; the 8th Division turned aside to clear the Crozon peninsula, west of the port. A few days after its arrival in the new sector, Colonel Fry rejoined his battalion. He had escaped from Brest in a rowboat.

About the time the 8th Division turned aside, the 29th Division on the west flank was approaching two ancient French forts, Fort Keranroux and Fort Montbarrey. The division captured Fort Keranroux on the afternoon of 13 September, mainly with the aid of heavy bombardment from planes and artillery. The reduction of Fort Montbarrey, a casemated fort with walls about twenty-five feet thick and surrounded by a fifty-foot moat, required intensive effort by the 29th Division's 121st Engineer Combat Battalion. The engineers first had to get close enough to the fort, in the face of withering fire from its ports, to place charges under the wall. Colonel Winslow, the VIII Corps engineer, planned to cover the ports with flame from flame-throwing tanks. He was able to obtain twelve such tanks—known as "Crocodiles"—from the British, but to get them close enough for their fire to be effective the engineers had to go out on the night before the attack and clear a path through a heavily mined and shell-pitted approach to the fort. This task, which Company B of the 121st Engineer Combat Battalion accomplished, was the first step of what turned out to be a classic siege operation.

The first attempt to get the tanks through failed. Of four Crocodiles that started out on 14 September, two wandered from the safe path through the mines; enemy fire destroyed another. The engineers again widened the path at night, and at 1500 on 16 September three Crocodiles, concealed by a smoke screen, were able to cover the entire west side of the fort with flames. Thus protected, engineers rushed to the outer wall and placed under it 2,500 pounds of TNT, creating a breach large enough for men to pass through. Then they placed 1,200-pound charge of TNT in a tunnel leading into the fort, causing the fort's reduction. Another party of engineers preceded the infantry, carrying scaling ladders that they set up against the fort. Scaling the roof, the assault party then used the ladders to get down into the courtyard. Within ten minutes the garrison surrendered.

Engineers of the 2d Engineer Combat Battalion, supporting the 2d Division approaching Brest from the east, also supplied scaling ladders as well as grappling hooks projected by rifle grenades for the infantry. But when the division came up against the ancient wall of the inner city, the engineers were unable to get close enough to blast a gap because the Germans had emplaced on the wall machine guns and a number of 88-mm. guns. The combat commanders called up the 8-inch guns that had been so successful at St. Malo. Firing from ranges as close as 5,000 yards, the big guns blasted a breach large enough for men to pass through; the engineers then widened it with explosives so that the hole would accommodate vehicles.

During the bitter house-to-house street fighting that followed, the 2d Engineer Combat Battalion made its most valuable contribution. The engineers became adept at blowing holes in the walls of houses at points where the entering infantrymen would not have to expose themselves to enemy fire in the streets. On the eastern side, away from the enemy, the engineers blew holes through inner walls to enable the troops to pass safely from building to building and in ceilings to allow the infantry to pass from floor to floor when the Germans defended stairways. The engineers also developed several methods of quickly overcoming obstacles in the way of the advancing troops. The engineers used TNT to cut steel-rail roadblocks and learned to fill craters and ditches quickly by blowing debris into them from the walls of adjacent buildings. In clearing debris from streets where sniper fire was prevalent, the engineers developed a new appreciation for the armored cab on D–4 angledozers.[24]

By the time Brest fell on 18 September, the Allies had the port of Antwerp. Brest was no longer required, and no effort was made to undertake extensive repair of the port facilities.

## The Seine Crossings

At the beginning of the third week in August, even before the siege of Brest had begun, U.S. Army engineers were helping American divisions to cross the Seine. Bridging operations began on 20 August when the 151st Engineer Combat Battalion put a treadway over the Seine at Mantes-Gassicourt, about thirty miles northwest (as the crow flies) of Paris. By the time they reached the Seine the engineers of both First and Third Armies had become adept at getting the combat troops across rivers. After First Army's breakthrough at Marigny–St. Gilles and Third Army's advance east from Fougeres (south of Avranches), bridge construction became the principal engineer mission. Roads across northern France were damaged in few places, and these could be quickly repaired or bypassed. The very speed of the advance prevented the Germans from either preparing extensive road demolitions or planting large minefields. Most bridges, however, were down—demolished either by the Germans or by Allied bombers.[25]

In supporting the advance of First Army's VII Corps, for example, corps and division engineers built twenty-nine bridges across the Seine between 31 July and 26 August. At several important crossing sites, such as those on the Seine immediately after the breakout and others on the Mayenne and Varenne Rivers during the closing of the Falaise Gap, the ground forces required four bridges at each crossing to provide adequate roadnets. Fortunately, in most cases not all the spans of existing stone bridges were down and most abutments were intact, permitting the rapid emplacement of treadway and Bailey bridging.[26]

Of particular interest to the engineers was a dual roadway Bailey built over the Varenne on 7 and 8 August at Ambrieres-le-Grand (about twenty miles southeast of Mortain), where only one arch of a 120-foot-long stone bridge remained in place. On the remaining pier, Company B of the 297th Engineer Combat Battalion began constructing a Class 40 Bailey at 0800 and by nightfall had completed it. That afternoon the 23d Armored Engineer Battalion quickly emplaced a treadway alongside, crossed the tanks of the 3d Armored Division, and then departed with the treadway. Two-lane traffic was still desired, but the abutments were not wide enough to carry two Bailey bridges side by side. The 297th Battalion converted the Bailey into a dual road structure by adding a second story to the central girder, building and launching a third girder, and then placing transoms and flooring for the second roadway. The two-lane bridge was

---

[24] Daily Opns Log, 2d Engr C Bn, Sep 44, in AAR, 2d Engr Bn, Jun–Dec 44.

[25] FUSA Rpt I, bk. V, pp. 224–25; TUSA Rpt, vol. II, p. Eng–3; Engr Opns VII Corps, vol. III, "Northern France and Belgium," p. 2.

[26] Engr Opns VII Corps, vol. III, "Northern France and Belgium," p. 2, and app. 3, Tabulation of Stream Crossing Data.

ready by 2000 on 8 August and proved sturdy enough to support not only a 1st Infantry Division regimental combat team crossing but also a week's continuous supply of traffic.[27]

Engineers with the convoys rolling eastward found northern France "something different from Normandy: the streets black with people, who seemed to do nothing twenty-four hours a day but stand there and cheer us and wave, and weep, some of them, and throw us flowers and fruits and vegetables, and stare wide-eyed at the trucks and jeeps and tanks. What always got them most were the tank retrievers that filled the whole road, with red lights blinking, and all armored up like something from Mars, and the Long Toms and 8 inch hows. They loved them!"[28]

While moving up to the XIX Corps' Seine River crossing at Meulan, a few miles northwest of Paris, the 1115th Engineer Combat Group's long, ungainly Brockway bridge trucks, carrying sections of steel treadways and lifting equipment, made a strong impression on the Germans. During the night of 26 August a convoy that included the 295th Engineer Combat Battalion ran into a company of German soliders. Uncertain of the enemy strength, the convoy held its fire. So did the Germans—a circumstance that mystified the Americans until two American prisoners of war, breaking away from their captors and jumping aboard the Ameri-

can convoy, supplied the reason. The Germans had been afraid to fire because they thought the Brockway truck was a new secret weapon—perhaps a rocket launcher.[29]

In the race across France the Seine River, not Paris, became the main objective. By mid-August enemy forces were fleeing the Argentan-Falaise pocket and concentrating along the lower Seine northwest of Paris. In the forefront of the pursuit, Third Army's XV Corps was to send its 5th Armored Division down the west bank of the Seine and put its 79th Infantry Division across the river to establish a bridgehead on the east bank near Mantes-Gassicourt.

A few hours before midnight on 19 August, receiving the order to cross, the commander of the 79th sent one regiment on foot across a dam near Mantes. A torrential rain was falling. In the blackness and rain the men walked single file, each man touching the one ahead. Another regiment, plus light equipment, crossed in engineer assault boats and rafts. The crossing seemed interminable—the river was from 500 to 800 feet wide. For the first bridge the 79th Division commander borrowed 700 feet of treadway from the 5th Armored Division. By the afternoon of 20 August the treadway was installed on rubber pontons, and another infantry regiment was crossing in trucks; by nightfall the bulk of the 79th, including tanks, artillery, and tank destroyers, was across the river. During the day enemy aircraft came over and attacked the treadway; its rubber pontons made the bridge vulnerable to bullets and bomb splinters. Next morning the division engineers began to construct a less

[27] Ibid., p. 3 and apps. 3 and 5; AAR, 297th Engr C Bn, Jun–Dec 44, Incl 3, Bridge Construction Rpt, 11 Aug 44. As insurance against the destruction of the Bailey (two enemy shells fell near the bridge on 7 August, though they did no damage), the 297th built a Class 40 floating treadway on pontons to the east of Ambrieres-le-Grand.

[28] MS, The XIX Corps History, p. 21, XIX Corps Engr, ML 2220, ETOUSA Hist Sect.

[29] Hist 1115th Engr C Gp, 29 Mar 43–Dec 44.

3D ARMORED DIVISION VEHICLES CROSS THE SEINE RIVER

vulnerable floating Bailey, supporting it on timber laid across four river barges. Finished at 0130 on 23 August, the improvised Bailey had to be used carefully because loads of more than forty tons caused the sides of the barges to spread apart. Nevertheless, the bridge served the division well.[30]

While elements of XV Corps, which temporarily passed to First Army control on 24 August, were using the Bailey over the lower Seine at Mantes-Gassicourt, engineers of Third Army's XII and XX Corps were preparing crossings south of Paris on the upper Seine. Typical was the effort by XX Corps engineers to cross the 7th Ar-

mored Division at Melun, twenty-five miles southeast of Paris. Hopes that the bridge at Melun could be captured intact were dashed on the morning of 23 August, when the Germans destroyed the span just as Combat Command Reserve (CCR) of the 7th Armored Division was about to attack. Because Combat Command Reserve had no assault boats and was receiving heavy fire from the opposite bank, the division commander brought up Combat Command A to cross downriver from Melun and attack the city from the north. Arriving the same morning at Ponthierry, a village about five miles downstream from Melun, Combat Command A, with the 179th Engineer Combat Battalion of the 1139th Engineer

[30] TUSA Rpt, vol. II, p. Eng–4.

FRENCH BARGES SUPPORT BAILEY BRIDGING OVER THE SEINE AT MANTES

Combat Group in support, found the bridge at Ponthierry demolished. Reconnaissance revealed two suitable assault crossing sites near Tilly, a hamlet a mile to the north. After a heavy artillery preparation at 1615, two companies of the 179th Engineer Combat Battalion, using seventy-six assault boats the 509th Engineer Light Ponton Company supplied, began crossing the armored troops at both sites. Initial waves went across without casualties, but succeeding waves met rifle fire that killed two of the engineers. The engineer battalion suffered even more heavily later in the evening when a German artillery shell hit one of its trucks, killing five men.

Meantime, elements of the 179th Engineer Combat Battalion had started construction of a treadway bridge at the northernmost site, aided by elements of the 7th Armored Division's organic 33d Armored Engineer Battalion. (During the fast pursuit the troops of the 33d had been riding on the outside of tanks acting as riflemen and had undertaken little engineer work.) By midnight the bridge was ready. Bulldozer operators, who prepared the approaches to the bridge as well as landing slips for a ferry operated at the south site, accomplished a particularly hazardous task under mortar, artillery, and rifle fire.

Engineers of V Corps had the enviable mission of assisting in the liberation of Paris. On 24 August reconnaissance parties of the 4th Engineer Combat Battalion, organic to the 4th Infantry Division, which with the 2d French Armored Division formed the bulk of V Corps, went forward to contact the French Forces of the Interior (FFI) and obtain data on Seine crossings. On the twenty-sixth, the combat engineers built a treadway bridge south of Paris and on that day and the next worked on the streets of Paris, clearing roadblocks and removing mines and booby traps. But the engineers had only two days to enjoy the riotous welcome given the liberators before the 4th Battalion moved east of Paris with its division. For the victory parade of the 28th Infantry Division down the Champs-Elysees on 29 August, engineers of V Corps' 1171st Engineer Combat Group improvised a reviewing stand for senior American and French officers, using a Bailey bridge turned upside down.[31]

### Beyond the Seine

After crossing the Seine, First Army's XIX, V, and VII Corps turned north and northeast in rapid pursuit of the fleeing and disorganized enemy. Fastest of all—"pursuit with a capital 'P' "—was the headlong 100-mile dash of XIX Corps to the Belgian border at Tournai on 1 and 2 September.[32] Crossing the Somme on bridges the British had captured intact with FFI help, the corps encountered no major water obstacles until it reached the Albert Canal and the Meuse River during the second week in September. In the "rather strange war" that developed, large pockets of the enemy were bypassed and Germans wandered into American bivouac areas. Two engineer task forces organized from elements of the 1104th Engineer Combat Group had the mission of rapidly clearing and maintaining roads and constructing the few bridges required.[33]

In the center of the First Army advance, the engineers of V Corps, supporting the 4th and 28th Infantry Divisions and the U.S. 5th Armored and 2d French Armored Divisions, constructed a series of floating and fixed bridges over the Aisne and the Oise and various small canals to the north of those rivers. Near Cambrai, south of the Belgian border, the corps (less the 2d French Armored Division) on 4 September turned to the right toward Luxembourg. During its march east, the corps encountered its first formidable water obstacle—the Meuse. The retreating Germans had destroyed all bridges along the line of advance from Charleville to Sedan. At Charleville on 6 September the 1171st Engineer Combat Group erected V Corps' first heavy ponton bridge, followed two days later by a second at Sedan. Because of the limited availability of floating equipment and of the need to keep treadway equipment with the forward elements, corps engineers rebuilt damaged bridges, including railway bridges, whenever possible. During these operations French civilians and members of the French Forces of the Interior provided helpful information concerning the status of bridges and the location of minefields.[34]

In the course of VII Corps' rapid

---

[31] Hist V Corps Engr Sect, Jun, Aug–Dec 44, Jan–9 May 45; *V Corps Operations in the ETO, 6 Jan 1942–9 May 1945,* p. 211, in CMH.

[32] Hewitt, *Work Horse of the Western Front,* p. 85.

[33] Hist XIX Corps Engrs, p. 11, ML 2220, ETOUSA Hist Sect.

[34] *V Corps Operations in the ETO,* pp. 214–36, in CMH; AAR, V Corps Engr Sect, Jun, Aug–Dec 44, Jan–9 May 45; Hist 112th Engr C Bn, 1944.

march northeast from the Seine the first important water barrier was the Marne, but it presented few problems to the corps engineers. The 3d Armored Division captured intact bridges at La Ferte and Chateau-Thierry, and one at Meaux, only partially destroyed, was quickly repaired. Elements of the 1120th and 1106th Engineer Combat Groups were over the border into Belgium before the end of the first week in September and made their most noteworthy contribution in bridging the Meuse in Belgium at Namur, Liege, and Dinant.

On the night of 6 September, the 1106th Group's 238th Engineer Combat Battalion constructed a record 564-foot treadway at Namur in five hours.[35] The next day the battalion spanned the Meuse with a 150-foot triple-double Bailey. Several shorter Baileys and treadways also had to be erected in the same neighborhood. The work went on under the protection of a corps antiaircraft battery; nevertheless, the battalion suffered two casualties. Beginning on 9 September the group's 237th Engineer Combat Battalion constructed a 550-foot treadway downriver at Liege and repaired a partially demolished bridge with Bailey equipment. Enemy bombing at the sites cost the battalion casualties consisting of three men killed and a number wounded. The most important effort of the 1120th Group took place upriver at Dinant, where the 297th Engineer Combat Battalion spent more than twelve hours on 9 and 10 September constructing a 287-foot, Class 40 floating Bailey, working most of the time in heavy fog.[36]

During Third Army's rapid dash to the Moselle from the Seine, where General Patton relinquished the Melun bridgehead to First Army, the principal water barriers were the Marne and the Meuse. On 28 August tanks of the 4th Armored Division, spearheading the advance of XII Corps, found the main bridge at Chalons-sur-Marne blown. The debris blocking the river formed a temporary dam, enabling the engineers of the 24th Armored Engineer Battalion to construct a hasty ford by which the entire task force crossed in 1 1/2 hours. As the water rose, the engineers constructed a treadway trestle bridge, and on the following day the 248th Engineer Combat Battalion of the 1117th Engineer Combat Group camped a few miles upstream at Vitry-le-Francois. By 31 August the 4th Armored Division was crossing the Meuse at Commercy over bridges seized intact. To the north the 1139th Engineer Combat Group, supporting the advance of XX Corps, found, on 29 August, two undamaged, permanent wooden bridges of unlimited capacity at Chateau-Thierry on the Marne. Treadways at other points were all completed the same day. At Verdun, where the main highway bridge crossed the Meuse, the Germans had installed mines, but the FFI was able to prevent demolition. On 31 August, XX Corps was over the Meuse in strength.[37]

Toward the end of August ominous entries had begun to appear in the journals of the engineer combat groups of First and Third Armies. Gasoline was running short, as were certain items of bridge-building equipment. The armies had outrun their supply depots, which

---

[35] Hist 1106th Engr C Gp, Jun–Dec 44.
[36] Engr Opns VII Corps, vol. III, "Northern France and Belgium," p. 4. See also histories of the units mentioned.

[37] TUSA Rpt, vol. II, p. Eng–6.

FRENCH CHILDREN WATCH THE 982D ENGINEER MAINTENANCE COMPANY WELD SIX-INCH PIPELINE

were far to the rear, most of them at the original invasion beaches. The problem was mainly one of transportation. The damage to railway lines and bridges had been extensive, principally as a result of Allied bombing. The installation of pipelines for petroleum, oil, and lubricants, an engineer responsibility, could not keep pace with the headlong advance of the combat forces, and trucks became the only means of getting supplies forward.[38] A particularly troublesome problem for the combat engineers was map supply—either because maps could not be sent forward in time to be of use or because the combat forces were moving into areas for which no maps were available. Leading elements of the 4th Armored Division, which during August traveled more than a thousand miles in less than thirty days, normally operated with road maps obtained from the FFI or captured German stocks. One of the first tasks of the engineers entering Verdun was to scour the city for German maps.[39]

For both U.S. armies, the pursuit ended the second week in September

---

[38] Hist 1139th Engr C Gp, Aug 44; MS, The XIX Corps History, p. 13, XIX Corps Engrs, ML 2220, ETOUSA Hist Sect; Ruppenthal, *Logistical Support of the Armies, Volume I,* pp. 500–16, 544–47.

[39] Hist 1139th Engr C Gp, Aug 44; Hist V Corps Engr Sect, Jun, Aug–Dec 44, Jan–9 May 45; Hist 24th Armd Engr Bn, Jul–Dec 44; TUSA Rpt, vol. II, p. Eng–5.

when Third Army met stiffening German resistance at the Moselle and First Army slowed down at the Siegfried Line in Belgium. By that time troops were exhausted, equipment was badly worn, and disturbing shortages in critical supplies had begun to appear. New offensives by both armies were authorized in mid-September, but it soon became apparent that stronger Communications Zone support was imperative.[40]

---

[40] Ruppenthal, *Logistical Support of the Armies, Volume I*, p. 583.

# CHAPTER XVIII

# Supporting a War of Movement in Northern France

Progress by American units after D-day depended on the maintenance of existing lines of communications. Fortunately, the French road and rail nets were highly developed and for the most part immediately usable by combat elements. ADSEC engineers were the first to tackle the damage from German demolitions and Allied bombing, turning over their responsibilities to their brethren in the COMZ area of operations as the front lines moved across France. Engineers constructed gasoline and oil pipelines simultaneously in a constant struggle to keep pace with the racing tactical units through the end of September.

## Highways

Immediately following the D-day landings in northern France, corps and First Army engineer combat battalions were to assume responsibility for road construction—corps engineers making emergency repairs only, and army engineers restoring bituminous surfaces. Bridging was to be of the military type, Bailey or treadway, to be replaced by timber bridges as rapidly as possible.[1] As soon as an army rear boundary became

established, road construction and maintenance were to be turned over to ADSEC. From D-day to D plus 90 the ADSEC engineer, Col. Emerson C. Itschner, planned to use four general service regiments, adding special equipment such as asphalt mixers and containers to their tables of equipment.

Road maps provided encouraging information about French roads to the engineers planning support of combat forces in northern France. The *Routes Nationales* were the French equivalent of numbered U.S. highways. Some of them dated from the Napoleonic era; all had a solid base of granite block surfaced with tarmac. The *Chemins Departmentaux,* comparable to numbered state roads in the United States were also of good quality, although the engineers knew little about their substructure. Both types seemed suitable for military traffic but were narrow by U.S. standards. The width of the national highways varied from twenty to twenty-six feet, that of the departmental roads from ten to twenty feet.[2] Route N–13,

---

[1] FUSA Rpt I, an. 9, p. 201 and an. 10, p. 208.

[2] OCE ETOUSA Hist Rpt 14, Road Maintenance and Highway Bridging, pp. 13–14; OCE ETOUSA Hist Rpt 12, Railroad Reconstruction and Bridging; OCE ETOUSA Hist Rpt 13, Petroleum, Oil, and Lubricants, Rpt of Activities, Engr Sect, ADSEC, COMZ, ETO, 7 Feb–30 Jun 44.

COLONEL ITSCHNER

which ran from Cherbourg southeast to Carentan and thence east behind the invasion beaches to Bayeux and beyond, received special attention in the planning. Another key route, N−800, led south from Cherbourg to Periers, where it turned southeast to St. Lo.[3]

The ADSEC general service regiments began landing on the Continent at the end of June, but because of the slow advance to St. Lo during the hedgerow fighting before the breakout on 26 July, combat engineers undertook most highway repairs inland of the beaches. (*Charts 4 and 5*) The two ADSEC engineer general service regiments landing at OMAHA (the 355th and 365th) spent their first month repairing roads leading to beach dumps. Those landing at UTAH (the 95th and 341st) undertook

the first ADSEC highway repairs performed on the Continent, beginning their work south of Cherbourg on 7 July. The 341st General Service Regiment was most experienced in road building and maintenance, having worked on the Alcan highway. To it went the difficult task of reconstructing N−13, running southeast from Cherbourg about fifteen miles to Valognes, and N−800, running south about the same distance to Bricquebec. These roads were sorely needed to move men, equipment, and supplies to the new battlefront after the fall of Cherbourg. Using crushed rock and asphalt, the men filled craters made by Allied bombs and shells and shored up the edges of pavement broken down under the pounding of heavy traffic. The work went on while the routes were carrying nearly 3,000 vehicles in a 24-hour period. To make up for the late arrival of some of its equipment the 341st Engineers improvised, using captured German equipment to assemble asphalt batching plants and a German cook wagon to heat tar.

Following the breakout at St. Lo and the formation of Third Army on 1 August, the 341st stayed close behind Third Army, repairing roads around Periers and maintaining those in the vital, narrow bottlenecks in the Coutances-Avranches area. In one ten-mile stretch of the main supply route running south from Periers to Avranches, the engineers laid more than 5,000 tons of stone in six days, working in shifts through daylight hours so intently that they "hardly saw armored division after division, the supply columns and a large part of the First Army move through the gap in the dust or mud."[4]

---

[3] Planned Road Net, Incl 25 to History of the ADSEC Engineer Section.

[4] Hist 341st Engr GS Rgt, 1944.

CHART 4—OFFICE OF THE CHIEF ENGINEER, ETOUSA, 1 AUGUST 1944

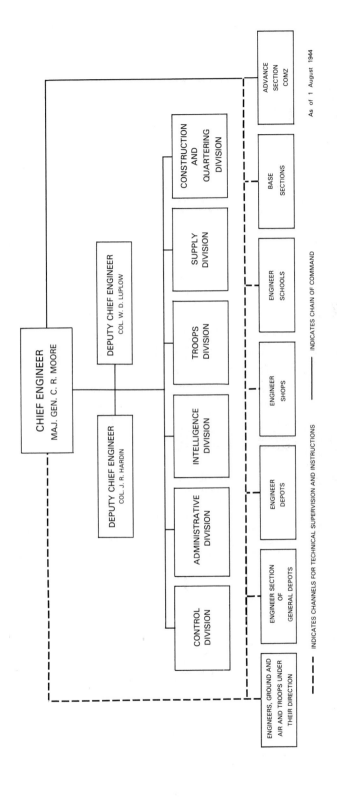

CHIEF ENGINEER
MAJ. GEN. C. R. MOORE

DEPUTY CHIEF ENGINEER
COL. J. R. HARDIN

DEPUTY CHIEF ENGINEER
COL. W. D. LUPLOW

CONTROL DIVISION

ADMINISTRATIVE DIVISION

INTELLIGENCE DIVISION

TROOPS DIVISION

SUPPLY DIVISION

CONSTRUCTION AND QUARTERING DIVISION

ENGINEERS, GROUND AND AIR AND TROOPS UNDER THEIR DIRECTION

ENGINEER SECTION OF GENERAL DEPOTS

ENGINEER DEPOTS

ENGINEER SHOPS

ENGINEER SCHOOLS

BASE SECTIONS

ADVANCE SECTION COMZ

As of 1 August 1944

————— INDICATES CHAIN OF COMMAND

– – – – INDICATES CHANNELS FOR TECHNICAL SUPERVISION AND INSTRUCTIONS

CHART 5—OFFICE OF THE CHIEF ENGINEER, ETOUSA, 1 OCTOBER 1944

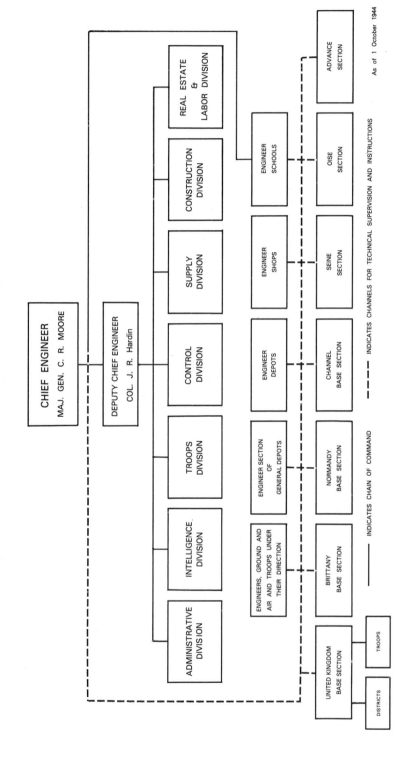

CHIEF ENGINEER
MAJ. GEN. C. R. MOORE

DEPUTY CHIEF ENGINEER
COL. J. R. Hardin

ADMINISTRATIVE DIVISION

INTELLIGENCE DIVISION

TROOPS DIVISION

CONTROL DIVISION

SUPPLY DIVISION

CONSTRUCTION DIVISION

REAL ESTATE & LABOR DIVISION

ENGINEERS, GROUND AND AIR AND TROOPS UNDER THEIR DIRECTION

ENGINEER SECTION OF GENERAL DEPOTS

ENGINEER DEPOTS

ENGINEER SHOPS

ENGINEER SCHOOLS

UNITED KINGDOM BASE SECTION

BRITTANY BASE SECTION

NORMANDY BASE SECTION

CHANNEL BASE SECTION

SEINE SECTION

OISE SECTION

ADVANCE SECTION

DISTRICTS

TROOPS

——————— INDICATES CHAIN OF COMMAND

– – – – – – INDICATES CHANNELS FOR TECHNICAL SUPERVISION AND INSTRUCTIONS

As of 1 October 1944

Except on the Cotentin peninsula south of Cherbourg to Avranches, highway reconstruction proved less difficult than ADSEC planners had expected. The primary roads stood up well under the pounding they received, and the Germans had not damaged highways or highway bridges to the extent feared. After the breakout, the armies moving across northern France encountered good roads that needed little work. Highway repair became mainly drainage and pothole filling on the Red Ball supply routes. Because of lessening requirements and the increased availability of prisoner of war and civilian labor, the four general service regiments earmarked for road building could be diverted to other work. The 365th transferred to hospital construction during most of the summer, and in mid-August the mission of the 341st, 355th, and 95th Engineer General Service Regiments changed from highway to railroad repair, which had by then become ADSEC's highest priority.[5]

### Railways

A 19 January 1944 agreement between the chief engineer, ETOUSA, and the chief of transportation made railroad reconstruction in northern France the responsibility of Colonel Itschner, the ADSEC engineer, to be performed at Transportation Corps request. Railroad reconstruction meant not only re-laying track but also reconstructing road culverts, bridges, and watering and coaling facilities. In southern France, responsibility for the construction and rehabilitation of railroads belonged not to the engineers, but to the 1st Military Railway Service (TC),

to which engineer units were attached or assigned.[6]

After the Normandy landings, priority went first to the tracks within Cherbourg and second to lines leading from Cherbourg to Lison junction near Isigny, about forty miles southeast. A line was then to be reconstructed leading southwest from Lison junction via Coutances, Folligny, Avranches, and Dol (in Brittany) to Rennes, the first major depot area. The British were responsible for the rail line running east from Lison junction.[7]

Planners estimated that 75 percent of the track and all the bridges would have been destroyed and that necessary reconstruction would require 55 percent new ties and 90 percent new bridging material. All this material was to be of British origin, not only for tracks (standard British 75-pound flat-bottom rail) but also for bridges, because the U.S. Army had developed no military railway bridges. British designs went into production both in the United States and in the United Kingdom. The types included in American planning were rolled steel joist (RSJ) spans, which came in lengths of 17, 21, 27, 31, and 35 feet; a 40-foot sectional girder bridge; a unit construction railway bridge (UCRB), in lengths from about 50 to 80 feet; and light steel trestling.[8]

The units earmarked for railroad construction included five engineer general service regiments, three engineer dump truck companies, and one engineer heavy ponton battalion for hauling materials and equipment. First

[5] Hists, 365th and 341st Engr GS Rgts.

[6] ETO Gen Bd Rpt 123, Military Railway Service, p. 2.

[7] Ruppenthal, *Logistical Support of the Armies, Volume I*, pp. 316–17, map 9.

[8] Moore, *Final Report*, p. 282.

Army was to lend the ponton battalion to ADSEC. The training and equipment of the five general service regiments left something to be desired. Only the 332d and 347th had attended the U.S.-British Railway Bridging School at King's Newton. The remaining three had to rely on a thirty-day intensive training program which was provided to several types of specialized units during April 1944. The training was not very effective, for railway tools and special track fixtures were scarce and much of the available material had already been packed for the cross-Channel attack.[9]

The chief of Colonel Itschner's Railroad Section, Lt. Col. A. D. Harvey, landed in Normandy on 11 June and immediately began reconnoitering railway lines near Isigny and Carentan, walking tracks when it was safe to do so. On 15 June he flew in a Piper Cub as low as 150 feet over the main line from Lison junction at Montebourg, a little more than halfway up the peninsula, to Cherbourg. He found that damage to tracks and yards, usually inflicted by Allied bombing, was much less than expected and that, except for a bridge over the Vire River near the Lison junction, the railway bridges would not be difficult to repair.[10] This and later reconnaissance trips showed that earlier estimates on the amount of material required could be revised downward. Two events after the landing also forced Itschner to alter the engineers' railroad reconstruction plan—the late capture of Cherbourg, which deferred railroad work there from mid-June to the end of the month, and the late

arrival of the engineer general service regiments earmarked for railroad repair.

Railroad rehabilitation on the Continent began at the Carentan yards on 17 June, with the 1055th Engineer Port Construction and Repair Group in charge. During the following week that group also furnished a detachment to direct a crew of civilians at the Lison junction yards, and the 342d Engineer General Service Regiment went to work on the line north from Carentan. The group also began repairing the Vire River railroad bridge. On 26 June the 1055th moved three locomotives from Lison to Isigny—the first U.S. railroad operation on the Continent.

The 332d Engineer General Service Regiment, scheduled to arrive on 14 June, did not land at UTAH Beach until the twenty-eighth. The regiment worked at Cherbourg on port reconstruction, while railroad work in that city became the responsibility of the 347th Engineer General Service Regiment, which arrived on the Continent about the same time. Other general service regiments earmarked for railroad work arrived soon thereafter, but not all were employed as planned. The 390th Engineer General Service Regiment performed track work between Cherbourg and Lison junction, but the 392d largely undertook engineer supply operations. The 354th worked on construction of the Couville railroad yards near Cherbourg, an assignment that original plans had not envisioned. The engineer heavy ponton battalion, hauling material and equipment, did not arrive until much later than planned, and when the unit reached France First Army assigned it another mission.[11]

---

[9] Ibid., pp. 154–55.

[10] Diary, Lt Col A. D. Harvey, D plus 5–D plus 49, app. 6, OCE ETOUSA Hist Rpt 12.

[11] For the railroad work at Cherbourg, see ch. XVII.

*After the Breakout*

Until the breakout at St. Lo on 26 July, railroad reconstruction received relatively low priority, for distances were short and trucks could do the hauling from beaches to dumps and from dumps to forward areas. After the breakout the tempo accelerated. Within a few days the general service regiment most experienced in railroad work, the 347th, came down from Cherbourg and took on the task of opening lines to St. Lo and beyond to Coutances. After the capture of Coutances on 29 July, urgent priority went to rebuilding the line south to Third Army's railhead at Folligny. In the fifty days following the St. Lo breakout, railroad reconstruction became the ADSEC engineer's primary mission.

First and most important was reconstruction of the yards at St. Lo, which Allied bombing had almost entirely destroyed. So complete was the destruction in one section that engineers had to obtain plans from the *Societe Nationale des Chemins de Fer* before they could start re-laying track. On 4 August two companies of the 347th began work at St. Lo, using rail, fittings, and ballast either salvaged from unused lines or hauled from beach dumps in trucks. On the same day, a third company of the 347th began rebuilding the double-track, three-span, masonry-arch railway bridge over the Vire River on the Lison–St. Lo line. Bombing had demolished the center span and damaged another. The engineers, who had not yet received any military bridging, replaced the center span with a timber trestle bridge—the first timber trestle the 347th Engineers built—and repaired the damaged span

by fitting face stone and keystones and filling in with concrete.[12]

Simultaneously with the jobs in the St. Lo area, the engineers began rehabilitating two single-track lines, one south of St. Lo and the other west. The track running to Vire, about twenty miles southeast of St. Lo, was to provide an alternate route behind the armies. The track on the west, from La Haye-du-Puits to Coutances, would bring forward supplies from Cherbourg. But the ADSEC engineer completed neither of these efforts. The Vire line, which a company of the 347th Engineers started to repair, was turned over to the British. The 2d Battalion, 390th Engineers, began work on the line to Coutances with engineers from the Transportation Corps' Military Railway Service (MRS), but before the line was complete MRS assumed full responsibility—ADSEC units were needed elsewhere, and ADSEC had to commit all its scarce railway troops to supplying ammunition and gasoline to Third Army.

The Third Army was already swinging east toward Paris when the 347th Engineer General Service Regiment began reconstruction of the Coutances-Folligny rail line. At Coutances, where Allied bombers had done considerable damage, Company D of the 347th encountered a damaged high viaduct railroad bridge—the first of many found in France. A six-span, single-track, masonry-arch structure with one span missing eighty feet over the Soulle River, the bridge provided the first opportunity to employ the British unit construc-

---

[12] Waldo G. Bowman, "Railroad Bridging in the E.T.O.," *Engineering News-Record* (July 12, 1945), 36–37.

tion railway bridge. Using the special launching nose, the engineers launched a fifty-foot unit to span the arch opening. Then they installed a timber strut just below the unit to resist thrusts from adjacent arches ·carrying the weight of heavy locomotives. In the meantime, the 347th Engineers had begun to repair a demolished concrete-arch railway bridge over a highway just south of Coutances, completing the work on 12 August.[13] On the same day General Patton put the engineers to a grueling test.

### Supporting Patton's Thrust Toward Paris

What was later described as "perhaps the most dramatic achievement of Engineers in railroad construction" began after sunset on 12 August when Colonel Itschner received surprising instructions from Third Army: "Gen Patton has broken through and is striking rapidly for Paris. He says his men can get along without food, but his tanks and trucks won't run without gas. Therefore the railroad must be constructed into Le Mans by Tuesday midnight. Today is Saturday. Use one man per foot to make the repairs if necessary."[14] The message meant that a railroad 135 miles long, with seven bridges down, three railroad yards badly bombed, track damaged in many places, and few, if any, watering and coaling facilities available, had to be reconstructed in seventy-five hours. Normally the job would have taken months.

Colonel Itschner had on hand only 2,000 men working on the line running from Coutances to Folligny—the 347th Engineer General Service Regiment and the 2d Battalion of the 390th. The latter had just begun restoring the yards at Formigny, a few miles south of OMAHA Beach, where the air forces had completely destroyed a large German troop train shortly after D-day. An additional 8,500 men were available to Itschner for his formidable task, but they were scattered widely, some as far away as Cherbourg. Moreover, the only means of communication with the widely separated units was by a messenger in a jeep.[15]

The first step was to fly over the railroad net from Folligny to Le Mans to select the lines that could be repaired in the shortest time. The most direct route led south from Folligny via Avranches, Pontaubault, and Fougeres to Vitre, where it turned east via Laval to Le Mans. Itschner had to rule out this route, for two bridges along it had been so badly bombed, piers as well as spans, that they could never be reconstructed in time. One was a forty-foot-high bridge over the Selune River at Pontaubault, the other a ninety-foot-high bridge over the Mayenne at Laval. To bypass both, the engineers planned to open a single-track line turning east just north of Pontaubault to St. Hilaire-du-Harcouet and then south to a point beyond Fougeres, from there east to Mayenne, and on south to La Chapelle-Anthenaise (beyond Laval). Here the line was to connect with the double-track railroad

---

[13] Ibid., pp. 37–38.

[14] Maj. Gen. Cecil R. Moore, "Engineer Operations in the European Theater, Informal Remarks . . . to SHAEF Correspondents, Friday, 6 October 1944," *The Military Engineer*, XXXVI (December 1944), 408; Col. Emerson C. Itschner, "Reconstruction of Western European Railroads," [July 1945], Bortz files.

[15] Itschner, "Reconstruction of W European Railroads"; Moore, "Engr Opns in the European Theater," p. 408.

to Le Mans. Five bridges were down along the planned route.[16]

Elements of eleven different engineer general service regiments worked simultaneously on the line. The experience of the 332d Engineer General Service Regiment illustrates the urgency with which the engineers moved to the scene. The 332d, then at Cherbourg, received orders at 0300 on 13 August to proceed to Mayenne. Two companies took the 0700 train to Carentan, then moved to Mayenne by truck. Upon arrival, the unit set up a pup tent bivouac in a hayfield nearby and quickly began work on the railroad. Some of the 9,000 engineer troops required to open the line did not arrive on the project until twenty-four hours before the deadline, and equipment moved slowly on the congested roads. Yet the work proceeded so swiftly that as the deadline approached Colonel Itschner had only one serious cause for concern—an eighty-foot single-track bridge at St. Hilaire-du-Harcouet.[17]

With a well-placed charge the Germans had blown the south end of the bridge from its abutment, dropping it into the Selune River. The 347th Engineer General Service Regiment cut off the damaged end, jacked up the bridge and placed it onto a pier built of ties in the form of a crib. This the unit accomplished in three days, during which many of the men had no sleep at all. When General Moore and Colonel Itschner flew over the St. Hilaire bridge site on an inspection trip six hours

before the deadline of midnight 15 August, they saw spelled out on the ground in white cement, "Will finish at 2000." The first gasoline-loaded train left the Folligny area at 1900 on 15 August, passed over the St. Hilaire bridge shortly before midnight, and after many delays was at Le Mans on 17 August. Thirty trains followed at thirty-minute intervals.[18]

Even while the emergency single-track line was being opened, engineers were working on the bridges at Pontaubault and Laval to provide a more permanent and serviceable line to Le Mans. These major bridges, which units of the 332d Engineer General Service Regiment reconstructed, were the most ambitious bridging projects yet undertaken. Each bridge had one badly damaged concrete pier that had to be replaced by a light steel trestling pier, and each bridge required two UCRB spans. The Pontaubault bridge was ready on 22 August, rebuilt in twelve days; that at Laval, where work continued at night under floodlights, was ready in fourteen days, and the first train crossed on 31 August.[19]

### The ADSEC Engineer Groups

About the time the rush job for General Patton was completed, the size of the ADSEC area and the increased volume of railroad reconstruction made it necessary for the ADSEC engineer's Railroad Division, which up to that time had handled all reconnaissance, plans,

---

[16] History of the ADSEC Engineer Section, figs. 23 and 24; OCE ETOUSA Hist Rpt 12, Railroad Reconstruction and Bridging, fig. 8; Ruppenthal, *Logistical Support of the Armies, Volume I*, p. 316, map 9.

[17] Itschner, "Reconstruction of W European Railroads."

[18] Interv, Col A. H. Davidson, Jr., in Memorandum to Files, 7 Mar 50, Bortz notes; Itschner, "Reconstruction of W European Railroads"; History of the ADSEC Engineer Section, fig. 21.

[19] History of the ADSEC Engineer Section, pp. 66–67 and figs. 23 and 24.

procurement, project assignments, and inspections, to delegate many of these responsibilities to subordinate units. Therefore, on 23 August ADSEC created three provisional engineer groups, ADSEC Engineer Groups A, B, and C. Each had an experienced general service regiment as a nucleus, with one or more additional regiments attached, and each was commanded by the senior regimental commander. Although each unit retained its identity for administrative functions, the group commander, aided by the staff of the nucleus regiment, handled all operational matters, including work assignments, supply, and reconnaissance.

The nucleus of Group A was the 332d Engineer General Service Regiment, whose commanding officer, Col. Helmer Swenholt, became group commander. Attached were the 392d, 375th, and 389th Engineer General Service Regiments. Group B, commanded by Col. Harry Hulen, had the 347th Engineer General Service Regiment as the nucleus, with the 377th Engineer General Service Regiment attached. Col. Edward H. Coe commanded Group C, whose nucleus was the 341st General Service Regiment, with the 355th and 95th attached. Of the nine general service regiments in the three groups, five had engineer dump truck companies attached, and one had an attached engineer welding detachment (provisional).

During the last week of August, elements of the three groups were working on almost all rail lines between Pontaubault and the Seine. Groups A and B set to repairing the main double-track Vire-Argentan-Dreux-Versailles-Juvisy line and a bridge crossing the Seine at Juvisy. Group C worked farther south in support of Third Army

to open the Chartres-Orleans-Montargis line. On 27 August the group received an urgent mission to open immediately a single-track line between Rambouillet and Versailles, the first line into Paris. Two companies of the 341st Engineer General Service Regiment, working twenty hours straight, completed the job the following day. Lt. Col. E. Warren Heilig of the 341st Engineers and his driver, Pvt. Harry Smith, were hailed by great crowds as the first Americans to enter Versailles on the heels of the retreating Germans.[20]

During the period of fast pursuit, Allied bombing and artillery fire caused most of the track damage. Until the engineers reached the area east of Metz, where German track destruction was severe—some of it occasioned by the "track ripper," a huge hook pulled by locomotives—the main problem was bridges.[21] The worst destruction Group A encountered was at a bridge over the Eure River near Dreux, about thirty miles west of Paris. All that remained of a five-span, 300-foot masonry-arch structure was a pile of splintered wreckage and two damaged abutments well over 200 feet apart. This bridge had a strange history. According to a story the engineers heard, the French had destroyed the bridge in 1939. Later, the Germans repaired it, replacing the masonry arches with steel beams and wooden piers. During the rush to the Seine, Allied bombers attacked the bridge repeatedly. Bombs falling wide of the mark became so dangerous to the local population that the French Forces of the Interior put demolition charges on the bridge and blew it up.

---

[20] Hist 341st Engr GS Rgt. 1944.
[21] Itschner, "Reconstruction of W European Railroads," p. 2.

Company F, 332d Engineer General Service Regiment, aided by elements of Companies C and D, rebuilt the bridge between 25 August and 9 September. The engineers placed five steel deck-type spans on four light steel trestle piers—seventy-foot-long unit construction railway bridge spans at each end and three I-beams in the center. The steel trestle piers in the center rested on existing concrete footings; those at the end of the bridge sat on footings the engineers made with compacted rubble. At first the bridge carried only a single track, but the engineers later completed a double-track bridge by increasing the width of the piers and building a duplicate superstructure on the widened section. The engineers assembled the additional spans on the ground and lifted them into place because the usual nose-launching method would have required halting traffic along the single-track line.[22]

For the first crossing of the Seine River south of Paris at Juvisy, the engineers faced the widest body of water they had yet encountered. (*Map 20*) No unit construction launching equipment was available for the four sixty-foot UCRB spans required to cover gaps in the existing bridge, gaps created when the Germans dropped two 120-foot lattice girder spans into the river. Group B's 347th Engineer General Service Regiment solved the problem by assembling the UCRB spans and towers for light steel trestling piers on shore. This procedure saved time in the long run, because it permitted superstructure assembly to proceed simultaneously with wreckage clearance and pier foun-

dation work. When the piers were ready, the engineers put the spans and towers aboard a French derrick barge, pushed it out to the site with tugs, and set the equipment in place in a matter of minutes. Speed was essential because until the bridge was in, Third Army operations east of Metz could not be supplied. The engineers completed the bridge on 6 September, forty-eight hours ahead of schedule.[23]

Bridge reconstruction east of Paris posed different problems. Bridges were usually longer and lower, so timber-pile trestles frequently could be erected on the debris of the old bridge, a distinct advantage. On the other hand, supply became more difficult because the long distance from the beaches made it impracticable to haul forward such material as UCRB spans. The engineers had to depend on materials obtained locally or captured from the Germans. The new conditions were exemplified in the reconstruction of the bridge over the Marne River Canal at Vitry. Two companies of Group C's 341st Engineer General Service Regiment repaired it in six days beginning 5 September, working around the clock and using floodlights at night. Two ninety-foot spans of the three-span masonry-arch bridge had received direct hits from Allied bombers as two German freight trains were crossing it on adjacent tracks. Cars, track, and stone were piled in the water. Instead of attempting to remove or build through the rubble, the engineers used the debris to carry wood sills upon which bents were set to support a stringer-type bridge. For spans, the engineers employed captured German

---

[22] Bowman, "Railroad Bridging in the E.T.O.," pp. 40–41 and figs. 11, 12a, and 12b.

[23] Ibid., pp. 39–40 and figs. 9 and 10.

Rotterdam

Maas R

NETHERLANDS

G E R M A N Y

Rhine R

Albert

Antwerp

Canal

COLOGNE

BRUSSELS

B E L G I U M

WEST

Tournai

Liege

Namur

Dinant

WALL

Cambrai

LUXEMBOURG

Somme R

Charleville

F R A N C E

Sedan

Meuse

Oise R

Aisne R

Verdun

Moselle R

Mantes-Gassicourt

Chateau-Thierry

Marne

Chalons-sur-Marne

PARIS

La Ferte

Marne R

Commercy

Meaux

Marne-

Canal

Melun

Vitry

Rhine

Ponthierry

Seine R

Yonne R

Orleans

Loire R

**BEYOND THE SEINE**
1944

| 0 | 25 | 50 Miles |
| 0 | 25 | 50 Kilometers |

*MAP 20*

I-beams and a prefabricated deck girder span found in a railroad yard.[24]

Fifty days after the breakthrough at St. Lo the rail net in the Third Army sector extended to Verdun on the Metz line and to Toul on the line to Nancy. In the First Army sector, the line was open from Paris northeast through Soissons, Laon, Hirson, Marienbourg, Charleroi, Gembloux, and Landen to Liege. (*Map 21*)

The first train to cross the border into Belgium was the regimental headquarters train of the 332d Engineer General Service Regiment. On 25 August Colonel Swenholt, the regimental commander (also commander of Group A), decided to move his headquarters and the administration section of Headquarters and Service Company to the La Hutte–Coulombiers area near Le Mans by train to save precious gasoline and tires. He used a German hospital train augmented with a few French cars and drawn by Transportation Corps locomotives. Pulling out of the village in some style after the townspeople had decked it with flowers, the train rolled over the Eure River bridge near Dreux on 9 September and continued to Paris via Versailles. Beyond Paris the engineers had to depend upon French locomotives and crews. Problems with the locomotives soon developed, and when the train reached the Belgian border more trouble arose, for the French crews objected to going into Belgium. Acquiring a German freight locomotive and recruiting crews from his own units, Colonel Swenholt got the twenty steel cars and five boxcars under way from Hirson shortly after midnight on 12 September and reached Charleroi,

Belgium, at 2000 the same day. After a stay of four days in Charleroi, during which the engineers were so mobbed by welcoming Belgians that the gendarmes had to be called out, the headquarters train arrived at Liege in the early morning of 17 September 1944.[25]

*Pipelines*

By 12 August 1944, the day General Patton demanded railroad reconstruction from Folligny to Le Mans to carry gasoline in the dash toward Paris, the pipeline designed to bring bulk POL forward from the ports ran only as far as St. Lo. ADSEC engineer units, whose mission was to construct pipelines, storage tanks, and pumping stations and then to operate them, began landing on OMAHA Beach shortly after D-day.[26] The largest unit in the POL organization was the 359th Engineer General Service Regiment, with Company A of the 358th Engineer General Service Regiment attached. Other components were seven engineer petroleum distribution companies—the 698th, 786th, 787th, 788th, 790th, 1374th, and 1375th; two engineer fire-fighting platoons; and a squad from an engineer camouflage battalion. The 358th and 359th General Service Regiments were not assigned to bulk POL supply on the Continent until well after their arrival in England in late 1943. The regiments were generally inexperienced in pipeline operations and had insufficient time and equipment for adequate training. On the other hand, the petroleum distribution companies had been

---

[24] Ibid., pp. 42–43 and fig. 13.

[25] Hist 332d Engr GS Rgt, 1 Jan–31 Dec 44.

[26] Ruppenthal, *Logistical Support of the Armies, Volume I*, p. 510. For early POL planning in the ETO, see Ibid., pp. 319–27.

recruited largely from oilfield workers
and had received specialized training
in the United States. In late spring of
1944 the 787th Engineer Petroleum
Distribution Company instructed the
two general service regiments in pipeline construction and operation.

Most engineer POL units had the
mission of installing and operating the
Major POL System at Cherbourg, constructing or rehabilitating facilities for
receiving, storing, and dispensing fuel.
Most POL was to be delivered dockside
by tankers, but some was to come in
through British lines laid on the floor
of the Channel from the Isle of Wight
to the Continent, a system called PLUTO
(Pipeline Under the Ocean). From Cherbourg south the engineers were to lay
three six-inch pipelines, two for motor
gasoline (MT 80) and one for aviation
gasoline (avgas), with pump stations,
tank farms, and dispensing facilities at
La Haye-du-Puits, Coutances, Avranches, Fougeres, and Laval. Lines for
motor fuel were to extend from Fougeres to Rennes and from Laval to Cha-
teaubriant. But because construction
for the major system could not begin
until Cherbourg was captured, the engineers were to put the Minor POL System into operation shortly after D-day
at two points east of OMAHA—Ste.
Honorine-des-Pertes, the easternmost
town in the American sector, and Port-
en-Bessin, at the edge of the British
beach area.[27]

### The Minor POL System

The first POL engineers ashore at

MAP 21

OMAHA were two companies of the
359th General Service Regiment and
two petroleum distribution companies,
the 698th and 786th. An advance party
of officers landed early in the evening
of 9 June and proceeded east to the
assigned bivouac area—an apple orch-
ard near the village of Huppain, somewhat inland and about halfway between
Ste. Honorine-des-Pertes and Port-en-
Bessin. In the next two days a convoy
with the rest of the first elements came
in over the narrow cliffside road to
Huppain. As the last men of the 786th

[27] Coll, Keith, and Rosenthal, *The Corps of Engineers:
Troops and Equipment*, pp. 417–37. See also Hists,
359th Engr GS Rgt, 1943–45, and 787th Engr Pet
Dist Co, 22 Feb 44–Dec 45.

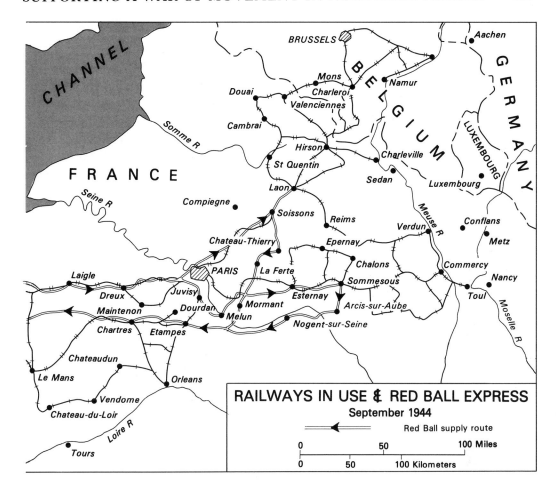

RAILWAYS IN USE & RED BALL EXPRESS
September 1944

Red Ball supply route

0          50          100 Miles

0      50      100 Kilometers

Engineer Petroleum Distribution Company landed at OMAHA on 11 June, they saw that the "wet, flat strip of sand was littered up and down the coast as far as the men could see. Machinery, guns, tools, clothes, and the innumerable odds and ends that came ashore with the assault were scattered and strewn as tho by some incredible wind. Broken landing boats [were] flung beside burnt-out tanks whose tracks were already bright with rust. [DUKWs,] bent like metal toys, spotted the foot of the sheer cliffs descending from the fortified hills." That night after the petro-

leum engineers had settled down in the bivouac at Huppain, German fighter-bombers roared low over them but dropped no bombs.[28]

At that time, the engineers had a scant ten days to get the first POL system in operation. Bulk deliveries of POL, which had been handled in cans during and immediately after the invasion, were scheduled to begin on D plus 15.[29]

At Ste. Honorine-des-Pertes the engi-

[28] Hist 786th Engr Pet Dist Co, Feb–Dec 44.

[29] Ruppenthal, *Logistical Support of the Armies, Volume I*, p. 322.

neers were to install two six-inch ship-to-shore submarine pipelines known as TOMBOLAs to receive gasoline and diesel fuel from tankers at a deepwater anchorage and carry it to five bolted steel tanks onshore. One tank, holding 10,000 barrels of gasoline, was for Army use; four 5,000-barrel tanks, one for gasoline and three for diesel fuel, were for the Navy. Pump stations and four-inch lines would carry the Army gasoline to an inland tank farm at Mt. Cauvin, a hill about two miles south of Huppain and equidistant from Ste. Honorine-des-Pertes and Port-en-Bessin. The Navy fuel was to go to the MULBERRY at OMAHA.

Port-en-Bessin had two moles where shallow-draft tankers could tie up. While the British used the easternmost, the engineers were to install two six-inch discharge lines at the other—one for motor gasoline and one for aviation gasoline—and to erect two 1,000-barrel tanks, one for each type. Two pump stations were required, as well as two six-inch delivery lines running to the tank farm at Mt. Cauvin.

Mt. Cauvin needed considerable work, including tankage for 30,000 barrels of motor gasoline, a six-inch gravity line and six tank truck filling risers, pump stations, and two four-inch lines connecting with British lines. In addition, one four-inch pipeline was to be constructed south to Balleroy, with a booster station on the way at Crouay. Balleroy, an important filling station, would have two terminal storage tanks (one holding 1,000 barrels and the other 5,000 barrels), dispensing lines and connections to permit loading six tank trucks simultaneously, and decanting connections where quartermaster troops could fill five-gallon cans.

Plans for expansion of the Minor POL System were partly shaped by the fuel needs of U.S. aircraft on the Continent. For aviation fuel, a four-inch line was to extend from Mt. Cauvin about twenty-eight miles west to Carentan, with booster stations on the way. At Carentan French fuel tanks with a capacity of 4,200 barrels were to be rehabilitated and dispensing facilities constructed. A similar line for motor vehicle gasoline was to run from Mt. Cauvin to St. Lo and Coutances, where the Minor and Major POL Systems would connect. At both St. Lo and Coutances, storage tanks and facilities to serve a quartermaster decanting station were to be constructed.[30]

Lack of supplies seriously handicapped the POL engineers who landed on OMAHA beginning 9 June. Construction materials expected to come in aboard a commodity-loaded coaster on 10 June did not arrive. By scouring OMAHA and UTAH beaches the engineers found enough scattered material to make a small start on 13 June. Two days later the first of eight LCTs, loaded with construction materials and sent forward when it became evident that the capture of Cherbourg would be delayed, arrived at Port-en-Bessin. Unfortunately, a storm that raged along the coast for three days wrecked two of the LCTs.

Mines the Germans had sown in the area also handicapped early operations. They had not been cleared because the combat engineers charged with this work had landed elsewhere. From one field

---

[30] OCE ETOUSA Hist Rpt 13, Petroleum, Oil, and Lubricants, app. 10c, POL Plan, OVERLORD, pp. 12–13; Ruppenthal, *Logistical Support of the Armies, Volume I*, pp. 316–17, map 9.

behind Ste. Honorine-des-Pertes the POL engineers removed more than a thousand mines, suffering six casualties, one fatal. Casualties would undoubtedly have been higher except for a "kindly, sharp-sighted little Frenchman," Eugene Le Garre, who had a summer home near the beach at Ste. Honorine-des-Pertes. From his front porch he had watched the Germans plant their mines and had noted their locations. On fishing trips he had discovered underwater mines near the beaches and furnished information for which Allied engineers were grateful.[31] The engineers also faced German snipers, whose bullets sometimes punctured pipelines. They often found that the elevations marked on their contour maps were incorrect, forcing drastic changes to the plans for tank sites. Nevertheless, by 23 June, the day the first tanker arrived at Port-en-Bessin, the POL engineers had their transmission, storage, and dispensing facilities ready. When the first TOMBOLA was launched at Ste. Honorine-des-Pertes three days later the engineers had extended a pipeline to the Balleroy storage area, where the POL troops had erected one tank and were installing dispensing facilities.[32]

After the capture of Cherbourg most POL engineers left work on the Minor POL System and proceeded toward Cherbourg via Bricquebec, where elements of the POL organization were already located. Company A of the 358th General Service Regiment and the 787th Engineer Petroleum Distribution Company, for example, did not

reach Huppain until 22 June and stayed only three days before moving west. After 1 July responsibility for the Minor POL System passed entirely to the 786th Engineer Petroleum Distribution Company, the only engineer POL unit remaining in the area.

As the transfer to Cherbourg began, the 786th was pushing pipelines westward, following a railroad bed that ran from Bayeux to Carentan via St. Jean-de-Daye. Although trucks and trailers negotiated the rough railroad bed with difficulty, it was the most direct and level route west. By 9 July construction had advanced to Govin, within five miles of St. Jean-de-Daye, but there enemy small-arms fire halted the work. St. Jean-de-Daye had not yet been captured, and the line that was to run through the town had to be abandoned. After a temporary suspension of all construction, the 786th Engineer Petroleum Distribution Company pushed a line for aviation fuel north from Govin to Carentan, arriving there on 24 July. South from Govin engineers constructed two pipelines, one for aviation fuel and another for motor gasoline, to tie in with the Major POL System at St. Lo. Early in August elements of the 1374th Engineer Petroleum Distribution Company, which had reached Huppain in mid-July, worked at Carentan repairing civilian gasoline tanks and at St. Lo building a 10,000-barrel tank.

### The Major POL System

Gasoline from the Cherbourg area began to flow into St. Lo on 11 August. While elements of the 359th Engineer General Service Regiment, with the 787th, 698th, and 1375th Engineer Petroleum Distribution Companies, recon-

[31] Hist 359th GS Rgt, pp. 145–46.
[32] Col A. G. Viney, Dep ADSEC Engr, Rpt to Engr Fwd Echelon, HQ, COMZ, 26 Jun 44, quoted in OCE ETOUSA Hist Rpt 13, Petroleum, Oil, and Lubricants, pp. 65–66.

structed POL facilities at Cherbourg, troops of the 359th General Service Regiment surveyed the pipeline route south.

Work on the pipelines to the front, beginning at the Hainneville tank farm in Cherbourg and undertaken mainly by the 2d Battalion of the 359th, proceeded expeditiously, thanks to an increase in supplies and manpower. Close behind the combat troops, the engineers extended the lines to La Haye-du-Puits and Lessay by the beginning of August. The route of the pipelines changed with the breakthrough. Instead of swinging south via Coutances and Avranches to Laval, the pipelines were to run southeast to St. Lo, Vire, and Domfront, and then east to Alencon, Chartres, and Dourdan, to cross the Seine near Corbeil and go to Coubert near Paris.

The major system consisted of three pipelines, two for 80-octane and one for 100-octane aviation fuel. Construction of the 80-octane lines got priority because of the greater demand for motor fuel. Except at highway and railroad crossings, where welded lines went underground, engineers laid the pipelines on the ground and connected each section with victaulic couplings. Whenever possible, the route followed a hard-surfaced road along which POL construction material could be transported. In the early days in Normandy the pipelines followed road shoulders because the engineers did not have time to break through the hedgerows and remove mines from the fields. But here the lines fell victim to errant drivers, and traffic accidents nearly always involved a section of the pipe. The engineers soon learned to lay the pipelines on the other side of the hedgerows,

where they escaped damage and still followed the line of communications.[33]

Construction from St. Lo went on simultaneously along three segments of the route: St. Lo to Vire, Vire to Domfront, and Domfront to Alencon. By the end of August the engineers had pushed one 80-octane line, the "Pioneer" six-inch line, as far as Alencon, eighty-one miles from St. Lo; a second 80-octane line had reached Domfront, and the aviation gas line was approaching Domfront. The need for speed and the inexperience of some of the POL engineers resulted, at times, in poor construction. Breaks occurred when the engineers were careless with couplings or left openings through which small animals entered the line or into which other troops threw such objects as C-ration cans. Breaks in the line north of Domfront on 29 August made it necessary for combat forces to draw all gasoline at St. Lo until repairs could be made. Interruptions to the work were inevitable when the engineers ran into minefields and suffered casualties or encountered pockets of enemy resistance. Fuel losses from holes punched in the line by black market operators and saboteurs became frequent as the lines moved east, while breaks resulting from ramming by trucks and tanks increased as the traffic built up.[34]

When the advance party of the 359th General Service Regiment reached the bombed-out city of Alencon on 20 August, it ran into clouds of dust from hundreds of vehicles rolling over the rubble in the streets. A tremendous acceleration of traffic came a week later with

[33] Moore, *Final Report*, pp. 312–13.
[34] Ruppenthal, *Logistical Support of the Armies, Volume I*, pp. 510–11 and map 16; History of the ADSEC Engineer Section, Incl 13.

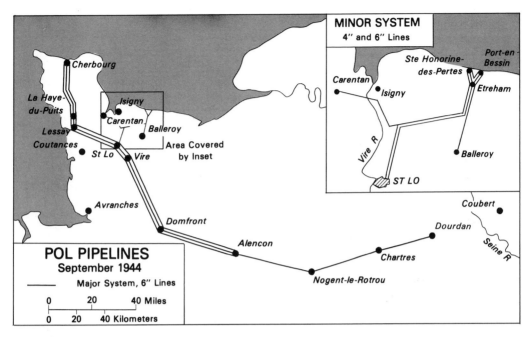

MAP 22

the inauguration of the Red Ball Express, an around-the-clock operation to carry supplies (except bulk POL) to the front. The engineers soon felt the effect of Red Ball on pipeline construction. Faced with the urgent needs of the advancing armies, COMZ chose to divert to Red Ball many truck units needed to carry pipeline construction materials to the POL engineers. At the end of August COMZ gave high priority to the rail movement of POL engineer materials, and within ten days the engineers received enough material in the Alencon-Chartres area to permit construction to continue. But by then the slowdown of pipeline construction had already contributed to the critical gasoline shortages that developed early in September.[35]

[35] Ruppenthal, *Logistical Support of the Armies, Volume I*, p. 513; Moore, *Final Report*, p. 313.

### New POL Organization

By the third week in August the engineer force working on the major and minor pipeline systems included three general service regiments, the 358th, 359th, and 368th; a battalion of a fourth, the 364th; and nine petroleum distribution companies, the 698th, 786th, 787th, 788th, 790th, 1374th, 1375th, 1376th, and 1377th. With attached truck companies, welding detachments, and firefighting platoons, the force numbered more than 7,000 men. On 23 August ADSEC organized this engineer force into the Military Pipeline Group (Provisional) under the command of Col. John L. Person of the 359th. (*Map 22*)

Enough troops were available to operate the systems, but by mid-September, after a brief spurt of moving construction materials by rail had ended, transportation to move the pipe forward was

DECANTING AREA ON THE OIL PIPELINE IN ANTWERP, BELGIUM

lacking. The Major POL System had advanced to Chartres, but the ADSEC engineer estimated that available trucks and trailers could deliver no more than seven to eight miles of pipe per day.[36]

The lack of transportation to move POL construction supplies made it increasingly difficult for the pipelines to keep up when ADSEC headquarters moved forward. This posed a problem of control. For a time, base sections operated parts of the system in their respective areas, but the division of responsibility was unworkable because the POL system was essentially an entity unto itself. When ADSEC moved to

Reims early in September, the entire POL system fell outside the ADSEC area and was likely to remain so for some time. Therefore, on 23 September 1944, the Military Pipeline Group (Provisional) passed to the control of Headquarters, Communications Zone, and was renamed the Military Pipeline Service (MPLS). Colonel Person continued as commander.[37]

COMZ instituted a number of helpful changes, dividing the pipeline area into districts, with commanding officers of the experienced engineer petroleum distribution companies in charge. COMZ also set up schools in each district for

---

[36] OCE ETOUSA Hist Rpt 13, Petroleum, Oil, and Lubricants, p. 88 and fig. 5; Hist 359th GS Rgt, p. 195.

[37] History of the ADSEC Engineer Section, p. 56.

the less experienced engineers of the general service regiments, took steps to reduce pilferage, and, most important, provided first a courier service and later a telephone service for better communications among the POL engineers who had hitherto been operating, as one expressed it, "by smoke signals." In addition, an airlift from the United States brought in a number of sorely needed spare parts.[38]

The problem of moving the construction materials forward remained vexing. By 6 October 1944, the Major POL System was in operation to Coubert, across the Seine about twenty miles southeast of Paris. The period of rapid pursuit was over, and other supplies, notably ammunition, had priority over POL. Planners then decided to terminate the major system at Coubert, at least for some time, and to concentrate on shorter pipelines based at Le Havre and Antwerp. Coubert remained the end of the line until January 1945.[39]

Farther east of Paris, Allied armies were approaching the German border by mid-September. The engineers expected formidable obstacles in the fortified belts of the Siegfried Line and in the Rhine River to say nothing of the terrain between them, heavily crisscrossed with watercourses large and small.

---

[38] OCE ETOUSA Hist Rpt 13, Petroleum, Oil, and Lubricants, app. 15, Military Pipeline Service: Individual and Unit History.

[39] Ruppenthal, *Logistical Support of the Armies, Volume I,* pp. 514–15. For construction of pipelines and supply of POL after January 1945, see Ibid., *Volume II,* pp. 193–209, 434–40, and map 11.

# CHAPTER XIX

# Breaching Germany's Barriers

Rolling into Eupen behind tanks on the afternoon of 11 September 1944, the engineers saw that "the 'fun' the boys had had in liberating all those towns and cities in France and Belgium was over."[1] They were greeted not with wild cheers but with hostile stares. Eupen was in Belgium, but it was only some five miles from the German border. All the signs were in German. From some windows hung Belgian flags, but from others were suspended white bedsheets signifying surrender. The engineers belonged to Company B of the 23d Armored Engineer Battalion and were supporting Combat Command B of VII Corps' 3d Armored Division, the spearhead tankers who, on 12 September, would be the first Americans to capture a German town.

General Eisenhower had long planned that as soon as enemy forces in France were destroyed the American armies would advance rapidly to the Rhine, First Army through the Aachen Gap on the north to Cologne and Third Army through the Metz Gap south of Koblenz.[2] On the northern battlefront in France artificial and natural barriers blocked the routes to the Rhine. The attackers would have to clear a path through the concrete fortifications that formed the Siegfried Line. They would also have to penetrate dense woods and forests, overcome fortifications protecting Aachen and Metz, and cross many rivers, some of them in flood. In the two months between the first breaching of the Siegfried Line and the start of the German counteroffensive in mid-December the deepest advance into Germany was only twenty-two miles.[3]

### The Siegfried Line

Begun in 1938, the Siegfried Line was a system of mutually supporting pillboxes, about ten per mile, extending along the German border from a point above Aachen south and southeast to the Rhine and thence along the German bank of the Rhine to the Swiss border. North of Aachen the line consisted of a single belt of fortifications, while south of that city it split into two belts, about five miles apart, known as the Scharnhorst Line and the Schill Line. Farther southeast, in the rugged terrain of the Eifel, the line was again one belt until it reached the region of

---

[1] Hist 23d Armd Engr Bn, 1944, p. 8.
[2] Msg, Eisenhower to Commanders, 4 Sep 44, quoted in Hugh M. Cole, *The Lorraine Campaign*, United States Army in World War II (Washington, 1950), p. 53.

[3] Charles B. MacDonald, *The Siegfried Line Campaign*, United States Army in World War II (Washington, 1963), p. 616. Unless otherwise cited, tactical details of the First Army penetration are from this source.

the Saar, where it split once more. *(Map 23)*

The pillboxes were set at least halfway into the earth. Walls and roofs were of reinforced concrete three to eight feet thick, sometimes covered with earth, grass, and trees and sometimes disguised as farmhouses or barns. Concealed steel doors led to rooms for quartering troops and storing arms and ammunition. The firing ports could usually accommodate only light machine guns and the 37-mm. antitank guns standard in 1938. Most heavier fire had to come from mobile artillery and tanks stationed near the fixed fortifications.

For protection against tanks the pillboxes often depended on natural barriers such as watercourses, forests, and defiles. In more open country the pillboxes had a shield of 45-foot-wide bands of "dragon's teeth"—small concrete pyramids, usually painted green to blend in with the fields. The pyramids had been cast in one piece on a concrete base, with steel reinforcing rods tied into the base's reinforcing rods. The teeth in the first two rows were about 2 1/2 feet high, those in the following rows successively higher until the last stood almost 5 feet tall. Between the rows were iron pickets imbedded in the bases, designed to take barbed wire. Wherever a road ran through the bank, the Germans blocked access with obstacles such as steel gates.[4]

In late August 1944 Hitler rushed in a "people's" labor force to strengthen the line. This effort bore fruit in the Saar, where the Third Army did not arrive at the Siegfried Line until early December; but in the First Army's Aachen and Eifel sectors, where VII Corps and V Corps reached the line almost simultaneously on 12 and 13 September, the Germans did not have time to accomplish much.[5] They had begun to dig antitank ditches in front of the dragon's teeth but had to abandon them, leaving picks and shovels behind; nor had they had time to string barbed wire on the iron pickets. In general, second-rate troops manned the pillboxes and other defensive works.

### VII Corps South of Aachen

By nightfall on 11 September two task forces of CCB—Task Force 1 commanded by Lt. Col. Wiliam B. Lovelady and Task Force 2 commanded by Lt. Col. Roswell H. King—and 3d Armored Division had passed through Eupen and encamped for the night east and northeast of the town. At 0800 next morning a reconnaissance force of infantry, tanks, and engineers of Task Force Lovelady began to move toward the German border, but the tanks bogged down on a forest trail. A second group set out along the main highway shortly before noon. Capturing some German machine gunners who surrendered without firing, the reconnaissance elements crossed the border shortly before 1500; the main body of Task Force Lovelady joined them about an hour later. The task force passed through the German town of Roetgen without opposition.

Beyond Roetgen, on a highway leading north, Task Force Lovelady ran into

---

[4] Engineer Operations by the VII Corps in the European Theater, vol. IV, "Pursuit Into Germany," app. 1, Initial Breaching of the Siegfried Line.

[5] Cole, *The Lorraine Campaign*, pp. 548–51. Unless otherwise cited, Third Army tactical details are from this source.

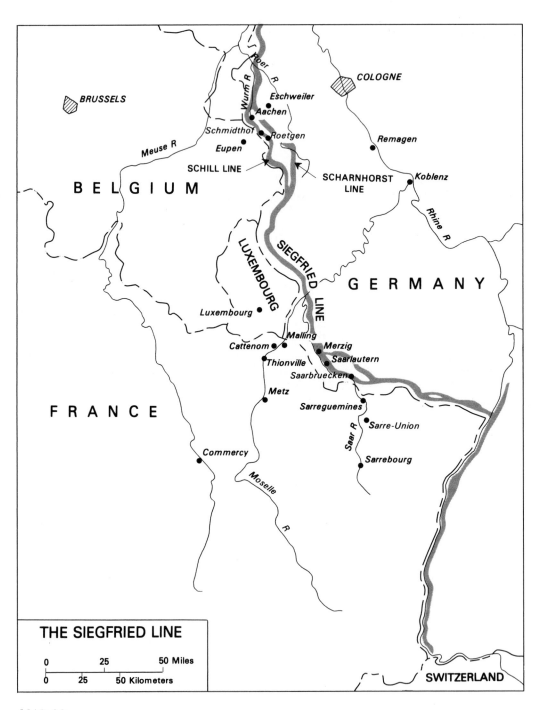

BRUSSELS

COLOGNE

*Roer R*

*Wurm R*

Eschweiler

Aachen

*Meuse R*

Schmidthof

Roetgen

Remagen

Eupen

SCHILL LINE

SCHARNHORST
LINE

Koblenz

B E L G I U M

*Rhine R*

L U X E M B O U R G

S I E G F R I E D   L I N E

G E R M A N Y

Luxembourg

Malling

Cattenom

Merzig

Saarlautern

Thionville

Saarbruecken

F R A N C E

Metz

Sarreguemines

Sarre-Union

*Saar R*

Commercy

Sarrebourg

*Moselle
R*

SWITZERLAND

**THE SIEGFRIED LINE**

| 0 | 25 | 50 Miles |
|---|----|----------|
| 0 | 25 | 50 Kilometers |

*MAP 23*

MEN OF THE 23D ARMORED ENGINEER BATTALION RIG CHARGES *to demolish dragon's teeth in the Siegfried Line.*

the first defenses of the Siegfried Line. Ahead was a crater the Germans had created by blowing a bridge over a dry stream bed, and behind the crater was a gate made of steel pipes. Left of the gate lay a band of dragon's teeth, extending for about a hundred yards and ending at a hill on which stood a pillbox. On the right rose a steep, almost perpendicular hill. Embedded in slots in this hill, just behind the gate, were steel I-beams that protruded across the road. This hill also boasted a pillbox.

Heavy fire from the two pillboxes stopped the advance about 1800. Darkness was falling, and the task force, whose vehicles stretched back beyond Roetgen, camped for the night. Dur-

ing the night the infantry began working its way behind the pillboxes, and after a fire fight early on 13 September both pillboxes surrendered. Then the engineers went to work. They filled in the road crater using a tankdozer, blew the gate with ten pounds of TNT, and removed the I-beams from the hill by hand. The attack columns began moving forward. After about three hundred yards they ran into another steel gate, which the engineers blew out about 1000. Task Force Lovelady was through the Scharnhorst Line.[6]

---

[6] Engineers in the Siegfried Line Penetration, CCB, 3d Armd Div, 12–22 Sep 44, pp. 3–6, in folder, Penetration of the Siegfried Line, 12–25 Sep 44, 3d Armd Div files.

During the afternoon of 12 September Task Force King bypassed Roetgen and headed toward the village of Schmidthof, about four miles to the north. King's unit encountered the same types of obstacles as Task Force Lovelady had faced. A crater, steel gates and I-beams, and dominating pillboxes in hilly, wooded terrain barred Task Force King's way. On the morning of 13 September tanks nosed out the first steel gate. A second gate was more formidable. In front of it lay a huge water-filled crater; behind it were I-beams embedded in concrete blocks. Moreover, the roadblock was under fire from 88-mm. artillery and the guns of tanks at Schmidthof. The shelling delayed the attack for hours. Unable to work on the roadblock under such fire, the engineers constructed bypasses wide enough to accommodate tanks. Tanks and artillery ultimately knocked out the guns at Schmidthof, and by the afternoon of 14 September Combat Command B's Task Force King had penetrated the line.[7]

Combat Command A of the 3d Armored Division, advancing on the north nearer Aachen where the countryside was open and rolling, ran into a belt of dragon's teeth extending from the edge of a forest on the Belgian border to the German town of Oberforstbach, a distance of about a thousand yards. Task Force X, commanded by Col. Leander LaC. Doan, began the advance about 1000 on 13 September. Doan sent infantry through the dragon's teeth; engineers of Company C, 23d Armored Engineer Battalion, followed with trip wires and demolition materials. Initially holding at the line of departure, the tanks were to move out as soon as the engineers had cleared a path for them. But the infantry and engineers ran into fire from a pillbox as well as heavy machine-gun and mortar fire from open emplacements that forced the forward troops to take shelter behind the dragon's teeth. Some way had to be found to get the tanks forward. At mid-afternoon reconnaissance discovered a passageway over the dragon's teeth— apparently, local farmers had filled in the spaces between the teeth with stones and earth. About a foot of each tooth was exposed, but engineers cut off these obstacles with explosives, and the tanks went through, neutralizing pillboxes at point-blank range.[8]

Having broken through the Scharnhorst Line, the 3d Armored Division pressed north toward Eschweiler, northeast of Aachen, and by 15 September came up against the dragon's teeth and pillboxes of the Schill Line. In this more thickly settled area pillboxes were often disguised as houses, ice plants, or power stations.

By the time VII Corps reached the Schill Line, the corps' units had learned that the best way to take out the pillboxes was to bring up tanks, tank destroyers, and self-propelled 155-mm. guns for point-blank fire. Even with a concrete-piercing fuse, high-explosive (HE) projectiles could seldom penetrate the thick walls; however, penetration was usually not necessary. The occupants of the pillboxes, suffering from concussion

---

[7] Ibid., pp. 8–12.

[8] Cracking the Siegfried Line, TF Doan, CCB, 3d Armd Div, 13–19 Sep 44, pp. 1–3, in folder, Penetration of the Siegfried Line, 12–25 Sep 44, 3d Armd Div files; Engr Opns VII Corps, vol. IV, "Pursuit Into Germany," app. 1, Initial Breaching of the Siegfried Line. The remainder of this section is taken from this latter source.

BULLDOZER SEALS BUNKERS IN THE FORTIFIED LINE OUTSIDE AACHEN

shock and choking on powdered concrete, would in most cases readily surrender.

Then the engineers' task began. In the VII Corps sector and farther south in the Schnee Eifel, where the V Corps had broken through the Siegfried Line in several places by mid-September, the Americans had learned that if a pillbox was not rendered unusable enemy patrols were likely to infiltrate the lines at night and reoccupy it. Although the simplest method was to blow up pillboxes, in many cases it was expensive—destruction of the larger pillboxes in VII Corps area required up to 1,000 pounds of TNT. In forward areas the noise and smoke of the explosions also attracted enemy fire. The VII Corps

engineers preferred to seal the pillboxes. Using a bulldozer, they would cover all openings with eight to ten feet of earth. In places where a bulldozer could not be employed, the engineers welded steel doors and embrasures shut. Between 11 September and 16 October in the VII Corps area only 36 pillboxes were completely destroyed with explosives as compared to 239 covered with earth and 12 closed by welding.

Most of this work was completed before the end of September. By October First Army had outrun supply lines, gas and ammunition were running low, the troops were exhausted, and their equipment was depleted. Bad weather prevented close air support. In addition,

German tanks and antitank guns, well positioned along the second band of the Siegfried Line, were inflicting heavy losses on American armor. At the end of September the advances of V and VII Corps halted, and both corps went on the defensive.

### XIX Corps North of Aachen

North of Aachen the Wurm River protected Siegfried Line pillboxes. The river rendered dragon's teeth superfluous except at a few points, and XIX Corps encountered none when attacking across a mile-wide front about nine miles north of Aachen. There the Wurm was about thirty feet wide and only three feet deep. The infantry could cross the stream easily, using duckboard footbridges or even logs thrown into the stream. But the Wurm was a real obstacle to tanks, for its banks were steep and marshy.[9]

The 30th Infantry Division was to spearhead the attack, followed by the 2d Armored Division. The infantry was in position on 19 September. The original plan was to push through the Siegfried Line next day and move south to relieve pressure on VII Corps near Aachen. But the weather did not permit an air strike deemed essential before the jump-off. To allow time for the bombing and for the arrival of supplies and reinforcements, the attack was postponed until 2 October.

During the fortnight's delay, the 105th Engineer Combat Battalion, organic to the 30th Division, reconnoitered the

---

[9] XIX Corps Special Rpt, Breaching the Siegfried Line; Hewitt, *Work Horse of the Western Front*, pp. 107–17. Unless otherwise cited, this section is based on these sources and the histories of the units mentioned.

Wurm River for the best crossing sites, and one of its companies constructed bridges for infantry and tanks. The tank bridges, which the engineers called culverts, were ingenious contraptions made of thirty-inch steel pipe, reinforced on the inside with smaller pipe and on the outside with a layer of six-inch logs bound with cable. The engineers constructed ten, to be divided equally between the two assault regiments. The method of emplacing the bridges, designed to protect the troops from small-arms fire, was also inventive. The culverts, laid lengthwise on improvised wood and steel sleds, were to be pulled to the crossing site by a tank moving parallel to the stream with a tankdozer following. At the site the tankdozer was to push the culverts into place and then cover them with dirt.

Two companies of the 105th Engineer Battalion were in direct support of the division's two assault regiments, with an engineer platoon attached to each infantry assault battalion and a three-man engineer demolition team, armed with bangalore torpedoes and satchel charges, moving out with each infantry platoon. The engineers supervised training of the infantry in the use of flame throwers, demolition charges, bazookas, and other weapons to be used against pillboxes.

D-day for the XIX Corps' attack on the Siegfried Line was 2 October. An air strike preceded the jump-off at 1100 but did little good. Nor did preparatory artillery and mortar barrages accomplish much beyond driving Germans holding outlying emplacements into pillboxes. Tank and tank-destroyer support was lacking, and wet weather proved too much for the culvert bridges. One of them became stuck in mud;

another could not be emplaced because its bulldozer became mired. The engineers abandoned the culverts and began constructing treadway bridges with the help of the 1104th Engineer Combat Group's 247th Engineer Combat Battalion. This work went forward under heavy enemy artillery fire, and after a treadway was ready at one regimental crossing half the tanks, as well as their recovery vehicles, bogged down in mud. In the other regimental sector the treadway was not in place until 1830—too late to permit a crossing.

Thus, the first day's assault on the pillboxes became entirely an infantry and engineer undertaking. The infantry had considerable success firing small arms and bazooka shells into apertures. Little use was made of flame throwers, pole charges, or satchel charges. When the pillboxes were small, located on flat or gently sloping ground, and lightly defended, the engineers preferred to seal them, bringing up a jeep-towed arc welder to weld shut the entrances and then bulldozing earth over the embrasures. When observed enemy fire was present, or when terrain or the tactical situation prevented the use of dozers, the engineers destroyed the pillboxes, placing TNT on the weaker portion of the walls and firing the charge electrically. The engineers found that a 400-pound TNT charge could destroy the average pillbox at this point in the line. Learning that a single explosion in the forward areas would bring down an accurate German artillery concentration, the engineers blew several pillboxes simultaneously.

When tanks arrived at the fortifications they assisted the infantry and engineers with covering fire. By blasting pillbox apertures and entrances with armor-piercing ammunition, the tanks sometimes could induce the occupants to surrender, but tank fire was effective only in knocking camouflage from the thick concrete. This was also true of most artillery fire. The only weapon that could achieve any significant penetration was the self-propelled 155-mm. gun.

*The Siege of Aachen*

By 7 October XIX Corps had breached the West Wall in its sector and was ready to join VII Corps in attacking Aachen. As the two corps moved to encircle the city, engineers served as infantry on the flanks, and when the assault commenced on 8 October both engineer groups sent battalions to the front lines. The XIX Corps wanted to free one regiment of the 29th Division to help the 30th Division in a drive south on 13 October to close the Aachen Gap. Thus, three days before the attack the 1104th Engineer Combat Group entered the line to contain the pillboxes near Kerkrade, west of the Wurm River. Corps headquarters attached to the group a company of tank destroyers and two batteries of self-propelled automatic weapons, actually half-tracks mounting .50-caliber machine guns. Lt. Col. Hugh W. Colton, commanding the group, combed his light ponton, light equipment, and treadway bridge companies to form an infantry reserve for the operation.[10]

Stiffening German resistance slowed the XIX Corps' advance south down both banks of the Wurm River. Not

---

[10] Hist 1104th Engr C Gp, Jun–Dec 44. Unless otherwise cited, this section is taken from this source and the histories of the units mentioned.

until late in the afternoon of 16 October was the corps able to link up with VII Corps elements north of Aachen. During the advance the 1104th Engineer Group patrolled its flanks and dispatched aggressive reconnaissance patrols in front of its position. On 17 October, after an artillery and mortar concentration, Colonel Colton sent the 172d and 247th Engineer Combat Battalions forward toward Aachen. Destroying pillboxes that blocked the way, the engineers, reinforced by a platoon of tanks, fought their way to the outskirts of the city but stopped as the town fell.[11]

Under VII Corps the 1106th Engineer Group during the last week of September moved to relieve the 18th Infantry, 1st Infantry Division, in positions on the heights south of Aachen so that the infantry could move north to link with XIX Corps. The group commander, Col. Thomas DeF. Rogers, began training his two combat battalions, the 237th and the 238th, in the use of 81-mm. mortars and organized a reserve of 150 men drawn from his light ponton and treadway bridge companies. As soon as the attachment to the 18th Infantry became effective on 29 September, Colonel Rogers sent his two combat battalions to occupy positions with the infantry battalions; the action proved so valuable in familiarizing the engineers with the operation that he strongly recommended an overlap period during any similar mission in the future.[12]

After the infantry began withdrawing on 2 October, the 1106th Engineer Group "became a real 'doughboy' outfit standing on its own feet in a front line fight." Supported by an armed field artillery battalion, the engineers laid booby traps and antipersonnel mines along the barbed wire protecting their front and sent out combat patrols to maintain contact with the enemy. Colonel Rogers learned that his group's tactical operations would act as a diversion for the 18th Infantry's assault on the city from the north.

The group's 238th Engineer Combat Battalion made an ingenious contribution to this mission on 8 October. Discovering several streetcars standing on tracks leading down a grade into Aachen, they loaded one of the cars with captured German shells and ammunition, a case of American explosives, and several time fuses. On its side they painted "V−13," inspired by a German V-bomb that had recently passed over the area. Then they sent their missile careening downhill toward Aachen. About 200 yards beyond a battalion outpost the car struck some debris on the track and exploded with a fine display of tracer shells. Next day the engineers tried again, loading a second streetcar with enemy shells and sending it down the track, but it hit the wreckage of the first and exploded. Clearing the wreckage from the track, the engineers sent a third car downhill on 16 October. It reached the city, but it could not be determined whether it did any damage. In any case, "Secret Weapon V−13" attracted swarms of newspaper correspondents. Colonel Rogers concluded that the greatest value of the V−13 was "in giving GI Joe

[11] Hist XIX Corps Engrs, p. 15, ML 2220, ETOUSA Hist Sect.

[12] 1106th Engr C Gp Opns Memo 9, Lessons Learned by the 1106th Engineer Combat Group during the Aachen Operation, 1 Nov 44, app. 9 to Engr Opns VII Corps, vol. IV, "Pursuit into Germany."

something amusing and bizarre to talk about."[13]

An all-out attack on Aachen began 11 October after the Germans refused to surrender. By that time, the 26th Infantry of the 1st Division was in position to attack from the east, its left wing tied in with the position of the 1106th Engineer Combat Group. The infantry began moving into the city in small assault teams that attacked block by block, building by building, even room by room; the engineers also sent patrols into the city.

Two men of the 238th Engineer Combat Battalion patrol, S/Sgt. Ewart M. Padgett and Pfc. James B. Haswell, were to play an important role in the surrender of Aachen. The Germans captured the two on 17 October in a clearing outside the city. After passing through several command posts the two Americans arrived on the third day at the garrison command post, a pillbox where the Germans held about thirty American prisoners. There, on the morning of 21 October, the German intelligence officer informed the American prisoners that the fort had tried to surrender but that two Germans carrying a white flag outside had been killed. He asked for a volunteer among the Americans to carry the flag. Haswell volunteered and Padgett insisted on going along.

Padgett took the flag, and the two men, followed by two German officers, ran out into the middle of the street and began waving it. Braving small-arms and mortar fire, they managed to reach an American officer who told them to bring out the entire German garrison. The two led out the Germans, including the commander of Aachen, Col. Gerhard Wilck. Before leaving the pillbox, the engineers asked Wilck for his pistol. He laid it on a table, smiled, and left the room. Thus they secured a prize souvenir of the occasion. Later, after surrender formalities were completed, Wilck shook hands with the two engineers, saluted, and thanked them for their "gallant bravery" in carrying out the surrender flag.[14]

### From the Moselle to the Saar

On 22 September General Bradley had stopped the Third Army advance to give priority to First Army's drive to the Ruhr in support of the 21 Army Group effort to capture Antwerp. At that time General Patton had been preparing to push through the Metz Gap to the Rhine. When Aachen fell on 21 October, Bradley lifted the restrictions on Third Army.

In the army's path lay some of the most formidable fortifications in Europe. West of Metz lay a chain of old forts, some dating from 1870, situated on ridgetops that gave every advantage to defenders. Next was the Moselle River, on whose east bank most of the city of Metz was located. The river had a swift current and steep gradients and was subject to autumnal flooding. Beyond the Moselle on the Lorraine plain, a region extending thirty miles to the Saar River, was the Maginot Line. At the Saar around Saarbruecken the main Lorraine gateway opened to the Rhine. There, on the east side of the Saar, was

[13] Ibid.; Combat Interv 4, 1106th Engr C Gp, South of Aachen, Battle of Aachen, 8–22 Oct 44, 1st Inf Div files.

[14] Interv, 238th Engr C Bn S–2 with Padgett, Experiences of Two American Prisoners of War Held in Aachen, Germany, Incl to Oct 44 Jnl, AAR, 238th Engr C Bn, Jun–Dec 44.

the strongest portion of the Siegfried Line.[15]

The plan was for XII Corps, in the area of Nancy thirty miles south of Metz, to start pushing north on 8 November. The XX Corps would follow the next day, advancing eastward north and south of Metz. About ten miles to the south, XX Corps' 5th Infantry Division already had a bridgehead over the Moselle at Arnaville. While that division turned north for a close envelopment of Metz, the 90th Infantry and 10th Armored Divisions were to make a wider encirclement, bypassing the forts around Metz by crossing the Moselle six miles northeast of the village of Thionville, about twenty miles north of Metz. At the same time, the 95th Infantry Division was to make a limited-objective crossing as a feint at a point about three miles south of Thionville.

### The Moselle Crossings at Malling and Cattenom

The bulk of the effort to get Third Army troops over the Moselle during the November attack fell to the engineers supporting the 90th Division. In rubber assault boats of the 1139th Engineer Combat Group, troops of the 359th Infantry were to cross near the village of Malling on the left (north) flank, supported by the 206th Engineer Combat Battalion. On the right, battalions of the 358th Infantry were to cross simultaneously near Cattenom, with the 179th Engineer Combat Battalion in support. At both crossings, where the water gaps were estimated to be 360 and 300 feet

wide, respectively, the engineers also were to construct an infantry support bridge, a treadway bridge, and a floating Bailey bridge, while the 90th Division's organic 315th Engineer Combat Battalion was to build a footbridge, operate ferries, and undertake far-shore work. As soon as the expanding bridgehead had cleared the far shore of Germans, the 160th Engineer Combat Battalion was to construct a double-triple fixed Bailey bridge at Rettel, northeast of Malling.[16]

By the night of 8 November the engineers had trained with the infantry in preparation for the crossing, demonstrating the proper way to carry and load an assault boat. For each boat the crew consisted of three engineers, one a guide. That night the river began to rise, and by the time the boats of the attack wave shoved off in drizzling rain at 0330 on 9 November, the infantry had to load in waist-deep water. In spite of a strong current the two leading infantry battalions were on the east bank of the Moselle by 0500. As they reached their destination the troops found that the high water had actually helped the crossings: extensive minefields the Germans had prepared on the far shore were flooded, and the boats passed over without danger. Also, the enemy had abandoned water-filled foxholes and rifle pits dug into the east bank.[17]

After daybreak, as succeeding infantry battalions crossed the racing yellow Moselle, enemy artillery fire fell so heavily on the east bank that many

---

[15] Cole, *The Lorraine Campaign*, pp. 28, 124–29. Tactical details in this section are from Cole.

[16] Combat Interv 364, Opns of 1139th Engr C Gp (8–17 Nov), Crossing of the Moselle River, XX Corps files.
[17] OCE ETOUSA Hist Rpt 10, Combat Engineering pp. 116–17.

crews abandoned their boats after debarking the troops, allowing the craft to swirl downstream to be lost. But the infantrymen made swift progress. At Malling, where they achieved complete surprise, troops of the 359th Infantry captured the town by noon. The 358th Infantry, after crossing from Cattenom, faced a more formidable objective—Fort Koenigsmacker, which had to be reduced before further progress could be made. There too the 90th Division achieved surprise. Assault teams of infantry and engineers (from the 315th Engineer Combat Battalion) ripped through bands of barbed wire and reached the trenches around the fort before an alarm was sounded. Braving mortar and machine-gun fire from the fort's superstructure, the teams reduced the fort, blowing steel doors open with satchel charges and blasting ventilating ports with thermite grenades or TNT.

By the end of November the 90th Division had eight battalions, including reserves from the 357th Infantry, across the Moselle. The division had advanced two miles beyond the river, overrun seven towns, and penetrated Fort Koenigsmacker.[18] Next day, as German resistance stiffened, little progress was made, but by midnight, 11 November, the 90th Division's leading units held a defensible position on a ridge topped with the Maginot Line fortifications. The division had knocked out or bypassed many of the line's weakly held pillboxes and had forced the surrender of Fort Koenigsmacker with hand-carried weapons and explosives, a few 57-mm. antitank guns ferried across the Moselle, and artillery fire from the west

bank. No tanks or trucks had yet been able to cross the river, and supply parties had to use rickety farm wagons and even abandoned baby buggies.

Attempts to bridge the flooding river, beginning early on 9 November, came to naught for two days. Before Fort Koenigsmacker surrendered, shellfire from the bastion had made the bridge site at Cattenom untenable and destroyed the bridging equipment. At Malling, harassing enemy machine-gun and mortar fire forced the 206th Engineer Combat Battalion to abandon its first attempt to build a footbridge. At 0600 on 9 November the engineers began constructing another and simultaneously put two ferries into operation. One, using boats lashed together and powered by outboard motors, carried ammunition and rations and evacuated the wounded around the clock. The other, using infantry support rafts to carry 57-mm. antitank guns, jeeps, and weapons carriers, was short-lived. A few antitank guns got across, but at 1100 a raft carrying a jeep ran into the infantry footbridge, broke its cable, and put the bridge out of action. The infantry support bridge, then about three-quarters finished, was carried downstream and lost.

Recovering some of the equipment, the engineers decided to build a treadway bridge at the site, and the 991st Engineer Treadway Bridge Company managed to complete the new span by dusk on 10 November. But the river's continued rise had now put the road leading to the bridge under nearly five feet of water. No vehicles could get through until the following afternoon when the floodwaters, having crested at noon on 11 November, began to recede. At 1500 the crossings began

---

[18] *The XX Corps: Its History and Service in World War II* (Osaka, Japan), p. 159.

TROOPS FLOAT FOOTBRIDGE SECTIONS INTO PLACE *on the flooded Moselle River in the 90th Division area.*

again. Ten supply-laden Brockway trucks, some jeeps, and a few light tanks and tank destroyers reached the far shore. Shortly after dawn next morning German artillery fire repeatedly hit the treadway, so weakening it that it could no longer bear the weight of a tank destroyer. It broke loose and went off downstream.

While waiting for more equipment to come up so they could rebuild the bridge, the men of the 991st Engineer Treadway Bridge Company used bridge fragments to construct a tank ferry. Employing a heavy raft made of pontons and treads and tying powerboats to the raft, the engineers manned the ferry, crossing a company each of

medium tanks and tank destroyers by dark. This work earned the 991st Engineer Treadway Bridge Company the Distinguished Unit Citation.[19]

Late on 12 November, the engineers were repairing the Malling bridge and building a bridge at the Cattenom site. But by now the XX Corps commander, Maj. Gen. Walton H. Walker, had decided on another site for heavy bridging to move his armored division across the Moselle.

### The Bridge at Thionville

The place was Thionville, where high

[19] OCE ETOUSA Hist Rpt 10, Combat Engineering, pp. 117–21; Cole, *The Lorraine Campaign,* p. 400.

retaining walls constricted the flood waters of the Moselle and where the Germans had built a timber bridge, long since down. On the near side two spans of the German bridge were usable, while on the far side part of an old stone-arch bridge, which the French had blown in 1940, was still standing. Third Army held the part of Thionville west of the river, but the Germans were on the other side; there, a canal paralleling the riverbank formed a secondary obstacle. Beyond the canal lay Fort Yutz, an old star-shaped stone fortification. On the west bank the 1306th Engineer General Service Regiment, which had been acting as an engineer combat group because no group headquarters was available, was preparing on 9 November to build a Bailey bridge as soon as the east bank was clear of enemy. Meanwhile, they could do nothing, for any movement near the river drew rifle and machine-gun fire from Germans on the far bank. In his pressing need to get his armor across the Moselle, General Walker gave the commanding officer of the 1306th Engineers, Col. William C. Hall, a hard assignment, changing "the routine job of constructing a support bridge into a weird operation of major importance to the advance of an entire corps."[20]

The first tactical task, to clear the east bank, General Walker gave to the 95th Division, which on 8 and 9 November had established a very small bridgehead across the Moselle at Uckange, a few miles south of Thionville. The commander of the 95th Division sent to Thionville two companies of the 378th

Infantry, supported by two companies of the 135th Engineer Combat Battalion. On the morning of 11 November the troops began to cross the Moselle at Thionville in powerboats. Enemy small-arms and mortar fire poured down on them. The engineer captain in charge of the boats was killed, as were a number of the crewmen, and all but one of the boats were lost. Nevertheless, by the morning of 12 November two platoons had crossed and cleared the south end of the island and had begun pushing north.

At 1030 that morning General Walker ordered the construction of the bridge, emphasizing that the success of the whole Third Army attack depended upon it. The 1306th General Service Regiment had already begun planning and from aerial photographs had determined that the gap to be bridged was about 165 feet long. The regiment decided upon a double-triple Bailey bridge, which could carry tanks. The 1306th had never built such a bridge, but one of its companies, Company C of the 1st Battalion, which had built a 100-foot double-single Bailey, took on the job. On the night of 10–11 November the regiment brought materials and equipment up to the bridge site and unloaded under blackout.

When the word came on 12 November to build the bridge, the engineers went into action. A party crossed the river in a powerboat, cleared the far span of mines, and prepared the far shore abutment. Then they discovered "a shocking fact"—the span to be bridged was 206 feet long instead of 165. The longest double-triple Bailey was 180 feet, and any lighter structure could not carry tanks. Engineers solved the problem by extending the near abutment

<hr>

[20] William C. Hall, "Bridging at Thionville," *Military Engineer*, XL (April 1948), 169. Unless otherwise noted, this account of the bridge at Thionville is taken from this source.

HEAVY PONTON BRIDGE AT UCKANGE, MOSELLE RIVER

about ten feet, moving the far bridge seat almost to the edge of the stone arch, and building a double-triple Bailey 190 feet long. It was a calculated risk that had to be taken.

Cranes began lifting the panels into place, and the launching nose moved out over the water. Then, at 1700, the bridge came under concentrated mortar fire. A direct hit killed one engineer and wounded six; within two minutes the Germans inflicted more than twenty casualties, and the entire company had to take cover. After dark work resumed, continuing all night with a second company relieving Company C. At dawn on 13 November a smoke generating company gave the men the protection of a smoke screen. Mortar fire

soon ceased as the infantry cleared the strip between the riverbank and the canal and advanced into Fort Yutz. Although 150-mm. guns began firing, the bridge escaped a direct hit, and no casualties occurred among the engineers climbing the superstructure clad in flak suits. Late that afternoon the engineers seated the far end of the bridge without difficulty.

About that time the near end ran into trouble, for one of six jacks failed to function. The bridge swayed and fell into the cribbing, and jacking up the near end took all night. A fresh company of engineers came up to the site. Despite heavy 150-mm. shelling which hit one man and ignited the remains of the German timber bridge, creating a glare that drew further artillery fire, they completed the bridge at 0930 on 14 November. The engineers believed it to be the longest single-span bridge ever launched as a unit.

On the afternoon of 14 November the tanks of Combat Command B, 10th Armored Division, began to roll over the Bailey bridge at Thionville, and by daylight next day all had crossed. Combat Command A used the treadway bridge at Malling and by dark on 15 November had two companies across. General Patton, who visited both sites, inspecting the Bailey bridge while it was still under enemy fire and crossing the treadway under a protecting smoke screen, later pronounced the 90th Division passage of the Moselle "an epic river crossing done under terrific difficulties."[21]

### Advance to the Saar

After envelopment to the north and south, coupled with a containing action west of the Moselle, Metz fell to XX Corps on 22 November. The lesser German forts in the area were left to "wither on the vine" (the last surrendering on 13 December) because scarce U.S. artillery ammunition had to be conserved to support the corps' advance to the Saar River.

The XX Corps was to make the main thrust, heading toward a crossing at Saarlautern, about thirty miles northeast of Metz at the strongest section of the Siegfried Line.[22] The XII Corps,

coming up from the south, was to drive with the bulk of its forces to Sarreguemines, about forty miles due east of Metz, where the Saar swung south out of the Siegfried Line and into the Maginot Line. One of the corps' two armored divisions, the 4th, was to cross south of Sarreguemines near Sarre-Union. The XX Corps' 95th Division was to cross the Saar at Saarlautern, followed by the 90th. Flank protection on the north would be provided by Combat Command B of the 10th Armored Division, which was to move toward Merzig, about ten miles north of Saarlautern. Ten miles north of Merzig, Combat Command A of the 10th Armored Division was to seize a bridgehead over the Saar at Sarrebourg, an important move because it pointed toward the ultimate axis of the Third Army effort—a Rhine crossing between Worms and Mainz. The 1139th Engineer Combat Group was to support the 10th Armored and 90th Infantry Divisions; the 95th Division was to have the support of the 1103d Engineer Combat Group.

In the path of XX Corps the Germans had demolished almost all the bridges over streams and culverts. Abutments, however, were seldom destroyed, making the use of fixed Bailey bridges or short fixed treadway sections both feasible and relatively easy.[23] Mud, rain, fog, and mines slowed the infantry more than did the Maginot Line, which was not very formidable. Crossing it, General Patton was "impressed by its lack of impressiveness."[24] Only in the path of the armor moving north

[21] George S. Patton, Jr., *War As I Knew It* (Boston: Houghton Mifflin, 1947), p. 172.

[22] Patton believed attacking the line where it was strongest not as foolhardy as it seemed, because "people are inclined not to occupy strong positions with as many men as they should." Ibid., p. 176.

[23] Combat Interv 44, Engineer Participation in the Metz Operation, p. 11, XX Corps files; Hist 315th Engr C Bn, 7 Mar 44–May 45.

[24] Patton, *War As I Knew It*, p. 181.

did effective field fortifications block the way.

On the night of 21 November Combat Command A of the 10th Armored Division came up against a strong line of fieldworks—a bank of antitank ditches, dragon's teeth, concrete pillboxes, and bunkers. American intelligence had provided little or no information about this formidable barrier. It was the Orscholz Switch Line (known to the Americans as the "Siegfried Switch"), constructed at right angles to the Siegfried Line and located at the base of the triangle formed by the confluence of the Saar and Moselle Rivers. The nineteen-mile-long triangle, ten miles wide at its base, was of vital concern to the Germans because at its apex lay the city of Trier, guarding the Moselle corridor, an important pathway to Koblenz on the Rhine.[25]

The Orscholz Line provided a bulwark for enemy forces withdrawing under pressure from XX Corps. The Germans manning its defenses poured artillery and mortar fire on the tankers and on engineers attempting to bridge the line's antitank ditches and deep craters. The 10th Armored Division was unable to drive through the fortifications, and an infantry regiment of the 90th Division had to reinforce the attack.

In three days of fighting the infantry suffered very heavy casualties, not only from enemy fire but also from exposure to cold, mud, and rain. Moreover, the bad weather forestalled American bomber support. At the end of November General Walker abandoned the attempt to penetrate the Orscholz Switch Line and to attack toward Sarrebourg. He sent the infantry regiment to the rear and directed Combat Command A of the 10th Armored Division to join Combat Command B near Merzig to protect the north flank of the XX Corps' drive on Saarlautern. By 2 December the armor had overcome all resistance in the Merzig sector.

On 1 December the weather had begun to clear—a good omen for the 95th Division's attack on Saarlautern— and on the morning of 2 December bombers blasted in and around the city. Shortly before noon the bombing lifted. The 2d Battalion of the 379th Infantry, the 95th Division regiment chosen to seize a bridgehead across the Saar, advanced into the city. By 1500 the troops had captured an enemy barracks on the western edge of Saarlautern, but as they converged on the center of the city they met heavy resistance. The Germans were fighting viciously, house by house and block by block.[26] To break through the strongly defended city and force a river crossing too seemed impossible, but fortune favored the attackers.

## The Capture of the Saarlautern Bridge

That evening Col. Robert L. Bacon, commanding the 379th Infantry, was handed a photograph taken from an artillery observation plane late in the afternoon. The picture showed a bridge, intact, spanning the Saar between the center of the city and a northern suburb. Colonel Bacon decided on a daring maneuver to capture the bridge

[25] For the Orscholz Switch Line, see Cole, *The Lorraine Campaign*, pp. 487–88 and map 43; *The XX Corps: Its History and Service in WW II*, p. 238.

[26] AAR, 95th Inf Div, 2 Dec 44.

before the Germans could blow it. He planned to send his 1st Battalion in boats across the Saar northwest of the city, where the river makes a loop, to seize the far end of the bridge while the 2d Battalion attacked toward the near (south) side.

Under cover of darkness, rain, and fog and with all sounds drowned out by the roar of American artillery, assault boats moved up to the crossing site, where the river was only 125 feet wide; the first wave of the commando-type operation was across at 0545. Led by an infantry battalion commander, Lt. Col. Tobias R. Philbin, the assault wave included a platoon from the 320th Engineer Combat Battalion under 2d Lt. Edward Herbert. On the far bank the column hurried down the road to the bridge, encountering only one German, an unarmed telephone operator. At the bridge was an armored car with a radio operator in it and a German soldier alongside. A company commander bayonetted the radio operator, and Colonel Philbin shot the other when he made a dash for the bridge to trip the switch that would blow it.[27]

Philbin's troops first cut all the wires they could find. Following closely behind the infantrymen, the engineers checked the bridge for mines and explosives. About halfway across they found four 500-pound American bombs, without fuses, laid end to end across the bridge. Without stopping, Herbert led his men to check the south end of the bridge. There they encountered a German officer and four enlisted men who refused an order to halt. All were shot.

A few minutes later the engineers saw a second party of several Germans coming toward the bridge dragging a rubber boat. They also refused to surrender and were shot. This gunfire brought on such a heavy concentration of German machine-gun fire that the engineers had to retreat to the north end of the bridge, where machine-gun and artillery fire pinned them down for hours. Not until 1600 were they able to return to the bridge and hoist the American bombs over the side and into the river. The engineers also managed to restore enough flooring to enable some tank destroyers and supply trucks to pass over the north side. After dark the Germans dispatched to the bridge some tanks loaded with explosives, but after the lead tank was hit they abandoned the attempt.

Next day the enemy resumed shelling and made determined efforts to retake or destroy the bridge. A party of German engineers came forward to blow it by hand because the 95th Division's artillery had knocked out the generators needed to blow the bridge electrically. The Germans were captured, and under questioning one of them revealed that the bridge was virtually a powder keg—channels bored in the piers were filled with dynamite and TNT. Herbert's platoon eventually removed three tons of the explosives.[28]

### Assaulting Pillboxes on the Far Bank

While the engineers were still trying to clear the bridge, fighting was already under way across the river in the suburbs of Saarlautern: Saarlautern-Roden and Fraulautern to the north and Ens-

---

[27] Details of the bridge capture are from interviews with 2d Lt. Edward Herbert et al., Combat Interv 205, XX Corps files, and AAR, 95th Inf Div, 2 Dec 44.

[28] Cole, *The Lorraine Campaign*, p. 518.

dorf to the east. Each regiment of the 95th Division had the support of a company of the 320th Engineer Combat Battalion. These suburbs boasted one of the strongest sectors of the entire Siegfried Line. Pillboxes of reinforced concrete were built into the streets and between houses, many extending two or three levels below ground, some with roofs and walls ten feet thick or steel turrets housing 88-mm. guns. The Germans had cleverly camouflaged the pillboxes. Some resembled manure piles or mounds of earth, others ordinary structures. One had been constructed inside a barn, and another was disguised as a suburban railroad station, complete with ticket windows. Ordinary buildings had been fortified with sandbags, wire, and concrete. "Every house was a fort," reported an officer from Saarlautern-Roden.[29]

The engineers who had the job of assaulting the pillboxes came under fire not only from the pillboxes themselves but from heavy German artillery emplaced on heights behind the three suburbs, outranging American artillery on the near bank of the river. Rain and overcast prevented air support. German tanks roamed the streets, and protection against them was available only in the two northern suburbs, where the Saarlautern bridge brought across American tanks and tank destroyers. The U.S. position in the southern suburb, Ensdorf, had to depend on bridges the engineers constructed, and German artillery knocked them out almost as soon as they were built. On 8 December artillery fire cost the 320th Engineer Combat Battalion more than $300,000 worth of bridging equipment.

To add to the hardships, the Saar River was rising rapidly. By 9 December, when assault boats were still supporting the Ensdorf attack, the river had swollen to a width of between 400 and 500 feet.

It became evident very early that the advance through the suburbs would be slow. Five German pillboxes, mutually supporting on each flank, held up an infantry battalion for two days at Saarlautern-Roden. Tank destroyers came up to fire directly at the pillboxes but without effect. On the afternoon of the third day, 7 December, T/5 Henry E. Barth of the 320th Engineer Combat Battalion's C Company volunteered to attack the first pillbox. Carrying a heavy beehive charge, he was unarmed but had the covering fire of eighteen infantrymen. Fifty yards from the target the infantrymen, who had suffered several casualties during the approach, took cover in a small building from which they kept up fire on the pillbox's machine-gun ports until Barth was close enough to rush forward, place his charge on a gun port, and detonate it. The Germans surrendered immediately. Another engineer, Pfc. William E. Farthing, captured a second pillbox singlehanded. Slipping out alone, Farthing crawled toward the pillbox and shoved an explosive charge into its gun port until it touched the gun muzzle, then detonated it.

Engineers advancing under infantry covering fire became the general pattern for taking out the pillboxes in the Saarlautern suburbs. Sometimes after a pillbox had fallen and the engineers and infantrymen inside were waiting for darkness to resume their advance, the Germans would counterattack and have to be driven off. The advance was

---

[29] AAR, 95th Inf Div, 2 Dec 44.

costly to the engineers. During December the 320th Engineer Combat Battalion had ten men killed in action and fifty-nine wounded, two so severely that they died in the hospital.[30] The pillbox-by-pillbox, street-by-street, house-by-house fighting in early December was so costly to the already depleted 95th Division that by mid-December XX Corps began withdrawing the unit to the west bank of the Saar, replacing it with the relatively fresh 5th Infantry Division.

The plan was for the 5th Division to drive north and ultimately advance alongside XX Corps' 90th Infantry Division. The latter had not been able to follow the 95th Division over the river but had had to cross some miles to the north. Its main objective was Dillingen, on the east bank of the Saar and covering the right flank of the Saarlautern defenses. Two battalions of the 1139th Engineer Combat Group were to ferry the 90th Division across the Saar. Since no bridge existed, the division selected two sites for assault boat crossings. The 179th Engineer Combat Battalion was to ferry the 357th Infantry over the river on the left (north) flank; the 206th Engineer Combat Battalion was to cross the 358th Infantry on the right. The engineers were to operate the assault boats for the infantry and, after the landings, to bring over supplies and evacuate the wounded. The 179th Battalion also had to construct an infantry support bridge, an M2 treadway for tanks, other vehicles, or both, depending on the outcome of the assault. Late on 5 December the engineers brought the boats down to the riverbank as a ninety-minute artillery barrage drowned the noise of the deployment.

The first boats shoved off at 0415. Darkness protected them from enemy fire, but they had to buck a strong current in the river, which had begun rising the day before. Almost half of the boats the 179th Engineer Combat Battalion operated swamped on the way over or back and went off downstream, smashing into the debris of a blown railroad bridge. Most of the first infantry wave got across without mishap, but for succeeding waves the crossings were progressively more difficult. At daybreak the enemy spotted the boats, and smoke seemed only to attract heavier fire. When the engineers attempted to put down footbridges that first day, the Germans knocked out the spans almost as soon as work started.[31]

On the far bank of the Saar a strong band of pillboxes barred the way eastward. The 357th Infantry made some progress on the north, but to the south the 358th was unable to cross railroad tracks separating the riverside village of Pachten from Dillingen. At Pachten one of the engineers of the 315th Engineer Combat Battalion, Sgt. Joseph E. Williams, won the Distinguished Service Cross for gallantry in action. Volunteering to breach a pillbox, he was wounded before he could reach it but crawled on and fired his charge. He refused to be evacuated, advanced on another pillbox, and although wounded for the second time succeeded in taking sixteen prisoners.[32] However, this

---

[30] Hist 320th Engr C Bn, 1942–11 Aug 45. Barth, Farthing, and seven other members of the 320th Engineer Combat Battalion were awarded the Silver Star for action in reducing pillboxes at Saarlautern-Roden from 4 to 7 December.

[31] Hists, 1139th Engr C Gp, Dec 44; 179th Engr C Bn, Aug, Nov, Dec 44; and 206th Engr C Bn, Jun–Dec 44.

[32] AAR, 358th Inf Div, 6 Dec 44.

and other acts of heroism by engineers and infantry were not enough to overcome the pillboxes. The only field gun the 90th Division had east of the river was a captured German 75-mm. piece. Frantic calls went back to the near bank for tanks and antitank guns.

To get the tanks and guns across the river the engineers tried to build M2 treadway bridges, but German artillery knocked them out. So intense was the enemy fire that the powerboats used to ferry supplies and evacuate the wounded could be employed only at night; at times ferry operations had to be suspended entirely. Not until 9 December were the engineers able to get heavy rafts into operation. That day the 179th Engineer Combat Battalion crossed tanks and antitank guns on an M2 steel treadway raft, and the 206th Battalion got some jeeps, antitank guns, and tank destroyers across. Later, the 206th had sole charge of the crossing operation.[33]

During the following week, despite chilling rain and snow, the engineers kept the vehicular ferry running, repeatedly repairing damage from heavy German artillery fire. As the river began to recede the engineers also built a corduroy road of logs on the far shore to keep the tanks from miring down when they rolled off the rafts.[34] By 15 December, after the tanks as well as the 359th Infantry had crossed the Saar, the 90th Division was penetrating fortifications protecting Dillingen. Then the attack halted for several days to give the 5th Division time to relieve the 95th in the Saarlautern bridgehead and come abreast of the 90th. The advance resumed on 18 December. Resistance proved surprisingly light, and in three hours most of Dillingen was captured.

### The Withdrawal

Next afternoon, on 19 December, General Patton ordered the 90th Division to give up its hard-won Dillingen bridgehead and withdraw west of the Saar. By that time German attacks in the Ardennes, beginning on 16 December, had been recognized as a full-scale offensive. After a conference with Eisenhower and Bradley at Verdun on the morning of 19 December, Patton committed to the American defenses the bulk of Third Army, including the 90th and 5th Infantry Divisions, leaving the 95th Division to hold the Saarlautern bridgehead—the only foothold left east of the Saar.

For the withdrawal the engineers had to depend on assault boats and the M2 treadway ferries because a heavy ponton bridge they had planned to erect was not yet in place. The first tanks and trucks went back west on the night of 19 December. After artillery fire knocked out one of the ferries during daylight operations, the crossings continued only at night. The 206th Engineer Combat Battalion was in charge of the withdrawal. By noon of 22 December the 90th Division had recrossed the Saar and was headed north to take its place in the hasty defense against the last great German counteroffensive in the west.[35]

South of Third Army's withdrawing elements, American and French forces also steeled themselves for the German

---

[33] Hists, 179th and 206th Engr C Bns.
[34] Hist 1139th Engr C Gp.

[35] Hists, 1139th Engr C Gp and 206th Engr C Bn.

blow. From mid-September on, Patton had been fighting with a new Allied army group on his flank in the south. Another seaborne thrust into German-occupied France on 15 August had rapidly cleared the southern tier of the country and linked with the 12th Army Group to form a continuous line from the Mediterranean to the English Channel. Mounted from the Mediterranean Theater of Operations, the assault and the subsequent advance north relied heavily on engineer elements for success.

# CHAPTER XX

# Southern France

As the Allied plans for the cross-Channel attack matured in January 1944, another staff headquarters in the Mediterranean began preparing for the last major seaborne thrust onto the European continent in World War II. Under the U.S. Seventh Army engineer, Brig. Gen. Garrison H. Davidson, the newly formed Force 163 moved into an unused French girls' school outside Algiers. Having briefly commanded the Seventh Army, then a headquarters organization with few troops assigned, General Davidson retained an interest in the planning of the invasion, Operation ANVIL, after Maj. Gen. Alexander M. Patch took over the army command on 2 March 1944. The predominantly engineer staff developed several alternate plans for the undertaking in southern France but at General Davidson's insistence and at the Navy Intelligence Board's recommendation, the planners concentrated on the forty-five mile coastline between Toulon and Cannes. There, the beaches offered a good gradient for amphibious operations and rapid access to the major port of Marseille and the naval base at Toulon. Two good roads into the French interior ran north from the area. One led up the Rhone River valley to Lyon, and the other through the Durance River valley to Grenoble. Having served as Napoleon's escape route from Elba in 1815, the latter was known as the Route Napoleon.[1]

ANVIL lived a precarious existence from the outset. It remained subordinate to the material demands of the projected Normandy invasion and the Italian campaign and subject to the voluble objections of Winston Churchill. Nevertheless, active planning continued at Seventh Army headquarters with the explicit endorsement of Lt. Gen. Jacob L. Devers, who had taken command of the North African theater at the turn of the year. Devers went so far as to freeze theater stocks necessary for ANVIL to preserve it as a viable operation. Not until 2 July did the Combined Chiefs of Staff finally direct the execution of ANVIL with a target date of 15 August. Churchill made a last-minute attempt to divert ANVIL forces to the west coast of France, but, because of General Devers' commitment to the project, planning for ANVIL at Seventh Army was uninterrupted.[2]

Planning sessions had hardly begun when the impetus for closer cooperation between Army and Navy planners

---

[1] Seventh U.S. Army, *Report of Operations, France and Germany, 1944–1945*, vol. I (Heidelberg: Aloys Graef, 1946), pp. 1–10. This chapter relies on this source for planning and tactical details pertaining to the Seventh Army, except where otherwise noted. It is cited hereafter as *Seventh Army Report*.

[2] Coakley and Leighton, *Global Logistics and Strategy, 1943–45*, pp. 365, 381–82.

made organizational innovation necessary. The experiences of the Sicilian and Italian landings showed the need for interservice coordination of the operation, while the near-debacle at Anzio provoked a reassessment of amphibious warfare practice. In March 1944 General Davidson recommended that General Patch establish two joint agencies, a Beach Obstacle Board and a Beach Control Board, to revise procedures for the combined operations phase of the forthcoming invasion.

To form the Beach Obstacle Board Seventh Army engineers joined Navy engineers and planners working under Vice Adm. H. Kent Hewitt, commander of the Western Naval Task Force, which would transport Seventh Army to the invasion area. Working through the summer of 1944 at the Invasion Training Center in and around Salerno, the board tested several devices that had arrived too late for use at Normandy. The Apex drone boats, the Reddy Fox explosive pipe, and the Navy "Woofus"—a rocket-firing LCM— engendered no great hopes among the board members, and they chose to rely primarily on demolition teams, each consisting of a naval officer and a balanced contingent of sailors and Army engineers.[3]

The Beach Control Board produced a similar new organizational element in the Beach Control Group, combining an Army engineer combat regiment, a naval beach battalion, and several smaller service units. Trained under the supervision of the Seventh Army G–4, Col. Oliver C. Harvey, one beach group was assigned to each of the three invading divisions with the job of moving supplies ashore in the assault, clearing any shore obstacles impeding deliveries to the troops moving off the beaches, and acting as an embryonic base section until the consolidation of the beachhead and the arrival of regular services of supply on shore.[4]

Tank-gapping teams were another successful innovation for ANVIL. An armored unit equipped with M4A4 tanks mounting bulldozer blades or scarifiers, the team was to breach the enemy beach minefields and sea walls serving as tank obstacles so that the armor in the first assault wave could move quickly off the open beaches in support of the advancing infantry. The engineers split the 6617th Mine Clearance Company to provide three teams, one attached to each of the engineer beach groups for the assault. Drivers from the regular armored forces were trained to manipulate the dozer blades to unearth buried mines as rapidly as possible.

By 19 June the major engineer combat unit assignments for the invasion were completed. Supporting the 3d Infantry Division as the nucleus for the 36th Engineer Beach Control Group, the 36th Engineer Combat Regiment operated with the 1st Naval Beach Battalion and various chemical, ordnance, signal, and military police units. Assigned to the 45th Infantry Division, the 40th Engineer Beach Control Group employed its core engineer regiment, the 4th Naval Beach Battalion, two quartermaster battalions, two port battalions, a medical battalion, and several smaller

---

[3] See ch. XIV; Morison, *The Invasion of France and Germany*, p. 241.

[4] Seventh Army, Engineer Section Reports, Engineer Historical Report, 1 Jan–30 Sep 44, pp. 1–2 (hereafter cited as Seventh Army, Engr Hist Rpt).

service units. With the 36th Infantry Division was the 540th Engineer Beach Control Group, comprised of the 48th Engineer Battalion, the 8th Naval Beach Battalion, two quartermaster battalions, two port battalions, a medical battalion, several detachments of service troops, and the three battalions of the 540th Engineer Combat Regiment.[5] Though the same mix of support units was employed as in OVERLORD, there was no provisional brigade headquarters such as the one that controlled activities during the cross-Channel attack.

Attached to Maj. Gen. Lucian K. Truscott's VI Corps, these units were accomplished veterans. The infantry divisions and engineers chosen for the first waves had all seen extensive action in the invasions of North Africa and Sicily and in the Italian campaign. The 36th Engineer Combat Regiment was preparing its fifth amphibious operation, and the 540th had had a distinguished career in two earlier landings. At the Invasion Training Center and around the Bay of Gaeta after the Seventh Army headquarters moved to Naples in early July, the engineer beach groups demonstrated demolitions, mine warfare, and small boat handling to infantry units. Since the engineers were well versed in tactics, their training centered on equipment—variations of the tank bulldozer and scarifiers, a new bridge-carrying tank, and other innovations.[6]

Enemy forces in the target area for Operation ANVIL looked formidable on paper but had major weaknesses in their organization and shortages in manpower and equipment. The local

GENERAL DAVIDSON

command, *Nineteenth Army*, three corps strong under Lt. Gen. Friedrich Wiese, had had to exchange several units with German commands in northern France following the Normandy invasion and emerged the loser in these transfers. Wiese's relationship with his senior command, *Army Group G*, was uncertain. The divisional commanders available to him were competent, but at least two were exhausted from their experiences on the Russian front. German strength in southern France, counting reserve aggregations, amounted to over 285,000 men, including weak naval and air support. Wiese had somewhere between 85,000 and 100,000 men in the immediate assault area to thwart an invasion that he knew was coming. German aerial reconnaissance over the Mediterranean had detected the Allied buildup of shipping; some agent reports even men-

---

[5] *Seventh Army Report,* vol. I, p. 81.
[6] Seventh Army, Engr Hist Rpt, p. 5.

tioned 15 August as the date set for the assault. The *242d Infantry Division,* defending nearly the exact area described in the Seventh Army assault plan, was one of the two best Wiese had. But like the other divisions along the coast from the Italian to the Spanish borders, it was understrength and lacked some equipment. Though relatively better off than other units for trained soldiery, the *242d* had unreliable ethnic German troops from eastern Europe reinforcing it, and its least effective regiment included a battalion of Azerbaijanis. To add to Wiese's difficulties, Hitler had personally decreed that the *242d* was to defend Toulon as a fortress and had given its sister division, the *244th,* the same assignment in Marseille. Under these conditions, the army commander could not use his two most effective divisions as a maneuver force.[7]

Obstacles to landing craft in southern France were not nearly as numerous as those sown on the Normandy beaches, but the Germans had not totally neglected their defenses. Beach sands and all the beach exits were heavily mined and covered with barbed wire. Heavy artillery pieces, some from scuttled French warships in Toulon harbor, commanded all the likely approaches to shore. Concrete geometric shapes of all kinds barred movement on major roads and intersections along the coast. But, lacking manpower and necessary supplies, the German defenders could not construct positions in great depth, though their orders called for networks extending eight miles inland. At German Navy insistence they left intact the

larger ports of Toulon and Marseille but completely wrecked some twenty smaller harbors in the invasion areas, including Ste. Maxime and St. Raphael. After 12 August, German forces along the coast were on constant alert.[8]

The main assault force assembled to strike this defensive shell loaded into attack craft with its contingents of engineers at Naples harbor between 8 and 12 August. Some of the slower vessels left the crowded anchorage early to coordinate their arrival off the beaches. By midnight 14 August, in calm weather and a light sea, over 950 vessels had gathered in assembly areas facing the Bays of Cavalaire, Pampelonne, and Bougnon and the shore east of St. Raphael. Before daybreak on 15 August commando raiders hit the suspected German gun emplacements on the Iles d'Hyeres off Cape Benat, and the Allied 1st Airborne Task Force began its drop into zones around the towns of Le Muy and Le Luc, some ten miles inland from the amphibious landing zones. As the sun rose at 0638 a furious naval bombardment was directed at the larger German guns on the mainland, now obscured in the light haze hanging over much of the shoreline in the early dawn.

### The Landings

Facing the 3d Infantry Division on the left were the Alpha beaches. Alpha Red, the westernmost, was an arc of smooth yellow sand on the Bay of Cavalaire, bordered by a thin, intermittent stand of pines thirty yards from the water. Six miles due east across the southern tier of the St. Tropez peninsula, Alpha Yellow stretched along

---

[7] MS R–103, Charles V. P. von Luttichau, German Operations in Southern France and Alsace, 1944: Army Group G Prepares to Meet the Invasion, 1957, p. 11, in CMH.

[8] Ibid.; *Seventh Army Report,* vol. I, pp. 37–40.

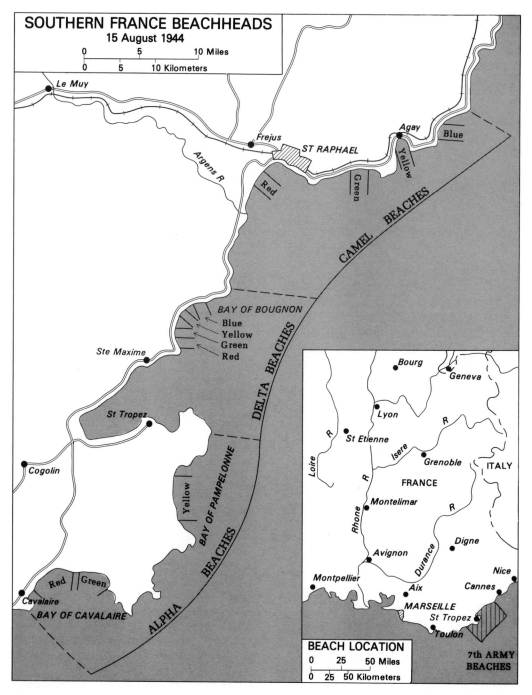

## SOUTHERN FRANCE BEACHHEADS
### 15 August 1944

0 ___ 5 ___ 10 Miles
0 ___ 5 ___ 10 Kilometers

Le Muy

Frejus

Argens R

ST RAPHAEL

Red

Agay

Blue

Yellow

Green

CAMEL BEACHES

BAY OF BOUGNON
Blue
Yellow
Green
Red

Ste Maxime

DELTA BEACHES

St Tropez

Cogolin

Yellow

BAY OF PAMPELONNE

BEACHES

Red | Green

Cavalaire

BAY OF CAVALAIRE

ALPHA

### BEACH LOCATION

Bourg

Geneva

Lyon

St Etienne

Loire R

Isere R

Grenoble

ITALY

FRANCE

Rhone R

Montelimar

Digne

Avignon

Durance R

Nice

Montpellier

Aix

Cannes

MARSEILLE

St Tropez

Toulon

0 ___ 25 ___ 50 Miles
0 ___ 25 ___ 50 Kilometers

7th ARMY
BEACHES

*MAP 24*

the Bay of Pampelonne, with restricted exits behind it leading to the resort town of St. Tropez to the north and over rolling farmland and rougher terrain to the west. (*Map 24*)

After 0710 minesweepers moved in under the cover of naval fire, clearing boat lanes to within 100 yards of the beaches. In the shallow water stood rows of concrete pyramids and tetrahedrons, most equipped with Teller mines. At 0730 eighteen Apex drones rumbled shoreward to blast clear the last 100 yards for the landing craft. Fifteen drones destroyed as many obstacles, but two circled aimlessly, and one roared back into the fleet area, damaging a sub-chaser when it blew up among the ships.[9]

By 0758, naval fire support shifted to the flanks of the beaches, and the first waves started shoreward. Three minutes later, the 7th Regimental Combat Team, 3d Infantry Division, struck Alpha Red, and the 15th Infantry drove onto Alpha Yellow. The tank-gapping team at Alpha Red immediately fell into five-foot surf off the beach, nearly drowning out the tank engines. Undeterred, their crews gunned the two engineer tanks up the sand, bulldozing a passage through the railroad embankment behind the beach and clearing a road through a mined, wooded area, all in less than ten minutes.[10] Elements

of the 1st Battalion, 36th Engineer Combat Regiment, came in with the first wave on Red, and immediately squads began probing for mines with bayonets and detectors.

The gapping team at Yellow landed some 1,500 yards to the left of its assigned point and had to wade the single tank through water five feet deep. But once ashore, the vehicle took only a quarter-hour to clear a 1,500-yard path through antitank and antipersonnel mines to a highway, silencing a German antitank gun in the process. The tank's dozer arm, partially severed by an exploding mine, finally buckled completely as the tank forded a stream to begin preparing a crossing site.

The 3d Battalion, 36th Engineer Combat Regiment, hit Yellow and, clearing paths through the mines, pushed vehicle tracks of reinforced matting through the serviceable beach exits. By 0920 the 36th Engineer Beach Group's command post was set up in the Hotel Pardigon in Cavalaire, off the left flank of Alpha Red. As the day progressed the 1st Battalion, leaving beach operations to the 3d Battalion, advanced inland with the infantry to clear roadblocks and minefields. The unit laid out dumps behind the troops moving to the beachhead line, leveled an airstrip for reconnaissance aircraft, and erected barbed-wire barricades for a prisoner enclosure.[11]

Alpha Yellow Beach closed down on 16 August; poor exits and a sandbar just off shore limited its supply flow. The 3d Battalion moved southwest across the St. Tropez peninsula on 18 August to relieve the crush of opera-

---

[9] Adm. H. Kent Hewitt, "Executing Operation ANVIL-DRAGOON," *U.S. Naval Institute Proceedings,* LXXX (August 1954), 903; Morison, *The Invasion of France and Germany,* p. 256; *Seventh Army Report,* vol. I, p. 199.

[10] Summary of Accomplishments, Tank-Gapping Teams, app. to Memo, Maj Thomas W. Wood for Joint Army-Navy Experimental and Testing Board, Ft. Pierce, Fla., 10 Sep 44, sub: Operation DRAGOON. All details on the operations of the tank-gapping teams are taken from this source.

[11] Hist Rpt, 36th Engr C Rgt, 1944, Report for August 1944.

tions on Alpha Red by opening Alpha Green opposite Red on the Bay of Cavalaire. Engineers quickly discovered that the exits off Green were heavily mined, and clearing them occupied much of the labor force until the end of the month. With these hindrances, service troops on the Alpha beaches had continual difficulty responding to the supply demands of the combat troops. Though the Alpha complex was the least efficient of the ANVIL beach operations, it continued to receive cargo until Marseille harbor came into full use.

Seven miles across the mouth of the Bay of St. Tropez from Alpha Yellow, beginning just east of rocky Cape Sardineau, the Delta beaches curved from south to northeast along the shores of the Bay of Bougnon. Delta Red and Delta Green lay contiguous, giving way to flat hinterlands. Delta Blue was separate, broken on its far right by a small river mouth and marked to its rear by rising slopes of the Maures. An eight-foot-high, three-foot-thick concrete wall stood along the back edge of Red and Green; behind it ran a paved road and a narrow-gauge coastal railroad atop a masonry embankment that also paralleled the shore behind Yellow and Blue.

No underwater obstacles hindered the Delta force, and at 0802 the 40th Engineer Beach Control Group, under Lt. Col. Oscar B. Beasley, touched down. Finding no mines on the beach, the 1st Battalion of the engineer regiment reduced concertina-wire defenses of Red and Green and set to work unloading over ponton causeways and landing craft that grounded several yards out on the steep gradient.

The gapping team at Delta Green had approached the beach 500 yards to the right of its intended landfall and immediately lost all three of its engineer tanks when they plunged almost out of sight into the water on leaving the landing craft. The crews dove to retrieve the wall-breaching charges in the forward racks on the tank hulls and blew out a sea-wall section large enough for troops, tanks, and supplies to move through. By nightfall the 1st Battalion had supply dumps laid out 500 yards inland.

At Delta Yellow and Blue, the 3d Battalion of the engineer regiment began limited operations. Landing craft nosed right into the beach here, but the exits at Blue were so constricted that it also closed on D plus 1. The 2d Battalion, 40th Engineer Combat Regiment, a later arrival, went to the aid of the 36th Engineer Beach Group on short-lived Alpha Yellow late in the afternoon of D-day. It then moved through St. Tropez in the face of stiff German resistance to clear mines and open over twenty new boat ramps on beaches christened Delta Red 2, at the head of the Gulf of St. Tropez and west of the town.[12]

Farther east the road and the railroad tracks that skirted the Delta beaches ran through the ancient Roman port of Frejus, still a major populated point although centuries-long silting had placed it a mile from the sea. At the head of the gulf that once led to its harbor was Camel Red, the best beach in the VI Corps assault area for its gradient, size, and access to the valley of the sluggish Argens River to the left. Its advantages as a lodgment had occurred to the Germans too, and they erected here the strongest and best-

---

[12] *Seventh Army Report*, vol. I, pp. 133–34.

organized defenses encountered in Operation ANVIL. The Navy and the Air Forces pounded the emplacements all morning, softening the defenses for a thrust ashore planned at 1400 on D-day, but minesweepers sent in at 1100 drew such heavy fire that they retreated. An air attack at noon rained 187 tons of explosives on the German positions.

The main assault in the Camel area came at 0803 on Green, a narrow 500-yard-long stretch of rocky shingle backed by rising cliffs scarred with quarries 1 1/2 miles east of the resort town of St. Raphael. Camel Yellow, to be taken indirectly rather than by immediate seaborne frontal attack, lay at the head of the Rade d'Agay across the base of the Drammont promontory from Green and was defended and blocked by obstacles and a net boom across the roadstead. At Antheor Cove, 2,000 yards east of Yellow, Camel Blue, a thin eighty-yard stretch, was the landing point of the troops of the 141st Infantry, 36th Division, who were to secure the easternmost flank of the beachhead line. The embankment of the coastal motor road ran thirty feet from the water's edge at Blue, and the narrow-gauge railroad crossed the back of the diminutive inlet on an eight-span masonry bridge a hundred feet above the water.

The 1st Battalion of Col. George W. Marvin's 540th Engineer Combat Regiment, leading the beach group, charged ashore on Green with two battalions of the 141st Infantry. Two engineer companies quickly organized the beaches, cleared mines, and set up dumps for the following assault waves. Company B crossed the Agay River with the 2d Battalion, 141st Infantry, and met infan-

try units coming from Camel Blue to take Yellow from behind in order to start supply operations there.[13]

The first wave on Camel Green went in without a tank-gapping team. Equipped with a rocket rack atop its turret, the tank intended for the first wave was aboard an LCT that broke down on the way to the invasion area. The tank arrived on another craft in a later infantry assault wave and moved to the beach wall to blast a hole. The rockets accomplished their purpose, but the backblast spewed a scorching sandstorm into the ranks of the unwary onlookers to the rear. After breaching the obstacle the engineer crew of the tank had no orders for other employment, though it occurred to them that they could have used their machine to help the regular engineer squads remove mines. Four D-7 bulldozers were damaged and several men wounded on Camel Green digging out mines by traditional methods.[14]

The Apex drones had their worst hour before the scheduled landing on Camel Red. Launched under a furious naval barrage about 1300, ten of the boats churned through the Gulf of Frejus. Three wrecked some mined tetrahedrons, one exploded on the far left flank of the beach, two ran up on the sand, and one made tight circles offshore. A destroyer blew another out of the water when it veered seaward, and sailors gingerly boarded the last two wayward robots to put them out of action. Navy intelligence later speculated that the Germans had stolen radio

---

[13] Ibid., p. 137; Hist 540th Engr C Rgt, p. 14.

[14] Summary of Accomplishments, Tank-Gapping Teams. The engineer tank crews on other beaches had complaints similar to those expressed in the aforementioned work about their inactivity after the assault.

control of the boats, a logical explanation of their dismal performance.

The volume of German fire during the foray of the drones forced a change in the plan to land the 142d Infantry, 36th Division, on Camel Red; the Navy placed the assault wave ashore on already secured Camel Green at 1515. Diverting the assault force doubtless saved needless casualties, but now the 540th Engineer Combat Regiment's overworked 1st Battalion, having moved the 141st and 143d Infantry regiments ashore at Green, received the men and equipment of the 142d as well. Work on the beach continued throughout the night, interrupted briefly at 2225, when several engineers joined rescuers swimming to the aid of the wounded on the striken LST–282 after a German glider bomb hit the craft. The vessel grounded in the shoals near Cape Drammont and lay smoldering with forty casualties aboard and half her cargo reduced to junk.[15]

The 540th's 2d Battalion, landing with the 142d Infantry, swept the right flank of Camel Green and then struck overland to organize Camel Yellow, at the same time relieving Company B. Yellow Beach became the principal supply beach in the Camel net, while troop and vehicular traffic moved over Green.

The 36th Division troops moving from these beaches carried the town of St. Raphael, lying between Red and Green, by evening of D-day and moved to reduce the formidable defenses of Red from the rear. After its relief on

Yellow, Company B led the engineer elements following the 36th Division into St. Raphael shortly after daybreak on 16 August. Scattered German sniper fire greeted the company's arrival on the outskirts of the town, but a short series of skirmishes eliminated the defenders, and the 540th Beach Group command post was set up in the town by noon. Joined later by Company A, Company B began the clearance of Camel Red, sweeping the western end of the beach, blasting out sections of seawall, and demolishing the seven-foot-high, three-foot-thick reinforced-concrete antitank blocks the Germans had strewn about the beach. The 1st Battalion less Company C, left behind to operate Camel Green, had Red open to traffic late in the afternoon of 17 August. Supply dumps behind the beaches had been operating for four hours, receiving laden trucks from the other Camel beaches.

Company F left Yellow on the eighteenth to begin clearing the dockside area and the quays of the town. Bulldozers had started to open the streets when one of the company machines engaged a row of blocks, concrete obstacles with hidden Teller mines. The engineer components of the 540th Beach Group, having sustained only one fatality since D-day, lost nearly a platoon when the detonation of one booby-trapped block killed four and wounded twenty-seven men. On the following day the remainder of the 2d Battalion abandoned Yellow Beach and came to St. Raphael to continue the harbor reconstruction that Company F had begun, and the little port began receiving incoming cargo on the twentieth.

While VI Corps consolidated the invasion beaches, the Seventh Army

---

[15] Morison, *The Invasion of France and Germany,* p. 270; Hist Div, WDSS, Invasion of Southern France, pp. 60–61, typescript copy in CMH. This source is based largely on the *Seventh Army Report* but is supplemented with additional material from after-action interviews.

MINE REMOVAL AT CAMEL RED. *Mines were used to blast a hole in the seawall at rear.*

Engineer Section, operating out of the Hotel Latitude Quarante-trois in St. Tropez, kept a close eye on the developing beach supply operations. The unexpectedly rapid advance off the ANVIL beaches soon forced the engineers to accelerate work schedules in two areas intimately connected with the forward movement of Seventh Army supply: rehabilitation of ports and repair of railroad lines and bridges. By 27 August General Davidson had completed personal reconnaissance of Marseille and Toulon as well as petroleum facilities at Port-de-Bouc. He was already revising engineer plans to speed up the influx of engineer units and supplies of all kinds.

The choice of ports for major cargo discharge became a bone of Army-Navy contention even before German resistance in Marseille and Toulon collapsed. From 25 August, General Davidson opposed the original Navy plan to refurbish both ports simultaneously. Spurred by the desperate need to get ahead of a mounting shipping crisis in the European theater, where two major amphibious invasions had taken place within two months, the Navy sought all means possible to turn ships around and keep a constant supply of empty vessels available. The Army's immediate concern was the movement of supplies; Toulon, a naval base with narrow wharves, constricted access, and only single-track rails to serve it, was unsuitable for bulk cargo movement except as a supplementary port. The railroad net in and out of Marseille was highly developed—capable of moving more than 350 boxcars a day—and followed the natural commercial route along the axis of advance of the Seventh Army. General Davidson recommended directing all salvage and clearance efforts at preparing Marseille for the twenty-five ships of the D plus 25 convoy. A conference on 1 September, chaired by Maj. Gen. Arthur A. White, Seventh Army chief of staff, resolved the impasse in favor of the Army's view but gave the Navy permission to assign Seabees to develop Toulon as a secondary port. After 1 September the French Navy also devoted most of its engineering efforts to the reconstruction of its former base.[16]

A successful French assault on the two cities, concluded on 28 August after a week-long fight, brought the headquarters and 2d Battalion, 36th Engineer Combat Regiment, and the 335th Engineer General Service Regiment into Marseille to prepare it for large-scale cargo operations. Assigned for the moment to Coastal Base Section established at Marseille, the troops undertook preliminary damage estimates, started mine and booby-trap clearance, and removed rubble in the dockside areas, with the 335th at first doing the mine clearance around the deepwater harbor and the 36th handling the Vieux Port area.

Many of the German mines were improvised, though the standard Schu antipersonnel and heavier Teller mines were plentiful. Larger charges meant to demolish entire docks and storage facilities were made locally of explosive-packed wooden barrels and 300-pound drums, casks of picric acid, and detonators. Equipped with timing mechanisms and set into the docks or warehouse walls, they blasted twelve-foot craters, making whole wharves temporarily impassable. The charges had flattened all warehousing in the dock area. The 335th dug out over thirty tons of explosives and removed 2,000 Teller mines, but had to detonate many of the big charges in place when the engineers discovered that the fuses had so decomposed that their safe deactivation was impossible.

Engineer regiments supervised by the headquarters organization known after 1 September as the 1051st Engineer Port Construction and Repair Group set about restoring enough of the port to serve the needs of the Seventh Army and the projected requirements of the 6th Army Group headquarters of Lt. Gen. Jacob L. Devers. The army group was scheduled to become operational on 15 September. On the landward side the engineers removed debris and repaired quay walls. Where German charges had blown holes in the tops and sides of masonry wharves, the engineers first reconstructed the dock walls. German prisoners, augmented by Italian labor gangs, did all of the heavy, disagreeable manual labor to clear the breaks and then to fill the craters, and they repaired wall sections with the rubble they carried from other parts of the city and the harbor.[17]

[16] Mins of Mtg, 6th Army Group Conference file 7, 25 Aug–1 Sep; Coakley and Leighton, *Global Logistics and Strategy, 1943–45*, p. 385; Official Diary for Commanding General Seventh Army, vol. II, 15 August 1944 to 31 January 1945, pp. 222–23, typescript copy in CMH.

[17] *CONAD History*, vol. I (Heidelberg: Aloys Graef, 1945), p. 40.

In the harbor channels the Germans had sunk over sixty-five ships in patterns that vitiated the methods the engineers had used at Naples harbor. At Marseille the enemy piled ships atop one another on the harbor floor at such odd angles to and distances from the quays that bridging over them was not feasible. Nearly all the 121 individual berthing spaces in the old and new sections of the 550-acre port were blocked; cranes serving the cargo wharves were toppled into the water to form additional blocks or were otherwise sabotaged. The Germans also had scuttled seven ocean-going vessels in a heap to close the mouth of the deepwater section of the port.

While Navy salvage teams attacked this key obstruction, French engineers and the 1051st tried to bypass it by blowing a passage in the breakwater protecting the harbor. The engineers moved in a well-drilling crew to bore holes in the jetty for charges. But then Navy divers managed to topple one of the seven hulks off the pile, allowing the passage of laden Liberty ships above the remainder of the wreckage. Once this blockage was eliminated, the Marseille port slowly came to life again. By 8 September, when the Coastal Base Section took control of the port, eight Liberty berths were operating around the clock; by month's end the port had received 188 ships carrying 147,460 men, 113,500 long tons of cargo, 32,768 vehicles, and 10,000 barrels of petroleum products of all kinds.[18]

In the area of Port-de-Bouc, a satellite port some twenty-five miles by sea northwest of Marseille, the engineers encountered similar, though much less extensive, destruction and harbor blockage. The center of the southern French petroleum traffic in peacetime, this port also had a daily capacity of 7,000 short tons of dry cargo; it was the hub of a canal system that funneled barge traffic between Arles, twenty-five miles up the Rhone River, and Marseille's Bargeline Harbor. Port-de-Bouc's dock system on the Mediterranean was constructed as an extension of a continuous commercial net winding along a narrow, 3 1/2-mile tidal strait passing through the town of Martigues, which sat astride the opening into a wide saltwater lake, the Etang de Berre. Its shore was lined with smaller wharves, canal entrances, and petroleum refineries.

Here the Germans had had little time for methodical destruction of facilities. They blasted loose large stones from the masonry docks to ruin them and to foul the berthing areas alongside. Company A, 335th Engineer General Service Regiment, arriving in the area on 27 August, replaced these stones easily and filled craters along the quays with the debris of the scattered German demolition charges. When the Navy finished sweeping mines from the approaches later in August and removed the single blockship in the harbor, three berths along the T-shaped jetty and on the quays became available for Liberties. The end of September saw the discharge of 36,837 long tons of regular cargo at Port-de-Bouc, little when compared to the tonnages of Marseille, but consistent with the port's real importance as the chief Allied POL entry point in southern France.[19]

---

[18] Ibid., p. 41; The Adm and Log Hist of the ETO, vol. VII, "Opening and Operating the Continental Ports," p. 127.

[19] The Adm and Log Hist of the ETO, vol. VII, "Opening and Operating the Continental Ports," p.

ENGINEER OFFICER PROBES FOR EXPLOSIVE CHARGE AT MARSEILLE

The main rail service through the area was a double-track system that paralleled the coast west of Marseille, crossed the narrow ship channel between Port-de-Bouc and Martigues at its center, swung east through Port-de-Bouc, and then veered north after bridging the Arles Canal. The Germans blocked both ship movement on the waterways and rail traffic by dumping the turn span that crossed the tidal strait into the ship channel and dropping the second rail bridge into the canal. The 1051st finally cleared the channel obstruction in October, blasting away the wreckage to allow heavy tanker traffic access to the Etang de Berre. Reconstruction of the rail overpass over the Arles Canal restored traffic on the line out of Port-de-Bouc in early December.[20]

### Base Sections and SOLOC

In the two weeks following the invasion, General Davidson made every effort to free engineer combat regiments on the beaches for work behind

---

134; Morison, *The Invasion of France and Germany*, p. 286; Unit Hist, 335th Engr GS Rgt, Hist Rpts for Aug–Sep 44. Company A was active around Port-de-Bouc until 27 September, when the 335th moved north. See also "POL Operations" below.

[20] OCE ETOUSA Hist Rpt 11, Port Reconstruction and Repair, app. 50, Port-de-Bouc.

the advancing armies. The Coastal Base Section, with an advance party ashore on 16 August, began assuming control of operations in Marseille and was in full control in the city by 8 September, a week ahead of schedule. The Coastal Base Section engineer, Lt. Col. Chauncey K. Smullen, agreed to release all engineers but one battalion of the 40th Engineer Combat Regiment from the beaches. Renamed Continental Base Section on 10 September, Coastal Base left Marseille to become the mobile section moving behind the 6th Army Group. On 26 September, when it was rechristened Continental Advance Section, the logistical command was at Dijon. *(Map 25)*

The Advance Section left behind at the port city a new support command, Delta Base Section (DBS), which ran the southern French ports until after V–J Day. The DBS Engineer Section, established 3 October under Lt. Col. William B. Harmon and among the largest components of the new base section, took over the 1051st Engineer Port Construction and Repair Group and the activities of over thirty other units providing fire protection, construction, water supply, and services in the port areas. By war's end in Europe the engineers had restored nearly 35 percent of Marseille's prewar harbor facilities, leaving the remainder for postwar reconstruction by the French government.[21]

With the relief of the engineers on the beaches, the over-shore operations began closing down. Supply-choked Alpha Beach closed 9 September, followed by the Deltas on the sixteenth

and the busy Camel Red on 25 September. By the end of the month the flow of supply had shifted to Marseille where Delta Base Section formed the southern end of 6th Army Group's line of communications in France.

Once 6th Army Group had met 12th Army Group in east-central France to form a continuous battle line facing the Reich, an adjustment in the administration of supply functions became necessary. SHAEF assumed tactical control of the 6th Army Group on 15 September, the day it began operations as a headquarters in France, but resolution of the question of command over the supply establishment in southern France was more gradual and complicated.

The complexities arose from the fact that two separate communications zone commands were now active in the ETOUSA area, an advance element of SOS, NATOUSA, that opened at Lyon on 11 September, and General Lee's COMZ, ETOUSA. Though the 6th Army Group's operational area was within Lee's preserve, it still drew its supply from massive reserves in the North African theater, which lay outside Lee's purview. COMZ was momentarily unprepared to handle requisitions and establish procedures for the Rhone valley supply net, but any accommodation would have to recognize the legal supremacy of COMZ on the European mainland. Conferences between the two parties proceeded throughout September. SHAEF was willing to allow General Devers as commander of 6th Army Group a fair degree of autonomy in his supply. In the compromise eventually worked out, ETOUSA would assume ultimate control of the Rhone supply route on 20 November while an inter-

[21] Seventh Army, Engr Hist Rpt, pp. 8–9; *History, Delta Base Section*, pp. 155–60, in CMH.

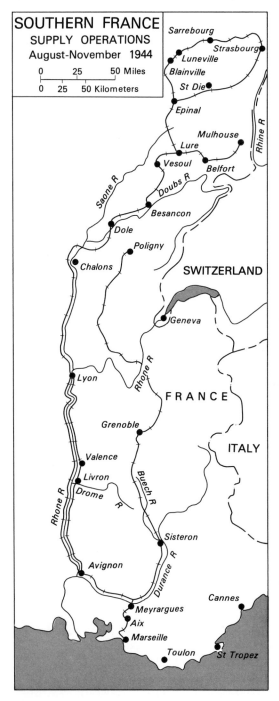

**SOUTHERN FRANCE**
SUPPLY OPERATIONS
August–November 1944

0    25    50 Miles

0    25    50 Kilometers

Sarrebourg

Strasbourg

Luneville

Blainville

St Die

Epinal

Mulhouse

Lure

Vesoul    Belfort

Rhine R

Saone R

Doubs R

Besancon

Dole

Poligny

Chalons

SWITZERLAND

Geneva

Rhone R

Lyon

FRANCE

Grenoble

ITALY

Valence

Livron

Drome R

Buech R

Rhone R

Sisteron

Durance R

Avignon

Cannes

Meyrargues

Aix

Marseille

Toulon    St Tropez

*MAP 25*

mediate command, the Southern Line of Communications (SOLOC), opened on the same day to handle supply in the south. Although a subsidiary of COMZ, ETOUSA, SOLOC was still authorized direct communication with NATOUSA on the matters of supply and personnel coming from Italy or North Africa. On 3 November, a COMZ general order named Maj. Gen. Thomas B. Larkin, former NATOUSA SOS commander, commander of SOLOC and deputy commander of COMZ, ETOUSA. This uneasy union of the two supply commands functioned acceptably, but SOLOC lasted only through the winter; on 6 February 1945, the command passed out of existence, six weeks before 6th Army Group crossed the Rhine.[22]

Engineer operations on the supply routes in southern France were under the SOLOC engineer, Col. Clark Kittrell, a career soldier with years of experience in civil works in the United States. Kittrell's Engineer Section was always understaffed and constantly working under two separate sets of procedures and policies, depending upon which theater's jurisdiction applied to matters touching on engineer operations. He continued to wrestle with shortages of spare parts and inadequate inventory methods that became worse as the demands of the sudden advance accumulated. Chief among the engineer concerns for SOLOC, however, were the functions affecting the supply of the pursuing army, railroad supply routes, and petroleum pipeline supply systems.[23]

---

[22] Ruppenthal, *Logistical Support of the Armies, Volume II,* pp. 41–45; History of SOLOC-ETOUSA, vol. I, Adm 600A, ETOUSA Adm files.

[23] Hist of SOLOC-ETOUSA, vol. II, Adm 600B, ETOUSA Adm files.

## Railroads

Allied rail supply operations in southern France began on 23 August with short-haul bulk service lines out of Frejus to points less than thirty miles inland. The 40th Engineer Beach Group had begun collecting empty rail cars at St. Tropez on D plus 2 and added this equipment to the twelve locomotives and eighty cars found intact at Carnoules, within the beachhead area. As Coastal Base Section took over Marseille, the Army engineers retained responsibility for roads and rail maintenance out of the city. Damage to roads was slight, and the rails were usually only blocked by fallen debris. Where Germans had torn up trackage, French railroad employees replaced rails and ties with no difficulty.

From a point above Aix-en-Provence, twenty-five miles north of Marseille, the French rail net divided into two routes traveling north: a multiple track link running up the Rhone valley on both sides of the river and a single track branching east and then north to Grenoble. More steeply graded, negotiating mountain terrain, and subject to deep snows and frequent flooding in the upland passes, the Grenoble route nevertheless had priority because there seemed to be far less damage along it than along the heavier duty Rhone alternate. The major breaks encountered in the southern end of the net were just southwest of Aix; at Meyrargues, ten miles north of Aix; and north of Sisteron at the confluence of the Buech and Durance Rivers.

The original plan for railroad repair left the entire job of major rehabilitation behind the armies to the engineers of the 1st Military Railway Service, scheduled for phasing into southern

France on D plus 30. When the advance up the Rhone valley got much ahead of schedule, bridge repair fell to the Seventh Army engineers, now forced to rely on their ingenuity and extensive stocks of locally procured materials. With heavy bridging steel sections still on convoys sailing from the United States or heading for Marseille from stockpiles within the Mediterranean, the engineers were working with a supply allotment adequate for D plus 14 operations when the combat elements had already taken D plus 60 objectives. General Davidson's construction regiments picked up what they could to improvise structures to span German demolitions in the rail supply line.

L−5 Cub planes gave the engineers a head start on surveying the damage. Engineer officers with Speed Graphic cameras flew low-level passes over blown bridges, some behind enemy lines, shooting oblique-angle photographs to give construction troops a means of computing their material requirements.[24]

The 343d Engineer General Service Regiment restored service to Aix in ten days by a strategem that saved days in repairing a 104-foot gap in the rail bridge. In the area the unit found a German 270-mm. railway gun. Hauling it to the site, the engineers stripped the gun and the rail trucks from the traverse base of the piece and, attaching a ten-foot steel extension, launched the platform as the stringers for the new span across the void, Bailey fashion. The Aix bridge work was complete on 29 August. At the same time engineers were restoring the bridge at

---

[24] *A Report on 7th Army Railroad Bridges during the Continental Operations 15 August 1944 to 9 June 1945,* pp. 5−8.

Meyrargues, a task made doubly troublesome by a rise in flood waters. After closing a 107-foot gap with the first Bailey railroad bridge in southern France, a quadruple-single span with a deck thirty-eight feet above the water's surface, they opened the bridge to traffic on 18 September.

The 40th Engineer Combat Regiment forged the last link in the rail chain on the eastern route. A Class 60 span covering two breaks over the Buech River north of Sisteron, the bridge used stocks of local lumber and steel sections. The engineers replaced a destroyed 91-foot-high central masonry pier with a vertically emplaced triple-single Bailey panel. Supply traffic, moving 1,500 tons per day over this point after 22 September, could travel to railheads in the Poligny-Mouchard area, 130 miles north of Grenoble, relieving some transport problems as the 6th Army Group crossed the Moselle River.[25]

When the director general of the Military Railway Service, Brig. Gen. Carl R. Gray, Jr., brought his headquarters from Rome to Lyon on 14 September, he immediately began a more complete reconnaissance of rail damage. He then revised original priorities, concentrating on the double-track system up the Rhone valley to Lyon. General Gray told General Devers four days later that the main breaks in this stretch were at Livron, Avignon, and Valence; two smaller rail bridges outside Lyon, one over the Rhone and one over the Saone River, would have to be reconverted from use as vehicular bridges. Save for

material shortages, the breaks at Valence and Avignon posed no problems.[26]

The 343d Engineer General Service Regiment, assigned the job of opening the Marseille-to-Lyon route, began work on the Livron bridge on 7 September. Where before the war a masonry-arch bridge had carried a single track across the shallow, muddy Drome, there was now a 310-foot break with all the masonry piles blown. The low height of the original structure and the river's slow current lessened engineering problems; the troops emplaced scarce steel I-beam stringers atop nine timber bents to open the line to railborne supply on 20 September, five days ahead of General Gray's estimates. This performance, together with the 343d's operation in the southern Rhone valley, earned the regiment Lt. Gen. Alexander M. Patch's commendation.

On 2 October, the 344th Engineer General Service Regiment repaired a 410-foot single-track structure over the Doubs River at Dole, using thirty-foot-high timber bents, with standard Bailey forming the span. Opening the Dole route brought the railheads north to Vesoul and Besancon.[27]

At that point in the restoration, with railheads moving into the rear of the 6th Army Group area, German demolitions at the bridges had become the smaller supply problem. By mid-September General Devers found that where railroads were concerned, the "bottleneck now is cars rather than bridges."[28]

---

[25] Ibid., pp. 16–17; 40th Engr C Rgt, Opns Rpt for Eastern France, sec. V, Reconstruction of Railroad Bridge, Sisteron, France, 6th Army Gp, G–3, Final Report, WWII, 1 Jul 45, p. 14.

[26] Memo, DG, MRS, for CG, 6th Army Gp, 18 Sep 44, sub: Resume of MRS Activities and Conditions of Railroads in Southern France.

[27] A Report on 7th Army Railroad Bridges, pp. 18–21; Hists, 343d Engr GS Rgt and 344th Engr GS Rgt.

[28] Lt Gen Jacob L. Devers, Diary entry 14 Sep 44.

THE AIX BRIDGE, WHICH USED THE CARRIAGE OF A GERMAN RAILWAY GUN

When the Allied drive slowed against stiffening German resistance at the Vosges Mountains and the defenses before the Rhine River, supply lines stopped growing. But the demand for ammunition rose alarmingly, and shortages persisted until the winter months. Trucks remained the principal means of transport until well into October, when new railroad rolling stock arrived at Marseille; in September trucks carried forward 222,000 tons of supply compared to 63,000 tons moving by rail. Engineer units had built eighty-eight highway bridges on the supply routes, mostly from local timber and steel stock.

After 30 October Seventh Army engineers divided responsibility for rail rehabilitation with the increasingly capable 1st Military Railway Service, whose units and equipment were now arriving more regularly. Army engineers reopened a northern loop in the rail service running from Epinal to Strasbourg through Blainville, Luneville, and Sarrebourg, while the 1st Military Railway Service worked on a southern leg running from Epinal through St. Die to Strasbourg. The Military Railway Service refurbished the military rail line behind the First French Army on an axis running from Vesoul through Lure and Belfort to Mulhouse. In supporting the drive up the Rhone, the 1st Military Railway Service supervised the construction of forty-two rail bridges and the repair of nine between Marseille and Dijon by early 1945. At various times, the work continued to involve the 40th, 94th, 343d, 344th, and 540th Engineer Regiments and the 1051st Engineer Port Construction and Repair Group.

With the winter lull in the advance, the engineers began to take up scarce Bailey panels laid down in the press of the rapid assault, replacing them with semipermanent timber bent, steel, and wood deck bridging along vital roads and rail lines. During the last half of October the engineers consolidated the hoarded reserves for the thrust through the Siegfried Line, over the Rhine River and into Germany itself.[29]

### Map Supply

The rapidity of the advance carried the assaulting American and French divisions into areas for which military maps were still in Italy. The two engineer units sent in with the invasion, the 1st Mobile Map Depot with VI Corps and the 2d Mobile Map Depot with the French, were merely clearinghouses for distribution. Their early stocks of 1:100,000, 1:50,000, and 1:25,000 maps reflected an invasion plan that did not project an Allied advance out of Provence until much later in the year. Small-scale maps for areas far up the Rhone valley were especially scarce; French units were even relying on the standard Michelin road maps and on information from local natives. By 1

September the demand for maps had inundated the two units, and the 1709th Engineer Map Depot Detachment flew in from Naples to help. In little more than a month these three units shipped over eight million maps to combat troops.

Map production in southern France began on 14 September with the arrival of the 661st Engineer Topographic Company and the 649th Engineer Topographic Battalion and reached a peak capacity within about two weeks. The demand for 1:25,000-scale maps also rose rapidly as the Allied offensive encountered the prepared German defenses at the Vosges Mountains and slowed down in late October and early November.[30]

### Engineer Supply for the First French Army

The establishment of 6th Army Group headquarters at Lyon on 15 September marked also the redesignation of the French Armee B as First French Army. Although now a formally organized field army operating on home soil, Lt. Gen. Jean de Lattre de Tassigny's command continued to labor under a notable lack of service forces, including engineers. French supply of all types funneled in part through Base 901, hastily transferred from Naples two weeks before the invasion to support Armee B. The organization had never functioned in its intended capacity in Italy, and it fared only slightly better in France. Attached to Coastal Base Section for the assault period, the command, under Brig. Gen. Jean Gross, was so lacking in basic equipment, trucks,

[29] Robert R. Smith, "Riviera to the Rhine," draft MS in the United States Army in World War II series, ch. XVI, passim; Msg, CG, 6th Army Gp, to CG, Seventh Army, CG, FFA, and DGMRS, 30 Oct 44, sub: Railway Plan, 6th Army Gp Transport Sect, Daily Rail Sitreps file, 15 Sep–30 Nov 44; *Seventh Army Report*, vol. II, p. 396.

[30] Seventh Army, Engr Hist Rpt, p. 16.

and trained staff personnel that it could not meet the demands made upon it. Divided in half in mid-October, Base 901 acquired a new commanding officer in Brig. Gen. Georges Granier as its headquarters moved to Dijon to work side by side with the Continental Advance Section in the city.

The establishment of the First French Army also occasioned the division of Seventh Army engineer stocks, nearly half of which were to go to the French. Brig. Gen. Henry C. Wolfe, 6th Army Group engineer, met with General Davidson on 20 September to apportion the materials, and Brig. Gen. Robert Dromard, First French Army engineer, received his allotment the following day. American sources supplied the French with sparing amounts of critical bridging parts and stream-crossing equipment and rationed what was found on the battlefields thereafter. The French also received maps from American topographic units until 1 November, when they organized their own printing operations.[31]

### POL Operations

The Seventh Army engineer POL plan for DRAGOON, formulated in early summer 1944 at Naples under Lt. Col. Charles L. Lockett, drew on the successful experience with pipelines gained in the North African and Italian campaigns. The engineers envisioned a pipeline system up the Rhone River valley, making use of the already exist-

ing refinery installations in Toulon, Marseille, and smaller ports at the river mouth.[32] Depending on the damage done by the retreating Germans, the engineers could easily support the troops battling in the beachhead area with a gallon of gasoline per man per day, the consumption rate established in earlier campaigns. But the rapid success of the invasion altered the sequence and timing of fuel depot construction and accelerated the schedule for laying of the pipeline north. Demands for gasoline skyrocketed; every truck moving forward off the beaches took with it as many jerry cans as it could hold, but advance units were still sending convoys on 300-mile round trips back to the beach dumps for resupply as the Seventh Army pursued the fleeing German *Nineteenth Army* to the north. *(Map 26)*

The 697th Engineer Petroleum Distribution Company was the first of its kind ashore, landing at Camel Green on D-day. Capt. Carl W. Bills, commanding the unit, was among the foremost POL experts in the theater, a man of wide prewar experience in the Oklahoma oil fields; despite his relatively low rank, he became the technical supervisor of the whole fuel pipeline system up the Rhone valley. The company entered St. Raphael as soon as the town was cleared, surveying for a pipeline in that area. Various detachments collected enough petroleum pumping equipment to begin construction and operations, but spent several days retrieving materiel coming to the invasion beaches in scattered lots on small

---

[31] Marcel Vigneras, *Rearming the French*, United States Army in World War II (Washington, 1957), pp. 186–90; Ruppenthal, *Logistical Support of the Armies, Volume II*, p. 379.

[32] *CONAD History*, vol. I, p. 234.

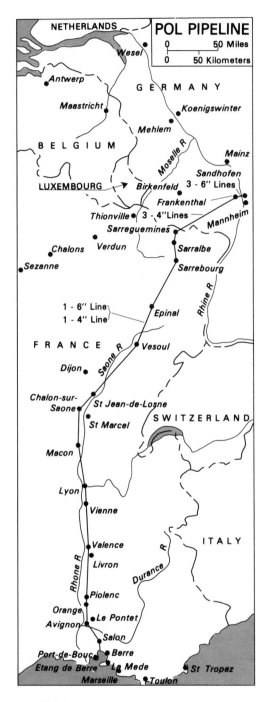

**POL PIPELINE**

0     50 Miles

0     50 Kilometers

NETHERLANDS

Wesel

Antwerp

GERMANY

Maastricht

Koenigswinter

Mehlem

BELGIUM

Mainz

Moselle R.

Sandhofen

LUXEMBOURG     Birkenfeld   3 - 6" Lines

Frankenthal

Thionville   3 - 4"Lines

Mannheim

Sarreguemines

Chalons   Verdun     Sarralbe

Sezanne     Sarrebourg

Rhine R.

1 - 6" Line     Epinal
1 - 4" Line

FRANCE     Vesoul

Saone R.

Dijon

Chalon-sur-
Saone     St Jean-de-Losne

St Marcel     SWITZERLAND

Macon

Lyon

Vienne

Valence     ITALY

Rhone R.     Livron

Durance R.

Piolenc

Orange   Le Pontet

Avignon

Salon

Port-de-Bouc   Berre

Etang de Berre   La Mede

Marseille   Toulon   St Tropez

*MAP 26*

landing craft. The company took four days to construct three 10,000-barrel tanks in the town. By the end of the month, St. Raphael was receiving bulk tanker discharge through one four-inch and one six-inch line connecting the facilities to the docks. Another four-inch aviation gas line covered the six miles from the larger tanks to a 1,000-barrel storage container at the airfield at Frejus. After the field was abandoned, the airfield tank served as a motor fuel storage point.[33]

Bypassing the embattled petroleum facilities at Marseille and Toulon for the moment, Captain Bills left a 79-man detachment in St. Raphael to run affairs and took the 697th to the next logical point for pipeline operations, the port area around Port-de-Bouc, 120 miles by road from St. Raphael. Arriving 25 August in Martigues, held only by FFI troops, the company rested for a day while the French overcame the last German sniper resistance. Rapid surveys with General Davidson at the scene revealed that, apart from a few bullet holes punched into the tanks by the U.S. XII Tactical Air Force, the prewar storage capacity of 250,000 barrels in the area was undiminished.

On 26 August the 697th began the construction of a nineteen-mile, four-inch-diameter victaulic pipe for 80-octane fuel to connect the refineries of L'Avera at Port-de-Bouc; La Provence at La Mede, three miles east of Martigues on the southern edge of the lake; and the large Bruni oil refining complex on the north shore of the Etang de Berre. A second four-inch line for 100-octane gasoline paralleled the first be-

[33] Ibid., p. 233n; Hist 697th Engr Pet Dist Co, Sep 44, p. 2–5.

tween Port-de-Bouc and La Mede, where the company built a 1,000-barrel storage tank.

In their four-year occupation the Germans had depleted the supply of coupling joints to match the French fittings within the refineries; the engineers were able to maintain an adequate supply only after the establishment of the engineer dump at Le Pas-des-Lanciers. The occupiers did leave behind a valuable source of expertise in the French former employees of the oil plants and the Vichy government fuel-rationing authorities. After the elimination of collaborators among them, these Frenchmen provided a ready and experienced supplement for Allied manpower and facilitated military and essential civilian fuel distribution.[34]

With the discharge areas intact and the first interterminal line wholly operational by 12 September, the company had already begun the pipeline covering the thirty-five miles between Berre and the Durance River. The line reached Salon, eight miles north of Berre and the site of a large convoy refueling and jerry can refill point, in the first week of construction and by 25 September was at the south bank of the Durance, five miles southeast of Avignon. Here, pushing the pipe across on a 1,480-foot timber trestle, the 697th passed the line to the 784th Engineer Petroleum Distribution Company, which linked it to their completed section. It covered the next thirty-two miles north to the French railroad tank car installation at Le Pontet, the second large decanting station for refueling of truck convoys. Accompanying the engineer pipeline along its whole length was a Signal Corps telephone net that permitted prompt reporting of pipeline leaks.

By early September, the press of operations forced the establishment of a provisional battalion-level supervisory headquarters to coordinate and control the pipelaying and operating activities of eight distribution companies, several attached companies from engineer combat regiments, and one dump truck company. First commanded by Maj. Charles B. Gholson, the unit finally was designated 408th Engineer Service Battalion (Pipeline) on 6 January 1945. It allowed the rapid transfer of supervisory talent among the operating battalion headquarters, the distribution companies, the Delta Base Section, and Continental Advance Section (CONAD) or SOLOC commands as the construction effort demanded. The headquarters also relieved the individual companies of the need to obtain their own supply of pipes, couplings, and pump gear from the harbors in southern France. The battalion tied its wholesale supply to the French rail net, placing stocks of pipe in rail sidings close to the line of construction at roughly twenty-mile intervals.[35]

After connecting the pipe on the north bank of the Durance, the 784th took responsibility for testing and operating the whole line from Berre to Le Pontet. Meanwhile, the 697th leapfrogged ahead to install the next section of pipe into the rehabilitated French storage tanks at Lyon, with dispensing points at St. Marcel, Vienne, and Lyon itself. By 9 November the pipe was moving nearly 13,000 barrels of fuel daily,

---

[34] *Logistical History of NATOUSA-MTOUSA*, p. 241.

[35] History of the 408th Engineer Service Battalion in the Southern Military Pipeline System (Aug 44–Aug 45), typescript [1947], p. 3; Adm Hist, 408th Engr Serv Bn, 10 Feb 45, p. 1.

a rate maintained until the end of the war on the Rhone River valley pipeline.[36]

Meanwhile, other petroleum engineer units arrived at Marseille and Port-de-Bouc to continue refurbishing and operating the bulk ports there. The 1379th Engineer Petroleum Distribution Company entered Marseille on 29 August after landing six days earlier at St. Raphael. The fierce battle for Marseille had done little damage to the petroleum facilities, and the company had pipelines running from the quays to the largest refinery at the Rue de Lyon within a week. One group left behind on Corsica to train French petroleum units rejoined the company on 17 September, With detachments in Port-de-Bouc, Marseille, La Mede, and Berre, the 1379th took over the whole tanker discharge operation in southern France and began the construction of a six-inch line around the Etang de Berre as the beginning of a new system to parallel the earlier four-inch pipe. The 696th Engineer Petroleum Distribution Company arrived at Berre on the twenty-first to carry the six-inch pipe to just above Avignon.[37] The 701st Engineer Petroleum Distribution Company, another highly experienced unit from the Italian campaign, arrived at Marseille on 9 October and moved the work ahead from Avignon to Piolenc; there, the 696th took over again to a point above Valence.

In late October the Rhone overflowed its banks after heavy rains. The two companies constructing the line up the riverbank south of Lyon had to float pipe into position by plugging one end of it and moving it into the heavy flood waters. A detachment of the 701st downstream repaired the severed four-inch line at Livron. In November, progress on both lines came to a temporary halt when an early freeze blocked the pipes and burst couplings on a stretch between Lyon and Macon—water used to test the pipe before pumping fuel through it had been left in the pipe during a sudden temperature drop. The 697th and the 701st backtracked, hastily thawed the line, and replaced broken sections, allowing operation to resume by 23 November.

The combined work of the 696th and the 697th Engineer Petroleum Distribution Companies and Companies E and F of the 335th Engineer General Service Regiment brought the operational four-inch pipe to the rear of the Seventh Army area at La Forge, near Sarrebourg, on 12 February 1945, although construction was slowed by heavy snow. The six-inch pipe lagged behind north of Vesoul, plagued by an inadequate supply of parts and faulty construction that had to be rechecked. The six-inch pipe became operational to the La Forge terminal on 3 April, while the 697th was overseeing the last leg of four-inch pipe construction in three parallel lines from La Forge through Sarreguemines and Frankenthal, Germany, and across the Rhine near Mannheim into the terminal at Sandhofen, a Mannheim suburb. Another seven miles of six-inch pipe, erected by the 1385th Engineer Petroleum Distribution Company under the supervision of the 697th experts and the 408th Engineer Service Battalion, connected the Frankenthal and Mannheim terminals.[38]

---

[36] OCE ETOUSA Hist Rpt 13, Petroleum, Oil, and Lubricants, app. 16.

[37] Unit Hist, 1379th Engr Pet Dist Co, Dec 43–Nov 45, pp. 3–4.

[38] Adm Hist, 697th Engr Pet Dist Co, Jan–May 45. Other constructing units on the lines between Sarreguemines and Sandhofen were the 1385th

On 26 February 1945, in the general consolidation of supply operations under ETOUSA, Lt. Gen. John C. H. Lee, commanding the Communications Zone (COMZ), ETOUSA, took under his ultimate authority the petroleum distribution net in southern France along with the pipelines constructed across the northern tier of the Continent. Operations records were turned over to the ETOUSA Military Pipeline Service after 26 February, and the 408th Engineer Service Battalion and its attached units came under the operational control of the ETOUSA staff, though still attached to CONAD for supply and administration. The construction companies remained relatively autonomous through all of the centralizing and remained in place to continue the operation of the 875 miles of four-inch and 532 miles of six-inch pipeline they had emplaced behind the 6th Army Group in the advance from southern France.[39]

### Preparing To Cross the Rhine

As the Germans fell back speedily upon their defenses before the Rhine in September and October 1944, 6th Army Group planners began to entertain the idea of crossing the river before the year was out. This possibility led the engineers to establish Rhine River crossing schools in late September. Seventh Army engineers, who would carry the brunt of the assault burden, treated the crossing as an amphibious operation complicated by the rapid current of the river—eight to ten miles per hour in the winter months. Once again General Davidson turned to his experienced engineer regiments, the 40th, the 540th, and the 36th, to form the central elements of combat groups capable of transporting assault troops and of organizing beachheads on the far bank as they had on the Riviera beaches.

On 26 September one battalion from each of the engineer regiments and two French engineer battalions began training in two crossing schools. The basic course was held near Dole on the Doubs River, usually slow and narrow in the autumn. Under the supervision of the 1553d Engineer Heavy Ponton Battalion, the combat engineers practiced with swift fourteen-foot storm boats and larger assault craft, both types powered with outboard motors. After four days of practice, the engineer trainees moved to the advanced-course site at Camp de Valbonne near Lyon on the Rhone River to gain experience with the same equipment in faster river currents.[40]

At Camp de Valbonne, under the direction of the 85th Engineer Heavy Ponton Battalion, the engineers also practiced bridge building over the rapid stream and experimented with heavier cable anchors for ponton treadway bridging and antimine nets to ward off explosives set adrift by the enemy to eliminate crossing structures. New means of launching and affixing cross-river cables were tested in efforts to provide guy wires for laden DUKWs negotiating the current with barely enough

---

Engineer Petroleum Distribution Company, the 2814th, Companies E and F of the 335th Engineer General Service Regiment, and a platoon of the 701st. Hist of the 408th Engr Serv Bn in the Southern MPS, p 2.

[39] OCE ETOUSA Hist Rpt 13, Petroleum, Oil, and Lubricants, app. 11, p. 3; Hist of the 408th Engr Serv Bn in the Southern MPS, p. 5.

---

[40] A Negro unit, the 1553d Engineer Heavy Ponton Battalion arrived in France 13 September 1944.

power to make headway against the river's flow.

As winter drew on and chances for crossing the last major water obstacle before the German heartland dwindled, the engineers concentrated on maintaining their equipment for the postponed operation. The equipment amassed for each crossing group counted 96 storm boats, 188 assault craft, 6 rafts, over 400 outboard motors, 1 heavy ponton bridge, and 150 DUKWs assigned to transport artillery pieces. All of this material was now mounted on wheels to take immediate advantage of any sudden breakthrough to the Rhine's edge. By early December, General Davidson decided to store the entire collection for the winter, and Army engineers moved their equipment to covered areas, factories, and the forests around Luneville.[41]

As the year ended, the engineers turned to face a different ordeal. In a final desperate attempt to stem the Allied advance to the Rhine, German forces along the western front launched a massive counteroffensive out of the Ardennes Forest. In the middle of December, the surprise blow put the entire Allied command in the west on the defensive for over a month and stretched engineer elements to their utmost.

---

[41] OCE ETOUSA Hist Rpt 10, Combat Engineering, pp. 235–39; Seventh Army, Engr Hist Rpt, p. 8.

# CHAPTER XXI

# The Ardennes: Engineers as Infantry

A cold rain was turning to snow on the afternoon of 8 December 1944, when the lead trucks of the 81st Engineer Combat Battalion pulled into the Schnee Eifel, a wooded ridge just inside the German border east of the Ardennes and southeast of Liege. The 81st Battalion had landed in France only a few days before with VIII Corps' 106th Infantry Division. The division, the newest on the Western Front and the youngest (the first containing a large number of eighteen-year-old draftees), had moved forward immediately after landing to take over a sector from the 2d Division, which was redeploying northward to reinforce a First Army attack on the Roer River dam.[1]

The Schnee Eifel landscape looked like a Christmas card, with snow-tipped fir trees dark against white hills. In the folds of the hills lay small villages set in hollows for protection against blizzards. Here the engineers found billets. The 81st Engineer Combat Battalion settled in at Heuem, on the road leading east toward the German border from St.-Vith, Belgium, an important road center and site of division headquarters. The battalion's Company B, supporting the 423d Infantry, bivouacked about 1 1/2 miles east at Schoenberg. Crossing the border into Germany, Company A found billets at Auw, only three miles as the crow flies behind the most forward position on the VIII Corps front, a six-mile stretch of the Schnee Eifel containing Siegfried Line pillboxes.

The first 20 miles of the 85-mile-long Ardennes front, beginning at Monschau, were held by V Corps' 99th Infantry Division. Also new to the theater, the division had arrived on the Continent during November 1944. The southern two miles of its portion of the front lay along a narrow, seven-mile-long valley known as the Losheim Gap. There the V Corps sector ended and that of the VIII Corps began. The next five miles of the Losheim Gap were held by the 14th Cavalry Group, a light reconnaissance unit that the 106th Division had inherited when the 2d Division moved north.

The 106th Division sector ended about five miles below the Schnee Eifel salient, at the village of Luetzkampen, and there the 28th Infantry Division area began. Near this point, where the nar-

---

[1] Hist 81st Engr C Bn, Dec 44; Hugh M. Cole, *The Ardennes: The Battle of the Bulge*, United States Army in World War II (Washington, 1968), p. 139 and map 1. Unless otherwise noted tactical information in this chapter derives from Cole.

row, swift Our River began to define
the border between Belgium and Germany, the American positions swung
southwest to the Belgian side of the
river along a high bluff carrying a road
(Route 16) known as the "Skyline Drive,"
which continued south through Luxembourg. Responsible for about twenty-
three miles of the front in Belgium and
Luxembourg, the veteran 28th Division
was resting and training replacements
for the more than 6,000 casualties it
had suffered during the battle of the
Huertgen Forest, more casualties than
any other division in that action.[2]

Beginning on 10 December, elements
of the 9th Armored Division, another
newcomer to ETOUSA, took over the
next six miles south along the front.
The bulk of the armored division, however, was in reserve fifty miles north.
Near the point where the Schwarz Erntz
River flowed into the Sauer River the
4th Infantry Division portion of the
front began. This division had also been
badly battered in the Huertgen Forest,
having suffered more than 4,000 casualties, second in losses only to the 28th.[3]
The 4th Division held the VIII Corps
front along the Sauer and the Moselle
to the border between Luxembourg
and France, where the First Army sector ended and that of Third Army
began.

The long front, manned by troops
weary from combat or not yet tested in
battle, was very lightly held in some
places. Along two miles of the Losheim
Gap, through which German armies
had poured westward in 1870, 1914,
and 1940, the Americans patrolled so
lightly that Germans on leave often

walked across to visit friends and rela-
tives behind the American lines. For
two months the front had been quiet
except for sporadic mortar and artillery fire. Across the narrow rivers or
from Siegfried Line positions American and German outposts watched each
other.[4]

### The Storm Breaks in the Schnee Eifel

It was snowing on the evening of 11
December when the 81st Engineer Combat Battalion relieved the 2d Engineer
Combat Battalion in the Schnee Eifel.
The 81st Battalion's foremost task was
road maintenance—removing snow and
filling shell holes. Behind the front road
maintenance was the responsibility of
the 168th Engineer Combat Battalion,
attached to VIII Corps. Operating quarries to provide crushed rock was part
of the road repair job, but engineers
also manned sawmills to provide lumber for a First Army winterization program, which called for wooden huts and
shelters.[5]

The crossroads village of Auw marked
the line dividing the 14th Cavalry Group
sector from that of the 422d Infantry,
106th Division. There Company A of
the 81st Engineer Combat Battalion
had comfortable billets, with headquarters men in one house and the three
platoons in three others. Before dawn
on 16 December heavy artillery fire
awakened the men. They found to their
surprise that the villagers were up,

---

[2] MacDonald, *Siegfried Line Campaign*, pp. 374, 493.
[3] Ibid., pp. 374, 474.

[4] John Toland, *Battle: The Story of the Bulge* (New
York: Random House, 1959), p. 4; Col. R. Ernest
Dupuy, *St. Vith: Lion in the Way* (Washington: Infantry
Journal Press, 1949), pp. 17–18.
[5] Hist 81st Engr C Bn, Dec 44; *First Army Report of
Operations, 1 August 1944–22 February 1945*, ans. 4–8,
p. 128.

dressed, and huddled in their cellars. Then they remembered that the evening before a young woman had been observed going from house to house, evidently carrying a warning. But there was no reason to suppose that this was more than a local attack, and when the artillery fire died away the company commander, Capt. Harold M. Harmon, sent out his platoons on road work as usual at 0800. The 1st Platoon under Lt. William J. Coughlin went to the 422d Infantry headquarters at Schlausenbach, about a mile away, the 3d Platoon under Lt. David M. Woerner to the 422d's 3d Battalion in the pillbox area, and the 2d Platoon under Lt. William E. Purteil to work in and near Auw. Captain Harmon then left for Heuem for the usual morning conference of company commanders.[6]

The engineers at Auw—the only troops in the town—heard rifle and machine-gun fire about 0930. It seemed close, but because the day was cloudy with drizzle and patches of heavy fog, nobody could find out what was happening. As soon as the engineers recognized the white-clad enemy, the 2d Platoon and the headquarters men took up positions in two buildings and began firing. At that point, the 1st Platoon, having heard the sound of battle from the direction of Auw, returned under heavy fire, dashed into the house where it was billeted, and began returning enemy fire coming from a barn across the road, using tracer ammunition to set the barn afire. Ten German infantry-

men ran out and were cut down by Company A cooks.

About 1000 Captain Harmon returned from Heuem, where he had learned that Lt. Col. Thomas J. Riggs, Jr., the battalion commander, had orders to employ the 81st Engineer Combat Battalion as infantry. The plan finally adopted was to commit the engineers with their respective regimental combat teams. Unable to find his men in Auw, Harmon started for the 422d Infantry area to locate his 1st Platoon. On the way he learned that the enemy had broken through the cavalry group defenses in the Losheim Gap and was attacking in great force. Returning to Auw, he was fired on by an enemy column but made a dash for it; although his jeep was riddled he managed to reach his 2d Platoon, which German tanks were about to encircle. He got the men on trucks and on the road back to Heuem.

Four German Tiger tanks came up the main street of Auw. Infantry was riding on the tanks, and most of the turrets were open; the tankers evidently expected little opposition. The engineers in their strongpoints opened up with rifles and machine guns, claiming "considerable" casualties before the Germans realized what was happening. The German infantry dropped to the ground, the tank turrets clattered shut, and the tanks opened fire with 88-mm. guns on the two houses that the engineers occupied. The headquarters men managed to escape, but then the full tank attack fell on Lieutenant Coughlin and his 1st Platoon. Eight rounds of point-blank 88-mm. fire burst in the building but miraculously caused no casualties, though small-arms fire wounded several men. Desperate,

---

[6] This account of the 81st Engineer Combat Battalion is taken from their unit citation, 25 May 1945, and the narrative, Baptism of Fire, both in Hist 81st Engr C Bn, 15 Mar 43–31 May 45; and Dupuy, *St. Vith: Lion in the Way,* pp. 32–34.

Coughlin decided to risk a dash across an open field behind the house. At 1500 he gave the order to withdraw. T/5 Edward S. Withee insisted on remaining behind to cover the withdrawal with his submachine gun. Captured after his heroic stand, Withee later was awarded the Distinguished Service Cross.

That afternoon in a sudden snowstorm Captain Harmon became involved in a 422d Infantry attempt to retake Auw. He moved thirty engineers to a point about a mile west of the town, but by that time American artillery was falling on Auw. Before the 422d could halt the American fire German artillery fire became so heavy that Harmon's party, having suffered ten casualties, had to withdraw to Heuem.

By the evening of 16 December it had become plain that the German attack, which the 106th Division had at first considered only an attempt to retake Siegfried Line pillboxes, was in fact an offensive on a grand scale all along the Ardennes front from Monschau to the Luxembourg border. In the Schnee Eifel the Germans committed the entire *LXVI Corps* of General der Panzertruppen Hasso von Manteuffel's *Fifth Panzer Army*. One of its divisions was to encircle and cut off the 422d and 423d Infantry regiments in the pillbox area and take St.-Vith. The other was to attack the 424th Infantry south of the pillbox positions, blocking the western and southern exits from St.-Vith.

The German pincer movement around the pillbox positions, successfully begun on the north with the capture of Auw, continued during the early morning hours of 17 December with the taking of Bleialf in the 423d Infantry's area to the south. The two German divisions rejoined at Schoenberg later that morning. At Heuem, only 1 1/2 miles to the west, the engineers on orders from the 106th Division withdrew at 0930 to a point about five miles west of St.-Vith. There they were fed and issued cigarettes, socks, galoshes, and ammunition. But they were to have little rest. At noon Colonel Riggs received orders to round up all the available men of the 81st and 168th Engineer Combat Battalions to halt a German attack on St.-Vith.

On a wooded ridge about a mile east of the town, astride the road from Schoenberg, Colonel Riggs assembled his little force, which had only a few bazookas and machine guns. In his 81st Engineer Combat Battalion, Company A, after losses on 16 December, had only sixty-five men; Headquarters and Service Company had only fifty, some of them clerks and cooks. The 168th Engineer Combat Battalion had the remnants of two companies and the bulk of a third. The men, with few tools, had hardly finished digging their foxholes when at 1600 three German self-propelled 88-mm. assault guns, supported by infantry, came down the road from Schoenberg. The Germans knocked out a divisional antitank gun in their path, forced a tank destroyer to withdraw, then turned their 88-mm. guns on engineers of the 168th Battalion in the most forward position, inflicting heavy casualties. Meantime, a forward divisional observer directed a P−47 fighter-bomber to the spot. After a number of passes the plane set one of the German gun carriages afire.

The defenders succeeded in delaying the enemy until dusk, when tanks of the U.S. 7th Armored Division began coming through the snow and mist

ENGINEERS DROP BARBED-WIRE ROLLS TO PREPARE DEFENSIVE POSITIONS

down the road from St.-Vith. By that time one of the German assault guns had broken through the 168th Battalion defenses and reached the 81st Engineer Combat Battalion's position. Jumping out of their foxholes, the engineers stopped the gun by pulling a chain of mines across the road. One of the 7th Armored Division tanks finally knocked the gun out.

Next morning, Company A, 81st Engineer Combat Battalion, and the tankers continued to hold against strong German attacks. In the afternoon a group under Colonel Riggs counterattacked, driving some German infantrymen out of hillside positions. The defenders could then consolidate their lines, but shortly after dark a message came from

division headquarters that signaled the beginning of the end. Threatened by German tanks that were outflanking the defenders on the Schoenberg road to the east, the 106th Division headquarters was withdrawing from St.-Vith ten miles west to Vielsalm.

The next two days, 19 and 20 December, were fairly quiet on the Schoenberg road, with German activity limited to patrol actions and intermittent shelling. During the night of the nineteenth the engineers laid hasty minefields along possible avenues of tank approach and covered foxholes with logs for protection from tree bursts. Patrols went into St.-Vith to salvage anything useful—food, blankets, clothing. From their foxholes on the Schoenberg road that night the engineers could see flashes in the distant sky—to the north where V Corps was trying to hold the *Sixth Panzer Army*; to the east beyond Schoenberg where the 422d and 423d Infantry regiments, hopelessly cut off, were making their last stand; to the south where the 424th Infantry, bolstered by a combat command of the 9th Armored Division, was successfully covering its withdrawal to Vielsalm. Far to the southwest flashes showed where the battle for Bastogne was raging.

By the morning of 20 December German successes in the Bastogne area had isolated the St.-Vith forces from the rest of VIII Corps. During the afternoon the 7th Armored Division commander received word that the 82d Airborne Division was on its way to help, but it was already too late. The Germans were impressed by the intensity of American artillery fire east of St.-Vith and by the number of American tanks—"tanks were everywhere," reported the *18th Volksgrenadier Division* on 20 December— and they assumed that the force blocking the Schoenberg road was stronger than it actually was. Nevertheless, the Germans were determined to break through the defenses as soon as they could extract their own artillery and tanks from a traffic jam that had built up around Schoenberg.

This the Germans accomplished by midafternoon on 21 December. Commencing at 1500 and continuing until well after dark, the enemy directed on the tankers and engineers a concentrated barrage of artillery, rocket, and mortar fire, inflicting heavy casualties. Company A, 81st Engineer Combat Battalion, for example, lost forty of its sixty-five men.

The engineers had not mined the road because of a promised 7th Armored Division counterattack. Without warning—the German barrage had knocked out all communications— shortly before midnight four Mark VI (Tiger) and two Mark IV tanks, with supporting infantry, came over a rise in the road, close to where some Sherman tanks were positioned at the American foxhole line. Firing a volley of illuminating flares that silhouetted the Shermans and blinded their crews, the German tanks picked off three of the Shermans and overran the foxholes. Colonel Riggs attempted to organize a defense at a ridge farther back, but it was hopeless. The Americans broke up into small parties. Wandering about in the heavy snow and darkness, most of the men, including Colonel Riggs, were captured. Only eight officers and enlisted men from Company A, 81st Engineer Combat Battalion, and thirty-three officers and men from the Headquarters and Service Company were able to reach Vielsalm.

Company C, with the 424th Infantry south of St.-Vith, protected the approaches to the town by guarding and blowing bridges; when 9th Armored Division tanks arrived on 20 December the company acted as infantry in support of the tanks. The bulk of Company B of the engineer battalion was lost when the enemy captured most of the 422d and 423d Infantry regiments.

For its first engagement the 81st Engineer Combat Battalion won the Distinguished Unit Citation. At St.-Vith from 16 to 23 December 1944, the battalion "distinguished itself in battle with such extraordinary heroism, gallantry, determination, and esprit de corps in overcoming unusually difficult and hazardous conditions in the face of a numerically superior enemy, as to set this battalion apart and above units participating in the same engagements."[7]

### Blocking Sixth Panzer Army's Drive to the Meuse

On the night of 16 December a heavy concentration of enemy artillery fire pounded and shook the eastern and southern flanks of V Corps' 99th Division. (*Map 27*) Under cover of this barrage, tanks of the German *Sixth Panzer Army* were advancing west toward the Meuse, creating the major threat in the northern sector of the Ardennes. At the extreme north, infantry of *LXVII Corps* attacked the Siegfried Line towns of Monschau and Hoefen on the morning of 16 December. These attacks failed, but in the Losheim Gap region (the central and southern portions of the northern sector) the Germans threw in considerable armor, and the tank columns broke through.[8]

Around midnight on 16 December a message came to V Corps' 254th Engineer Combat Battalion, which was repairing roads in support of the 2d and 99th Divisions. The unit was bivouacked in the woods near Buellingen at the southern end of the corridor along which the 2d Division was attacking through the 99th toward the Roer River. The engineers were on a two-hour alert to act as infantry. But in the darkness the roads around the bivouac became so jammed with American tanks and other traffic that the battalion's commanding officer was not able to reach 99th Division headquarters and return with orders until 0230. Engineer Companies A, B, and C were to form a defensive line south and east of Buellingen to protect American tanks and tank destroyers withdrawing under pressure from German forces coming up the road from Honsfeld, three miles to the southeast.

At 0600 the engineers of Company B, stationed on the road to Honsfeld, saw white and red flares about eight hundred yards away and heard tracked vehicles approaching. When they heard shouts in German, the engineers opened fire with rifles, rifle grenades, and machine guns. The German infantry riding on the lead tank and in six half-tracks jumped down and attacked, but they were driven back. The vehicles withdrew. Twenty minutes later the German infantry reappeared, followed by tanks. The tank fire was ineffective against the dug-in engineers, and the attackers were again repulsed. Ten minutes later, as the sky was getting light, a third force came up the road. This time tanks were in the lead, and they overran Company B's position, crushing two machine guns. They also passed over foxholes where engineers were crouching, but injured only three Americans.

The engineers continued to fire on the German infantry, but the 254th Engineer Combat Battalion's position was now hopeless. The men were ordered to fall back on Butgenbach while fighting a delaying action through Buellingen.[9] Many of the men were cut off, and the situation at Buellingen was so confusing because communications were out that when the commanding

---

[7] Citation in Hist 81st Engr C Bn, 15 Mar 43–31 May 45.

[8] Maj. Gen. Walter E. Lauer, *Battle Babies: The Story of the 99th Infantry Division in World War II* (Baton Rouge: Military Press of Louisiana, 1951), pp. 16–28.

[9] Hist 254th Engr C Bn, Jul–Oct–Dec 44.

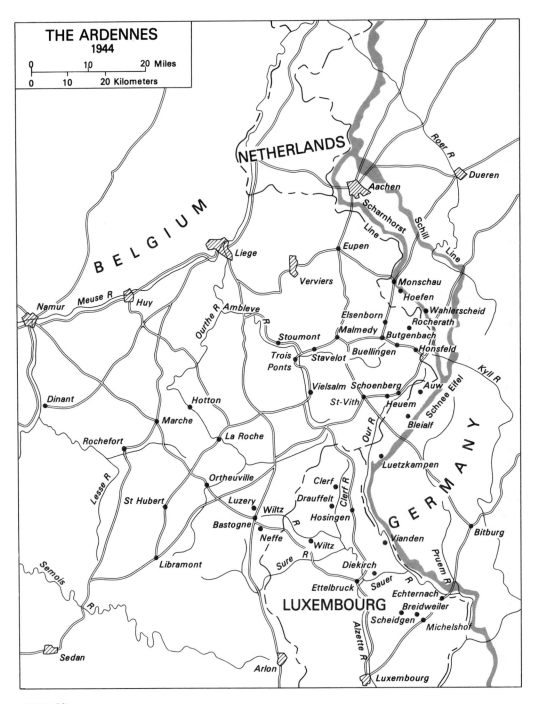

# THE ARDENNES
## 1944

0     10     20 Miles

0    10    20 Kilometers

NETHERLANDS

BELGIUM

GERMANY

LUXEMBOURG

Roer R

Dueren

Aachen

Scharnhorst Line

Schill Line

Eupen

Verviers

Monschau

Hoefen

Wahlerscheid

Liege

Rocherath

Elsenborn

Namur    Meuse R    Huy

Ourthe R   Ambleve R

Malmedy

Butgenbach

Honsfeld

Stoumont

Buellingen

Trois Ponts

Stavelot

Kyll R

Vielsalm   Schoenberg

Auw

Schnee Eifel

St-Vith

Heuem

Dinant

Hotton

Bleialf

Marche

Rochefort

La Roche

Luetzkampen

Ortheuville

Clerf

Lesse R

Drauffelt

Clerf R

St Hubert

Luzery

Wiltz

Hosingen

Bitburg

Bastogne

Neffe

Wiltz

Vianden

Sure R

Diekirch

Pruem R

Libramont

Ettelbruck

Sauer R

Echternach

Semois R

Breidweiler

Scheidgen

Michelshof

LUXEMBOURG

Alzette R

Sedan

Arlon

Luxembourg

Our R

**MAP 27**

officer of the 254th arrived at Butgen-bach he reported to Maj. Gen. Walter E. Lauer, commanding the 99th Division, that his battalion had been destroyed. According to Lauer, "It was a dramatic moment at my C. P. at about noon that day when the details of the action were reported. I awarded the battalion commander then and there the Bronze Star Medal, and gave him my lunch to eat."[10] Later the engineer officer discovered that he had not lost his entire battalion. Although many men had been killed or captured, others, in groups of two or three, made their way back to Butgenbach or Wirtzfeld.[11]

The tanks that came up on the Honsfeld road early on 17 December belonged to Obersturmbannfuehrer Joachim Peiper's *Kampfgruppe Peiper*, the armored spearhead of *I SS Panzer Corps*, the strongest fighting unit of *Sixth Panzer Army*, which had broken through at the Losheim Gap. By 1030 on 17 December Peiper's tanks were rolling into Buellingen, but instead of continuing northwest to Butgenbach as the Americans expected, most turned southwest out of the town. Although Buellingen was a target of the *12th SS Panzer Division*, Peiper had detoured through the town to avoid a stretch of muddy road between Honsfeld and Schoppen, his next objective to the west. He had also learned that there were gasoline dumps in Buellingen, and he filled his tanks from American dumps, using American prisoners as labor.[12]

Buellingen was an important supply area, with dumps and service troops.

Headquarters Company and Company B of the 2d Engineer Combat Battalion, part of the 2d Infantry Division, were billeted there. Ordered to hold the town at all costs, Company B put up a determined defense, but once in the town German tanks took up positions at intersections and cut all traffic. The engineer company split into platoons, fought until its ammunition was gone, and then had to withdraw. Four officers and fifty-seven enlisted men of Headquarters Company were surrounded. From the basement of their billet they fired at all the enemy infantry that came in view, but they had no bazookas to use against tanks. Nevertheless they were still reported to be holding out on the night of 18 December, when advance elements of the *12th SS Panzer Division* began arriving in the town to direct a coming fight at Butgenbach. After that, nothing more was heard from Headquarters Company, and the men were assumed to be either killed or captured.[13]

The arrival of Peiper's tanks at Buellingen on the morning of 17 December brought the first realization of the scale of the German offensive, because communications had gone out when the Germans hit the 99th Division regiments stationed along the West Wall on 16 December. On the morning of the seventeenth Maj. Gen. Leonard T. Gerow, commanding V Corps, decided to pull his corps back to a defensive position on the Elsenborn ridge northwest of Buellingen. Two infantry regiments of his 2d Division were attacking West Wall positions about five miles to the northeast near Wahlerscheid, sup-

---

[10] Lauer, *Battle Babies*, p. 34n.

[11] Hist 254th Engr C Bn, Jul–Oct–Dec 44.

[12] Cole, *The Ardennes: The Battle of the Bulge*, pp. 91–92, 260–61.

[13] Hist 2d Engr C Bn, 2d Inf Div, Jun–Dec 44.

ported by a regimental combat team composed mainly of the 99th Division's 395th Infantry. The withdrawal route of these forces ran south from Wahlerscheid to the twin villages of Krinkelt and Rocherath, then northwest of Elsenborn through Wirtzfeld. Infantry of the collapsing 99th Division was also passing through the twin villages on the way to Elsenborn. The Germans had made deep penetrations along the roads leading west and could be expected to attack Krinkelt and Rocherath.

During the dangerous withdrawal the engineers supporting both divisions played an important part. The 99th Division's 324th Engineer Combat Battalion was with the 395th Regimental Combat Team in woods east of Wahlerscheid. When the combat team received the task of covering the 2d Division's move south, the engineers assumed defensive positions as infantry. At one time on 17 December the battalion was cut off and surrounded by the enemy, but managed to escape and join the forces at Elsenborn.[14]

At dusk on 17 December Company C of the 2d Engineer Combat Battalion, organic to the 2d Infantry Division, was working behind the infantry to block the road to the east. The infantry felled trees and created abatis, which the engineers mined and booby-trapped. By the time the company reached the twin villages enemy riflemen were close behind, but thick fog that lay close to the snow-covered ground concealed the unit. When Company C reached Rocherath the village was burning, and traffic on the road was completely blocked. The company turned off the main road and moved west along for-

est trails to Elsenborn, on the way clearing from the trails abandoned trucks and guns and putting down matting, brush, and even abandoned bed rolls to get the unit's vehicles through to Elsenborn. Next day, 18 December, the engineers worked on the Elsenborn defenses, placing mines and wire, but that night part of the company had to return to Krinkelt. Under heavy pressure the last U.S. unit in the town, the 38th Infantry, was getting ready to pull out, and engineers were needed to set up roadblocks behind the regiment to protect its withdrawal.

The road to Krinkelt was under heavy artillery fire. More than once the engineers had to jump from their trucks and run; several trucks were damaged. They arrived at Krinkelt in the blackness, discovering next day, 19 December, that the enemy was edging closer, obviously preparing for a final night attack. At 1730, in darkness and fog, the 38th Infantry began to pull out. The engineers, who could not set up their roadblocks until all the tanks of the covering force had withdrawn, were the last Americans left in the town. "Under the very noses of the pressing SS troopers," they went to work installing roadblocks at all important corners. Enemy tank, artillery, and small-arms fire killed a number of men, but the survivors managed to finish the job and withdraw to Elsenborn.[15]

By 20 December a regiment of the 1st Infantry Division had reinforced the 2d and 99th Divisions at Elsenborn. On the north, the 9th Division took over the Monschau-Hoefen sector. These two positions held. At the Elsenborn ridge, which the Germans called the

---

[14] Hist 324th Engr C Bn, 9 Nov–31 Dec 44.

[15] Hist 2d Engr C Bn, 2d Inf Div, Jun–Dec 44.

"door posts," the *12th SS Panzer Division* gave up the fight on 23 December when the unit ran into a fresh 1st Division regiment.[16] Thereafter the Germans would not risk at Elsenborn anything better than second-line troops capable only of defensive action.

About the time the *12th SS Panzer Division* was moving against Krinkelt and Rocherath, Peiper's *Kampfgruppe* swung west toward its objective, a Meuse crossing at Huy, about fifteen miles upriver from Liege. At dusk on 17 December Peiper's lead tanks were approaching Stavelot, on the northern bank of the Ambleve River forty-two miles short of Huy. Peiper was already deep into the area where First Army's service troops were working behind the combat zone. A few miles west of Stavelot at Trois Ponts on N−23, Peiper's route to the Meuse, was the headquarters of the 1111th Engineer Combat Group, whose battalions were supporting First Army's winterization program. The 291st Engineer Combat Battalion was operating a sawmill just west of Trois Ponts and a company of the 202d Engineer Combat Battalion another at Stavelot.

The first news of the enemy breakthrough came to the 1111th Group commander, Col. H. W. Anderson, at 1005 on 17 December, when he learned that the Germans were near Butgenbach. This posed a serious threat to Malmedy, five miles northeast of Stavelot. At Malmedy Anderson had about two hundred men of the 291st Engineer Combat Battalion, aided by the 962d Engineer Maintenance Company, building a landing strip for liaison planes

near First Army headquarters at Spa. He sent the commanding officer of the 291st, Lt. Col. David E. Pergrin, to Malmedy to take charge of the group's units there. Later in that day they were augmented by the 629th Engineer Light Equipment Company, which had been doing road work near Butgenbach but had managed to extricate itself ahead of the German advance.[17]

Anderson ordered his engineers at Malmedy to prepare to defend the town. Prospects for defense looked bright soon after Pergrin's arrival, especially when elements of the 7th Armored Division rumbled into the town. But the armor was only passing through on its way to St.-Vith, and as the vehicles disappeared down the road most of the First Army rear units, according to an engineer account, fled in panic, leaving behind food, liquor, documents, footlockers, clothing, and all sorts of equipment. The engineers, armed only with mines and a few bazookas, stayed.[18] When Colonel Pergrin was asked later why his men did not leave with the other units, he said the reason was "psychology." Combat units moving up to the front had taunted the road builders they passed, "You engineer so-and-sos! Why don't you come on up there and fight?"[19]

By noon of 17 December the engineers had set up roadblocks on the edge of town. An hour later, patrols reported seeing sixty-eight enemy armored vehicles including thirty tanks on a road a few miles to the southeast. About 1430 Colonel Pergrin was standing on a hill

---

[16] Cole, *The Ardennes: The Battle of the Bulge*, p. 578.

[17] Hist 1111th Engr C Gp, Jun, Nov, Dec 44.
[18] Hist 291st Engr C Bn, Dec 44.
[19] Helena Huntington Smith, "A Few Men in Soldier Suits," *American Heritage* (August 1957), 30 (account from interview with Pergrin).

near town when he heard "an awful lot of noise" in the valley below; then four American soldiers ran toward him, screaming.[20] They were survivors of the "Malmedy massacre" in which Peiper's men shot up a convoy of field artillery observers that crossed their path, then rounded up about eighty-five prisoners, marched them into a field, and at a signal shot them down with machine-gun and machine-pistol fire. Pergrin brought the four survivors back to Malmedy in his jeep. Their story did not shake the determination of his engineers to defend Malmedy "to the last man."[21]

On the chance that Peiper would bypass Malmedy (as he did) and head for Stavelot, Pergrin sent a squad of his engineers equipped with twenty mines and one bazooka south to set up a road-block at Stavelot. They emplaced a hasty minefield at the approach to a stone bridge leading into the town and waited. At 1900 three Mark IV tanks came toward the bridge. The first struck a mine that blew off its treads; the others withdrew. Two of the engineers, Pfc. Lorenzo A. Liparulo and Pvt. Bernard Goldstein, tried to follow the tanks in a jeep. They were wounded by German fire, Liparulo fatally, but the Germans did not attack again until early next morning. By that time a company of the 526th Armored Infantry Battalion, towing 3-inch antitank guns, had reinforced the engineer roadblock. The armored infantry managed to repulse a German infantry attack but was no match for the 88-mm. guns on German tanks that began rumbling over the bridge into the town about 0800.[22]

While the fighting was still going on inside Stavelot, Peiper turned some of his tanks west toward Trois Ponts, the next town on his route to the Meuse. In his own words, "We proceeded at top speed towards Trois Ponts in an effort to seize the bridge there. . . . If we had captured the bridge at Trois Ponts intact and had had enough fuel, it would have been a simple matter to drive through to the Meuse River early that day."[23]

Trois Ponts, as its name suggests, boasted three bridges—one over the Ambleve that provided entry to the town; another over the Salm within the town, carrying the main highway west; and a third over the Salm southeast of town. By the time Peiper turned his lead tanks toward Trois Ponts the 1111th Engineer Combat Group had prepared all three bridges for demolition. Company C of the group's 51st Engineer Combat Battalion, ordered the night before to defend the town, had placed charges on two of the bridges, and a detachment of the 291st Engineer Combat Battalion had prepared the third. The engineers were armed only with bazookas and machine guns, but during the morning a 57-mm. antitank gun with its crew, somehow separated from the 526th Armored Infantry Battalion, turned up in the town and was used to block the road from Stavelot.

At 1115 on 18 December, when the first enemy tank came into sight, the engineers blew the bridge over the Ambleve. Half an hour later the lead tank ran into the roadblock. The 57-mm. gun immobilized it, but fire from other tanks knocked out the gun and killed four of the crew. Finding the bridge

---

[20] Ibid., p. 29.

[21] Hist 291st Engr C Bn, Dec 44.

[22] Hewitt, *Work Horse of the Western Front*, p. 174.

[23] Cole. *The Ardennes: The Battle of the Bulge*, p. 267.

blown, Peiper's men hesitated for about forty-five minutes. Though the tanks could not cross, the narrow, shallow Ambleve offered no obstacle to infantry. The defenders expected an infantry attack, and Company C spread out for 500 yards along the steep far bank. The Germans apparently decided not to risk an infantry crossing at that point, but they did attempt to cross at the bridge southeast of town, which the 291st Engineer Combat Battalion blew while two German soldiers were on the span.

Peiper's lead tanks then turned north, seemingly probing for a way to outflank the town. Colonel Anderson had the bridge over the Salm within Trois Ponts destroyed. In midafternoon he departed for First Army headquarters, leaving the defense of Trois Ponts in the hands of a new arrival on the scene, Maj. Robert B. Yates, the 51st Engineer Combat Battalion's executive officer.

As darkness fell at 1700, Major Yates drew his men back to the center of Trois Ponts where they could hear the sound of enemy armor and vehicles all night. Yates employed several ruses to hide his weakness in men and weapons from the enemy. He moved small groups of riflemen, firing, from point to point; he had a heavy truck driven noisily around the streets to mimic the sound of arriving artillery; and to create the impression that reinforcements were coming in from the west, all night he ran his five trucks out of town with lights out and back in town with lights on. Also, he received an unexpected assist from a tank destroyer that his men had set afire to keep it out of enemy hands—the 105-mm. shells within the burning vehicle continued exploding for some time. These deceptions apparently worked, for the Germans did not attack. Just before midnight their tanks moved north up the road toward Stoumont.[24]

That day, 18 December, infantry of the 30th Division arrived to man the defenses at Malmedy and Stavelot. One of the division's regimental combat teams went into position to interrupt Peiper's tanks at Stoumont, but the engineers were the sole defenders of Trois Ponts all that day and the next.[25] Late on 19 December a small advance party of paratroopers arrived from the west. They were from the 82d Airborne Division, elements of which Maj. Gen. Matthew B. Ridgway, commanding general of the XVIII Airborne Corps, had rushed forward to help stop Peiper. The newcomers did not know that the critical bridgehead of Trois Ponts was in friendly hands, much less that it was held by a single engineer company. Greeting the paratroopers, Major Yates joked, "I'll bet you guys are glad we're here."[26]

Next afternoon, following an enemy artillery barrage that killed one engineer and wounded another, a company of the 505th Parachute Infantry Regiment arrived at Trois Ponts with a platoon of airborne engineers. But when the infantrymen took up a position on a hill east of town they were surrounded, and troops of the 51st Engineer Combat Battalion had to provide covering fire to extricate the airborne

---

[24] Hist 51st Engr C Bn, Jun–Dec 44, and Jnl entry, 18 Dec 44; Hists, 291st Engr C Bn and 1111th Engr C Gp, Dec 44.

[25] Hewitt, *Work Horse of the Western Front*, pp. 174–77.

[26] Cole, *The Ardennes: The Battle of the Bulge*, p. 351.

force. Not until dusk on 21 December were Yates' men able to withdraw from the defensive positions they had held for five days and journey to their battalion headquarters at Marche, far to the west. Exhausted and numb from the bitter cold (the temperature had dropped to 20° F.), they had been "spurred to almost superhuman effort" by the "heroic example and leadership of Major Yates."[27]

Combined elements of the 82d Airborne, 30th Infantry, and 3d Armored Divisions stopped Peiper on the Ambleve near Stoumont. The deepest penetration in the Battle of the Bulge was to be made not by the *Sixth Panzer Army* but by the *Fifth Panzer Army* to the south.

### *Delaying Fifth Panzer Army from the Our to the Meuse*

On the Skyline Drive in Luxembourg it had been snowing or raining off and on throughout the first two weeks in December. Clearing away accumulations of snow and icy slush was the principal task of Company B of the 103d Engineer Combat Battalion, quartered at Hosingen. The company was supporting the 28th Division's 110th Infantry, located in the center of the division's frontline positions. Other companies of the same engineer battalion were supporting the 112th Infantry on the north and the 109th Infantry on the south.

Because the 28th Division could not hope to defend every mile of its 23-mile-long front, the division commander had set up a series of strongpoints; Hosin-

gen was one. Garrisoned by Company K of the 3d Battalion, 110th Infantry, Hosingen overlooked two roads from Germany that crossed the Our River, wound over the Skyline Drive, descended to the Clerf River, and then continued west for fourteen miles to the important road center of Bastogne. One road, crossing the Skyline Drive about two miles north of Hosingen, was a paved highway, the best east-west route in the sector. About two miles west of the drive the road ran through the castle town of Clerf on the Clerf River, where the 110th Infantry had its headquarters. The other road, muddy and winding, crossed the Skyline Drive just south of the outskirts of Hosingen. The engineers knew this secondary road well. They had accompanied infantry over it on several small raids into Germany, using rubber boats to cross the Our, and on it they had emplaced an abatis and planted a minefield.

At 0530 on 16 December, a German barrage of massed guns and rockets reverberated over the Skyline Drive for about half an hour. As dawn broke, cloudy and cold with patches of ground fog, infantry of the *26th Volksgrenadier Division* came up the muddy road. Some troops bypassed Hosingen, but one battalion entered the town. Company K, 110th Infantry, and Company B, 103d Engineer Combat Battalion, put up a strong defense. House-to-house fighting continued all day, but no German tanks appeared until the morning of the seventeenth—German engineers had failed to erect heavy bridging at the nearest Our River crossing. When the tanks reached Hosingen they set the town afire, but the defenders held out until the evening of the seventeenth, after Clerf had surrendered.

---

[27] Hist 51st Engr C Bn, Oct, Nov, Dec 44, and Jnl entry, 20 Dec 44.

Communications had been out since the heavy opening barrage on the sixteenth, so the headquarters of the 103d Engineer Combat Battalion at Eschdorf, twelve miles to the southwest, had no word from this last bastion until 0050 on 18 December. Then an officer got through to report that the evening before, the troops at Hosingen had still been fighting. Out of ammunition and beyond the range of American artillery, they were withdrawing from house to house, using hand grenades. After that nothing more was heard.[28]

During the night of 17 December the Germans, having secured two bridges over the Clerf River at Clerf and farther south at Drauffelt, moved swiftly west in several columns. One turned south toward the 28th Division command post at Wiltz, twelve miles east of Bastogne.

The defenders of Wiltz included 600 men of the 44th Engineer Combat Battalion. This unit, along with the 168th, the 159th, and the 35th Engineer Combat Battalions and Combat Command Reserve of the 9th Armored Division, made up General Middleton's VIII Corps reserve. Until noon of 17 December the 44th Battalion had been working in the corps area as part of the 1107th Engineer Combat Group, maintaining roads and operating two sawmills, a rock quarry, and a water point. Then General Middleton sent the battalion to Wiltz and attached it to the 29th Infantry Division, whose commander, Maj. Gen. Norman D. Cota, gave the engineers the mission of defending the town. Cota's plan called for securing Wiltz and covering all approaches to the town. Supporting the

PLACING CHARGES TO DROP TREES *across roadways.*

engineers were remnants of the 707th Tank Battalion with six crippled tanks and five assault guns; four towed 3-inch guns from a tank destroyer battalion; a depleted battalion of 105-mm. divisional artillery; and a provisional battalion of infantry organized from headquarters troops. The 105-mm. howitzers went into battery along a road leading southeast from Wiltz, while the rest of the defense force manned a perimeter north and northeast of town, north of the Wiltz River.

About noon on 18 December tanks and assault guns of the *Panzer Lehr Division's Reconnaissance Battalion* struck the forward outposts, overrunning a section of tank destroyers. The engineers held their fire until the German infantry arrived behind the tanks and then cut it down. But the weight of armor

___
[28] Hist 103d Engr C Bn, Dec 44.

proved too strong, and the engineers had to withdraw to a second line of defense.

During the night activity on both sides was limited to intense patrolling and harassing fire. Next morning the defenders were able to dig in and generally improve their positions, but in the middle of the afternoon the Germans attacked strongly from the north, northeast, and east with tanks accompanied by infantry armed with machine pistols. The three-hour attack cut the engineers' Company B to pieces. At dusk the 44th Engineer Combat Battalion was forced to withdraw into Wiltz, having suffered heavy casualties.

The engineers still felt confident, believing that the attack had cost the Germans dearly and gained them little ground. They also felt safer after they blew the bridge over the Wiltz. But about 1800 a new German column was reported approaching from the southeast, on the same side of the river as the town. A few hours later the enemy had cut all roads to Wiltz, and ammunition was running low. At 2130 the defense force received orders to pull back toward American lines to the rear. It was a grueling and bloody withdrawal through German roadblocks and a gauntlet of fire. The 44th Engineer Combat Battalion suffered heavily during the evacuation, losing 18 officers and 160 enlisted men.[29]

While the 44th Engineer Combat Battalion was defending Wiltz, two of the VIII Corps' reserve engineer battalions were engaged elsewhere. On the north the 168th, supporting the 106th Division, was astride the road from

Schoenberg to St.-Vith; on the south the 159th, attached to the 4th Division, was preparing to bar the way to Luxembourg City. Thus, by 1500 on 17 December, General Middleton had only one reserve engineer battalion, the 35th. Relieving the battalion of attachment to the 1102d Engineer Combat Group, he assigned it to the defense of Bastogne.[30]

By then Bastogne was in great danger. In midafternoon the commander of Combat Command Reserve of the 9th Armored Division (spread out along the paved road leading into the city from Clerf) reported that the Germans were overrunning his most advanced roadblock. The enemy was then less than nine miles from Bastogne. General Middleton was expecting reinforcements—the 101st Airborne Division from SHAEF reserve and Combat Command B of the 10th Armored Division from Third Army—but these units could not arrive until 18 December. In the meantime, the engineers would have to guard the approaches to Bastogne. At the suggestion of the VIII Corps engineer, a second engineer combat battalion was committed. It was the 158th, not a part of Middleton's formal reserve but part of First Army's 1128th Engineer Combat Group, which was working in his area and could be called upon "in dire circumstances."[31]

The 158th Engineer Combat Battalion received orders at 1730 on 17 December to take over the 35th Engineer Combat Battalion's 3,900-yard left flank extending from Foy, a town on the main paved road (N−15) leading into Bastogne from the north to Neffe, a

[29] Hist 44th Engr C Bn, Oct. Nov, Dec 44.

[30] Hist 35th Engr C Bn, Oct 44−Apr 45.
[31] Cole, *The Ardennes: The Battle of the Bulge*, p. 310.

ROAD MAINTENANCE OUTSIDE WILTZ, BELGIUM

town just south of the main paved road (N−28) from the east—the most likely direction of the German advance. The VIII Corps engineer advised that a takeover in the blackness of the winter night would be too difficult, and the commander of the 158th, Lt. Col. Sam Tabet, postponed the arrival of his battalion at the perimeter until daybreak at 18 December. Company A began to dig in on the left near Foy, Company B near Neffe, and Company C near Luzery, just north of Bastogne. To help hold his line of defense astride the roads along which the Germans were advancing, Tabet obtained 4 tank destroyers mounting 105-mm. howitzers, 8 light tanks, and 2 Shermans, all taken from ordnance shops and manned by

ordnance mechanics. The battalion also managed to round up 950 antitank mines.[32]

During the daylight hours of 18 December the engineers sent out reconnaissance parties and set up roadblocks, using chains of mines, bazookas, .50-caliber machine guns, and rifle grenades. Late that evening they were attached to the 10th Armored Division, whose Combat Command B was expected to arrive momentarily. Around midnight they heard rifle and automatic weapons fire to the east, and Germans overran one of the engineer roadblocks a

---

[32] Hist 158th Engr C Bn, 17 Dec−20 Dec 44. Unless otherwise cited, this account of the 158th is taken from this source.

few miles down the road from the command post.

At 0600 next morning tanks of the *Panzer Lehr Division* hit the engineer roadblock at Neffe, manned by Company B's 2d Platoon under a young lieutenant, William C. Cochran. Cochran could not tell in the darkness and fog whether the approaching tanks were German or American, so he went forward to get a better look. He was quite close to the first tank when he called back to his men, "These are Germans." From the tank someone replied in English, "Yes, we are supermen" and fired. Cochran fired back, killing two men riding on the tank.[33]

Pvt. Bernard Michin, waiting at the roadblock with a bazooka, peered at the advancing tank. Never having fired the weapon before, he let the vehicle come within ten yards of him to be sure of his target. At that range the explosion seared Michin's face and totally blinded him. He rolled into a ditch, stung with pain. A German machine gun stuttered nearby, and he tossed a hand grenade in the direction of the firing, which stopped abruptly. Still blind, he ran toward American lines where willing hands among the platoon guided him to the rear. His sight returned only after another eight hours, but his heroism had earned him the Distinguished Service Cross.[34]

By the evening of 19 December, infantry of the 101st Airborne Division had relieved the 158th Engineer Combat Battalion, and the battalion was back in a bivouac area well to the west. But the engineers were to be allowed only the briefest respite. Beginning at 2200

the 158th was alerted to defend a Bailey bridge at Ortheuville, about ten miles west of Bastogne. This bridge, which carried the VIII Corps' main supply route (N−4, from Namur via Marche) over the western branch of the Ourthe River, was threatened by reconnaissance tanks of the *2d Panzer Division.* Advancing southwest along Route N−26, which intersected N−4 about seven miles west of Bastogne, they were probing for a route west to bypass that city.[35]

The 299th Engineer Combat Battalion had prepared the Bailey bridge at Ortheuville for demolition and with detachments of the 1278th Engineer Combat Battalion had been setting up roadblocks and mining bridges in a wide arc behind Bastogne to bar the way to Germans bypassing the city to the north or south. Because the Ortheuville bridge was vital to the supply route the engineers had not yet demolished it. As the Germans began to attack toward the bridge during the early hours of 20 December, defenses consisted of not more than a platoon of the 299th Engineer Combat Battalion, reinforced by eight tank destroyers the 705th Tank Destroyer Battalion had left behind on its way to Bastogne.[36]

Arriving in Ortheuville at daybreak on 20 December, the 2d Platoon of the 158th's Company B found that German machine-gun and rifle fire had driven the 299th Battalion's platoon off the Bailey bridge and that the Germans had seized it. The 158th's platoon separated into squads, crossed the Ourthe on a

---

[33] Smith, "A Few Men in Soldier Suits," p. 31.
[34] Ibid.; see also Hist 158th Engr C Bn.

[35] Cole, *The Ardennes: The Battle of the Bulge,* pp. 319−20 and map VI.
[36] Hists, 299th Engr C Bn, 16−22 Dec 44, and 5th Engr C Bn (formerly 1278th Engr C Bn), 16−24 Dec 44.

small wooden bridge, and attacked the Germans' right and left flanks. The engineers pushed the plunger to blow up the bridge, but nothing happened; presumably German fire had cut the wiring. Tank destroyers stopped an enemy tank column attempting to cross the bridge, and at noon the Germans withdrew.[37] With the arrival of the 1st and 3d Platoons, Company B, 158th Engineer Combat Battalion, advanced down Route N−4 to the intersection with N−26, clearing the road and setting up roadblocks. Elements of Companies A and C joined later in the afternoon, bringing forward four 105-mm. tank destroyers. By the end of the day the 158th had made Route N−4 safe for convoys of gasoline and ammunition to roll into Bastogne from depots at Marche.

At 1800, Company B, which had done most of the battalion's fighting for the past two days, withdrew to a bivouac area, but an hour later it was alerted again. The Bailey bridge at Ortheuville was under heavy artillery fire, and at 2000 German armor overran the roadblock at the intersection of Routes N−4 and N−26, continuing up N−4. As soon as the 2d Platoon of Company B arrived on the scene some of the men crossed to the enemy side of the bridge and planted antitank mines across the road, but they failed to stop the Germans and had to withdraw across the wooden bridge.

In three attacks, one involving a party of four Germans dressed as civilians or U.S. soldiers, the enemy tried to seize the wooden bridge but was repulsed. Then, after a second attempt to blow

the bridge failed, a fourth German attack was successful. The enemy infantry forded the river and picked off the defenders silhouetted against the glare of the burning houses beyond. At midnight German armor began clanking across the Bailey bridge. After a parting shot from one of their four tank destroyers caused a gratifying (but inconclusive) explosion, the engineers withdrew about eight miles southwest to St. Hubert, where in the early afternoon they were ordered to take over the defense of Libramont, another eight miles to the south.

The German armored column crossing the Bailey bridge at Ortheuville ran into roadblocks established by the 51st Engineer Combat Battalion, sent down from Marche. This was the battalion that had contributed its Company C to the defense of Trois Ponts. On 21 December the other two companies were guarding a barrier line along the eastern branch of the Ourthe River from Hotton, about six miles northeast of Marche, to La Roche, nine miles southeast of Hotton, and were manning roadblocks south of Marche on Route N−4 and southwest of Marche as far as Rochefort.[38]

The defense of Hotton, at the western end of an important Class 70 bridge over the Ourthe, was in the hands of a squad from Company B and half a squad from Company A. The *116th Panzer Division*, attacking from the northeast in an attempt to get to the Meuse north of Bastogne, shelled Hotton at daybreak on 21 December and then struck with about five tanks and some armored infantry—the spearhead of an

---

[37] OCE ETOUSA Hist Rpt 10, Combat Engineering, pp. 24−25.

[38] AAR, 51st Engr C Bn, Jun−Dec 44, and Hist 51st Engr C Bn, Oct, Nov, Dec 44. Unless otherwise cited, this account is taken from these two sources.

armored brigade. In the ensuing fire-fight the American defenders included half a squad of Company A, the squad of Company B, ten men of the battalion's Headquarters and Service Company, and two 40-mm. gun sections from the battalion's attached antiaircraft battery. They were joined by several bazooka teams, a few 3d Armored Division engineers with a 37-mm. gun, and a Sherman tank with a 76-mm. gun that the engineers discovered in an ordnance shop on the edge of the town and had commandeered along with its crew. This scratch force, under the command of Capt. Preston C. Hodges of Company B, managed to hold the town until shortly after noon, when a platoon of tanks of the 84th Infantry Division arrived from Marche and a task force of the 3d Armored Division came in from the east.[39]

### Stopping the German Seventh Army

At the southernmost portion of the VIII Corps front the Our flowed into the Sauer and the Sauer formed the boundary between Luxembourg and Germany. There General der Panzertruppen Erich Brandenberger's Seventh Army, composed of two infantry corps, attacked on 16 December. This army was the "stepchild of the Ardennes offensive," lacking the heavy support accorded the two powerful panzer armies on the north.[40] Its mission was to guard the flank of the Fifth Panzer Army. Its northernmost corps (the LXXXV), with the 352d Volksgrenadier Division,

was to cross the Our north of its juncture with the Sauer and advance on a westward axis parallel to the Fifth Panzer Army. The southernmost corps, the LXXX, with the 276th and 212th Volksgrenadier Divisions, was to establish a bridgehead at the town of Echternach on the Sauer and make a limited advance to the southwest in the direction of Luxembourg City.

Guarding the line of the Our on the north was the 28th Division's 109th Infantry. It was attacked by the 352d Volksgrenadier Division and the Fifth Panzer Army 5th Parachute Division, which was driving a wedge between the 109th and the 110th Infantry regiments to the north. Most of the 28th Division's meager reserves had gone to the hard-pressed 110th Infantry, in the path of the powerful Fifth Panzer Army. Among the few reserves allotted to the 109th Infantry was Company A of the 103d Engineer Combat Battalion, which was attached to the 109th on the evening of 16 December.[41]

By the end of the sixteenth elements of the German parachute division on the extreme north had crossed the Our at Vianden (about thirteen miles southeast of Wiltz) on a prefabricated bridge emplaced in about an hour, broken through to the Skyline Drive, and cut off several 109th Infantry outposts. The rapidity of this advance, threatening Wiltz, caused the 28th Division commander to request some of the 109th Infantry's reserves. A platoon of tanks with an infantry platoon aboard and a few engineers started north, but could neither stop nor penetrate the northern wing of the 352d Volksgrenadier

[39] Theodore Draper, The 84th Infantry Division in the Battle of Germany (New York: Viking Press, 1946), p. 90; Spearhead in the West: The Third Armored Division, p. 111.

[40] Cole, The Ardennes: The Battle of the Bulge, p. 258.

[41] Hist 103d Engr C Bn, Dec 44, S–2 and S–3 Jnls.

*Division;* they joined the withdrawal westward toward Wiltz. The southern wing of the *352d*, on the other hand, encountered Americans dug in on heights in a triangle formed by the confluence of the Our and the Sauer. On the night of 17 December the *Volksgrenadier Division* received some bridging equipment and, with its increasing strength in heavy weapons including Tiger tanks, was able to break through the defenders' roadblocks and take Diekirch, six miles southwest of the Our crossing, on 20 December. That night the division advanced nearly three miles farther to take Ettelbruck, a German objective for 16 December. By delaying the German division four days, the outnumbered defenders had disrupted enemy plans. The engineers who established roadblocks and manned outposts had made a considerable contribution. One platoon patrolling roads in the forward area captured twelve Germans before it was forced to withdraw.[42]

Just to the south, where the *LXXX Corps* was attacking, the 60th Armored Infantry Battalion of the 9th Armored Division, an untried unit sent to this quiet sector for combat indoctrination, held about six miles of front. When the *276th Volksgrenadier Division* attacked the armored battalion, the 9th Armored Division commander sent forward reinforcements of tanks, tank destroyers, and artillery; the infantry reinforcements consisted of a company of divisional engineers. The new strength enabled the armored infantry battalion to fight as a combat command and to put up strong resistance to the *276th*. Least effective of the three *Seventh Army* divisions committed to the battle, the *276th*

---

[42] Hist 103d Engr C Bn, Dec 44.

had no tanks, and American shelling effectively interfered with its attempts to get heavy weapons over the Sauer. The division had to pay heavily for the three or four miles it was able to advance from the Sauer—a more limited penetration than that of any other *Seventh Army* division.

General Brandenberger sent his best division, the *212th Volksgrenadier*, across the Sauer about twelve miles southeast of Vianden into a hilly area around the town of Echternach known as "Little Switzerland." This was the northern portion of the 35-mile-long front, bordered by the Sauer and the Moselle, and held by Maj. Gen. Raymond O. Barton's depleted 4th Infantry Division.

Crossing the narrow, swift Sauer at several points in rubber boats, the German troops quickly overcame forward elements of the 12th Infantry, the only troops in the Echternach area. Here, as in other sectors, the preliminary German artillery barrage cut wire communications; in this sector, held by a regiment battered in Huertgen Forest, radios were scarce and had very limited range in the broken terrain. Thus, it was around noon before General Barton, at division headquarters near Luxembourg City about twenty miles southwest of Echternach, had a clear picture of what was happening. From the meager stocks of his 70th Tank Battalion he allotted the 12th Infantry eight medium and ten light tanks, making possible the formation of tank-infantry teams to aid the hard-pressed infantry companies at the front. With one of these teams, Task Force Luckett, the 4th Engineer Combat Battalion went forward to hold high ground near Breidweiler, about five miles southwest of Echternach, but when no enemy appeared part of the battalion returned to engineer work.[43]

On the afternoon of 16 December General Barton telephoned General Middleton, the VIII Corps commander, to ask for reinforcements. All Middleton could offer was the 159th Engineer Combat Battalion, which was working on roads throughout the corps area as far north as Wiltz and Clerf. Middleton told Barton that "if he could find the engineers he could use them."[44]

Barton found the headquarters of the 159th in Luxembourg City. The engineers were ready for orders to move to the front, for two of their trucks on a routine run to pick up rock at Diekirch in the 28th Division area had returned with the news that the rock quarry was under German fire. On 17 December the battalion was attached to Task Force Riley from Combat Command A of the 10th Armored Division, whose objective was the village of Scheidgen, some four miles south of the Sauer on the Echternach–Luxembourg City road. The Germans had already overrun Scheidgen, bypassing roadbound U.S. tanks by going through the woods.[45]

On the morning of 18 December, wet and cold with heavy, low-hanging clouds, the engineer battalion drew ammunition and grenades and moved forward from Luxembourg City. Company B remained in reserve several miles to the rear. Accompanied by light tanks and tank destroyers, Companies A and C advanced toward Scheidgen, the engi-

neers through woods south of the town and the tanks on a road from the west. They took the town without much opposition, though part of Company C received heavy small-arms fire from Hill 313, about a mile north. After a night in Scheidgen under heavy German shelling the two engineer companies secured Hill 313, which overlooked the Echternach–Luxembourg City road. They dug foxholes and waited. They could see Germans moving around at the foot of the hill, and next morning, 20 December, they received a barrage of enemy artillery, mortar, and rocket fire. Then two parties of Germans tried to come up the hill, but were repulsed. That day, Company B (minus one platoon) came up, assuming positions on high ground about 800 yards west of Hill 313, while Companies A and C took turns going into Scheidgen for hot food and a little rest. The engineers kept hearing reports that infantry was coming up to relieve them, but none arrived.

On the morning of 21 December the Germans attacked again. Some charged up Hill 313 screaming and firing automatic weapons, but the main force hit Company B on the left, drove a wedge between two platoons, killed the company commander, and occupied the company's positions. The tactical value of Hill 313 was lost, and Scheidgen had become a shambles from heavy pounding by German artillery. Companies A and C withdrew to positions slightly southeast of Scheidgen toward Michelshof, while the remnants of Company B went to the rear.

Michelshof, a crossroads town on the road to Luxembourg City, formed part of the main line of resistance. The two engineer companies, accompanied by

[43] Hist 4th Engr C Bn, May–Dec 44.

[44] Cole, *The Ardennes: The Battle of the Bulge*, p. 243.

[45] *The 159th Engineer Combat Battalion* (Antwerp: De Vos van Kleef, Ltd., 1945), pp. 17–19. The account of the action around Scheidgen is taken from this source.

two medium tanks and a tank destroyer and commanded by Capt. Arthur T. Surkamp, the battalion S–3, dug in there on 22 December. Nothing lay between them and the enemy on the north but a badly mauled company from the 12th Infantry, a patch of woods, and some open fields. During the day they came under rocket and artillery fire, but supporting artillery of the 10th Armored Division put a stop to most of it.

About 1700, as dusk was falling, enemy troops moved out of the woods in V formation and advanced across the fields toward the engineers. Captain Surkamp, alerting the artillery to "drop them in close" when signaled, ordered the engineers to hold their fire. When the leading soldiers were 150 yards away, the engineers, the tankers, and the artillery opened fire. Most of the enemy in the formation were killed or wounded.

On the morning of 23 December the engineers woke to find that the heavy clouds were gone. Soon they heard the drone of motors, and American fighter and bomber planes passed over. "This was the thing we had sweated out for days and there they were, you then knew that the jig for Herr Hitler was up."[46]

The next morning, Christmas Eve, Third Army infantry relieved the men of the 159th Engineer Combat Battalion. General Patton was swinging the bulk of his troops north to pound the German southern flank, relieve Bastogne, and help end the Battle of the Ardennes.

General Middleton credited the engineers with doing a "magnificent job" as infantry in repulsing the Germans in the Ardennes. On the other hand, the VIII Corps engineer and various engineer group commanders believed that the engineer combat battalions could have done more to impede the German advance had they been employed not in the front line but in a tactically unified second line of defense in the rear. Going a step further, the official Army historian of the Battle of the Ardennes states that "the use of engineers in their capacity as trained technicians often paid greater dividends than their use as infantry" and points out that Field Marshal Walter Model issued an order on 18 December forbidding the use of the German pioneer troops as infantry.[47]

Yet on the defensive in the Ardennes General Middleton had to depend on the engineers. At crucial points on the front, such as Auw, divisional engineers were the only troops on the scene when the Germans struck. Because there was thought to be little danger of an attack in this quiet sector, aside from a single armored combat command General Middleton's only reserves consisted of four engineer combat battalions—the 44th, 35th, 168th, and 150th. They fought in defense of Wiltz, Bastogne, St.-Vith, and Michelshof. Several First Army engineer combat battalions which were operating sawmills in the area— the 291st, 51st, and 158th—distinguished themselves at Malmedy, at Trois Ponts and Hotton, and at Bastogne and Ortheuville. The engineers were able to upset the German timetable, delaying the onrushing columns long enough for American reinforcements to be brought to the five main pillars of

---

[46] *The 159th Engineer Combat Battalion*, p. 20.

[47] Cole, *The Ardennes: The Battle of the Bulge*, p. 329.

resistance—Elsenborn ridge, the fortified "goose egg" area around St.-Vith, Bastogne, Echternach, and Marche.[48]

### Engineers in NORDWIND

When the German Ardennes offensive fell on 12th Army Group in full fury in mid-December 1944, General Devers estimated that it was only a matter of time before German forces would strike 6th Army Group to prevent its advancing to aid the 12th Army Group to its immediate north. At the end of the month the Seventh Army held a broad salient, eighty-four miles of front that wound into the northeastern corner of Alsace from Saarbruecken to the Rhine River, with limited bridgeheads across the German border. The right flank of the Seventh Army line ran south along the Rhine to a point below Strasbourg. There, the First French Army zone began, running farther south and including a vise closed on the pocket of German divisions pinned in their positions around Colmar. A German plan, Operation NORDWIND, developed by Christmas Day, called for a massive double envelopment to catch the entire Seventh Army. Converging German attacks, one to the north out of the Colmar Pocket, would join another arm driving south near the Maginot Line town of Bitche. They would meet around Sarrebourg, twenty to thirty miles behind the Seventh Army lines. The offensive was set for 31 December 1944.

By 28 December, General Devers had ordered a phased withdrawal through three defensive lines, the first along the

Maginot Line and the others marking a progressive pullout to strong positions in the Low Vosges Mountains. These orders changed repeatedly as the German thrusts failed and as French protests about the surrender of Alsatian territory reached SHAEF headquarters, but regardless of the changes, the construction of the defenses fell to the engineers.

In the last two weeks of December the three veteran engineer combat regiments, the 540th, the 40th, and the 36th, began extensive work in the VI Corps area, the most exposed northeastern corner of Alsace, which the Germans now proposed to isolate. Basing much of the fortification on the Maginot structures assigned as the first defense line, the engineers supplemented their construction with roadblocks, usually employing concealed 57-mm. antitank gun positions. Across the rear of the corps and the army area they prepared all bridges for demolition.

The 1st Battalion, 540th Engineer Combat Regiment, extracted itself from a precarious position at the start of the German drive. Assigned to VI Corps, the regiment was alerted as early as 18 December against German attacks expected over the Rhine, but no serious threats had developed by Christmas Day on the regimental front, and the engineers spent a peaceful holiday. The unit was busy through the end of 1944 extending Maginot Line positions, laying mines, and constructing bridges around Baerenthal, fifteen miles south of Bitche.

In the early morning hours of New Year's Day 1945, the 1st Battalion of the 540th Engineer Combat Regiment assembled at Baerenthal, organizing as infantry to help meet the enemy ad-

---

[48] John S. D. Eisenhower, *The Bitter Woods* (New York: Putnam, 1969), pp. 462–63.

vance into the unit's general area. Small units joined counterattacks or rescue attempts through the morning. Company B stood with the 117th Cavalry Reconnaissance Squadron in the line. Before sunup, two platoons of Company A assaulted German positions to open a path for isolated elements of the 125th Armored Engineer Battalion. Two platoons of Company C went into the main line, flanking elements of the 62d Armored Infantry Battalion.

By midmorning the rescued 125th Armored Engineer Battalion took positions in the main line with Company C, 540th Engineer Regiment, in the face of the rapidly developing German onslaught. The hastily collected defenses of widely disparate units sagged under the weight of the German drive and finally broke at noon, sending Company C retreating upon the 1st Battalion headquarters. Just as the headquarters detachment finished burning its unit records, the Germans overran the area, and the engineers joined the general withdrawal.

By mid-January, the 1st and 2d Battalions, 540th Engineer Combat Regiment, were again in the line as infantry in 45th Division positions around Wimmenau and Wingen, twenty-five miles south of Bitche and twenty miles southeast of 1st Battalion's former positions around Baerenthal. The regiment's major concern other than combat was the construction of works near the towns of Haguenau and Vosges, a defensive line intended to contain other German thrusts across the Rhine.[49]

On VI Corps' left the 36th Engineer Combat Regiment relieved the 179th Infantry, 45th Division, on 1 January 1945 and continued to operate as infantry until 7 February. The regiment began withdrawing from positions north of Wissembourg on the Franco-German border to the main line of resistance in the Maginot bunkers and trenches and sent aggressive patrols through inhabited points well forward of this line to prevent a solid enemy front from taking shape.[50]

When the German drives on the whole Seventh Army front had spent themselves by mid-January, the 36th Engineer Combat Regiment moved to relieve the 275th Infantry. The engineers occupied the right flank position of the 157th Infantry in the 45th Division line while the infantry regiment led the division's counterattack on the enemy salient from Bitche toward the south on 14 January. In this case the 36th Engineer Combat Regiment witnessed a disaster.

As part of a double envelopment to clear the enemy from the Mouterhouse-Baerenthal valley, the 157th Infantry had advanced one battalion against the positions of the *6th SS Mountain Division* in the valley and the woods around it, but the unit was pinned down and then surrounded. In eight days of heavy fighting, the regiment attacked with its remaining battalions to extricate the surrounded unit. On the fifteenth two more companies drove their way into the encirclement, only to find themselves trapped with the surrounded battalion. After five concerted assaults on the German lines, the 157th had to abandon the effort, and the regiment

[49] Hist 540th Engineer Regiment [11 Sep 42–14 Feb 45], pp. 21–24.

[50] Hist Rpt, 36th Engr C Rgt, Jan 45.

SEVENTH ARMY ENGINEERS INSTALL A BRIDGE ON THE ILL RIVER

left the line on 21 January; breakout attempts from within the pocket gained the freedom of only 2 men of the original 750 engulfed in the German net. Engineer attacks to relieve the pressure on the 157th's right were of no avail. The five companies were annihilated.[51]

The beginning of January found the 40th Engineer Combat Regiment spread out on VI Corps' right flank, supporting the three infantry divisions facing a German thrust across the Rhine River in the vicinity of Gambsheim, fifteen miles north of Strasbourg. The bulk of the regiment was with the 79th Infantry Division, with one battalion supporting the 3d Division. By early February

the 40th Engineer Combat Regiment, reinforced with the 111th Engineer Combat Battalion, fell in behind the 36th Infantry Division, involved in clearing the west bank of the Rhine.[52]

While this clearing operation was being completed, Seventh Army was already moving to reverse the tide of Operation NORDWIND and to straighten its front in preparation for its own assault on the Siegfried Line and for crossing the Rhine. The first of these operations was the elimination of the Colmar Pocket, which had held out all winter despite determined French assaults. General Devers gave the XXI Corps, under Maj. Gen. Frank W.

---

[51] Seventh Army Report, vol. II, pp. 588–90; Hist Rpt, 36th Engr C Rgt, Jan 45.

[52] Hist Rpt, 40th Engr C Rgt, Jan 45.

Millburn, to the operational control of the First French Army for the mop-up. The 3d, the 28th, and the 75th Infantry Divisions, the 12th Armored, and the 2d French Armored Divisions had their own organic engineers, supplemented by numerous attached special units whose services were needed to keep open main supply routes for the troops cleaning out the remnants of German resistance around Colmar. The 1145th Engineer Combat Group, attached to XXI Corps, was the parent organization for these units. The lack of treadway bridge units in the 6th Army Group area was partially alleviated by the attachment of the 998th Treadway Bridge Company from 12th Army Group and a detachment of the 196th Engineer Dump Truck Company, converted into a bridge unit.

American engineers repeatedly went into the line as infantry during the Colmar action. The 290th Engineer Combat Battalion spent the whole period of its assignment to XXI Corps in direct contact with the enemy and aggressively pursued retreating German units in maneuvers with the 112th Infantry, 28th Infantry Division.[53]

The elimination of the Colmar Pocket in mid-February released the XXI Corps for action on the left flank and center of the Seventh Army line. The attached

engineer units reverted to Seventh Army control for use in a series of limited objective assaults which eventually brought French and American divisions to the Siegfried Line. After crossing the Saar and the Blies Rivers, Allied forces were on German soil and in front of the city of Saarbruecken. The 6th Army Group troops did not reach the Siegfried Line until mid-March, long after the Allies to the north had overcome that obstacle in the late fall of 1944.

*Seventh Army Through the Siegfried Line*

The 6th Army Group engineer, General Wolfe, had the benefit of engineer intelligence gathered on the famous Siegfried Line defenses farther north in the 12th Army Group zones. By early December, Seventh Army engineers had detailed studies of the nature of the defenses and the best means of breaching them. Farther to the north, along the traditional east-west invasion corridors, the West Wall defenses ran in thicker bands, presenting layers of fortifications sometimes twelve miles deep. In the 6th Army Group sector the line was formidable but generally less deep than in the 12th Army Group's zone. The 6th Army Group planners in fact developed designs to break through it and to jump the Rhine River, using the troops that had trained for that eventuality through the previous autumn.[54]

General Patch's Seventh Army opened an assault on the line on 15 March. Central in the drive was the XV Corps which, because of the planned approach to the Rhine behind the Ger-

---

[53] Unit Hists, 1145th Engr C Gp, 196th Engr Dump Truck Co, 998th Engr Treadway Bridge Co, and 290th Engr C Bn. The 6th Army Group attached seven other units to the French Army's operational control in January and February 1945. Among them were the 677th Light Maintenance Company, 1271st Engineer Combat Battalion, Company B of the 1553d Engineer Heavy Ponton Battalion, the 25th and the 286th Engineer Combat Battalions, and the 3d Battalion of the 40th Engineer Combat Regiment. The 3d Armored Engineer Battalion was attached to the 2d French Armored Division. 6th Army Gp Sitreps, Jan–May 45.

[54] AAR, Seventh Army Engr, Dec 44, sub: Breaching the Siegfried Line; *Seventh Army Report*, vol. III, p. 695.

man defenses, had the 540th and the 40th Engineer Combat Regiments attached. Both units now had a 35-mile train of vehicles and trailers with river-crossing equipment retrieved from the forests and factories of Luneville. To keep the main arteries clear for combat elements, the long lines of laden engineer vehicles moved mainly on secondary roads, a feat for the accompanying pile-driving equipment and cranes.

Engineer troops set the pace of the attack in many places. Each regiment of the 63d Division, whose men were the first to reach the far side of the Siegfried defenses in the XXI Corps area, had one company of the 263d Engineer Combat Battalion attached. In a performance repeated all along the assaulting line, these engineers used primacord explosive rope and the heavier tank-launched "Snake" to clear paths through minefields. Hastily erected treadway bridges carried assaulting Shermans over the antitank trenches, while engineer satchel charges extracted dragon's teeth to make paths for vehicles. Engineers moved with infantry teams to demolish concrete casemates, forestalling the enemy's attempts to return and use pillboxes again. Many of the bunker entrances were simply sealed with bulldozed earth. The 263d Engineer Combat Battalion alone used fifty tons of explosive on the German fortifications. The Seventh Army had four full divisions through the vaunted line on 23 March.

### After the Ardennes

During the Allied offensive that began 3 January, following the German repulse in the Ardennes, engineer units were generally released from their infantry role and reverted to the task of helping the combat troops to move forward. The weather turned bitter cold, and snow or ice covered the roads. Working sometimes in blinding snowstorms, the engineers scattered cinders and gravel on the roads, aided in some areas by German civilian laborers. Frozen ground and deep snow made mine removal all but impossible. At one time in the XIX Corps sector, for example, thirteen bulldozers were lost to mines buried deep in snow. Since normally fordable streams were too icy for wading, the engineers had to build footbridges or use assault boats. At the little Sure River, during XII Corps' advance in late January, the engineers turned the frozen riverbank to advantage by loading men into assault boats at the top of the bank and shoving the boats downhill like toboggans.[55]

A thaw during the first week of February, far more extensive than usual, presented worse problems than the cold. Roads disintegrated into deep mud. The engineers laid down crushed stone, sometimes on a bed of dry hay, and when this did not work they corduroyed the roads with logs, using prisoner of war labor. The engineers had to build highway bridges strong enough to withstand the rushing streams flooded by melting ice and snow.[56]

By mid-February engineer units were again being drawn from their normal duties to train for the major engineer effort on the European continent—the crossing of the Rhine.

---

[55] Hist XIX Corps Engrs, p. 16, ML 2220, ETOUSA Hist Sect; Charles B. MacDonald, *The Last Offensive,* United States Army in World War II (Washington, 1973), p. 49.

[56] OCE ETOUSA Hist Rpt 14, Road Maintenance and Highway Bridging, pp. 39–40; Engr Opns VII Corps, vol. VI, "The Roer River Crossings and Advance to the Rhine," pp. 3–4.

# CHAPTER XXII

# The Roer Crossing and the Remagen Bridgehead

The ETOUSA chief engineer, Maj. Gen. Cecil R. Moore, considered the Rhine crossing nearly as important as the D-day Channel crossing. Beginning early in October 1944 he met often with SHAEF engineers from all British and American army group and army command levels and with members of the British and American navies. The planners decided that after the first waves of infantry had crossed in assault boats, larger LCVPs and LCM landing craft under Navy control would ferry tanks, trucks, and supplies and enough troops to build up the bridgehead rapidly. The engineers would then string stout cable from one bank to the other to guide DUKWs, smaller landing craft, and amphibious tanks. Once established on the far bank, engineers would construct the first heavy ponton and steel treadway bridges.[1] But in January 1945 no Allied army yet stood on the Rhine, and the force most likely to reach it still had to cover difficult terrain and cross another river that provided unexpected delays.

Sitting tight through December 1944 and January 1945, Lt. Gen. William H. Simpson's Ninth Army was already perched on the west bank of the Roer River behind Aachen, holding a salient on the German northern flank. General Simpson was searching for the opportunity to act on plans developed the previous October to sweep from the Roer to the Rhine and past it, if possible. Ninth Army had three corps arrayed on a thirty-mile front on the Roer's west bank from Dueren in the south to Roermond at the confluence of the Roer and the Meuse. There the Germans still held a bridgehead west of the Roer in the first week of February 1945. On Ninth Army's right was the XIX Corps with the 30th and 29th Infantry Divisions in the assault and the 83d Infantry and 2d Armored Divisions in reserve; in the center was XIII Corps with the 102d and 84th Infantry Divisions on the line and the 5th Armored in reserve. On the left, occupying a good half of the Army front, was XVI Corps, operational only since 7 February. The corps consisted of the 35th and 79th Infantry Divisions and the 8th Armored Division.

In Operation GRENADE, originally conceived as a thrust due east to envel-

---

[1] Moore, *Final Report*, p. 170; OCE ETOUSA Hist Rpt 20, Forced Crossing of the Rhine, pp. 5–6, and apps. 1–6.

op Cologne on the Rhine, American forces were to advance northeast toward Wesel, converging there with a First Canadian Army attack, Operation VERITABLE, to smash the weakened elements of German *Army Group H*. Set for 10 February 1945, the Ninth Army offensive was to seal the northern border of the Ruhr industrial complex, while the British Second Army, on Ninth Army's northern flank, struck out northeast across the northern German plain. On the very eve of the attack, the Germans hastily played one last defensive card to forestall the Ninth Army's expected assault.[2]

Already the subject of a Ninth Army engineer study in January 1945 was a complex of seven dams on the Roer River and its tributaries. Impounding a flood of 111 million cubic meters of water, the two largest dams, the Urfttalsperre and the Schwammenauel, represented a constant threat to future operations. Air attacks on the Schwammenauel had failed to rupture it, and the German Ardennes offensive had interrupted First Army's ground attacks through November and December 1944. On 4 February 1945, First Army troops captured the Urft Dam with no difficulty, but as the 309th Infantry, attached to the 9th Infantry Division, First Army, moved in late on the ninth to take the Schwammenauel Dam, the Germans, leaving the face intact, blew out all the dam's discharge valves. No wall of water sped down the Roer valley; rather, the cumulative flow caused

a slow, steady rise in the Roer, and the stream overflowed its banks in the lowlying areas north of Dueren. Usually averaging ninety feet in width, the river formed lakes twelve hundred feet across in places and achieved velocities that made military bridging impossible. Based on the observations of engineers posted on the banks and aerial photographs that recorded the slow withdrawal of the waters, Col. Richard U. Nicholas, Ninth Army engineer, finally predicted that operations could proceed on 24 February. The inundation forced the impatient Simpson to delay the assault for the better part of two weeks, time spent making additional preparations and revising plans.

On the supposition that the Germans would not expect a Roer crossing until after 24 February, the day when the dams would probably empty and the river return to normal, General Simpson had decided to achieve surprise by ordering the crossing before daylight on 23 February. Colonel Nicholas advised Simpson that the river by that time would have receded enough to make a crossing possible and that the Roer's swift current would have subsided somewhat. Preceded by a tremendous 45-minute artillery preparation, the Roer crossings of XIX Corps' 30th and 29th Divisions and XIII Corps' 102d and 84th Divisions (supported respectively by the 1115th, 1104th, 1141st, and 1149th Engineer Combat Groups) began at 0330 on 23 February from Linnich on the north to a point below Juelich on the south.

*The Roer Crossings*

General Simpson later called the Roer crossings a "rehearsal for the Rhine,"

---

[2] MacDonald, *The Last Offensive*, pp. 135–45; Col. Theodore W. Parker and Col. William J. Thompson, *Conquer, The Story of the Ninth Army, 1944–1945* (Washington: Infantry Journal Press, 1947), pp. 114–60. Tactical detail on the GRENADE operation is taken from these two sources.

ENGINEERS EMPLACE MATS TO STABILIZE THE BANKS OF THE FLOODED ROER

but actually little of the experience gained at the Roer would prove applicable to the Rhine.[3] The rivers were quite different; even in flood, for example, the Roer was narrow. For such a river, engineer doctrine dictated that after the assault boat crossings prefabricated footbridges would be used to move troops to the far bank and infantry support, heavy ponton, treadway, and Bailey bridges quickly thrown across. In the Roer crossings no naval landing craft of the type so important in plans for the Rhine crossings were required.[4] LVTs were available from the hundred earmarked for the Rhine crossings, but they were not to be used except in special circumstances, where muddy banks or unexpectedly heavy enemy fire on the far shore were encountered.[5]

The artillery barrage that began at 0245 on 23 February was the heaviest yet laid down in Europe. The engineers waiting with their assault boats and footbridge material in the fields along the west bank of the Roer or in cellars saw in the pink sky to the rear lightning-

[3] Lt. Gen. W. H. Simpson, "Rehearsal for the Rhine," *Military Review*, XXV, no. 7 (October 1945), 20.
[4] Interv, Maj Edward L. Waller, S–2, 1141st Engr C Gp, 12 Feb 45; Folder, Bridging the Roer: The

Contribution of the Engineer Combat Groups in Ninth U.S. Army, 23 Feb–10 Mar 45, CI 371, ETOUSA Hist Sect. Subsequent references to contents of this ETOUSA Historical Section folder will be cited as: Bridging the Roer.
[5] Hewitt, *Work Horse of the Western Front*, p. 218.

like flashes from the big guns. In the dark sky above they observed long red ribbons of tracer rounds from machine guns, and on the east bank ahead exploding shells illuminated ruined houses or bare tree branches and sodden fields. (*Map 28*)

On the right, about three miles upstream from Juelich, engineers supporting the 30th Division crossed some combat troops before the barrage lifted. They soon found that they were to suffer more from the swift current than from enemy fire. The rushing waters carried assault boats downstream, capsizing them and breaking cables when the engineers tried to anchor footbridges. At the site where the 82d Engineer Combat Battalion was trying to get the 120th Infantry across, friendly artillery fire falling on the far bank until 0330 cut a footbridge. Thereafter the current, as strong as seven miles an hour in this sector, aborted six efforts to replace the bridge. Only by transferring the work downstream where the current was slower were the engineers able to build a footbridge at all, and it was not ready for use until 1730. In the meantime, the 234th Engineer Combat Battalion, assigned to the 1115th Group, carried men and supplies over the Roer in ten LVTs that made a total of fifty-four trips beginning at 0330. Other infantrymen of the 120th Infantry crossed via a footbridge the 295th Engineer Combat Battalion put in downstream for the 119th Infantry. The current caused trouble for treadway bridges at both sites. Delays occurred with a treadway the 295th was erecting when boats carrying the cable to the far bank overturned or swamped; the cable was not anchored until 1400. In the 120th Infantry sector upstream, the 82d Engi-

neer Combat Battalion anchored its first treadway to the piles of a demolished German bridge.

Elsewhere, heavy German fire added to the hazards of the current. On the east bank at Juelich, an old Prussian garrison town where XIX Corps' 29th Infantry Division was to cross, the enemy held commanding positions in the ruins of the town and at an ancient, thick-walled fortress, the Citadel. Near Linnich on the west bank, two XIII Corps infantry divisions, the 102d and 84th, had to cross on a narrow two-mile front because the area to the north and south was flooded. Crossing at Juelich and Linnich, which the Germans would undoubtedly expect, had obvious disadvantages. But considering the problems the swampy flats elsewhere posed, General Simpson decided that the advantage of paved roads leading into and away from the towns justified the risk.[6]

The paved roads leading into Juelich from the west determined the location of the first bridges the engineers built. On the right, where the road from Aldenhoven came in, the narrowness of the river and the height of the far bank—offering protection against small-arms fire—dictated a reversal of the usual assault procedure. Rather than crossing in boats, most assault troops of the 175th Infantry were to cross on footbridges built by the 1104th Engineer Combat Group's 246th Engineer Combat Battalion. At 0430 on 23 February at this site the group's 247th Engineer Combat Battalion was to start construction of two tactical bridges— one heavy ponton and one treadway. About the same time the 246th, having completed three footbridges, was to

---

[6] Simpson, "Rehearsal for the Rhine," p. 24.

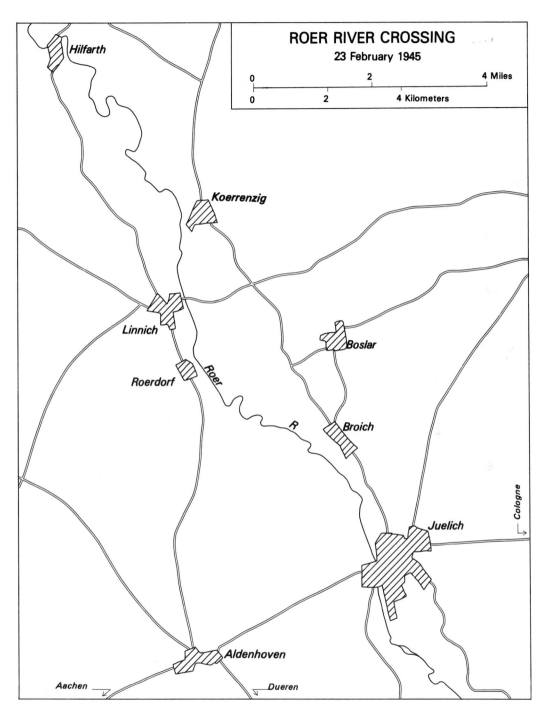

ROER RIVER CROSSING
23 February 1945

MAP 28

move downstream to build an infantry support bridge at a point where a paved road from Boslar entered the city. This was expected to be the first vehicular bridge into Juelich, although the site lay under the guns of the Citadel. North of Juelich, where the river was wider, no bridges were to be built until the floodwaters subsided. There, where a paved road ran from Boslar to the riverbank and on the other side to the village of Broich, troops of the 115th Infantry were to ferry to the far bank in assault boats and LVTs.[7]

Half an hour before the opening barrage lifted on 23 February three assault boats filled with divisional engineers of the 121st Engineer Combat Battalion and covering troops of the 175th Infantry got across at the Aldenhoven road site against scattered German machine-gun fire. These troops spread out along the far bank, and at 0330 the 246th Engineer Combat Battalion began work on a footbridge under a smoke screen. Although making it difficult for the engineers to see what they were doing, the smoke protected them from rifle, machine-pistol, and machine-gun fire from the far bank. Again, the greatest problem was the racing current. After some difficulty in anchoring the cable, the engineers completed the first footbridge on schedule at 0424. But a few minutes later an assault boat, swept downstream by the current, rammed into the bridge and buckled it. As day broke, cloudy, damp, and chilly, repairs to this bridge went on simultaneously with the construction of two additional footbridges. The engineers completed one footbridge by 0600; the first troops to use it were two Germans who ran

out of a bunker on the far side and surrendered to the engineers. By 0700 all three footbridges were in place, and the infantrymen were dashing across to clean out German strongpoints in houses on the far bank.

Around 0900, small-arms fire ceased to harass the 247th Engineer Combat Battalion which, since 0430, had been constructing the heavy ponton and treadway bridges at the Aldenhoven site. But now German mortar and artillery fire began to fall, with tragic results at the treadway, where seven rounds of heavy artillery fire killed six engineers and wounded eighteen. The fire also destroyed the bridge. Work began on a new bridge twenty-five yards upstream at 1400, but observed artillery fire and the swift current delayed completion until late the following morning. The engineers working on the heavy ponton bridge were luckier and had the span in operation by 1600 on D-day. Before darkness fell on 23 February tanks and bulldozers were clanking across.[8]

At the Boslar-Juelich site downstream the beach party started out at 0300 in two assault boats. One capsized and the other was caught by the current and thrown on the east bank near a minefield, where several men were injured. These two incidents cost the party more than half its strength. The 246th Engineer Combat Battalion suffered a series of misfortunes when it tried to build an infantry support bridge at the downstream site. The engineers had swept the approach for mines, but their metal mine detectors were ineffective on the plastic Topf mines in the road and on the shoulders. After the Topf mines

---

[7] Section on 1104th Engineer Combat Group, Bridging the Roer; Ewing, *29 Let's Go!*, pp. 225–27.

[8] Bridging the Roer; Ewing, *29 Let's Go!*, pp. 228–31.

2D ARMORED DIVISION TANKS CROSS THE ROER INTO JUELICH

destroyed a wrecker, two tractors, and two dump trucks, the engineers spent six hours checking the road by probing. When construction finally began, heavy mortar fire from the Citadel drove off the working crews. Some crew members infiltrated to the bridge from a stadium on the near bank; others were guided by an artillery observation plane that flew overhead, signaling to the men to take cover when the observer saw the muzzle flash of enemy mortars. The mortar fire stopped when the Citadel fell in midafternoon, but when the engineers at last reached the site the swift current made it impossible to stretch anchor cables across the river. Not until 1000 on 24 February were the engineers successful, and it was midafter-

noon before the bridge was open to traffic.[9]

By that time the current downstream had subsided enough to enable the engineers to build bridges for the 115th Infantry. In spite of trouble with plastic mines on the near bank and the hampering effect of heavy smoke, which blinded and sickened the engineers, by daylight they had most of two infantry battalions across the river in assault boats and LVTs. On the east bank minefields held up the infantry for a time, and although one infantry battalion had little trouble in taking and clearing Broich, heavy fire from houses and bunkers on high ground north of Juelich

---

[9] Bridging the Roer.

held the second from its objective until late in the evening. The third infantry battalion, routing its companies through Broich, reached its first-day objective, a hill northeast of the town. There it made contact with the 102d Infantry Division on the left.[10]

Troops of the 102d Division, which the 1141st Engineer Combat Group supported, crossed the Roer downstream at two sites where there had once been bridges (hence paved roads) —one at Roerdorf (nearest Juelich) and another at Linnich. At Roerdorf two companies of the group's 1276th Engineer Combat Battalion were to cross the leading waves of the 405th Infantry in assault boats, then emplace an antimine boom and build a treadway for vehicles. Simultaneously with the assault boat crossings a third engineer company was to build two footbridges upstream from the treadway site. Standing by in case the bridges could not be built or were knocked out were some LVTs manned by members of a tank battalion. As the American artillery barrage began, the engineers carried the assault boats and footbridges to the riverbank, a hazardous operation because German artillery had all roads leading to the river well targeted.

The first wave of assault boats, moving off at H-hour on 23 February, received direct hits from enemy fire on the way over; several boats were riddled by shell fragments and sank. The swift current carried many empty boats downstream during the return trip.

The engineers dragged some back, but other boats were swept over a dam and capsized. By the time the second wave had reached the far bank, so many of the original twenty assault boats had been lost—most hit by enemy fire—that twenty more were called for. German mortar fire knocked out the second twenty along the road to the launching sites, and these, too, had to be replaced. Of the total of sixty boats ultimately committed only two were still usable when ferrying ended about 0700. By then the engineers had managed to ferry across most of two infantry battalions. An hour later several LVTs arrived on the scene, but they were in such poor shape mechanically that they could not be employed.

The engineers had bad luck with the footbridges from the start. The men carrying them down to the river came under heavy artillery and mortar fire and had to scatter. When the engineers were able to begin working they had to battle the current. One footbridge overturned and could not be rebuilt; the other parted in the middle when its cable lines snapped. The engineers repaired the bridge, only to see it collapse again when a tree fell across it; it was not in operation until 1300. In the meantime, divisional engineers had been able to get an infantry support bridge across, and the troops used this span instead of the footbridges. Work on a treadway began at 0930 at a site immediately upstream from the demolished bridge where the river was narrowest. That site was relatively free from artillery fire because the enemy had not expected a crossing there. Nevertheless, the swift current made anchoring and guying difficult, while marshiness on the far bank caused fur-

[10] Ewing, 29 Let's Go!, pp. 223–31; Joseph Binkoski and Arthur Plaut, The 115th Infantry Regiment in World War II (Washington: Infantry Journal Press, 1948), pp. 282–83, 292–93.

ther delay. The bridge was not open for traffic until 2200.[11]

At the Linnich site and just to the south the 1141st Engineer Combat Group's 279th Engineer Combat Battalion was to cross the 102d Division's 407th Infantry. There the same hazards prevailed as at the Roerdorf site—rapid current and enemy fire. One treadway was in place at 1800, but low-flying German aircraft bombed it, wrecking all but one of the floats. All traffic during the night of 23–24 February had to be rerouted over the Roerdorf treadway, which for a time was the only vehicular bridge in the XIII Corps area. This bombing raid demonstrated the importance of placing high priority on getting antiaircraft weapons across the river.[12]

German bombs also fell on the Linnich bridges less than a mile north, where troops of the 84th Infantry Division were crossing the Roer with the support of the 1149th Engineer Combat Group's 171st Engineer Combat Battalion. In this narrowly restricted area plans differed from those the 30th and 102d Divisions followed—instead of two engineer battalions crossing two infantry regiments abreast, one engineer battalion was to cross the infantry regiments in succession.[13] After getting the first wave—a battalion of the 334th Infantry—over in assault boats, the 171st Engineer Combat Battalion was to build at Linnich three footbridges,

an infantry support bridge, and two treadways. Meantime another of the 1149th Group's battalions, the 292d, was to build a Class 70 Bailey bridge at an autobahn crossing about four miles north of Linnich near the town of Koerrenzig.[14]

The 334th Infantry characterized the crossing of its lead battalion as smooth, marred only by a burst of enemy machine-gun fire that killed five men, but attempts to build footbridges for the succeeding battalions were more frustrating here than anywhere else in the entire XIII Corps area. The current immediately tore out the first footbridge, empty assault boats racing downriver from the 102d Division crossings destroyed the second, and enemy mortar fire broke the cables of the third. Not until 1100 did the infantrymen have a footbridge they could use. In the meantime the 171st Engineer Combat Battalion had suffered a number of casualties from enemy fire.

All 84th Division bridging was delayed. The engineers could not complete an infantry support bridge until 1630, and the treadway bridge was not in until much later. At daylight a pocket of enemy troops that the 334th Infantry had bypassed fired on anyone who went down to the river at the treadway site; work could not even begin until the pocket was cleared around noon on 23 February. The engineers then went ahead without interference and had the bridge almost ready to take traffic at 2000 when enemy aircraft flew over, causing casualties and damaging the far side of the bridge. This was, in the words of the 84th Infantry Division

---

[11] Section on 1141st Engineer Combat Group, and Interv with its CO, Col William L. Rogers, 26 Feb. 45, both in Bridging the Roer; Hist 1276th Engr C Bn, Jan–May 45.

[12] Section on 1141st Engineer Combat Group, Bridging the Roer; Simpson, "Rehearsal for the Rhine," p. 26.

[13] Draper, *The 84th Infantry Division in the Battle of Germany,* p. 141; Hist 171st Engr C Bn, Jan–May 45.

[14] Section on 1149th Engineer Combat Group, Bridging the Roer.

FOOTBRIDGE ON THE ROER

historian, "perhaps the most critical moment of the first day," because it meant that no tanks or tank destroyers could get across the river to help the infantry on D-day. Using material intended for the second treadway, the engineers were able to replace the bridge by noon on 24 February. At dusk the same day work started on a heavy ponton bridge at the site originally selected for the second treadway, and the ponton span was operational before dawn of 25 February. Over the heavy ponton and treadway crossed the entire 84th Infantry Division, elements of the 5th Armored and 35th Infantry Divisions, and corps units, including artillery.[15]

The most ambitious effort in the XIII Corps sector was the construction of a Class 70 Bailey bridge across the Roer at the former autobahn crossing north of Linnich near Koerrenzig. Having repaired and strengthened an existing 120-foot trestle bridge over a creek west of the river to accommodate Class 70 loads, the 292d Engineer Combat Battalion began work on 25 February to bridge the 220-foot gap over the Roer. This involved placing a pier seventy feet from the near shore and then closing a 150-foot gap with a triple-triple Bailey and the last 70-foot gap with a triple-single. Open to traffic at 0830 on 26

---

[15] Cpl. Perry S. Wolff, *A History of the 334th Infantry* (Germany, 1945), p. 81; Hist 171st Engr C Bn, Jan–

May 45; Draper, *The 84th Infantry Division in the Battle of Germany*, pp. 151–52; Section on 1149th Engineer Combat Group, Bridging the Roer.

February, this bridge became the main crossing for XIII Corps.[16]

Once on the far bank, XIII Corps' troops made such good progress that General Simpson decided not to hold them back to provide a bridgehead for XVI Corps. Instead, he directed XVI Corps to seize its own bridgehead at Hilfarth, about five miles downstream from Koerrenzig. Spearheading this crossing, the 35th Infantry Division moved out in the evening of 25 February. Next morning some elements of the 134th Infantry were crossing the Roer on two footbridges and an infantry support bridge a short distance downstream from Hilfarth, while others were attacking the town. Many infantrymen were wounded in enemy minefields that the Germans covered with small-arms and machine-gun fire. Clearing the town, the troops found that although the highway bridge there was somewhat damaged, it was still usable; by early afternoon the bridge was carrying XVI Corps tanks across the Roer. During the afternoon corps engineers built two treadway bridges to ease traffic problems.[17]

The Roer crossings had consumed large amounts of bridging equipment and numerous assault boats. This was the price General Simpson had expected to pay for the surprise he achieved by attacking while the river was still swollen, and he considered "one of the essential factors in our success" the quick replacement of boats and bridging materials from engineer parks close to the river.

Initial waves of combat troops had gone across the Roer with small loss of life; the first day's casualties throughout Ninth Army amounted to 92 killed and 913 wounded. In proportion to the number of men involved the casualties among the engineers, who had been forced to go on working at the bridge sites after the Germans recovered from their surprise, were high. The four engineer groups supporting XIX and XIII Corps during the Roer crossings lost 31 men killed and 226 wounded.[18]

### The Ludendorff Bridge

Though Ninth Army planners had proceeded on the assumption that the Germans would destroy all eight of the Rhine bridges in their area, they also made determined efforts to capture at least one usable span intact. On 2 March German-speaking American troops in captured German tanks failed in an attempt; by the fifth no bridge was left standing. Field Marshal Montgomery vetoed a Ninth Army proposal for a quick assault crossing near Wesel while the Germans were still regrouping across the Rhine. On 6 March he set the date for the 21 Army Group crossing at 24 March. Montgomery could not foresee the good fortune that would befall First Army troops moving south of the Ruhr on Ninth Army's right.

First Army made good progress on 6 March, with VII Corps entering Cologne and III Corps, farther south, approaching Bonn near the Ahr River, which flows into the Rhine just upstream of

---

[16] Section on 1149th Engineer Combat Group Bridging the Roer.

[17] Parker and Thompson, *Conquer, The Story of the Ninth Army*, pp. 174, 176; *History of the XVI Corps* (Washington: Infantry Journal Press, 1947), pp. 24–26.

[18] Simpson, "Rehearsal for the Rhine," p. 26; Parker and Thompson, *Conquer, The Story of the Ninth Army*, p. 171. Figures on engineer casualties are in Bridging the Roer and Hist XIX Corps Engrs, p. 18, ML 2220, ETOUSA Hist Sect.

that city. This crossing would block the Ahr River valley, the main escape route of the enemy. Cologne had several bridges, but by the time the city was cleared on the afternoon of 7 March, the Germans had destroyed them all.[19]

In the III Corps zone was an important highway bridge over the Rhine at Bonn. About twelve miles upstream from Bonn lay a railway bridge at Remagen, built during World War I and named for one of the German heroes of that war, General Erich Ludendorff. On the evening of 6 March, Maj. Gen. John Millikin, the III Corps commander, asked the First Army air officer to forbid bombing of the Bonn and Remagen bridges on the very slim chance that both might be captured intact. Neither had figured seriously in III Corps planning, and the Bonn highway bridge had to be eliminated entirely from the corps' plans early on 7 March, when First Army transferred responsibility for Bonn to VII Corps. The III Corps all but discounted the Ludendorff Bridge—it had been under Allied air attack since September 1944, and in late December the air forces claimed four direct hits. During January and early February the bridge strikes had intensified, but the Germans had proved adept in making repairs. In mid-February American air reconnaissance reported that the bridge was back in service. Thereafter a cloud cover had protected the span from attack. It seemed inconceivable that the Germans would not destroy the bridge before it could be captured.[20]

When III Corps' spearhead, the 9th Armored Division, moved east on 7 March, its main effort was directed toward the Ahr River crossings, Combat Command A to cross at Bad Neuenahr and one column of Combat Command B at the point where the Ahr flows into the Rhine, a little more than a mile upstream from Remagen. Another column of Combat Command B, organized as a task force under Lt. Col. Leonard Engeman, commanding the 14th Tank Battalion, was to turn aside and take the towns of Remagen and Kripp, the latter near the Ahr-Rhine confluence. Orders said nothing about capturing a bridge.[21]

Led by a platoon from Company A of the 27th Armored Infantry Battalion, riding on half-tracks, and a platoon of four new T−26 90-mm. tanks from the 14th Tank Battalion, Task Force Engeman left Meckenheim at 0820 on 7 March for Remagen, ten miles away. With it was the 2d platoon of Company B, 9th Armored Engineer Battalion, under 1st Lt. Hugh Mott.

The column moved out in a cold drizzle. The men, having pushed from the Roer toward the Rhine with little rest since 28 February, were groggy from lack of sleep. The engineers were particularly weary. On the march they had built treadway bridges over three rivers, one under heavy German artillery fire. The bridging work was more difficult because the T−26 tanks had wider treads than the M−4 Shermans. The new M2 treadway bridge could accommodate the T−26s but was not satisfactory for other vehicles, notably trucks. The engineers had found a number of bridges standing, but had

[19] Engineer Operations by VII Corps in the European Theater, vol. VII, "Crossings of the Rhine River and the Advance to the Elbe," p. 1, and app. II.

[20] Ken Hechler, *The Bridge at Remagen* (New York: Ballantine Books, 1957), pp. 69−75. Unless otherwise cited, this section is based on this source.

[21] Combat Interv 300, 9th Armd Div, 7−8 Mar 45.

THE LUDENDORFF RAIL BRIDGE AT REMAGEN

to search carefully for explosives and to remove mines and roadblocks along the roads.[22]

After leaving Meckenheim the column made good time, meeting little resistance. At 1300 the leading infantry platoon commander was standing on a bluff at Apollinarisberg, overlooking Remagen and the 700-foot-wide Rhine rushing through a gorge. About a mile upstream the Ludendorff Bridge was still standing and the infantry officers could see it plainly through field glasses. It was a steel-arch bridge a little more than a thousand feet long and wide enough to carry two railroad tracks. Two castle-like stone towers with windows guarded each end. Beyond the towers on the far side the two railroad tracks entered a tunnel cut into a rock cliff. By the morning of 7 March the last train had gone over. One of the tracks on the bridge the Germans had covered with planking; over it streamed a procession of soldiers, trucks, horse-drawn wagons and guns, civilians, and cattle.

Colonel Engeman sent infantrymen down the hill to take Remagen and ordered the leader of the 90-mm. tank platoon "to barrel down the hill and go

---

[22] Hist 9th Armd Engr Bn, 1944–45 and AAR for Mar 45; Memo, for 6th and 12th Army Gps, 15 Mar 45, sub: Widened Bridges for the T–26 Tank, OCE ETOUSA, 823-Bridges, 1944–45. For the development of the widened treadway, see Coll, Keith, and Rosenthal, *The Corps of Engineers: Troops and Equipment*, pp. 490–95.

through and cover the bridge with tank fire, and if anybody attempted to repair or demolish the bridge to liquidate them."[23] The Combat Command B commander, Brig. Gen. William M. Hoge, came forward. Although Hoge had no specific orders to take the bridge, he had an informal understanding with the commanding general of the 9th Armored Division that if the bridge was intact it should be seized. When he arrived on the scene, Hoge had to weigh the chance that the Germans would blow the bridge while Americans were on it or trap part of his forces by letting some units get across before blowing the bridge.

At 1515 a courier arrived from Combat Command B's other column, south of Remagen at Sinzig, with information from a German civilian that the Ludendorff Bridge was to be blown at 1600. The story later proved fictitious, but the prospect of forty-five minutes' grace made up General Hoge's mind. He immediately ordered Colonel Engeman to emplace tanks and machine guns on the Remagen approach to the bridge, to fire smoke and white phosphorus, to bring up engineers to pull firing wires and fuses, and to make a dash across the span.[24]

Engeman's tankers were already at the bridge. His messenger found the young engineer platoon leader, Lieutenant Mott, at a hotel near the river and passed on Hoge's orders to rip out demolitions and to find out whether the bridge would support tanks. Mott

took along two of his sergeants, Eugene Dorland and John A. Reynolds. As they neared the bridge the three were shocked by a tremendous explosion that blew a thirty-foot crater into the Remagen approach. This, for the time being at least, would deny the bridge to any vehicles, including tanks.

Mott and his men jumped down into the crater for protection against a second blast, but when they saw the commander of the 27th Armored Infantry Battalion talking to 1st Lt. Karl Timmerman, commanding the leading infantry company and pointing toward the bridge, the engineers climbed out and went forward to join the infantrymen. Just as they did so there came a second explosion, this time about two-thirds of the way across the bridge. The structure groaned and seemed to raise itself ponderously; timbers flew and a huge cloud of dust and smoke ascended. But when the smoke cleared the men saw that the bridge was still standing. Obviously the few German defenders moving about on the far side had set off only one charge in a vain attempt to drop the span. Mott decided that his main job would be to locate and cut the wires to other charges before the Germans could detonate them. The three engineers ran out on the bridge just as Timmerman and his lead scouts were beginning to cross.

Machine-gun fire came from the far towers and from a barge on the river, but with the help of covering fire from the tanks on the Remagen side the infantrymen made their way cautiously along a catwalk around the hole in the bridge. The engineers searched for demolition charges and wires. Finding four thirty-pound packages of explosives tied to I-beams under the decking,

[23] Interv, Lt Col Leonard Engeman, 14 Mar 45, in The Remagen Bridgehead, Seizure and Expansion, 6–11 Mar 45, 9th Armd Div, ML 888, ETOUSA Hist Sect.

[24] Interv, Gen Hoge, 14 Mar 45, in The Remagen Bridgehead, Seizure and Expansion.

they climbed down and cut the wires, sending the packages splashing into the Rhine.[25] Climbing back onto the bridge, Sergeant Dorland blasted a heavy cable apart with his carbine. The engineers apparently did not locate the wiring fuse that would have set off all the charges—the Germans had enclosed it in a thick pipe laid underneath the tracks to protect it from American shells. As soon as the infantry had cleared the towers on the far side, Dorland found the box that housed the master switch and shot out the heavy wires leading from it. A few minutes later the three engineers came upon a large explosive charge of from 500 to 600 pounds correctly wired and prepared for detonation but with its fuse cap blown.

Fuse damage was one possible solution to the mystery that continued to puzzle historians, American and German, for years: why the main charge that would have dropped the bridge had failed to explode when, at 1530 after Americans were seen approaching from Remagen, the German engineer at the bridge, Capt. Karl Friesenhahn, turned the key to set it off. One explanation for the failure was sabotage, either by a German soldier or a foreign worker, but this theory could not be substantiated and Captain Friesenhahn and the German commandant at the bridge, Capt. Willi Bratge, dismissed it as impossible because the mechanism was carefully guarded at all times. Most German officers and historians believed that the wires were severed by a lucky hit from an American tank gun. Jacob Klebach of Remagen, a sergeant-major working with the German engineers on the bridge that day, offered another

explanation. Interviewed twenty years later, Klebach said, "The truth is that the concussion damage of all the months before just made it a toss-up whether the fuses would function when needed."[26]

Calling up the rest of his platoon to help remove the demolitions, Lieutenant Mott reported to Colonel Engeman that he could have the bridge ready to take tanks in two hours if he could obtain enough timber to repair the damaged planking. While Engeman was trying to find the timber, the armor, at Mott's request, brought up a tank-dozer to fill the crater at the Remagen end of the bridge.[27] Fear of a German counterattack spurred efforts to get tanks across. Lumber for the planking was difficult to locate, but General Hoge rounded up enough, instructing his S-4 and civil affairs officials to "tear down houses in Remagen if necessary."[28]

By 2000 that evening the news of the capture of the Ludendorff Bridge had traveled from combat command through division, corps, army, and army group to General Eisenhower at SHAEF. Maj. Gen. Harold R. Bull, Eisenhower's G-3, could not see the value of the bridge. The terrain on the other side was miserable and, he told General Bradley, "You're not going anywhere down there at Remagen"; nor did the effort fit into plans to cross farther north.[29] But Bull's opinion was the exception. Command-

---

[25] Hechler, *The Bridge at Remagen*, pp. 66–67.

[26] Interv in New York *Times*, "Rhine Crossing: Twenty Years Later," March 21, 1965. Hechler in *The Bridge at Remagen* discusses the probability of sabotage or damage from a tank shell; see pp. 212–20.

[27] Engeman interv in The Remagen Bridgehead, Seizure and Expansion.

[28] Hoge interv in The Remagen Bridgehead, Seizure and Expansion.

[29] John Toland, *The Last 100 Days* (New York: Random House, 1966), pp. 214–15.

ers from Eisenhower down were elated and enthusiastically approved reinforcements. Lt. Gen. Courtney H. Hodges that same evening relieved III Corps of its mission to drive south across the Ahr and approved exploiting the Rhine crossing. General Millikin made plans to motorize the reserve elements of his 9th and 78th Infantry Divisions and rush them to Remagen.

Col. F. Russel Lyons, the III Corps engineer, followed plans First Army had already worked out for a Rhine crossing in its area, based on topographical and terrain studies. Engineers were to erect a treadway bridge downstream from the Ludendorff Bridge and a ponton bridge upstream. While they were being built, ferries were to carry men, supplies, and vehicles to the far bank and bring back the wounded. Nets and booms would have to be emplaced upstream to protect the bridges from underwater attack by small submarines and frogmen carrying explosives. (In September the Germans had used specially trained and equipped swimmers in an attempt to blow up the Nijmegen bridge in the British area.)[30] Since these preparations required resources III Corps did not have, First Army turned over to the corps' operational control the units and equipment needed. Two First Army engineer combat groups that had been supporting the 9th and 78th Infantry Divisions were to be employed, the 1111th to build the treadway and landing sites for three ferries, the 1159th to construct the ponton bridge and operate the ferries, using DUKWs and Navy LCVPs. The 164th Engineer

Combat Battalion was to emplace the nets and booms to protect the Ludendorff Bridge from underwater attack.[31]

While these engineers stood alert during the rainy night of 7 March, 9th Armored Division engineers on the scene were working on the approaches and the planking to get tanks across the bridge. All afternoon infantry had been moving across, walking very fast or running to escape sniper fire, movement which slowed the engineers' work. Although the crater at the approach was filled in by dusk, not until 2200 was Mott able to tell Engeman that the bridge was ready to take tanks. The engineers had laid down white guide tapes to enable the tanks to bypass dangerous places. In the blackness shortly after midnight nine Shermans started across, their passage over the planking "accompanied by an ominous and nerve-wracking creaking." They got across safely, but when a tank destroyer, following them at a slightly faster pace, came to the point at which the Germans had blown their charge, its right tread fell into the hole. For the rest of the night the engineers worked to jack up the tank destroyer, which was blocking the passage of all vehicles, but they were not successful until 0530.[32]

Among the nearly 8,000 men who crossed the bridge in the first twenty-four hours after its capture was the remainder of the 9th Armored Engineer Battalion's Company B. During the early hours of 8 March Company C

---

[30] Brig. Gen. P. H. Timothy, *The Rhine Crossings; Twelfth Army Group Engineer Operations* (Fort Belvoir, Va., 1946), pp. 11, 24.

[31] Intervs, Col F. Russel Lyons, 21 Mar 45, and Lt Col H. F. Cameron, CO, 164th Engr C Bn et al., 26 Mar 45, in The Remagen Bridgehead, Seizure and Expansion; III Corps Hist, 314.7, file 1; Hists, 1111th and 1159th Engr C Gps, Mar 45.

[32] Intervs, Engeman, 14 Mar 45, and Capt George P Soumas, CO, Co A, 14th Tank Bn, 15 Mar 45, both in The Remagen Bridgehead, Seizure and Expansion.

relieved Company B on the bridge. After making an intensive search for German demolitions, which turned up 1,400 pounds in wells of the piers, the men of Company C assumed the job of repair and traffic control just as enemy bombers and artillery began to hit the bridge. The *Luftwaffe* was relatively ineffective, but the artillery did considerable damage. Company C estimated that during the forty-eight hours it worked on the bridge, the Germans scored at least twenty-four direct hits. At times, when panic-stricken drivers abandoned their vehicles, the engineers drove the vehicles off the bridge, and when first-aid men refused to set foot on the bridge the engineers acted as medics.

Late on the afternoon of the ninth, shells from heavy artillery tore a fifteen-foot hole in the decking and set fire to an ammunition truck on the far bank, blocking all traffic. Amid exploding ammunition, an engineer of Company B in an armored bulldozer safely pushed the blazing truck off the road. But when squads of Company C tried to repair the hole in the decking, two officers and nine enlisted men were wounded by a shell exploding in the superstructure near them. Then the engineers spread out in two-man teams, repairing the hole by laying steel treadways over planks. On the morning of the tenth the 276th Engineer Combat Battalion, one of the III Corps units sent to Remagen, relieved Company C. Before leaving, Company C put up a sign: "Cross the Rhine With Dry Feet, Courtesy of the 9th Armored Division."[33]

*The Ferries*

The III Corps' engineer units arrived late because of traffic jams on narrow winding roads, the blackout in which they had to feel their way forward, and enemy shellfire near Remagen. Thus, the 86th Engineer Heavy Ponton Battalion, which was to operate ferries while tactical bridges were being built, did not arrive until around 0330 on 9 March. Under intermittent shelling, the weary men immediately began to construct the first raft at the site selected for the crossing, downstream from the Ludendorff Bridge. The engineers lowered five boats into the water and lay balk and planking over them. Before noon next morning three five-boat rafts had been built, and the approaches at Remagen and at Erpel on the east bank were ready. At 1100 on 9 March in a cold wind and lashing rain, without waiting for a cable to be emplaced, the first ferry chugged across the Rhine, propelled by two outboard motors and two powerboats—a 22-horsepower motor fastened to each of the end engineer boats and a powerboat lashed to the second and fourth. Headed upstream at a 45-degree angle because of the swift current, the ferry took less than eight minutes to reach the far shore.[34]

The Remagen-Erpel ferry, the only one in operation on 9 and 10 March, became a vital factor in support of the bridgehead across the river. At noon on the tenth a gasoline truck on the Ludendorff Bridge had been hit and set afire; all ammunition and gasoline

[33] Hist 9th Armd Engr Bn, 1944–45; Interv, Capt Ellis G. Fee, CO, Co C, 9th Armd Engr Bn, 14 Mar 45, in The Remagen Bridgehead, Seizure and Expansion.

[34] Interv, Lt Col Robert O. Hass, CO, 86th Engr Heavy Ponton Bn, 25 Mar 45, in The Remagen Bridgehead, Seizure and Expansion.

convoys were ordered ferried across for two days. The second ferry was constructed upstream of the Ludendorff Bridge, from Kripp to Linz, but enemy opposition near Linz caused delays and the ferry did not begin operation until late on the afternoon of 11 March. Work on the third ferry (downstream of the treadway), from Unkelbach to Unkel, was so slowed by very accurate (probably observed) artillery fire that it could not be finished in time to be of much use. By noon on 12 March the treadway and ponton bridges had been completed. Then the need for the rafts diminished, although that day and the next the ferries made a further important contribution to the far shore bridgehead when they crossed four heavy Pershing tanks to Erpel and thirty-one Shermans to Linz.[35]

From the beginning, plans for a Rhine crossing had included LCM, LCVP, and DUKW ferry operations (the DUKWs to carry ammunition, gasoline, and rations). Early during the Remagen operation the Transportation Corps' 819th Amphibian Truck Company, which had distinguished itself at OMAHA on D-day, came forward and was attached to the 1159th Engineer Combat Group. The company's DUKWs were late getting into operation because it was hard to find a suitable site to launch the trucks. Then, when they began ferrying at a site near Kripp, the DUKWs had to travel some twelve miles to the rear to pick up their loads because First Army disapproved of setting up dumps for them closer to the river. Men on the scene generally believed that a river crossing under conditions like those at

Remagen, involving a long land haul and short water haul, was uneconomical for DUKWs.[36]

No LCMs came forward because First Army considered that capture of the bridge rendered them unnecessary, but LCVPs were needed to ferry troops and evacuate the wounded. The LCVPs arrived in the Remagen area at midnight on 10 March, sent forward in flatbed trailers together with cranes for launching them. They proved highly useful—each craft could ferry thirty-six soldiers faster and more efficiently than the troops could march across a footbridge. This speed was demonstrated on 15 March, when four LCVPs transported a regimental combat team of VII Corps' 1st Division across the Rhine at a site not far downstream from the Ludendorff Bridge and leading to Unkel on the far shore. A round trip required not more than seven minutes, enabling the LCVPs to put ashore 2,200 infantrymen in three hours. The immediate job of the first boats that arrived, however, was to aid in the construction of the heavy ponton bridge.[37]

*The Treadway and Ponton Bridges*

On 9 March under cold, rainy, and overcast skies, two engineer units that had distinguished themselves during

---

[35] Ibid.; Folder, Crossing the Rhine Operation "Varsity," OCE files.

[36] Diary, III Corps Engr, 25 Mar 45, and Interv, Capt John C. Bray, CO, 819th Amphib Truck Co, 25 Mar 45, both in The Remagen Bridgehead, Seizure and Expansion.

[37] On LCMs, see Ltr, Cmdr, TG, 122.5 to CinC, U.S. Fleet, 16 Apr 45, sub: Operations Rpt, copy in OCE files; Opns Rpt, LCVP Unit No. 1, 12th Army Gp Naval Opns Rpt, copy in OCE files. The Navy's LCVP Unit No. 1, with twenty-four boats, was assigned to First Army. Sixteen boats were in the first contingent arriving at Remagen; the remaining eight came up later.

the Battle of the Ardennes in the Mal-medy−Trois Ponts area began arriving at Remagen, the 291st Engineer Combat Battalion under Lt. Col. David E. Pergrin to work on a treadway bridge from Remagen to Erpel and the 51st Engineer Combat Battalion under Lt. Col. Harvey R. Fraser to build a heavy ponton bridge upstream, from Kripp to Linz. Arriving before dawn, the 291st had to wait until 0830 for the 998th Treadway Bridge Company to bring up bridging equipment. This company, the only unit available, had been working with First French Army. By 1030 Colonel Pergrin had a platoon clearing the approach on the near bank.

The men had just started to cut away the bank when an enemy artillery shell hit the site, injuring seven. There were no more direct hits that day, and by dusk the engineers had extended the treadway 200 feet, with good prospects of reaching the far shore next morning. Then, shortly after midnight, German tanks on high ground at the east end of the bridge began to rake the bridging with direct fire. They knocked out two cranes and twenty-six rafts assembled with treadway and caused a five-hour delay. Work resumed although enemy shelling continued, intensifying just after noon on 10 March, when the treadway began receiving a round of heavy artillery every five minutes. At 1230 a direct hit at the west end damaged fifteen rafts. The treadway held them in place, enabling the engineers to finish the bridge. Reaching the far shore at 1710 the engineers could claim to have built the first tactical bridge over the Rhine and, at 1,032 feet, the longest yet constructed in Europe. But repairs to the rafts delayed the opening of the bridge to traffic until 0700 on 11

March. That morning the 988th Engineer Treadway Bridge Company replaced the 998th, which had run out of equipment. The building of the treadway bridge had been costly, with one man killed and twenty-four wounded during construction.

By the time the bridge was finished, German artillery fire was letting up. A German artillery observer with a radio had been captured in Remagen, a heavy concentration of U.S. artillery had laid down a smoke screen, and the advance of the combat forces on the far shore was pushing the German guns back. During its first two days of operation, the eastbound traffic count for the treadway was 3,105 vehicles. At noon on 13 March the bridge began carrying a heavy volume of westbound traffic as eastbound traffic transferred to the ponton bridge located upstream.[38]

Building the heavy ponton bridge from Kripp to Linz had to be postponed until the enemy was cleared from a high hill across the river. When the order to begin construction came at 1600 on 10 March, the executive officer of the 51st Engineer Combat Battalion, Maj. Robert B. Yates (who had distinguished himself at Trois Ponts during the Bulge), had everything ready, including six smoke pots on a 3/4-ton truck. Despite the smoke screen, six rounds of heavy artillery, variously described as 170-mm. and 88-mm., immediately hit the near shore and bridge site, but did no damage. The equipment for the bridge, which the

[38] Interv, Lt Col David E. Pergrin, 22 Mar 45, and Col F. Russel Lyons, 21 Mar 45, and Diary, III Corps Engr, all in The Remagen Bridgehead, Seizure and Expansion; Hists, 291st Engr C Bn, Jan−Apr 45, May 45, and 111th Engr C Gp, Mar 45.

HEAVY AND PNEUMATIC PONTONS LOADED FOR TRANSPORT TO REMAGEN

181st and 552d Heavy Ponton Battalions provided, consisted of fourteen four-boat rafts and seventy-five feet of trestle, reinforced by pneumatic rubber floats between each raft. The 51st used a total of sixty boats and fifty-seven rubber floats. Next day, 11 March, with the current at the site swift and the river rising, the engineers had such trouble maneuvering the parts into position with powerboats that they called for LCVPs. Slipping crossways in the current, one of the LCVPs on the upstream side rammed into a section of the bridge and might have swept it into the treadway if three LCVPs downstream had not held the section in place until the engineers could safely anchor it to a barge on the far shore.

While this work was going on, German planes came over, bombing and strafing in pairs. At the far shore abutment three men were killed, two were seriously wounded, and several suffered light wounds from bomb fragments. An hour before midnight on 11 March the bridge was open for traffic and next day was reinforced to carry 24-ton loads, but possibly because it was easy to spot from the air, the ponton bridge continued to come under attack from German bombers and strafers. On 13 March five waves flew over; one in midafternoon killed Maj. William F. Tompkins, Jr., commanding officer of the 552d Heavy Ponton Battalion, for whom the bridge was named. When the weather cleared on 14 March the Germans stepped up air attacks. A river barge on the far shore near the anchor barge received a direct hit from a 500-pound bomb that killed two of its engineer guards; on the bridge itself five men were wounded by shell and bomb fragments. This marked the end of the low-level, daylight attempts to destroy the Remagen bridges from the air. With clearing weather American fighters could rise to meet the enemy, and by 14 March a heavy concentration of American antiaircraft guns on both banks of the river rendered daylight attacks too costly to the dwindling *Luftwaffe*.[39]

### Collapse of the Ludendorff Bridge

On 12 March, after the treadway and ponton bridges were in operation, the engineers closed the Ludendorff Bridge for repairs. The fixed span was considered worth repairing because artillery could not knock it out as readily as the tactical bridges—an ordinary shell would not damage its structure but only rip the flooring. Moreover, the tactical bridges could not as easily carry heavy loads such as the new Pershing tanks.[40]

The Germans had certainly tried to knock out the Ludendorff. On the night of 10 March, just as the 276th Engineer Combat Battalion had begun construction of a 140-foot double-double Bailey at the near shore to make possible two-way traffic, a direct enemy artillery hit killed Maj. James E. Foley, the battalion executive officer, and wounded nineteen men. On the days following, enemy shells continued to fall as the 276th worked on the approaches, completing them under cover of darkness on 12 March. A team from the 1058th Port Construction and Repair Group undertook the heavy steel work on the bridge.[41]

In the meantime, preparations were under way to protect the bridge from waterborne or underwater attack. Five hundred yards upstream the engineers were to string a net across the river to catch floating mines, boats loaded with explosives, torpedoes launched from one-man submarines, and frogmen. The next barrier to be emplaced was an impact boom 600 yards from the bridge, the third a log boom at 900 yards. Responsibility for installing these devices went to the 164th Engineer Combat Battalion, a First Army unit that reported directly to the corps engineer. The 164th arrived on the evening of 8 March and started work next morning, but it soon became evident that the construction site, on the far shore at the river's edge, was in the direct line of enemy artillery fire. That afternoon enemy shells killed three men and wounded two, and on the afternoon of 10 March four men were killed when German artillery hit a truck; three others were wounded. The intensity of enemy artillery fire as well as the lack of powerboats delayed the placement of floats. Nevertheless, at 2200

[39] Intervs, Lt Col Harvey R. Fraser and Maj Robert Yates, 20 Mar 45, Col F. Russel Lyons, 21 Mar 45, and Diary, III Corps Engr, all in The Remagen Bridgehead, Seizure and Expansion; Hists, 51st Engr C Bn, Jan–Jun 45; 1159th Engr C Gp, Mar 45 and 26 Jun 44–20 Aug 45; Opns Rpt, LCVP Unit No. 1.

[40] Interv, Gen Hoge, 14 Mar 45, in The Remagen Bridgehead, Seizure and Expansion.

[41] Hist 1159th Engr C Bn, Mar 45 and 26 Jun 44–20 Aug 45; Intervs, Lt Col Kenneth E. Fields, CO, and Maj Francis E. Goodwin, S–4, 1159th Engr C Gp, 21 Mar 45, in The Remagen Bridgehead, Seizure and Expansion; Jnl, 276th Engr C Bn, Feb, Mar, Apr, May 45.

on 11 March the impact boom's anchorage of angle iron and railroad bumpers was in place, as were four sections of the boom.

Then orders came to protect the heavy ponton bridge newly installed at Kripp. Work at the new site began next day, 12 March, but was hampered by nightly air raids, which two days later killed three and wounded two engineers. The difficulty of towing over water the heavy material required to erect and anchor the protective booms also slowed progress, for powerboats and LCVPs—both of which had been adequate in constructing floating bridges—had insufficient power. The most satisfactory work boats were 38-foot Army tugboats known as Sea Mules. With a detachment of the 329th Harbor Craft Company (TC) to operate them, the tugs came forward on flatbed trailers on the evening of 14 March.[42]

For further protection against waterborne attacks, guards with rifles stood on the Ludendorff Bridge with orders to shoot at suspicious objects. Tanks of the 738th Tank Battalion with brilliant searchlights called canal defense lights took positions on the banks to illuminate the river, the first use of such tanks during the war. Three LCVPs were launched upstream of the antimine boom at noon on 14 March. They patrolled the river every night, dropping fifty-pound depth charges at five-minute intervals, with good effect. Two German swimmers found lying exhausted on the far bank a few days later said they had been stunned by the

depth charges, as well as numbed by the cold water.[43]

On 16 March the Germans began their strongest effort yet to bring down the Ludendorff Bridge. That morning shells larger than 88-mm. came over, and on 17 March several rounds of giant projectiles from a tank-mounted piece called the Karl howitzer landed in Remagen. On the same morning a German rocket unit in the Netherlands fired eleven V–2s at the bridge—the only tactical use of V-weapons during the war. About 1220 one rocket hit a building in Remagen serving as command post for Company B of the 284th Engineer Combat Battalion (a unit the 1159th Engineer Combat Group had brought up for road work west of the Rhine), killing three men and seriously injuring thirty-one, among them the company commander.[44] Another rocket hit a house east of the bridge, killing three American soldiers and wounding fifteen. The rest of the rockets landed harmlessly in the river or open country.[45]

Soon the rocket barrage and the shelling ended. All was quiet on the clear, windless spring day. Capt. Francis E. Goodwin, S–4 of the 1159th Engineer Combat Group, walked out onto the bridge from the Remagen side around 1400 and found the engineers of the 276th Engineer Combat Battalion and

---

[42] First U.S. Army Report of Rhine River Crossing, pp. 28, 31–32, 44; Diary, III Corps Engr, in The Remagen Bridgehead, Seizure and Expansion.

[43] Hist 164th Engr C Bn, 5 May 43–2 Sep 45; Opns Rpt, LCVP Unit No. 1, p. 5; Diary, III Corps Engr, and Interv, Lt Col H. F. Cameron, CO, 164th Engr C Bn et al., p. 5, in The Remagen Bridgehead, Seizure and Expansion.

[44] Hists, 284th Engr C Bn, Feb, Mar–May 45, and 1159th Engr C Gp, 26 Jun–20 Aug 45 and Mar 45.

[45] MacDonald, The Last Offensive, p. 228, quoting SHAEF Air Defense Div, Summary of Casualties and Damage from V-Weapon Attack, Rpt for the Week Ending 19 Mar 45.

the 1058th Engineer Port Construction and Repair Group making good progress.[46] The 276th was finishing the deck repair. The Germans had placed decking only on the upstream half of the bridge; the engineers were decking the downstream half, as well as repairing damage from the enemy shells that had fallen almost every day.[47] The new flooring was complete except for a gap at the Remagen approach and another where the Germans had attempted to blow the bridge. Goodwin passed a squad loading pieces of lumber on a truck. At the point where the Germans had tried to blow the bridge he found Maj. William S. Carr and the 1058th Port Construction and Repair Group with a crane and steel cable. They were preparing to repair the most critical spot, the bottom chord on the upstream arch truss, which the German demolition charge of 7 March had broken. Carr said he expected to have the repairs completed next day. Captain Goodwin crossed to the east bank of the Rhine. It was then about 1445.

A few minutes before 1500 Lt. Col. Clayton A. Rust, commanding the 276th Engineer Combat Battalion, was walking over the bridge on his way to inspect the new approach on the far side, accompanied by his executive officer. When he was about halfway across, he heard a sharp crack like the report of a rifle. It was a rivethead shearing. He saw a vertical hanger ahead of him breaking loose and then heard another sharp report behind him. The whole deck trembled, dust rose, and he knew the bridge was collapsing. Turning around, he ran toward Remagen as fast as he could, but found himself running uphill because the far side of the bridge was falling. The next moment he was in the water.

At 1500 Captain Goodwin was riding a motorcycle around the east abutment of the bridge on his way to cross back over the treadway, when a sound he could not identify made him look up. To his horror he saw that the arch of the Ludendorff Bridge had crumbled. The east abutment was falling. The assistant S–3 of the 1058th Port Construction Repair Group, 1st Lt. F. E. Csendes, was in the tunnel on the far side, where he had gone with a sergeant to pick up some clamps, when he heard someone yell. He looked out and saw the center span of the bridge twisting counterclockwise and buckling; then it fell into the river and the adjacent spans with it.

Captain Goodwin raced his motorcycle over the treadway and told the men on the west bank to pick up the survivors and protect the treadway from heavy bridge iron and timbers that might float downstream. From Remagen he sent ambulances to the scene, then continued to the forward command post of the 1159th Engineer Combat Group at Kripp, arriving there at 1512. After instructing the sergeant in charge to round up all the medical aid available, he rode back across the ponton bridge to the east bank and sent

---

[46] Goodwin statement in Summary of Statements of Witnesses, Incl 2 to Lt Col K. E. Fields, CO, 1159th Engr C Gp, Report on the Collapse of the Ludendorf [sic] Bridge, 19 Mar 45, in Hist 1159th Engr C Gp, Mar 45.

[47] Waldo G. Bowman, *American Military Engineering in Europe from Normandy to the Rhine* (New York: MacGraw-Hill, 1945), p. 83. Bowman, editor of *Engineering News-Record*, inspected the bridge on 16 March 1945. Also see Jnl, 276th Engr C Bn, Mar 45, entries for 151755 and 161830.

WRECKAGE OF THE LUDENDORFF BRIDGE AFTER ITS COLLAPSE

powerboats downstream for rescue work.[48]

Colonel Rust and his companion were pulled out of the river at the treadway bridge, both shaken but not badly hurt. Few of the men working on the bridge at the time were as lucky. Six members of the 276th Engineer Battalion were killed in the collapse of the bridge, 11 were missing (presumably drowned), and 60 were injured, 3 so severely that they died. The commander of the 1058th Port Construction and Repair Group, Major Carr, was killed; seven of his men were missing and six injured.[49]

The main reason for the collapse of the Ludendorff Bridge, most engineers believed, was the break in the bottom chord of the upstream truss from the German demolition charge of 7 March. This forced the downstream truss to carry the whole load and subjected the entire bridge to a twisting action. The strain on the truss was increased by the weight of the timber decking American engineers had added to the flooring, by continuous bridge traffic between 7 and 12 March, and by engineer repairs between 12 and 17 March—ham-

---

[48] Statements of Goodwin, Rust, and others, in Summary of Statements of Witnesses, Incl 2 to Fields' Report on the Collapse of the Ludendorf [sic] Bridge; Operations and Reconnaissance Journal, Forward CP Vic Kripp; both in Hist 1159th Engr C Gp, Mar 45.

[49] Fields Rpt and Rust statement in Hist 1159th Engr C Gp, Mar 45.

mering, welding, and moving heavy cranes and trucks.

The immediate cause of the collapse was thought to be vibration from artillery fire. The enemy fired very heavy artillery shells beginning on 15 March and culminating on 17 March with the Karl howitzer and the $V-2$ rockets. Some of the shells actually hit the bridge. Perhaps even more damaging vibration came from American artillery fire. Only 2,000 yards from the bridge an 8-inch howitzer battalion had fired more than a thousand rounds in the previous five days, and just before the bridge fell a battalion of giant 8-inch guns and another of 240-mm. howitzers were firing constantly.[50]

### The III Corps Bailey Bridge

At 1800 on 17 March, only three hours after the collapse of the Ludendorff Bridge, the commanding officer of the 148th Engineer Combat Battalion, Lt. Col. William J. Irby, received orders from First Army to build a Class 40 floating Bailey bridge at Remagen. The floating Bailey was regarded as a "semitactical" bridge, normally used to replace treadway bridges and requiring considerably more time to construct than either treadways or pontons. The battalion was one of three operating a Bailey bridge park at Weilerswist about ten miles west of Bonn, under the 1110th Engineer Combat Group, First Army's Bailey bridge and mine boom experts.

Colonel Irby lost no time. Ordering his men to begin loading the bridging equipment on about one hundred trucks, most of them borrowed from quartermaster units, he sent two of his officers to reconnoiter for a site and instructed his company commanders to move their men to the Remagen area and to meet him at this advance command post at Remagen at 0200 on 18 March. Then he hurried to group headquarters, where he was told that he would have the help of Company C, 291st Engineer Combat Battalion, and sixty men of the 501st Light Ponton Company.

Irby had not expected orders to build a Bailey bridge over the Rhine so soon, and his planning had focused on a 25 March target date. Nevertheless his men were ready, having practiced on the Meuse near Liege for months. Most important, the equipment was ready, neatly laid out along the roadnet at Weilerswist in the order in which it would be used, landing bay equipment in one stack, floating Baileys in another.

Work began at 0730 on 18 March at the site where the heavy ponton ferry had operated from Remagen to Erpel (downstream from the treadway bridge). While the company from the 291st Engineer Combat Battalion prepared approach roads to connect with the existing roadnet, the 148th Battalion built the bridge. Here, as with the treadway and ponton bridges, the swift river current made it difficult to tow components into position. Repaired civilian Rhine tugboats were too slow and clumsy, but three U.S. Navy LCVPs proved excellent. The rushing waters of the Rhine also complicated anchorage, but the engineers solved this problem by dropping five 1,500-pound an-

[50] Ibid.; Interv, Col V. F. Burger, XO, III Corps, FDC et al., 10 Mar 45, in The Remagen Bridgehead, Seizure and Expansion; Bowman, *American Military Engineering in Europe from Normandy to the Rhine* (quoting Capt. James B. Cooke, structural expert in the OCE ETOUSA), pp. 84–87.

chors upstream and sinking two rock-filled barges to which cables were attached.

Artillery fire occasionally landed near the bridge but did no damage. Men worked around the clock; the coxswain of one of the LCVPs, for example, remained at the wheel for twenty-nine hours without a halt. By 0715 on 20 March the 1,258-foot floating Bailey was ready to take traffic—twenty-four hours earlier than First Army had expected.[51]

*VII Corps, First Army, and V Corps Crossings*

By 16 March VII Corps' 1st and 78th Infantry Divisions (the latter transferred from III Corps on 16 March) had crossed the Rhine on the III Corps' bridges and ferries at Remagen and were driving north and northeast to seize the line of the Sieg River, which entered the Rhine from the east near Bonn. The time had come to build tactical bridges in the VII Corps area, and equipment was available for two steel treadways and one heavy ponton.

During site selection the roadnet on the opposite bank was an important consideration but not the only one. The best of four good roads leading to the Cologne-Frankfurt autobahn lay opposite Bonn, but sites there had to await the clearing of the area by the 78th Division, headed north along the Rhine. Therefore, the first tactical bridges were to be constructed in the southern part of VII Corps' zone. Not far downstream from the site of III Corps' float-

ing Bailey, the 1120th Engineer Combat Group was to build an M2 steel treadway at Rolandseck, and about five miles farther downstream at Koenigswinter the same group was to build a heavy ponton bridge. At the southern fringe of Bonn the 1106th Engineer Combat Group was to construct an M2 treadway. Corps engineer units were to build bridges and operate ferries, using heavy ponton rafts and all LCVPs not required as powerboats or guard boats.[52]

Special security precautions were taken as a result of the enemy harassment that bridge builders in the Remagen area had suffered. To cover both banks at each site the 80th Chemical Smoke Generating Company provided smoke, thickened as necessary by boat-mounted smoke generators. First Army engineers built protective booms, and two Navy LCVPs patrolled the river during darkness. At each site, corps artillery furnished a battery of 155-mm. howitzers, two forward observers, and an artillery liaison plane. Corps antiaircraft artillery, in addition to providing 90-mm. antiaircraft protection, turned searchlights on clouds to provide artificial moonlight at night.

In building the bridge at Rolandseck, the 297th Engineer Combat Battalion had the help of a company from the 294th Engineer Combat Battalion and two treadway bridge companies, the 988th and 990th. Work on the west bank began at 1930 on 16 March at a spot where a civilian ferry had operated. During the night the battalion S-3,

---

[51] Interv, Lt Col William J. Irby, 23 Mar 45, in The Remagen Bridgehead, Seizure and Expansion; Rpt of Rhine River Crossings, First U.S. Army, pp. 14–16; Timothy, *The Rhine Crossing*, p. 10; Hist 148th Engr C Bn, Jan–Apr 45; Opns Rpt, LCVP Unit No. 1, p. 7.

[52] Rpt of Rhine River Crossings, First U.S. Army, pp. 16–20; Engr Opns VII Corps, vol. VII, "Crossings of the Rhine River and the Advance to the Elbe," pp. 1–6, and app. 8, Engr FO 6, 16 Mar 45. Unless otherwise cited this section is based on these two sources.

Maj. Matthew J. Sweeney, was wounded by artillery fire and had to be evacuated. On the east bank heavy traffic and the slow pace of blackout driving delayed the arrival of bridge equipment, and construction did not start until 0745 on 17 March. That afternoon floating debris from the Ludendorff Bridge halted work at Rolandseck for more than an hour. All these factors slowed construction time to 23 1/2 hours.[53]

Work on the ponton bridge at Koenigswinter, which the 294th Engineer Combat Battalion built with the help of the 181st, 86th, and 552d Engineer Heavy Ponton Battalions, began at 2210 on 18 March and was completed in less than seventeen hours. The treadway at Bonn, which the 237th Engineer Combat Battalion built with the help of a company each from the 238th Engineer Combat Battalion, the 23d Armored Engineer Battalion, and the 990th Engineer Treadway Bridge Company, went even more rapidly. At 1,340 feet the longest bridge yet built across the Rhine, it was completed in record time. For one thing, construction started in daylight. Also, the men of the 237th had a powerful incentive. The VII Corps commander, Maj. Gen. J. Lawton Collins, who urgently needed the bridge near Bonn, offered to buy beer for every man working on it if the total construction time did not exceed ten hours. Work began at 0615 on 21 March and the first vehicle crossed at 1625—ten hours and ten minutes later. That was good enough for General Collins. The following day he hosted a party in a hall at Bonn to celebrate with

the engineers the completion of the "Beer Bridge."[54]

The VII Corps operated three heavy ponton ferries, one upstream of the Rolandseck bridge, another downstream of the Koenigswinter bridge, and a third at Bonn. These ferries carried not only vehicles that convoy jams at the bridges had delayed but also Pershing tanks, each ferried on a Navy LCVP-propelled, six-ponton raft. First Army had long planned for at least a semi-fixed bridge that could accommodate heavy tanks. Accordingly, on 25 March the engineers began work at Bad Godesberg, about five miles upstream from Bonn, on a bridge designed for two-way Class 40 or one-way Class 70 traffic. Vehicles began crossing this bridge on 5 April.[55]

At a conference with First and Third Army commanders at Luxembourg on 19 March, General Omar N. Bradley told General Hodges, First Army commander, to be prepared by 23 March to break out of his bridgehead, drive southeast, and link up with Third Army in the Lahn River valley. The objective was a corridor running from Frankfurt (across the Rhine from Mainz, about 100 miles upstream from Remagen) to Kassel, about 160 miles to the northeast. Patton was told to "take the Rhine on the run."[56]

Hodges ordered his V Corps, the southernmost unit which shared a boundary with Third Army, to cross the Rhine. Early on 21 March the corps commander, Maj. Gen. Clarence R. Huebner, sent elements of his 2d and

[53] App. 1, Summary of Data on Rhine Bridges, in Engr Opns VII Corps, vol. VII, "Crossings of the Rhine River and the Advance to the Elbe."

[54] Hist 1106th Engr C Gp, Jan–May 45, and fig. 16, Engr Opns VII Corps, vol. VII, "Crossings of the Rhine River and the Advance to the Elbe."
[55] Timothy, *The Rhine Crossing*, p. 33.
[56] Bradley, *A Soldier's Story*, p. 519.

69th Infantry Divisions across the river on III Corps bridges and ferries. By the evening of 22 March, V Corps had a bridge of its own. Using the only bridge equipment available, the corps engineers constructed a Class 40 M2 steel treadway about ten miles upstream from the III Corps bridges. Victor Bridge was 1,372 feet long, designated "the longest tactical bridge in the world" by the men of the 254th Engineer Combat Battalion, who built it with the help of the 994th and 998th Engineer Treadway Bridge Companies and, as the sign beside the bridge proclaimed, "U.S. Navy"—a detachment from the Navy's LCVP Unit No. 1.

Work began on both banks at 0800 on 22 March. The engineers used no smoke screen, nor was artillery support deemed necessary. The principal protective effort was directed against water attack, to which, farthest upstream, the Victor Bridge was especially vulnerable. Infantry and cavalry patrolled the banks; the engineers emplaced three protective booms, using a locally procured steam tug; and at night tanks threw the beams of their canal defense lights over the rushing waters to seek out enemy swimmers and floating mines. Though the booms were not ready immediately, the bridge was finished in twelve hours and was opened to traffic at 2000 on 22 March. The V Corps used the bridge entirely for vehicles and crossed the infantry in LCVPs.[57]

In the meantime, far to the north and south of the V Corps crossing site, the Ninth, Third, and Seventh Armies were in position for their own assault crossings of the Rhine.

_____

[57] *V Corps Operations in ETO*, pp. 404, 406, in CMH.

CHAPTER XXIII

# The Assault Crossings of the Rhine

The Remagen bridgehead had made headlines as a spectacular and fortuitous jump across the last major water barrier in the western Reich. Once formed, though, it received only sparse sustenance from SHAEF. General Eisenhower still focused upon the larger preparations of 21 Army Group and Ninth Army north of Remagen to cross the Rhine in an area where terrain favored mutually supporting offensives into the heartland of Germany. Much to the disgust of Lt. Gen. Courtney H. Hodges, First Army commander, the supreme commander kept the nine divisions in the bridgehead on a short leash, tying down weak German forces in the area while the Ninth, Third, and Seventh Armies to the north and south crossed the Rhine.

### Ninth Army at Rheinberg

Ninth Army was ready. On 19 February, even before the Roer operation, General Simpson had delegated to Maj. Gen. John B. Anderson, commanding the XVI Corps, the job of planning a Rhine crossing at Rheinberg, some fifteen miles south of Wesel, under the code name FLASHPOINT. Though the operation did not begin as early as General Simpson had hoped, the plans governed Ninth Army's move across the river in late March. Col. John W. Wheeler,

the XVI Corps engineer, had already staged a general planning session on 12 February with the commanders and staffs of the two corps engineer combat groups, the 1153d and the 1148th. The engineers discovered that they had on hand only 150 storm boats, plywood craft powered by a 55-horsepower motor with a combat load of seven prone infantrymen. Most of the assault force would thus have to move in slower, fifteen-man single assault boats, either paddled across or propelled by 22-horsepower outboard motors. Of the 500 single assault craft rounded up, exactly half had motors. The engineers planned to ferry tanks on rafts of floating Bailey bridge sections. To guarantee the rapid transfer of heavier weapons, vehicles, and supply, they availed themselves of the services of Naval Landing Unit No. 3, which furnished twenty-four LCVPs and twenty-four LCMs. Another hundred LVTs were available to handle special missions, especially to transfer entire beach parties to the far shore. To exploit the assault, the engineer groups would have ready on the west bank one heavy ponton bridge set and three floating treadways; twelve Sea Mule tugs would help emplace the bridge components. To counteract German air attacks, the army command attached to the engineers an automatic antiaircraft weapons battalion for the operation.[1]

Training for the operation continued until 10 March at two centers on the Meuse River in the Netherlands, where conditions approximated those at the Rhine crossing site. Col. David C. Wallace, commanding the 1153d Engineer Combat Group, established his school at Echt, about twenty miles south of Liege. Col. Ellsworth I. Davis of the 1148th Engineer Combat Group set up a second training site at Sittard, farther south. The group engineers trained with the troops of two relatively fresh infantry divisions they would support in the assault, the 30th and the 79th Divisions. As part of XIX Corps, the 30th had crossed the Roer against only light resistance and the 79th against none at all. Neither engineer group had any assault experience, though several of the engineer officers had seen action. The commanding officer of the 1104th Engineer Combat Group took up a temporary assignment under the more experienced Col. John W. Wheeler, the XVI Corps engineer. Wheeler also temporarily assumed direct control of the intelligence sections of the two engineer groups in the assault. They remained in positions from which they could constantly reconnoiter the river at Lintfort, six miles southwest of Rheinberg, throughout the period before the attack.[2]

Colonel Wallace assembled the river-crossing equipment and operators in the training area and organized his 1153d Group into eight task forces. Task Force Assault, consisting of the 258th Engineer Combat Battalion reinforced by 200 powerboat operators from the 1153d and Ninth Army, was to furnish and operate all storm and double assault boats for the initial crossings. Task Force Heavy Boats, the 202d Engineer Combat Battalion reinforced by U.S. Navy Task Unit 122.5.3, was in charge of the LCMs, LCVPs, Sea Mules, and rafts to be used in ferrying operations. Task Force Roads, the 280th Engineer Combat Battalion, was to do road work up to the Rhine. The remaining five were Task Forces M2 Treadway, Heavy Ponton Bridge, Boom (to construct debris and antimine booms), M1 Treadway, and LVT.

Colonel Davis of the 1148th Engineer Combat Group organized his engineer troops differently. His 149th Engineer Combat Battalion was to support one infantry regiment of the 79th Division, controlling and operating assault and storm boats and all types of ferrying equipment. The 187th Engineer Combat Battalion was to provide the same support to the other assault infantry regiment. The 1276th Engineer Combat Battalion was to support the two engineer battalions by launching Bailey rafts, Sea Mules, LCMs, and LCVPs, erecting an M2 treadway bridge, and installing mine booms.

One of the most difficult problems was moving the large, cumbersome boats to be used in the ferrying operation over the roads from Echt to the Rhine, especially the LCMs and Sea Mules, which had to be carried on tank transporters. The 202d Engineer Combat Battalion, responsible for moving forward all the heavy equipment of

---

[1] Hist 1153d Engr C Gp, Mar–May 45; Hist 1148th Engr C Gp, Mar 45; Timothy, *The Rhine Crossing*, pp. 7–8; Hewitt, *Work Horse of the Western Front*, p. 235.

[2] *Conquer, The Story of the Ninth Army*, pp. 190–91; Hewitt, *Work Horse of the Western Front*, pp. 231–33; Combat Engineers' Rhine-Ruhr-Elbe Operation, 24 Mar–1 May 45, CI 372, ETOUSA Hist Sect; Hist XIX Corps Engrs, p. 19, ML 2220, ETOUSA Hist Sect; Hists, 1153d Engr C Gp, Mar– May 45, and 1148th Engr C Gp, Mar 45.

both groups, sent a demolition crew and a bulldozer along the eighty-mile route from Echt to Lintfort, the initial assembly area, to widen roads and remove obstacles.[3] At Lintfort, all XVI Corps' assault craft and bridging materials were to be stored in the large railroad yard of a coal mine. The engineers made elaborate preparations to camouflage the equipment with garnished fish nets, chicken wire, and cotton duck blackened with coal dust. At the same time, XIII Corps engineers constructed a dummy depot near Krefeld as part of Operation EXPLOIT, an elaborate scheme designed to trick the Germans into expecting a crossing at Uerdingen, some fifteen miles south of Rheinberg.[4]

By 20 March both engineer combat groups, having completed a week of training along the Maas, were moving the river-crossing equipment forward to Lintfort. From there to the crossing sites at Rheinberg the two groups had exclusive use of one road, over which the LCMs, LCVPs, DUKWs, and Sea Mules moved at night to conceal them from the Germans.[5] By nightfall on 23 March the engineers had reconnoitered their crossing areas, paying particular attention to unloading sites for the heavy craft. The bridging equipment, loaded on vehicles at Lintfort, was ready to go forward as soon as the engineers had breached a twelve- to fifteen-foot winter dike along the riverbank. Camouflaged assault and storm boats were in place behind the dike, their motors warmed for the early morning start by

chemical heating pads borrowed from hospital units.[6]

The 1153d Engineer Combat Group had made thorough arrangements for an orderly crossing of the 30th Division. There were to be three beaches—Red, White, and Blue—one for each of the division's infantry regiments, with Red on the left, or north, opposite Buederich; White in the center; and Blue on the right, or south, opposite Rheinberg. The first boats over, guided by machine guns firing tracer ammunition, were to mark the boundaries of their beaches with red, white, or blue aircraft landing lamps. Thereafter the assault elements would show the heavy boats where to land by emplacing ten-foot stakes on which were wired flashlights with a red covering, no covering (white), or a blue covering to designate the beach. Lights were arranged one above the other (two for LCVPs, three for LCMs, four for duplex-drive tanks) or in a design (three forming a triangle for Bailey rafts). The beachmaster wore a white helmet; those of the engineer guides, boat crews, and others were marked with white paint in identifying patterns.

### Over the Rhine

The night was clear and the riverbanks almost dry at 0100 on 24 March when the Ninth Army artillery preparation erupted into the sky. An hour later the 30th Division's first wave of storm boats, each carrying two engineers and seven infantrymen, pushed off. The second wave consisted of storm and double assault boats constructed by bolting together two single craft, stern to stern; the third of LVTs and double

[3] Hist 202d Engr C Bn, 1 Jan–1 Jun 45; *History of the XVI Corps*, p. 39.

[4] Engineer Operations in the Rhine Crossing, Ninth U.S. Army, pp. 51, 55.

[5] Cover Narrative, 79th Div, FLASHPOINT Operation, CI 159, ETOUSA Hist Sect.

[6] *Conquer, The Story of the Ninth Army*, p. 245.

assault boats; and the fourth of LCVPs. Troops of the first wave were able to rig the lights on the far shore three minutes after hitting the beach. *(Map 29)*

German shells killed one man, wounded three others, and knocked out two Red Beach storm boats, but elsewhere the Americans encountered little or no resistance. The artillery barrage had stunned or daunted the few Germans on the far shore, and the artillery had cut enemy telephone wires, making it impossible for the Germans to call up artillery fire immediately. By 0243 the engineer of the 30th Infantry Division could report that all the assault battalions were across and that resistance had been negligible; by 0600 the bulk of the 30th Division's three infantry regiments was on the far shore.

Upstream, around a bend in the Rhine, the first wave of the 79th Infantry Division's two assault regiments started off at 0300 in storm and assault boats. By that time fog and smoke had settled on the water and on both banks of the river. Here the width of the steep banks and swampy areas on the far shore restricted the crossing sites. Some of the assault boats failed to get across. Three swamped because the engineers of the 149th Engineer Combat Battalion had not built bow extensions high enough. But the men swam to shore, and none were lost in the assault crossings. By 0600 at the upstream or southernmost site, the 187th Engineer Combat Battalion had crossed its infantry regiment, and by 0730 the 149th Engineer Combat Battalion had put ashore all men of the second regiment at the northern site. The remaining infantry regiment of the 79th Division ferried across next day, 25 March, the two engineer battalions sharing the work.[7]

At both the 30th and 79th Infantry Division sites the LVTs were in action early and saw extensive service throughout D-day. The LVTs, victims of the current, tended to drift downstream and could not manage direct crossings to a small, defined bridgehead at the outset of the assault. Later, however, they ferried load after load of tanks, which did not need specially prepared points of debarkation on the far bank. The DUKWs also proved excellent both as ferry craft and as general utility boats during bridge construction. The heavier ferry craft had trouble getting forward over the congested roadnet in the darkness, the LCVPs on flatbed trailers, the LCMs and Sea Mules on tank transporters. At 0130 these cumbersome loads caused a traffic jam that was not cleared until 0300.

In the 30th Infantry Division zone enemy fire hampered construction of hardstandings at the launching sites, and the LCVPs and LCMs could not begin ferrying operations until daybreak. By noon eight LCVPs and nine LCMs were hauling men, weapons, light tanks, and tank destroyers across the Rhine. The landing craft also helped during the construction of the three bridges—M2 treadway, heavy ponton, and M1 treadway. By afternoon several treadway rafts and two Bailey rafts, propelled by powered storm boats, were carrying Sherman tanks across.

In the 79th Infantry Division's area ferrying assumed increasing impor-

[7] Engineer Operations in the Rhine Crossing, Ninth U.S. Army, p. 19 and map, Incl 3. Unless otherwise cited, this section is based on this source, pp. 18–31, and also on the histories of the 1153d and 1148th Engineer Combat Groups. Engineer Study of the Rhine River Crossing made by the 79th Inf Div, Exhibit D, CI 160, ETOUSA Hist Sect.

89TH DIVISION INFANTRY CROSS THE RHINE AT OBERWESEL

tance after enemy fire slowed work on the divisional bridge. The 1276th Engineer Combat Battalion, with the mission of launching the ferry craft, was also responsible for the M2 treadway bridge and the mine booms. The unit was not only overburdened with work but was also unlucky. German phosphorous shells set the battalion command post ablaze at 0230, and a few minutes later enemy mortar fire added to the confusion. No one was hurt, but the unit struggled to move its equipment through the congested area. Tractors had to pull the LCM-laden transporters across the last yards of soft riverbank, but once there the transporters could back into the water and float their cargoes off with the assistance of crawler cranes at the site. By 0700 two LCMs were carrying tanks to the far shore, but German fire hit one and seven more craft remained on the west bank until 1900. The engineers launched the LCVPs more easily, and nine were in operation by noon. The Sea Mules bogged down on their transports short of the bank and got into the river only after the men finished a plank road to the water at noon on 25 March.[8]

Engineers supporting both the 30th and 79th Infantry Divisions recognized that ferry sites should be located downstream of tactical bridges to avoid the

---

[8] AAR, 1276th Engr C Bn, Jan–May 45.

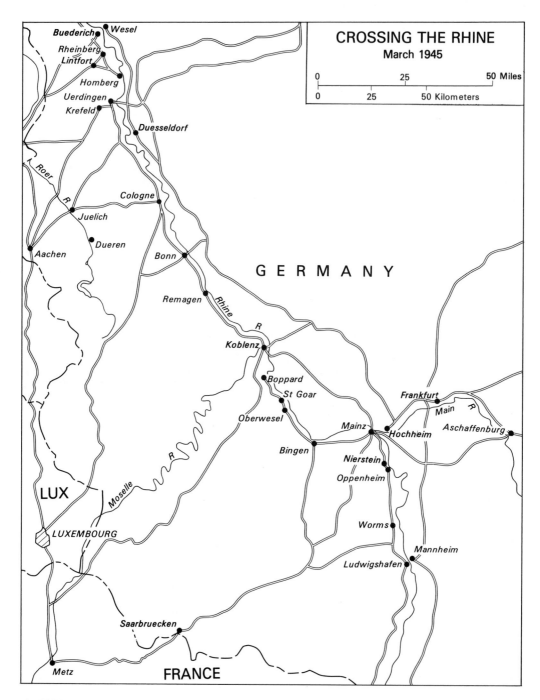

**CROSSING THE RHINE**
March 1945

0          25          50 Miles

0          25          50 Kilometers

Buederich    Wesel
Rheinberg
Lintfort
Homberg
Uerdingen
Krefeld
Duesseldorf

Roer
R
Cologne
Juelich
Dueren
Aachen    Bonn

G E R M A N Y

Remagen    Rhine

R
Koblenz

Boppard
St Goar    Frankfurt
Oberwesel    Main    R
Mainz    Aschaffenburg
Bingen    Hochheim
Nierstein
Oppenheim

Moselle    R
LUX    Worms
LUXEMBOURG    Mannheim
Ludwigshafen

Saarbruecken

Metz    **FRANCE**

*MAP 29*

possibility of ramming, but in several cases the best ferry sites—those not requiring extensive preparation—were located immediately upstream. So they equipped the ferries with two anchors each, to be cast overboard if the power failed, to prevent the ferries from floating downstream with the current.

Another deviation from planning was the timing of bridge construction. Because only a 50 percent reserve of bridge material was available, planners had not intended that bridge construction start before bridgeheads on the far shore had been seized. Firm, substantial bridgeheads would forestall observed enemy fire against bridging operations. But enemy resistance seemed to be so light and smoke so effective for concealment that work on all three 30th Division bridges began by 0630 on 24 March and on the 79th Division bridge at 0800.

However, after the wind changed and the smoke lifted, enemy fire hit the treadway bridges in both zones. Moreover, ferries that swept downstream when anchors failed to hold (or crews neglected to use them) rammed the treadways. Intermittent artillery fire hit the northernmost bridge, the M2 treadway in the White Beach area, several times. Then shortly after the bridge opened to traffic at 1600 a Bailey raft loaded with a Sherman tank crashed into it, causing so much damage that the bridge could not be reopened until 0200 on 25 March. At the M1 treadway in the Blue Beach area enemy fire interrupted work for an hour in the morning and knocked out 144 feet of the bridge during the afternoon. The bridge opened for traffic at 0830 on 25 March, but a little more than an hour later a Sea Mule drifted against the

treadway and buckled it. The M2 treadway built in the northern part of the 79th Division's zone was the southernmost of the three treadways. It was hit first by light enemy fire and then at 2330 by three LCMs that broke the bridge about 240 feet from shore; it could not be repaired until noon on D plus 1. By that time heavier artillery fire was falling, which killed the commander of the engineer treadway bridge company, wounded several men, and knocked out seven floats. That evening the XVI Corps engineer, Colonel Wheeler, turned the bridge work over to the 1153d Engineer Combat Group, whose 208th Engineer Combat Battalion completed the repairs late on the afternoon of D plus 2, 26 March. In the meantime, the 79th Division was able to use the 30th Division's M1 treadway. To protect the bridges against debris, floating mines, barges, explosive-filled motorboats, submarines, and underwater swimmers, five booms were to be installed and covered by tanks with canal defense lights, but group engineers could not complete the task primarily because powerboats needed to emplace the booms were not available.

Far to the south (upstream) of the 79th Division's area, near Homberg, 75th Infantry Division engineers constructed an excellent cable boom in darkness on the morning of D-day. Then a direct artillery hit severed the cable, setting the boom adrift, and enemy strafing eliminated a rebuilt boom next morning. Lacking booms, XVI Corps depended on antitank guns and tank destroyers placed in dikes along the riverfront and on patrol boats equipped with an underwater listening device. The enemy attempted no water-

ENGINEERS SLIDE BAILEY BRIDGING INTO PLACE AT WESEL

borne or underwater attacks.

The tactical units were satisfied with the crossing. The 30th Infantry Division considered the Rhine "much less of a problem than the swollen, racing Roer had been."[9] Though 1,100 feet wide in the 30th Division's zone, the Rhine was slow moving and easy to work in. Enemy resistance there and in the 79th Division's zone was negligible compared with that at Remagen, and the Germans in the XVI Corps' area may well have been deceived by camouflage and the diversionary operations at Krefeld and Uerdingen. In both division zones assault troops had crossed quickly and with very few casualties. By 0600 the engineers had moved eight infantry battalions of the 30th Division and five of the 79th over the Rhine; by the end of D-day three tank battalions, two field artillery battalions, and two tank-destroyer battalions were also on the far bank. One field artillery battalion managed to cross the treadway at White Beach before the bridge was rammed; the rest of the heavy weapons went across on ferry craft. By nightfall engineers were ferrying one Sherman tank over the Rhine every ten minutes. The crossing had cost XVI Corps 38 men killed, 426 wounded, and 3 missing. Ninth Army considered the operation a complete success.[10]

---

[9] Hewitt, *Work Horse of the Western Front*, p. 235.

[10] Ibid., p. 242; *History of the XVI Corps*, pp. 42–46; *Conquer, The Story of the Ninth Army*, p. 247.

Farther south, the two other American field armies in the line jumped the Rhine between 23 and 26 March. The techniques employed in the crossings of Third and Seventh Armies varied. General Patton got six battalions across with a fair degree of surprise by restricting artillery and air bombardment in his assault zones around Oppenheim and the Rhine gorge. Seventh Army, on Patton's right flank, made comparatively heavier use of artillery in its assault near Worms. Common to all these efforts, however, was extensive engineer preparation beforehand.

### The XII Corps Crossing at Oppenheim

For months the engineers of XII Corps, scheduled to make Patton's first crossing, had considered Oppenheim a good site. Because the Third Army operation was to be a surprise, a crossing at a town was essential to conceal the movement of the assault boats to the river's edge. The engineers favored Oppenheim because it straddled one of the main roads to Frankfurt am Main, some twenty miles to the northeast. The bridge carrying the road over the river could not be counted on, but at that spot the Rhine was not more than a thousand feet wide and fairly slow, while its sandy banks were firm enough to support amphibious vehicles. For building rafts and launching LCVPs the protected Oppenheim boat basin on the near bank was ideal.[11]

As planning progressed it became evident that some 560 assault boats would be available. This made it necessary to expand the plans to include a neighboring town, Nierstein, 1,500 yards downstream. During the assault

at 2200 on 22 March, engineers of the 1135th Engineer Combat Group's 204th Engineer Combat Battalion were to cross two battalions of the 5th Division's 11th Infantry in column at Nierstein and the third battalion at Oppenheim. As soon as the 11th Infantry had cleared the far bank, the group's 7th Engineer Combat Battalion was to put across the 5th Division's 10th Infantry at Oppenheim.[12]

On the morning of 22 March German planes bombed and strafed Nierstein, but nothing indicated that the enemy expected an immediate crossing there. The only activity the Americans could see on the far bank was a party of soldiers digging mine holes in the dike about fifty yards from the river's edge. After dark on the twenty-second the 204th Engineer Combat Battalion brought assault boats down to the river's edge. No artillery barrage was fired, nor did the boats use their motors. Three engineers manned each boat, which carried twelve infantrymen. As silently as possible, the boats paddled across in the blackness. The first boat from Nierstein drew a single burst of machine-gun fire, but the infantry replied with automatic rifles and before the boat unloaded five Germans came down from the dike and surrendered. The first infantry company was ashore in eight minutes, and by 0130 on 23 March all three battalions of the 11th Infantry were over the Rhine with only twenty casualties. Strongest resistance had occurred in the Oppenheim cros-

---

[11] *XII Corps: Spearhead of Patton's Third Army*, p. 360.

[12] Interviews with officers of the 150th, 204th, and 7th Engineer Combat Battalions and 88th Engineer Heavy Ponton Battalion on 25 and 31 March and 5 April 1945, CI 44, ETOUSA Hist Sect. Details of the crossing are from this source.

sing, during which one engineer was killed.

At 0200 the 7th Engineer Combat Battalion began crossing the 10th Infantry in a column of battalions. Just at daylight, as the last wave was paddling across, shells from a German self-propelled 105-mm. gun hit the water, splashing and swamping some of the boats but causing no casualties. The gun could not be driven off or silenced until the ferries went into operation to carry across heavy weapons. Meanwhile, enemy shelling, bombing, and strafing interfered with the work at the Oppenheim boat basin where the 88th Engineer Heavy Ponton Battalion was constructing four Class 40 rafts. The first raft, pushed downstream to Ferry Site 1 near Nierstein, did not begin operating until 0700, when it carried a bulldozer to the far shore; it was 0830 before tank destroyers could raft across to attack the self-propelled gun. During the night a party of engineers had marked beaches for the landing of DUKWs, LCVPs, and Weasels using blinking white, red, and green lights and setting up vertical panels of corresponding colors for daytime use. Some LCVPs were working by dawn on 23 March, but DUKWs and Weasels did not arrive until the next day.

The 2d Infantry of the 5th Division crossed to the east bank on rafts and LCVPs next morning, and by midafternoon an attached battalion of the 90th Infantry Division had also crossed. Two of the big rafts could accommodate six jeeps at a time; they operated continuously for two days and nights, one pushed by an LCVP, the other by two powerboats. The rafts continued supply and evacuation operations even after bridges were in, a treadway at 1800 on 23 March and a heavy ponton bridge at 0700 the next morning. The raft operations permitted the 4th Armored Division to employ the treadway as a one-way crossing, and the division used the bridge continuously for twenty-four hours beginning at 0900 on the twenty-fourth.[13]

In one respect the engineers of the 1135th Engineer Combat Group showed more foresight than had their colleagues in the First and Ninth Army crossings. When the construction of the heavy ponton bridge began, all ferries moved to Ferry Site 2, downstream of all bridges. There, the U.S. Navy was operating LCVPs, and DUKWs began operations on the twenty-fourth. This movement downstream assured that the ferries would not crash into the bridges.

The 150th Engineer Combat Battalion began bridge work at 0330, but German artillery fire at dawn and strafing and bombing during the morning interrupted the work. American combat troops on the east bank soon silenced the artillery piece, and although the bombing and strafing wounded one man, the air attacks did little damage to the bridge material.[14]

About the time bridge building began, a detachment of the 1301st Engineer General Service Regiment, experienced in boom construction, started emplacing an antimine floating log boom and an antipersonnel boom made of admiralty netting, both upstream of the bridges. The engineer detachment completed the log boom by 1400 on 23 March. The more troublesome antipersonnel boom was only half completed

---

[13] AAR, 5th Inf Div, CI 43, ETOUSA Hist Sect.
[14] Hist 150th Engr C Bn, 16 Oct 44–12 May 45; Annex E, AAR, 1135th Engr C Gp, Jan–Apr 45.

by nightfall, but during the night two German frogmen were caught in its meshes. Each carried two disc-shaped magnetic mines, both set to explode at 0600. The Germans said they were two of a party of five frogmen who dropped into the river about eleven kilometers upstream with orders to place mines on either a ferry site or a bridge. They had almost immediately lost contact with the other three, who were never picked up. The two captives were soldiers who had been sentenced to three months' service in a naval diving school for offenses committed in Russia and in Greece. On this penal service, they revealed, they could not handle explosives and received their mines only when they were actually in the water upstream of Rheinberg. The officers had also told them that they had little chance of returning from the mission.[15]

### The VIII Corps Crossing at the Rhine Gorge

The area selected for the VIII Corps crossings, between Koblenz on the north and Bingen on the south, was the famous Rhine gorge, where the river runs swiftly between rock cliffs. There had lived the river barons, who from their castles on the heights had exacted tribute from passing ships. At a point near St. Goar stands the Lorelei, the huge rock formation from which the golden-haired maiden of Heine's poem enticed sailors to their deaths on the shoal below. This stretch of the Rhine was the worst possible for an assault crossing. For that very reason Patton had selected it in the belief that "the impossible place is usually the least well defended."[16] He was wrong. Boatmen on

the river were at the mercy of those on the heights above. At the 87th Infantry Division's crossing site near Rhens, a mile or so upstream from Koblenz, fire from machine guns, mortars, flak guns, and artillery emplaced on the rocky cliffs above fell on a 347th Infantry launching site six minutes before H-hour, scheduled for 0001 on 25 March. This caused such disruption that an hour passed before a second try could be made; this time the men succeeded. At another site a few hundred yards downstream, the leading assault boats moved out on time but had scarcely touched down on the east shore when German flares lit up the river. Following boats drew heavy fire. After daylight the attack battalions tried smoke cover, but damp air in the gorge kept it from rising much above the surface of the river. By early afternoon, with resistance continuing, units waiting to cross at Rhens moved upriver four miles to Boppard. The crossing attempts at Rhens had been costly: the 347th Infantry had sustained casualties of 7 killed and 110 wounded. In proportion, its supporting 35th Engineer Combat Battalion had suffered even more, with 9 men killed, 6 missing, and 19 wounded.[17]

The 1102d Engineer Combat Group, supporting the 87th Division crossings, had set up headquarters at Boppard. There the assault wave achieved a measure of surprise, pushing out into the river shortly after midnight on 25 March. The 159th Engineer Combat Battalion, after moving the 345th Infantry across the river, considered the crossing "not tough at all, that is, not like we expected it to be."[18] A smoke screen laid down

---

[15] Merzweiler interv, 25 Mar 45.
[16] Patton, *War as I Knew It*, p. 275.

[17] Hist 35th Engr C Bn, Oct 44–Apr 45.
[18] *The 159th Engineer Combat Battalion* (Antwerp, 1945), p. 30.

for the crossing of succeeding waves proved effective. Although artillery and mortar fire continued sporadically during the morning, six LCVPs were in the water transporting infantry, and rafting soon began, the first tank crossing at noon. Enemy fire slowed the work of the 44th Engineer Combat Battalion on a treadway bridge until 0930 on the overcast, rainy morning of 26 March. Shortly before the bridge opened, the men working on it saw evidence of the 89th Infantry Division's bloody crossing upstream at St. Goar during the night. An assault boat came hurtling downstream; only one of its four passengers had escaped injury—another was dead and two were wounded.[19]

The night before the 89th Division's crossing, scheduled for 0200 on 26 March, the 1107th Engineer Combat Group set up headquarters in a 13th-century castle on a cliff overlooking St. Goar. Three sites had been selected for the assault. Five companies of the division's 354th Infantry were to be divided between St. Goar and a wooded area downstream, while a battalion of the 353d Infantry was to cross at Oberwesel, upstream of St. Goar. The 168th Engineer Combat Battalion was to support all assault crossings, the 188th Engineer Combat Battalion to construct rafts and take charge of all ferry equipment, and the 243d Engineer Combat Battalion to build a treadway bridge at St. Goar.[20]

The troops expected trouble at St. Goar because the day before the Germans had announced on their radio

that the Americans had tried to cross there. The opposition proved even stronger than anticipated. In fading moonlight the first assault boats pulled away from the shadowy western shore at 0200. American artillery was quiet because a surprise operation like that at Oppenheim had been ordered, but the Germans were already shelling from St. Goarshausen across the Rhine. A German 88-mm. gun hit three of the thirty-one boats taken down to the riverbank at St. Goar before they could be launched. One shell killed three motorboat operators, injured six other men of the 168th Engineer Combat Battalion, and killed the 89th Division's chemical officer. The rest of the assault boats had gone about a third of the way across the river when heavy enemy fire came down, mostly from 20-mm. antiaircraft guns. Then a shell ignited a gasoline barge anchored in midstream near St. Goar. By the light of the leaping flames the anxious watchers on the near bank saw boats exploding "in a geyser of flying wood and sprawling bodies."[21]

Two hours later, at 0400, none of the boats had returned. Group engineers considered it unlikely that many of them had been swept downstream by the swift current, since they had provided some of the boats with motors to tow those that had none. They concluded that all the boats had been lost and that the assault engineers who had been able to get across were fighting alongside the infantry. During the night small-arms fire could be heard from St. Goarshausen; when dawn came U.S. troops could be seen advancing toward the center of town, cleaning it out house

[19] VIII Corps Intervs, 25–26 Mar 45, CI 44, ETOUSA Hist Sect.

[20] Hist 1107th Engr C Gp, Jan–May 45. Unless otherwise cited, the details of the crossing are from this source.

[21] Hist 1107th Engr C Gp, Jan–May 45.

MEN CONNECT BRIDGE SECTIONS NEAR ST. GOAR

by house. Daylight also revealed shattered assault boats lining the far bank.

The crossing at the wooded area downstream from St. Goar was also bloody; there too German 20-mm. antiaircraft guns and heavy machine guns played a leading role. Most of the 89th Division's casualties—29 killed, 146 missing, and 102 wounded—were men of the 354th Infantry. At Oberwesel, although the Germans used a castle on an island in midriver as a strongpoint, firing from slits in the walls, the crossing went well. During the morning DUKWs went into service. In contrast to the forty-five minutes required for assault boats to get to the far bank and return, the engineer-manned DUKWs carried eighteen infantrymen and made the round trip in five minutes.[22] With reinforcements and help from artillery and self-propelled guns brought up to the near bank, by noon enemy fire was almost eliminated at Oberwesel, which then became the main crossing site. In the afternoon six LCVPs and six LCMs ferried enough troops and equipment over to clear St. Goarshausen by early evening.[23]

Raft construction began at St. Goar at 1800. Work on a treadway bridge started there at 1930, but the swift current

[22] *The 89th Infantry Division, 1942–1945* (Washington: Infantry Journal Press, 1947), p. 107.
[23] AAR, Third U.S. Army, 1 Aug 44–9 May 45, vol. II, Staff Sect Rpts, p. Eng–32.

M2 TREADWAY BRIDGE *on the Rhine at Boppard.*

washed out anchors. A cable had to be strung across the river, and the treadway was not completed until early on the morning of 28 March. In the meantime, two 89th Division task forces crossed the Rhine on the 87th Division's bridge at Boppard.[24]

General Patton could have used the bridges at Boppard and Oppenheim to send Third Army's XX Corps across the Rhine. Instead he chose to make an assault crossing at Mainz, between Boppard and Oppenheim, on 28 March, probably because he considered Mainz, centrally located and with a good road and rail net, the best place for permanent rail and highway bridges.

---

[24] Hist 1107th Engr C Gp and *The 89th Infantry Division,* p. 108.

## The XX Corps Crossing at Mainz

At Mainz the Rhine is almost 2,000 feet wide—one of its widest points. Directly opposite the city, which lies on the west bank of the Rhine, the narrower and slower Main River empties into the Rhine from the east. Parallel to the Main's north bank an excellent road ran to Frankfurt am Main and beyond, into the heart of Germany. Elements of the 4th and 6th Armored Divisions, having broken out of the Oppenheim bridgehead, tried to cross the Main near Frankfurt between 25 and 27 March. At three places railway bridges were found still standing, but the only one that would take tanks was at Aschaffenburg, fifteen miles up the Main from Frankfurt. Demolitions had so weakened the other two bridges that only foot soldiers could get across; heavy shelling from Frankfurt prevented engineers from repairing the bridges.

Although the width of the Rhine at Mainz would place a heavy strain on XX Corps' bridging equipment, the city had a number of advantages as a crossing site: the banks were flat, the enemy lacked high ground for observation, and buildings extending to the water's edge would protect the attackers from small-arms fire and shell splinters as they embarked in the assault boats. As at Oppenheim, boat basins with slips were available to provide concealment for launching naval craft.

The XX Corps decided on two assault crossings, both of which the 80th Infantry Division was to undertake. The division's 317th Infantry was to cross the Rhine at Mainz, where engineers were to build a treadway bridge; the 319th Infantry, using the Oppenheim bridge over the Rhine, was to cross the

Main from Bischofsheim to Hochheim, three miles upstream from Mainz. At Hochheim, where the Main was less than 700 feet wide—a favorable circumstance in view of an increasing shortage of bridging material—engineers were to build a second treadway, allowing more tanks to cross to reinforce the XII Corps' armor.

In the early hours of 28 March the 1139th Engineer Combat Group's 135th Engineer Combat Battalion paddled the first assault wave over the Rhine at Mainz. From an island in midriver and from the far bank came small-arms and machine-gun fire and some 20-mm. antiaircraft shells. The second wave, crossing in LCVPs and LCMs, encountered heavier shelling. During the assault crossing 10 men were killed, 18 wounded, and some 55 reported missing. Small-arms fire falling on the bridge site delayed a start on the treadway. Because there was no reserve bridging material, the 160th Engineer Combat Battalion, which had the treadway project, was reluctant to run the risk of losing what equipment it had. But on orders from the XX Corps commander, Maj. Gen. Walton H. Walker, the engineers began work at 0900.

At the Main River site there was little or no opposition to the assault crossings, which the 1139th Group's 179th Engineer Combat Battalion supported. By 0900 the 206th Engineer Combat Battalion's heavy rafts were ferrying tanks to help clear the far bank, and at 1855 the battalion completed a 624-foot bridge. Next day around noon, the Mainz bridge over the Rhine was ready for traffic. The XX Corps engineers were especially proud because they believed the 1,896-foot span to be the longest tactical bridge built under combat conditions in the European theater.[25]

### The Seventh Army Crossings

About fifteen miles south of Oppenheim lay Worms, where the Seventh Army was to cross the Rhine. The fact that operations there and at the Oppenheim bridgehead would be mutually supporting outweighed the disadvantages of the terrain at Worms. On the far bank, some eight miles east of the Rhine, the hills of the Odenwald rose sharply. On those heights the Germans could make a stand and contain the bridgehead—if they had men and weapons to do so. Enemy strength was difficult to estimate, but Seventh Army intelligence indicated that the Germans had not more than fifty men per riverfront kilometer and no large guns permanently emplaced east of the Rhine.[26]

Early Seventh Army plans and preparations, begun in September 1944, had envisioned a Rhine crossing about twenty miles upstream from Worms and south of Mannheim. For that reason a good deal of the engineer planning concerned the possibility that the Germans might open power dams upstream from Basel to create flood waves that could wash out tactical bridges as far north as Mannheim, leaving American assault troops stranded on the far shore. To provide warning of approaching floods so that floating bridges could be safeguarded, the ETOUSA chief engineer established a flood protection service in his office; engineers at the headquarters of the various armies set up similar

[25] Hist 1139th Engr C Gp, Mar 45; Third Army Rpt, vol. II, pp. Eng–32–33; *The XX Corps: Its History and Service in World War II*, pp. 331–33.

[26] *Seventh Army Report*, vol. III, pp. 746–47. Unless otherwise cited, this section is based on that source.

organizations. To collect planning data, 6th Army Group engineers experimented with hydraulic models of the dams between Basel and Lake Constance.[27] This effort decreased in importance when 6th Army Group learned that the Swiss were prepared to protect the dams along their border with Germany. Moreover, Seventh Army changed its crossing site to Worms, north of Mannheim.

The 40th and 540th Engineer Combat Groups, both amphibious veterans, were available to put Seventh Army's XV Corps across the Rhine on a nine-mile front extending north and south from Worms. Training had begun in September 1944, when Seventh Army's rapid advance inland through southern France made a November or December Rhine crossing appear likely. During those months the Rhine current is swift, usually from eight to ten miles per hour. Accordingly, the Seventh Army engineer, Brig. Gen. Garrison H. Davidson, felt that hand-paddled assault boats would be out of the question. He would need the services of boat operators who had trained at sites on the Rhine and Doubs rivers to pilot motor-driven boats. To prepare for a swift-current crossing the engineers also experimented with stringing cable to help DUKWs take artillery across promptly and with anchoring ponton bridges.[28]

In the event, much of the time spent preparing for a swift-current crossing

was wasted. By the 26 March crossing date, the current was only three or four miles per hour, slow enough to use paddle-powered assault boats. In the sector north of Worms, where XV Corps' 45th Infantry Division supported by the 40th Engineer Combat Group crossed the river, using powered boats actually proved detrimental because motor noise alerted the enemy. In addition, the engineers found that DUKWs and duplex-drive tanks could cross without the aid of cables.[29]

Around midnight on 25 March a four-man patrol of the 180th Infantry, 45th Division, paddled across the Rhine in a rubber boat to reconnoiter the east bank. The patrol saw some German soldiers but was not fired upon and, after searching fruitlessly for gun emplacements and mines, returned safely to the near bank in time to take part in the assault crossing at 0230.[30] The heavy storm and assault boats, brought to the riverbank on carts borrowed from the Chemical Warfare Service, were launched on schedule from stone-paved revetments. Mist rising from the river hid the moon. To achieve surprise the attackers used neither smoke nor any preliminary artillery barrage. However, after the Germans heard the roar of the motors, small-arms, 20-mm. antiaircraft, and mortar fire hit the boats as they reached the far bank. This fire was heaviest in the 180th Infantry's sector, where 60 percent of the boats were damaged; the 179th Infantry lost only 10 percent of its boats. All fourteen of the duplex-drive tanks in the assault went across safely. With the help of the tanks and of artillery ferried over

[27] Lt. Col. Stanley W. Dziuban, "Rhine River Flood Prediction Service," *The Military Engineer*, XXXVII, no. 239 (September 1945), 348–53; and "Hydraulics Model Experiments," in Ibid., XXXVIII (May 1946), 189–93.

[28] Brig Gen Garrison H. Davidson, The Crossing of the Rhine, Incl 3 to Hist Rpt, Mar–Apr 45, Office of the Engr, Seventh Army.

[29] River Crossing Notes, 29 Mar 45, in Hist 40th Engr C Gp, 16 Feb–31 Mar 45.

[30] Hist 180th Inf Rgt, 1–31 Mar 45.

in DUKWs or on infantry support rafts, the infantry overran the Germans and made good progress on the ground. During the crossing the 2831st Engineer Combat Battalion, piloting the storm and assault boats, suffered eighteen casualties; the 2830th Battalion, which operated rafts and ferries, sustained none.[31]

Just south of Worms, the 3d Division made two feints across the Rhine below Mannheim on the evening of 25 March which alerted the enemy. When the 540th Engineer Combat Group's 2832d and 2833d Engineer Combat Battalions began moving toward their assembly areas at 2000 hours—the former to support the 7th Infantry on the south, the latter the 30th Infantry—they came under German artillery and mortar fire. This fire continued while the engineers pulled the storm and assault boats over the steep, revetted banks and into place for the crossing. In the 7th Infantry zone flames from a barn set on fire by a German incendiary shell lit up the crossing area, silhouetting the men and boats.[32]

At 0152 friendly artillery began a massive barrage that continued until H-hour, 0230. Four minutes before the barrage lifted, 7th Infantry boats began moving across the river, and by 0340 both assault infantry battalions were over. In the 30th Infantry's zone, where opposition was lighter, the two assault battalions were across by 0330. The artillery barrage, as well as the use of smoke, kept the loss rate of storm boats to only 10 percent. Ten of fourteen du-

plex-drive tanks reached the far shore. About H plus 2 the first DUKW crossed the river safely without cables. The engineers also found that cables were not necessary for the rafts, which by 0700 were ferrying tanks and vehicles across the Rhine. Nevertheless, since the ferrying operations lay upstream from where floating bridges were being built, the engineers strung cables and used them to keep ferries from being swept downstream to crash into the bridges.

The engineers who were to build a mine barrier and patrol the river to protect the bridges from floating mines, frogmen, and other menaces reached their assembly area, farthest upstream of all, at 0300. The fire from German antiaircraft guns, ranging in caliber from 8-mm. to 128-mm. and emplaced on an island in the Rhine, drove the engineers off. Heavy fire from the island, a fortress that had apparently escaped the notice of Seventh Army planners, continued throughout much of D-day, harassing the 7th Infantry's crossing site and holding up the barrier work. It was late afternoon when a battalion of the 15th Infantry assaulted the island from the east bank of the Rhine and silenced the guns. On D plus 1 the engineers erected the mine barrier, and the river patrol went into operation with searchlights, artillery, and DUKWs mounting quad-50 machine guns. The patrol sank a number of barges that might have destroyed the downstream bridges.

Fire from the German guns on the island also delayed construction of the nearest floating bridge, a treadway south of Worms. The 163d Engineer Combat Battalion began work at 0600 on D-day but did not complete the

[31] Hist 40th Engr C Gp, 16 Feb–31 Mar 45.
[32] Hist 540th Engr C Gp, Mar 45; Taggart, *History of the Third Infantry Division*, p. 339. Unless otherwise cited, the story of the 3d Division crossing is from these two sources.

HEAVY PONTON BRIDGE IN THE SEVENTH ARMY AREA

treadway until 1850. The first usable bridge was a heavy ponton span at Worms, about two hundred feet downstream from the site of the Ernst Ludwig highway bridge, which the Germans had demolished. In just over nine hours the 85th Engineer Heavy Ponton Battalion built the 1,047-foot ponton; open to traffic at 1512 on D-day, it was named the Alexander Patch Bridge for the Seventh Army commander. Although the handsome stone tower of the Ernst Ludwig Bridge, still standing on the far bank, harbored enemy snipers, ruins of the span provided good anchorage for the bridge builders. The Alexander Patch Bridge carried 3,040 vehicles eastward during its first twenty-four hours of operation.[33] Because of its early completion and excellent location, Seventh Army preferred the Alexander Patch Bridge to a ponton bridge the 1553d Engineer Heavy Ponton Battalion erected downstream near Rheinduerkheim in the 45th Division's sector. As a result, that bridge operated at only half its capacity.[34]

On 29 March, General Davidson, the Seventh Army engineer, instructed the 85th Engineer Heavy Ponton Battalion to build a bridge to take tanks and vehicles over the Rhine to Mannheim. With the help of aerial photographs a recon-

---

[33] *Seventh Army Report*, vol. III, p. 887.
[34] Hist 40th Engr C Gp, 16 Feb–31 Mar 45.

naissance party found a suitable site at Ludwigshafen, on the west bank opposite Mannheim. Eight bulldozers worked six hours clearing rubble from the streets and preparing the site, and the 1553d Engineer Heavy Ponton Battalion brought pontons down from the Worms area on its trailers. Construction started at daylight on 30 March. The bridge opened to light traffic at 1500, but tanks and heavy vehicles had to wait until 1900 because of a delay in obtaining two-inch decking. The engineers dubbed the span the Gar Davidson Bridge to honor the Seventh Army engineer.[35]

### The Rhine Crossings in Retrospect

No two assault crossings of the Rhine during March 1945 were exactly alike. Conditions ranged from the haste and improvisation of First Army's Remagen bridge crossing to the long, careful planning involved in Ninth Army's crossing near Rheinberg. Moreover, Ninth Army's massive artillery preparation, which eliminated surprise and necessitated fast assault boats and speedy rafting of heavy weapons, contrasted sharply with Third Army's dispensing with preliminary bombardment and achieving surprise with a night crossing in paddle boats.

Engineer planning had allowed for diversity. Working during the fall of 1944 before the Battle of the Ardennes, planners had assumed a winter crossing and made provisions for bad weather and excessive flooding. Such conditions did not arise. Crossings were also easier than expected because the Germans did not seriously try to destroy

bridges with mines, midget submarines, or boats laden with explosives.[36]

Looking back, corps and army engineers saw no reason to revise engineer doctrine. Rather, a study of the Rhine operations provided several examples of the folly of deviating from doctrine. Perhaps the most outstanding instance was disregard of the rule that all heavy boats and rafts should operate downstream of bridges, even if launching and landing sites downstream were inferior to those upstream. For example, at Wallach the 1153d Engineer Combat Group's achievement in installing a treadway bridge by 1600 on D-day was nullified when a Bailey raft crashed into the bridge, knocking it out for more than seven hours.

Almost all of the standard streamcrossing equipment provided for the Rhine crossing—assault and storm boats, utility powerboats, outboard motors, rafts, and bridging material—had already been used, most of it successfully. The principal criticisms were that the infantry support rafts tended to swamp in the Rhine's swift current and that utility boats were not powerful enough to serve efficiently as general work boats for building bridges, emplacing heavy boom material, or towing heavy rafts.

The engineers also obtained material from sources other than standard engineer stocks. Two of the most important types of equipment, LCVPs and LCMs, the U.S. Navy furnished to First, Ninth, and Third Armies. The engineers generally considered the LCVPs invaluable. They ferried troops at a rapid rate, faster than the men could walk over footbridges, and returned the

---

[35] Hist 85th Engr Heavy Ponton Bn, Jan–May 45.

[36] OCE ETOUSA Hist Rpt 20, Forced Crossing of the Rhine.

wounded quickly. The LCVPs also performed excellent service as patrol boats and even acted as work boats and tugboats, although they did not have enough power to handle the heavy reinforced rafts required for ferrying tanks. Opinions on the value of LCMs varied. Ninth Army engineers felt that the craft did not contribute enough to the crossings to warrant the effort involved in transporting and launching it. On the other hand, the Third Army engineer found LCMs extremely useful, citing an instance during which six LCVPs and six LCMs crossed an entire division with all its vehicles and equipment in forty-eight hours.

Other special nonengineer equipment employed during the Rhine crossings included DUKWs, LVTs, and Sea Mules. In all crossings except at Remagen (where DUKWs were subjected to an excessively long land haul) they performed valuable service, not only in carrying shore parties and artillery to the far bank but also in working around bridges and dropping bridge anchors. LVTs were well liked, especially LVT4s, which could load jeeps through drop doors. Although a good work boat, the Sea Mule was bulky to transport, hard to handle in a rapid current, and susceptible to damage in shallow water because of exposed propellers and rudders. For these reasons, most engineers thought it should be replaced in river crossings by a new and more powerful engineer power utility boat.[37]

In sustaining surprise during the Rhine crossings, dummy bridging of wood and burlap played an important part. So convincing from the air were Ninth Army's decoy preparations near Uerdingen that on the night of D plus 2 German planes strafed the area. During the Seventh Army crossings engineers threw two dummy bridges across the Rhine upstream and downstream of real bridges. Made of wooden frames resting on steel drums, the spans seemed so real even at ground level that guards had to be stationed at their approaches to prevent crowds of refugees from using the dummies to flee over the Rhine.[38]

---

[37] Ibid.
[38] Ibid.

# CHAPTER XXIV

# Into the Heart of Germany

"No one slept, no one ate, no one did anything but attack and push on, attack and push on." So the tankers of XIII Corps' 5th Armored Division described their dash from the Rhine to the Elbe.

Passing to Ninth Army control on the morning of 31 March, the 5th's tankers crossed the Rhine that same day over a ponton bridge at Wesel, where the British Second Army's bridges had just been turned over to Ninth Army on orders from Field Marshal Montgomery. By the time the last elements of the armored division reached the bridge night had fallen, and as the men crossed the river they entered a nearly surreal atmosphere. Floodlights split the darkness and shone on the water; antiaircraft guns pointed toward the sky. In the glare of the lights barge-mounted pile drivers were pounding, while plumes of smoke from busy tugboats silhouetted huge cranes.[1] Two important bridges were under construction. Ninth Army engineers were driving piles for a fixed highway bridge, and ADSEC engineers were building a railroad bridge. All were working around the clock so that the combat forces, racing across tactical bridges, would not run out of supplies before they could reach the heart of Germany.

Months before, Colonel Itschner and his ADSEC staff had established dumps of material for the railroad bridge, planned as a single-track span on steel girders supported by light steel trestles and timber-pile piers. The planners had intended to use the site of a destroyed German railroad bridge downstream from where the Lippe River entered the Rhine. When the engineers reconnoitered the far bank, however, they found the damage there too extensive for quick repair and had to settle on a site upstream near a wrecked highway bridge to which the Germans had added a single-track rail line. This substitution meant a very long bridge since it added to the Rhine section of twenty-three spans (1,753 feet) a section of six spans (463 feet) over the Lippe. Luckily, the supply of meter-depth I-beams needed for girders had been assured when the Hadir Steel Mill in Luxembourg became operational in October 1944.

On 29 March a large force under Col. James B. Cress began work. The organization consisted of the 1056th Port Construction and Repair Group; elements of the 341st, 355th, and 1317th Engineer General Service Regiments; and an engineer construction battalion, a dump truck company, an engineer maintenance company, and a welding detachment. Several nonengineer units

---

[1] *The Victory Division in Europe: History of the Fifth Armored Division*, pp. 49, 63.

were included—a Signal Corps battalion to provide communications, a Transportation Corps harbor craft company to control water traffic, and a U.S. Navy detachment to assemble barges. The around-the-clock work was hard and dangerous, and the construction cost the lives of three men of the 355th Engineer General Service Regiment. This first railroad bridge across the Rhine opened to traffic at 0100 on 9 April, only ten days, four hours, and forty-five minutes after the first pile was driven; it was named the Major Robert A. Gouldin Bridge for an officer of the 355th Engineer General Service Regiment who lost his life during the construction.[2]

Ninth Army's fixed timber-pile highway bridge was placed about seventy-five yards upstream of the wrecked German bridge (the railroad bridge was about the same distance downstream) to take advantage of existing roadnets.[3] The span was to carry three lanes—two-way Class 40 and one-way Class 70 traffic. The builder was the 1146th Engineer Combat Group, using the 250th, 252d, and 1256th Engineer Combat Battalions, aided by detachments from ADSEC's 1053d and 1058th Port Construction and Repair Groups and a U.S. Navy Seabee maintenance unit.

The first step was to construct an embankment on the near side of Wesel to carry an approach road. To obtain the needed fill, the engineers demolished old Fort Blucher and carted the rubble to the site. Work on the bridge

itself began on 31 March. Like the railroad bridge, the highway bridge was very long, spanning the Rhine (1,813 feet) and the Lippe (411 feet). The western and eastern approaches to the two rivers totaled more than 2,000 feet. Open to truck traffic during the early afternoon of 18 April, the span was called the Roosevelt Bridge in memory of President Franklin D. Roosevelt who had died less than a week before.[4]

### Ninth Army's Dash to the Elbe

Rolling over the ponton bridge at Wesel with the 5th Armored Division on 31 March was the division's organic 22d Armored Engineer Battalion. To get the armor over streams on the way to the Elbe, the engineers carried a truckload of lumber to refloor bridges and treadway to use at crossing sites where bridges were down.

On the route along the northern edge of the Ruhr Pocket, the first water barrier in the 5th Armored Division's path was the Dortmund-Ems Canal. The original plan had been to bridge the canal at Muenster, from which good roads led eastward; but south of Muenster near Senden, on the right flank of the advance, Combat Command Reserve ran into fire from German 20-mm. flak guns, bazookas, small arms, and tanks. The armored division commander, Maj. Gen. Lunsford E. Oliver, decided to cross the canal at Senden and move south, skirting the pocket of resistance. The task of getting the tanks across the canal fell to CCR's engineers, Company

[2] ADSEC History, pp. 71–73, 75–76; Maj Gen C. R. Moore, "Rhine River Railroad Bridges," app. 12 to OCE ETOUSA Hist Rpt 12, Railroad Reconstruction and Bridging; *Bridging the Way to Victory with the 355th Engineers* [355th Engr GS Rgt, 1945].
[3] See photograph, Timothy, *The Rhine Crossing*, p. 43, fig. 76.

[4] Engineer Operations in the Rhine Crossing, Ninth U.S. Army, pp. 44–49; Hist 1146th Engr C Gp, Jan–May 45, and MS, 1146th Engr C Gp, A Report on the Roosevelt Rhine and Lippe River Bridges . . . April 1945, OCE files.

C of the 22d Armored Engineer Battalion.

Orders came at 2100 on 31 March for CCR's armored infantry to establish a bridgehead on the far bank of the canal to protect the engineers working on the bridge, but no mention was made of how the infantrymen were to get across. After two men making their way down the bank in the dark found some rowboats, the infantry rowed over the canal to set up a defensive perimeter. At 0400 on Easter, the engineers began installing treadway. Four hours later in a light rain the tanks started to cross the canal, and by the morning of 2 April all Combat Command Reserve was over. The bridge also carried Combat Command B and the motorized 84th Infantry Division, which was following the armor. Later XIII Corps engineers came up and repaired a German bridge over the canal; the 5th Armored Division's Combat Command A used this span after it cleaned out the German pocket south of Muenster.

Racing northeast in the rain through the spring-green countryside on the morning of 2 April, the tank columns began to encounter roadblocks. Some were merely logs stacked on the road; others consisted of two emplaced cylinders, one on either side of the road. These the Germans made by driving a circle of wooden piles in the ground, filling the center with dirt or crushed rock, and blocking the gap between the cylinders with a truck or wagon. There was also the "rolling roadblock"—a huge drum filled with gravel or dirt. None of the roadblocks delayed the advance for very long; few were manned and some had not even been completed. When the Germans did man the blocks, the Americans could normally eliminate

the covering fire, and then the engineers with the help of tanks could destroy all but the most elaborate obstacles in fifteen to twenty minutes.

On 3 April the engineers became involved in an attempt to seize bridges across the Weser River. Small assault teams of engineers, tanks, and infantry were organized to take the bridges by surprise, but they found all bridges blown. There followed five days of effort to seize bridges, and the tankers, pounding swiftly down the autobahn, at one point got close enough to see a bridge intact, only to hear a dull boom and watch the girders falling into the river. All efforts failed. On 8 April Combat Command Reserve was ordered to cross the Weser over a bridge in the XIX Corps zone at Hameln of Pied Piper fame.

Once across the Weser CCR's tanks ran into increasing enemy resistance. Although the engineers lost some of their trucks to 20-mm. flak fire, they managed to keep up with the attack, filling craters in the roads and removing mines and roadblocks from the path of the fast-moving armored columns. The attack proceeded so swiftly that soon bridges were being captured intact. The engineers' main tasks then became removing bombs (some of them American 500-pound aerial bombs) buried in bridge abutments and emplacing flooring that would carry tanks.

On 12 April Combat Command Reserve reached the Elbe. After two days of searching for bridge sites the engineers started to install a bridge at Sandau, but while they were assembling bridge equipment orders came that no bridge would be built.[5]

---

[5] *The Victory Division in Europe*, pp. 50–58; Interv, Capt Frank Perlman, CO, Co C, 22d Armd Engr Bn,

South of XIII Corps in the dash to the Elbe was the bulk of XIX Corps, which also sent some elements even farther south to aid in reducing the Ruhr Pocket. Its rapid sweep to the Elbe was spearheaded by the 2d Armored Division and its 17th Armored Engineer Battalion. By the end of the first week of April the 2d Armored Division had crossed the Weser on treadway bridges its engineers had built and the Leine River on bridges captured intact. On 11 April, after taking the great Hermann Goering Steel Works southwest of Braunschweig, the tankers made a 73-mile march in a single day to reach the Elbe just southeast of Magdeburg at Schoenebeck. There, as the armor drew within a few feet of a still standing bridge, heavy German antiaircraft shelling demolished it.

The tankers then sent for DUKWs. After nightfall on 12 April the DUKWs carried two battalions of armored infantry across the river just south of Magdeburg and before daylight next morning crossed an infantry battalion of the 30th Division. No antitank guns, tanks, or tank destroyers could get across because the water on the near side was too shallow for vehicular ferries.

After dark on 12 April the 17th Armored Engineers began to build a treadway bridge, but shelling from large guns at Magdeburg, increasing with daylight, slowed the work. The engineers set out smoke pots and by noon

---

3 May 45, CI 43, ETOUSA Hist Sect; Intervs, Lt Col Fred E. Ressegieu, CO, and Maj Albert M. Brown, XO, 22d Armd Engr Bn, 4 May 45, CI 278, ETOUSA Hist Sect; Intervs, Lt Col John H. Morave, 85th Div Engr; Lt Col Marvin L. Jacobs, CO, 309th Engr C Bn; and Capt Seymour S. Deutsch, Asst 85th Div Engr, 9 Apr 45, CI 188, ETOUSA Hist Sect.

on 13 April had advanced their bridge to a point within twenty-five yards of the far bank. Two hours later German shellfire destroyed it. Enemy fire also defeated an effort to construct a ferry. The engineers deposited rubble in the river to form a loading ramp and managed to anchor a guide cable to the east bank. Then, as the first raft carrying a bulldozer approached the far bank, German artillery severed the cable, and the raft careened downstream.

The XIX Corps was unable to get tanks across to the precarious bridgehead, where the infantry was being attacked by tanks and assault guns of the new *Twelfth Army*, which the Germans had hastily formed of young men from army schools, overaged conscripts, and other remnants. Accordingly, the XIX Corps commander ordered the infantry to abandon the bridgehead and withdraw. Tanks and infantry of the 2d Armored Division then moved south to use a XIX Corps crossing over the Elbe at Barby, five miles upstream and out of range of the artillery at Magdeburg. There the 83d Division's 295th Engineer Combat Battalion, supported by the 992d Engineer Treadway Bridge Company, had built the first bridge over the Elbe on 13 April. The engineers named the span the Truman Bridge in honor of the new commander in chief. Two days later the 234th Engineer Combat Battalion built another treadway in the same area. The Germans tried in every way, including the use of frogmen, to destroy both bridges but were unsuccessful.

The engineers called their Truman Bridge "Gateway to Berlin"; but it had hardly been built when they learned that it was, in fact, a gateway to nowhere. On 15 April the word came that there was to be no drive to Berlin and no advance beyond the Elbe.[6]

### First Army's Drive to Leipzig and Beyond

On 5 April, after the attack to seal off the Ruhr ended, First Army's V and VII Corps began a drive east to the Leipzig area, where most of the remaining German industrial capacity was concentrated and where General Eisenhower believed the German government was fleeing.[7] The 3d Armored Division, leading the VII Corps advance, was delayed two days by resistance at numerous roadblocks. The V Corps' leading infantry division, the 69th, ran into determined resistance at Hann-Muenden on the Weser and also was stalled for two days. But V Corps' other spearhead unit, the 2d Infantry Division, had a comparatively clear route and by nightfall on 6 April was crossing the Weser in assault boats, thus gaining a bridgehead only one day after Ninth Army had crossed.

On 7 April V Corps engineers built a treadway over the Weser at Hameln for the rest of the 2d Infantry Division and next day helped the 69th Division cross the narrow Werra River via another treadway. On 8 April the engineers built a second treadway over the Weser, this time for the 9th Armored Division at Hann-Muenden, an industrial center where the engineers uncovered a Panzer Pioneer School with a supply of all types of land mines—including Russian ones—as well as German building equipment and tools.

On 10 April General Bradley removed restrictions on eastward movement. That day the 9th Armored Division, once over the Weser, passed through the 2d and 69th Infantry Divisions and raced ahead. Its leading elements were accompanied by V Corps engineers, who undertook reconnaissance and erected signs with the distinctive, pentagonal V Corps insignia.[8]

With little rest during the long drive after the Rhine crossing at Hoenningen, the V and VII Corps engineers were as weary as the tankers and infantrymen who, according to correspondent Hal Boyle,

threw themselves down in fields for a nap whenever the columns paused. They are moving across wide rolling farm lands along roads blanketed with blinding yellow dust. Trucks going back for supplies occasionally drive with their lights on so that the vehicles moving forward won't crash into them in the yellow fog. Black pillars of smoke from enemy vehicles can be seen on the horizon as the tanks smash slowly forward against stiffening resistance from German troops who fight until surrounded or they are out of ammunition and then surrender and say amiably, "The war will be over in two weeks."[9]

Approaching the Saale River on 12 April, the 9th Armored Division ran into an area known to the Allied airmen as "flak alley"—one of the heaviest concentrations of antiaircraft guns (mainly 88-mm.) in Europe. Emplaced in an arc around Leipzig to protect neighboring synthetic oil refineries and related industries, including Germany's

---

[6] MacDonald, *The Last Offensive*, ch. XVII; Hist 17th Armd Engr Bn, Jul 44–May 45; *Thunderbolt Across Europe*, pp. 89–91; Hist XIX Corps Engrs, pp. 19–20, ML 2220, ETOUSA Hist Sect.

[7] Dwight D. Eisenhower, *Crusade in Europe* (Garden City, N.Y.: Doubleday, 1948), p. 400.

[8] AAR, Engr Sect, V Corps, Jan–9 Mar 45.

[9] As quoted in *V Corps Operations in ETO*, p. 426, in CMH.

largest synthetic rubber plant, were about a thousand antiaircraft weapons, depressed for ground fire. The armored division's leading task force on the north lost nine tanks when it came up against the first German position. (*Map 30*)

Because of the flak guns, the V Corps commander, Maj. Gen. Clarence R. Huebner, ordered the 9th Armored Division to bypass Leipzig and push on to the Mulde River. Coming up to the Saale River at Weissenfels on 13 April, part of the armor crossed on a bridge captured intact, the rest on a 240-foot treadway that corps engineers constructed the next day. The infantry divisions following in the wake of the armor crossed on the treadway and in assault boats. The 9th Armored Division drove east toward the Mulde, crossing the Weisse Elster near Zeitz on bridges the Germans did not have time to destroy. The two infantry divisions turned north to attack Leipzig, the 2d moving against the city from the west, the 69th from the south. On 15 April leading elements of the armor reached the Mulde at Colditz, twenty miles southeast of Leipzig. Combat Command Reserve crossed the river on a railroad bridge and released 1,800 prisoners of war at a camp there, but did not advance much beyond the Mulde.

The two infantry divisions moved cautiously against Leipzig, hoping at this late stage of the war to keep casualties down. On the west the 2d Infantry Division launched night attacks to surprise the crews of the flak guns. Because these crews were unaccustomed to ground combat the tactic usually worked, but in this case the infantry suffered heavy casualties before breaking into Leipzig from the west and the

south on 18 April. Prolonged negotiations for surrender ended on 20 April, and the 2d and 69th Infantry Divisions moved on to the Mulde to relieve the 9th Armored Division.

At Leipzig the main concern of V Corps engineers was the water system, damaged by Allied bombing and shelling. Although the water supply was low, it was adequate until German water works employees could undertake repairs, supervised by American engineers. In addition, V Corps engineers took on a job that was normally not their function—repairing a railroad. Reconnaissance showed that the 150-mile railroad line from Muehlhausen to Leipzig could be opened for traffic if about 2,000 feet of bomb-cratered line were refilled, ballasted, and laid with track. The 1121st Engineer Combat Group's 254th Engineer Combat Battalion accomplished the work, taking great pride in naming the repaired road the "Snortin' Bull Express." The rail service carried to Leipzig gasoline for the spearhead units, thereby freeing for normal engineer duties the companies that the 1121st Engineer Group had furnished to haul fuel to the front. On the return trip to Muehlhausen the train carried to the rear German prisoners of war and Allied soldiers released from German prison camps.[10] Following the linkup of U.S. and Russian forces on 25 April, V Corps engineers erected a Bailey bridge over the Mulde at Eilenburg so that the American commanders could cross the river and meet the Russians at Torgau on the Elbe River.

---

[10] AAR, Engr Sect, V Corps, Apr 45; *Dozer Blade* (a weekly newpaper published by the 1121st Engineer Combat Group), 21 Apr 45, copy in Hist 1121st Engr C Gp, Mar–Dec 45.

Sandau

BERLIN

Braunschweig

Magdeburg

Barby

Schoenebeck

Elbe R

Dessau

Torgau

Hameln

Leine R

Muenster

Senden

Eilenburg

Nordhausen

Leipzig

Dresden

Gieselwerder

Weissenfels

Colditz

Hann-Muenden

Werra R

Muehlhausen

Zeitz

Saale R

Mulde R

Chemnitz

Eder R

Fulda R

Gotha

Ohrdruf

GERMANY

CZECHOSLOVAKIA

Frankfurt

Schweinfurt

Lohr

Main R

Aschaffenburg

Oppenheim

Wuerzburg

Worms

Fuerth

Nuremberg

Naab R

Regen R

Jagst R

Altmuehl R

Regensburg

Sulzbach

Mosbach

Danube R

Heilbronn

Crailsheim

Deggendorf

Kocher R

Rhine R

Danube R

Passau

FRANCE

Neckar R

Stuttgart

Isar R

Landshut

Moosburg

Strasbourg

Inn R

AUSTRIA

Freudenstadt

Horb

Ulm

Haigerloch

Hechingen

Ehingen

Munich

Wasserburg

Bisingen

Tailfingen

Dietenheim

Salzburg

Rosenheim

Iller R

Lech R

Garmisch-Partenkirchen

Saalach R

*MAP 30*

The men of VII Corps' 3d Armored Division, swinging eastward in early April north of the V Corps drive, came to feel that "there was always one more river."[11] Col. Mason J. Young, the VII Corps engineer, had long since learned that he could not count on finding German bridges still intact. Therefore, when VII Corps' combat units approached the Weser River on 7 April, he was prepared for a crossing. The organic divisional engineers—the 1st Engineer Combat Battalion supporting the 1st Infantry Division on the left of the 3d Armored Division and the 329th Engineer Combat Battalion supporting the 104th Infantry Division on the right—had assault boats, storm boats, infantry support rafts, and material for footbridges so that they could make an assault crossing and establish a bridgehead. Then VII Corps' 1106th Engineer Combat Group was to build the bridges the 3d Armored and 1st Infantry Divisions would require and the 1120th Engineer Combat Group those needed at the 104th Infantry Division's crossing.[12]

Reaching the Weser at Gieselwerder at midafternoon on 7 April, the leading elements of the 104th Division saw an arched iron bridge still standing. As the Americans dashed toward it, the Germans blew the span. A German tank and about fifty infantrymen left in the town put up a fight, but by dark resistance was over. All night trucks carrying assault boats rolled into Gieselwerder, and before dawn two battalions were crossing in the boats and on a footbridge the 329th Engineer Combat Battalion had built. By noon on 8 April the combat engineers were constructing treadways and infantry support bridges at this and other sites. Late that night the 3d Armored Division's tanks began crossing; before sunset on 9 April the combat commands had crossed the river and, branching out, had captured twenty-two towns beyond the Weser.

At dusk on 11 April assault elements of two task forces of Combat Command B, 3d Armored Division, one commanded by Col. John C. Welborn, the other by Lt. Col. William B. Lovelady, entered Nordhausen. Here, on the eastward route nearest to the Harz Mountain area, Hitler was attempting to mount a counteroffensive to relieve his forces in the Ruhr Pocket, using troops of the newly formed *Twelfth Army*. General Huebner ordered the 3d Armored Division to block exits from the Harz Mountains and sent his 1st Infantry Division and part of his 104th Infantry Division into the mountain redoubt.

Nordhausen was also a place of utter horror. In a concentration camp with a capacity of about 30,000, the tankers discovered the pathetic remnants of a slave labor force used in huge underground factories, one for manufacturing V−2 rockets. Many of the living, in the last stages of starvation and too weak to move, were lying alongside the emaciated dead. The tankers of the 3d, their historian recorded, "were in a savage mood as they went on to the final battles."[13]

The armor fought the last battles between the Saale and the Mulde without infantry support, except from their

---

[11] *Spearhead in the West*, p. 145.

[12] Engr Opns VII Corps, vol. VII, "Crossings of the Rhine River and the Advance to the Elbe," app. 10, Engineer Plan for Weser River Crossing, 6 Apr 45.

[13] *Spearhead in the West*, p. 150.

Men of the 234th Engineer Combat Battalion Haul a Tank Across the Saale River

organic armored infantry units. The 104th Division had orders to stop on the way and capture Halle, the tenth largest city of Germany, which held out until 19 April. Meantime most of Combat Command B, still in the lead, stalled in front of strong enemy panzerfaust positions and antitank fire. Only Task Force Welborn, which hit the softest spot in the German defenses, was able to keep up its momentum. This task force soon reached an autobahn leading north, and by the evening of 14 April one of Welborn's infantry patrols arrived at the point where the autobahn crossed the Mulde on a steel-girder, two-span bridge two miles south of Dessau. The infantrymen found the

autobahn bridge still standing, but before the rest of the task force could come up, the Germans destroyed it. Colonel Welborn thereupon ordered engineers to bring up boats for an assault crossing. The 294th Engineer Combat Battalion sent forward fourteen boats, but by the time the boats arrived early in the afternoon Welborn had decided that the infantry could cross on the destroyed autobahn bridge. The infantry started crossing at 1600, protected by a smoke screen.

Building a new bridge alongside the autobahn bridge did not appear too difficult at first, for the river was narrow and required not more than 150 feet of treadway. But the engineers had hardly begun to inflate pontons when enemy artillery fire fell on them, killing one and wounding three. This fire was so accurate that it stopped the work in midafternoon. Next morning, 16 April, after a crane had put a powerboat into the water to tow pontons to the far bank, German artillery fire hit and set afire a truck arriving with pontons. Two engineers dragged from the blazing truck were seriously burned. All that day and into the moonlit night, enemy shellfire forestalled all bridging work.

On 17 April work resumed under a smoke screen. By afternoon about fifteen pontons were in the water, but then enemy artillery scored a direct hit, killing one engineer, wounding eight, and knocking many more into the water. Arriving on the scene, the commander of Combat Command B suspended operations, and shortly after dark orders came to pull back to the near bank of the Mulde.[14]

### Third Army Reaches Austria

After crossing the Rhine at Oppenheim, Third Army's spearheading XII Corps crossed the Main on battered bridges still standing between Aschaffenburg and Frankfurt am Main. Then the corps left the Rhine-Main plain and headed through rolling forested hills and open farmlands, using the Frankfurt-Dresden autobahn toward the corps' next objective, Chemnitz, south of Leipzig and ten miles beyond the Mulde.

Leading the advance, Combat Command A of the 4th Armored Division struck its first obstacle on 1 April at the Werra River. Bridges were down, and next morning when the 24th Armored Engineer Battalion began to build treadways at two towns, German planes swooped low to attack, while direct fire came from the east bank. The armored infantry finally managed to cross despite small-arms fire; next day the tanks crossed the Werra and were again rolling east along the autobahn.[15]

At Leina the tankers came to a blown overpass that forced them off the autobahn. In any case the 4th Armored Division received orders to backtrack, swing north, and assist in an attack on Gotha. After the town fell, the armor moved south to Ohrdruf, finding a small but gruesome concentration camp. There Combat Command A remained six days. Starting east on 12 April the 4th Armored Division tankers—having by then come under the command of XX Corps—found that demolitions made using the autobahn too dangerous and took to the fields on either side.[16]

For infantry vehicles the Frankfurt-Dresden autobahn was literally the backbone of Third Army's push east during the first half of April. Engineers found that their largest task was not spanning rivers but building bridges over or around the autobahn's damaged overpasses and underpasses. At the rivers the enemy occasionally delayed construction, not only at the Werra but also at the Elster, where the bridge site was dominated for a time by a battery of 88-mm. guns. Yet the Ful-

---

[14] Interv, Capt G. E. Conley, CO, Co B, 23d Armd Engr Bn, 2 May 45, CI 270, ETOUSA Hist Sect.

[15] Hist 24th Armd Engr Bn, Kyll River to Chemnitz, 5 Mar–20 Apr 45, CI 275, ETOUSA Hist Sect.

[16] Interv, Capt Roland G. Ruppenthal with Lt Col Hal C. Pattison, XO, CCA, 4th Armd Div, 22 Apr 45, sub: CCA from the Crossing of the Kyll to Chemnitz.

da, Werra, Saale, and Elster Rivers presented few engineering problems because they were low, making nearly all fordable.[17]

Bridges on the autobahn were normally quite large. Fortunately the Germans usually blew only one span, and when a Bailey could not bridge the gap the engineers would construct a treadway bypass. But so many bridges were down that the engineers began to run out of material. One very wide gap they simply filled with earth; at another site that required a large amount of Bailey bridging, the engineers used bents to make a Class 40 double-single Bailey. Elsewhere, the Germans had buckled two center stringers of a four-stringer bridge and had blown holes in twenty-five feet of the roadbed. Here, building piers to strengthen the buckled stringers was especially difficult because the slope beneath was so steep. Unable to use a bulldozer, the engineers had to work with picks and shovels, and the bents had to be constructed on level ground and moved into position with block and tackle.[18]

On 13 April the 4th Armored Division, leading the XX Corps, reached the Mulde and by nightfall had seized four bridges intact. During the sweep to the Mulde the engineers of the 1154th Engineer Combat Group, supporting the XX Corps drive, carried out reconnaissance of roads and minor road clearance and repairs. The Germans were being pushed back so rapidly that they were unable to do enough damage to slow the advance.

The XX Corps expected to go on to Dresden, but a directive from General Eisenhower on 15 April brought about a radical change in plans.[19] Having decided not to go to Berlin, Eisenhower directed the 12th Army Group to hold along the Elbe-Mulde line with the First and Ninth Armies and sent the Third Army southeast down the Danube valley into Austria for eventual linkup with the Russians.[20]

New plans required the reshuffling of corps. The VIII Corps went to First Army, to remain along the Mulde; III Corps' six divisions, having completed operations in the Ruhr, turned south to take over the right flank in Patton's drive; XX Corps was to move forward in the center and XII Corps on Third Army's left. Third Army was to be strengthened to fifteen divisions, many of them newcomers to battle. Because the regrouping took time, the drive in force could not begin until 23 April although XII and XX Corps actually started to advance three or four days earlier.

By 22 April forward troops of XX Corps were southeast of Nuremberg, only forty miles from the Danube. Leaving the Berlin-Munich autobahn, the corps turned southeast toward Regensburg, where the Danube turns almost at a right angle to flow southeast, paralleling the Czechoslovakian border. On 24 April a task force of the 3d Cavalry Group (Mechanized), leading the XX Corps advance, reached the Danube southwest of Regensburg. Supported by a company of the 245th Engineer Combat Battalion, the cavalry task force began crossing in assault boats the following night.

---

[17] *Third Army Report*, vol. II, Engr Sect, p. Eng–37; Hist 1154th Engr C Gp, 26 Mar–30 Apr 45.

[18] Hist 1107th Engr C Gp, Jan–May 45.

[19] Opns Rpt, 1154th Engr C Gp, 26 Mar–30 Apr 45.

[20] MacDonald, *The Last Offensive*, ch. XVIII. Tactical details on Third Army's drive are from this source.

The 1139th Engineer Combat Group built the first bridge over the Danube to support XX Corps' 71st Infantry Division, newly arrived at the front. By 2215 on 26 April the group's 160th Engineer Combat Battalion had completed an M2 treadway at Sulzbach, just east of Regensburg. While the bridge was being built, group engineers also helped the 71st Division's organic 271st Engineer Combat Battalion to move infantry across in assault boats.[21]

Three Danube tributaries—the Isar, Inn, and Enns Rivers—impeded the drive southeast down the broad Danube valley. At the Isar the engineers found the current too swift for paddled assault boats. Instead, some of the infantry crossed in motor-driven storm boats, while other troops used a damaged railway bridge, at one place climbing hand over hand.

Arriving on 2 May at the Inn River, which marked the border with Austria, 71st Division scouting parties found all bridges down but discovered two large dams that might be used for crossings. In a determined effort to seize the dams before the Germans could blow them, infantrymen of the 71st Division fought their way across, captured German demolition crews just in time, and cut wires that would have set off explosions. By midnight the 71st Division had two bridgeheads across the dams, thereby becoming the first Allied unit to enter Austria from the west.

Late on 3 May XX Corps gave all units the mission of establishing contact with the Russians at the Enns River. Moving over two bridges captured intact beyond Lambach, motorized patrols of the 71st Division on 7 May encountered the headquarters of the Russian 5th Guards Airborne Division near St. Peter, Austria. That day the American patrols withdrew behind the Enns after they received the orders that ended hostilities in Europe.[22]

Advancing to the left of XX Corps down a narrow corridor between the Czechoslovakian border and the Danube, XII Corps had to cross the Naab and the Regen, both tributaries of the Danube. Engineers of the 1135th Engineer Combat Group, supporting XII Corps, found that assault crossings were unnecessary, for resistance was light, mainly scattered small-arms and panzerfaust attacks. The engineers quickly installed tactical bridging and almost immediately replaced such spans with fixed bridges. On the extreme left of the XII Corps advance, in rolling, pine-covered, upland country near the Czechoslovakian border, an armored task force found the Naab so shallow that tanks and other armored vehicles were able to ford it.

On 30 April, an overcast day with some snow, the 1135th Group received orders to plan for an assault crossing of the Danube at Passau; it was canceled when orders came to remain north of the Danube. On 4 May the group completed a ponton bridge at Passau and two days later had a treadway over the Danube at Deggendorf. The XII Corps, arriving just ahead of XX Corps, captured an intact highway bridge over the Danube at Linz, but had hardly

---

[21] AAR, 1139th Engr C Gp, Apr 45.

[22] Fred Clinger, Arthur Johnston, and Vincent Masel, *The History of the 71st Infantry Division* (Munich, 1946), pp. 83–98. For engineer support of XX Corps' 13th Armored Division and 80th Infantry Division in the drive down the Danube after 28 April, see Hist 1154th Engr C Gp.

PONTONS HEADED FOR THE DANUBE

begun to press southeast when word came of the German surrender.[23]

On Patton's right III Corps, with the 86th and 99th Infantry Divisions and the 14th Armored Division, drove south through a corridor between the XX Corps zone and the Berlin-Munich autobahn. Here as in the other zones, the only real obstacles were rivers, first the Altmuehl, then the Danube, and beyond the Danube the Isar and the Inn. All bridges were down.

The 99th Infantry Division, whose own 324th Engineer Combat Battalion had the support of the 1159th Engineer Combat Group's 291st Engineer Combat Battalion, met heavy enemy opposition at the Altmuehl. The division undertook several night assault crossings and by the evening of 26 April was on the banks of the Danube—not the blue Danube the men had imagined, but "a muddy, dirty, yellow colored, fast flowing, smelly river."[24] The division's heavy equipment and supplies arrived promptly, thanks to a treadway the divisional engineers had quickly built over the Altmuehl.

Shortly before noon on 27 April the troops began to move across the Danube in assault boats from four sites. One

---

[23] AAR, 1135th Engr C Gp, Jan–Apr 45; Lt. Col. George Dyer, *XII Corps: Spearhead of Patton's Third Army* (Baton Rouge: Military Press of Louisiana, [1947]), p. 420; *Third Army Report*, vol. II, Engr Sect, p. Eng–43.

[24] Lauer, *Battle Babies*, p. 297.

site was hit by heavy small-arms and artillery fire from well dug-in and concealed enemy positions. But at the other three the troops met little opposition, and the 324th Engineer Combat Battalion, with the help of the 291st, began constructing a ponton bridge near Kienheim at an old boat landing. The road seemed to the division's commanding general "ideal for our purpose."[25]

So it might have been in good weather. But it rained during the afternoon, and when heavy engineer trucks began to haul bridging equipment down to the banks of the Danube, the roadbed disintegrated into a seemingly bottomless marsh. By putting down gravel and stone and corduroying the road with logs cut from nearby forests, the engineers were able to move pontons down to the river. Working all night and all the next day, part of the time under German artillery fire, the engineers completed the bridge before dark on 28 April. The division's trucks and tanks began to roll toward the bridge, then bogged down so badly that the engineers had to use tractors to tow them out of the marsh and onto the bridge apron. The work of reinforcing the road resumed, continuing after dark by turning on truck headlights. This was the first time in the war the engineers supporting the 99th Infantry Division had been permitted to use lights at night. No hostile fire fell because infantry had crossed the bridge on foot and had driven the German artillery out of range.

By nightfall of 29 April elements of the 99th Division had reached the Isar at two towns, Moosburg on the near bank and Landshut astride the river.

At Landshut, where the enemy put up a stiff fight, the 99th Division infantry climbed over the debris of a blown bridge at Moosburg, ran across on a dam nearby, and paddled over the Isar in assault boats. To get the 14th Armored Division tanks in position to help in the fight required strenuous engineer effort. Working under artillery fire the engineers built a short treadway from the near side of the Isar to an island in the river. From there the tanks fired on Landshut, which fell early on 1 May. By dark all elements of the 99th Division had crossed the Isar.

Advancing toward the Inn River in a light snowfall, the infantry soon outdistanced the armor, roadbound because of soggy fields and stopped by blown bridges. The 99th Infantry Division was the first III Corps element to reach the Inn, but it was to go no farther. Just before noon on 2 May, corps ordered the division to halt and await new orders. Within sight of the Bavarian Alps, the division received the news that Germany had surrendered.[26]

### Seventh Army to the "Alpine Fortress"

Breaking out of its Rhine bridgehead near Worms with the mission of protecting 12th Army Group's right during its drive toward Leipzig, Seventh Army advanced on a 120-mile-wide front—more than double the width of the army sectors within 12th Army Group. The Seventh Army commander, General Patch, gave XV Corps the main role on the left, ordered XXI Corps to drive east in the center, and sent VI

[25] Ibid., p. 304.

[26] Ibid., pp. 297−318; Hist 1159th Engr C Gp, 26 Jun 44−20 Aug 45; Hist 291st Engr C Bn, Jan−Apr 45, May 45.

Corps to the south on the right. When the drive began early in April the 6th Army Group commander, Lt. Gen. Jacob L. Devers, restricted the VI Corps drive because he did not have strength for an all-out advance. The weak link was the First French Army, which had to keep some troops on the west bank of the Rhine facing the Black Forest, others along the French-Italian frontier, and still others at ports along the French Atlantic coast.[27]

Making the main thrust on the north, XV Corps advanced rapidly. Although some of the towns in the corps' path, notably Aschaffenburg, were resolutely defended, the combat units met only sporadic resistance while marching to their objective, the Hohe Rhoen hill mass, during the first week in April. The Germans derisively called their own roadblocks 61-minute blocks because, they said, "It will take the Americans sixty-one minutes to get past them. They will look at them and laugh sixty minutes and then tear them down in one."[28]

More troublesome to the engineers was debris on the roads—German vehicles that American tanks, artillery, and planes had destroyed.[29] Debris also filled the streets of the fire-scarred towns, and the engineers went in to clear the streets while fighting was still going on. The 14th Armored Division, leading the XV Corps advance, met its first serious resistance at Lohr. The engineers entered the town at nightfall to find it "afire from the shelling, the flames leaping through the darkness

and crackling through the madness of the firing; the smoke was in your eyes and nose, and the weird shadows of the men running, and of the tanks, and of nothing at all (at night, in a burning town, in war) leapt and jumped along the walls."[30]

Moving along with the combat troops during the rapid march, the engineers had some strange encounters. One occurred near Lohr. Lt. Melvin O. Robinson of the 125th Armored Engineer Battalion, reconnoitering in his jeep with his driver, Pfc. George A. Bartels, saw a Mark VI tank by the road. The two men were approaching it cautiously to see whether it was mined, when all at once they were surrounded and fired upon by a party of twenty-one German soldiers. Neither American had time to fire, and both were wounded. Then the Germans threw down their weapons and surrendered. Toward the end of the week, two jeeploads of engineers starting out one night to look for a bivouac ran into an ambush at a roadblock. A mortar round killed one man and wounded another. The rest of the men were taken prisoner, but before the night was over tankers of the 14th Armored Division found and released them.[31]

Resistance decreased as the troops reached the narrow, winding roads of the Hohe Rhoen. On 8 April Seventh Army's armor established contact with Third Army, and the time had come for XV Corps to turn southeast.

Through the zones of both XV and XXI Corps meandered the Main River, making so many loops and turns that it had to be crossed not once but several

---

[27] MacDonald, *The Last Offensive*, p. 430. Unless otherwise cited, tactical details are from this source.

[28] Taggart, *History of the Third Infantry Division*, p. 346.

[29] Ibid., p. 350.

[30] Capt. Joseph Carter, *History of the 14th Armored Division*, ch. XII.

[31] Ibid.

times—when XV Corps' 3d Infantry Division turned south on 11 April the division crossed the Main for the fourth time.[32] Most of the bridges over the Main were down, but the crossings presented no special engineer problems. The river was fordable in places, and Seventh Army had plenty of DUKWs to help in the crossings.

In the XXI Corps sector a regiment of the 42d Infantry Division and a combat command of the 12th Armored Division reached the Main opposite Wuerzburg on the night of 2 April to find the three bridges across the river down. Unwilling to wait for the 142d Engineer Combat Battalion to arrive with assault boats, a party of Rangers crossed just before dawn in a rowboat they had found along the bank. They reached the far bank unobserved and sent the boat back for another load. The two boatloads of Rangers had established a small bridgehead by the time the engineers came up.

Daylight revealed a surprising scene. Across the river rose the ramparts of the huge Marienburg Castle. On one of the retaining walls the Germans had painted in large white letters "Heil Hitler!"

As the first engineer assault boat of eleven infantrymen and three engineers reached midstream, the Germans opened fire with rifles and 20-mm. antiaircraft guns. The guns were not very accurate, possibly because the Germans were unable to depress the barrels sufficiently, but throughout the day shells fell around the boats. In spite of enemy fire and a swift current, the engineers managed to get an entire infantry battalion across before the day was over. While the infantry enlarged the bridgehead the engineers built a ferry for jeeps, ambulances, and radio equipment and began constructing a Bailey across a hole the Germans had blown in a substantial stone bridge leading into the castle area.

Before dawn on 4 April foot troops (but not vehicles) were able to use the Bailey bridge. To bring armored aid to the infantry the engineers erected a treadway bridge. While the fight was raging in the city early next morning, a party of about two hundred Germans made a desperate, last-ditch attempt to reach and destroy the treadway and to demolish the Bailey, which was still not complete. The attack stalled a hundred yards short of the Bailey bridge, and by the end of the day the battle for Wuerzburg was over.[33]

On the following day, 6 April, the 42d Infantry Division moved northeast toward the corps' next objective, Schweinfurt, the center of the German ball-bearing industry. The main problem was 88-mm. guns ringing the city. These weapons had made Schweinfurt one of the costliest of all targets for Allied bombers and, because the guns could be depressed for ground fire, would very likely make it costly for ground troops as well. The plan was to encircle the city with the 42d's three regiments. No assault river crossing was required, but to enable a combat command of the 12th Armored Division to swing south of Schweinfurt and cut the enemy's escape route to the east, the 142d Engineer Combat Battalion built a treadway over the Main at Nordheim. The

---

[32] Taggart, *History of the Third Infantry Division*, p. 351.

[33] *42d "Rainbow" Infantry Division: A Combat History of World War II (1947)*, pp. 58–70.

encirclement was successful, and with the close support of medium bombers most of the 88-mm. guns were destroyed. By 13 April XXI Corps was ready to turn southeast and help XV Corps capture Nuremberg by attacking the suburb Fuerth.

Nuremberg lay in a broad valley veined by three rivers with confusing names. The Rednitz, flowing from the south, and the Pegnitz, from the east, joined at the northern boundaries of Fuerth to form the Regnitz. The river crossings were not difficult. For example, in the XV Corps' zone, under cover of darkness the 3d Infantry Division made unopposed crossings of both the Regnitz and a man-made stream paralleling it, Ludwigs Canal; the 45th Infantry Division crossed the Pegnitz over a bridge captured intact. Within the city, through which the Pegnitz and the canal ran, all bridges were down, but troops could cross on the twisted girders of blown bridges.

The engineers' hardest task was removing roadblocks, which were numerous and strong and included streetcars derailed and placed sideways, barriers of logs, and huge chunks of scrap iron and steel. Another engineering task that was to prove increasingly important went to the 40th Engineer Combat Group's 2831st Engineer Combat Battalion, attached to the 3d Division. As the infantry progressed through the city the engineer battalion assumed the guard of enemy installations, not only the usual railroad yards and factories but also important Nazi Party offices in Nuremberg. Eighty-six such installations had been discovered by the time Nuremberg fell on 20 April.[34]

The XV Corps' next objective was Munich. Then the corps was to plunge into an area the Germans called the *Alpenfestung* ("Alpine fortress") and the Americans called the National Redoubt, presumably located in the mountains of southern Bavaria, western Austria, and northern Italy. General Eisenhower believed that the Germans intended to withdraw into this mountain fortress. To block such a move, he directed 6th Army Group to advance into a wide area containing the passes into the Italian Alps, including the famous Brenner Pass. The Alpine fortress region extended from Salzburg on the right, in the XV Corps line of march, to Lake Constance on the left, where VI Corps was heading.[35]

While XV and XXI Corps were making grand sweeps to Nuremburg, VI Corps, on the right of the Seventh Army sector, halted early in April before strong German resistance at the Neckar and Jagst Rivers. About ten miles north of Heilbronn, an important communications center, the Neckar forks. Its right fork, the Jagst, flows northeast, then southeast through the town of Crailsheim. Along the arc of the Jagst between Heilbronn and Crailsheim, the enemy unexpectedly delayed VI Corps for about ten days.

Combat commands of the 10th Armored Division, spearheading the 63d and 100th Infantry Divisions, found the bridges over the Neckar and Jagst down. While the bulk of the armor waited for

---

[34] *Rpt of Opns, The Seventh United States Army in France and Germany 1944–1945*, vol. III, pp. 792–96; Tag-

gart, *History of the Third Infantry Division*, p. 353; *42d "Rainbow" Division*, p. 85; Opns Rpt, 40th Engr C Gp, 1 Apr–25 Aug 45.

[35] Eisenhower, *Crusade in Europe*, p. 397; Toland, *The Last 100 Days*, pp. 262–63. For a map of the German National Redoubt area, see *Seventh Army Report*, vol. III, opposite p. 807.

bridging at the most important objective, Heilbronn, the 63d Division crossed the Neckar on a treadway downstream at Mosbach and began reconnoitering the north bank of the Jagst.

Considered the gateway to Bavaria and the Alps, Heilbronn was strongly defended. On 4 and 5 April three battalions of the 100th Division managed to cross the Neckar and establish tenuous bridgeheads in a factory area on the far bank, but German artillery on heights above the city prevented the construction of a treadway bridge and destroyed ferries that might have taken tanks across.

The 10th Armored Division had to use the 63d Division's bridge downstream at Mosbach and so was unable to help in the attack on Heilbronn. Instead, it became involved in a battle for Crailsheim. The town fell on 6 April, but the Germans succeeded in cutting its line of communications and continued to counterattack strongly. Crailsheim became "another Bastogne." By 11 April Maj. Gen. Edward H. Brooks, commanding VI Corps, decided it was not worth the effort to hold the town; that night the armored division withdrew. The tankers turned west, forded the shallow headwaters of the Kocher River, and headed for a meeting with the infantry east of Heilbronn.[36]

In the meantime, the infantry of the 100th Division was putting up a desperate fight for Heilbronn. By the afternoon of 7 April the 31st Engineer Combat Battalion had almost completed a treadway when German artillery scored a direct hit on it. The following morning the engineers emplaced a second treadway. Some tanks and tank destroyers managed to cross before the Germans destroyed the span at noon, but even with the help of tanks the 100th Division was unable to push east of Heilbronn until 14 April.[37]

By 17 April engineers of the 540th Engineer Combat Group, in close support of VI Corps, were building bridges over the Neckar, the Jagst, and the Kocher to get men and supplies forward for a push across the Danube and into the Alpine fortress.[38] Leaving Stuttgart to the First French Army, VI Corps raced toward the Danube. The first crossings the corps made came around midnight on 23 April. The 10th Armored Division used three bridges captured near Ehingen, while the 44th Division employed a treadway south of the town. Part of the infantry division turned north to assist in the capture of the medieval city of Ulm, astride the Danube. In the path of this force lay the Iller River, flowing into the Danube near Ulm. In the swift current the infantry's assault boats capsized, forcing one company to cross on cables, hand over hand, while engineers placed heavy logs across blown bridges for catwalk crossings.

Two combat commands of the 10th Armored Division, racing more than twenty miles ahead, reached the Iller during the night of 24 April, and a company of the division's 55th Armored Engineer Battalion built a treadway bridge near Dietenheim. An incident at this bridge typified the fluidity of pursuit warfare. A trapped German column attempted to escape over the tread-

[36] Lester M. Nichols, *Impact: The Battle Story of the Tenth Armored Division* (1954), pp. 221–70.

[37] *Seventh Army Report*, vol. III, pp. 782–89.
[38] Jnl, 540th Engr C Gp, Jan–May 45.

way in the darkness, using a captured American truck to lead it. The Germans almost succeeded. When the Americans discovered that the column was German, a wild firefight erupted, during which an engineer bulldozer operator used his blade to bring down a German officer.[39]

Although disorganized, the enemy was still capable of placing dangerous obstacles in the path of tanks. As the 10th Armored Division moved into the Bavarian Alps, it found bridges over deep gorges destroyed, huge craters blown in the roads, and fields mined. At one point the Germans had rolled down the hairpin curve of a mountain road a 200-yard-wide avalanche of boulders, gravel, and logs.

On 30 April the armor halted at the resort town of Garmisch-Partenkirchen; infantrymen of the 44th and 103d Divisions took up the advance through the Alpine passes to the Inn River valley, nestling between the precipitous mountain ranges of the Bavarian Alps on the north and the Tyrolean Alps on the south, along the border with Italy. The 44th Division, heading for Resia Pass on the Austrian-Italian border, slowed early at a point where the enemy had blasted away a cliffside road.[40] A bypass had to be found. Then the troops were hindered by snowbanks blocking the roads and falling rain, mixed with snow. On 5 May, when surrender negotiations began and all advances in the VI Corps sector halted, the division was still more than twenty miles short of its goal.

The 103d Infantry Division, commanded by Maj. Gen. Anthony C. McAuliffe and headed for Innsbruck and the Brenner Pass, had better luck. By the evening of 3 May the division was in Innsbruck, and one of its motorized regiments was on its way to the Brenner Pass, headlights blazing; at 0150, 4 May, McAuliffe's men took the pass. Later in the morning advance parties sent over the border into Italy met Americans from the U.S. Fifth Army, thus fulfilling a prediction made by General Eisenhower when he left the Mediterranean for the European theater late in 1943 that he would meet the soldiers of the Mediterranean command "in the heart of the enemy homeland."[41]

The last Alpine pass to be captured was at Salzburg, important because the Germans fleeing from Patton's Third Army might attempt to use it. On 1 May XV Corps, in position to move swiftly down the Munich-Salzburg autobahn, was assigned to capture Salzburg. After assault crossings of the Danube and Lech Rivers on 26 April, XV Corps took Munich by nightfall of the thirtieth. Through the city ran the Isar River, which might have delayed the advance, but with the help of German anti-Nazi resistance forces ten bridges within the city were seized intact. Leaving the 45th Infantry Division to garrison Munich, Maj. Gen. Wade H. Haislip, the XV Corps commander, assigned the capture of Salzburg to the 3d Infantry Division with the 106th Cavalry Group attached and the 20th Armored Division, a newly arrived unit that had

---

[39] Nichols, *Impact: The Battle Story of the Tenth Armored Division*, p. 278.

[40] See photograph, *Seventh Army Report*, vol. III, p. 842.

[41] Eisenhower, *Crusade in Europe*, p. 418. For tactical details of the drive for the passes, see *Seventh Army Report*, vol. III, pp. 840–47.

replaced the 14th Armored Division. The 42d Infantry Division was to secure crossings for armor at the Inn River, the last major barrier to the Alpine fortress area. The advance was to begin on 2 May.[42]

One task force of the 3d Infantry Division was already moving on 1 May. In an unseasonable May Day snowstorm, whipped by a cold wind from the Alps, the force sped down the autobahn to cut off escaping Germans and secure bridges across the Inn. At Rosenheim the Americans found three bridges. Two they captured without difficulty, but the third—the most strategically located and the only one capable of carrying tanks—was defended briefly by a small party of Germans. The infantry task force took the offensive, but stopped at the bridge, which had mines strewn along its flooring. Then the task force commander noticed a smoldering fuse beneath the bridge and cut the primacord just in time to prevent the detonation of a huge amount of explosives. This bridge not only took the divisional tanks over the Inn but also enabled the 3d Division to win the race for Salzburg—the advance of the 20th Armored Division had slowed when the 42d Infantry Division was unable to find an intact bridge in its area. Not until late on 3 May did tanks of the 20th Armored cross the Inn, using a dam near Wasserburg.

By nightfall on 3 May elements of the 3d Infantry Division, racing down the autobahn, had reached the Saalach River, only five or six miles southwest of Salzburg.[43] In the lead was the 2d

Battalion of the 7th Infantry. The regiment was an old one with a great deal of esprit de corps—its crest and colors carried a cotton bale, symbolizing service under Andrew Jackson at the Battle of New Orleans, where it had used such bales as breastworks. It had landed in North Africa on 8 November 1942 and had been fighting ever since. Finding all three bridges over the Saalach down, the 10th Engineer Combat Battalion crossed the 2d Battalion, 7th Infantry, in assault boats. By dawn on 4 May the infantry was entering Salzburg. The city quickly capitulated. By then it was plain that German resistance in the Alpine fortress, or National Redoubt, was no more than a mirage.

### Support of Alsos

In the last half of April, with German armies collapsing, Allied technical teams moved into Germany in the VI Corps area to capture German scientists, documents, and equipment in order to assess their contributions to the German war effort. Because of the progress the United States had made in achieving nuclear reactions in the Manhattan Project, the most urgent of these efforts sought intelligence on how close the German scientists were to building a fission bomb that, even at that late hour, might change the course of the war. An investigation team of nuclear scientists had already been active in Alsace, capturing almost 1,000 tons of uranium ore and various equipment in the 6th Army Group area. Associated with the American nuclear research effort in the United States and operating under the code name ALSOS, the team, commanded by Col. Boris T. Pash, now sought to seize the remain-

---

[42] AAR, XV Corps, 31 Jul 44–31 May 45.
[43] Taggart, *History of Third Infantry Division*, pp. 369, 371.

ing uranium supply, the research documents and laboratories, and the brains behind German nuclear science.[44]

To support these scientific teams, SHAEF assigned each army group command a so-called T-Force headquarters to which scientific personnel were assigned when they arrived in the theater. The technical experts and theoretical scientists usually were accompanied by a complement of combat troops to protect them and by combat engineers who could serve that purpose but whose main task was to dismantle captured equipment and laboratories. In General Devers' headquarters, the 1269th Engineer Combat Battalion provided combat engineer support for the 6th Army Group T-Force.

Intelligence gathered in ALSOS operations before the 6th Army Group crossed the Rhine pointed to the existence of a dispersed research complex centered on the villages of Hechingen, Bisingen, and Tailfingen nestled at the eastern edge of the Black Forest.

Colonel Pash's target area lay in a broad valley laced with the tributaries of the Neckar River, a region of charm and natural beauty. At the western end of the valley lay Freudenstadt, some twenty-five miles east of the Rhine at the same latitude as Strasbourg in Alsace. From Freudenstadt southeast curved a rough arc of small towns that marked the scientific mission's line of advance across thirty-five miles of German countryside. Denied an airborne operation to secure this area, Pash decided instead on an unsupported thrust into the hills, risky as it was in the face of small and scattered, but still combat ready, groups of German soldiers and SS troops.

Colonel Pash's difficulties were compounded by the sudden successes of the First French Army. On 16 April the 6th Army Group had drawn army boundaries in the area to leave the city of Stuttgart in the Seventh Army zone of operations. French forces had cleared the east bank of the Rhine opposite Strasbourg by that date and General Jean de Lattre de Tassigny, ignoring General Devers' restrictions on his movements, exploited his advantage to thrust north and seize Stuttgart by 22 April. This forced Colonel Pash to move his team across a French rear area, a feat that took resolution, considerable bluff, and occasional strong language with French soldiery. The French Provisional Government never knew the nature of the search missions, but suspected that General Devers hoped to capture the remnants of the Vichy French regime, which had taken refuge in the German city of Sigmaringen, some fifty miles south of Stuttgart.

The 1269th Engineer Combat Battalion less its Company B, left behind with the 6th Army Group T-Force, joined the ALSOS team at Freudenstadt on the morning of 21 April; the engineer contingent became Task Force White, after its commander, Lt. Col. Willard White. The entire command of scientists, engineers, and British technicians was known as Task Force A.[45]

---

[44] The mission was called ALSOS, the Greek word for "grove" (as in olive grove), as a play on the name of then Maj. Gen. Leslie R. Groves, the military head of the U.S. Manhattan Project. This account of the activities of the investigation team in Germany relies on the unit records of the 1269th Engineer Combat Battalion for April and May 1945 and on Col. Boris T. Pash's *The ALSOS Mission* (New York: Award Books, 1969), pp. 204–41.

---

[45] Unit Records, 1269th Engr C Bn, Jan–May 45. The 1269th replaced its own Company B with

The same morning Task Force A set out on Colonel Pash's Operation BIG from Freudenstadt through the quiet town of Horb to Haigerloch, twenty miles east of Freudenstadt. Here the elated scientists made their first big discovery. As the engineer troops consolidated the group's position in the town, the ALSOS team shot open a bolted door sealing the entrance to a cave in the side of a cliff. Inside, the team found a large chamber and several smaller rooms crammed with instruments, control boxes, and an array of cylinders described by a frightened German technician as a uranium machine. Though missing its uranium element, the device was an operating atomic pile, captured undamaged.

While the scientists, with engineer help, spent two days dismantling the equipment, Colonel Pash led most of the engineers to the Bisingen-Hechingen area, the next populated complex. Spurred by statements of Germans captured at Haigerloch, the force went in search of the missing uranium and other German scientists in the vicinity. Early engineer patrols ran into increasing signs of enemy small unit activity. Bisingen itself was quiet when the engineer column snaked into the town, but as the scientists left to explore Hechingen four miles to the north, a skirmish between engineers remaining in Bisingen and some German stragglers set off a show of resistance to the American troops by the hostile inhabitants. Colonel White put the whole battalion on alert, and the incident passed without further development, though the men advancing into the last town occu-

pied during Operation BIG were considerably more edgy for this experience.

Early on 24 April, Company A, bayonets fixed, moved on Tailfingen, ten miles by road southeast of Bisingen. In Bisingen and Hechingen some twenty-five noted German nuclear physicists and their staffs had surrendered and under interrogation had revealed the location of other German technical facilities in the town Task Force A now approached. Although expecting resistance, the engineer column pulled into Tailfingen after encountering little more than a roadblock on the way. By noon the troops had established Task Force A in Tailfingen and had surveyed the area for signs of German military activity. The atmosphere here contrasted sharply with that in Bisingen the day before. The laboratory staff of nuclear physicist Dr. Otto Hahn was cooperative as was the burgermeister, and the task force soon had the information it needed.

The last discoveries of Operation BIG were at hand. In a cesspool in the town the team found a large metal container holding the valuable secret research papers of the Hahn laboratory. The Allied technicians then moved to a plowed field outside the town to supervise a hastily impressed German excavation crew, whose digging uncovered a large wooden platform. Drawing back this cover, they found a neat stack of dark ingots—the missing uranium from the pile at Haigerloch. A nearby gristmill yielded up three large drums of heavy water, used to control the reaction in the pile.

The engineers loaded this treasure aboard the battalion's trucks with some strain, the scientists hardly concealing

Company B of the 163d Engineer Combat Battalion to fill its ranks. Colonel Pash incorrectly identifies Colonel White as Wilbur White.

their amusement at the surprise of the troops as they loaded the trucks. The deceptively light-looking stack of ingots, about two cubic feet in size, weighed over two tons, uranium being among the densest elements.

With the entire supply of German uranium in Allied hands, Operation BIG ended, as did the 1269th Engineer Combat Battalion's association with the ALSOS team. The battalion returned to the 6th Army Group T-Force at Munich in the closing days of the war.[46]

Engineer units were a central element in the last six weeks of the war against crumbling German forces in the heart of the Reich. In the war of pursuit that eventually cut Hitler's dwindling territory in half, the race to the Elbe in the north and into Austria and Czechoslovakia in the south was a matter of bridges and open roads. Along lines of communications from French and Dutch ports to the most forward fighting front, engineers supported the advance that contributed to the final collapse of the Nazi regime.

---

[46] Among the later discoveries made by the men of Company A of the battalion around Munich was the cache of stolen art treasures hidden in a mine outside the city. The erstwhile owner of this collection was Reichsmarschal Hermann Goering.

# CHAPTER XXV

# Conclusion

U.S. Army engineers unquestionably fulfilled their traditional mission in the Mediterranean and European theaters in World War II. In their massive construction program in England, they housed the Allied armies preparing for the main thrust against German forces in the west. In combat zones in both theaters, engineer work on beaches and in bridging, rail and road construction, and mine clearance permitted the tactical advance of combat elements. Diverse specialty units from water purification to engineer pipeline companies also contributed to the success. In the communications zones, constant rehabilitation of harbors and of lines of communications guaranteed the movement of Army supply in unprecedented volume and provided facilities for other service branches. Of course, none of these accomplishments was without drawback or fault. Like the rest of the Army throughout the war, the engineers learned and relearned lessons constantly, often in the face of enemy fire.

During the interwar period the Corps of Engineers had acquiesced in the almost inevitable allocation of limited funds to combat arms at the expense of combat support elements. In the small American Army of the 1930s, training had consistently favored combat engineering and the quick engagement of

the enemy to produce a decision in a short time, all at the expense of a thorough grounding in administrative functions and the methods of building and maintaining a rear area service of supply. When the first engineers went overseas, the want of properly schooled supply personnel and of a comprehensive system of supply management compounded the material shortages that plagued them. The engineers in England in 1941 wrestled with their early logistical problems without much application of one of the chief American contributions to warfare: a business sense of organization, efficiency, and planning foresight. The lack of trained depot troops and of an adequate and standardized inventory procedure continued on the Continent later in the war and contributed to the shipping crisis of the fall of 1944. Improvement was slow, and at the close of the war the ETO chief engineer called for a revamping of engineer supply doctrine, policy, and operating procedures.

A problem as basic as the supply shortages was the alarmingly low level of engineering and construction experience among new engineer officers and troops arriving in England after 1942. Though aviation engineer units could learn their jobs by doing them in England, combat and construction engineers had barely enough time during the BOLERO buildup to learn the rudiments of their trade as they would practice it under fire. Officers in the theater perforce absorbed an education in the technical side of their work and at the same time in the art of leadership. The training of engineers overseas also suffered from the uncertainties of strategic direction through 1942 and 1943; the TORCH operation committed many of the most accomplished engineers to the war in North Africa.

The ETOUSA command structure that first evolved in England with the theater chief engineer subordinate to the theater services of supply echelon persisted to the end of the war in northern Europe. Though the peculiarities of that arrangement placed General Moore at an organizational level from which he could advise General Eisenhower on engineer affairs only through General Lee, he, like the other technical chiefs in the theater, accommodated himself to this system, and it never exercised an untoward effect on engineer operations. Similarly, the sometimes tangled lines of authority for the engineers in North Africa saw resolution only in the last year of the war, but here too other considerations were more important to engineer performance than the top-level organization.

The evolution and the employment of major new engineer organizations and units in the theaters met with mixed success. With the enemy in possession of ports on the Continent and with North African harbors of any consequence under Vichy control, gaining a foothold in either area involved amphibious operations. The amphibian brigades the engineers developed to meet the demands of seaborne inva-

sion were original in concept, but only partially realized their true potential in European and North African operations. In contrast to the Pacific, where engineers retained their boat regiments, the truncation of the brigades in Europe limited their performance; when the Navy insisted on running all the landing craft to be employed in beach operations, the Army brigades lost their organic boat elements. The division of labor remained, however; all activities on the seaward side of a landing operation were the responsibility of the Navy and everything on shore remained the province of the Army. No single authority controlled the entire expanse between the ships offshore and the inland supply dumps. The history of amphibious operations after TORCH saw continuous efforts to provide this control by placing on the beach an organization whose writ would extend seaward and landward from the traditional division point of Army and Navy authority during an assault landing—the high-water mark on the beach. In subsequent invasions, joint Army-Navy organizations were formed to manage traffic from offshore and to move supply across the beaches quickly. These arrangements brought ashore not only naval demolitions experts with Army engineers, but also an entire self-contained organization, the engineer special brigade, with the functions of obstacle demolition, fire fighting, ordnance disposal, medical service, quartermaster duties, vehicle maintenance, signals, and traffic management. Despite the loss of the boat regiments, the engineers adapted to an amphibious doctrine and an assault function with organizations unknown in the Army before the war.

Through the war in Europe, as in

other theaters, the engineers struggled with demands of unprecedented complexity on their unit structure. The triangular division with its assigned engineer battalion proved itself in battle in North Africa, Italy, and northern Europe. But the introduction in the theaters of other new and specialized engineer functions during the press of combat created command and organizational problems that began to see some resolution only toward the conflict's end. The evolution of units along the group concept reflected efforts to tailor engineer commands to meet the exigencies of modern war. The direct borrowing of techniques and manpower from the national industrial base brought the latest industrial methods and devices into military use rapidly, but the absorbing of these features into a regular military organization involved trial, error, and time.

The engineer group concept forsook the traditional regimental structure for one based on function and extreme flexibility. As a tactical headquarters with its engineer battalions attached rather than assigned to it, the group was a loose organization that allowed the rapid transfer of specialty units in and out of the command for specific tasks. Heavy equipment belonging to the group's battalions was generally concentrated in a separate supply pool that took the place of the regiment's headquarters and service company so that the individual battalions could travel light.

The pronounced advantages in flexibility and mobility achieved by the engineer battalions in this fashion were not entirely unqualified. The rapid introduction of the group concept produced widely disparate ideas as to the command arrangements between headquarters and subordinate attached units; doctrine on group tactics was lacking, and the shifting of units from one group to another frequently caused more administrative confusion and morale problems than were acceptable. The burden on independent battalion commanders for planning and carrying out work was too great for the staffs they had available to them. The group concept was also so unevenly applied in the field that widely divergent practices held sway in Italy and in northwestern Europe. Though this did not affect the performance of the units as much as other factors such as shortages of manpower, engineers in the European theater who gathered after the war to discuss their experiences decided that the concept had been overused and imperfectly applied; they voted to retain the desirable features of the engineer group in a more formal military unit with a regimental designation.[1]

Quite aside from the problems of new engineer functions to be performed, some lack of technical experience also surfaced among officers as the war progressed despite an excellent engineer reserve establishment. The rapid expansion of the officer corps and the often hasty training of candidates at home produced situations in the field in which engineer troops had more technical know-how than some of their officers. Highly specialized organizations such as port construction and repair groups and petroleum distribution companies at first benefited from

---

[1] ETO Gen Bd Rpt 71, Engineer Organization, p. 12.

the crash recruiting campaigns among the marine technicians and wildcatters of civilian industry. As with the general service regiments first sent to England, the result was often a concentration of scarce talent in a few units. Units formed later had the pick of the draft and of qualified officers, but, however well motivated, these men had to learn much of their work after they had reached the theaters of operations.

Though the petroleum distribution companies also suffered this disadvantage, the reasons for their sometimes slow progress lay elsewhere. Pipeline construction could never keep up with the tactical units in their race across northern France after the breakout from the lodgment area of Normandy. The unexpectedly rapid advance from southern France likewise outran the pipeline that was to carry fuel forward to the combat elements. Even with more manpower and a surplus of pipeline material, a rapidly changing tactical situation imposed impossible construction demands upon the petroleum distribution companies in the field. Gasoline-starved armored divisions were sending truck convoys on 250-mile supply runs to the closest pipehead through August and early September 1944.

The systems nevertheless proved themselves. Without them, POL supply lines would have relied on truck and road capacity that was equally taxed during the pursuit warfare of late summer 1944. In the slower moving Italian campaign, pipeline troops had more success in keeping pace with the fighting units they were supplying despite the rugged terrain. The chief engineer of the Mediterranean theater considered them among the best special engi-

neer troops in the Peninsular Base Section.[2]

The engineers in Europe and North Africa quickly learned the value of modern heavy equipment in combat support and in rear area operations. The versatile engineer bulldozer, which became the symbol of the American ability to tackle seemingly impossible jobs, was indispensable in all aspects of road and airfield construction. Supplemented by graders and rollers that leveled roads and fields in short order and by huge rock crushers to provide aggregate from quarries, the dozer consistently enabled the engineers to rehabilitate older lines of communications or to create new ones at great speed. Without their large and powerful machinery, in fact, the engineers could not have coped with their assignments. Constant revision of the standard TOEs for equipment through the war reflected the trend toward ever heavier machinery. At the war's end, engineer officers recommended that the D−7 Caterpillar dozer be standard in all units, replacing any lighter machines.

Similar sentiments prevailed on the use of trucks, which grew larger and heavier in American and British inventories as the war went on. The humble 2 1/2-ton dump truck was always in short supply for the engineers. Adaptable to a number of uses, including the easy transport of oil pipeline sections, the dump trucks were valuable enough to prompt demands for their substitution for cargo vehicles of the same size. The Brockway trucks issued to engineer heavy ponton units to transport bridge sets and floats also contributed

[2] Coll, Keith, and Rosenthal, *The Corps of Engineers: Troops and Equipment,* p. 437.

to the trend toward larger and heavier vehicles.

The tactical bridging with which the American Army experimented in 1940 in imitation of German examples proved itself in combat, but one of the most rewarding measures of the war was the adoption of the British Bailey bridge. Besides providing a common heavy bridge for both British and U.S. Armies, the Bailey was far more versatile than any American design and proved itself even as a floating ponton structure. In another application of modern technique to an engineer function, the use of light aircraft for observation and photographic surveillance added much to the process of estimating bridging and road-building requirements along projected lines of advance that still lay in enemy territory. In Europe, the engineers could also harness a steel production capacity to their own use. Contracts with French firms supplemented the American supply, especially of I-beam stringers for heavy railway bridging.

In one area, mine warfare, German practice continued to excel until the end of the war. American methods were inferior by comparison; standard U.S. Army mines were usually smaller and far less ingenious in design than the German variety. The Teller antitank mine had twice the explosive charge of the American M-1 antitank mine, which did little damage to German tank hulls, though it could wreck tracks that struck it. Smaller American antipersonnel mines were often unstable and dangerous to the engineers implanting them. Engineer training in mine warfare theory was more than adequate, but the men lacked the experience that would have made them experts. Captured or swept ordnance was always too danger-

ous to transport to the United States, and as a result many engineers came to the battlefield without having seen the devices they were to unearth and disarm. The engineers established countermine schools in the theaters and shared their own experience with the troops of other arms in an attempt to save lives and to establish standards for American mine warfare. The SCR-625 detector and such innovations as the Snake proved of more value than devices like the Scorpion flail, but the war ended with the engineers still relying on the one method of mine sweeping used from the start: a sharp-eyed veteran probing with a bayonet held at a thirty-degree angle. Units emplacing minefields were also notably absent-minded about passing along specific detail on the location and the dimension of mined areas, leaving enemy and Allied troops to negotiate the field later. The Germans routinely recorded all minefields in minute detail and collected this information at the field army level with identical records going to a central land mine office in Germany. A postwar engineer investigating board recommended the American imitation of the German system, at least in establishing a centralized theater-level mine information network.[3]

Several considerations affected mapping throughout the operations in the Mediterranean and European theaters. Map quality was usually sufficient to satisfy the needs of the using combat elements during the hostilities. Maps obtained from British sources under wartime agreements and from French or even captured German stocks sup-

[3] ETO Gen Bd Rpt 73, Engineer Technical Policies, p. 13; Ottinger, "Landmine and Countermine Warfare," North Africa, 1940–1943, p. 260.

ported planning and tactical operations; these sources were supplemented by maps derived from aerial photographs by American air forces. All of these methods had drawbacks, but served the purposes of Allied armies well enough.

Less satisfactory, although never an obstacle to operations, was the problem of map issue to using units. Each field army had difficulty in moving map stocks to the forward battalions, but the causes of the problem varied. Inevitably, pursuit warfare led to situations in which troops advanced into areas not depicted on the maps they carried for immediate operations. Pursuit operations also demanded more small-scale maps—those above 1:50,000, which was the preferred tactical map in Europe. Static or siege operations required larger scale renditions of 1:25,000 or even 1:5,000.

Distribution units in the field handled more than 210 million maps of all sizes in the European theater alone, with the bulk of this number coming from presses in the United States; over 28 million maps were from the French Institut Geographique National. Troops used commercial road maps where they were available, and the theater sought to supply each vehicle with a local road map. Engineer authorities assembled at the end of the war estimated, however, that had the demands for any category of maps been even minimally higher, the strained distribution nets would not have met requirements.

Though highly publicized by both enemy and Allied sources, fortifications in Europe proved less formidable than anticipated. In the cases of the Atlantic Wall and the Siegfried Line, engineers proceeded with infantry teams to re-

duce bunkers or, sometimes, to seal their defenders inside. Assaults on fortified positions showed that aggressive, well-trained engineer and infantry parties supported by flat-trajectory artillery fire or close tactical air cover could reduce the most forbidding German casemates. Engineers examining coastal defenses after assault landings discovered that naval fire was effective against concrete emplacements, but only direct hits or an impact close enough to shower the bunker interior with fragments brought decisive results.

Engineers performed well when they went into action as infantry. General Moore remarked after the war that the use of engineers in combat had been more frequent than he had anticipated. Although their celebrated performance in the German Ardennes offensive received considerable public attention, engineers were committed as infantry during tactical emergencies everywhere in Europe and North Africa. Their combat doctrine proved sound in the heat of battle. Engineers established perimeter defenses around bridgehead construction sites and served in active combat with infantry and as covering forces at roadblocks and minefields throughout the war.

Engineer strengths in the Mediterranean and in northern Europe varied as the strategic importance of the northern European campaigns grew and that of the Italian campaign declined. Nevertheless, the proportion of engineer troops to combat elements at the end of the war was not widely divergent in the two theaters. In the European theater there were 323,677 engineers— some 10.5 percent of the total theater strength of 3,065,505 on 30 April 1945. One man in nine in the ETO was an engineer. In the Mediterranean the ratio was one in eleven. Engineers there numbered 44,467, or about 9 percent of the theater aggregate of 493,876 in the last month of the war. These figures can be contrasted with those for the Southwest Pacific, where one man in seven was an Army engineer. Despite the usual shortages in their numbers, the engineers were the largest single component of the divisional slice outside of regular combat troops.[4]

---

[4] Extracts, *Staff Officers' Field Manual Planning Data,* Draft FM 101–10, 1 Sep 47, pp. 406–07.

Their frequent shortages in men and equipment notwithstanding, the engineers met the exacting demands of the campaigns against German and Italian arms in North Africa and Europe. In a war calling for the closest integration of all combat and support arms for success in battle, the engineers were a competent and motivated force. They facilitated the concentration of Allied armies in England, helped move combat forces and their supply across hostile beaches, and supported the final decisive drives into the very heart of the Reich.

# Bibliographical Note

*Documentary Sources*

Documentary sources for the history of engineer operations in Europe and North Africa during World War II consist of records generated in the various theater command headquarters, in staff sections, and in active combat, general, or special service engineer units. Now housed in the General Archives Division of the Washington National Records Center, Suitland, Maryland, they include daily journals, memorandums, correspondence, general and special orders, and periodic reports for commands and units in both theaters. The author has supplemented information drawn from these sources by soliciting comments from engineer participants in the events described through interviews, correspondence, and submission to them of early drafts of the manuscript for elaboration or correction.

Several major collections were of special value in the preparation of this account. The military series of the central files of the Office of the Chief of Engineers, War Department, contains materials on the engineer preparation for war and the later broad supervision of engineer technical affairs overseas. A wartime Historical Branch in OCE gathered a separate documentary file during the war and, as the Engineer Historical Division, later supplemented the collection with additional documentary and interview files. Ancillary collections include the Army Map Service wartime records. This material has also been retired to the Washington National Records Center.

The files of the European Theater of Operations, U.S. Army, contain the records of the chief engineer and the stated theater policies and procedures governing engineer activities in England and on the Continent. The ETO Historical Division files also deal extensively with the history of engineers in the war in Europe. The files of the base sections and the advance section likewise contain material central to the engineer support of combat operations.

North African—Mediterranean theater files, also in the Washington National Records Center, are similarly organized by command and cover engineer activities in North Africa and Italy. Records of numerically designated units are filed individually by unit number in the records center.

The amount of unpublished material on engineer units in the two theaters is also voluminous, though it is uneven in quality. The more important works are the following:

1. Twenty Engineer Historical Reports were prepared by the Liaison Section of the Intelligence Division, OCE, ETOUSA, late in 1945. Each report deals exhaustively with a single broad aspect of engineer endeavor in England and on the Continent and includes extensive appendixes that contain some basic documents, detailed drawings, technical guidance, and occasional interview transcripts. This series is filed under the heading ETO Administrative File in the General Archives Division, Washington National Records Center. There is no comparable collec-

tion for the North African and Mediterranean theaters, though a short series of histories of base sections exists for North Africa and Italy, the latter on file at the Center of Military History. Engineer affairs are included as appropriate in these volumes.

2. A multi-volume history of the Mediterranean theater's Allied headquarters, History of AFHQ, also has numerous references to engineer activities and to command problems involving engineers.

3. Of the 131 ETO General Board Reports, the results of investigations by specially appointed teams of ETOUSA veterans, four deal directly with engineer organizations, technical and tactical policies, and engineer equipment. Others deal with matters affecting engineer operations such as theater organization, supply policy, maintenance, and the structure of SOS, ETOUSA, and COMZ, ETOUSA. A complete set of the reports is at the Center of Military History.

4. The eleven-volume Administrative and Logistical History of the European Theater of Operations also contains considerable engineer information. Intended as a series of preliminary monographs for a major history of ETOUSA, the works were completed in the theater early in 1946. Of importance for engineer operations are the following: The Predecessor Commands: The Special Observers (SPOBS) and United States Army Forces in the British Isles (USAFBI) by Henry G. Elliott; Organization and Command in the European Theater of Operations by Robert W. Coakley; Operations TORCH and the ETO; Neptune: Training for Mounting the Operation, and Artificial Ports by Clifford Jones; Open-

ing and Operating the Continental Ports by Elmer Cutts and Robert L. Davis; Survey of Allied Planning for Continental Operations by Howard L. Oleck, Henry J. Webb, and Vernon W. Hoover; The Local Procurement of Labor and Supplies, United Kingdom and Continental by Henry G. Elliott; and Troop and Supply Buildup in the United Kingdom Prior to D-day by Herbert French.

### Published Sources

Important published sources include Maj. Gen. Cecil R. Moore's comprehensive *Final Report of the Chief Engineer, European Theater of Operations, 1942–1945* and the published histories of the First, Third, Fifth, and Seventh Armies, and of the 12th Army Group. A general treatment of logistical—and engineer—problems in North Africa and Italy is in the *Logistical History of NATO-USA-MTOUSA* (Naples, 1946). Of special value were the following volumes in the official United States Army in World War II series: Blanche D. Coll, Jean E. Keith, and Herbert H. Rosenthal, *The Corps of Engineers: Troops and Equipment* (Washington, 1958); Roland G. Ruppenthal, *Logistical Support of the Armies, Volume I* (Washington, 1953) and *Logistical Support of the Armies, Volume II* (Washington, 1959); Richard M. Leighton and Robert W. Coakley, *Global Logistics and Strategy, 1940–1943* (Washington, 1955) and Robert W. Coakley and Richard M. Leighton, *Global Logistics and Strategy, 1943–1945* (Washington, 1968). The campaign histories in the series also provided a comprehensive background for this account of engineer operations.

The chief commercially published

works used in the preparation of this book were General of the Army Omar Nelson Bradley's *A Soldier's Story* (New York: Henry Holt and Co., 1951), Brig. Gen. William F. Heavey's *Down Ramp! The Story of the U.S. Army Amphibian Engineers* (Washington: Infantry Journal Press, 1947), General of the Army Dwight D. Eisenhower's *Crusade in Europe* (Garden City, N.Y.: Doubleday, 1948), General George S. Patton, Jr.'s *War as I Knew It* (Boston: Houghton Mifflin Co., 1947), and Wesley F. Craven and James L. Cate's *The U.S. Army Air Forces in World War II* (Chicago: University of Chicago Press, 1948–1958), 7 volumes.

Numerous articles on engineer operations appeared during and after the war in service journals. Among the best of these were those in *Military Review, The Military Engineer*, the *Engineering News-Record*, and the *Industry Journal*.

# Glossary

| | |
|---|---|
| AAA | Antiaircraft artillery |
| AAF | Army Air Forces |
| ABC-1 | Agreements reached at Washington Conference, January–March 1941 |
| ABS | Atlantic Base Section |
| ACofS | Assistant Chief of Staff |
| ADSEC | Advance Section |
| AEF | Allied Expeditionary Force (World War II) |
| AEF | American Expeditionary Forces (World War I) |
| AFHQ | Allied Force Headquarters |
| AFSC | Air Force Service Command |
| AGF | Army Ground Forces |
| Alsos | Code name for an Allied intelligence mission that sought information on German developments in nuclear fission |
| AMGLO | Allied Military Government Labor Office |
| Anvil | The planned 1944 Allied invasion of southern France in the Toulon-Marseille area (later Dragoon) |
| AP | Troop transport |
| AP | Antipersonnel mine |
| Apex | A remote-controlled drone boat |
| ASF | Army Service Forces |
| AT | Antitank mine |
| AUS | Army of the United States |
| Avalanche | Code name for the invasion of Italy at Salerno |
| Avgas | Aviation gasoline |
| Backbone | An assault plan which called for a foray, into Spanish Morocco should Spain change its nominally neutral position |
| Bang | Shipping code name for Zone III, Northern Ireland |
| Barracuda | Assault plan aimed directly at the harbor of Naples |
| Baytown | Assault plan that called for the British to move across the Strait of Messina to Reggio di Calabria |
| Belgian gates | Nickname of Element C, a beach obstacle emplaced on northern French beaches |
| Big | Assault plan to move nuclear intelligence teams from Freudenstadt through Horb to Haigerloch in southwest Germany |
| Blackstone | A subtask force of Western Task Force whose mission was to capture Safi, a small port 150 miles south of Casablanca |

| | |
|---|---|
| Blade Force | Belonging to the British 78th Division; resembled a U.S. armored combat command and included an American armored battalion |
| BOLERO | Code name for the buildup of U.S. forces and supplies in United Kingdom for cross-Channel attack |
| Bouncing Betty | German antipersonnel S-mine |
| BRIMSTONE | Plan for the capture of Sardinia, canceled |
| BRUSHWOOD | Subtask force of Western Task Force for the attack on Fedala, Morocco |
| CCA | Combat Command A |
| CCB | Combat Command B |
| CCR | Combat Command Reserve |
| CCS | Combined Chiefs of Staff |
| CE | Corps of Engineers |
| CENT | Task force in Sicily assault landing (45th Infantry Division); also the code name for beaches assaulted by this force |
| CG | Commanding general |
| Chocolate bars | Precast concrete units with scored checkerboard surface |
| Class I | Rations |
| Class II | Organizational equipment |
| Class III | Fuels and lubricants such as gasoline and coal |
| Class IV | Construction supplies |
| Class V | Ammunition and explosives |
| Class 30, 40, 70 | Designation indicating weight-bearing capacities of military bridges and roads |
| CO | Commanding officer |
| COBRA | Code name for the operation launched by First Army on 25 July 1944, designed to break out of the Normandy lodgment |
| CofEngrs | Chief of Engineers |
| CofS | Chief of Staff |
| COMZ | Communications Zone |
| CONAD | Continental Advance Section, Communications Zone |
| COSSAC | Chief of Staff to the Supreme Allied Commander |
| COWPUNCHER | Amphibious exercises before invasion of Italy |
| CTF | Center Task Force, North African invasion |
| D-1 | Vierville exit, OMAHA Beach, Normandy |
| D-3 | Les Moulins leading to St. Laurent, OMAHA Beach |
| DBS | Delta Base Section |
| DIME | Task force for Sicily assault landing (1st Infantry Division); the beaches assaulted by the task force |
| DRAGOON | Final code word for the invasion of southern France |

| | |
|---|---|
| DUKW | A 2½-ton, 6-by-6 amphibian truck |
| E–1 | Easy Red, leading up between St. Laurent and Colleville, OMAHA Beach |
| E–3 | Colleville draw, OMAHA Beach |
| EAC | Engineer Amphibian Command |
| EAF | Eastern Assault Force, North African invasion |
| EBS | Eastern Base Section |
| ETF | Eastern Task Force, North African invasion |
| ETIT | Engineer technical intelligence team |
| ETOUSA | European Theater of Operations, U.S. Army |
| EUCOM | European Command |
| EXPLOIT | An elaborate deception scheme designed to trick the Germans into expecting a crossing of the Rhine River at Uerdingen, some fifteen miles south of Rheinberg |
| F–1 | Draw leading off Fox Red, OMAHA Beach |
| FABIUS | Amphibious landing exercises of all assault forces except Force U, early May 1944, southern England |
| FEC | French Expeditionary Corps |
| FECOMZ | Forward Echelon, Communications Zone |
| FFA | First French Army |
| FFI | French Forces of the Interior |
| FLASHPOINT | A plan to cross the Rhine at Rheinberg, fifteen miles south of Wesel |
| G–1 | Personnel officer of division or higher staff |
| G–2 | Intelligence section |
| G–3 | Plans and operations section |
| G–4 | Logistics and supply section |
| GANGWAY | Assault plan aimed at the beaches immediately north of Naples |
| GHQ | General Headquarters |
| GLUE | Mailing code name for Zone II, Bristol and London |
| GOALPOST | Task force for assault landing in Mehdia–Port-Lyautey area, North Africa |
| GOOSEBERRY | Partial breakwater formed off the Normandy beaches by the sinking of blockships |
| GPA | General Purchasing Agent |
| GPB | General Purchasing Board |
| GRENADE | Code word for a Ninth U.S. Army assault crossing of the Roer followed by a northeastward drive to link with the First Canadian Army along the Rhine, February 1945 |
| Hards | Short for hardstandings |

| | |
|---|---|
| HE | High-explosive |
| HHC | Headquarters and Headquarters Company |
| HUSKY | Code name for Allied invasion of Sicily in July 1943 |
| | |
| IBC | Iceland Base Command |
| IBCAF | Iceland Base Command, Air Force |
| IBS | Island Base Section |
| INDIGO | Code name for occupation of Iceland |
| ISIS | Inter-Service Information Series (British) |
| ISS | Identification of Separate Shipments to Overseas Destinations |
| | |
| JOSS | Task force for Sicily assault landing (3d Infantry Division); the beaches assaulted by the task force |
| | |
| KOOL | Task force for Sicily assault landing (2d Armored Division less Combat Command A); the beaches assaulted by the task force |
| | |
| LBV | A fifty-ton self-propelled barge |
| LCA | Landing craft, assault |
| LCI | Landing craft, infantry |
| LCM(I) | Landing craft, mechanized, Mark I |
| LCM(III) | Landing craft, mechanized, Mark III |
| LCP | Landing craft, personnel |
| LCT | Landing craft, tank |
| LCVP | Landing craft, vehicle and personnel |
| LSI | Landing ship, infantry |
| LST | Landing ship, tank |
| LVT | Landing vehicle, tracked |
| | |
| MAGNET | Plan for shipment of American forces to Northern Ireland |
| MAMD | Marshaling area mapping depots |
| MBS | Mediterranean Base Section |
| MP | Military police |
| MPLS | Military Pipeline Service |
| MRS | Military Railway Service |
| MSR | Main supply route |
| MT 80 | Motor gasoline |
| MTO | Mediterranean Theater of Operations |
| MULBERRY | The artificial harbor constructed off the Normandy beaches |
| MUSKET | Assault plan that would bring Fifth Army into Taranto, Italy |
| | |
| NAAF | Northwest African Air Forces |

| | |
|---|---|
| NAAFI | Navy-Army-Air Force Institution (British equivalent to post exchange) |
| NAASC | North African Air Service Command |
| NATOUSA | North African Theater of Operations, U.S. Army |
| NCDU | Naval combat demolition unit |
| NEPTUNE | Actual 1944 operations within OVERLORD. The code name was used for security reasons after September 1943 on all OVERLORD planning papers which referred to the target area and date. |
| NIBS | Northern Ireland Base Section |
| NIF | Northern Ireland Forces |
| NORDWIND | Code word for a German counteroffensive launched on New Year's Eve 1944 near the southern end of the Allied line in Alsace |
| NYPOE | New York Port of Embarkation |
| OCE | Office of the Chief of Engineers |
| OMAHA Beach | Landing beach in Normandy |
| OVERLORD | Plan for the invasion of northwest Europe, June 1944 |
| PBS | Peninsular Base Section |
| PBS (Main) | Leghorn half of Peninsular Base Section |
| Pensouth | Naples half of Peninsular Base Section |
| PLUTO | Pipeline Under the Ocean |
| POE | Port of Embarkation |
| POL | Petroleum, Oil, and Lubricants |
| PROCO | Projects for Continental Operations |
| QUADRANT | Quebec Conference, August 1943 |
| RAF | Royal Air Force |
| RAINBOW−5 | A U.S. war plan designed to implement that portion of ABC−1 which applied to the United Kingdom in the event of U.S. entry into the war |
| RCT | Regimental combat team |
| ROUNDUP | Plan for major U.S.-British attack across the Channel in 1943 |
| RSJ | Rolled steel joist |
| SBS | Southern Base Section |
| SCR−625 | U.S. mine detector |
| SEXTANT | International conference at Cairo, November and December 1943 |
| SHARK | Task force (II Corps), Operation HUSKY |
| SHAEF | Supreme Headquarters, Allied Expeditionary Force |
| SHINGLE | Code name for the Anzio landing, 22 January 1944 |
| SLEDGEHAMMER | Plan for a limited-objective attack across the Channel in 1942 |
| SOLOC | Southern Line of Communications (Rhone Valley) |

| | |
|---|---|
| SOS | Services of Supply |
| Soxo | Mailing code name for Zone I, northern England |
| SPOBS | Special Observer Group |
| | |
| TAG | The Adjutant General |
| TBA | Table of Basic Allowance |
| TC | Transportation Corps |
| TERMINAL | A special landing party |
| TIGER | Code name for an amphibious rehearsal for OVERLORD |
| TOE | Table of Organization and Equipment |
| TOMBOLA | A flexible six-inch underwater pipeline designed to discharge POL tankers anchored offshore at Ste. Honorine-des-Pertes |
| TORCH | Code name for the Allied invasion of Northwest Africa, 1942 |
| TPP Section | Transportation, Plant, and Personnel Section |
| TRIDENT | Washington Conference, 1943 |
| | |
| UCRB | Unit Construction Railway Bridge (British) |
| UGLY | Shipping address code name for United Kingdom |
| USAAF | U.S. Army Air Forces |
| USAFBI | U.S. Army Forces British Isles |
| USANIF | U.S. Army Northern Ireland Forces |
| USMC | U.S. Marine Corps |
| USFET | U.S. Forces in the European Theater |
| UTAH Beach | Landing beach in Normandy |
| | |
| VERITABLE | A 21 Army Group plan for a Canadian attack between the Maas and the Rhine, January–February 1945 |
| | |
| WBS | Western Base Section (England) |
| WEBFOOT | Code name for a practice landing preparatory to Anzio landings |
| WNTF | Western Naval Task Force |
| Woofus | A rocket-firing LCM |
| WTF | Western Task Force (North African invasion) |
| | |
| XO | Executive officer |
| | |
| ZA | Zone of the Advance |
| ZI | Zone of the Interior |

# Basic Military Map Symbols*

Symbols within a rectangle indicate a military unit, within a triangle an observation post, and within a circle a supply point.

## Military Units—Identification

| | |
|---|---|
| Antiaircraft Artillery . . . . . . . . . . . . . . . . . . . . . . . . . . . . . . . . . . . . | ▲ in rectangle |
| Armored Command . . . . . . . . . . . . . . . . . . . . . . . . . . . . . . . . . . . . . | ⬭ in rectangle |
| Army Air Forces . . . . . . . . . . . . . . . . . . . . . . . . . . . . . . . . . . . . . . . | ∞ in rectangle |
| Artillery, except Antiaircraft and Coast Artillery . . . . . . . . . . . . | • in rectangle |
| Cavalry, Horse . . . . . . . . . . . . . . . . . . . . . . . . . . . . . . . . . . . . . . . . | ╱ in rectangle |
| Cavalry, Mechanized . . . . . . . . . . . . . . . . . . . . . . . . . . . . . . . . . . . | ⬿ in rectangle |
| Chemical Warfare Service . . . . . . . . . . . . . . . . . . . . . . . . . . . . . . . | G in rectangle |
| Coast Artillery . . . . . . . . . . . . . . . . . . . . . . . . . . . . . . . . . . . . . . . . | ◇ in rectangle |
| Engineers . . . . . . . . . . . . . . . . . . . . . . . . . . . . . . . . . . . . . . . . . . . . | E in rectangle |
| Infantry . . . . . . . . . . . . . . . . . . . . . . . . . . . . . . . . . . . . . . . . . . . . . | ⊠ |
| Medical Corps . . . . . . . . . . . . . . . . . . . . . . . . . . . . . . . . . . . . . . . . | ⊞ |
| Ordnance Department . . . . . . . . . . . . . . . . . . . . . . . . . . . . . . . . . . | ⚙ in rectangle |
| Quartermaster Corps . . . . . . . . . . . . . . . . . . . . . . . . . . . . . . . . . . . | Q in rectangle |
| Signal Corps . . . . . . . . . . . . . . . . . . . . . . . . . . . . . . . . . . . . . . . . . | S in rectangle |
| Tank Destroyer . . . . . . . . . . . . . . . . . . . . . . . . . . . . . . . . . . . . . . . | TD in rectangle |
| Transportation Corps . . . . . . . . . . . . . . . . . . . . . . . . . . . . . . . . . . | ⊛ in rectangle |
| Veterinary Corps . . . . . . . . . . . . . . . . . . . . . . . . . . . . . . . . . . . . . . | ▽ in rectangle |

Airborne units are designated by combining a gull wing symbol with the arm or service symbol:

| | |
|---|---|
| Airborne Artillery . . . . . . . . . . . . . . . . . . . . . . . . . . . . . . . . . . . . . | ⬐ |
| Airborne Infantry . . . . . . . . . . . . . . . . . . . . . . . . . . . . . . . . . . . . . . | ⊠ |

*For complete listing of symbols in use during the World War II period, see FM 21–30, dated October 1943, from which these are taken.

# Size Symbols

The following symbols placed either in boundary lines or above the rectangle, triangle, or circle inclosing the identifying arm or service symbol indicate the size of military organization:

Squad . . . . . . . . . . . . . . . . . . . . . . . . . . . . . . . . . . . . . . . . . . . . ●

Section. . . . . . . . . . . . . . . . . . . . . . . . . . . . . . . . . . . . . . . . . . . ●●

Platoon . . . . . . . . . . . . . . . . . . . . . . . . . . . . . . . . . . . . . . . . . ●●●

Company, troop, battery, Air Force flight . . . . . . . . . . . . . . . . I

Battalion, cavalry squadron, or Air Force squadron . . . . . . . . . II

Regiment or group; combat team (with abbreviation CT following identifying numeral) . . . . . . . . . . . . . . . . . . . . . . . . . III

Brigade, Combat Command of Armored Division, or Air Force Wing. . . . . . . . . . . . . . . . . . . . . . . . . . . . . . . . . . . . . . . . . . . X

Division or Command of an Air Force. . . . . . . . . . . . . . . . . . . . XX

Corps or Air Force . . . . . . . . . . . . . . . . . . . . . . . . . . . . . . . . . . . XXX

Army. . . . . . . . . . . . . . . . . . . . . . . . . . . . . . . . . . . . . . . . . . . . . . XXXX

Group of Armies. . . . . . . . . . . . . . . . . . . . . . . . . . . . . . . . . . . . XXXXX

## EXAMPLES

The letter or number to the left of the symbol indicates the unit designation; that to the right, the designation of the parent unit to which it belongs. Letters or numbers above or below boundary lines designate the units separated by the lines:

Company A, 137th Infantry . . . . . . . . . . . . . . . . . . . . . . . . . . A⊠137

8th Field Artillery Battalion. . . . . . . . . . . . . . . . . . . . . . . . . . ⊡8

Combat Command A, 1st Armored Division. . . . . . . . . . . . A⬭1

Observation Post, 23d Infantry. . . . . . . . . . . . . . . . . . . . . . . ⧍23

Command Post, 5th Infantry Division . . . . . . . . . . . . . . . . ⊠5

Boundary between 137th and 138th Infantry . . . . . . . . . . . —|||— 137 / 138

# Weapons

Machine gun . . . . . . . . . . . . . . . . . . . . . . . . . . . . . . . . . . . . . . ●→

Gun. . . . . . . . . . . . . . . . . . . . . . . . . . . . . . . . . . . . . . . . . . . . . . . ●

Gun battery . . . . . . . . . . . . . . . . . . . . . . . . . . . . . . . . . . . . . . . ⊥⊥⊥

Howitzer or Mortar . . . . . . . . . . . . . . . . . . . . . . . . . . . . . . . . . ◀●

Tank . . . . . . . . . . . . . . . . . . . . . . . . . . . . . . . . . . . . . . . . . . . . . . ◇

Self-propelled gun . . . . . . . . . . . . . . . . . . . . . . . . . . . . . . . . . . ▣

# UNITED STATES ARMY IN WORLD WAR II

The following volumes have been published or are in press:

The War Department
 *Chief of Staff: Prewar Plans and Preparations*
 *Washington Command Post: The Operations Division*
 *Strategic Planning for Coalition Warfare: 1941–1942*
 *Strategic Planning for Coalition Warfare: 1943–1944*
 *Global Logistics and Strategy: 1940–1943*
 *Global Logistics and Strategy: 1943–1945*
 *The Army and Economic Mobilization*
 *The Army and Industrial Manpower*
The Army Ground Forces
 *The Organization of Ground Combat Troops*
 *The Procurement and Training of Ground Combat Troops*
The Army Service Forces
 *The Organization and Role of the Army Service Forces*
The Western Hemisphere
 *The Framework of Hemisphere Defense*
 *Guarding the United States and Its Outposts*
The War in the Pacific
 *The Fall of the Philippines*
 *Guadalcanal: The First Offensive*
 *Victory in Papua*
 *CARTWHEEL: The Reduction of Rabaul*
 *Seizure of the Gilberts and Marshalls*
 *Campaign in the Marianas*
 *The Approach to the Philippines*
 *Leyte: The Return to the Philippines*
 *Triumph in the Philippines*
 *Okinawa: The Last Battle*
 *Strategy and Command: The First Two Years*
The Mediterranean Theater of Operations
 *Northwest Africa: Seizing the Initiative in the West*
 *Sicily and the Surrender of Italy*
 *Salerno to Cassino*
 *Cassino to the Alps*
The European Theater of Operations
 *Cross-Channel Attack*
 *Breakout and Pursuit*
 *The Lorraine Campaign*
 *The Siegfried Line Campaign*
 *The Ardennes: Battle of the Bulge*
 *The Last Offensive*

# The U.S. Army Center of Military History

The Center of Military History prepares and publishes histories as required by the U.S. Army. It coordinates Army historical matters, including historical properties, and supervises the Army museum system. It also maintains liaison with public and private agencies and individuals to stimulate interest and study in the field of military history. The Center is located at 20 Massachusetts Avenue, N.W., Washington, D.C. 20314.

# Index